Peace and World Order Studies

A Publication of the Five College Program in
Peace and World Security Studies
(PAWSS)

Michael T. Klare, Director
Conn Nugent, Coordinator of Five Colleges, Inc.

Amherst College

Hampshire College

Mount Holyoke College

Smith College

University of Massachusetts at Amherst

FIFTH EDITION

Peace and World Order Studies

A CURRICULUM GUIDE

EDITED BY

Daniel C. Thomas
and Michael T. Klare

Five College Program in
Peace and World Security Studies,
Hampshire College

WESTVIEW PRESS
Boulder, San Francisco, & London

Published in 1989 in the United States of America by Westview Press, Inc., 5500 Central Avenue, Boulder, Colorado 80301, and in the United Kingdom by Westview Press, Inc., 13 Brunswick Centre, London WC1N 1AF, England

Library of Congress Cataloging-in-Publication Data
Peace and world order studies : a curriculum guide / edited by Daniel
   C. Thomas and Michael T. Klare. — 5th ed.
      p.   cm.
   ISBN 0-8133-0730-9. ISBN 0-8133-0731-7 (pbk.).
   1. Peace—Study and teaching. 2. International organization—
Study and teaching. I. Thomas, Daniel C. II. Klare, Michael T.,
1942–   .
JX1904.5.P39   1989
327.1′72′07—dc20   89-32205
                                                                              CIP

Printed and bound in the United States of America

The paper used in this publication meets the requirements of the American National Standard for Permanence of Paper for Printed Library Materials Z39.48-1984.

10   9   8   7   6   5   4   3   2   1

Contents

ESSAYS

III. Strategies for Curriculum Development   73

SYLLABI

IV. Introductions to Peace and World Order Studies   111

V. War and International Conflict   181

Foreword

As the president of a liberal arts college, I believe that the field of peace and world order studies constitutes an essential part of the undergraduate curriculum. From an intellectual viewpoint, peace studies provides students with entry into a critical dimension of human thought and behavior: the causes and consequences of war and the centuries-old struggle to diminish international violence. For this reason alone, peace studies should command the attention of college faculty and administrators. But peace studies entails more than this. By educating students about the basic "facts of life" in the nuclear age, we can better prepare them to serve as informed and capable citizens when, later in life, they are confronted with critical issues of war and peace. Finally, by examining these issues in the classroom, we create the possibility for conceptual breakthroughs in the search for peace and world security. In these varied ways, peace studies supports the academy's historical role as a crucible for democracy and as a laboratory for human betterment.

To perform these roles in a rapidly changing world, the field of peace and world order studies must continually expose itself to new and vital challenges. In 1984, when I wrote an introduction to the fourth edition of the *Curriculum Guide*, we in the field were still struggling to incorporate material about peace and world order into the undergraduate curriculum. In that year, the *Wall Street Journal* ran a lead editorial opposing undergraduate peace studies programs, and the president of the United States continued his denunciation of the Soviet Union as an "evil empire." The challenge then was difficult but clear: We had to make the case to our colleagues in higher education that U.S.-Soviet relations, North-South relations, and the impact of technology and culture on war and peace are important matters to our students. Furthermore, as complicated as these matters are, we had to impress upon them the idea that these are issues with which undergraduates can struggle, and that from this exercise they can learn a great deal.

Today, we have a different but equally difficult task before us. Almost every college and university in the country offers some course relating to peace and world order in the nuclear age. Peace studies has gained acceptance, but we must still guard against being lulled by our very success into believing that individual courses, while vital, are in themselves sufficient. As the president of a college, I feel that all administrators must acknowledge the necessity for a broad program of peace and world order studies within the liberal arts curriculum and act to promote a hospitable atmosphere for its development.

Another challenge to success is the requirement of ensuring that the bountiful courses being offered today are of high quality and that they accomplish the educational purposes for which they are intended. How do we ensure that the courses offered in our colleges and universities address the truly critical issues? How do we guarantee that all points of view are fully considered and discussed? How do we encourage students and faculty to look beyond the obvious questions to the more subtle and troubling ones?

Students tend to prefer questions for which there are obvious answers, but peace studies, by its very nature, pursues problems and questions that have long defied easy solutions. Issues related to the control of low-intensity conflict around the world, for example, do not have easy answers. We could call for an end to arms transfers to the Third World, and perhaps persuade the major powers to adjust their economies to make this possible, but that solution would fail to address the growing arms industry in the Third World itself. We might reduce tensions between the superpowers and slow or even halt the nuclear arms race, but that alone would not help the millions of people victimized by regional wars and their consequences—homelessness, hunger, disease, and ravished economies. Part of the challenge of exploring difficult questions is the requirement that we consider fundamentally new types of solutions; many of today's problems—such as widespread nuclear proliferation and massive threats to the global environment—transcend national borders and therefore defy traditional, exclusively national solutions. Undergraduates, who frequently show such invigorating ingenuity in problem solving, can deal productively with these complicated issues.

This field is both expanding and maturing. In that context, we must reaffirm our commitment to scope and to quality, breadth, and diversity as we introduce today's students to the complex global issues with which they will struggle for the rest of their lives as policymakers, as citizens, and as human beings. The syllabi included in this edition demonstrate our faculties' vigorous response to this challenge. Many of the introductory courses encompass a broad spectrum of issues, including the causes and ethics of war and peace, the characteristics of the nuclear age, and related problems of human rights and development, as well as a range of alternative solutions. Moreover, a variety of sophisticated upper-level courses are currently addressing regional conflicts, authoritarianism and repression, social movements and revolution, and Third World development, among other topics. The syllabi also sample teaching on a variety of innovative and constructive solutions, including arms control and disarmament, alternative security, conflict resolution, and international law and organization.

The years since the fourth edition was published have been marked by another important change. A field that was once dominated by historians, political scientists, and physicists now involves representatives of the arts, anthropology, psychology, philosophy and religious studies, and literature, to name just a few of the participating disciplines. At Hampshire College, for instance, a multidisciplinary theater event held in the spring of 1988 included plays and choral performances dealing with war and peace across time and in different cultures. This fifth edition is an important step in reaching out to faculty and students across the United States and in other parts of the world to explore ways in which peace and world order studies can be incorporated into all fields and departments in our colleges and universities.

The fifth edition of *Peace and World Order Studies: A Curriculum Guide* demonstrates conclusively that educators in the field have responded with great energy and imagination to the new challenges facing peace studies. The syllabi included herein not only encompass a broader range of issues and perspectives than previous editions; they also exhibit a strong commitment to intellectual growth and rigor. Much of the credit for this evolution goes to the faculty from all over the country who have devoted themselves to the advancement of scholarship and teaching in the field. Special recognition is also due to the editors, Daniel Thomas and Michael Klare, who have commissioned essays and gathered syllabi that reflect the breadth and quality of work on campuses around the United States.

This edition of the *Curriculum Guide* exhibits a new maturity in the field of peace and world order studies. It is clear, however, that the field is still growing and expanding. I am confident that the next edition—the sixth—will reflect this ongoing commitment to intellectual progress.

Adele Simmons
Hampshire College

Preface and Acknowledgments

The four previous editions of *Peace and World Order Studies: A Curriculum Guide* are a testament to the evolution and vitality of our field. Many of the essays and syllabi in those volumes have become classics, setting the standard for teaching and curriculum development in peace studies. To undertake a fifth edition, therefore, was to accept a double challenge: to chronicle the breadth and diversity of teaching in the field, while providing materials that will inspire and inform faculty who seek to make their courses more current, compelling, and rigorous. In responding to this challenge, we consistently sought to demonstrate the intellectual and pedagogical richness of the field as it has evolved over the past five years.

If peace studies is to continue to prosper, we in the field must draw on the best and most relevant work in the disciplines with which we have long been associated, such as political science, history, sociology, and psychology. We must also seek out and involve people from other disciplines, thereby introducing additional areas of expertise and new approaches to education. Most important, we must pursue the new analytical perspectives that will broaden our horizons and bring us closer to understanding and solving the pressing global problems of our time. This collection of essays and syllabi has been prepared with these goals in mind.

The essays in this collection were designed to illustrate not only the range of substantive approaches to peace studies but also the various ways in which faculty have sought to translate these visions into actual curricular endeavors. As the reader will note, these essays present a variety of intellectual and curricular perspectives. What their authors share is a belief that institutions of higher education must devote some of their vast research and pedagogical energies to the pursuit of peace, and that such efforts should be characterized by a commitment to creativity, rigor, and respect for fundamental human values.

In selecting the ninety-three course syllabi incorporated into this edition of the *Curriculum Guide*, we attempted to provide a broad cross-section of teaching in peace and world order studies in all of its aspects and to highlight courses given at a wide range of institutional settings—from community colleges to major research universities. In beginning this search, we attempted to solicit materials from as broad a constituency as possible: Six thousand copies of a "Call for Syllabi" were mailed to faculty in peace studies, international relations, and many other disciplines; in addition, notices were inserted into various academic newsletters, and numerous individuals were contacted for contributions. In the end, approximately one thousand syllabi were received from faculty at colleges and universities all across the United States. An Editorial Advisory Committee composed of leading figures in peace studies was formed to assist in planning the *Curriculum Guide* and in assessing the vast quantity of materials submitted. As editors, we can attest to the quality and diversity of materials presented herein; however, all views expressed in the syllabi and essays are solely those of the authors and should not be understood to represent the editors' prescription for what should constitute teaching in this field.

The first four editions of *Peace and World Order Studies: A Curriculum Guide* were published between 1973 and 1984 by the World Policy Institute (formerly the Institute for World Order) of New York City. In September 1986, complete responsibility for editing and producing the *Curriculum Guide* passed to the Five College Program in Peace and World Security Studies (PAWSS) based at Hampshire College in Amherst, Massachusetts, which established its National Curriculum Resources Project to conduct this and other outreach efforts. Special thanks are therefore due to Adele Simmons, president of Hampshire College, and to the staff of the World Policy Institute, especially its president, Archibald Gillies, and the editor of the fourth edition, Barbara Wien, for making this transition possible.

Preparation of this volume entailed consultations with many individuals. While a complete list of all those involved would read like a "who's who" of teaching and research in the field, we wish to express special thanks to the members of the Editorial Advisory Committee: Robert Elias of Tufts University, Vincent Ferraro of Mount Holyoke College, Angela Gilliam of the State University of New York at Old Westbury, Ted Herman of Cornwall, Pennsylvania, Jerome King of the University of Massachusetts at Amherst, George Lopez of the University of Notre Dame, Carol Rank of the University of California at Berkeley, Betty Reardon of Columbia University, Patricia Washburn of Earlham College, Barbara Wien of the Institute for Policy Studies, and Nigel Young of Colgate University. We also give great thanks to Mary Schultz, who persevered through the typing of this unwieldy manuscript and contributed many helpful suggestions based on her own college teaching experience.

Finally, we take special pleasure in thanking those individuals whose assistance and support have been essential to the success of the PAWSS Program and its Curriculum Project. This roster properly begins with the presidents of the Five College consortium—Peter Pouncey of Amherst College, Adele Simmons of Hampshire College, Elizabeth Kennan of Mount Holyoke

College, Mary Maples Dunn of Smith College, and Chancellor Joseph Duffy of the University of Massachusetts at Amherst, along with the coordinator of the Five College consortium, Conn Nugent. Equally important are the members of the Steering Committee of the PAWSS program: Jan Dizard, William Taubman, and Ronald Tiersky of Amherst College; Allan Krass and Brian Schultz of Hampshire College; Joseph Ellis, Vincent Ferraro, and Anthony Lake of Mount Holyoke College; Thomas Derr, Deborah Lubar, and Thomas Riddell of Smith College; and James Der Derian, Jean Bethke Elshtain, Jerome King, and George Levinger of the University of Massachusetts at Amherst.

Finally, our deepest gratitude is extended to Ira and Miriam Wallach for their great interest in and unwavering support of this important endeavor.

Daniel C. Thomas and Michael T. Klare
Five College Program in
Peace and World Security Studies

Talloires Declaration of University Presidents

We, the presidents of 45 universities from all regions and many cultures of the world, having convened at Talloires, France, from September 12 to 16, 1988, believe that the universities of the world bear profound moral responsibilities to increase understanding of the awful risks of the nuclear age and to reduce those risks. Charged by our societies to prepare our students for life, we are committed as educators to prevent global death.

In a world that is plagued by war, hunger, injustice, and suffering, we believe that universities nurture life through the creation and transmission of knowledge. We join in supporting research and teaching programs that will increase our common understanding of the causes of conflicts and their resolution, the relationship between peace and development, and the sources of injustice and hunger. In so doing, we shall better discharge our responsibilities to educate the men and women who will lead our societies into the twenty-first century.

Although differences in regional perspectives and academic traditions will necessarily create a diversity in our teaching and research, we aspire to a commonality in our educational programs. We hope that the sixty million students and two million teachers engaged in higher education throughout the world will join us in these endeavors.

To achieve these goals, we recognize the importance of the following local, regional, and global measures:

1. Language, history, culture, and the methods to create peace must be integral parts of the subjects that we teach. Peace as a concept must be in our students' imaginations, in their intellects, and in their lives.

2. Research and teaching in this area should incorporate contributions from many fields of knowledge, including the natural sciences, the humanities, medicine, the social sciences, philosophy, theology, and law. We recognize

For more information, contact President Jean Mayer, Tufts University, Medford, MA 02155.

that many universities have agreed to conduct only research, the results of which may be made public, and we encourage this approach.

3. Universities should support the development of courses and research on arms control, negotiation and conflict resolution, peace and development, and related subjects while providing for the training of teachers and scholars interested in incorporating these topics into their regular courses.

4. In making every effort to support regional academic associations, universities should encourage the development of regional centers that assist in the organization of research, the exchange of information and curricula, and faculty development in the areas of our concern.

5. In order to maximize the global impact of local and regional programs, universities should design and implement an international information center and communications consortium. These facilities will support the exchange of information, provide communication based on relatively low-cost technologies, offer access to computer networks, and afford one- and two-way television linkages among university classrooms in various parts of the world and thereby create a truly "Global Classroom."

6. In support of these local and regional initiatives, we, the presidents assembled at Talloires, have established a coordinating body in the form of a steering committee and a permanent secretariat.

Talloires, France
September 15, 1988

Hachemi Alaya
University of Tunis
Tunisia

Ayo Banjo
University of Ibadan
Nigeria

Boonrod Binson
Chulalongkorn University
Thailand

Bhaskar Ray Chaudhuri
Calcutta University
India

Yuri L. Ershov
Novosibirsk State University
USSR

James O. Freedman
Dartmouth College
USA

Mario Ojeda Gomez
College of Mexico
Mexico

Paul Edward Gray
Massachusetts Institute of
   Technology
USA

Francis Sheldon Hackney
University of Pennsylvania
USA

Frederic P. Herter
American University of Beirut
Lebanon

Theodore M. Hesburgh, C.S.C.
University of Notre Dame
USA

Martin H:son Holmdahl
Uppsala University
Sweden

J. P. Kubilyus
Vilnius V. Kapsukas State
  University
USSR

Eduardo Lopez de la Osa
University of Madrid
Spain

Norio Matsumae
Hokkaodo Tokai University
Japan

Shigeyoshi Matsumae
Tokai Educational System
Japan

Jean Mayer
Tufts University
USA

N. A. Medvedev
Kaliningrad State University
USSR

Calvin Hastings Plimpton
American University of Beirut
Lebanon

Avelino Jose Porto
University of Belgrano
Argentina

Moonis Raza
University of Delhi
India

Akilagpa Swayerr
University of Ghana
Ghana

Bruno Rodolfo Schlemper
University of Santa Catarina
Brazil

John Fraser Scott
La Trobe University
Australia

Adele Smith Simmons
Hampshire College
USA

Paulo Renato Costa Souza
State University of Campinas
Brazil

David W. Strangway
University of British Columbia
Canada

Justin Thorens
United Nations University
Switzerland

Juan Oscar Usher
Catholic University
Paraguay

Tapio Variz
University for Peace
Costa Rica

G. P. Vyatkin
Chelyabinsk Polytechnic Institute
USSR

Xie Xide
Fudan University
China

ESSAYS

I

Introduction

Elise Boulding
Professor Emerita and Dickey Senior Fellow,
Dartmouth College

In 1972, when the first edition of *Peace and World Order Studies: A Curriculum Guide* was published, there were but a few dozen fledgling peace studies programs at colleges and universities in the United States. Faculty were beginning to teach courses on peace, conflict resolution, and world order, often on overtime, because they felt the urgency of preparing the next generation to deal with problems not adequately covered in existing departments. Supporting the development of peace studies during that time were some of the leading figures in the social sciences. Included in this pioneer band were sociologists Robert Angell, Jessie Bernard, and Louis Kriesberg of the United States, and Johan Galtung and Alva Myrdal of Norway and Sweden, respectively, both of whom did some teaching in the United States at this time; economists Emile Benoit and Kenneth Boulding; psychologists Jerome Frank, Harold Guetzkow, Herbert Kelman, Robert Lifton, and Ralph White; political scientists Chadwick Alger, John Burton, Berenice Carroll, Inis Claude, Carl Deutsch, Bruce Russett, Gene Sharp, and David Singer; international law and organization specialists Richard Falk, Roger Fisher, Oscar Schachter, and Lewis Sohn; anthropologists Margaret Mead, Raoul Naroll, and Sol Tax; historians Charles Barker, Charles Chatfield, Blanche Wiesen Cook, Sandi Cooper, and Merle Curti; and mathematicians and systems engineers Norman Alcock, Seymour Mehlman, Anatol Rapoport, and Thomas Schelling. Of course I have omitted from that roster many other prominent individuals!

Clearly, some of the most creative minds of the post–World War II period were turning to new paradigms for the study of war and peace systems and processes. For many of their contemporaries, however, peace studies (as it came to be called in shorthand) was considered an intellectual aberration, involving a regressive emotional tendency that undercut the scientific objectivity so important to the increasingly policy-relevant social sciences. Peace researchers pointed out that it was no more unscientific to value peace while doing research on war/peace processes than it was to value health while doing research on disease, but the analogy was not widely accepted.

Sixteen years later, the involvement of the social sciences in policy issues has greatly expanded, and schools of public policy have been established across the United States. Discussion of the extent to which social scientists should try to improve the existing system of administering goods and services in the public domain is now taken for granted among academics, professionals, and civic leaders.

Unquestionably, peace and world order studies have benefited from this development. Although the legitimacy of the systems modification debate is a little slower in being accepted when applied to national security issues, many have come to realize that a systematic rethinking of peace, security, and defense strategies is required. Clearly, the increasingly lethal nature of modern warfare, both nuclear and non-nuclear, has helped bring about this new openness regarding public scrutiny and debate on defense options. What peace studies programs offer, among other things, is a consideration of a whole range of previously unexamined options for the maintenance of international peace and security. The concept of *alternatives*, which has been so useful in futures studies, can now be applied to *alternative security.*

Foundations, true to their function of looking for creative new thinking about the social order, have discovered the importance of peace and security studies and are now providing significant funding for university programs and for individual scholars. In placing particular emphasis on projects that move beyond traditional academic disciplines, and on academic "retooling" for faculty who seek to develop competence outside their own disciplines, foundations are bringing their all-important resources to bear on precisely the functions that peace studies came into existence to perform—namely, the development of interdisciplinary capabilities for a new analysis of the existing international system, and the exploration of processes, structures, and mechanisms that can create the conditions for a more just and stable world order. Joining the foundations in this endeavor is the U.S. Institute for Peace, established by the United States Congress in 1984 to initiate and support research, training, and education toward the peaceful resolution of international conflict.

At this juncture the critical question is, Will scholars using the broader frame of reference of peace studies be able to interact productively with scholars using the narrower frame of reference of traditional security studies? By choosing to focus on the *conditions* of peace, scholars in the new peace studies field deal with security issues by additionally examining the related topics found in the table of contents of this curriculum guide: world political economy and social justice, ecological balance, peacemaking and conflict resolution, nonviolence theory and action, social movements and social change, the role of women, the role of teachers, religious and ethical perspectives, and the treatment of war and peace in literature, the arts, and the news media. These topics do not preclude the more direct considerations of war and militarism, regional conflicts, arms control, international law and organization, which are also covered in this volume.

The conditions-of-peace approach facilitates the identification of interrelationships between military and nonmilitary factors in international relations, and allows for the possibility of developing a conflict-reducing, problem-solving diplomacy that draws on resources in American society not previously thought relevant to the maintenance of peace. The conditions-of-peace approach also identifies interrelationships between domestic and international security in the process of examining how socioeconomic, political, and cultural issues are handled at home and how we deal with them abroad. It is precisely the exclusion of such factors from traditional international relations analysis that frustrates the search for alternatives to the existing world system with its persistent recurrence of war.

Given the amount of intellectual and financial resources that goes to support the narrower study of national security, and the powerful influence that this older national security tradition has on national policy, it would appear that the interaction between the two frames of reference is crucial if we are to develop alternative security options. This cannot happen unless U.S. colleges and universities have strong peace studies programs. The national security community believes that security is attainable through the efforts of unilateral military organizations such as the United States Department of Defense and its counterparts, and that these institutions can create national power and international peace through deterrence. On the whole, the peace studies community sees deterrence as a long-run illusion and views the emphasis on military strength as eroding national vitality, both economically and culturally. *Both* groups are concerned with maintaining the viability of the United States and the world of which it is a part.

Imaginative university administrators will see how important it is to develop and maintain a strong program in peace studies if new approaches to international security policy are to be developed. If foundations are moving in this direction, and if Congress itself has underwritten the legitimacy of peace studies, then universities cannot afford to lag behind.

It cannot be emphasized enough that the situation facing us today differs completely from that during the period when peace studies programs were first being developed in the 1960s and 1970s. The situation has changed with respect to the status of interdisciplinary studies as an academic enterprise, the status of new approaches to national security, the rapidly developing field of impact assessment, and the changing character of the international system itself as new intergovernmental and nongovernmental networks arise to address global problems from perspectives that encompass a diversity of national and human interests. Each of these developments is considered below.

1. Interdisciplinary studies *per se* have gradually built up a new legitimacy stemming, in part, from calls by the federal government in the late 1960s for the formation of mission-oriented multidisciplinary academic task forces to deal with pressing social problems such as urban maldevelopment and the isolation of minorities from the socioeconomic mainstream. Campus programs in urban, environmental, and minority (including women) studies evolved concurrently with other responses to that call. Peace studies can be seen as part of that broader movement toward multidisciplinary, mission-oriented research and education.

2. The legitimacy of debate on the efficacy of warmaking as a means of national defense has been enhanced by recent work on nonoffensive defense (NOD), civilian-based defense, and other alternative forms of defense. For example, the two leading U.S. theorists of alternative defense, Gene Sharp (1985) and Randall Forsberg (1984), are now being heard in the United States security community, and the newsletters *Alternative Security* and *Defense and Disarmament Alternatives* are gaining in importance. In Europe, the newsletter *NOD*, published by a network of scholars based at the University of Copenhagen, reports that a number of peace researchers have received research contracts from governments to develop NOD models for European security. The establishment of the U.S. Institute for Peace and of comparable institutions in other countries such as Austria, Canada, the Netherlands, Norway, Sweden, and West Germany has also contributed to the growing legitimacy of this inquiry.

3. Social impact assessment became an important part of the methodology of the policy sciences in the 1970s, and environmental impact assessment followed closely behind. However, the congressionally mandated environmental impact assessments of different weapons systems had relatively little effect on security policy discussions until the prestigious International Council of Scientific Unions (ICSU) stepped in. The three-year study of "nuclear winter" undertaken by the Council's Scientific Committee on Problems of the Environment (SCOPE, 1985–1986) involved interdisciplinary collaboration among scientists on every continent and across all political barriers, and has been widely studied by governments. This study, which made no policy recommendations, nevertheless showed the importance for sound security analysis of bringing together data from a wide variety of disciplines relating to the biosphere, the atmosphere, and the hydrosphere in order to evaluate the impact on the planet and its inhabitants of the use of a given set of weapons systems—in this case, nuclear weapons. Security specialists, who ordinarily focus on short-term outcomes, were compelled by these data to shift their attention to the long-run consequences of military policy.

4. The ICSU example illustrates not only the importance of multidisciplinary impact studies but also the relevance for peace studies of another development: the capability of increasing numbers of international nongov-

ernmental organizations (INGOs) to launch research projects that represent world interests rather than national interests. Shortly after the ICSU study was begun, the International Social Science Council (ISSC) established a multidisciplinary issues group on peace in 1984 to provide for an ongoing effort to stimulate research on peace and conflict. Its first major project was a book on war and its consequences in human communities (Vayrynen 1987) that contains studies from each of the social science disciplines represented in the ISSC. The next step will be collaborative behavioral research among the disciplines.

The work of these scientific INGOs represents only a small part of the efforts being made by the 18,000 INGOs that have evolved since the beginning of this century to pursue a variety of transnational goals including peace, development, and human welfare. Taken together with the 2,000 intergovernmental organizations (IGOs) that have evolved bilaterally and multilaterally to deal with political, social, and environmental problems that cross national borders, and the United Nations system with its globe-spanning infrastructure of specialized agencies and associated organs, they represent an extraordinary transformation in the type of transactions that are now taking place in the international system. The global rise in unilateral military capabilities and an apparent decline in the status of the United Nations must be viewed against this empirical phenonmenon of an ever more closely meshed set of transnational governmental and nongovernmental networks to deal with human problems. The very rise of concepts such as the international information order and the international cultural order, to say nothing of the international economic, security, and environmental orders, reflects new understandings of the resources that the peoples of the 167 self-governing societies of the modern world bring to the challenge of living together on the Earth (Boulding 1988).

None of these developments are adequately accounted for in standard university programs in international relations or security policy. But they are central to peace studies, which examines all forms of contemporary social change in search of peace processes that will work. The nineteen different categories of courses found in this *Curriculum Guide* reflect all those dimensions. They also reflect a commitment to a workable social order for all of humanity.

The fifth edition of *Peace and World Order Studies: A Curriculum Guide* represents the state of the art in teaching in a field with vital contributions to make to international security and peace policy. It will certainly be widely used by faculty and students at many schools—including, I hope, on the campuses of West Point, Annapolis, the Air Force Academy, and in the halls of the U.S. Institute of Peace. It will also be read by university administrators who have the responsibility to allocate resources to programs at their institutions. The time for peace studies is here and now.

References

Boulding, E. (1988). *Building a Global Civic Culture: Education for an Interdependent World*. New York: Teachers College Press.

Forsberg, R. (1984). "The Freeze and Beyond: Confining the Military to Defense as a Route to Disarmament." *World Policy Journal*, Vol. 1.

Scientific Committee on Problems of the Environment (1985–1986). *Environmental Consequences of Nuclear War*, Vol. I; *Physical and Atmospheric Effects*, Vol. II; *Ecological and Agricultural Effects*. Chichester, England: John Wiley & Sons, Ltd.

Sharp, G. (1985). *Making Europe Unconquerable: The Potential of Civilian-Based Deterrence and Defense*. Cambridge: Ballinger Publishing Company.

Vayrynen, R., ed. (1987). *The Quest for Peace: Transcending Collective Violence and War Among Societies, Cultures and States*. London and Beverly Hills, California: Sage Publications Ltd. Published for the International Social Science Council.

II

Perspectives on the Curricular Agenda

1. The Evolution of Peace Studies

Carolyn M. Stephenson
University of Hawaii–Manoa

Peace studies is commonly defined as the systematic interdisciplinary study of the causes of war and the conditions of peace. It arose as an academic field in the aftermath of World War II, for many of the same reasons that the field of international relations had started in the aftermath of World War I. This paper will argue that there have been three distinct "waves" of peace studies. The field was initially developed during the 1950s and early 1960s, primarily at research institutes and a few graduate schools. In the early 1970s, following the Vietnam War and the civil rights movement in the United States, the second wave of peace studies began to focus on the development of undergraduate education. With the third wave, in the 1980s, the field can be said to have come of age, with a massive increase in both undergraduate and graduate programs, and a massive expansion of private and state funding for research and education in the field.

Despite differences of opinion within the field on important topics such as the nature of "peace," there is general agreement that peace studies is interdisciplinary, international, and policy oriented—that is, intended to have some impact on the real-life political environment of both policymakers and peace movements. While both peace research and peace studies are inter-disciplinary, peace *research* is concentrated largely within the social sciences, having begun with a positivistic, behavioral data-based approach to the study of conflict and having later expanded to embrace a wide variety of research methods. Peace *studies* (which is generally defined in the United States to include both research and education), on the other hand, has a broader disciplinary base, drawing on all of the social sciences, as well as history, anthropology, psychology, philosophy, physics, biology, religion, art, linguistics, and other fields.

Peace studies courses and programs often have titles that suggest the differentiation within the field, and the relationship of the central core of peace studies to other fields. Thus, in addition to just "peace studies," they include "peace and security studies" (or global or world security studies), "peace and justice studies," "peace and world order studies," "peace and global studies," "peace and conflict studies," and "peace and conflict resolution studies." Even though most would agree that the central core of peace studies includes the study of peace as the absence of violence, there is disagreement as to what constitutes "peace" and "violence." While it is not the province of this paper to analyze each of the various approaches to peace studies, a basic recounting of this debate is necessary for understanding the historical evolution of the field. (Other essays, as well as an examination of the syllabi provided in this book, will illustrate the variety of approaches.)

Debates on "Peace"

Probably the most significant division in the field of peace studies concerns the definition of peace. The major debate has been whether to define peace simply as the absence of war (often called "negative peace") or whether the concept encompasses both the absence of war and the presence of social and economic justice (often called "positive peace"). Those who argue that peace should be defined narrowly hold that broadening the concept reduces its clarity; those who favor the broader conception argue that the violent life-threatening characteristics of various forms of systemic repression and underdevelopment often approach or exceed that of overt warfare. Just as there is no consensus in political science regarding the concepts of "power" or "politics," the disagreement in peace studies over the central object of our study contributes to the vitality of the inquiry.

To some degree this division in peace studies can be traced geographically: In northern Europe and much of the Third World, the concept of positive peace is more widely accepted; in the United States, a larger number of peace researchers limit their inquiry to negative peace. The two individual researchers most often associated with the poles of this debate are Johan Galtung (1975) of Norway, who is credited with inventing the term "positive peace" in the mid-1960s, and Kenneth Boulding (1977) of the United States, among whose "twelve friendly quarrels" with Galtung include this one.

In practice, however, there is probably more consensus than this conceptual schism would seem to suggest. For example, few scholars would contest the argument that there is a relationship between the absence of war and the presence of other social values such as justice and freedom, even if we cannot articulate those relationships precisely in a general theory acceptable to the whole of the field. Also, most would not be satisfied with a notion of peace that did not imply some degree of long-term stability. As Karl Deutsch put it, a security-community is one in which there are "dependable expectations of peaceful change" for the foreseeable future (1957, p. 5). Similarly, in advocating the "negative peace" definition, Herbert Kelman includes in that definition "the absence of systematic, large-scale collective violence, accompanied by a sense of security that such violence is improbable" (1981, p. 103). Although he makes the case that peace as "the preservation of human life and the avoidance of violence and destruction are *extremely high values*" in their own right (p. 105), he also sees justice as having a strong bearing on the feasibility, stability, universality, and quality of peace (p. 109).

If one accepts Kelman's definition, as well as his ancillary advice that the study even of negative peace requires also the study of justice, as this author suspects the majority of the field does, then one is left with the notion that peace studies as a field must focus its teaching and research on the various possible relationships between "negative" and "positive" peace, rather than being doctrinaire in definitional matters. In the end, it may be clearer to *define* peace as the absence of organized violence; but to limit one's study to this formulation alone would not be productive in advancing either the theory or the practice of the field.

A final important point of definition regards the inevitability and the desirability of conflict. By and large, peace researchers reject the commonly shared public definition of peace as the absence or suppression of conflict. Rather, they accept conflict (which, of course, is not the same as violence) as a normal part of human life and international relations. The challenge for peace analysts is to determine how to manage and resolve conflict in ways that reduce the possibility or the level of violence without diminishing other values, such as justice or freedom.

Distinctions Between Peace Studies and Its Sister Fields

It is important to clarify some of the characteristics that separate peace studies from other closely related fields such as security studies, international relations, and conflict resolution. In fact, some would argue that these areas are totally different from peace studies, while others would argue that one is a branch of the other. These arguments aside, there are at least five features of peace studies that distinguish it from the "sister" fields: (1) Peace studies generally focuses on the security of the whole international or global system, while security studies scholars tend to focus on the security of a single state or alliance. (2) Peace studies covers the full continuum of violent versus peaceful activity (from the individual to the group to the global level), with the primary emphasis at the group and global levels, while international relations focuses on relations between states, and conflict resolution focuses primarily on individual and group conflict, usually in the domestic arena. (3) Peace studies tends to focus on a longer time period than international relations. Whereas the study of international relations generally covers the period since the creation of the nation-state system in 1648, peace studies goes both further back in history and further "forward" through a systematic study of the future. Accordingly, international relations accepts the nation-state and the existing international system as givens whose fundamentals are unalterable, while peace studies examines as well a wide variety of potential alternative world order systems, centralized and decentralized, hierarchical and nonhierarchical. (4) Peace studies incorporates the social sciences, the humanities, and the natural and physical sciences, while international relations tends to be limited to the social sciences, and especially to political science. (5) Peace studies is explicitly policy oriented in the sense that it aspires to describe, explain, and recommend policy relating to the conditions of peace to both governments and social movements, while a substantial number of those in international relations see themselves as limited to description and explanation. (6) Finally, peace studies is value-explicit, while in international relations research, values tend to be more hidden; indeed, some international relations scholars still claiming that research can be "value-free," a conception that most of the sciences have rejected for more than a decade. The most notable consequence of this difference is that the dominant paradigm in international relations tends, at least in practice, to be more accepting of the utility of coercive power and threat systems than is peace studies. The value of conflict, integration, disintegration, equality, justice, freedom, and the relative trade-offs between these factors, as well as the appropriateness of various methods for achieving those valued positively, are widely debated within as well as between both fields.

The Origins of Peace Research and Peace Studies

The origins of peace research can be traced as far back as the writings of Thomas Hobbes and John Locke, if not to Plato and Thucydides. Hobbes' characterization of war as originating from a combination of the greed and equality of human beings, with the solution being a social contract dependent on the creation of authoritative institutions, has been a thread in both realist and idealist strands of peace research ever since. A second equally important strand in the field has been informed by Locke's assertion of the right of popular revolution against the tyranny of authoritarian institutions. For the purposes of this discussion, however, the origins of peace research as a separate field of inquiry are more productively traced within the twentieth century only. One can discern three primary waves of peace studies since its emergence between the two world wars.

The First Wave

Quincy Wright and Lewis Richardson are widely considered the forefathers of modern peace research. Working independently in the United States and the United Kingdom in the 1930s, they were among the first to do quantitative analyses of war. Believing that the outbreak of war was due largely to policymakers' ignorance of what might be the consequences of their decisions, Wright and Richardson both concluded that improving and then evaluating the relevant knowledge base was a necessary part of dealing with the problem of war.

Wright, in his analysis of the causes of war, found that each of six great wars over the course of more than twelve centuries showed a combination of idealistic, political, psychological, and juridical causes. Richardson looked at the attributes of nation-states (among other factors), and found that homogeneity in culture, language, and religion did not preclude the occurrence of war among them. Richardson's and Wright's analyses, like the more sociologically and culturally based theories of Pitrim Sorokin in the 1920s, did much to illuminate the motives for initiating war—both for men and for states—and the attributes of states and the relationships between them that lead to war.

Peace studies as an academic field really began in earnest in the late 1940s and early 1950s with the establishment of two groundbreaking research institutes. In France, the Institut Français de Polaemologie was founded in 1945 by a number of individuals, including Bert Roling, a well-known international jurist who considered polymologie (war research) essential to the development of international law. In the same year, Theodore Lentz founded the Lentz Peace Research Laboratory in St. Louis, Missouri, to encourage the mobilization of social scientists for the development of a science of peace. A letter published in April 1951 by Athur Gladstone and Herbert Kelman in the *American Psychologist*, arguing that pacifist challenges to the assumptions underlying conventional foreign policy deserved the systematic attention of psychologists, led in 1952 to the formation of the Research Exchange on the Prevention of War and its *Bulletin*. In 1954–1955, Kelman joined Anatol Rapaport, Kenneth Boulding, and Stephen Richardson (the son of Lewis Richardson) as the first group of Fellows at the Center for Advanced Studies in the Behavioral Sciences at Stanford. This pioneering group was made aware of the writings of the elder Richardson and arranged for their dissemination. It also split the functions of the Research Exchange and reestablished the prewar Society for the Psychological Study of Social Issues (SPSSI). They also replaced the *Bulletin* with the more formal *Journal of Conflict Resolution: A Quarterly for Research Related to War and Peace*, which began publication in 1957 at the University of Michigan (where both Rapaport and Boulding were then located). The Center for Research on Conflict Resolution and the Correlates of War Project were also organized at Michigan to examine some of the systemic factors thought to be associated with the frequency, severity, magnitude, and intensity of war.

Several prominent centers for peace research were founded in 1959. A Peace Research Institute was established in Dundas, Canada, by Hannah and Alan Newcombe to conduct studies in the negative peace tradition; it now publishes *Peace Research Reviews* and *Peace Research Abstracts*. In Norway, the Peace Research Institute Oslo (now known as PRIO) was established by Johan Galtung as part of the Institute of Social Research. It became independent in 1966. In the late 1960s, the radical critique of peace research and Galtung's concept of "positive peace" were predominant at PRIO, constituting a central focus of its *Journal of Peace Research* (JPR), which began publication in 1964. *JPR* was later joined by the *Bulletin of Peace Proposals*, designed to publish more short-term analyses and policy prescriptions. In Britain, the Lancaster Peace Research Centre, which later became the Richardson Institute for Peace Studies, was also formed in 1959. The other major center founded at this time was the Stockholm International Peace Research Institute (SIPRI), established in 1966 and still noted for its research and publications on armaments and disarmament.

International organizations of peace researchers also arose at this time. The Peace Research Society (International), which now prefers the term "peace science," was set up at a meeting in Sweden in 1963 by Walter Izard of the United States. The Polemological Institute at the University of Groningen in the Netherlands, established in 1961, became the first site of the International Peace Research Association (IPRA) when it was founded in 1964. IPRA, which is now regarded as the major international professional organization in the field of peace research, meets every two years in different regions of the world and publishes selected *Proceedings* of those meetings as well as a *Newsletter*.

National associations of peace researchers also came into being. The Conference (now Council) on Peace Research in History (CPRH) was formed at the December 1963 meeting of the American Historical Association, following the assassination of John F. Kennedy and the beginning of heavy U.S. involvement in the Indochina war. Another, more fundamental, inspiration for the establishment of CPRH was the realization by many historians that their discipline had tended to focus on war to the exclusion of social movements against war. In 1972, CPRH began publishing the journal *Peace and Change*, which is now cosponsored by the Consortium on Peace Research, Education, and Development (COPRED). The Canadian Peace Research and Education Association was formed in 1966.

The Second Wave

The second wave of peace studies, which arose in the late 1960s and early 1970s, can be understood as the democratization of peace research. In Europe, the reaction to the Vietnam War led to the development of critical or radical peace research, and in the United States it led to peace education. In contrast to the first wave of peace studies, which consisted primarily of peace research (with a touch of education at the graduate level), the second generation emphasized peace education, especially at the undergraduate level. Peace researchers came to realize that their research had relevance for the undergraduate curriculum, and even more so for the troubled campuses of the Vietnam era.

The first undergraduate peace studies program in the United States had been established in 1948 at Manchester College in Indiana, but it was not until the early 1970s that a significant number of peace studies programs were created at colleges and universities. Among the earliest to do so was Colgate University, where the first chair in Peace Studies in the United States was created in 1971. Other early programs were established at Bethel College, Earlham College, Gustavus Adolphus College, Manhattan College, Kent State University, Syracuse University, and the University of Akron. As with the Manchester program, many of the early programs began in small church-affiliated liberal arts colleges. Supporting these developments were two organizations: the Institute for World Order (now known as the World Policy Institute), established in 1966, which published the first four editions of this *Curriculum Guide* and now publishes two journals in the field, *Alternatives* and *World Policy Journal*); and COPRED, founded in 1970. In England, the first chair in peace studies was established in 1973 at the University of Bradford, offering both graduate and undergraduate programs.

Unlike the educational efforts of the 1950s and 1960s, including programs at Northwestern University, Stanford, and Yale in the United States, and Lund, Gothenburg, and Uppsala in Sweden, the new programs of the 1970s were primarily oriented toward undergraduate teaching rather than toward research and specialized graduate training. By the end of the 1970s, there were more than 100 institutions in the United States with curricula in peace studies (some with full majors), up from only a handful at the beginning of the decade.

Along with educational programs, more national and international associations were established during this period. COPRED was established in 1970 to link peace research, peace education, and peace action, and to meet the needs of both policymakers and peace movements in the United States and Canada. The Peace Education Commission of IPRA was founded in 1973 to make peace research more accessible by combining a participatory—action—research tradition with an emphasis on process, on experiential learning, and on democratic pedagogy. In the United States, professional academic organizations such as the International Studies Association and the American Sociological Association began to form subsections on peace studies. Several regional scholarly organizations were also formed during this period, such as the Latin American Council on Peace Research (CLAIP), headquartered in Mexico, and the Asian Peace Research Association (APRA), formed in 1974 and headquartered in Japan. While the quantitative and behavioral approach continued to be important in peace research, other research traditions took their places beside it and peace education joined peace research as an important component of the field.

The Third Wave
The phase of peace studies that began in the 1980s is, in one sense, the culmination of earlier phases; in another sense, it constitutes a different phenomenon. In this phase, the impetus for innovation did not come so much from within the peace studies community as from widespread public

concern over the nuclear arms race. Because many college faculty and administrators shared these concerns, there arose during the 1980s a large number of undergraduate and graduate-level programs focused more specifically on questions of nuclear war and superpower relations than on the broader questions that peace studies had examined before. As they have evolved, some of these programs, including that of the Five Colleges, have incorporated into their curricular agenda many of the structural, cultural, and psychological inquiries common to peace research. They have also begun to identify themselves with the broader peace studies community.

Other programs, such the Institute on Global Conflict and Cooperation (the statewide program of the University of California), have explicitly excluded such issues from their mandate, concentrating instead on problems more directly related to the prevention of nuclear war. Only where non-superpower conflicts in the Third World show a risk of escalation to a nuclear "third world war" are they considered relevant for study under this definition of peace studies. In fact, however, most peace researchers in the United States do not limit themselves to this nuclear war–prevention approach, which they would consider more closely associated with national security studies or strategic studies than with peace research.

A second component of this third wave has been the tremendous increase in the study of third-party conflict resolution, or mediation. Supported by several large foundations, a number of universities have initiated programs of research and education, for the most part beginning at the graduate or post-graduate level and then extending slowly into the undergraduate curricula. Although conflict resolution is considered by some to be a sister field to peace studies rather than part of the peace studies core, it has had a strong influence on peace studies, and many programs now incorporate it into their curricula.

Institutions with leading programs in this area include the Program on Negotiation, a consortium of Boston-area projects based at the Harvard Law School, and programs at the Universities of Colorado, Hawaii, Michigan, Minnesota, Syracuse, Wisconsin, and at George Mason and Syracuse Universities, among others. Some of these are located in law schools while others are interdisciplinary programs. The National Institute for Dispute Resolution (NIDR) has helped to develop and monitor curricula in this area, especially in law school–based programs. Although many conflict resolution programs focus largely on individual or domestic conflict, some, including those at Colorado, Hawaii, and Syracuse, define more explicitly the linkages between conflict resolution and peace studies. For example, The University of Hawaii has both a Program on Conflict Resolution and an Institute for Peace, both formed in 1985, with linkages between the fields including an M.A. in Peacemaking and Conflict Resolution. The object of the National Conference on Peacemaking and Conflict Resolution (NCPCR), which held its first conference in 1982, was to link conflict resolution with other parts of the field, and to link professional conflict resolvers with researchers and educators.

A third important influence on the curricular and research dimensions of peace studies in the 1980s has been the new inquiry into alternative international security systems, and into the related but previously neglected area, the conditions of peace. As nonviolent struggles took place in Poland and the Philippines, and to some degree in Iran, researchers began to devote new attention both to nonviolence and to transarmament, or the process of transition from violent to nonviolent struggle. One of the leaders in this area is Gene Sharp's Program on Nonviolent Sanctions in Conflict and Defense at Harvard, which was established more than a decade earlier. The aggravation of European security concerns through the deployment of Pershing, cruise, and SS-20 missiles led researchers first in Western Europe, and later in Eastern Europe and the United States to explore concepts of "nonoffensive" or "defensive defense." Among the earliest was the Alternative Defence Commission, housed at the University of Bradford School of Peace Studies in the United Kingdom. This commission was joined later in the United States by a Working Group on Alternative Defense initiated by Randall Forsberg's Institute for Defense and Disarmament Studies (IDDS) in Boston and by the broader-focused Exploratory Project on the Conditions of Peace (EXPRO), located at Boston College. A distinction must be made between work on *alternative defense* and work on *alternative security*, as the latter has a much broader agenda. These areas of study have just begun to join the well-researched "causes of war" themes as central issues for curricula.

A fourth noteworthy trend of peace studies in the 1980s is the sudden burst of government-sponsored institutions and educational initiatives. The states of California, Hawaii, New Jersey, Ohio, and Wisconsin, and the government of New Zealand, among many others, have begun to support peace education. National institutes have been formed: the Austrian Peace Research Institute (1983), the Canadian Institute for Peace and International Security (1984), the Australian Peace Research Centre (1984), the U.S. Institute of Peace (1984), and the Scientific Research Council on Peace and Development in the Soviet Union (1979), followed by similar councils in Bulgaria (1981) and Hungary (1982), and a Peace Research unit in the Academy of Sciences in Czechoslovakia (1982). The United Nations also participated in founding a University for Peace in San Jose, Costa Rica.

College faculty, too, have begun to take more direct responsibility for the institutional and intellectual progress of the field. In the United States, regional consortia have begun to proliferate, with Indiana, Hawaii, New England, New York, Ohio, Oregon, and Wisconsin among the first. In 1987, a group of directors of college and university peace studies programs met at the University of California at Irvine to establish the Peace Studies Association (PSA). Articulated as "An Organization of College and University Academic Programs for the Study of Peace, Conflict, Justice, and Global Security" and based at Bethel College, PSA seeks to support the further development of the field by providing resources and advice to new faculty and by making other efforts to enhance the academic quality of all programs.

This trend toward the institutionalization of peace studies brings with it both old debates and new strengths.

Evaluating the Evolution

It is now clear that peace studies is not a passing fad, but an important and thriving part of the academic landscape. What is not clear is how the field will continue to evolve. Suffice it to say that while all would agree that there is an intellectual core to the field that centers on the causes and prevention of war, there remains severe disagreement as to what the outer boundaries of the field should be.

It is our questions, rather than our answers, that best define the academic field of peace studies today—as is true of any healthy field of inquiry. In truth, we do not yet know whether arms races will continue to lead to war, or whether they are the best way to avoid war in a nuclear age. We have no firm evidence of whether military strength leads to peace or war. We have conflicting evidence as to whether individual aggression is related to group violence, or domestic violence to international violence. We do not know whether Hobbes, Lenin, and Eisenhower were correct in identifying human greed, imperialism, and the military-industrial complex, respectively, as the major cause of war. Nor do we know whether certain kinds of political regimes or organizational systems are more or less prone to repression or violence or war; there is contradictory evidence as to whether democracies do or do not go to war less often than other types of regimes. There is little evidence to tell us whether tearing down highly centralized state bureaucracies will reduce exploitation, repression, violence, and war or lead us into a Hobbesian state of anarchic violence. We do not yet know what role male, female, and other individual differences play in determining propensities toward violence.

In other words, all our research—on decisionmaking theory, on bureaucratic and systems theory, on international law and organization, on social movements, on conflict and third-party conflict resolution, on nonviolent struggle and sanctions, on nonoffensive defense and other alternative security systems, on human rights and development—has not yet given us unassailable answers to the problems of violence and war. What we *do* know is that these inquiries address important questions that merit further research and teaching.

The maintenance of creative tensions and diversity in the field is the sign of a healthy, growing process of inquiry. At some point attempts will likely be made to define the subject matter, processes, and purpose of the field in such a way as to include some elements of this diversity and to exclude others. Such an attempt would probably weaken the field; there is intellectual and organic strength in the maintenance of diversity—disciplinary diversity, diversity in process, pedagogy, paradigm, and purpose, as well as diversity in orientation to various constituencies and to the short versus the long term. To a large extent, it is the confrontations of ideology with ideology, methodology with methodology, and disciplinary paradigm with disciplinary paradigm that provide intellectual strength to the field of peace studies. Linkages do need to be made between parts of the field, but the development of a single unified field of inquiry would probably lead peace studies away from its original purposes, and we would need to recreate it with another name.

References and Bibliography

Alternative Defence Commission (1983). *Defence Without the Bomb.* London: Taylor and Francis.

Boulding, Kenneth (1977). "Twelve Friendly Quarrels with Johan Galtung." *Journal of Peace Research*, Vol. 14, pp. 75–86.

Chatfield, Charles (1979). "International Peace Research: The Field Defined by Dissemination." *Journal of Peace Research*, Vol. 16, No. 2, pp. 161–179.

Dedring, Juergen (1976). *Recent Advances in Peace and Conflict Research.* Beverly Hills, Calif.: Sage.

Deutsch, Karl (1957). *Political Community and the North Atlantic Area.* Princeton, N.J.: Princeton University Press.

Galtung, Johan (1975). *Essays in Peace Research*, Vol. 1. Copenhagen: Christian Ejlers.

Kelman, Herbert C. (1981). "Reflections on the History and Status of Peace Research." *Conflict Management and Peace Science*, Vol. 5, No. 2 (Spring), pp. 95–110.

Korany, Bahgat (1986). "Strategic Studies and the Third World. *International Social Science Journal*, Vol. 35, No. 4, pp. 547–562.

Mack, Andrew (1985). *Peace Research in the 1980s.* Canberra: Australian National University.

Richardson, Lewis F. (1960). *Statistics of Deadly Quarrels.* Pittsburgh, Pa.: Boxwood.

Sharp, Gene (1985). *Making Europe Unconquerable.* Cambridge, Mass.: Ballinger Publishing Co.

Singer, J. David (1981). "Accounting for International War: The State of the Discipline." *Journal of Peace Research*, Vol. 18, No. 1.

Stephenson, Carolyn M., ed. (1982). *Alternative Methods for International Security.* Washington, D.C.: University Press of America.

Varis, Tapio. "Introduction," in Liparit Kiuzadjan, Herberta Hogeweg-de Haart, and Werner Richter, eds. (1986). *Peace Research: A Documentation of Current Research.* Moscow: European Coordination Centre for Research and Documentation in the Social Sciences.

Wiberg, Hakan (1983). "The Peace Research Movement," paper delivered at the Tenth General Conference of IPRA, Gyor, Hungary.

Wright, Quincy (1965). *A Study of War*, 2 vols. Chicago: University of Chicago Press, revised edition (originally published in 1942).

2. Pedagogical Approaches to Peace Studies

Betty Reardon
Columbia University

The field of peace studies has come a long way since the first editions of this *Curriculum Guide* were published in the mid-1970s. However, despite numerous scholarly conferences on the nature of the field and nearly two decade's experience with establishing programs and designing curricula, relatively little attention has been paid to the *pedagogy* of peace studies— that is, to its learning goals and teaching methods.

This essay is an attempt to encourage more intentional and systematic consideration of the pedagogy of peace studies by examining what I consider to be the major current approaches in terms of substance, purposes, and teaching practices. Most curricula, including peace studies courses and programs, are heavily influenced by the world views of the practitioners. With this in mind, I have identified three broad approaches to the pedagogy of peace studies, which I classify as *reformist, reconstructionist,* and *transformational.*

While each approach has political significance in that it seeks to enable students to make informed judgments on policy matters, none, when responsibly practiced, advocates particular political positions. All, however, do assume that the various forms of international violence are problems on which academic institutions should focus in both research and teaching. In posing the questions for student research and study, the world view, values, and assumptions of the instructor are crucial. Just as most peace studies practitioners advocate the development of student awareness of political choices as an educational goal of the field, I believe that developing consciousness of one's own world view is an important professional goal for educators and a fundamental starting point in curriculum planning. Only through integrating such self-awareness into the curriculum planning and teaching processes can we honestly hope to offer students an authentically open inquiry into the issues about which they should be forming their own critical consciousness.

The common assumptions of peace studies are subject to various interpretations and stem from somewhat different assumptions. Some reflections on these differences are offered below in the hope that all peace educators and peace studies advocates will question them as they plan courses and programs.

Although my own assumptions and purposes incline more toward one of these approaches than to the other two, I do not hold any to be superior to the other. Each can be equally effective if it is appropriate to the needs of the students and consistent with the substantive and normative purposes of the instructor. The point here is to try *to direct attention toward as much intentionality in the selection and development of approaches and methods as is exercised in that of content.*

It also bears noting that these three categories are not precisely distinct one from another, nor is it possible or even desirable to categorize particular peace studies courses or programs within one of them to the complete exclusion of the other two. They are, as indicated, only general approaches intended to provoke further discussion. And because, for reasons of length, these descriptions will be based solely on approaches to *negative peace* (i.e., the prevention and elimination of war), this brief essay will not deal fully with the pedagogical implications of other topics represented in this *Curriculum Guide* related to the concept of *positive peace* (i.e., the conditions of social justice, economic well-being, democratic participation, and ecological balance).

As John Hurst argues in his article on pedagogy in the *World Encyclopedia of Peace*, all branches of peace studies have as their ultimate educational purpose making a contribution "to a peaceful and just world that can be sustained over time."[1] Each of the three approaches outlined here can be identified by its assumptions about the causes of war (and, in the case of "positive peace," about the causes of poverty, oppression, and ecological damage), its inclinations toward particular types of solutions, its assumptions about the normative and political changes needed to achieve that goal, its sources of knowledge, and its learning objectives.

The Reformist Approach

The earliest and most widely practiced approach to peace studies is identified, for the purposes of this essay, as "reformist." Its social and political goals are policy changes intended to prevent war and reverse the arms race. These purposes incline this approach to concentrate on the problems and possibilities of arms control, conflict resolution, and other forms of behavioral change.

The most significant potential for behavioral change is deemed to lie with the views and actions of nation-state elites. Among such changes would be a reduced reliance on the threat and use of force to achieve political and economic purposes in the international system, and the emergence of a tendency to rely more on negotiation, international institutions, and political solutions to international conflict. Concomitant, supportive, and perhaps impelling attitudinal changes among the citizenry are also sought.

Attitudes of tolerance and understanding, as well as a more profound knowledge of cultural and ideological differences and of the causes of conflict, are seen as vital to this process—and education is directed accordingly. A knowledge of international institutions and international law, and a critical understanding of foreign policy and security issues (including official policy and alternatives proposed by citizen activists), are also considered essential.

The learning goals of the reformist approach derive from some general assumptions about the causes of war, the frequency of military actions, and the dynamics of arms races. The causal factors are seen to lie mainly in the behaviors of the international actors, influenced by misinformed policies, flawed ideologies, hypernationalism, and unchecked impulses toward aggression. These causes in turn are often seen as conditioned by distortion of positive concepts such as independence, freedom, and patriotism, or by adherence to such negative values as ethnocentricism and imperialism.

The knowledge base from which "reformist" curricula seek to derive an understanding of these causes and a capacity for reflection on proposed solutions is to be found, for the most part, in the social sciences (particularly policy sciences) and in some of the other traditional disciplines that can be adapted to the educational purposes of peace studies.[2] Insights from the relevant disciplines are brought to bear on the problems of war, conflict, and aggression in a multidisciplinary fashion. Where this approach characterizes an entire academic program, virtually every discipline featured in the curriculum can offer a course in peace studies, thus illustrating the relevance of peace studies to the traditional disciplines and its adaptability to traditional forms of pedagogy.

The traditional university teaching methods of reading, reflection, lecture, and discussion adapt very well to reformist assumptions about the significance of information to changing attitudes and world views. Reformist peace studies, in fact, shares with most social education the assumption that ignorance is a major cause of social and political problems. Because these curricula emphasize the importance of well-informed policy choices and often rely on information that is not widely available, increased student proficiency in gathering and weighing evidence and analyzing arguments are pursued. Students are also encouraged to apply relevant ethical and normative criteria to the analysis of policy alternatives. This process is not in any way divergent from the fundamental purpose of liberal education, but it does augment and specify its goals so as to make them more relevant to responsible citizenship in the nuclear age. Finally, given the nature of contemporary warfare and the costs of preparation for war, this educational process is intended to lead to citizen action. Indeed, preparation for empowerment and action on global problems is a common goal of all approaches to peace studies.

The Reconstructionist Approach

The "reconstructionist" approach considers the reconstruction of the international system as a *sine qua non* to the achievement of a just and lasting peace. In practice, this approach tends to consider some of the "reformist" solutions as desirable transition steps toward a reconstructed world system. However, overcoming patterns of militarization inextricably linked to the arms race are deemed impossible without the eventual obsolescence of the military option, and such obsolescence is deemed to require drastic changes in the structures and processes that determine international security matters. Indeed, some who embrace the reconstructionist approach project the ultimate goal as a significant limitation of national sovereignty in relation to international conflict and security. Sovereignty is seen as a major obstacle to the development of the global institutions needed for peacekeeping and peacemaking. Greater emphasis is placed on systemic questions than on the behavior of individuals or individual governments because their actions are understood to be substantially constrained by more profound systems and structures. Still, individual attitudinal and value changes are considered by most reconstructionists to be essential prerequisites to structural change.

The knowledge base upon which reconstructionist curricula are built includes much from critical peace research and futures research, some of it in an admittedly utopian vein. In addition, the traditional disciplines and policy sciences are adapted to pursuing an inquiry into the characteristics of a truly just and peaceful world society, into the kinds of structural changes most necessary to realize such a society, and into the pragmatic strategies for implementing them.

This form of inquiry problematizes the obstacles to achieving the preferred world structures so that the substance of much reconstructionist curricula is based upon a global problematique involving issues of war and conflict as well as the interrelated problems of poverty and development, repression and social justice, resource depletion and ecological balance. All of these problems are seen to be interconnected and fundamentally rooted in inadequate and unjust international structures. The policy sciences and traditional disciplines are applied to the study of problems in an interdisciplinary, global, problem-centered manner rather than in the multidisciplinary issue-oriented fashion favored by the reformist approach. Reconstructionist course designs often focus on a particular global problem (e.g., disarmament) or problematique (e.g., international security) and include materials from various disciplines as well as from peace research.

The learning objectives of the reconstructionist approach tend to emphasize capacities for involvement in structural change. Teaching methods involve extensive structural analyses and often employ simulation exercises based on proposals for alternative security systems or models for preferred world orders.[3] The most specific pedagogical method of the reconstructionist approach is derived from world order models research, moving from problem diagnoses through the projection of a preferred system to consideration of transition strategies. This approach often also involves students in their own world order modeling projects and research into preferred futures, as well as in various forms of action research and experiential learning.

The Transformational Approach

The most recent and most comprehensive of the three peace studies teaching approaches described here is the "transformational" one. It espouses as its overarching goal nothing short of profound cultural change. This approach puts equal emphasis on behavioral and structural change, but it views as the most essential development a transformation of consciousness, asserting that the fundamental causes of violence, war, and oppression lie in the way we think. Only through fundamental changes in values and modes of thinking, this approach posits, can we achieve a comprehensive global peace that rejects all forms of violence and coercive authority in favor of a social order held together by communal values and consensual politics.

In the view of transformationalists, contemporary human consciousness is deeply conditioned by rationalism and reductionism, and is therefore not capable of grasping the full complexity of the problems that produce war and violence. Thus we tend to deal with these problems in discrete components, more often addressing symptoms rather than fundamentals. As seen by the transformationalists, the consciousness that perpetuates war is one that views human beings as being aggressive and greedy, and accordingly has produced a fabric of political and economic systems and personal and social relations characterized by competition, threat, and, not infrequently, violent conflict.

The knowledge base from which a transformational approach to peace studies derives its curricula is both catholic and iconclastic. As the task deals with changing human thinking, it delves into the critical literature of all relevant disciplines. Although it employs traditional modes of inquiry where appropriate, it is not bound by them. With its heavy emphasis on the creation of new knowledge, it inclines toward trandisciplinarity, synthesizing and extending established scholarly methods and, where necessary, inventing new ones. It makes use of such innovations as macro-history, feminist scholarship, human ecology, process theology, and action research in developing its content and pedagogy.

The transformational approach uses traditional and radical teaching methods, along with other innovative learning designs. Standard forms are combined with experiential, communal, and cooperative learning. Skills of analysis are balanced by those of interpretation, and there is a strong tendency toward praxis and holistic learning. The students' experiences are reflected upon, and the experiences of those in other systems and cultures are interpolated into a curriculum that considers the human as well as the structural and political dimensions of the problems under study.

The primary learning goals pursued through the transformational approach are (1) awareness of the significance of consciousness and culture to problems of structure and policy, and (2) the development of capacities to bring about social and cultural change. Such capacities involve the valuing and analytic skills pursued in the reformist approach, the projections and design skills of the reconstructionist approach, and—the most prized skill of the transformationists—a creative imagination that views problems as tasks and issues and policies as components of a total process for achieving the most fundamental change.

Commonalities in Instruction and Teaching

It was postulated at the outset of this essay that the pedagogic styles of all three approaches are heavily influenced by the normative purposes of the inquiry and by the analytical framework in which the inquiry is conducted. To the extent that observation is accurate, each of the generalized approaches suggests a different pedagogy. Before examining the differences among those pedagogical styles, however, we must identify some of their fundamental similarities.

The most widely shared aspects of a peace studies pedagogy are the emphases on values clarification and analysis, and the prominence of participatory modes of learning. By and large, the field rejects most of the traditional notions about value-free social science, choosing instead to define and assess explicitly the values inherent not only in all policies and data bases but also in the perspectives from which they are examined, including that of the instructor. When a teacher acknowledges his or her own normative perspective, and encourages students to identify the perspectives, assumptions, and values of all sources being applied in the course of study, students more readily learn how to weigh evidence objectively and to develop their own critical capacities.

The point, of course, is not to convince students of any particular perspective but, rather, to facilitate a more honest exploration of the topics under study and to encourage explicit consideration of the purposes of the inquiry. Teachers using this approach are especially responsible for presenting material from a range of perspectives and for creating a classroom environment open to consideration of any and all students' beliefs.

Lectures are still used by most peace educators to present concepts and data. However, participatory modes of learning such as dialogue and discourse are considered by many to be a more effective instructional method. Given the "applied" nature of peace studies, its practitioners have always been among those who advocate "learning by doing" as one of the most effective routes to understanding and empowerment. This preference has many manifestations, including independent research projects, internships related to classroom material, and student-led courses, the latter two of which are discussed in other essays in this volume.

Pedagogical Distinctions: Various Teaching Styles

While most peace studies are normative and participatory, there are some pedagogical distinctions among the three approaches that attest to the range and diversity of the field and stand as evidence of the rich methodological possibilities to be explored. One area in which such differences can be seen is the conduct of the participatory classroom, where various styles of discussion characterize the three approaches. The exemplars described here refer to the particular modes that appear to be emphasized by each, which I define as "dialogue," "discourse," and "conversation."

In many cases, the responsibility of scholarship to clarify and deepen analysis requires that the discussion mode tends to be "dialogic" or "socratic," whereby students may question and exchange ideas with each other, but the essential flow of dialogue is between student and teacher, and the central questions are posed by the teacher. This teaching mode is especially common in the classes pursuing the "reformist" approach, due to both its *multi-disciplinary* nature and its reliance on the substance and methods of the various disciplines.

In the "discourse" mode, the instructor serves as guide to a wider involvement of students, the purposes being to encourage as much student participation as possible, to explore as many points of view as possible, and to attend to the questions brought to or derived from the inquiry. In addition to the transfer of substance, the discourse is guided so as to deepen the understanding and assessment of various analyses, to ensure that students appreciate underlying assumptions, concepts, and values and how they differ, and to include cultural, gender, or other perspectives often excluded from the exploration of social and political issues. It therefore involves more student-to-student interaction. As this discourse style lends itself well to examination of alternative international structures, it is frequently practiced within the approach to peace studies earlier labeled "reconstructive."

In the "conversational" mode, the inquiry derives from questions posed by the entire group. Each student bears responsibility for her or his own learning and for contributing to that of others. The role of the instructor is primarily that of initiator and "facilitator." This latter role can be rotated among all class members from session to session. In any case, the conversation is assumed to take place among equals. Differences in learning (i.e., experience, age, expertise) will enrich the conversation; but when differences are mediated in ways that permit more influence of one participant over others, they limit the potential breadth of learning that occurs when all contribute equally. This mode is most characteristic of the transdisciplinary inquiry of the transformational approach, wherein learners from different disciplines search for common questions about the fundamental problems of peace.

Dialogue, discourse, and conversation are but three pedagogical methods among many that need to be more deeply explored and experimented with by all involved with peace studies as we attempt to maximize the appropriateness of our pedagogy to the substance of our field.

Conclusion

Few courses or programs fall completely within the boundaries of any one of the three approaches outlined above. Most, however, are predominantly influenced by the reformist approach. Others combine the reformist and reconstructionist approaches, and a few aspire to be transformational. The importance of these identifications is related not so much to classification as to their usefulness in promoting awareness of assumptions and encouraging intentionality about pedagogy in curriculum planning.

Peace and conflict research have made significant strides in defining the purview of the substantive field. However, the methodologies that help undergraduate students learn how to think about this substance, how to pursue the inquiry, and how to act upon the conclusions of the inquiry are just now becoming a major topic of discourse among academics in the field. The contributions of such educators as John Hurst and Michael Nagler of the University of California–Berkeley and Carol Cohn of the New School for Social Research have been invaluable initial contributions to such discourse.[4]

It is now incumbent upon all peace studies practitioners to become seriously involved in such questions as "What is it that undergraduate students need to know?" as we design course content; "Why do they need to know it?" as we analyze the assumptions that underlie our curricular choices; "How can we help them to learn it?" as we try to devise an effective and relevant pedagogy; and "What should be done in the light of this knowledge?" as we probe the values that lead us, students and teachers, to choose among policy options, alternative structures, and modes of learning.

Notes

1. John Hurst, "A Pedagogy for Peace," *World Encyclopedia of Peace* (New York: Pergamon Press Ltd., 1986).

2. David Johnson, ed., *Education for Justice and Peace* (Maryknoll, N.Y.: Orbis Books, 1985).

3. World Order methodology is discussed in more detail in Betty Reardon, "Transformations in Peace and Survival Programs in the 1970s," in *Education for Peace, Focus on Mankind*, edited by G. Henderson (Washington, D.C.: Association for Supervision and Curriculum Development, 1973).

4. For more information, consult the introductory essay in the Report of the Peace and Conflict Studies Program, University of California, Berkeley, and the text of Carol Cohn's presentation on the pedagogy of peace studies, available from the International Institute on Peace Education, c/o Department of Secondary Education, University of Alberta, Edmonton, Canada.

3. A Values-Based Approach to Peace Studies

Robin J. Crews
Bethel College

The goals of peace studies include, among other things, the pursuit of knowledge about peace and its development. Approaches to the study of peace are as varied as approaches to the pursuit of knowledge in general. In this essay, I develop an approach to the study of peace that is informed by sociological analysis, principles of Gandhian nonviolence, and notions of epistemology.

The Role of Peace Studies in the University

It is sometimes assumed that there is such a thing as purely theoretical learning—learning wherein one investigates reality at the level of theory without affecting reality itself. This assumption (which is closely associated with the Cartesian delineation between mind and matter, and which underlies the belief that learning should not be involved with the application of knowledge, i.e., with social change) contradicts the fact that our familiarity with reality is based upon our perceptions of it. As we comprehend existing symbols or create new theoretical constructs to help explain the world around us, that world changes because our perceptions of it are no longer the same. When a student understands relativity theory in physics, the physical world has changed for that student forever.

Thus all learning contributes in essential ways—some enormous, some minute—to a restructuring of the human experience. Peace studies specifically and intentionally constitutes such learning. It is generally accepted that at the heart of the undergraduate educational process is the goal of learning about the world in which we live. In this way the formal training of the university experience contributes to the universal and ultimate human quest for meaning.

Fundamentally, the role of peace studies in the university is to assist in the human quest for meaning—and to do so in such a way that the world benefits from this search in the process. This quest has many manifestations, including the empirical pursuit of physical "truth" entailing the scientific measurement and interpretation of sensate perceptions; the pursuit of metaphysical "truth" through faith; the search for social linkage by belonging to a community of others; and the elemental process of growth by choosing among alternative futures, both immediate and distant. A key aspect of peace studies is the examination of these images—an enterprise that the field approaches in many diverse ways.

Examining and Challenging Values

Underlying the search for modes of learning that lead to constructive social change and a more peaceful world is a consensus about the inadequacy of present directions—a shared belief that we will not achieve a peaceful world in the future if we continue down the road we are on now. Because the future reality that humanity will create depends upon our *image* of that reality, we must develop new, more humane visions of the future. And because those visions depend upon our culture, a fundamental task for peace studies is the critical examination of our values, beliefs, and assumptions as well as of our hopes and fears, our rituals and our traditions.

The objectives of this examination are liberation from those parochial ideologies and provincial dogmas of the past that prevent us from envisioning and creating a peaceful world, and the development, in their place, of those value constellations that contribute to the full potential of peaceful coexistence in life. The controversial questions about what we leave behind and what we take with us from the past into the future are difficult to formulate and often more difficult to articulate. They are at the heart of peace studies.

Human values—and the methods by which they are shaped—are central to our quest for meaning. We teach them through actions and words, through role modeling, through traditions and rituals. As noted earlier, they underlie our images of meaning, which include, among others, our images of truth, belonging, and choosing.

Images of Truth

In Western scientific culture, we have historically chosen to pursue knowledge about physical reality through the use of scientific methods. This knowledge has often been equated with immutable "Truth." We have also pursued metaphysical dimensions of truth through faith. Both avenues of understanding have contributed much to our larger pursuit of truth. Yet the assumption that these are the only two avenues available to us, and that they are intrinsically antithetical and mutually exclusive of each other, has contributed to a competition for ideological primacy between them—a competition that has persistently hindered the search for truth.

Truth Through Science. The assumptions that objectivity is an achievable goal, that the pursuit of knowledge is *a priori* beneficial, that value-neutrality is possible, that "Truth" can be discovered through the scientific pursuit of knowledge in the physical world, that scientific inquiry can exist in a vacuum apart from social reality, that increased material well-being is an inevitable result of economic and technological growth, and that it is inherently useful and appropriate to seek technological solutions to social problems—these are all tenets of the social institution of science that contemporary society has come to accept and demand as it waits passively for its scientists to solve the problems that loom ever larger on our ecological and economic horizons.

These assumptions of the Newtonian, mechanistic world view are in part responsible for the unthinkable massacres that transpired on August 6 and 9, 1945. And it is these assumptions that contribute to the current research, development, testing, and deployment of space weapons and chemical munitions that threaten to rival existing technologies of mass destruction. It is these values that allow young scientists at Livermore and Los Alamos, and in weapons development firms in all industrial societies, to rationalize that their work on weapons is a noble and humane endeavor.

To alter fundamentally the course of the arms race requires a willingness to examine the values that underlie our society's pursuit of truth. After centuries of perceiving and defining reality almost exclusively in terms of the sensate world, we are finally coming to understand that science and empiricism are social institutions based upon historically and culturally specific social values.

In the teaching of Mohandas Gandhi, we are told that truth cannot be attained without love—truth, or the overcoming of injustice, is not possible unless we transform our adversaries through loving nonviolence. Indeed, for Gandhi, nonviolence is the pursuit of truth through love. Quite to the contrary, Western scientific culture has sought to separate truth and love through science. Not only does this result in a cultural acceptance and fascination with the implements of mass destruction, but it has also created an intellectual framework that has paralyzed alternative modes of seeking truth and conducting international relations. This framework has denied the legitimacy of viewing peace as the pursuit of truth through love. Many people accept our current prostitution of science as its only identity and as an historical inevitability. However, as science is a social institution—something we create—it is also something we can transform.

The challenge, then, is to critique the ethical and logical dimensions of science, to contribute to the rebirth of sciences that pursue truth through love, rather than through the design of weapons of mass destruction. The task is to reintegrate ethics and other critically essential social values into new ways of teaching science; to alter our own images of truth so as to include other ways of knowing; to assume responsibility for the development of technology in society; and to be more selective and humane in those technologies that we do elect to design and build. In other words, the role of peace studies is to comprehend more fully this empowering knowledge and to assist in the transformation of scientific approaches to truth.

In order to treat the empirical pursuit of truth through science appropriately, peace studies faculty should inject as much natural and physical science as is possible into the curriculum—and not just in "nuclear war" courses. Courses should be designed and team-taught by natural and physical scientists as often as teaching schedules allow. Peace studies faculty outside the "hard" sciences should also seek to be included in the teaching of science courses.

An understanding of scientific methods and competency in analytical problem-solving are essential if peace studies is to maintain intellectual rigor and to progress at a sufficient rate and in the appropriate directions for it to make a difference in the world of tomorrow. Therefore, scientific research methods and theory construction should be taught and used in peace studies courses as well as in physical science courses. Once introduced, logic and analytical approaches to understanding can then be employed in examinations of the assumptions of science; in other words, the methods and rules of science can be used in an examination of science itself.

Although some of this agenda must wait for students at the upper division and graduate levels, introductory courses can and should include units on science that introduce it as a social institution, and that identify it as one of *a number of* legitimate approaches to perceiving and understanding the world (rather than as the only legitimate approach). To succeed in this task, teachers should demystify images of science and technology that reinforce the "leave it to the expert" syndrome regarding policy choices, examine how the compartmentalization of science obscures social and ecological consequences, and explore the nature of "pure" versus "applied" science, including the development of civilian and military technologies.

It is important that science not be perceived as a target at which faculty in the social sciences and humanities can direct unwarranted criticism. We must examine fully the contributions of science to war (especially the history of the Manhattan Project and the resulting arms race up until the present), but such critiques should be balanced with an appreciation of the constructive uses of modern science. Finally, students should gain an understanding of the difficulty in making choices about science and technology, of the problems involved in applying ethical and moral criteria to those choices, and of the absolute necessity of doing so.

Truth Through Faith. Another way that humanity has pursued truth is through faith. In its more organized forms, this search has taken place through the development and maintenance of religious ideologies. Our religious images are based upon values taught to us through the process of inculcation as we are socialized into the world in which we live. Nothing else explains the fact that Jews produce children with an understanding of Jewish ritual and tradition, while Catholics somehow have children that understand Catholic ritual and tradition; nothing else explains the fact that Mennonites perceive an image of god significantly different from that of Muslims.

Despite the fact that few of us are specifically capable of completely and comprehensively describing our images of the divine, these images are somehow communicated to the young and then shared throughout a lifetime with others of their faith. Somehow we know how to create an image of god in our children, yet we cannot put that image into words. Clearly, these images are incredibly powerful.

However, we do use words to convey what we mean when talking about god; and the words we use to generate images of our god are often quite limiting—that is, exclusive of others' images. If this is indeed the case, then our faiths—even though they are fundamentally important and constructive for us—stand between us and a peaceful world. It is a cliche, but also a truism, that more blood has been shed in the name of god than for any other reason. This is so because our images of god are so powerful, so primary in our belief systems. And so long as some peoples' images of god exclude the viability of other people's images of god, then we will continue to live in a world beset by bloody and intractable conflicts between Protestants and Catholics, Jews and Muslims, and Sikhs and Hindus, to mention a few.

Peace will remain a fantasy as well as a slogan for the initiation of combat so long as our images of god do not allow for others to have their images of god, and so long as the agenda is social conformity and missionary conversion rather than tolerance of diverse images. Accordingly, one role of peace studies is to identify and examine beliefs that contribute either to exclusiveness or inclusiveness. This does not mean that we need to abandon our images of god. It only means that we need to transform them into images that benefit from the knowledge that peace is predicated on tolerance, not on its antithesis. We will achieve peace when our religious ideologies and dogmas allow us to value diversity and to accept the sanctity of other people's spiritual paths.

Peace studies curricula can improve their treatment of the pursuit of metaphysical truth by examining the nature of "truth" as such. Here, secularly oriented programs need to balance their agendas by incorporating units on religious contributions to peacemaking. On the other hand, programs predicated on primarily theological world views should seek as ecumenical a perspective on religion as possible. In so doing, such programs must examine the assumptions and values of religious belief systems, describe the many images of god, assess the implications of these values, assumptions, and images for the production and management of conflict in the world, and address the issues of inclusiveness, diversity, and tolerance.

Images of Belonging

There are many different types of human communities, some less voluntary than others. All of them contribute to a sense of belonging in the world; many, however, foster a desire to exclude the rest of the world. In this way, most communities offer the benefits of relationship, as well as the potential for exclusiveness, intergroup competition, ethnocentricity, xenophobia, intolerance, discrimination, and unnecessary conflict. This is true of prisons and the military as well as of gender, family, ethnicity, and the nation-state. Put differently, the obverse of belonging has many faces and regularly contributes to the violent conflict and structural violence we see in the world today. The dynamics and ideologies of "us" versus "them" (as expressed, for instance, in nationalism and excessive patriotism, gender-based chauvinism, religious self-righteousness, and racial prejudice) are antithetical to the development of peace. Thus an important role of peace studies is to explore new ways of creating community that value uniqueness while minimizing exclusiveness and unnecessary competition.

Peace studies has already progressed far in this dimension. Robert Jay Lifton's (1987) seminal research into the concept of a "species self" is a major recent contribution in the field of psychology to the evolution of a global identity. Elise Boulding's new book, *Building a Global Civic Culture* (1988), is a profoundly important treatise on the creative and cooperative work involved in learning about species identity, in discovering our commonalities, and in building a shared global community. Boulding's book is essential reading for everyone in the field, because it comprehensively addresses so many aspects of the role of peace studies. Hence, in this area, we in the field of peace studies are challenged with the exciting task of building upon the work of Lifton, Boulding, and others.

College and university curricula can address problems inherent in the more traditional images of belonging in at least three basic ways: (1) by helping students identify their own images of belonging (an endeavor that includes assessments of the origins of identities, and expectations of and responsibilities to the communities involved); (2) by presenting information about communities of belonging not familiar to most students (e.g., public interest groups, the various agencies of the United Nations, peace organizations and their national and local chapters, cultural exchange programs, and so on); and (3) by jointly (with students) developing or "mapping" new constellations of communities (from local to global) that allow for overlap and mutual identification without exclusiveness or inherent competition for primacy.

Images of Choosing

"Images of choosing" is a metaphor for the ways in which we exist in the present and create our future out of it. Within the systemic limitations of genetics and history, we—as individuals and as a society—*choose* our future. The amount of freedom available for choice varies considerably with individuals and social groups, but even the poorest of the poor make choices.

Images of choosing are important to the field of peace studies because they allow for an examination of the degree of human empowerment that competes with systemic limitations. Apathy, monolithic power models, belief in technological determinism or in salvation through armageddon, and ideologies which proclaim that violence is the outcome of instinctual human characteristics all share a denial or devaluation of the element of human choice and human potential. Peace studies can and should explore the ways in which we create the future, and how we might expand that potential for creation over time. This field of inquiry involves the subject of our choices, as well as our means and structures of choosing, the role of creativity and cooperation in choice, and the consequences of refusing to acknowledge that choices exist.

Specifically, we need to ask questions about how we make these choices now, within our political and economic systems. What is democracy? How closely does our current system approach this ideal? How does this system work? Does it require participation? What form of socioeconomic organization of society is most compatible with democracy? Is the use of military force to coerce others into organizing their societies in certain ways congruous with the basic tenets of democracy? Is the possession of thermonuclear weapons of mass destruction—or the threat to use them to protect that which we choose to define as our national interests—in accordance with the principles and purposes of democracy? We also need to ask similar sorts of questions about other political systems and about the international system as a whole.

At the same time, peace studies should develop methods for *imaging the future*—that is, it should encourage students to visualize multiple world futures that incorporate new and visionary modes of social and political organization. In developing such techniques we can draw on Elise Boulding's "Imaging a World Without Weapons" workshops, which encourage a multiplicity of alternative futures and allow for new visions of practical, peaceful worlds to be created "outside" the realm of today's dominant world views.

There are many ways for images of choosing to be incorporated into peace studies curricula.

- First, the apathy and alienation that appear as normative aspects of our culture, and that result in large part from the "psychic numbing" produced by our inability to deal with the ever-present risk of nuclear holocaust as well as from the compartmentalization of our complex and technical society, must be named and confronted. Connections to, and responsibility for, our lives and the world of which they are part have to be re-identified and rediscovered as important individual and social values.
- Second, students must be given the opportunity to entertain the notion that social reality is constructed, and that many of the limits to what is possible that were previously assumed to be valid are in fact arbitrary and outmoded; in other words, they are the products of dogma and ideology, rather than of "truth." Here, curricula need to incorporate experiential learning through "imaging the future" exercises.
- Third, the learning process needs to examine the dynamics of action. Clearly, the relationship between means and ends is an essential theme that relates in important ways to our processes of choosing. Simple slogans such as "peace through strength" should be examined logically and their influence on society assessed. At the same time, curricula need to include units on our knowledge of conflict and its resolution, and to provide training in specific skills for conflict resolution, negotiation, and mediation.
- Finally, curricula need to be designed in such a way that students are empowered as they learn about the complex problems we face in the world today, rather than frightened into acquiescence—indeed, into careers with ostrich-like characteristics.

The Pedagogical Importance of Values

It is neither useful nor appropriate to ask whether values should be taught. In one way or another they are taught or shaped in every social interaction and institution, including those whose goal is formal learning (i.e., schools). The disciplines we emphasize, the curricula we select, the authors we choose for our students to read and analyze—all of these choices impart values. The more appropriate question is to ask *how* we can teach about values in a positive, pluralistic, and empowering way. In this regard, the most important single thing we can do is to train students to ask critical epistemological questions, rather than to accept dominant ideas as "given," as "the truth," or as "the way the world is."

In this context, peace studies is especially challenged to teach about values ethically and honestly. We can do so by incorporating into our curricula the rigorous examination of competing normative positions, with an eye toward understanding how they underlie all policies and world views. When students learn to challenge and examine values successfully, at least three essential pedagogical transformations will have transpired. First, they will have learned to critically examine ideas and values, and to evaluate them on their own merit. Second, they will have come to appreciate the existence of relationships between ideas and values. Finally, and perhaps most important, they will be better prepared to select from among the examined values and ideas for themselves—better prepared to shape a philosophy of life that reflects sound ethical and logical inquiry.

To teach values by examining and challenging them is critical because the values assumed by each new generation are the essential ingredients of our common future. Drawing on metahistory and deconstructionism, we are now learning that much of the power of those who perpetuate the arms race may be hidden in the cognitive and emotive images of discourse. We must be willing to unravel those images if we wish to create new thought-worlds.[1] At the heart of old and new thought-worlds are values.

Of course, peace studies curricula must be designed so that those entering the field do not seek to exploit it as a forum for political, ideological, or religious proselytizing. When abused as such, peace studies invites criticism and loses legitimacy in the eyes of its students. Value formation and selection on the part of students should come from an examination of various ideologies about the pursuit of truth, not from their inculcation *as* truth.

Practicing a New Process

In addition to analyzing the relationship between cultural content (as it exists today or as we envision it in the future) and truth, peace studies has the potential to offer a profoundly alternative view of the search for truth. Not only does this view require further definition and articulation, but its validity is predicated upon *practice*. To identify cooperation, tolerance, holistic analysis, interdisciplinary examination, and metacultural critique as elements of the search is not sufficient: Those in the field must challenge themselves with the experience of actually *practicing* the processes they seek to institutionalize in the future. What matters here is neither content nor rhetoric about process, but *process itself.* Getting beyond the dogmas of Western scientific culture that have allowed for the illogical separation of means and ends can be accomplished only by perceiving and practicing the means as ends-in-process.

The success of peace studies is dependent upon the ability of faculty in the field to (1) become cooperative in their shared endeavors; (2) minimize competition among disciplines, ideologies, and affiliations; (3) learn enough of the language, theories, and methods of other disciplines to apply interdisciplinary approaches in their own teaching and research; (4) respect different perspectives and others in the field; and (5) seek multiple alternatives rather than singular prescriptions.

Ultimately, faculty are charged with the task of learning to get beyond ideological labels in order to respect, if not to love, others. For those researching the phenomenon of nonviolence, this means interaction with arms control analysts; for devotees of international relations, it means identification with those focusing on themes of justice, gender, or environmental respect; for theologically inspired faculty, it means active listening to secular colleagues (and vice versa).

The practicing of process also may entail renaming the concepts of "negative" and "positive" peace, so as to avoid denigrating those who focus on the former, while retaining the substantive distinction between peace as the absence of war and militarism (i.e., "negative peace") and peace as the presence of justice (or "positive peace"). Whether individuals in the field choose to focus their inquiry and their curricula on ways to reduce violence in the international system, or on the conditions and characteristics of peace, all perspectives are valid and constructive, and must be pursued through cooperative interaction.

Another challenge to the field of peace studies is to fulfill the potential of its interdisciplinary character. Although some progress has been made here, that quality is still predominantly latent. Most research and teaching in peace studies is conducted within one discipline or another, or it is conducted in a superficially interdisciplinary fashion—that is, the sociologist contributes a sociological perspective in tandem with the psychologist who offers a psychological one, and so on. To the extent that it is humanly and professionally possible, individuals in the field must seek to develop their own interdisciplinary competencies and perspectives while still enhancing their specific areas of expertise and interest.

The practicing of process also suggests that those in the field focus on the development of means suitable to the development of peace. Pedagogically, the emphasis on means implies imparting healthy modes of seeking knowledge, rather than inculcating specific values or ideas as content. Intellectually, it denotes the search for a balanced relationship between traditional academic teaching styles and new experiential modes of learning. Beyond these manifestations of an emphasis on means, the practicing of process ultimately means creating learning structures that contribute to seeking truth through love and exposing those which separate the means from the end.

Seeing the world from as many vantage points as possible is a fundamental task of peacemakers. Therefore, the practicing of process also means developing the ability to engage in what might be called "transperceptual learning"—that is, the learning that comes from perceiving reality from the perspectives of others to the degree possible. Ultimately, the best solutions to our common challenges are the product of joint visualization and cooperative response. This is so because good solutions represent the truth we collectively seek, which in turn is the result of our ability to visualize the perceptions, identify the needs, and respect the rights of others. The sorts of solutions we seek are those that result from cooperative interaction, and that honor the perceptions and needs of others. Transperceptual learning, then, is the dynamic process that comes on the heels of love and precedes the discovery of truth through love.

Conclusion

Relationships between means, ends, meaning, truth, and values inform this approach to the construction of peace studies curricula and to the formulation of their role in the Academy. This perspective is only one of many. Peace studies invites the participation of all those whose vision affirms peace as a positive goal and as a concrete process requiring the development of specific social and technical knowledge. The field is open to all who are willing to challenge and transform outdated world views through the creation of new visions of what is necessary, desirable, and possible.

Notes

1. "Thought-world" was a metaphor used by Pam Solo in a talk given at a conference on "The New Security Debate: Challenges and Strategies for the Peace Movement" sponsored by the Institute for Peace and International Security in Cambridge, Massachusetts in January 1987.

References

Boulding, Elise (1988). *Building a Global Civic Culture: Education for an Interdependent World*. New York: Teachers College Press.

Lifton, Robert Jay (1987). *The Future of Immortality: And Other Essays for a Nuclear Age*. New York: Basic Books.

4. A Third World Approach to Peace and World Order Studies

M. Francis Abraham
Grambling State University

In recent years, minority schools—especially the historically black colleges and universities—have taken a keen interest in peace and world order studies. This is particularly true of many church-related schools that perceive a natural link between religion and peace. As part of this trend, minority scholars have begun to examine the evolving peace studies curriculum from a Third World perspective. In this essay, I attempt to take a fresh look at some of the concepts and concerns that have a special meaning or relevance for minority students. I do not mean to suggest that this perspective is of no consequence to others; nor is it my intention to imply that other issues and concerns are of no relevance to Third World or minority students. Ideally, all curricula in peace and world order studies, regardless of whether they are designed for a largely minority student body, will integrate many of the issues I raise.

Let us begin with a standard definition of peace.

> Peace is a world in which neither the overt violence of war nor the covert violence of unjust systems is used as an instrument for extending the interests of a particular nation or group. It is a world where basic human needs are met, and in which justice can be obtained and conflict resolved through nonviolent processes and human and material resources are shared for the benefit of all people.

This definition of peace, developed by the National Council of Churches, points out the premises and rationale as well as the content of peace and world order studies. Peace is defined both negatively, as the absence of manifest conflicts, and positively, as the creation of a new social order based on justice and the fulfillment of basic needs. Thus any viable peace studies program must first analyze the sources of conflict in society before it begins to address the question of building a just world peace. What, then, are the imperatives entailed in designing a peace studies curriculum for minority students? What do they perceive as significant threats to peace, and how do they visualize a peace-world? How can their perceptions, concerns, and hopes be integrated into a peace and world order studies curriculum?

38

Prejudice and Discrimination

I believe that issues of prejudice and discrimination must form a significant component of the agenda for curriculum development in peace studies. Racial and ethnic prejudices—actual, alleged or presumed—often prompt discrimination and frequently lead to conflicts. Moreover, the life experiences of many minority students leads them to see most social problems and conflicts as manifestations of prejudices that are deeply rooted in the social system. Theoretical notions of race, ethnicity, and pluralism, as well as issues pertaining to race and ethnic relations in contemporary society, must be analyzed within the context of existing socioeconomic and political frameworks. Pluralism in contemporary society must mean more than tolerance and coexistence; it must involve an active appreciation of ethnic differences and cultural variations.

Poverty

Peace cannot be advanced or sustained without the elimination of systemic poverty, which, by definition, is a negation of human rights and, therefore, an ever-present source of conflict. Poverty in the midst of plenty suggests social exploitation, especially when it is experienced disproportionately by particular racial or ethnic minorities. Thus race, poverty, and exploitation constitute an entangled web that contains seeds of distrust, hatred, and antagonism. Poverty is an affront to human dignity; it prevents the realization of the human potential, and it feeds violent revolution. Quite simply, poverty and peace cannot coexist. To many students of Third World origin, this relationship is not merely a theoretical proposition; it is a matter of existential reality.

Therefore, curricula in peace studies must critically evaluate conceptual and empirical analyses of the "poverty establishment." In so doing, it must examine the question of the right to food not only as a moral or human rights issue, but also as a national policy imperative. How do we guarantee the social and economic rights of every individual while preserving their political and civil freedoms? Can we strike a balance between individualistic free enterprise and collectivistic social welfare? What does the notion of equity imply about how the system serves the interests of its constituent parts? These and similar issues pertaining to basic human needs, social welfare, and public policy must be examined in a peace studies program.

The Concept of Justice

Discussion of potential conflicts is as important as that of actual conflict. Since many forms of conflict arise from perceptions of injustice, the concept of justice needs to be analyzed in all its ramifications. Notions of justice range from the actual fairness of a system to the perception of its fairness in the administration of justice. As the old adage goes, it is not enough that justice is done; all must *feel* that justice is being done. There are always questions about the fairness of a system that is perceived as perpetuating injustice in myriad subtle ways. Studies in criminal justice show that members of the minorities receive harsher punishment than those of the majority for similar offenses. Equal access to resources, equal opportunity in education, and equitable representation in democratic processes are other essential ingredients of justice, and must be considered as part of the peace studies curriculum.

Human Rights

Although it is generally agreed that real peace does not exist where human rights are violated, and although most political elites around the world emphatically affirm their commitment to the advancement of human rights, the concept itself poses definitional problems. The First World (i.e., the network of industrialized capitalist countries) emphasizes political and civil freedoms. These Western liberals preach political rights but are generally not anxious to concede the legitimacy of calls for economic rights or a restructuring of the global economic order. On the other hand, leaders in the Second World (i.e., the industrialized socialist countries) tend to emphasize the pursuit of socioeconomic rights for their societies, while shunting calls for political and civil freedoms. Many in the Third World and the Nonaligned Movement attempt to strike a compromise between these two views by stressing economic self-reliance and political self-determination as they pursue development amidst an interdependent world. However, some of the same Third World leaders who clamor for a new international economic order and an end to military intervention by the northern powers maintain semifeudal economic and political systems in their own countries. In other words, although all nations pay lip-service to freedom and justice, few pursue policies motivated by a global conception of human rights as mapped out, for example, in the Universal Declaration of Human Rights, adopted by the United Nations in 1948.

Therefore, curricula in peace and world order studies must provide for a lively debate on the rhetoric and practice of fundamental human rights policy. Easily accessible starting points for this discussion are the texts of the reports of the Universal Declaration and Amnesty International (AI) on human rights abuses/observation in every country; indeed, to illustrate how the human rights issue is applied and often twisted for political purposes, students can contrast the AI literature with the U.S. State Department's annual human rights country reports. And since students of Third World origins tend to identify with victims of exploitation, the curriculum selected for peace and world order studies must provide for the critical examination of all human rights, including the rights of women and minorities, workers and peasants, and all the less-privileged sectors of the United States and global population.

Disarmament

Although everyone is concerned about the threat of nuclear war, the arms race is of primary concern to many people as a question of national priorities and human welfare. The crucial link between disarmament and the quality of life is felt by all, but it is of special significance to disadvantaged Third World and minority communities, on whom the arms race places the greatest burden. For these students, disarmament is a crucial pocketbook issue: Defense spending reduces the funds available for critical public services, including education and student financial aid.

In many countries, governments spend much more on the military than on education and health combined. As Ruth Leger Sivard points out in the annual *World Military and Social Expenditures*, the world's average expenditure per soldier is approximately sixty times that per school-age child, and there are seven soldiers for every doctor in the world. Similarly, the vast majority of the world's annual expenditures for research and development go to support military activities, with only a tiny fraction left for economic and social development. All peace and world order studies curricula should treat armament/disarmament issues in this light; Sivard's annual report is a good tool with which to initiate this inquiry, and it is accessible to students.

Minority Religions

A curriculum in peace studies for Third World students must also examine the special relevance of minority religions, especially the black churches, to the pursuit of peace and justice. As notions of peace, justice, and welfare are deeply ingrained in the teaching of most minority religions, a concern for these values is considered a natural extension of religious belief. Thus, the Negro Spiritual—though born of suffering—is infused with compassion and radiates the joy of peace. The peace studies curriculum must also show how the black churches and their ministers have always been in the forefront of social movements for peaceful change. Finally, the curriculum must explore how the unique value systems and the cultural mosaic of minority religions can be drawn upon to initiate and sustain a grassroots movement for peace and social justice.

Gandhi's Concept of Nonviolence

Mohandas Gandhi's theories of the political and spiritual dimensions of nonviolence are treated extensively in most peace studies curricula, and no reiteration is needed here. All of these concepts are very important and should be included in any peace and world order studies curriculum; but two central ideas of Gandhi are particularly relevant to Third World students.

The Spiritual Dimensions of Nonviolence
Gandhi firmly believed that nonviolence is impossible without a living belief in God. His concept of nonviolence entails complete fearlessness and absolute

readiness to suffer without retaliating. Thus Gandhi firmly believed that nonviolence is impossible without a living belief in God. He suggested that this sort of supernatural courage—which demands nothing short of the ability to face death—is obtainable only by prayer and spiritual discipline. Students should explore the illuminating parallels between the spiritual bases of nonviolence expounded by Gandhi and the black churches' view of religion as the source of solace and strength in the face of adversity.

The Concept of *Sarvodaya*

Gandhi's concept of *sarvodaya* meant the well-being and progress of the whole being and community—that is, the welfare of all, including "the poorest, the lowliest and the lost." He considered the well-being of the lowest strata of society to be the real test of the greatness of society. The primary purpose of Gandhi's constructive program was to create a moral and just social order. These are the ideas that inspired the Reverend Martin Luther King in his campaigns for freedom, justice, and peace.

Martin Luther King

Most peace studies curricula already include some attention to the life and writings of Martin Luther King, Jr., particularly his philosophy of nonviolence and his methods and techniques of conflict resolution. However, these curricula must stress the point that King struggled not merely for civil rights for blacks; he also sought a just social order based on equality, peace and progress. When he spoke out against hunger in the United States and slaughter in Vietnam, he was speaking for all underprivileged peoples, regardless of color or creed, and against a political establishment that had come to represent exploitation and injustice.

Social Justice Today

Finally, a peace studies curriculum for Third World and minority students must reflect the salient concerns of the contemporary social order. It must pay adequate attention to the demands for equality, power, and progress that have emerged as the dominant objectives of political activism in today's minority community. Members of minority groups are no longer interested in "tokenism" or favored treatment; they seek absolute equality on the basis of merit. Likewise, they are no longer content with the passive—and often inconsequential—experience of voting rights or a token voice in government; they seek real power with which to effect change. Eradication of poverty is no longer the main plank; overall progress is. These aspirations, inspired by new conceptions of justice, are an important part of today's social justice agenda, and they need to be addressed as well in peace studies courses.

5. Research Frontiers for Peace Studies: New Inquiry and Curriculum Development

Daniel C. Thomas and Nigel Young
Five College Program in Peace and World Security Studies
and Colgate University

Peace studies is about to enter its third decade as a major presence in higher education. During this period, faculty in the field have maintained a remarkable commitment to curriculum innovation, as evidenced by the evolution of syllabi over the five editions of *Peace and World Order Studies*. If this process of innovation is to continue, those who are developing new courses must take advantage of the ground-breaking inquiry now under way in our field. Because there are many more areas of new research relevant to peace studies than could possibly be discussed in this essay, we have chosen to highlight those that represent new interdisciplinary combinations not readily accessible through traditional disciplinary channels. Specifically, we will examine current research on

- peace movements;
- cognition, war, and peace;
- alternative security;
- militarism and development;
- language and media;
- feminism and militarism; and
- conflict resolution.

These research frontiers suggest new perspectives on familiar issues, identify new issues that had previously been neglected, and advance the search for solutions to pressing global problems. We will explore these research frontiers, pinpoint some of the leading scholars and writings in each area, and consider the uses of this work for curriculum development.

The reader should understand at the outset that there has always been an ambiguous, if not distant, relationship between formal *peace research* (as manifested in graduate and postgraduate scholarship, and in the field's professional journals and associations) and undergraduate teaching in the field of *peace studies*. This relationship is due partly to the fact that peace studies, as currently practiced in American colleges and universities, draws more from the traditional disciplines and from contemporary political analyses than from work identified as "peace research." While such *ad hoc* innovation has been remarkably successful in filling some glaring gaps in the standard curriculum, our teaching would be immeasurably strengthened by more systematic integration with the field's own research frontiers.

The first challenge is to determine where such "frontiers" of research are located. Most innovative research in the peace studies field is produced and disseminated by one of the four sources delineated below.

1. First we consider the scholars, institutes, journals, and associations that constitute the peace research community. The scholarly journals most useful for accessing this work are the *Bulletin of Peace Proposals, Journal of Peace Research, Journal of Conflict Resolution, Current Research on Peace and Violence,* and *Peace and Change,* as well as the *International Peace Research Association Newsletter.*

2. Next we consider the peace studies programs that, while not necessarily part of the peace research community *per se,* nevertheless regularly sponsor innovative research conferences and publications in addition to their curricular activities. In the United States, such programs include those at Colgate University, Cornell University, the University of Colorado at Boulder, George Mason University, Syracuse University, the University of California system, John Jay College of the City University of New York, and the Five Colleges (Amherst, Hampshire, Mount Holyoke, and Smith colleges and the University of Massachusetts at Amherst).

3. We must also consider the accumulated body of unanswered questions that have arisen out of the experience of teaching in the field. These questions regularly arise at gatherings of faculty in the field, such as the annual meetings of the Peace Studies Association (PSA), the Consortium on Peace Research, Education, and Development (COPRED), and the National Conference on Peacemaking and Conflict Resolution (NCPCR), as well as the peace studies sections of the various discipline associations. In fact, many of the course syllabi contained in this volume exemplify this quest for new answers, and even for new questions.

4. Finally, we consider the research conducted by scholars beyond the institutional boundaries of peace studies that is nonetheless directly relevant to the concerns of the field, including innovative research in anthropology, history, political science, psychology, and women's studies.

In addition to these relatively formal sources of intellectual development in the field, it is important that we recognize the contributions made by more spontaneous and informal sources. For example, one of the field's most significant pieces of *samizdat* resulted from feminist scholar Carol Cohn's participation in a well-known strategic studies seminar; pirated copies of Cohn's (1987b) analysis of the latent structures of nuclear discourse and security language had a tremendous impact on the field well before its official publication.

In the early 1970s, when the first generation of undergraduate peace studies programs was established, one outstanding research frontier pertained to transnationalism and the rise of nonstate actors in world affairs, including nongovernmental organizations, multinational corporations, and paranational movements. But because much of the peace research community was still preoccupied with the intellectual spin-offs and disputes arising from the Indochina War, the bulk of this other ground-breaking research took place instead on the margins of established International Relations. Consequently, this controversial new research remained primarily in International Relations circles and failed to provide intellectual impetus for the emerging under-graduate curriculum in peace studies at a time when that input would have been important.

In the 1980s, the direction and agenda of research in peace studies has been influenced most notably by the resurgence of peace movement activity and by trends in global politics. A large number of peace researchers assumed leadership roles in the peace movement during the past decade, in the process becoming participants instead of onlookers; as such, they were compelled to acknowledge the weaknesses of the movement's historical consciousness and policy prescriptions. This acknowledgment led to a concern with the sociology and history of peace movements, a search for demilitarized security concepts, the quest for a new language of peace not perverted by strategic discourse, the integration of feminist theory as elaborated by the women's peace movement, attention to the psychological dynamics of nuclear despair, and a reappraisal of the linkage of disarmament with global ecological and developmental issues.

In addition, heightened international tension at the beginning of the decade—as manifested in the sharp acceleration of the nuclear arms race, the Soviet occupation of Afghanistan, and the U.S. militarization of Central America—focused new attention on the East-West conflict and on the dynamics of superpower competition in the Third World. Furthermore, dynamic nonviolent political struggles in the Philippines, Poland, the West Bank and Gaza Strip, Southern Africa, Latin America, and several Pacific nations compelled many scholars to devote increased attention to the goals, tactics, and political consciousness of these movements. And as the news media responded to increased popular interest in war and peace with increased programming, some peace researchers began to question their representation of these issues.

The declining political and cultural hegemony of the superpowers as well as the increasing prominence of grassroots movements around the world are also reflected in the renewed attention being given the sort of episte-mological and theoretical questioning that arose in the 1960s. Whether anarchist, feminist, post-Marxian, "Green," deconstructionist, or part of some other emerging critical paradigm, this questioning is helping to open the new intellectual and political space needed for fundamental reappraisals of the human condition. For example, the so-called Europeanization of Europe, as manifested by many politicians' increased suspicion of the superpowers and by the development of a transnational grassroots "civil society," is simultaneously a cause and a consequence of these intellectual reorientations.

Research Frontiers

On Peace Movements

Over the past two centuries, mass-based peace movements have had a significant impact both on peoples' attitudes toward war and on governments' willingness to initiate or continue militaristic policies. They have also been active in articulating alternative visions for society and in devising policy options whose emphasis on transnationalism and decentralization made them quite different from those proposed by governments. Hence, in the context of the renewed activism of the last decade, they have become increasingly central to the research and curriculum of peace studies.

To speak of a *single* peace movement over time contradicts the massive historical evidence of great diversity in objectives, methods, and constituencies. Nevertheless, the ideal concept of "peace movement" may be a useful reminder that—despite all the variations, multiplicity of organizations, sections of movements, breaks and discontinuities—something has existed, and has been perceived as existing, that transcends all these fragments and changes. The study of peace movements must thus account for both the amorphous category known as "the peace movement" and the historically unique character of each component, each group, each phase, at each moment in time.

Scholars today tend to employ one of four basic methodologies in the study of peace movements. One method, as seen in the work of Bob Overy (1982) and Nigel Young (1976, 1984, 1988), is to classify peace movements in terms of their objectives—for example, in terms of the abolition of conscription, nonintervention, disarmament, and so on. Another method, also developed by Young (1986) and closely related to the study of political ideology and intellectual history, is to identify "peace traditions" that persist over time within various political cultures. A third method, pioneered especially by scholars such as Charles Chatfield (1973) and Peter Brock (1970), may be described as one of *periodization*. This method analyzes cycles of peace movement activity in terms of popular support, organizational strength, and political action; it also explores their correlation with the incidence of wars and arms races, fluctuations in military spending, variations in public opinion, and particular events such as international crises or the introduction of compulsory military service.

Today, scholars are exploring a broad range of peace movement activity and thought, and employing a variety of methodologies and analytical perspectives. Taken together, these endeavors have allowed peace studies to repossess substantially the history and political sociology of peace movements as an important project in itself. This inquiry also contributes to our understanding of a long-term process of social evolution that could significantly transform many of the assumptions and institutions that dominate contemporary political life.

The diversity in this inquiry is represented, for example, by Zsuzsa Hegedus's (1987) critical work on the literature of new social movements, by the theoretical and comparative historical studies done by Katsuya Kodama (1988) and Nigel Young (1986, 1987), and by the work of Chadwick Alger and Saul Mendlovitz (1987) on the challenge of developing global linkages and consciousness among grassroots movements. The late historian Charles DeBenedetti's two recent books on American peace movements (1980, 1988) and Taylor and Young's (1987) edited volume *Campaigns for Peace* are significant contributions to the field of peace history that serve as accessible texts for classroom use. E. P. Thompson (1982), leading scholar and visionary in the European peace movement, has stressed the importance of such peace histories in placing cycles of activism within a larger time-frame. In addition, the incorporation of such research by the peace movements themselves has contributed to the growing intellectual maturity they require if they are to be sustained through periodic cycles of rise and decline.

Scholars tend to divide contemporary peace movement activity into two analytically distinct categories or traditions: the antinuclear movements and the so-called new social movements. Movements in the first category tend to pursue a relatively narrow agenda, most often arguing for nonradical solutions to the immediate problem of the nuclear arms race. The second category of peace movement activity in the 1980s is part of a wider holistic/globalist/ecological orientation that also includes the "Green" and "New Age" movements. Important work in this latter area has been undertaken by scholars such as Alain Touraine (1985) and Joyce Mushaben (1985).

Another key area of developing research on peace movements deals with the movements' language and relationships with the media. Through the work of researchers on media and language (as subsequently discussed), researchers on peace movements have incorporated a greater understanding not only of the importance of the symbols and language of these movements but also of their relationship with the dominant language and the media. This process is reflected in the greater self-knowledge and sophistication of the peace movement itself.

This greater reflexivity of the peace movement in its analysis of news and in its awareness of its own public projection has also attracted scholarly attention to such questions as whether the movement, by participating in the security debate and employing its arcane language, might actually legitimate the dominant assumptions of that debate. The work of Glen Hook (1986) and Robin Luckham (1984) and *Deadline,* the newsletter of the Center for War, Peace, and the News Media at New York University, point to the need to understand peace movements as both image-producers and media-products. Insofar as the peace movement is both consumer and consumed, the fact that nuclear language and security discourse may go unchallenged tends to legitimate them, leaving intact political assumptions about national security, deterrence, and defense.

Much of this new scholarship has been pioneered by members of the study group on peace movements of the International Peace Research Association (IPRA), the Council on Peace Research in History (CPRH), the World Order Models Project (WOMP), and by several smaller groups. Samples of this work can be found in the *Journal of Peace Research, Peace, and Change* (which is co-published by CPRH and COPRED), and WOMP's *Alternatives,* among other journals. But despite great improvements in the quality of scholarship in this field, there remains a shortage of both comparative historical work and the creative use of survey data. Another major challenge confronting scholars is to take advantage of the intellectual rapprochement taking place between the historians of peace movements and those analysts who are exploring new social movements and alternative futures. This development, by anchoring our work in a larger time-frame, has great potential for enriching our curricula.

Both the quantity and quality of courses on peace movements are slowly increasing as new research is disseminated. Courses tend to include the social analysis of current social movements, comparative studies of movements through history, and the lessons of violence and nonviolence as tools for social change. Some faculty in the field have come to believe that experiential learning (via field placements with citizen action groups) is an important element in the study of social movements.

On Cognition, War, and Peace

Peace studies has been greatly enriched by the work of scholars from a range of disciplines who explore the cognitive dimensions of human and social behavior as it relates to war and peace. Three important subjects of inquiry in this subfield are the origins of human aggression, the effects of the "nuclear shadow," and the dangers of miscalculation leading to war.

The origins of aggression and violence have long been a central concern of peace research and education. Educators in the field draw on the pessimistic works of Konrad Lorenz (1966) and Edmund Wilson (1978), as well as on the work of Margaret Mead (1940), Albert Bandura (1973), and others who have argued more recently that war is not an inevitable part of the human condition. Although the tension between these theories is far from resolved, the preponderance of expert opinion suggests that the practice of warfare is not biologically determined even if humans have a genetic capacity for aggression. For example, the International Society for Research on Aggression stated in 1986 that it is

> scientifically incorrect to say that we have inherited a tendency to make war from our animal ancestors, . . . that war or any other violent behavior is genetically programmed into our human nature, . . . that in the course of human evolution there has been a selection for aggressive behavior more than for other kinds of behavior, . . . that humans have a "violent brain," . . . [or] that war is caused by "instinct" or any single motivation.

"War is biologically possible, but it is not inevitable," the International Society concluded, adding that "the same species who invented war is capable of inventing peace." As distinct from basic aggressive tendencies (which can be manifested in interpersonal violence or channeled into constructive outlets), war is a social institution requiring sophisticated choices and planning. The understanding of warfare as a socially organized and sanctioned use of mass violence, rather than as an unavoidable human activity, is reinforced by the work of individuals such as David Fabbro (1978), who has compared the social habits and structures of various peaceful societies.

Regardless of how war comes about, the omnipresent threat of nuclear holocaust has significantly affected the psyche of every individual, according to such prominent scholars as Jerome Frank (1982), Joel Kovel (1983), and Joanna Macy (1983). These scholars and others have identified the phenomenon of "nuclear numbing," whereby one's ability to deal with the external world is overwhelmed by the specter of nuclear war. This phenomenon results, they argue, in various forms of personal and political apathy, and sometimes in the systematic denial of the threat itself. Indeed, we are all plagued at some level by the simultaneous obsession with and denial of the nuclear threat; research shows that even very young children are tormented by images of cataclysm that they have absorbed from parents, friends, and popular culture.

Robert Jay Lifton (1982), best known for his studies of Nazi doctors and Hiroshima survivors, has taken the lead in exploring the macro-level psychological implications of the "nuclear shadow." Lifton (1987b) has identified a social condition he calls "nuclear normality," which points to the fact that society has grown accustomed to living with nuclear weapons, due in part to repeated government campaigns designed to instill complacency in the face of nuclear terror. Lifton (1987a) has also investigated the nature and value of a developing social-psychological concept—the "species self"—that inspires individuals to transcend their apathy through an understanding that the self-concept is inseparable from that of humanity as a whole.

At the forefront of the growing subfield of political psychology are works by scholars such as Robert Jervis (1976), Richard Ned Lebow (1981), and Jervis, Lebow, and Janice Stein (1985), which have pointed out the structural and cognitive reasons why reliance on the rationality of nuclear decisionmakers can be very dangerous. For example, Jervis, Lebow, and Stein have studied the process by which societies project mirror-images of their self-identities onto their adversaries, thus justifying their own aggressive actions on the presumption of their adversaries' aggressiveness. They have also explored the way in which nations' misperceptions of each other's intentions make crises more likely and the tendency of leaders to make short-sighted decisions under the pressure of extreme crisis, thus precipitating uncontrollable escalation. Herbert Kelman (1987), a pioneer of peace research in the United States, has published several political-psychological analyses of the Israeli-Palestinian conflict that suggest that only face-to-face negotiations between the parties can break down the mutual denial of each other's identity and right to exist.

These inquiries into the cognitive dimensions of war and peace issues have established their place in the peace studies curriculum and have helped push the research frontiers of peace studies in new disciplinary directions. Nonetheless, the field will be even further enriched as more and more psychology faculty adopt this material for teaching and develop new upper-level courses on the cognitive dimensions of war and peace.

On Alternative Security

Few areas of human endeavor are more central to the peace studies inquiry than the measures taken by states in pursuit of security for their populations. Today, a broad range of scholarship under the rubric of "alternative security" is setting forth new ways of understanding the nature of "security" and developing new approaches to security policy appropriate to those under-standings. This entire spectrum of thought rests on the belief that the unilateral threat and use of offensive military force is becoming increasingly dysfunctional and dangerous. It affirms a positive-sum theory of security, whereby the security of one society or nation within the global system can be achieved only by promoting the security of the entire system (in contrast to the traditional zero-sum theory whereby one state guarantees its security through military measures that reduce the security of its rivals). This approach also posits a more complex definition of "security," taking into account such nonmilitary factors as the economic well-being of populations and the ecological health of the planet.

For purposes of discussion, this broad inquiry can be divided into two schools of thought: (1) "alternative defense" (also known as "nonoffensive defense" and "defensive defense"), or the process of restructuring military postures so as to optimize their capacity for *defensive* deterrence in such a way that one's adversary feels less threatened and is therefore less likely to engage in arms racing or preemptive strikes; and (2) "common security," or the development of a new global security system stressing multilateral action to avert interstate warfare and to overcome the underlying causes of violence.

Although this collection of ideas has been explored in the research community for many years, it first achieved worldwide political currency in 1982 with the publication of *Common Security* by the Independent Commission on Disarmament and Security Issues. Popularly known as the Palme Commission, after its chair, the late prime minister of Sweden, Olof Palme, this international group of analysts and political leaders argued that in the nuclear age countries cannot achieve security at each others' expense, nor can they achieve security through military strength alone. The path to "common security," they affirmed, consists of an active arms control and confidence-building process, a reinvigorated United Nations system, and a strengthened commitment by the industrialized nations to Third World development.

The *alternative defense* school of thought suggests that relying on the threat of offensive retaliation undermines a nation's security by producing insecurity in rival countries, thereby increasing the likelihood of arms races and preemptive strikes. A nonoffensive defense (NOD) posture, on the other hand, would consist of doctrine and forces designed to be optimally effective for defensive operations, yet structurally incapable of cross-border power projection. If adopted incrementally, it is argued, such a posture would be inherently less threatening to other states and therefore less conducive to escalation during a crisis.

This school of thought was first developed in Europe, where it is viewed by some politicians and peace activists as a way to prevent war, dismantle the bloc system, and promote greater independence from the superpowers. Leading European analysts in this field include Albrecht von Muller and Lutz Unterseher (1987) of West Germany, who have developed bilateral and unilateral strategies for implementing a nonprovocative defense of Western Europe. Representing another significant trend in this field—namely, the pursuit of East-West scholarly collaboration on security matters—von Muller has also worked with Andrzej Karkoszka (1987, 1988) of Poland to develop ways in which the two blocs could take complementary steps toward nonprovocative military postures.

In England, the Alternative Defence Commission, based at the University of Bradford's School of Peace Studies, has published three studies of non-nuclear, nonprovocative defense postures for the United Kingdom. Elsewhere in Europe, several governments have supported feasibility studies of such proposals. Official Soviet policy now stresses many precepts of common security and defensive defense, as demonstrated by Mikhail Gorbachev's unilateral cuts in Soviet conventional forces in Europe, including many formations with clearly offensive functions. In the United States, Michael MccGwire (1988) of the Brookings Institution is just one of many analysts now suggesting that a fundamental reassessment by the Soviets of their military doctrine has provided the West with an unprecedented opportunity to pursue a mutual security regime based on arms reductions and defensive restructuring. Randall Forsberg (1984) of the Institute for Defense and Disarmament Studies has argued that the only realistic way to end the arms race and achieve security is through a combination of defensive defense and nonintervention that would confine the military forces of the major powers incrementally to more-defensive missions. An accessible and comprehensive survey of nonoffensive defense thinking by scholars from East and West was published in September 1987 as a special issue of the *Bulletin of the Atomic Scientists*.

Another body of alternative defense thinking, known as "civilian-based defense" (CBD), represents an even more significant departure from traditional approaches to security. Pioneered by Gene Sharp of Harvard University's Program on Nonviolent Sanctions, this approach proposes that civilian populations be trained in nonviolent resistance as a way of deterring invasion and resisting domestic tyranny. In Sharp's latest work, *Making Europe Unconquerable* (1986), he applies the knowledge gained from numerous historical case studies to a contemporary security concern—the defense of Western Europe against potential aggression. Furthermore, Sharp's colleagues Christopher Kruegler and Patricia Parkman (1985) have argued strongly that peace studies ought to devote more attention to nonviolent struggle and civilian-based defense as practical alternatives to political violence.

The allied field of "common security" often incorporates many of the elements of alternative defense but looks beyond the particular problem of national self-defense against an aggressive adversary. This school suggests that it could be difficult to distinguish between threatening and nonthreatening defense postures during a crisis. In any case, these theorists argue, NOD postures cannot ensure the security of smaller countries or uphold international norms against aggression, intervention, and genocide. This school further argues that defensive defense by itself does not provide mechanisms either for the resolution of conflicts once they have started or for the implementation of international peacekeeping. Hence, common security proposals seek to correct the deficiencies of defensive defense by incorporating institutions for conflict resolution and peacekeeping with the sort of global norms that would facilitate genuine global disarmament and demilitarization. In the United States, one of the pioneers of this approach is Robert Johansen (1983, 1987), who has proposed alternative security strategies as a pragmatic replacement for nuclear deterrence.

Some researchers have expanded the notion of "common security" even further, seeking to address a broad range of contemporary political, cultural, and environmental trends. Chadwick Alger (1985), Elise Boulding (1988), and Richard Falk (1987), for example, have called attention to the expanding political role of sub- and transnational actors in world affairs and to the resulting increase in what is sometimes called "peoples' detente." In Europe, E. P. Thompson (1982) of Britain and George Konrad (1984) of Hungary have emphasized the growth of a trans-European "civil society," including the new popular consciousness that many observers believe is spanning the East-West divide and making the military division of the continent between antagonistic blocs increasingly anachronistic. Other analysts affiliated with the Worldwatch Institute, including Lester Brown (1986) and Daniel Deudney (1983), have articulated theories of whole-earth ecological and economic security, suggesting that massive environmental threats can be overcome only through a cooperative global effort.

This broad range of scholarship on the meaning and pursuit of security is still quite new, and it requires considerably more work. Nonetheless, it has grown so fast in the past few years that Bjorn Moller of the Center of Peace and Conflict Research at the University of Copenhagen was recently able to publish a 53-page bibliography of the literature in the field in the *Non-Offensive Defence International Research Newsletter* (1987). Alternative security scholarship has also attracted interest and criticism from more traditionally minded national security analysts. For example, *Fateful Visions* (Nye et al., 1988), the latest book from Harvard University's Avoiding Nuclear War Project, critiques ten alternative security proposals—from nonprovocative and civilian-based defense to "Star Wars" to world government. It concludes that this range of alternative visions and strategies can contribute only marginally to more traditional policies of nuclear deterrence, crisis management, and international cooperation.

Alternative security thinking has gradually begun to influence the curriculum not only in peace studies but in international relations and other relevant fields as well. Nearly a dozen syllabi in several sections of this

Curriculum Guide attest to the growth and diversity of undergraduate teaching in this area. Still, much more remains to be done if the innovations of alternative security thinking are to be integrated into college curricula.

On Militarism and Development

As the field of peace studies broadens its focus to include not only the East-West conflict but also North-South and South-South conflict issues, researchers are beginning to examine the critical link between militarism and underdevelopment in the Third World. It is here, more than anywhere else, that the field's dual concerns with the elimination of military violence ("negative peace") and the alleviation of so-called structural violence ("positive peace") seem to come together. This perception is based on mounting evidence that spreading militarism in the Third World (as reflected by data on military production and expenditures, frequency and intensity of armed conflicts, and military intervention in domestic politics) is contributing to the economic indebtedness and stagnation of Third World countries as well as to the misery and repression of their populations.

A basic reference tool in this general field is Ruth Leger Sivard's *World Military and Social Expenditures,* an exhaustive compendium of relevant data that is updated annually. Additional useful data and analyses have been published in the *SIPRI Yearbook* and other specialized volumes published by the Stockholm International Peace Research Institute (SIPRI). Two other Scandinavian research centers—the Peace Research Institute, Oslo (PRIO), in Norway, and the Tampere Peace Research Institute (TAPRI) in Finland have also supported considerable research in this field. Much of this work (as well as that of other specialists in the field) is accessible in the *Bulletin of Peace Proposals,* published by PRIO.

One aspect of this problem that has received particular attention in recent years is the international arms trade and its impact on the Third World. SIPRI has just released a three-volume series edited by Michael Brzoska and Thomas Ohlson (1986) that incorporates the work of many prominent researchers in this area. Josef Goldblat (1987), also of SIPRI, has published a concise discussion of the challenge of demilitarization in the developing world. In the United States, important work has been conducted by James Katz (1984, 1986), Michael Klare (1985), and Miles Wolpin (1985), among others. Some scholars, including Eqbal Ahmad (1980), Nicole Ball (1988), and George Lopez and Michael Stohl (1986), have studied the effect of the pervasive influence of the military in many Third World states on their sociopolitical evolution, especially with respect to human rights abuses, state terror, and the denial of democracy. This topic has also received considerable attention from researchers at institutes and universities in the Third World. Ball (1982) has also compiled a useful guide to this whole range of literature.

As a result of increased interest by many governments and nongovernmental organizations, the United Nations launched a major research effort in the early 1980s on the links between disarmament and development. It has since published several reports on the social and economic consequences of global militarization, and UN official Liviu Bota (1985) has authored a special report calling for the establishment of an international disarmament fund for development. Other relevant UN findings are available in *Disarmament* (a periodic review published by the UN Department for Disarmament Affairs) and in the report of the United Nations' 1987 International Conference on the Relationship Between Disarmament and Development.

In addition to being a rich area for new research, the field of militarism and development is a vital component of courses that seek to explore the wider context of international conflict and violence. Some of the syllabi in this volume, including Jean Stern's "Third World Arms Races" course and others in the Human Rights and the World Political Economy sections, show how these connections between disarmament and development can be drawn. Nevertheless, much room for innovative curriculum development remains in this area.

On Language, Communications, and the Media

One of the most vigorous new areas of research in the peace studies field examines language, social discourse, and other forms of communication in terms of war and peace issues. Because modes of public communication have a tremendous influence on people's understanding of war and peace, on their propensity to be politically active, and on the course of the policy debate itself, this work is highly germane to peace studies. As a result of the work of individuals such as Crispin Aubrey (1982), Paul Chilton (1987), Carol Cohn (1987a), Glen Hook (1985), and R.B.J. Walker (1986), we now recognize that people's perception of the nuclear dilemma has been shaped considerably by the very language used in public discourse on this matter. Those scholars who delve into "nuke speak"—the language of nuclear war analysis—have shown how this discourse serves to make nuclear weapons easier to live with by obscuring the reality of their destructive powers. In recognition of this phenomenon, Hook and others are taking steps to develop a vocabulary more conducive to widespread public understanding of, and hence participation in, these debates. In addition, an international network of scholars working on these topics has been organized by James Skelly, a sociologist at the University of California at San Diego. These studies of language as an integral part of nuclear culture are slowly influencing the peace studies curriculum, as more and more courses on the nuclear age begin to focus critical attention on the actual terminology and texts of the debate.

On a parallel track, scholars of the media such as Robert Karl Manoff are studying how the peace movement and the defense debate are presented to and perceived by the public, how the "war and peace news" packages and slants these phenomena, and how these media actually affect events through their tremendous powers of persuasion. In the United States, this close analysis of the media has been publicized through *Deadline*, the newsletter of Manoff's Center on War, Peace, and the News Media at New York University. The "Press and the Arms Race" syllabus in this volume by David Rubin at NYU is just one example of the many new courses being taught across the United States that assess media coverage of war/peace issues. In the United Kingdom, similar assessments have been developed by the researchers of the Glasgow University Media Group (1985).

Another area in which narrative and discourse analysis also comes into play is the study of war/peace imagery in the arts, literature, and film. For example, Paul Boyer (1985) and Spencer Weart (1988) have studied artifacts of popular culture in order to uncover societal attitudes toward nuclear war. This general topic lends itself well to both advanced courses and general education curricula, in which such diverse materials as Benjamin Britten's "War Requiem," Virginia Woolf's *Three Guineas*, and Stanley Kubrick's *Dr. Strangelove* can be creatively employed. Other productive options might include close textual analysis of novels and poetry, the study of poster art (especially from the early twentieth century), or multimedia presentations on war/peace imagery in the visual arts such as that developed by Dick Ringler of the University of Wisconsin at Madison.

While the new scholarship on semiotics, discourse, and narrative should be used selectively at the undergraduate level, some entirely new courses— such as the syllabi in this volume by Sandi Albertson, Curtis Hinsley, and Dick Ringler—provide models for the intensive study of the impact of war and peace on literature and the arts. To aid scholars and educators in this field, Paul Brians, a professor of English at Washington State University, has begun publishing a research newsletter, *Nuclear Texts and Contexts*.

On Feminism and Peace

A sixth notable area of inquiry is the application of feminist analyses to a wide range of topics related to peace studies, including the causes of war and other forms of violence, nonviolence and social change, and traditional pedagogies. This field, sometimes called "feminist peace research," has been led by such theorists and educators as Elise Boulding (1977), Birgit Brock-Utne (1985), and Betty Reardon (1985). Moreoever, as Barbara Roberts (1984) and others have argued, feminist peace research serves as a corrective to the traditional peace research agenda, which has largely been set by men. For example, it adds to the research agenda such neglected topics as violence against women, emphasizes that women tend to suffer disproportionately from various forms of structural violence, and incorporates feminist research methodologies.

The central theoretical debate of this field concerns the question as to whether women are inherently more "peaceful" than men. Most scholars in the field would agree with Christine Sylvester (1987) that patriarchy is an important but not sufficient explanation for social violence, as evidenced by the range of attitudes among women regarding the acceptability of violence. Nonetheless, the distinction between male and female behavior patterns remains a key organizing concept for work in this area. The sociologist Jessie Bernard (1981), for example, suggests that within the male-dominated world there exist a "male ethos" of competition and power and a "female ethos" of love and duty. Similarly, the psychiatrist Jean Baker Miller (1982) points to a difference in the way that men and women conceptualize power, whereby men understand it as the ability to control or limit the actions of others whereas for women it is more closely related to creativity.

In their search for archeological and anthropological data on the origins of the male domination of society, Riane Eisler and David Loye (1986) concluded that human culture appears initially to have been oriented toward a system of male-female "partnership" rather than toward a male-dominated system. They also suggest that early societies were not characterized by much organized violence, whether structural or overt. Such analyses suggest that violence cannot be significantly diminished until political life is transformed by the increased participation of women.

Drawing on these interpretations of gender differences and their relationship to the use of violence, many feminist scholars and activists have concluded that nonviolence is the most appropriate method for a feminist transformation of society. This conclusion has also been inspired and informed by various women's experiments with nonviolence as an active tool for social change, including especially the women's peace encampments of the 1980s. Pam McAllister (1982) and Robert Cooney and Helen Michalowski (1987), for example, have edited useful collections of essays on feminist theories of nonviolence and case studies of its use by women's movements.

The emerging praxis of alternative pedagogies is another area of new work coming largely out of feminist scholarship but directly relevant to peace studies. Educators have developed teaching-learning methods that emphasize discussion and experiential learning over more traditional pedagogic forms. By deemphasizing the teacher's role as "expert," these pedagogies are designed to foster the independent thinking, freedom of expression, and applied knowledge necessary for student empowerment. (For further discussion of this approach to pedagogy, see the essays in this volume by Betty Reardon and Dale Bryan and by Dominic Kulik and David Yaskulka.)

The cross-fertilization of feminist scholarship and peace studies holds great potential for research on both peace and women, as well as for studies of the causes of war, social movements and the state, security discourse, and alternative futures. In the area of teaching, too, there is much joint work to be done between Women's Studies and Peace Studies programs, especially at the undergraduate level. As illustrated by the curricula in this volume, educators in the field are just beginning to answer this challenge.

On Conflict Resolution

A final area of new research is the broad field of conflict analysis and conflict resolution. According to one of its pioneers (Burton, 1986), this field is "the facilitated analysis of the underlying sources of conflict situations by the parties in conflict . . . [and] the process whereby institutional and policy options are discovered that meet the needs of the parties, thus establishing the basis for a resolution of the conflict." Recent activity in this area has been considerable. Some has been directed at building theories of conflict and its resolution, and some has been focused on developing and testing practical means for resolving disputes. Although, in practice, conflict resolution has focused more on the domestic than the international sphere, it is beginning to have a considerable impact on curriculum development in the field of peace studies.

Pioneers in the general field include John Burton (1969, 1986), a political scientist who has argued that a permanent settlement to any conflict must account for each party's basic needs; Roger Fisher (1981), a lawyer who advocates "principled negotiation"; and Herbert Kelman (1972, 1979), a social psychologist known for his work on the Middle East conflict. Burton and Kelman have developed an innovative workshop process designed to involve members of adversarial communities in the exploration of hypothetical solutions that all parties could accept. Louis Kriesberg (1982), author of one of the leading textbooks on conflict analysis and resolution, *Social Conflicts*, is also active in the field of peace studies.

Paralleling the rise of conflict resolution as a field for research and professional practice has been the steadily increasing number of curricula in graduate and professional schools and, more recently, at the undergraduate level. The syllabi on conflict resolution included in this volume have been chosen to reflect not only the diversity of inquiry in this field but also its relevance to peace studies.

Conclusion

During the 1980s, the frontiers of peace research have once again become more theoretically and historically grounded, and the curricula in the field are slowly following suit. But the field can do still more to integrate historical perspectives. Pedagogically, the use of history in peace studies is both sobering and empowering: Students come to understand better the enormity of the task of eliminating war while gaining a better appreciation of sustained resistance and social activism. After all, encouraging an awareness among students of the struggle for peace as a long-term human project is at the core of our pedagogical strategy. Accordingly, courses on the Vietnam War and the history of draft resistance in the United States are included in this volume.

In terms of curriculum development, these new research frontiers challenge those of us in peace studies to continue incorporating new disciplinary, interdisciplinary, and transdisciplinary perspectives. Cross-disciplinary collaboration not only improves the quality of research and curricula; it also facilitates a rapprochement between fields that have traditionally been divided. For example, courses on the language and imagery of war and peace can involve faculty from the arts, film, communications, journalism, literature, and linguistics. Likewise, courses on new social movements can bring together sociologists, historians, and political scientists.

As the title of this introductory essay suggests, teaching and curriculum development in peace studies should both push and draw on the frontiers of research. One of the most positive features of peace research in the 1980s is that much of the intellectual work initiated by scholars is part of a longer-term exploration and not just a reflection of or a reaction to current events and pressing policy concerns. In this sense, peace studies remains a field whose agenda is both utopian and practical, visionary and immediate. If this process is to remain vibrant, however, peace studies and peace research must develop ahead of new crises in the political and intellectual mainstream, rather than merely analyzing them after the event.

One of the most important strengths of peace studies is its prescience—its ability to educate for the future without losing touch with the past or being overwhelmed by the present. In fact, the evolution of the field's curricula through the many editions of this *Curriculum Guide* attests to that dynamism and openness. Today's intellectual innovations will be reflected in tomorrow's syllabi and programs. Indeed, the very nature of our field ensures that the next edition of the *Curriculum Guide* is already in the making.

Bibliography

On Peace Movements

Alger, Chadwick F., and Saul H. Mendlovitz (1987). "Grass-Roots Initiatives: The Challenge of Linkages." In Saul H. Mendlovitz and R.B.J. Walker, eds., *Towards a Just World Peace.* London: Butterworth.

Brock, Peter (1970). *Pacifism in the Twentieth Century.* New York: Van Nostrand Publishers.

Chatfield, Charles, ed. (1973). *Peace Movements in America.* New York: Schocken Books.

Center for War, Peace, and the News Media. *Deadline.* A newsletter that analyzes media coverage of the arms race and related issues.

DeBenedetti, Charles (1980). *The Peace Reform in American History.* Bloomington: Indiana University Press.

——— (1983). "On the Significance of Citizen Peace Activism: America, 1961–1975," *Peace and Change,* Vol. 9 (Summer).

——— (1988). *Peace Heroes in Twentieth-Century America.* Bloomington: Indiana University Press.

Hegedus, Zsuzsa (1987). "The Challenge of the Peace Movement: Civilian Security and Civilian Emancipation." In Saul H. Mendlovitz and R.B.J. Walker, eds., *Towards a Just World Peace.* London: Butterworth.

Hook, Glenn (1986). "The Evolution of Anti-Nuclear Discourse in Japan." Paper presented at the XIth Meeting of the International Peace Research Association, Sussex, U.K.

Kodama, Katsuya (1988). "A Paradigm of the New Peace Movements." Paper presented at the International Peace Research Association's annual meeting, Rio de Janeiro, August 14–19, 1988.

Luckham, Robin (1984). "Of Arms and Culture," *Current Research on Peace and Violence,* Vol. 7, No. 1.

Mendlovitz, Saul H., and R.B.J. Walker, eds. (1987). *Towards a Just World Peace: Perspectives from Social Movements.* London: Butterworth; Committee for a Just World Peace. Includes essays by Chadwick F. Alger, Richard Falk, Zsuzsa Hegedus, Saul H. Mendlovitz, R.B.J. Walker, and Nigel Young.

Mushaben, Joyce (1985). "Cycles of Peace Protest in West Germany: Experiences from Three Decades," *West European Politics,* Vol. 8, No. 1 (January).

_____ (1986). "Grassoots and Gewaltfreie Aktionen: A Study of Mass Mobilization Strategies in the West German Peace Movement," *Journal of Peace Research*, Vol. 23, No. 2 (June).

Overy, Bob (1982). *How Effective Are Peace Movements?* Eugene, Oreg.: Harvest House.

Taylor, Richard, and Nigel Young (1987). *Campaigns for Peace: British Peace Movements in the Twentieth Century.* New York: St. Martin's Press.

Thompson, E. P. (1982). *Zero Option.* London: Merlin Press.

Tourraine, Alain (1985). "An Introduction to the Study of Social Movements," *Social Research*, Vol. 52, No. 4 (Winter).

Young, Nigel (1976). *War Resistance and the Nation State.* Ann Arbor, Mich.: University of Michigan.

_____ (1984). "Why Do Peace Movements Fail?: An Historical and Social Overview." *Social Alternatives.*

_____ (1986). "The Peace Movement: A Comparative and Analytical Survey," *Alternatives*, Vol. 11, No. 2.

_____ (1987). "Peace Movements in History." In Saul H. Mendlovitz and R.B.J. Walker, eds., *Towards a Just World Peace.* London: Butterworth.

_____ (1988). "Scholarly Books and Articles on Peace Movements." A comprehensive bibliography. In progress. Available from the author, c/o Colgate University.

On Cognition, War, and Peace

Bandura, Albert (1973). *Aggression: A Social Learning Analysis.* Englewood Cliffs, N.J.: Prentice-Hall.

Fabbro, David (1978). "Peaceful Societies: An Introduction," *Journal of Peace Research*, Vol. 15.

Frank, Jerome (1982). *Survival and Sanity in the Nuclear Age.* New York: Random House.

International Society for Research on Aggression (1986). "Statement on Violence." Drafted at the UNESCO Conference on Aggression and the Brain, Seville, Spain, May 1986. Reprinted in *International Peace Research Newsletter*, Vol. 25, No. 1 (January 1987).

Jervis, Robert (1976). *Perception and Misperception in International Politics.* Princeton, N.J.: Princeton University Press.

Jervis, Robert, Richard Ned Lebow, and Janice Gross Stein (1985). *Psychology and Deterrence.* Baltimore: Johns Hopkins University Press.

Kelman, Herbert C. (1987). "The Political Psychology of the Israeli-Palestinian Conflict," *Political Psychology*, Vol. 8, No. 3.

Kovel, Joel (1983). *Against the State of Nuclear Terror.* Boston: South End Press.

Lebow, Richard Ned (1981). *Between Peace and War: The Nature of International Crisis.* Baltimore: Johns Hopkins University Press.

Lifton, Robert Jay (1987a). *The New Psychology of Human Survival: Images of Doom and Hope.* Occasional Paper 1. Center on Violence and Human Survival, John Jay College, City University of New York, New York.

_____ (1987b). "False Normality in the Nuclear Age." In Proceedings of a Conference on *Nuclear Normality: The Ethics of Annihilation*, held in May 1987 at the Center on Violence and Human Survival, John Jay College, City University of New York, New York.

Lifton, Robert Jay, and Richard Falk (1982). *Indefensible Weapons: The Political and Psychological Case Against Nuclear Weapons.* New York: Basic Books.

Lorenz, Konrad (1966). *On Aggression.* New York: Harcourt, Brace and World.

Macy, Joanna (1983). *Despair and Personal Power in the Nuclear Age.* Philadelphia: New Society Publishers.

Mead, Margaret (1940). "Warfare is Only an Invention—Not a Biological Necessity," *Asia*, Vol. 40, No. 8. Reprinted in Charles R. Beitz and Theodore Herman, *Peace and War*. San Francisco: W. H. Freeman and Co.

Wilson, Edmund (1978). *On Human Nature*. Cambridge, Mass.: Harvard University Press.

On Alternative Security

Alger, Chadwick (1985). "Creating Local Institutions in the United States for Sustained Participation in Peacebuilding," *Peace and the Sciences*, No. 1/2.

Alternative Defence Commission (1987). *The Politics of Alternative Defence: A Role for A Non-Nuclear Britain*. London: Paladin Books.

Boulding, Elise (1988). *Building a Global Civic Culture: Education for an Interdependent World*. New York: Teachers College Press.

Brown, Lester (1986). "Redefining National Security." Ch. 11 in Linda Starke, ed., *State of the World Report 1986*. New York: W. W. Norton. Each annual edition of *The State of the World Report* contains useful data and analysis on redefining national and global security.

Bulletin of the Atomic Scientists (September 1988). Special issue on Non-Offensive Defense.

Deudney, Daniel (1983). *Whole-Earth Security: A Geopolitics of Peace*. Worldwatch Paper No. 55, Worldwatch Institute, Washington, D.C.

Falk, Richard (1987). "The State System and Contemporary Social Movements" and "The Global Promise of Social Movements." In Saul H. Mendlovitz and R.B.J. Walker, eds., *Towards a Just World Peace*. London: Butterworth.

Forsberg, Randall (1984). "Beyond the Freeze: Confining the Military to Defense as a Route to Disarmament," *World Policy Journal*, Vol. 1, No. 2.

Independent Commission on Disarmament and Security Issues (1982). *Common Security: A Blueprint for Survival*. New York: Simon and Schuster.

Johansen, Robert C. (1983). *Toward an Alternative Security System*. World Policy Working Paper 24. New York: World Policy Institute.

———— (1987). "Global Security Without Nuclear Deterrence," *Alternatives*, Vol. 12, No. 4.

Konrad, George (1984). *Antipolitics*. Translated by Richard E. Allen. New York: Henry Holt and Co.

Kruegler, Christopher, and Patricia Parkman (1985). "Identifying Alternatives to Political Violence: An Educational Imperative," *Harvard Educational Review* (February 1985).

MccGwire, Michael (1988). "A Mutual Security Regime for Europe?" *International Affairs*.

Moller, Bjorn (1987). "Bibliography of Non-Offensive Defence," *NOD International Research Newsletter*. Copenhagen: Centre of Peace and Conflict Research, University of Copenhagen.

Nye, Jr., Joseph S., et al. (1988). *Fateful Visions: Avoiding Nuclear Catastrophe*. Cambridge, Mass.: Ballinger Publishing Co.

Sharp, Gene (1986). *Making Europe Unconquerable: The Potential of Civilian-Based Defense*. Cambridge, Mass.: Ballinger Publishing Co.

Thompson, E. P. (1982). *Beyond the Cold War*. New York: Pantheon Books.

Unterseher, Lutz (1987). *Defending Europe: Toward a Stable Conventional Deterrent*. Working Paper SB-2, Center for Philosophy and Public Policy, University of Maryland.

von Muller, Albrecht, and Andrzej Karkoszka (1988). "A Modified Approach to Conventional Arms Control," *Defense and Disarmament Alternatives*. Institute for Defense and Disarmament Studies (May).

———— (1987). "An East-West Negotiating Proposal," *Defense and Disarmament News*. Institute for Defense and Disarmament Studies (May).

On Militarism and Development

Ahmad, Eqbal (1980). "The Neo-Fascist State: Notes on the Pathology of Power in the Third World," IFDA Dossier 19. Reprinted in *Toward a Just World Order*, edited by Richard Falk, Samuel Kim, and Saul Mendlovitz (Boulder: Westview Press, 1982).

Ball, Nicole (1982). *The Military in the Development Process: A Guide to the Issues*. Claremont, Calif.: Regina Development Books.

———— (1988). *Security, Economy, and the Third World*. Princeton, N.J.: Princeton University Press.

Bota, Liviu (1985). "The Establishment of an International Disarmament Fund for Development," *Bulletin of Peace Proposals*, Vol. 16, No. 1. Preface to a report by the same name published in 1984 by the UN Institute for Disarmament Research in Geneva.

Brozska, Michael, and Thomas Ohlson, eds. (1986). *Arms Production in the Third World, SIPRI*. Philadelphia and London: Taylor & Francis.

———— (1987). *Arms Transfers to the Third World, 1971–1985, SIPRI*. Oxford and New York: Oxford University Press.

———— (1988). *Arms Transfer Limitations and Third World Security, SIPRI*. Oxford and New York: Oxford University Press.

Goldblat, Josef (1987). "Demilitarization in the Developing World," *Journal of Peace Research*. Vol. 24, No. 1.

Katz, James E. (1984). *Arms Production in Developing Countries*. Lexington, Mass.: Lexington Books.

———— (1986). *The Implications of Third World Military Industrialization*. Lexington, Mass.: Lexington Books.

Klare, Michael T. (1985). *American Arms Supermarket*. Austin: University of Texas Press.

Lopez, George, and Michael Stohl, eds. (1986). *Governmental Violence and Repression: An Agenda for Research*. Westport, Conn.: Greenwood Press.

———— (1987). *Dependence, Development, and State Repression*. Westport, Conn.: Greenwood Press.

Sivard, Ruth Leger, ed. (annual). *World Military and Social Expenditures*. Washington, D.C.: World Priorities, Inc.

United Nations (1981). *Development and International Economic Cooperation: A Study of the Relationship Between Disarmament and Development*, UN document A/36/356 (the "Thorsson Report").

———— (1987). *Report of the International Conference on the Relationship Between Disarmament and Development*. UN document A-CONS 130/39.

———— (1986). *Disarmament*, Vol. 9, Nos. 1–2. UN Department for Disarmament Affairs, New York. Two-part special issue on disarmament and development.

———— (1982). *The Relationship Between Disarmament and Development*. UN Disarmament Study Series No. 5. London and Philadelphia: Taylor & Francis.

Wolpin, Miles (1985). *Militarization, Repression and Social Welfare in the Third World*. London: Croom Helm.

On Language and Media

Aubrey, Christin (1982). *Nukespeak: The Media and the Bomb.* London: Comedia Publishing Group.

Boyer, Paul (1985). *By the Bomb's Early Light: American Thought and Culture at the Dawn of the Atomic Age.* New York: Pantheon.

Chilton, Paul (1987). "Metaphor, Euphemism and the Militarization of Language," *Current Research on Peace and Violence,* Vol. 10, No. 1, Tampere, Finland.

Cohn, Carol (1987a). "Sex and Death in the Rational World of Defense Intellectuals," *Signs* (Summer).

———— (1987b). "Nuclear Language and How We Learned to Pat the Bomb," *Bulletin of the Atomic Scientists,* Vol. 43, No. 5.

Deadline. A research newsletter from the Center for War, Peace, and the News Media, New York University, 10 Washington Place, New York, N.Y. 10003.

Glasgow University Media Group (1985). *War and Peace News.* Milton Keynes, England: Open University Press.

Hook, Glen (1985). "Making Nuclear Weapons Easier to Live With: The Political Role of Language in Nuclearization," *Bulletin of Peace Proposals,* Vol. 16, No. 1.

Nuclear Texts and Contexts. A research newsletter available from Paul Brians, English Department, Washington State University, Pullman, Wash. 99164-5020.

Walker, R.B.J. (1986). "Culture, Discourse, and Insecurity," *Alternatives,* Vol. 11, No. 4.

Weart, Spencer (1988). *Nuclear Fear: A History of Images.* Cambridge: Harvard University Press.

On Feminism and Peace

Bernard, Jessie (1981). *The Female World.* New York: Free Press.

Boulding, Elise (1977). *Women in the Twentieth-Century World.* New York: Halsted Press.

Brock-Utne, Birgit (1985). *Educating for Peace: A Feminist Perspective.* New York: Pergamon Press.

Cooney, Robert, and Helen Michalowski, eds. (1987). *Power of the People.* Philadelphia: New Society Publishers.

Eisler, Riane, and David Loye (1986). "Peace and Feminist Theory: New Directions," *Bulletin of Peace Proposals,* Vol. 17, No. 1.

Miller, Jean Baker (1982). "Women and Power." In *Work in Progress,* Stone Center for Developmental Services and Studies, Wellesley College, 82-01.

McAllister, Pam, ed. (1982). *Reweaving the Web of Life: Feminism and Nonviolence.* Philadelphia: New Society Publishers.

Reardon, Betty A. (1985). *Sexism and the War System.* New York: Teachers College Press.

Roberts, Barbara (1984). "The Death of Machothink: Feminist Research and the Transformation of Peace Studies," *Women's Studies International Forum,* Vol. 7, No. 4.

———— (1985). "Research and Resources for Feminist Peace Studies." Paper presented to the Annual Meeting of the Canadian Women's Studies Association (May 28).

Stiehm, Judith, ed. (1983). *Women and Men's Wars.* New York: Pergamon Press.

Sylvester, Christine (1987). "Some Dangers in Merging Feminist and Peace Projects," *Alternatives,* Vol. 12, No. 4.

On Conflict Resolution

Burton, John (1969). *Conflict and Communication: The Use of Controlled Communication in International Relations.* New York: Free Press.

―――― (1986). "The Theory of Conflict Resolution," *Current Research on Peace and Violence,* Vol. 9, No. 3. Special issue on Conflict and Conflict Resolution.

Fisher, Roger, and William Ury (1981). *Getting to Yes.* Boston: Houghton Mifflin Co.

Kelman, Herbert C. (1972). "The Problem-Solving Workshop in Conflict Resolution." In *Communication in International Politics,* edited by R. Merritt. Urbana: University of Illinois Press.

―――― (1979). "An Interactional Approach to Conflict Resolution and Its Application to Israeli-Palestinian Relations," *International Interactions,* Vol. 6.

Kriesberg, Louis (1982). *Social Conflicts,* 2nd edition. Englewood Cliffs, N.J.: Prentice-Hall.

6. Peace Studies in the 1990s: Assessing Change in the Global War/Peace System

Michael T. Klare
Five College Program in Peace and World Security Studies

A key distinguishing characteristic of peace studies is its goal-oriented nature; that is, we seek not merely to comprehend the dynamics of war and militarism, but also to identify processes by which to reduce their incidence and severity. As a result, we are naturally concerned with international developments that bear on the frequency and intensity of armed conflict, civil repression, and mass human suffering. It is only by studying these phenomena that we can develop the analytical tools that will enable us to conduct a search for workable solutions. Hence, the study and analysis of international affairs is a critical dimension of peace studies.

In studying world affairs, moreover, our approach is inherently inter- or transdisciplinary in nature. Because violence in the global system (whether military or "structural") results from a combination of political, economic, social, and cultural factors, any comprehensive analysis of the subject must draw upon the methodologies and the accumulated wisdom of many fields, including history, economics, psychology, anthropology, sociology, and political science. As suggested by some of the other essays in this volume, we seek "meta-analyses" that combine the findings of *all* of these fields in order to understand the dynamics of the global war/peace system.

One method for conducting this search is to look *backward*, to study the historical record in order to derive some hypotheses about the causes of war and the relative effectiveness of various approaches to the prevention and termination of war. For this reason, most introductory peace studies courses devote considerable attention to past conflicts (typically, World War I or II), and to such experiments in peacemaking and disarmament as the League of Nations and the Baruch Plan of 1946. Much of the advanced work in peace research, moreover, involves the comparative analysis of past wars and disarmament efforts.

But peace studies also recognizes a need to look *forward*, to examine current international developments in order to identify worrisome trends (so that appropriate corrective action can be taken) and to assess the effectiveness of current peacemaking efforts (with a view to their improvement). For this reason, most peace studies programs include courses that examine such ongoing phenomena as the superpower arms race, nuclear proliferation, regional conflict, Third World underdevelopment, and civil repression. Typically, students in such courses are required to study one or more of these phenomena as part of a required research project, and to propose possible means for their solution. It is assumed (correctly, one hopes) that these students will someday put these analytical and problem-solving skills to work as they proceed onward in their professional careers.

Many of the syllabi that have been assembled for this volume incorporate this problem-oriented approach to international war/peace phenomena. Almost all of the introductory courses provide students with some exposure to the current literature on the nuclear arms race, and most include some discussion of other contemporary issue areas—the economics of global militarism, the abuse of fundamental human rights, the role of the United Nations, and so on. These, and other current issues, are also addressed in many of the more advanced courses in the field.

This focus on international conflict dynamics helps account for the growing popularity of peace studies among students, as well as for the growing recognition by university faculty and administrators that it constitutes a significant addition to the undergraduate and graduate curriculum.

We know, from polling data, that young people are acutely aware of the threat of nuclear annihilation. Some students respond to this peril through denial, by escaping into hedonism, self-absorption, and careerism; others, however, respond in a positive manner, by seeking to understand the causes of war and by engaging in constructive action to diminish the risk of catastrophe. These latter are the students who have been drawn to peace studies, and who, in many ways, represent the world's best hope for a safe and peaceful future. Perhaps the most important contribution of peace studies in the 1980s has been to provide thousands of young people with a positive alternative to nuclear fatalism and despair.

Similarly, by placing its focus squarely on some of the most significant and threatening phenomena of the modern era, peace studies has earned grudging respect from many initially skeptical faculty and administrators. At many schools, peace studies programs made their initial appearance with courses on the nuclear arms race. These courses (a sampling of the best of which are included in this volume) provided large numbers of faculty and students with their first opportunity to examine and discuss this critical concern in the classroom. Often launched on an experimental basis, these courses have been accorded a permanent place in the undergraduate curriculum as colleges and universities have acknowledged their responsibility to include teaching on critical international issues as part of a comprehensive liberal arts education.

Following on these initial successes, many peace studies programs have been able to thrive and grow on campuses where committed faculty have been able to demonstrate to colleagues and administrators that they possessed a capacity for examining a fundamental concern of modern life (i.e., international conflict and its prevention) and that existing courses and disciplines were not adequately addressing this topic. On those campuses where this process has occurred, the basic course on the nuclear age has been joined by courses on such topics as regional conflict and revolutionary war, militarism and human rights, arms control and disarmament, famine and underdevelopment, the ethics and morality of international affairs, and contemporary social movements and social change.

This approach has also been reflected in many of the graduate programs in peace studies that have emerged in recent years. Here too, the key to success has been a perception that peace studies (or peace and security studies, as it is often termed at the graduate level) constitutes a distinctive and important *field* of inquiry, and one that has heretofore been neglected by other academic programs and disciplines. This field of inquiry has also proved a very rich source of subject matter for research by graduate students and faculty—much of which has subsequently been published in the academic literature, thereby adding increased legitimacy to peace studies.

In short, peace studies has made great strides in the 1980s in terms of establishing a significant presence on the academic horizon. Much of this success, I would argue, is the result of the field's ability to lay claim to the scholarly study of a significant array of critical international phenomena. If peace studies is to grow and mature in the years ahead, therefore, it must enhance its exploration of these phenomena and further demonstrate the validity of its analyses. Furthermore, in keeping with its problem-solving orientation, peace studies must show that its analyses can contribute to the search for constructive solutions.

In part, we accomplish this by doing better what we are doing already. We must probe more deeply into the causes of war, enrich our assessment of war-averting strategies, and widen our focus to include additional manifestations of global violence. Many of the syllabi included in this edition of the *Curriculum Guide* were selected precisely because they help steer us in this direction.

But it is not enough to improve our understanding of the world as it is. Because the international system itself is changing rapidly, we must develop our analyses so as to account for new and altered circumstances. More than this, we must develop an *analysis of change*. In other words, if we are to maintain our expertise in the area of global conflict and peacemaking, we must develop analyses that will enable us to anticipate and account for the ways in which the global war/peace system is changing. Only by understanding the nature of these changes will our analyses of conflict remain valid; and only by enriching our analyses will we be able to help in the search for viable methods of peacemaking.

The Changing War/Peace System

How is the global war/peace system changing? We cannot answer this question fully, of course, as more time is needed to plot the outcome of many current trends. But at least some of the most important factors of change can now be identified.

1. *The U.S.-Soviet rivalry appears to be diminishing in intensity.* Following extremely high levels of tension in the early 1980s, reforms in Soviet domestic and foreign policy as well as popular mobilization against the renewed cold war seem to have led to a softening of U.S.-Soviet antagonism, as evidenced by the signing of the Intermediate Nuclear Forces (INF) Treaty in December 1987 and by the subsequent Reagan-Gorbachev summit in Moscow. On his return from the summit, Reagan declared in London, "Quite possibly, we are beginning to take down the barriers of the postwar era"—an extraordinary statement from a president who commenced his administration with talk of the "evil empire" and an accompanying call for massive increases in U.S. nuclear and conventional forces. If such a statement is followed by substantial new agreements in the area of arms control and regional cooperation, the post-Reagan era could see a historic decline in U.S.-Soviet hostilities. And while mutual fear and suspicion between the superpowers is not likely to disappear altogether—indeed, we must constantly be on the lookout for a flareup in tension—the world could experience a significant reduction in the risk of global nuclear war.

2. *North-South and South-South tensions appear to be escalating.* Although conflict between East and West appears to be subsiding, conflict between the industrial powers of the North and the largely agrarian nations of the South appears to be intensifying, as is conflict among Third World countries. Similarly, there appears to be an increase in "low-intensity conflict"—that is, guerrilla war, counterinsurgency, terrorism, border skirmishes, ethnic conflict, and so-called police operations by the major powers.[1] It is possible, of course, that this intensification of North-South and South-South hostility is more apparent than real, in that we in the North naturally tend to become more aware of conflict in the South at times when East-West conflict is at a low ebb. But it also appears that the 1980s have witnessed unusually high levels of violence in such areas as Central America, Southern Africa, the Gulf region, Southwest Asia, and Israel/Palestine. Whether this is due to the relaxation of superpower domination, or to the sharpening of economic competition between North or South, or to other factors entirely, cannot at this time be satisfactorily determined. But if current trends continue, it seems likely that the 1990s will be a time of considerable conflict and tension in the Third World.

3. *Third World countries are acquiring increasingly powerful arsenals of modern weapons.* At one time, most Third World countries were armed with the obsolete hand-me-downs of the major industrial powers. Today, as a result of the booming arms trade, many such countries are equipped with substantial arsenals of modern high-tech weapons.[2] Clearly, the acquisition of such capabilities has greatly enhanced the capacity of belligerent states to sustain combat at high levels of intensity—a capacity that has been woefully evident in the continuing Gulf conflict. Moreover, it is not just established governments that are acquiring such capabilities: Through the

flourishing black market arms trade, many insurgent groups and terrorist formations have gained access to modern guns and missile systems.[3]

Equally worrisome is the fact that many of the more advanced Third World countries have acquired the capacity to design and manufacture modern arms on their own—including, in several notable cases, the capacity to produce nuclear weapons. According to the U.S. Arms Control and Disarmament Agency (ACDA), Third World countries now account for 15 percent of international arms exports, up from 6 percent in 1975.[4] Moreover, several Third World producers, including Argentina, Brazil, China, Israel, and the two Koreas, have become major suppliers of modern conventional arms to other Third World countries, including the belligerents in the Gulf region.[5] Accompanying this flow of conventional arms-making technology is the continuing proliferation of nuclear and chemical weapons technology. At present, five Third World countries—China, India, Israel, Pakistan, and South Africa—are believed to possess at least a rudimentary arsenal of nuclear devices, and several other countries have taken at least some steps in this direction.[6] Clearly, the acceleration of these technology flows in the years ahead would lead to a very ominous future regarding regional conflict in the Third World.

4. *The interplay between global economic developments and global military developments appears to be increasing.* Economic factors have, of course, always figured significantly in the causation of international conflict. For most of the cold war period, however, ideological factors have tended to play a more conspicuous role—especially in the case of the U.S.-Soviet competition. Now, with the ebbing of U.S.-Soviet hostilities, we appear to be entering a period in which economic factors will again be significant. Signs of this trend include growing unrest in the Third World and Eastern Europe prompted by domestic austerity programs imposed by international lending agencies; multinational naval operations in the Gulf region intended to safeguard the international oil flow; opposition in Congress to the transfer to Japan of advanced U.S. military technology (out of fear that the Japanese will divert the technology to their export-oriented civilian economy); and the growing use of food as a weapon in internal conflicts. The outcome is unclear; but the likelihood is that economic issues of this sort will figure significantly in the global conflict environment of the 1990s.

5. *Non-state actors are playing an increasing role in world affairs.* Much of the traditional literature on international peace and conflict tends to assume that all significant action in this field is undertaken by governments, serving as representatives of the nation-state. In the 1980s, however, both peace- and warmaking activities have increasingly been conducted by nonstate actors, including insurgent movements, mercenary bands, religious agencies, grassroots citizen action groups, and so on. Such formations have played key roles in many of the major conflicts of the 1980s, including those in South Africa, Central America, Lebanon, the Philippines, Afghanistan, Israeli-occupied Palestine, and South Korea. Wherever one looks in the Third World, moreover, there are minority or separatist groups engaged in struggle

for greater freedom and autonomy. At the same time, we have seen a significant increase in peacemaking efforts undertaken by citizens' groups, religious agencies, and other nongovernmental organizations (NGOs). Both of these developments—the proliferation of internal and regional conflicts fought largely by irregular forces, and the peacemaking initiatives of the NGOs—are likely to gain further momentum in the 1990s.

6. *The number and type of peacemaking efforts are growing at an extraordinary pace.* It used to be, as noted in the fifth point above, that peacemaking was the exclusive prerogative of national governments (especially the richest and most powerful ones). Today, although traditional diplomacy is still an important part of international peacemaking, many nonstate actors are also making an important contribution to world peace and security. At the same time, we have seen a significantly increased diversity in the *methods* of peacemaking. Among the new approaches that have become conspicuous in recent years are the "citizen diplomacy" undertaken by grassroots groups to overcome ethnic and ideological barriers; the hostage-release efforts undertaken by individuals and religious groups; the "sister city" projects linking communities in East and West, North and South; the nonviolent "witnesses" employed in areas of conflict, intended to separate warring parties and deter attack; the interparliamentary initiatives designed to promote arms control and human rights; the permanent women's encampments situated at nuclear weapons sites; and the citizen boycotts and divestment campaigns intended to pressure corporations that do business in countries ruled by undemocratic and repressive regimes (e.g., South Africa and Chile). Such endeavors made a significant impact in the 1980s and are likely to play an even greater role in the years ahead.

This renaissance in the art of peacemaking is being reinforced by creative new proposals for alternative modes of international security and national defense. Variously termed nonoffensive defense, defensive defense, and citizen-based defense, these approaches to security seek to reduce the likelihood of international conflict by replacing countries' offensive military capacities with forces armed and trained for purely defensive missions. Theoretically, such methods are more successful at preventing war than existing modes because they would remove the stimulant for arms racing by rival countries while still deterring outright attack by an aggressively minded neighbor.[7] Alternative security thinking has already made great progress in government and peace movement circles in Europe, and it is likely to gain increasing prominence in the United States as well in the years ahead.

7. *Countries are likely to rely increasingly on the United Nations and other inter- and transnational agencies for solutions to global problems.* Despite recent difficulties arising from disputes over UN financing, current trends suggest an expanding role for international organizations in world affairs. The Soviet Union has recently promised to lend greater support to the United Nation's peacekeeping efforts, and both the UN-negotiated ceasefire in the Gulf war and the pullout of Soviet forces from Afghanistan have restored world

confidence in the organization's efficacy. As we look toward the 1990s, a more prominent role for the United Nations seems likely on a wide range of peacekeeping issues, including the civil war in Angola, the South African withdrawal from Namibia, the Vietnamese withdrawal from Kampuchea, and the possible international monitoring of arms-reduction treaties and nonintervention pacts.

Furthermore, the United Nations and other international bodies are likely to play an increasing role in managing global environmental problems that exceed the capacity of any single nation to solve. Such problems—the depletion of the ozone layer, the "greenhouse effect," widespread deforestation, and pollution of the oceans, for example—acquired new urgency in the late 1980s and demonstrated the need for international cooperation in overcoming threats to global security. It is possible that such cooperation will legitimize concepts of "common security," and thereby increase the willingness of countries to cooperate in other areas, including disarmament and international peacekeeping.

These are but a few of the global trends that are likely to have a major impact on the international war/peace system of the 1990s. In all likelihood, they will develop and interact in hard-to-predict but significant ways. Although we cannot anticipate all of their likely effects, it is essential that we address them in our teaching and research work.[8]

Curricular Implications

Most critical, in my view, is the need to integrate these phenomena more carefully and effectively into the course offerings of the peace studies curriculum. Because today's students will have to live with the consequences of these phenomena in the decades ahead, it is essential that we provide them with the information and analytical tools they will need for this purpose. Moreover, as teachers in the field, we need to study these trends if our analyses of global phenomena are to remain valid in the future. And, as I suggested earlier, such integration is necessary if we are to retain our claim of expertise in the field of global conflict and cooperation.

Our first task, therefore, is to incorporate analyses of these changing world conditions in the courses we teach. But we face a more fundamental challenge as well: to structure our teaching and research in such a way as to participate constructively in the search for new modes of peacemaking and conflict resolution. It is already evident, from the assessments drawn above, that the international system will face severe stresses and strains in the 1990s, and that the existing methods for coping with such pressures are likely to become less and less effective. New solutions to global problems are clearly needed—and peace studies should serve as a laboratory for their development. Specifically, we should explore new approaches to peace and world security with our students in the classroom. In the process we should seek to involve and build upon the visionary work now under way in alternative security and peace research (see the essay by Daniel Thomas and Nigel Young in Part II of this volume). By creating "laboratories" of this sort, we and our students will have an extraordinary opportunity to participate directly in the global struggle for peace.

As I have outlined them, these challenges and opportunities suggest the following considerations for curriculum development:

- Courses on nuclear weapons and East-West issues need to be balanced by courses (or course-segments) on conventional arms and North-South conflict. In particular, we need to increase our curricular attention to such topics as the increase in "low-intensity conflict" and regional combat in the Third World; the global trade in sophisticated weapons and arms-making capabilities, including nuclear weapons; the changing interventionary policies and practices of the superpowers; and the negotiation and verification of arms-reduction pacts.
- Courses on war and the arms race should stress the complexity of international conflict issues. Specifically, this entails addressing both nuclear and non-nuclear weapons issues; examining the interplay between East-West and North-South conflict situations; assessing the role of both state and nonstate actors in peace- and warmaking activities; and analyzing the characteristics and consequences of both "low-intensity" and "high-intensity" conflict.
- Courses on arms control and disarmament should include segments on "alternative security" thinking and nonprovocative defense.
- Courses on peace and peacemaking should stress the multiplicity of methods available for the minimization of violence and the resolution of international conflict, including those available to nonstate actors such as citizens groups and transnational social movements. Increased attention should also be paid to the role of the United Nations and other international bodies.
- New courses should be developed, or old ones revised, to examine nonmilitary forms of violence in the international system, such as economic underdevelopment, famine, and human rights abuses. This category includes the study of aggravating factors such as ethnic, religious, and ideological schisms, the competition for scarce resources, and ecological destruction.
- Upper-level courses should be developed to provide committed students with the advanced research and analytical skills needed to study issues of global conflict, and to prepare them for related research and analysis careers in government, academia, or public interest organizations. (The syllabus of a course of this type, "Current Problems in Peace and Conflict Studies," is included in this volume.)

Such initiatives, if undertaken in the years ahead, will infuse our peace studies programs with new excitement and creativity. It will force us to broaden our own knowledge and understanding of current international developments, to search out new texts and teaching materials, to *create* new teaching materials to fill critical voids in the existing peace studies literature, and to develop new courses and course segments. A broadened and enriched curriculum, moreover, will attract new interest and enthusiasm from the student population. Most important, such efforts will enhance our potential contribution to the continuing search for meaningful alternatives to the global war system.

Notes

1. For discussion of this phenomenon, see Michael Klare and Peter Kornbluh, eds., *Low-Intensity Warfare* (New York: Pantheon, 1988).

2. Between 1980 and 1987, Third World countries ordered $352 billion worth of conventional arms and actually took possession of $322 billion worth (in constant 1987 dollars). Included in these acquisitions were 35,702 tanks and armored troop carriers, 21,447 artillery pieces, 4,102 combat planes, 584 surface ships and submarines, and 38,316 surface to air missiles. See Richard F. Grimmett, *Trends in Conventional Arms Transfers to the Third World by Major Suppliers, 1980–1987* (Washington, D.C.: Congressional Research Service, 1988), pp. 46, 56, 65.

3. For discussion, see Michael T. Klare, "The Arms Trade: Changing Patterns in the 1980s," *Third World Quarterly* (October 1987), pp. 1257–1281.

4. U.S. Arms Control and Disarmament Agency, *World Military Expenditures and Arms Transfers, 1986* (Washington, D.C., 1987), p. 101.

5. See Klare, "The Arms Trade"; and Michael Brzoska, "Profiteering on the Iran-Iraq War," *Bulletin of the Atomic Scientists* (June 1987), pp. 42–45.

6. On nuclear proliferation, see Leonard S. Spector, *Going Nuclear* (Cambridge, Mass.: Ballinger, 1987).

7. For discussion, see Robert C. Johansen and Saul Mendlovitz, eds., *Contending Approaches to National Security* (Boulder, Colo.: Lynne Rienner Press, 1989). For a bibliography on this topic, see the syllabus in this volume for "Beyond the Arms Race."

8. For an earlier perspective on the state of the field and the range of global issues requiring attention from peace studies faculty, see George Lopez, "A University Peace Studies Curriculum for the 1990s," *Journal of Peace Research*, Vol. 22, No. 2 (1985), pp. 117–128.

III

Strategies for Curriculum Development

1. Conceptual Models for Peace Studies Programs

George A. Lopez
University of Notre Dame

No two peace studies programs are exactly alike. The nature of any individual program is influenced by a number of choices faculty must make regarding the substantive dimensions of the field they wish to emphasize and the institutional structure they judge would be most appropriate for introducing that material to their campus. After working for ten years at quite a few campuses with faculty who were in the process of developing peace studies programs, I have reached a clear and relatively simple set of conclusions regarding this challenge.

This essay is designed to help those who are new to the field to negotiate this process in such a manner as to develop a curriculum that is academically rigorous, appropriate to the tenor of their campus, and structurally sustainable. I will focus on the substantive dimensions of the field as the primary consideration, noting, where appropriate, other factors that come into play as a program develops. I will also give special attention to decisions regarding the organization of courses, debates on the content of an introductory course, senior seminars, and experiential education. In the conclusion, I will discuss briefly the recent emergence of graduate-level programs in peace studies and offer some suggestions regarding the implications of this development.

Reflections on Curriculum Development

For a peace studies program to "get off the ground," leadership must come from a dedicated committee of hard-working faculty, administrators, and students who are willing to study the pedagogical and substantive issues embodied in the field.

In the 1970s, before the field had much historical data on program development, those interested in developing university-level peace studies programs had to rely on the perspectives and challenges posed by a few scholarly analyses. Wehr and Washburn (1976) articulated a variety of strategies for the establishment of what they called a "Peace and World Order Systems" curriculum at colleges and universities. Their study addressed the logistical dimensions of how an institution could build from single course offerings, to minors, and ultimately to a fully developed peace studies major within the college or university. Their work also advocated a particular conceptual direction to peace studies education: one in which students would be taught the centrality of global security rather than just national security, and in which courses would focus on the development of those world order values, policies, and institutions necessary for creating a better world.

At about the same time, John Vasquez (1976) explored a number of the theoretical and methodological issues raised by a peace pedagogy. Vasquez highlighted the "two cultures problem"—a situation in which university educators seemed caught in the tension between a behavioral science/international relations approach to peace studies problems, on the one hand, and a more activist, experience-based, and often normative approach to the field, on the other. It might appear to some that this tension was much less relevant to program development than originally stated by Vasquez (see Lopez, 1985: 120–122). Nonetheless, this debate about the focus of the field and the structure of programs remains very much alive today, albeit in new forms.

At the beginning of this decade Dennis Carey (1980) argued for a discipline-like approach to peace studies, in which the study of various forms of conflict, violence, and their regulation would be the conceptual underpinning of a program. Shortly thereafter, Douglas Sloan (1982) argued that solid education in peace studies ought to focus on nuclear issues and the search for serious policy alternatives to existing nuclear policies. Sloan also asserted that part of the difficulty in teaching peace studies in the 1980s was that too many educators assumed the need for technical skills and in-depth background in strategic thought as the only manner in which the education about nuclear issues and peace could be conducted. To the contrary, Kohn and Badash's (1988) recent study of university efforts in nuclear education across the United States illustrates that there is actually a marked diversity in courses and disciplinary approaches to dealing with the nuclear dilemma.

In the late 1980s, new insights about and prescriptions for education in peace studies have emerged from a number of challenging inquiries into the conceptual boundaries of the field. For example, the discourse analysis work of Carol Cohn (1987) and others regarding nuclear language and the thought patterns of defense intellectuals has identified at least two "new" areas for peace studies education: an approach based on linguistic analyses and a feminist approach to the study of peace and security issues. (For more information on this and other "research frontiers," see the essay in this volume by Daniel Thomas and Nigel Young.)

Kruegler and Parkman (1985) raise a rather different set of conceptual issues that also have great significance for curriculum development. Strongly influenced by the work of Gene Sharp, they maintain that peace studies scholarship has focused so much attention on violence that the history and tactics of the nonviolent resolution of conflict remain virtually unknown. It is essential, they argue, that peace studies commit itself to educating about the history, theory, and practical mechanics of nonviolent struggle, defense, and conflict resolution.

Whereas Cohn focuses on nuclear issues, and Kruegler and Parkman address nonviolence, Rivage-Seul (1987) broadens the debate by challenging peace education to help students avoid the political disempowerment fostered by a world of harsh bureaucratic decisionmaking, violence, and injustice. Taking issue with the approach advocated by Sloan and others calling for courses that would make students *knowledgeable* about nuclear issues, she asserts that courses about and *experiences with* those lacking power in the political system are most essential. Not the least of the reasons supporting this claim is the fact that students themselves often have a sense of powerlessness. Her suggestion for peace studies, then, is that it adopt the approaches of Paulo Freire—that is, that it include course content and skills that empower people to change the quality of their lives through their own efforts.

Developing a Conceptual Map
of Peace Studies

In light of this diverse literature (to which must be added the "traditional" literature of international relations and the now extensive literature on conflict resolution), how can faculty who are eager to undertake serious work in peace studies go about developing a comprehensive curricular model? Experience has shown that the colleges and universities that have been successful in this enterprise are the ones that sketch for themselves a full conceptual map of the field and then debate the relative merits and priorities embodied therein. A *sample* conceptual map of the field is the nine-cell matrix presented in Map A. Map B is another way of mapping the field. The three perspectives discussed by Betty Reardon in her essay in this volume suggest yet another conceptual map for peace studies. (This essay's discussion will refer solely to Map A.)

In considering the conceptual perimeters of the peace studies field, faculty committees have tended to see the substantive focus of their program as lying within one of three broadly defined categories.

Areas of Substantive Focus

Levels of Human Interaction	Causes and Consequences of Violence -1-	Methods for Reducing or Resolving Violent Conflict -2-	The Values, Norms, and Institutions of Peace -3-
Individual -- A --	• Aggression • Socialization • Bigotry • Inter-personal violence	• Communication skills • Negotiation • Mediation • Education	• Nonviolence as a lifestyle • Ethical/religious perspectives
Social Group and Intranational -- B --	• Economic disparity • Repression • Revolution	• Arbitration • Negotiation • Mediation • Conflict resolution workshops	• Nonviolent direct action • Social movements • Justice • Freedom
International -- C --	• War • Arms race • Arms trade • Xenophobia • Intervention • Nuclear War	• Diplomacy • International peacekeeping • Mediation • Crisis management	• International law and organization • Nonoffensive defense • Global cooperation

Conceptual Map A of Peace Studies

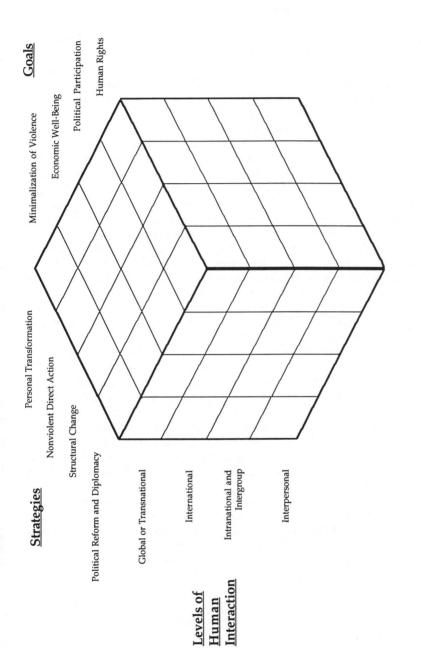

Goals

Human Rights

Political Participation

Economic Well-Being

Minimalization of Violence

Strategies

Personal Transformation

Nonviolent Direct Action

Structural Change

Political Reform and Diplomacy

**Levels of
Human
Interaction**

Global or Transnational

International

Intranational and
Intergroup

Interpersonal

Conceptual Map B of Peace Studies

In the first, *the causes and consequences of violent conflict,* a program would focus on such issues as the nature of aggression, the conditions under which conflict becomes violence, and the effects of violent conflicts on victims, perpetrators, and the wider environment.

The second area of substantive focus, *the theories and skills for managing, reducing, and/or resolving conflict,* may be the most dynamic during the 1980s. This theme includes the study of various forms of negotiation, arbitration, conciliation, and mediation. It also addresses areas of communication theory, conflict analysis, and areas of law.

In the third area, the study of those *values, norms, and institutions necessary for building a significantly less violent world,* the normative and prescriptive dimensions parallel the descriptive. Because it is based more explicitly on normative criteria, this approach is somewhat more controversial than the first two models.

Cutting across these three substantive areas of inquiry in peace studies are three distinct levels of analysis: that of the individual, the social group, and the national/international system. Experience has shown that successful programs are those which quickly recognize that the nine distinct cells resulting from this matrix provide marvelous opportunities for faculty from a variety of disciplines to make contributions to program development. Each individual sector of the matrix, of course, constitutes a legitimate subfield within peace studies and is sufficiently rich with content and importance to warrant further exploration by a university program.

Based on the outcome of this deliberation about the parameters of the field (which should include an honest assessment of the substantive strengths of the faculty involved), a peace studies committee should decide which of the nine cells to address in the program's curricular offerings. To emphasize subfields A1, A2, B1, and B2, for example, implies a significant role for faculty in psychology and sociology. To pursue program development in subfields A2, B2, and C2, on the other hand, would imply a focus on law, international relations, communications, and history, as well as sociology and psychology. Other possible combinations and contributions are readily apparent.

It should also be apparent from Map A that few campuses are likely to be able to offer courses in each of the nine subfields. Rather than worrying about accusations of bias, a peace studies program must make honest choices about what it can and cannot accomplish without sacrificing quality of instruction. If necessary, one can always point out that such decisions are commonplace in higher education, especially at small and middle-sized colleges and universities. Thus, when the faculty in a department cannot adequately cover all the subfields of their discipline, they prudently elect to concentrate on those areas that they consider to be of highest priority based on their interpretation of the discipline and the competence of the department's faculty. For example, an English department may opt for two courses on Shakespeare rather than one on Elizabethan and one on Victorian literature. Similarly, a department of history may have neither the interest nor the expertise to offer courses on all regions of the world and periods of history. In neither case are they any less departments of English or history for having made tough decisions about their areas of specialization. By the same token, peace studies programs—when constructed with a rigorous conceptual map in mind—are not inadequate to the task of systematic education in the field when they opt for a particular area of specialization. The logical corrolary to this flexibility in the choice of specialization is the notion that if a faculty committee recognizes its own shortcomings in a particularly vital area, and no appropriate colleague can be found, it should identify one of its own members to develop the necessary competence in that area.

The Process of Program Development

No faculty committee will succeed in creating, much less sustaining, a successful peace studies program unless it proceeds with the development and evaluation of a conceptual map of the field with a high degree of rigor and energy. In fact, an analysis of the experience that hundreds of faculty have had while developing programs over the years indicates certain lessons that, when adapted to a particular campus, can go a long way toward ensuring coherence and sustainability, and thus respectability, for a university peace studies program (see Lopez, 1986).

A visible and hard-working group of faculty, administrators and students should be assembled to serve as the peace studies "vanguard." The special task of these committee members is to investigate the viability and contours of a peace studies program at their institution, which they accomplish by thoroughly investigating the conceptual map and its relation to existing faculty strengths, interests, and course offerings. To begin this process, the committee should explore the nature of the field itself, considering it as a whole and in terms of the relationship of each part to the others. The next step is to compile an inventory of existing faculty and institutional resources in order to identify areas of strength as well as those that will require development in the future. Finally, the committee should construct a plan for particular aspects of the program's curriculum and institutional form, encompassing such issues as whether to offer a major or a minor, the role of the introductory course, the place of internships and experiential learning, and so on. In this latter task, the committee should be especially concerned about the management and sustainability of the program over time. Finally, the committee should produce a clear statement of purpose for the program that can be distributed to appropriate campus bodies, including the faculty and administrative entities responsible for academic affairs, the various departments, and the school newspaper.

Experience has shown that the programs which have been successful over time are those that were able, whether by design or not, to locate the issues they wanted to focus on in the classroom in one or more of the cells of the conceptual map of the peace studies field.

Relating to the Institution's Mission Statement

In many cases, the wider mission of the host institution is an important consideration in deciding on which part of the field a peace studies program should focus. This factor is too often underestimated both in the work of the campus committee and in the translation of the committee's conceptual scheme into a vibrant and respected curricular endeavor. If a faculty group cannot find some congruence between the definition of peace studies it has adopted and the purpose and role of its home institution, it will be much more difficult for peace studies to "catch on" as a plausible part of the curriculum. In practice, then, the faculty members working on the development or expansion of a program must be able to deduce from their institution's statement of purpose a way in which to demonstrate to their colleagues that peace studies assists in fulfilling the mission of the institution.

It is not surprising that a number of surveys (Everts, 1972; Lopez, 1978) reveal that peace studies programs have been much more successful at smaller, Church-affiliated liberal arts colleges than at larger state institutions or urban universities. With the former, it is much easier to identify the expressed purpose of the institution and to demonstrate a reasonably high degree of congruence between peace studies and that purpose.

This challenge is more difficult in larger state and urban institutions, where the core values and mission may be more elusive, or at least less likely to play a determining role in the academic life of the school. Furthermore, as many colleges and universities struggle with enrollment and attempt to be all things to all people, the place of peace studies can become quite ambiguous. Nevertheless, the better able a faculty group is to articulate a definition of peace studies that is consistent with the cells of Map A and with the core values and mission of its institution, the more likely it is that its endeavors will succeed.

Models for Program Development

Colleges and universities have pursued a variety of schemes for translating the pedagogical literature and the conceptual map into the process of actually instituting a peace studies program. Four particular curriculum models seem to dominate the field: (1) the introduction of a regular major; (2) the organization of a minor or curricular "concentration"; (3) the infusion of peace studies into a broad segment of the liberal arts curriculum; and (4) the placement of peace studies within an existing interdisciplinary or general education framework. Although I will not delve at length into each of these approaches, it is important that I show how a committee's decision with regard to the conceptual map can affect the curriculum model they choose.

The development of the "major model" may seem to be the most desirable goal, but it has been pursued by only a minority of programs in the field. Moreover, institutions have arrived at this point after traveling a number of different paths. At smaller liberal arts institutions such as Colgate University and Earlham College, some programs introduced majors in peace studies after a substantial amount of faculty development and curriculum infusion had occurred throughout the school. In these cases the peace studies committee elected to involve a large number of disciplines and to pursue various levels of analysis. In the end, however, both the Colgate and the Earlham programs developed a primary emphasis on the national and international system levels.

At other institutions, including Kent State University and Syracuse University, program development proceeded on the assumption that a full major would focus primarily on the second vertical column of the conceptual map: conflict management, reduction, and resolution. This observation should not be taken to mean that teaching on international relations and the causes of war did not exist at either institution, for it did; rather, the faculty committee selected the aforementioned emphasis in order to allow for comprehensive study of a particular area in both its theoretical and practical dimensions. Extracurricular components, such as internship placements and skill training workshops that involve students with conflict resolution professionals, were also developed in accordance with the subfield commitment made by the program.

The second scheme for the organization of a peace studies curriculum, and by far the most popular approach, is the development of a defined set of courses that constitute a certificate, a curricular concentration, or a minor in peace studies. The decision to opt for this form of organization does not *necessarily* imply that the institution lacks the resources for a full-scale major, nor does it indicate that the committee charged with developing peace studies on the campus failed to win sufficient academic or political support. Rather, it is usually preference regarding transdisciplinary education and the conceptual map that influences faculty to pursue a nonmajor format for peace studies. For example, the faculty at some institutions have chosen to attempt to expose a larger number of students to peace studies than would be possible by focusing on a major. Therefore, even when a large enough number of faculty are participating in the program to cover most of the cells on the conceptual map, a minor or certificate structure is opted for so that students from a variety of discipline-based majors can take cognate courses through a peace studies minor. Given sufficient administrative resources, of course, a program could pursue this strategy *and* offer a major to interested students.

The third curricular pattern entails the infusion of peace studies themes into as many campus courses as possible. Where this model is successful, it reflects a faculty decision that the issues addressed by peace studies are so important that the goal must be to expose as many students to those issues as possible. Much like the minor or certificate strategy, this approach requires that a great many courses be offered in the numerous cell areas of the conceptual map. In its optimal form, the infusion approach provides students with an opportunity to pursue a traditional education in the natural sciences, humanities, and social sciences, while also learning about the various substantive areas that inform peace studies as a field. Campuses that have succeeded in this venture have explicitly pursued faculty development across a variety of disciplines in order to facilitate the introduction of peace studies issues and perspectives into a broad range of courses. The faculty at Gustavus Adolphus College, for example, decided to organize their faculty development efforts around the theme that "peace is development." With the support of a grant from the U.S. Department of Education, more than 70 percent of the faculty participated in the program and developed an area of expertise related to the challenge of development. Their commitment was sustained over time through an ongoing series of "brown bag" lunches and frequent reappraisals of the entire curriculum.

Faculty at the University of Ohio began to explore the role of peace studies on their campus at a time when the institution as a whole was in the process of assessing the future of its general education curriculum. In this environment, the peace studies committee members were able to demonstrate to the entire faculty and administration that the courses they proposed would foster improved cross-disciplinary integration and thereby advance the entire general education curriculum. Of course, the very process of infusion can dissipate the focus of peace studies and thereby make this approach the most difficult to sustain over time. However, as its advocates argue, it also prevents the "ghetto-ization" of peace studies and, by its very nature, develops a self-sustaining momentum that can influence faculty and curricula long after the original impetus is gone.

Finally, the development of peace studies on a number of campuses has emerged as "a rose by other names." For a number of different reasons, some faculty groups spearheading peace studies enterprises have decided that neither of the three curriculum strategies outlined above fits their situation. In finding a home for peace studies, then, these groups often decide to make peace studies a "track" within a larger multidisciplinary framework that has already proven successful at the institution. This approach is pursued more often in large universities than in small colleges, reflecting the fact that a great deal of peace studies–related activity is already taking place at most large institutions. Thus, after a great deal of faculty effort at West Virginia University had been devoted to the development of a transdisciplinary educational enterprise in international studies, the peace studies committee chose to locate its program within the international studies track rather than to create a competitive structure. A similar pattern developed at Wittenberg University, where peace studies flourishes within the context of an existing international studies program. Of course, in these sorts of institutional settings, a faculty committee may have somewhat less flexibility in the boundaries of the peace studies conceptual map.

The lessons that those seeking to organize their own peace studies programs might take from this sketch of alternative schemes ought to be clear. First, almost any particular curriculum model for peace studies can succeed if the faculty involved have properly examined the dimensions of the field and have devoted considerable attention to the means by which to operationalize its key frameworks, concepts, and queries. The committee must also have determined an appropriate locus for peace studies within the larger institutional mission, and it must have selected a structure conducive to accomplishing that function. Some would argue that the only structure able to do full justice to the content of the field and to ensure survival in a harsh academic environment is the development of a full department and major with tenured faculty, institutional budget lines, support staff, and the like. However, dozens of schools have found that the development of a minor or certificate program, or the opting for a strategy of infusion or of locating peace studies in an existing transdisciplinary venture, can also be equally productive.

Finally, it is not entirely clear whether the field of peace studies would be better served by graduating a relatively small number of peace studies majors or by graduating a large number of students who have had substantial exposure to peace studies issues while in pursuit of more traditional majors. Until this question is answered conclusively, it is fair to say that a variety of options have worked in the past and are likely to work well in the future.

Central Questions in Program Development

A serious examination of the conceptual map of the field is is also essential when deciding on such questions as the design of an introductory course, the design of a senior seminar, and the inclusion of an experiential component in the curriculum. An ongoing debate in the field, and one that takes on very special meaning in the early stages of program development, concerns the question of what constitutes an adequate "introduction to peace studies." The fact that there are so few "intro texts" in the field—and that there are none that are widely used or that reflect the breadth of the conceptual map—reflects this lack of consensus.

This issue is especially important because educators usually impose on the introductory course the burden of surveying the entire terrain of a field—its critical concepts, theories, and methodologies. In peace studies, it is the very breadth of the field that produces such a diversity of approaches to the introductory course. For example, how much time should be devoted to the study of Gandhi or King in a program that specializes in the "causes of war" cell? Should this be a course that examines not only the causes of war but also the conditions of peace? How can and should an instructor integrate "hands on" techniques and case studies in the area of conflict resolution? These are just a few of the dozens of critical questions and choices that influence the design of an introductory course in peace studies.

Different colleges and universities have attempted to deal with this issue in a number of ways, but most still believe that the basic introductory course should encompass as many areas of the conceptual map as possible. It was toward this end that Colgate University premiered a model in the early 1970s that has been used in numerous other locales—namely, a large introductory course staffed by faculty from five or six different disciplines. Although the course focused largely on global war and peace issues, the diversity of disciplines often spread the approaches throughout the nine various cells.

At Earlham College, the introductory curriculum was organized quite differently. The faculty there felt that any serious introduction to peace issues ought to take seriously the means by which these issues are addressed in a number of disciplines. Their solution was to develop a four-course introductory sequence known as Peace and Conflict Studies I–IV. Students in this program complete four distinct introductory courses that address peace and conflict issues from the perspectives of anthropology ("Culture and Conflict"), politics ("Political Violence and World Order"), Economics ("Equity and Efficiency"), and Philosophy ("Ethics and the World Food Problem"). (The syllabi featured in this volume provide examples of several approaches to the introductory course.)

A second vital issue in the minds of many peace studies faculty concerns the mix of disciplines, topics, and learning objectives that ought to constitute a senior seminar in the field. This challenge, which parallels that of the introductory course, is especially critical for those institutions committed to a major in peace studies. Should the seminar devote some time to each of the nine subfields of peace studies? Should the course replicate the disciplinary perspectives of earlier courses or attempt to develop an appreciation of transdisciplinary peace research? Should students undertake a significant research project? Should the course seek to empower students on the verge of graduation by including an experiential component such as an internship? These are some of the questions that must be addressed in the process of designing a capstone course in the field. (The syllabi by Neil Katz, Michael Klare, and John Ratcliffe sample a range of approaches to the senior seminar.)

A third unresolved challenge regards the proper place of experiential education in a peace studies program. Over a decade ago, Jerry Folk (1978) argued that one of the distinctive aspects of peace studies was that it permitted students to move outside the classroom in an observer-participant role such that they could examine first-hand the dynamics of conflict, social change, and conflict resolution that they had studied in the classroom. Nonetheless, for financial, bureaucratic, and political reasons, the place of experiential education—whether it be foreign study in a conflict locale, an internship in a government agency or public interest organization, or a volunteer placement in a community action group—still remains unclear for most programs. Aside from Tufts University and the University of California at Berkeley, only those schools with a long tradition of support for both experiential learning and peace studies—such as George Fox, Earlham, and Manchester Colleges and Colgate University—include serious "experiential" components in their peace studies curriculum. Nonetheless, faculty at many other colleges and universities are grappling with the question of experiential education. (The essay in this volume by Dale Bryan details the evolution of the Tufts program's experience with internship curricula.)

The Challenge of Graduate Programs in Peace Studies

It seems appropriate to close this discussion of conceptual models for program development in peace studies by referring to the most notable current trend in the field: the emergence of graduate-level programs. This evolution in the institutional character of the field was barely discernible a few years ago. In 1985, I noted that peace studies in the 1990s would be faced with particular opportunities and challenges in the areas of cross-cultural and international education, future imaging, and the relationship between peace and justice. Although these substantive concerns remain, it is the steady increase in the number of universities offering masters- and doctorate-level programs that will probably have the greatest impact on the field over the next decade. It is still too early to predict the specific conseqences of this evolution, but it is likely to affect the substantive definition of the field, clarify its relationship to the disciplines, and influence the field's undergraduate curriculum. To illustrate this trend, I will profile briefly a few representative graduate programs.

One of the leaders in graduate-level peace studies has long been Syracuse University, where the Program for Nonviolent Conflict and Change has offered interdisciplinary Ph.D. and M.A. degrees for more than a decade. However, Syracuse is virtually unique in its long-standing commitment to interdisciplinary graduate study. The University of Colorado at Boulder and Cornell University, on the other hand, have pursued a discipline-based approach by housing their peace studies Ph.D. programs in the Sociology and Political Science departments, respectively. (Both programs naturally permit and encourage their graduate students to take advantage of courses and faculty in other fields.) The University of Notre Dame recently introduced a Masters program in Peace Studies that includes, by conscious design, twelve to fifteen students from countries outside the United States who have demonstrated an interest in peace, development, and human rights.

The 1980s have also witnessed a significant increase in graduate programs in conflict resolution. The leading institution in this area is George Mason University, which now offers a professional M.A. in Conflict Management and a research-oriented Ph.D. in Conflict Analysis and Resolution; George Mason also offers mid-career programs for diplomats, military officers, and other public servants. Meanwhile, a number of law schools in the country have developed curricula in "alternative dispute resolution" (i.e., mediation, arbitration, and negotiation) in an effort to increase the professional competence of lawyers in this area and thereby to broaden their role in family, community, labor, and environmental disputes. (For more information on graduate programs in peace studies and conflict resolution, see Thomas, 1987.)

In this context, the future of peace studies in higher education may no longer rest solely on debates about undergraduate curricula and pedagogy. It now seems likely that the field will have to grapple with new issues such as credentialing, opportunities for graduate research, and the insertion of peace studies into other graduate and professional fields. As peace studies expands and gains increased recognition, our real challenge is to remain true to the field's tradition of basing its curricula and research on an honest appraisal of peace and violence in society, rather than succumbing to the temptations of even greater prominence.

References

Carey, Dennis (1980). "A Discipline Development Model for Peace Studies," *Peace and Change*, Vol. 6, Nos. 1 and 2, pp. 90–98.

Cohn, Carol (1987). "Nuclear Language and How We Learned to Pat the Bomb," *Bulletin of Atomic Scientists* (June), pp. 17–24.

Everts, Philip P. (1972). "Developments and Trends in Peace and Conflict Research, 1965–1971: A Survey of Institutions," *Journal of Conflict Resolution*, Vol. 16, No. 4, pp. 477–510.

Folk, Jerry (1978). "Peace Studies Programs: Towards An Integrated Approach," *Peace and Change*, Vol. 5, No. 1, pp. 56–61.

Kohn, Walter, and Lawrence Badash (1988). *The University and the Nuclear Predicament*, IGCC Policy Paper No. 6, University of California, San Diego, La Jolla, Calif. 92093.

Kruegler, Christopher, and Patricia Parkman (1985). "Identifying Alternatives to Political Violence: An Educational Imperative," *Harvard Educational Review*, Vol. 55, No. 1, pp. 109–117.

Lopez, George A. (1986). "Making University Peace Studies Viable," *Christian Science Monitor*, Special Supplement on Peace Education (January 31).

———— (1985). "A Peace Studies Curriculum for the 1990s," *Journal of Peace Research*, Vol. 22, No. 2, pp. 117–128.

———— (1978). "The Status of Peace and World Order Studies in U.S. Colleges and Universities: A Survey Analysis," *International Peace Studies Newsletter*, Vol. 7, No. 3, pp. 3–8.

Rivage-Seul, Marguerite (1987). "Peace Education: Imagination and the Pedagogy of the Oppressed," *Harvard Educational Review*, Vol. 57, No. 2, pp. 153–169.

Sloan, Douglas (1982). "Towards an Education for a Living World," *Teachers College Record*, Vol. 84, pp. 1–14.

Thomas, Daniel C. (1987). *Guide to Careers and Graduate Education in Peace Studies*. Amherst, Mass.: Five College Program in Peace and World Security Studies.

Vasquez, John A. (1976). "Toward a Unified Strategy of Peace Education," *Journal of Conflict Resolution*, Vol. 20, No. 4, pp. 707–728.

Wehr, Paul, and Michael Washburn (1976). *Peace and World Order Systems*. Beverly Hills, Calif.: Sage Publications.

2. The Interdisciplinary Challenge of Peace Studies

Carol Rank
University of California–Berkeley

Ever since the first significant generation of peace studies curricula was established in U.S. colleges in the wake of the Vietnam War, the impetus behind this field has been the need to fill a gap in the university curriculum and to present new perspectives on the global problematique. The faculty and students who pushed for the creation of these new programs felt that conventional courses on international relations and political science, emphasizing a *realpolitik* approach to the pursuit of exclusively national interests, offered few insights into the construction of a more peaceful and just world community. New courses and programs had to be created, it was determined, to include critical topics such as the dynamics of peace movements and nonviolent social change, relationships between militarism and underdevelopment, and alternative methods of conflict resolution.

In developing peace studies to address perceived social needs, many educators and scholars came to see interdisciplinarity as a way to transcend the shortcomings of narrowly defined, specialized disciplines. A well-known example of this critique is contained in Roy Preiswerk's landmark essay, "Could We Study International Relations as if People Mattered?" According to Preiswerk, by fragmenting humanity into a *homo economicus, homo sociologicus,* etc., the social sciences fail to grasp "the totality of real human beings." Narrowness in the scope of inquiry is considered a measure of serious academic work; yet, though specialization is necessary, it can also result in esoteric research of primary use to *other* social scientists. Such research is dangerous, Preiswerk said, to the extent that it "blurs the pathological direction of mankind's development" and the need to explore alternatives.[1]

Although peace studies was originally a reaction to the traditional practice of political scence and international relations, the field now encompasses a number of disciplinary perspectives and has developed a research and curricular agenda of its own. Peace studies is concerned not only with relations between states but also with the conditions within societies that produce violence. In the words of Tord Hoivik, former director of the Peace Research Institute in Oslo, Norway (PRIO):

The guiding force of peace research, its concern for nonviolence, justice, and deep social change, requires a grasp of whole societies. Political institutions are parts of the whole. Political science applied to the whole gives only a partial understanding. . . . Peace research has always seen itself as multi-disciplinary.[2]

In its broadest sense, peace studies addresses such diverse topics as the links between technological and social evolution, the influence of religious and ethical values on the shaping of cultural attitudes toward violence, and feminist perspectives on militarism. Peace studies can expand into these and other areas, but it remains focused on the goal of reducing violence within and between societies. Its ability to focus in this way is its strength. Its aim is not to advance any one particular discipline but, instead, to draw insights from a number of disciplines into the means by which to create a more peaceful world.

The challenge posed by peace studies to the teaching and research agendas of these disciplines has been taken up by many in the academic community. For example, the International Studies Association, the Social Science Research Council, and the International Social Science Council have in recent years devoted considerable energy to the fostering of peace research.[3] In addition, the American Sociological Association, Political Science Association, and Psychology Associations have established peace studies–related sections, and an international community of historians regularly convenes a Conference on Peace Research in History and co-publishes the journal *Peace and Change*. Organizations such as the Peace Studies Association (PSA), the Consortium on Peace Research, Education, and Development (COPRED), and the International Peace Research Association (IPRA) involve researchers and educators from a wide range of fields.

The problem with being so broadly interdisciplinary is that the boundaries of the field are difficult to determine. Some peace studies scholars argue that it must attempt to distinguish itself from related fields. Others believe that it should be more concerned with having an impact on as many disciplines as possible than on carving out a distinct niche for itself.

In practice, peace studies programs are a means of drawing together existing courses on peace-related issues. Many peace studies programs have, in fact, been created through the gathering together of relevant courses from a number of different departments. This collection of courses is then augmented with new peace studies courses that integrate various perspectives or focus on specific topics not previously available in the curriculum. These programs also serve as catalysts for the introduction of new courses into established departments, and as supportive environments for students and faculty who wish to pursue inquiry into peace-related issues.

This process of bringing together and integrating research and researchers around an emerging body of questions is usually one of the first stages in the birth of a new field. As Paul Wehr points out in his book, *Conflict Regulation*,[4] literature on conflict is scattered throughout the disciplines and should be gathered together to advance the field of peace research. As this process proceeds, and the pieces are brought together, they begin to form a new field with a life and identity of its own.

The need for such interdisciplinary peace studies programs is being increasingly recognized by university presidents and administrators, a large number of whom have voiced their support for peace studies during the 1980s. Former University of California president David Saxon, for example, wrote in the *Journal of Higher Education* that the social, economic, and ideological forces that fuel the arms race have not been "considered in as interrelated and coherent a way as they need to be." He claimed further that in the pursuit "of a peaceful world we have an important ally in our universities—the power of an open and inquiring intelligence to clarify, to interpret, to illuminate."[5]

While such statements are encouraging signs of the growth and development of the field, the reality is that most peace studies programs are extremely difficult to establish and maintain, in large part *because* of their interdisciplinarity. The interdisciplinary challenge of peace studies lies in its requirement for intellectual cooperation across disciplinary boundaries and for an administrative structure flexible enough to allow this cooperation to take place. If we are to advance and strengthen the field of peace studies, therefore, we must examine and overcome the problems that arise from its interdisciplinarity.

Is Peace Studies a Discipline?

In examining obstacles to peace studies that result from its interdisciplinarity, we should first examine the nature of disciplines and consider how interdisciplinary programs can function on a par with established disciplines. We also must seek to establish a common understanding of what it means to be interdisciplinary, multidisciplinary, or transdisciplinary. This process is critical to the goal of clarifying our objectives and revealing implicit assumptions, which often go unexamined.

Ideally, peace studies seeks to be "transdisciplinary," meaning that it embodies concepts and principles which overlap disciplinary boundaries. As explained by Johan Galtung, "we used to say 'interdisciplinary' and 'international.' We now say 'transdisciplinary' and 'global.'"[6] Environmental problems, for example, are best described as global, inasmuch as the ecosystem transcends the boundaries of nation-states and cannot therefore be considered exclusively an "inter-*national*" problem. In like manner, the issues addressed by peace studies transcend disciplinary boundaries.

Another term that is sometimes used, "multidisciplinary," implies merely a juxtaposition of disciplines. Interdisciplinarity is a step beyond that, because it considers the relationship between disciplines. In practice, interdisciplinary programs or courses are often more "multidisciplinary" than "interdisciplinary," as little comparative work is accomplished. Transdisciplinarity is the next stage in that it aims to explicate concepts woven throughout a number of disciplines.

Although transdisciplinarity may be the aim, peace studies is still most accurately described as an *interdisciplinary* field because that term reflects the reality that faculty in peace studies generally bring their disciplinary perspectives to bear on the issues and because they have been only partially successful in the pursuit of transdisciplinary analyses. More important, many would argue that peace studies should not aim to become a discipline unto itself but, rather, should remain open as a meeting ground for various disciplinary perspectives. Thus it has come to be known as a *field* rather than as a discipline.

Acknowledging that it may not be desirable for peace studies to become a discipline unto itself, many involved in the field nevertheless recognize the importance of defining the extent to which it has progressed according to the evolutionary stages of a new discipline. For example, Dennis Carey, professor of Peace Studies at Kent State University and currently a consultant on peace studies to the governor of Ohio, identifies these stages as the development of substantive and syntactic structures, and the institutional-ization of the field. Concepts in conflict resolution, arms control and disarmament, human rights and other areas form part of peace studies' "substantive structure." The use of methodologies appropriate to these research topics contributes to the development of peace studies' "syntactic structure." Institutionalization includes such factors as resources allocated to programs, granting of degrees, staffing and tenure, and so on. There is great evidence of peace studies' progress in all these areas.[7]

William Keeney, also from Kent State University, lists the following as constituting a discipline: a body of knowledge; a literature to support that body of knowledge; a focused area of study; and a methodology for study of the field. Peace studies has developed "an increasing body of knowledge about violence, conflict, and the range of options to meet the problems associated with violence and conflict," he argues. The field of peace research and peace studies has also generated a substantial body of literature, including books, journals, and periodicals. The focus of the field is the reduction of violence at all levels of society, and its research methodologies are drawn mainly from the social sciences.[8]

Strictly speaking, disciplines are branches of knowledge, each of which claims its own distinct concepts, methods of inquiry, and tests for truth. [9] They are a reflection of the analytic, reductionist mode of thought, which requires a delimitation of realms of phenomena, a breaking down into parts for the purpose of precise analysis. Because disciplines are products of reductionist thinking, "progress" in disciplinary research entails a process of the "fission" of knowledge, in which phenomena are broken into smaller and smaller units. In contrast, interdisciplinary and transdisciplinary research involves a reversal of this process, not "fission" but "fusion," a synthesis or integration of interrelated elements.[10]

According to these definitions, peace studies does not aim to become a separate discipline but is instead a field of knowledge that utilizes methodologies, concepts, and "tests for truth" drawn from various disciplines. Nonetheless, even if peace studies aims neither to become a discipline unto itself nor to be described as such, it should still be able to *function* on a par with established disciplines.

Paradoxically, if we accept a functionalist definition of what constitutes a discipline, we can say that peace studies already *is* a discipline. The functionalist definition of a discipline, which does not necessarily discount the one above, merely outlines the elements operant in an active field of study. For example, in discussing the criteria for recognition of a discipline, Kenneth Boulding, a prominent economist and peace researcher, once asked somewhat facetiously, "Is there a bibliography? Can you teach a course in it? If so, it must be a legitimate field of study."[11]

According to Joseph Kiger's functionalist definition in *The Encyclopedia of Education* of what constitutes a discipline in the United States, criteria include "the number of persons interested in and devoted to its study, the relative importance of such persons, its generally reputed significance in the academic structure," and the existence of a "national learned society devoted to the discipline."[12] While some of Kiger's criteria are obviously quite subjective, it would not be hard to demonstrate that peace studies also meets these functional standards for disciplinary status.

The argument that peace studies *functions* as a discipline is made in a publication of the Department of Peace and Conflict Studies at Lund University in Sweden that focuses on the field's research credentials.

> If we consider the establishment of professional journals, university departments and international associations as the birthmarks of a new discipline, we may say that peace research was born in the late fifties and was fully established by the late sixties. The first journals appeared in 1957 and 1959, international organization took place in 1963–1964 (International Peace Research Association, IPRA), and by 1965 there were, according to UNESCO statistics, some 100 institutions in the world that devoted at least some effort to peace research. . . . The UNESCO statistics show that by 1978 there were 310 institutions of peace and conflict research in the world.[13]

Although peace studies clearly meets the requirements for recognition as a legitimate field of study on a par with established disciplines, it has not yet achieved equal status. Peace studies faculty do not negate the necessity of disciplinary teaching and research; they merely desire that peace studies acquire the stability and respect enjoyed by the traditional disciplines, and that it function as a complementary part of the curriculum. Ideally, the aim is not only a peaceful coexistence but a fruitful cooperation between peace studies and the disciplines.

Finding a Home for Peace Studies

In *The Aims of Education,* Alfred North Whitehead argued that knowledge is advanced through the creation of new areas of inquiry.[14] That proposition is as true today as it was when Whitehead made it in 1929. Our categories of knowledge, the boundaries of disciplines, are continually in flux as researchers venture into new realms: biochemistry, microbiology, social psychology—the list is long and always evolving. Disciplines are "products of historical accretion," says Karl Jaspers, shifting according to the progress of research and the meeting of society's needs.[15]

The shifting nature of knowledge, however, is often not reflected in the administrative structure of the university. Knowledge is rigidly fragmented into disciplines and housed in academic departments, each with its own intellectual and bureaucratic turf. Tenure and professional advancement depend on the extent to which faculty prove themselves within the established disciplines. Rewards are not meted out to those who attempt to break new ground *between* the disciplines. On the contrary, faculty who engage in interdisciplinary efforts often jeopardize their standing within their home departments.

In this environment, peace studies has difficulty finding a permanent home in the university inasmuch as it lacks the status and therefore the resources of established disciplines. Faculty involved in peace studies often must develop and teach such courses on their own time. Many, if not most, peace studies programs run on what one director called "sweat equity"— the voluntary and often unremunerated efforts of dedicated faculty.[16] Particularly in times of limited budgets, interdisciplinary programs such as peace studies are difficult to initiate and maintain, since they compete with established departments for available resources.

In fact, peace studies programs are often caught in a "blame-the-victim" syndrome; they are criticized for conceptual and administrative weaknesses but are not given adequate support to overcome them. Hence, the theoretical development of the field as a whole is impeded by the university structure. As described by one peace studies director:

> Although we have established ourselves and have made great progress, like most peace studies programs we have been under-supported, marginalized, not considered a central part of the university curriculum. Our particular weaknesses have been lack of administrative time and lack of resources to encourage faculty interaction, growth, and support. Similar to other nontraditional programs, our faculty maintain their scholarship and employment base in separate disciplines. [This] creates dispersion and lack of curricular cohesion. . . . Peace studies has suffered from lack of faculty time and administrative support to capitalize on our diverse talents. The organizational work of creating and sustaining peace studies has been done without reimbursement. . . . We have innovated, and have paid the price for over-extension into multiple discipline areas.[17]

Such obstacles to peace studies program development are encountered by most other interdisciplinary fields as well. These stumbling blocks are in fact built into the university structure itself. Understanding the difficulties involved with interdisciplinary scholarship and teaching can help faculty and students make the case for special consideration when trying to convince administrators to free faculty time and resources for interdisciplinary programs.

Support from the university administration for peace studies can take many forms, including the augmentation of interdisciplinary groups in which faculty get release time from their home departments and are able to obtain tenured positions within the interdisciplinary field. This, of course, requires confidence on the part of the university administration that resources thus invested will bear fruit. Michael Heyman, now chancellor of the University of California at Berkeley, once commented, regarding the augmentation of interdisciplinary groups, that "a university has a moral responsibility to seek new ways to confront in rational ways great contemporary issues. We must take some chances, even with our most precious resources."[18]

Certainly peace studies is worth the risk of allocating at least a small share of the university's resources. By supporting research and teaching on peace, colleges and universities fulfill their traditional role as the developers and purveyors of new areas of knowledge. And if peace studies, in however small a measure, does help generate and transmit ideas that can reduce violence and promote peace and justice, the university does indeed have a moral and social responsibility to foster the development of this field.

Notes

1. Roy Preiswerk, "Could We Study International Relations as if People Mattered?" in Preiswerk, *International Relations in a Changing World* (Geneva: Graduate Institute of International Studies, 1977). Reprinted in Gordon Feller et al., eds., *Peace and World Order Studies: A Curriculum Guide*, 3rd ed. (New York: Institute for World Order, 1981), and in Richard Falk, Samuel S. Kim, and Saul H. Mendlovitz, eds., *Toward a Just World Order* (Boulder, Colo.: Westview Press, 1982).

2. Tord Hoivik, "Peace Research and Science," *Journal of Peace Research*, Vol. 20, No. 3 (1983) p. 265.

3. See Kenneth Prewitt, "Security, Peace and Social Science," *Society*, Vol. 23, No. 1 (November/December 1985); and Raimo Vayrnen, ed., *The Quest for Peace: Transcending Collective Violence and War among Societies, Cultures and States* (Beverly Hills: Sage Publications/International Social Science Council, 1987).

4. Paul Wehr, *Conflict Regulation* (Boulder, Colo.: Westview Press, 1979), preface.

5. David Saxon, "A Role for the Universities in Ending the Arms Race," *Chronicle of Higher Education* (July 6, 1981).

6. Johan Galtung, interviewed by the author, University of California at Los Angeles, March 1987.

7. Denis Carey, "A Discipline Development Model for Peace Studies," *Peace and Change*, Vol. 6, Nos. 1 and 2 (Winter 1980), pp. 90–93.

8. William Keeney, Center for Peaceful Change, Kent State University, "Is Peace Studies a Discipline?" Consultation at St. Johns and St. Benedict Colleges. Unpublished document.

9. See P. H. Hirst, "Liberal Education and the Nature of Knowledge," in Reginald Archambault, ed., *Philosophical Analyses of Education* (London: Routledge and Kegan Paul, 1965); and David Aspin, "The Epistemological Status of Peace Studies," Working Paper No. 11, Peace Research Center, Australian National University, Canberra, 1987.

10. Robert Scott, "Personal and Institutional Problems Encountered in Being Interdisciplinary," in Joseph Kockelman, ed., *Interdisciplinarity and Higher Education* (University Park: Pennsylvania State Press, 1979), p. 310.

11. Kenneth Boulding, Consultation with the Peace Studies Committee of the University of California, Berkeley, 1982.

12. Joseph L. Kiger, "Disciplines," *The Encyclopedia of Education*, Vol. 3 (Austin: University of Texas Press, 1978), p. 130.

13. Department of Peace and Conflict Studies, Lund University, Sweden. Extract found in Barbara Wien, ed., *Peace and World Order Studies: A Curriculum Guide*, fourth edition (New York: World Policy Institute, 1984), p. 4.

14. Alfred North Whitehead, *The Aims of Education* (New York: Macmillan, 1929), pp. 37–38.

15. Karl Jaspers, *The Idea of the University* (Boston: Beacon Press, 1959), p. 81.

16. Howard Richards of the Earlham College peace studies program (Indiana) used this term to describe the voluntary efforts of faculty upon which his program and others must rely. Interview by Carol Rank, Earlham College, March 1987.

17. Duane Campbell, "Peace Studies and Civic Responsibility in Higher Education," Document on Peace/War Studies at California State University, Sacramento, pp. 2–3.

18. Michael Heyman, memo to Chancellor Bowker on the Augmentation of Interdisciplinary Groups, University of California, Berkeley, 1975.

3. Internship Education in Peace and Justice Studies: The Tufts University Experience

Dale A. Bryan
Tufts University

Teaching for the realization of global peace and justice means educating students to be able to challenge institutions that deny the possibility of full human and social development. As educators this means helping students to acquire knowledge that integrates the wide diversity of human cultures and to think critically about society. It is important to recognize, however, that a conviction for and a commitment to constructing a just world peace cannot be taught, cannot be transferred by technique. It must be experienced by the learner in actual social contexts and action beyond the classroom.

Internships with public and private organizations—including advocacy groups, government agencies, and research institutes, especially those that emphasize the critical role of active citizen participation in a democracy—contribute significantly to the learning objectives of peace studies. The action-learning pedagogy of experiential education, of which internships are a part, is one of the most effective means for teaching and learning academic content, and for generating critical and integrative thinking skills as well as a sense of social responsibility. By engaging students and learning activities directly in the phenomena being studied, internships can effectively integrate new knowledge with an enhanced sense of social responsibility. Internships also help to create links between the peace studies curriculum and the realities of citizen participation and public policy in related areas.

The guided internship curricula at Peace and Justice Studies (PJS) differs from many traditional internships in that faculty/staff and students routinely interact and reflect on both the campus and community experience, instead of leaving students entirely responsible for gleaning from the experience whatever educational value they might. In addition to acquiring formal knowledge on social movements and popular participation, students benefit from the emphasis placed on developing organizational skills and a sense of political empowerment. At PJS they are free to work with any organization or agency that promotes citizen action on issues that she or he deems relevant to "peace and social justice."

For emerging and established programs in peace studies or any other field that are considering a systematic internship or similar experiential component for their curriculum, our experiences with internships may provide some useful lessons. Before examining the details of the PJS internship curriculum, however, we must explore further the pedagogical theory that underlies it.

The Theory and Process of
Dialogic Supervision

Peace a 1d justice educators should not be satisfied merely with helping students become "well informed" about social issues, even if they are more critically and integratively aware. Students must also be empowered with practical and strategic skills to transform social conditions and their relationship to the rest of the world, or else they will not be prepared for the responsibilities of living humanely in an age of increasing global interdependence and ecological fragility.

This concern has been well articulated by the question of "whether it is preferable to act one's way into new ways of thinking or to think one's way into new ways of acting" (Byron, 1986). Given society's present dilemmas, it is clear that students must do more than learn to *think about* social problems and relationships in new ways; they must also *act* in new ways to create new, more preferable conditions for humanity. The PJS experience with internships suggests that experiential learning in specific social change contexts facilitates both approaches to developing knowledge.

Through dialogic interaction with students while they are doing their internships, educators are able to maximize their students' opportunity for reflection on both their concrete experience and its relation to relevant theories and data (Shor and Freire, 1987). In other words, active faculty/ staff involvement in a student's internship experience promotes the integration of the "thinking about" and the "acting for" dimensions of learning.

Each student meets weekly with the internship coordinator to discuss his or her journal observations about the placement and assigned readings. The journal's primary function is to help students reflect on the links between academic concepts and their actual experiences. By drawing on their initial analyses of academic and action components, the guided dialogue provides students further opportunity for developing and applying critical thinking skills.

The pedagogic objective is to move students' subjectivity to the center of the learning experience, and to encourage the development of their own capacities for creative thinking about peace and justice (Collins, 1986; Simon, 1987). As the students share the experiences and challenges of people involved in public interest work, they develop a grounding from which their own theories, concepts, and problem-solving rationales can emerge (Glaser and Strauss, 1967). Through this process, including the dialogue with faculty, the students' own words, views, and experiences become the "objects of study," the things to be thought about (Shor and Freire, 1987). They are encouraged, and consequently empowered, to remake formal theory, concepts, facts, and ideas by drawing on their intimate and intuitive experiences with the very social forms—the words, thoughts, actions, and feelings expressed among the people and organizations of their placement—in which content has a real life beyond the textbook. From their practical experiences with public interest work, students begin to develop the knowledge and skills needed to understand and participate actively in democratic society.

The Substantive Orientation

At PJS, the substantive focus for guided internships is the study of social movements and social change. In talking with students about their plan of study, we encourage them to consider the role that collective citizen action plays among the obstacles, conditions, and paths to a just world peace. Students are asked to investigate the ebb and flow of popular movements and their relationship to peace and conflict, justice and domination, change and repression. As educators *for* peace and justice, we locate students' academic preparation within social forces that demand structural reform and contest normative expressions and interpretations for human and social development, for both the individual and the community (Touraine, 1988).

During their internships with groups that compose the "new social movements," with public agencies whose mandate relates to the concerns of these movements, or with groups who oppose them, students can grapple with some of the theoretical debates current to the topic of their study. For example, students might reflect on the desirability and efficacy of mass organizations, with their division of labor and internal discipline, as compared to those of community groups that attempt to model consensus decision-making and exemplify nonhierarchical and egalitarian values. Similarly, students can compare various traditional change strategies such as public education, lobbying, and elections with more direct action strategies such as nonviolent civil disobedience.

The Service Dimension

Furthermore, student involvement in public interest activities empowers them with the critical thinking and applied skills necessary for moral responsibility and community leadership. As such, peace and justice education furthers the traditional university mission to promote human and social development.

Students who have an active commitment to social responsibility and who are both knowledgeable and practiced in these areas stand to enhance the strategic efficacy of community groups as these students enter the labor force in positions of responsibility. The evidence that students gain from these placements—and that employers value their experience—is found in the number of students who have found entry-level jobs with similar organizations. Of the forty-six Tufts graduates who have participated in this project to date, eleven have gone on to such positions. During a telephone interview with a potential employer of one student, I learned that she was impressed that the student came to her "knowing the language we use, and not just from books!" More thorough longitudinal data would help to better assess not only these internships' benefits to the community and these organizations but also the achievement of other learning objectives.

The PJS Internship Requirement

At Tufts, an internship is part of the required core for the Certificate in Peace and Justice Studies, which is awarded to undergraduates who complete a multidisciplinary program of study—five core courses and three electives. Four broad areas of concern are emphasized within the program: peace, human rights, global movements and change, and future studies.

The program presently offers three options for completing the internship requirement. Students are encouraged, but not required, to take their internship placement concurrent with an elective course that surveys sociological perspectives on social movements. This arrangement is deemed to facilitate best their integration of and critical reflection on both practice and theory. Students who elect to forgo the survey and case study course while they complete the internship must then choose between either taking the course at a later time or completing a content-specific, academic regimen as part of their placement. The latter choice also emphasizes the study of social movements and social change and involves a readings-and-review component, two five-page analytical essays, a journal for both personal and academic reflections, and a series of guided discussions with the internship coordinator. Students not enrolled in the PJS Certificate Program may also take the internship placement with faculty supervision for a pass-fail grade. Every student taking an internship, regardless of program status, must maintain a journal and participate in discussions about her or his experience.

The current option and academic format have evolved from a combined seminar-field placement course, where students had to volunteer a minimum of eight hours work per week with a local organization as well as attend a three-hour seminar that featured guest presentations by staff members of similar groups. Class requirements included a weekly journal, a two-stage term paper, and a class presentation. By the end of the semester, students were actively lobbying for an extra credit for the large time commitment required by this format.

The next semester's expectations for both in-class and in-the-field time were considerably revised. A small number of the weekly seminar meetings were canceled altogether, and students were given an option for the amount of necessary field placement time. For students willing to spend at least eight hours per week at the site, two five-page essays were required along with a weekly journal. Students could instead choose a six-hour placement, but they were then expected to complete three essays and the journal. This seminar-field placement arrangement is demanding on faculty and difficult to administer at times, but its basic format was retained for the third semester as well.

Throughout these first three semesters, and despite the administrative complications and time demands, student evaluations were consistently highly favorable. Students described the course as a dynamic and rewarding learning experience, and especially valued its unique blend of "academic" and "activist" components. For example, social science literature was complemented with organizations' newsletters, and class discussion involved both types of literature as well as reflection on the analyses and oral histories presented by guest speakers. In-class analysis of social movements was informed by concrete practice with placement organizations.

The course ranked highest on two dimensions of student empowerment: enhanced social responsibility and critical thinking. Toward the first objective students consistently scored the statement, "class discussion has encouraged analytical thinking," with a nearly perfect mark. On criteria for the objective of social responsibility, suggested by the perceived contribution of the course to their "overall learning experience" and by its contribution to their "academic and/or professional plans," the score was similarly high.

During the third year, increasing numbers of students expressed interest in the internship placements and advisory structure arranged by the program, but not in attending a seminar. Although we accommodated these students, it quickly became clear that their learning experience was less valuable than when they participated in the internship-seminar combination. This trial period suggested that new hands-on, practical experience is not necessarily educational learning, nor will it always affect attitudes and action (Conrad and Hedin, 1977). Without an academic regimen through which the students could evaluate their placement experiences, the biweekly meetings with staff became little more than friendly check-ins to see that all was well. However, where students were willing to read literature relevant to their site observations and journal reflections, the discussions became more animated, substantive, and provocative. And because this group was able to spend more time (at least twelve hours per week) at the internship, both the students and the placement supervisors were pleased with the greater degree of project involvement and productivity.

In planning the internship course's curriculum and advising structure for 1988 (the fourth and most recent year), the program committee was convinced of the value of dialogic supervision within the action-reflection process, of the substantive orientation on social movements and social change, and of the multiple benefits from the increased degree of involvement at the site organization. The present separation of seminar and internship will attempt to maximize the process, content, and service dimensions of action-learning.

Administrative Challenges

From the perspective of curriculum development, it is important to consider carefully the most appropriate timing for integrating the internship within a student's plan of study. In our experience, the optimal design entails the upper-level student's use of the simultaneous placement experience and seminar to prepare and/or gather data for the senior project, which formally completes the PJS Certificate. In that sense the internship can serve as an experiential and research capstone for the total academic regimen. For example, students researching the future impact of citizen advocacy on a particular government policy could use their internship to assess their placement organization's strategy to mobilize public opinion and action, or to effectively lobby political elites. With the results of such action-research in hand, the students can bring their analyses to the senior seminar, where they compare academic interests and projects with their peers. In pursuit of this particular arrangement, most students take their internship-seminar option in the fall term of their senior year and the final integrative seminar in the spring semester.

In some instances, students complete the internship, with or without the complementary seminar, in their sophomore year. We have found that when the internship experience is taken at this stage in the students' course sequence, their interest in the academic content of peace and justice studies is heightened and their motivation and responsibility for their learning experience is enhanced. Many students have continued to volunteer time with their chosen organization long after their placement is completed; others have promoted campus awareness of pressing social issues; and several have been motivated to join the faculty-student administrative structure of our program. Despite the lost opportunity to integrate the internship with advanced research, many of our students have argued that an internship taken in the second year tends to have a more significant and lasting impact on their overall learning experience. On the other hand, definite advantages accrue to students who undertake the internship or field experience just prior to completing their course of study. Among the benefits is the opportunity provided by a recent action-reflection experience for strengthening a student's senior project. This experience, in turn, increases the possibility that their final papers will enhance their chances for success in obtaining entry-level employment with similar organizations or admission to advanced levels of study. In the end, each student's choice is negotiated in the context of the program advisor's knowledge of the entire curriculum and assessment of the individual student's interests.

As might be expected, a primary administrative responsibility is the development and oversight of the actual internship opportunities. Chief among our concerns in selecting placements are adequate and responsible supervision throughout the semester, sufficient training as needed, the relationship of the work to the program's curriculum, the degree to which a student is involved in group decisionmaking, an accessible and hospitable work environment, and willingness to support the student's pursuit of her or his academic objectives.

Students can either locate internship sites on their own or choose from among those already negotiated by the program and listed in an office catalogue. In every case, once the placement is agreed upon, an internship contract is completed and signed by the student, the site supervisor, and program staff. Evaluation of the placement is accomplished through the faculty-student meetings and student journal entries and, when necessary, through questionnaires, telephone contact, and visits to the site.

Future Directions

The environment at Tufts is generally hospitable to action-learning pedagogy. As such, it reflects faculty and administrative acceptance of and commitment to experiential education as a useful part of the undergraduate curriculum. In fact, Tufts students may take two internships for academic credit, and they can usually apply both toward their degree requirements.

Nonetheless, some administrators and faculty remain skeptical about the curricular value of experiential education and seek to impose budgetary constraints on our efforts to meet increased student demand. Of course, the lack of support from some sectors over the years has not prevented us from making great strides in understanding how best to integrate action-learning into the peace and justice studies curriculum. Therefore, we plan to continue innovating and refining our work in this area. Inspired by the advice and support of other academic programs and several community groups, we are now in the process of developing an experiential-learning center devoted to fostering student internships, volunteer community service placements, and action-research projects.

References

Byron, William J. (1986). "Economics." In David J. Johnson, ed., *Justice and Peace Education*. Maryknoll, N.Y.: Orbis Books.

Collins, Patricia Hill (1986). "Learning from the Outsider Within: The Sociological Significance of Black Feminist Thought," *Social Problems*, Vol. 33, pp. S14–S32.

Conrad, Dan, and Hedin, Diane (1977). "Citizenship Education Through Participation." In Frank Brown, ed. *Education for Responsible Citizenship*. New York: McGraw-Hill.

Glaser, Barney G., and Strauss, Anselm L. (1967). *The Discovery of Grounded Theory*. Hawthorne, N.Y.: Aldine Publishing.

Johnson, David M., ed. (1986). *Justice and Peace Education*. Maryknoll, N.Y.: Orbis Books.

Livingston, David W., ed. (1987). *Critical Pedagogy and Cultural Power*. South Hadley, Mass.: Bergin and Garvey.

Shor, Ira, and Freire, Paulo (1987). *A Pedagogy for Liberation*. South Hadley, Mass.: Bergin and Garvey.

Simon, Roger I. (1987). "Work Experience." In David W. Livingston, ed. *Critical Pedagogy and Cultural Power*. South Hadley, Mass.: Bergin and Garvey.

Touraine, Alain (1988). *Return of the Actor*. Minneapolis: University of Minnesota Press.

4. Student-Initiated Curricula in Peace Studies: The Williams College Experience

Dominic Careri Kulik and David Yaskulka
Center for Common Security*

A central question in curriculum development concerns the means by which students can become prepared to take leadership in a democratic society. Encouraging students to take *leadership in the classroom* is one way to meet that challenge. Since 1983, students at Williams College have successfully developed an innovative model for full-credit, student-run courses on non-violence, social change, and alternative security. These courses have become sustainable and reproduceable models of participatory education. They allow students to study important contemporary issues not found elsewhere in the curriculum while developing leadership skills through a unique student-facilitated format.

Following our graduation from Williams, we spent a year traveling to dozens of campuses across the country, systematically describing our experience with student-initiated curricula to college students, faculty members, and administrators. This experience has led us to believe that the Williams model can contribute significantly to curriculum development in peace studies and in other liberal arts fields. We present this approach here in the hope that it may inspire others to adapt and develop the model at their own institutions.

The Williams Model

At Williams, we developed a student-run, discussion-oriented classroom to complement the traditional faculty-led model. The students themselves take turns leading each class. Faculty do not attend these classes but, instead, serve as advisers for final projects through a dialogue that occurs outside of the classroom.

---

*More information about student-run curricula, including sample syllabi from the Williams College courses, can be obtained from the authors of this essay at the Center for Common Security, P.O. Box 275, Williamstown, MA 01267.

This model began as the brainchild of our colleague Jeff Sultar, who organized and developed it during his junior and senior years at Williams. Since then, it has evolved from an independent study course to a group-independent study course to a complete student-run course—all fully accredited. Throughout its seven years, various groups of student leaders have developed and expanded this model to accommodate numerous sections and new student-run courses. The model has also become a part of the foundations of two new academic programs. Since 1983, nearly a quarter of the Williams College faculty have served as advisers to twenty-four class sections.

These courses have acquired a reputation for academic rigor which equals or exceeds that of many traditional courses. In many ways the model on which they are built represents a "politics of possibility" in education: It is continuously undergoing development and revision, and it has been adapted for student-initiated courses at other colleges throughout the United States. This success, we believe, merits attention from educators and students alike.

Student-Student Pedagogy

A primary concern of any pedagogical approach must be the degree to which it prepares students for effective participation in a democratic society. This challenge requires that we address two broad and interacting aspects of curricula: *what* we learn, and—though far less often examined—*how* we learn.

What we learn must not exclude students' voices. This pedagogy requires students to formulate their own syllabi and classroom agendas. It introduces new and valuable subject matter for accredited work and treats the experiences and perspectives of students as legitimate sources of knowledge.

The first premise of *how* we learn is that empowerment is an essential goal of education. Knowledge gained in the classroom, when paired with empowerment to act, leads to responsible citizenship. Conversely, passive learning models (even when they confer a great deal of knowledge) can engender citizen disenfranchisement.

To ensure the active application of knowledge, educators must challenge socialized classroom patterns that engender passivity. We must explore how and to what degree students participate in the educational process; we must explore our modes of speech (how, and to whom, we direct our ideas); and we must even reconsider such seemingly mundane issues as the optimal seating arrangement for a learning environment.

Student-student pedagogy involves a rethinking of the traditional roles of teachers and students. When students reposition themselves as facilitators of classroom knowledge, they experience their own creative powers. Moreover, they tend to appreciate faculty more fully, even as they look more critically at their own classroom behavior.

In the process of facilitating—or leading—a class, students must be able to identify significant points and questions in the assigned readings; they must also ensure that these points and questions are addressed in discussion. In addition, they must mediate classroom discussion so as to equalize participation throughout the class. Rather than merely competing with each other, the students participating in this model of classroom organization must draw together as a community of learners—building trust and sharing the responsibilities of learning.

Integrating Content and Process: Studying Nonviolent Sanctions

Significant benefits result when both the process *and* the content of education move students from conditioned passivity to critical thinking, participation, and the creation of practical alternatives. A leading advantage of student-run courses is that they address pedagogical problems by experimenting with functional alternatives to standard modes of education.

We have had great success in applying this pedagogic model to a wide range of topics, including the study of nonviolent action. As an active, democratic, and *democratizing* means of wielding social power, nonviolent action promotes citizen initiative, the decentralization of power, and movements for social justice. In the form of nonviolent civilian-based defense, it offers a complement—or even an alternative—to military defense.

Just as student-run education thrusts students into positions of leadership and promotes equitable participation, nonviolent action overcomes citizen passivity and challenges traditional political assumptions. It encourages diverse individuals to participate in the normally exclusive security debate, and it leads to the development of a positive peace agenda (rather than a reactive, nay-saying agenda). We have found that, when explored together, the strategies of student-run education and citizen nonviolence create a democracy-increasing symbiosis between education and politics.

How to Begin

The first step in developing a student-initiated course is to assemble a core group of interested students and then to determine the subject(s) to be studied. This process calls upon students to identify the most compelling and challenging topics they can imagine—topics that are likely to inspire the high degree of commitment required for such courses, and that are not offered elsewhere in the curriculum. Once an appropriate topic has been chosen, a coherent and rigorous syllabus must be compiled. This process often entails extensive library research, consultations with interested faculty and students, and contact with relevant off-campus organizations such as the Center for Common Security and the National Curriculum Resources Project of the Five Colleges.

It is best to begin by taking advantage of the existing opportunities for student curricular initiatives, such as the independent study option. A sympathetic faculty member who respects a student's dedication and ability will usually agree to sponsor an independent study that surveys the chosen body of literature. Many faculty will prove supportive of projects that have as one objective the design of syllabi for other interested students.

Ideally, a small group of students (the core group) will undertake a group independent study for which each student has his or her own faculty sponsor. These students meet twice a week without faculty supervision, taking turns leading the discussion based on a common reading list. This process lays the groundwork for the next step in that it serves as a *de facto* student-run classroom; when both faculty members and students can attest to the high quality of work generated by a student-run course, additional institutional support for student-student pedagogy is more easily gained.

In pursuing this innovative approach to their education, students must build strong alliances with many segments of the campus community and solicit input from faculty in many departments and across the political spectrum—namely, department chairs and key committee members, deans and presidents, as well as a diverse group of students, staff, clergy, and community leaders. Broad, strategically placed support can help ensure that a high-quality proposal for curricular innovation will be reviewed and accepted by the appropriate college authorities; it will also contribute significantly to the educational value of the project.

Anticipation of Potential Obstacles

New and innovative endeavors will naturally provoke some fears and objections, but these can be addressed through proper planning. Typical concerns include the following:

1. Students may lack the qualifications to lead classes, and faculty supervision is often absent. This concern is addressed by actively involving faculty in the planning process, by emphasizing the goal of self-learning (to which most universities subscribe), and by making it clear that this initiative affects only one or two courses within an entire curriculum.
2. Academic standards may suffer. This concern is addressed by means of a well-conceived and rigorous syllabus, and with assurances that faculty advisors will monitor their students' progress in the course.
3. The faculty may be overloaded with work. This concern is addressed by having the student organizers doing almost all the work, and by dividing the remaining responsibilities among many faculty.
4. The student organizers may be overloaded with work. This concern is similarly addressed by dividing the work among many students, and by pursuing course credit and paid teaching assistantships for the course organizers.

Nuts and Bolts

There are many logistical challenges involved in creating and maintaining student-run courses. Students should plan ahead as best as possible, but they should also expect pitfalls. We have found that most mistakes simply add new dimensions to the learning process. The following tips, which were gleaned from several years of trial-and-error experience at Williams College and from our consultations throughout the country, can be adapted to the needs of each institution.

Class Size and Distribution. Class size must promote discussion. The number of students should be large enough to encompass a diverse range of experience and ideas but small enough to create a supportive space conducive to listening and friendship. The classes at Williams are generally limited to fifteen students.

As student-designed courses present the opportunity for granting special attention to the personal dimensions of students' backgrounds, not only class size but also the distributions of gender, race, age, and academic concentration of participants should be balanced whenever possible.

Leading a Student-Run Course. The students who assume primary responsibility for organizing the class (namely, the teaching assistants, or TAs) and the students who enroll out of subsequent interest can avoid potential tensions by (1) providing a structure that guides the course efficiently and allows room for democratic input and reform; (2) developing a course that satisfies both administrators' demands for academic rigor and students' desire for autonomy; and (3) avoiding the reintroduction of traditional roles of authority and dominance into the class, including the preeminent roles often assumed, for example, by men, by "expert" students, or by the TAs themselves.

As there are no faculty present in student-run courses, students take turns leading ("facilitating") class discussion on a number of occasions throughout the term. By this means, students can increase their understanding of the educational process from a totally new vantage point—that of the teacher.

We suggest that two students serve as facilitators for each class session, dividing their responsibilities between "content" and "process." The content facilitator is responsible for keeping the discussion focused on the material, whereas the process facilitator recognizes requests to speak and helps balance the patterns of participation within the class. These facilitators should meet with the TAs prior to each class in order to review the material and questions to be discussed. They will also find it helpful to devote one or two sessions early in the term to group process theories and techniques. Every student should experience the challenge of each facilitation role at least once during the semester.

Grading. Where possible, we recommend that student courses employ the little-used option of a descriptive final grade. These written evaluations are generally composed of three distinct parts (all of which must be approved by a faculty sponsor): (1) a standard course description; (2) an evaluation of the students' in-class performance written by the course organizers, two of the student's peers, and the student in question; and (3) an evaluation of the final project written by the faculty adviser. Other options include a pass/fail system and the traditional A-B-C scale. When using these more traditional grading methods, the faculty advisers should be encouraged to accept input from the course organizers, the student's peer-study group, and the student.

Conclusions and Results

As demonstrated by the Williams College model, student-initiated courses represent an important complement to the traditional classroom and serve as a productive component of the peace studies agenda. Students taking these courses devoted unusually high levels of energy and participation while developing critical leadership skills. Many graduates asserted that these courses were among their most important learning experiences at college. It is inspiring to know that students at college campuses all across the country are now adapting this model to suit their interests and academic environments.

Participatory education fosters student leadership and citizen involvement, and participation in just one student-run course can begin the process. As more and more students assume leadership roles in their own educations, U.S. colleges and universities will increasingly contribute to the emergence of a generation with the knowledge, skills, and confidence necessary to realize our country's democratic ideals.

SYLLABI

IV

Introductions to Peace and World Order Studies

1. Introduction to Peace Studies: Violence and Nonviolence

Nigel Young and John Crist   *Fall 1987*
Peace Studies Program, Colgate University,
Hamilton, NY 13346

This course is an initial survey of major themes, approaches, and issues of
the Program. It gives students an opportunity to understand the scope and
focus of the field, and to select areas for further specialization in later years,
in more depth. It is required for major and minor concentrations in Peace
Studies.

The intention of the class sessions is to summarize and introduce the
following key components of the study of peace: (1) the analysis of the
predominance of violent and threatening conflict, including the possibility
of nuclear war in contemporary states and societies, (2) the delineation of
proposals and attempts to introduce more equitable, harmonious, and nonviolent societies, (3) the analysis of the methods of constructive and nonviolent
group and individual action to transform unjust, violent, or oppressive
situations, and the conditions for success of such an activity, and (4) the

111

role of social transformation in preventing outbreaks of destructive violence and removing the causes of such outbreaks.

The course is also intended as an indication of (1) the breadth and depth of the peace field, (2) the intellectual issues to be taken up in other peace studies courses, (3) the relationship with other programs, (4) the field of peace research and peace studies as it has developed over the past 25 years, (5) the relationship of different peace topics and disciplines to each other and to certain ideas and perspectives developed in the field, and (6) how the other courses in the program fit into the general framework of peace studies.

Summary of Course—Topics to Be Covered

This survey of key issues in the study of war and violence, peace ideas and actions, includes the philosophy and techniques of nonviolence.

During the first weeks, lectures will introduce peace education as a recognized field of study encompassing various approaches within the field, define peace and peace studies, and address key issues in the development of peace and conflict analysis and theory relating to (a) violence and nonviolence, (b) war and social justice, (c) peace and disarmament plans and proposals, (d) alternative perspectives on war, its evolution, and its replacement, (e) the threat of nuclear war, and (f) the means of peaceful social change and conflict resolution.

Starting with the challenge of the arms race and the possibilities of World War III, the course deals with issues of conflict, aggression, territoriality, and other sources of violence from a transdisciplinary perspective. The other sections of the course include:

- The relationship between war, patriarchy, conquest, the state, and other forms of social repression; the tension between global, national, and local loyalties.
- A history of peace ideas and proposals—as well as a survey of peace activity—counterposed to the development of war and militarism, both in its origins and in its contemporary forms.
- Alternatives to the arms race, including civilian-based defense and dispute resolution.
- Disarmament, enemy images, as well as the arguments for and against deterrence: the East/West conflict and the Cold War.
- The role of social transformation and development in creating positive peace and nonviolent, free, and just society—the tension between North and South.
- Methods of resolving conflict creatively and equitably, without recourse to violence or threats of exploitation.

The contemporary context of peace studies will be a main focus of the first and final sessions, including both (a) the concern with peace as an intellectual problem, and (b) the concern with peace as a moral or political problem. However, the course will also deal with the historical development of peace ideas and actions—namely, the following traditions and views:

1. The religious peace traditions
2. Liberal internationalism
3. Socialist anti-militarism and internationalism
4. Women's peace perspectives (feminist traditions)
5. Nonviolence (Gandhian traditions)
6. War resistance and conscientious objection
7. The Communist approach to war/peace issues
8. Nuclear disarmament approaches since 1945
9. The new peace movements and the new arms race
10. Conflict resolution and alternative dispute resolution movements.

Required Readings
Manual of Readings.
Overy, Bob. *How Effective Are Peace Movements?*
Young, Nigel J. *Studying Peace: Problems and Possibilities.*
Sivard, Ruth. *World Social and Military Expenditures* (may alternatively use J. Turner and SIPRI, *Arms in the 1980s*).
Cooney, R., and H. Michalowski. *The Power of the People.* (C&M)
Sharp, G. *Power and Struggle* (Vol. I of *The Politics of Nonviolent Action*).
Mendlovitz and R.B.J. Walker. *Towards a Just World Peace.* (M&W)
Evan, W., and S. Hilgartner. *The Arms Race and Nuclear War.* (E&H)

Strongly Recommended Readings
Dyer, Gwynne. *War.*
Woito, Robert. *To End War.*
Weston, Burns. *Towards Nuclear Disarmament and Global Security.*
Brock, Peter. *20th Century Pacifism.*
Kokopeli/Lakey. *Off Their Backs and On Their Own Feet.*
Sharp, Gene. *Politics of Nonviolent Action*, Vol. II.

Course Requirements and Assessment
Attendance at lectures, discussion groups and films is a requirement of the course, and attendance will be monitored. Class participation will, with attendance, constitute 20% of the assessment. The rest of the assessment will be based on the following scheme: two-part midterm exam (one essay section and one other written assignment)—30%; in-class quizzes—10%; two-part final exam (one take-home section and a one-hour exam)—40%.

COURSE OUTLINE AND SCHEDULE

Sept. 9—Introduction to the Course: What Is Peace Studies?

Sept. 11—Peace Studies at Colgate University
- Joseph J. Fahey, "Parameters, Principles, and Dynamics of Peace Studies," *Educators for Justice and Peace*, O'Hare, ed. (San Francisco: Harper and Row Publishers, 1983), pp. 172–185.

Sept. 15—Origins and Scope of Peace Studies
- Sivard, pp. 1–52.
- Young, all.
- *M&W*, pp. 3–14.
- Christine Arber, "Towards a Redefinition of Peace in Education and Research."

Sept. 16—What Are "Positive Peace" and "Negative Peace"?
Film: First Contact.
- Christine Arber, "The Concepts of 'Negative' Peace and 'Positive' Peace with Reference to the Development of the Peace Movement Before and After 1945."
- (Recommended) *M&W*, pp. 213–300.

Sept. 18—Discussion of Structural Violence, Colonialism and "First Contact"
Video: Dead Birds. (Sept. 17)
- Nigel J. Young, "Educating the Peace Educators," *Bulletin of Peace Proposals*, Vol. 12, No. 2, 1981; PRIO, pp. 123–135.

Sept. 22—War: Its History and Causes
- Dyer, ch. 1.
- Gardiner and Heider, "Violence," *Gardens of War*, pp. 135–144.

Sept. 23—Video: Dyer Series on War, Part 1: "The Road to Total War"
- Thomas C. Schelling, "The Diplomacy of Violence," *Peace and War*, Charles R. Beitz and Theodore Herman, eds. (San Francisco: W.H. Freeman, 1973), pp. 74–90.

Sept. 25—Discussion of World War I and Films
Films: All Quiet on the Western Front and Kameradschaft. (Sept. 24)
- Margaret Mead, "Warfare Is Only an Invention, Not a Biological Necessity," *Peace and War*, Charles Beitz and Theodore Herman, eds. (San Francisco: W.H. Freeman, 1973).

Sept. 29—War, Aggression and Conflict
- T.B. Bottomore, "Force in Social Life," *Sociology: A Guide to Problems and Literature* (London: George Allen and Unwin, Ltd.) pp. 217–228.
- *C&M*, ch. 1.

Sept. 30—State, Violence and Territoriality
- Robert L. Carneiro, "A Theory of the Origin of the State," *Science*, Vol. 169 (August 21, 1979), pp. 733–738.
- *M&W*, pp. 15–48.

Oct. 2—History of Peace: Ideas and Action
- *C&M*, Introduction.
- *M&W*, pp. 137–170.

Oct. 6—The Peace Traditions: Perspectives on Peace
- *C&M*, ch. 4.

Oct. 7—Obedience, Resistance, Violence and Nonviolence: The Work of Gene Sharp
Film: Gandhi (Oct. 8).
- Sharp, all.
- *C&M*, ch. 6.
- Gene Sharp, "Examples of Nonviolent Resistance," *Politics of Nonviolent Action: Part One: Power and Struggle* (Boston, 1973), pp. 86–90.

Oct. 9—Gandhi and the Politics of Mass Nonviolent Action
- Krishnalal Shridharani, "War Without Violence," *Reader in Political Sociology*, Frank Lindenfeld, ed. (New York: Funk and Wagnalls, 1968), pp. 444–456.
- Joan Bondurant, "Satyagraha as Applied Socio-Political Action," *Conquest of Violence: Gandhian Philosophy of Conflict* (Berkeley: University of California Press, 1985), pp. 36–55.

Oct. 13—War Resistance, Conscientious Objection and Civil Disobedience
- *C&M*, chs. 1, 4, 5.
- Henry David Thoreau, "Civil Disobedience" (revised), *Pacifist Conscience*, Peter Mayer, ed. (Chicago: Henry Regnery Co., 1966).

Oct. 14—Peter Tarnoff, Council on Foreign Relations

Oct. 20—King: Nonviolence, Social Justice, and Human Rights
Video: Eyes on the Prize.
- *C&M*, ch. 8.
- *Eyes on the Prize* (text), pp. 77–100.

Oct. 23—Discussion of Civil Rights Movement and Nonviolence
- Martin Luther King, Jr., "New Day in Birmingham, Alabama," *Why We Can't Wait* (1963), pp. 30–39.

Oct. 27—War, Liberation and Social Justice
- Barbara Deming, "On Revolution and Equilibrium," *Revolution: Violent and Nonviolent.*

Oct. 28—Vietnam: The War's Effect on Peace Studies
Film: In the Year of the Pig (Oct. 29).
- Björn Hettne, "Peace and Development Contradictions and Compatibilities," *Journal of Peace Research*, Vol. 20, No. 4 (1983), pp. 333–342.

Oct. 30—Responses to the War: A Discussion
- *C&M*, ch. 10.

Nov. 3—The Cold War
- *E&H*, ch. 27.

Nov. 4—Video: *Faces of the Enemy*
Film: The Atomic Cafe (Nov. 5).
- *E&H*, pp. 223–231.
- David Barash, "Nuclear Psychology," ch. 14, *The Arms Race and Nuclear War* (Belmont, CA: Wadsworth, 1987).

Nov. 6—Discussion of the Psychology of the Arms Race
- *E&H*, part I, and ch. 5.

Nov. 10—The Nuclear Era: Politics and Society
Video: Hiroshima/Nagasaki.
- *E&H*, part II, and chs. 6, 9.
- *M&W*, pp. 171–190.

Nov. 11—Disarmament and Arms Control
- *E&H*, pp. 259–86.
- "Negotiated Agreements," ch. 10 in Barash.

Nov. 13—The Nuclear State and Democracy
Film: Half-Life (Nov. 12).
- Nigel J. Young, "War Resistance, State and Society," *War, State and Society*, Martin Shaw, ed., 1985, pp. 95–113.

Nov. 17—Anti-Nuclear Movement
- *E&H*, ch. 13.

Nov. 18—The New Peace Movement
Slides on peace movement.
- *E&H*, ch. 11.
- *C&M*, ch. 11.
- *M&W*, pp. 191–212.

Nov. 20—Central America and the Peace Movement: Discussion of Salvador
Film: Salvador (Nov. 19).
- Review part V ("Globalism, the Nonaligned Movement, and Social Change") of *Manual of Readings* (Hettne, Deming, Fanon and Young).

Nov. 24—Discussion: Globalism and Transnationalism
- *M&W*, pp. 333–386.

Dec. 1—Conflict and Social Life
- A. Rapoport, "A Taxonomy of Conflicts," and "Some Aspects of Endogenous Conflicts," *Conflict in Man-Made Environment*, pp. 174–196.

Dec. 2—Communication and Conflict Resolution Skills

Neil Katz, Director, Program on Nonviolent Conflict Resolution, Syracuse University.
* Optional weekend workshop on creative conflict management.

Dec. 8—Feminism and Peace Studies

* Betty Reardon, "A Gender Analysis of Militarism and Sexist Repression," *IPRA Newsletter*, Vol. XXI, No. 2 (1983), pp. 3–9.
* C&M, pp. 213–222.

Dec. 9—Careers in Peace Studies

Film: Seven Days in May (Dec. 10).

Dec. 11—Review of Semester: Peace in the Future?

* Roy Preiswerk, "Could We Study International Relations as if People Mattered?" *Peace and World Order Studies,* Institute for World Order, New York, New York, 1981, pp. 2–23.
* C&M, ch. 11.

ADDITIONAL READINGS

I. The Study of War and Conflict

Brock, Peter. "Varieties of Pacifism at the Outset of the Twentieth Century." *Twentieth Century Pacifism*, pp. 1–13.
Mayer, Peter. *The Pacifist Conscience.* Introduction. Chicago: Gateway Edition.
Curle, Adam. "Human Nature." From a lecture at Bradford University.
Kreisberg. "Essentials, Settings, and Implications." *Social Conflicts,* 2nd ed. Prentice-Hall, 1982, pp. 317–336.
Coser, Lewis. "Some Social Functions of Violence." *The War System: An Interdisciplinary Approach.* R. Falk and S. Kim, eds. Boulder, CO: Westview Press, 1980, pp. 334–346.

II. The Origin, Development, and Future of States

Young, Nigel J. "Transnationalism." *World Encyclopedia of Peace,* Vol. 2. Linus Pauling, ed. New York: Pergamon Press, 1986.
Krippendorff, Ekkehart. "The State as the Focus of Peace Research," *Peace Research Society, Papers,* XVI, The Rome Conference, 1970, pp. 47–59.
Hamilton, Charles. *The State.* Introduction (May 1975), pp. iii–xx.

III. Deterrence, Diplomacy, and the Military Industrial Complex

Geyer, Alan. "Deterrence and Counterforce."
McNamara, Robert S. "Mutual Deterrence." *Peace and War.* Charles R. Beitz and Theodore Herman, eds. San Francisco: W.H. Freeman, 1973, pp. 91–97.
Johansen, Robert C. "Salt II: A Symptom of the Arms Race."

Pilisuk, Mark and Tom Hayden. "Is There a Soviet Military Industrial Complex that Prevents Peace?" *Peace and War.* Charles Beitz and Theodore Herman, eds. San Francisco: W.H. Freeman, 1973, pp. 288–315.

IV. The Cold War, The Soviet Threat, and the Breakdown of Negotiations

Kaldor, Mary. "Is There a Soviet Military Threat?" *Debate on Disarmament.* Michael Clark and Marjorie Mowlam, eds. Boston, 1982, pp. 29–43.

Morganthau, Hans. "The Origins of the Cold War." *The Origins of the Cold War.* Lloyd C. Gardner, Arthur Schlesinger, and Hans Morganthau, eds. Massachusetts: Ginn and Co., 1970, pp. 79–102.

Churchill, Winston. "'Iron Curtain' Speech," "Vital Speeches of the Day," XII, March 1946, pp. 329–332.

Lasch, Christopher. "The Cold War, Revisited and Re-visioned." *New York Times.* January 14, 1968, pp. 1–13.

Halliday, Fred. "The Sources of the New Cold War." *Exterminism and Cold War.* Edited by New Left Review. London: Verson, 1982, pp. 289–328.

Myrdal, Alva. "Arms Control and Disarmament Agreements, 1959–1975," from "The International Control of Disarmament." *Scientific American Progress in Arms Control.* San Francisco: W.H. Freeman.

Blackaby, Frank. US-Soviet Negotiations." *SIPRI Yearbook,* 1985.

Excerpts from The Charter of the United Nations.

European Nuclear Disarmament (END) Campaign Appeal.

V. Globalism, the Nonaligned Movement, and Social Change

Fanon, Frantz. "The Wretched of the Earth." *Reader in Political Sociology.* Frank Lindenfeld, ed., pp. 486–505.

Young, Nigel J. "On War, National Liberation, and the State."

VI. Nonviolence in Theory and Practice

Lacefield, Pat, and Scott Kennedy. "An Introduction to Nonviolence." *Fellowship.* March/April 1980, pp. 3–6.

Boulding, Kenneth. "Power in Society." *Ecodynamics: A New Theory of Societal Evolution.* Beverly Hills: Sage, 1978, pp. 240–252.

Gandhi, Mohandas K. "On Nonviolence." *Peace and War.* Charles Beitz and Theodore Herman, eds. San Francisco: W.H. Freeman, 1973, pp. 345–348.

Horsburgh, H.J.N. "The Bases of Satyagraha." *Nonviolence and Aggression.* Oxford, 1968, pp. 27–40.

Bondurant, Joan. "The Salt Satyagraha." *Conquest of Violence: The Gandhian Philosophy of Conflict.* Princeton University Press, 1958, pp. 88–102.

Deming, Barbara. "Nonviolence and Casualties." *Peace and War.* Charles Beitz and Theodore Herman, eds. San Francisco: W.H. Freeman, 1973, pp. 375–377.

Schelling, Thomas C. "Some Questions on Civilian Defense." *Peace and War.* Charles Beitz and Theodore Herman, eds. San Francisco: W.H. Freeman, 1973, pp. 368–374.

Ostergaard, Geoffrey. "Resisting the Nation-State: The Pacifist and the Anarchist Traditions." *The Nation State.* L. Tivey, ed., pp. 171–195.

Shaw, Martin. "Socialism Against War; Remaking a Tradition." *Socialism and Militarism*, pp. 1–33.

VII. The Peace Movement, Social Change and Future Orientations and Prospects for Peace

Carroll, Sue, et al. "Organizing for Social Transformation." *Peace and War.* Charles Beitz and Theodore Herman, eds. San Francisco: W.H. Freeman, 1973, pp. 415–424.

Spretnak, Charlene. "Naming the Cultural Forces that Push Us Toward War." *Journal of Humanistic Psychology* (1983), pp. 43–54.

Galtung, Johan. "Towards a Definition of Peace Research." United Nations University Project, Geneva.

Vayrynen, Raimo. "Transnational Coordination and Development of Peace Research." IPRA presentation at meeting.

Galtung, Johan. "Twenty-Five Years of Peace Research: Ten Challenges and Responses." *Journal of Peace Research*, Vol. 22, No. 2, 1985, pp. 141–158.

Young, Nigel J. "Transnationalism and Communalism." *Gandhi Marg*, No. 32, July 1983, pp. 191–208.

Rotblat, J. "The Pugwash Movement." *UNESCO Paper*, 1983.

2. Introduction to World Order

Richard Falk   *Fall 1986*
Politics Dept., Princeton University, Princeton, NJ 08544

This course seeks to explore the prospects for strengthening the quality of world order. Quality can be understood in relation to some idea of justice or by reference to a series of world order values that are set forth and defended by reference to some source of authority or by their claimed consequences.

The underlying theme of world order inquiry challenges students to fashion their own understanding of the potential for global reform under present historical circumstances.

As an approach to international relations the world order orientation includes the following distinctive features: that morality counts in all dimensions of human experience (as compared to power politics); that the study of future prospects and alternatives illuminates present political choices; that the study of the past organization of international political life is illuminating; that visions, utopias, prospects, and prophesies are relevant to the study and appreciation of international politics; and that it is useful to develop the perspective of particular individuals, groups, and nations and of holistic, encompassing interpretations.

Required Readings

Devall, Bill, and George Sessions. *Deep Ecology.* Peregrine Books, 1985. (paper)

Falk, Richard, Samuel S. Kim, and Saul H. Mendlovitz, eds. *Toward a Just World Order.* Westview Press, 1982. (paper)

LeGuin, Ursula. *The Dispossessed.* Avon, 1974. (paper)

Soroos, Marvin S. *Beyond Sovereignty: The Challenge of Global Policy.* University of South Carolina Press, 1986. (paper)

Recommended Readings

Foell, Earl, and R. Hennemann. *How Peace Comes to the World.* MIT Press, 1986. (cloth)

Lifton, Robert Jay, and Richard Falk. *Indefensible Weapons: The Political and Psychological Case Against Nuclearism.* Basic Books, 1982. (paper)

COURSE OUTLINE

Lectures and precept discussions will be correlated with assigned readings except under special circumstances; an asterisk (*) denotes recommended reading.

An Introductory Diagnosis

- Ursula LeGuin, *The Dispossessed* (1974).
- Doris Lessing, *Memoirs of a Survivor* (1975), pp. 3–217.
- *Doris Lessing, *Shikasta* (1979).
- *Doris Lessing, *Briefing for a Descent into Hell* (1971).
- *R.A. Falk, *This Endangered Planet: Prospects and Proposals for Human Survival* (1971).
- *Theodore Roszak, *The Unfinished Animal* (1977).
- *William Irwin Thompson, *Pacific Shift* (1986).

An Orientation Toward International Political Life

- Soroos, pp. 3–19 (1986).
- *Samuel S. Kim, *The Quest for a Just World Order* (1983).
- *Louis Rene Beres, *People, States, and World Order* (1981).
- *Ian Clark, *Reform and Resistance in the International Order* (1980).
- *Charles Beitz, *Political Theory and International Relations* (1979).
- *R. Kothari, *Footsteps into the Future* (1974).

Fashioning a Response
- Soroos, pp. 120–160 (1986).
- Falk et al., pp. 1–54 (1982).
- *Saul H. Mendlovitz, ed., *On the Creation of a Just World Order* (1975).
- *John McMurtry, *The Structure of Marx's World-View* (1978).
- *"Manifesto of the Communist Party," in R.C. Tuckery, ed., *The Marx-Engels Reader*, 2nd ed., pp. 469–511 (1978).
- *Grenville Clark and Louis B. Sohn, *World Peace Through World Law*, 2nd ed., rev. (1960).
- *Warren Wager, *Building the City of Man: Outlines of a World Civilization* (1971).
- *Pierre Teilhard de Chardin, *The Future of Man* (1969).

The Challenge of Nuclear National Security
- Soroos, pp. 163–194 (1986).
- Lifton and Falk, pp. ix–xi, 3–22, 100–110, 128–169, 244–273 (1982).
- *Michael Mandlebaum, *The Nuclear Future* (1983).
- *Gywn Prins, ed., *The Nuclear Crisis Reader* (1984).
- *Dietrich Fischer, *The Prevention of War in the Nuclear Age* (1984).
- *Joseph Nye, *Nuclear Ethics* (1986).
- *Harvard Nuclear Study Group, *Living with Nuclear Weapons* (1983).
- *The United Methodist Council of Bishops, *In Defense of Creation: The Nuclear Crisis and Just Peace* (1986).
- *Jonathan Schell, *The Fate of Earth* (1982).
- *Bruce Russet, *The Prisoners of Insecurity* (1983).
- *Avner Cohen and Steven Lee, eds., *Nuclear Weapons and the Future of Humanity* (1986).
- *Robert Jervis, *The Illogic of American Nuclear Strategy* (1984).
- *Russell Hardin et al., eds., *Nuclear Deterrence: Ethics and Strategy* (1985).
- *George Kennan, *The Nuclear Delusion* (1982).

Assessing the Role of the Sovereign State as World Order Actor
- Falk et al., pp. 55–97 (1982).
- *James Mayall, ed., *The Community of States* (1982).
- *Hedley Bull, *The Anarchical Society: A Study of Order in World Politics* (1977).
- *Hans J. Morgenthau, *Politics Among Nations*, 5th ed. (1973).
- *Robert C. Johansen, *The National Interest and the Human Interest* (1980).
- *Stanley Hoffman, *Primacy or World Order: American Foreign Policy Since the Cold War* (1978).
- *Robert Keohane and Joseph Nye, *Power and Interdependence* (1977).
- *William Applemann Williams, *Empire as a Way of Life* (1980).
- *John Herz, *The Nation-State and the Crisis of World Politics* (1976).
- *Michael Donelan, ed., *The Reason of State* (1978).
- *Stanley Diamond, *In Search of the Primitive* (1974).

- *Anthony D. Smith, *Theories of Nationalism*, 2nd ed. (1983).
- *Eric Nordlinger, *On the Autonomy of the Democratic State* (1981).

Enhancing the Quality of World Order
- Falk et al., pp. 141–216 (1982).
- *F.H. Hinsley, *Power and the Pursuit of Peace* (1963).
- *Barrington Moore, Jr., *Reflections on the Causes of Human Misery* (1972).
- *R.B.J. Walker, ed., *Culture, Ideology, and World Order* (1984).
- *Robert Gilpin, *War and Change in World Politics* (1981).

The Challenge of World Poverty
- Soroos, pp. 195–226 (1986).
- Falk et al., pp. 289–358 (1982).
- *J. Bhagwati and John Gerard Ruggie, eds., *Power, Passions, and Purpose* (1984).
- *H. Magdoff, *The Age of Imperialism* (1969).
- *The Brandt Commission, *Common Crisis* (1983).
- *Jacques Loup, *Can the Third World Survive?* (1980).
- *Marc Nerfin, ed., *Another Development* (1975).

The Challenge of Oppressive Politics
- Soroos, pp. 227–260 (1979).
- Falk et al., pp. 365–434 (1982).
- *George Konrad, *Antipolitics* (1984).
- *U.S. Department of State, Country Reports on Human Rights, annual series.
- *Falk, *Human Rights and State Sovereignty* (1981).
- *Petra Kelly, *Fighting for Hope* (1984).
- *Pam McAllister, ed., *Reweaving the Web of Life: Feminism and Non-violence* (1982).
- *Carol Gilligan, *In a Different Voice* (1982).
- *Margaret Randall, *Sandino's Daughters* (1981).
- *Francis Jennings, *The Invasion of America: Indians, Colonialism, and the Cant of Conquest* (1976).
- *Virgil J. Vogel, ed., *This Country Was Ours: A Documentary History of the American Indian* (1972).
- *Eric R. Wolf, *Europe and The People Without History* (1982).
- *Rex Weyler, *Blood of the Land: The Government and Corporate War Against the American Indian Movement* (1982).
- *Milan Kundera, *The Book of Laughter and Forgetting* (1980).

The Challenge of Ecological Decay
- Soroos, pp. 294–322 (1979).
- Falk et al., pp. 435–496 (1982).
- *William Ophuls, *Ecology and The Politics of Security* (1977).
- *Andre Gorz, *Ecology as Politics* (1980).
- *Rudolph Bahro, *Building the Green Movement* (1986).

- *Harold and Margaret Sprout, *The Context of Environmental Politics: Unfinished Business for America's Third Century* (1978).
- *Lester Brown and others, *State of the World*, annual series since 1984.
- *"Bhopal," special section, *Alternatives*, Vol. IX, pp. 134–165 (1986).

The Path of Ecological Reconstruction

- Bill Devall and George Sessions, *Deep Ecology* (1985).
- *Gary Snyder, *Earth House Hold* (1969).
- *Peter Russell, *The Global Brain* (1976).
- *David Spangler, *Towards a Planetary Vision* (1977).
- *David Bohm, *Wholeness and the Implicate Order* (1983).
- *Jose Arguelles, *The Transformative Vision* (1974).
- *Jerome Rothenberg and Diane Rothenberg, eds., *Symposium of the Whole* (1983).
- *Paul Taylor, *Respect for Nature: A Theory of Environmental Ethics* (1986).
- *Jonathon Porritt, *Seeing Green* (1985).
- *Fritjof Capra and Charlene Spretnak, *Green Politics* (1984).
- *Wendell Berry, *The Unsettling of America* (1977).

The Path of Social and Political Reconstruction

- Falk et al., pp. 559–662 (1982).
- Eric Foell and R. Hennemann, *How Peace Comes to The World*, selections to be announced.
- United Nations University, *Peace and Global Transformation Project: Toward a Liberations Peace*, mimeographed (1987).
- *Baha'i Universal House of Justice, *The Peoples of the World: Statement on Peace* (1986).
- *Marcus G. Raskin, *The Common Good* (1986).
- *Report of the Alternative Defence Commission, *Defence Without the Bomb* (1983).
- *Hanna Newcombe, *Design for a Better World* (1983).
- *Gandhi, *All Men Are Brothers* (1980).
- *Gene Sharp, *The Politics of Nonviolent Action* (1973).
- *Frank E. Manuel, ed., *Utopias and Utopian Thought* (1967).
- *Martin Buber, *Paths in Utopia* (1949).
- *E.P. Thompson, *Beyond the Cold War* (1982).
- *Eleonora Masini, ed., *Visions of Desirable Societies* (1983).
- *Frantz Alt, *Peace Is Possible: The Politics of the Sermon on the Mount* (1985).

3. Introduction to Peace and Conflict Studies

Anatol Rapoport   *Fall 1987*
Peace and Conflict Studies Programme,
University College, University of Toronto,
Toronto, Ontario M5S 1A1, Canada

This is a core course in a four-year undergraduate programme in peace and conflict studies. It is designed to give first-year students who may desire to enroll in the programme an overview of an approach to peace and conflict studies based on four different perspectives. The *psychological perspective* focuses on the human individual, his/her motivations, thinking habits, attitudes, and predilections to the extent that these are relevant to conflict and conflict resolution. The *ideological perspective* focuses on the same factors characterizing entire populations or cultures. The *strategic perspective* involves a critical examination of notions related to "rational" conduct of conflict. It focuses mainly on modes of thought prevalent in military and political circles. The *systemic perspective* examines the dynamics of large-scale social events generated by massive effects such as fluctuations of economic indices, arms races, political upheavals, and the like. Peace keeping, conflict resolution, and integrative processes are examined in the light of the above four perspectives.

Course Requirements
The course outline follows A. Rapoport's *Approaches to the Study of Conflict* (forthcoming). Evaluation is based upon: class participation—20%; four Book Reviews—10% each; Final Examination—40%.

COURSE OUTLINE

Session 1—Introduction: The Four Dimensions of Conflict

Part I. The Psychological Dimension
Session 2—On "Aggression"
• K. Lorenz, *On Aggression.*

Session 3—The Evolutionary Perspective
- R. Axelrod, *The Evolution of Cooperation.*

Session 4—The Behavioural Perspective
- J. Dollard et al., *Frustration and Aggression.*
- L. Berkowitz, *Aggression: A Social Psychological Analysis.*

Session 5—The Attitudinal Perspective
- G.W. Allport, *The Nature of Prejudice.*

Session 6—Use and Limitations of the Psychological Approach

Part II. The Ideological Dimension

Session 7—Ideology: The Substrate of Collective Thought
- K. Mannheim, *Ideology and Utopia.*
- K. Marx and F. Engels, *The Communist Manifesto.*

Session 8—The Idea of Freedom and the Cult of Property
- Excerpts from M. Adler, *The Idea of Freedom.*
- A. Smith, *The Wealth of Nations.*
- Inaugural addresses of American presidents.

Session 9—Perpetual Struggle as an Outlook and Violence as a Way of Life
- T. Hobbes, *Leviathan.*
- V.I. Lenin, *Materialism and Empiriocriticism.*
- E. Hyams, *Terrorists and Terrorism.*

Session 10—Addiction to Power
- H. Arendt, *The Origins of Totalitarianism.*
- N. Machiavelli, *The Prince.*
- Excerpts from A. Hitler, *Mein Kampf.*

Session 11—Ideological Issues of the Cold War
- A. Rapoport, *Strategy and Conscience.*
- A. Rapoport, *The Big Two.*

Session 12—The End of Ideology?
- D. Bell, *The End of Ideology.*
- H. Morgenthau, *Politics Among Nations.*

Part III. The Strategic Dimension

Session 13—Militarism
- A. Vagts, *A History of Militarism.*

Session 14—Formal Theory of Decision
- H. Raiffa, *Decision Analysis.*
- A. Rapoport, *Two-person Game Theory.*
- A. Rapoport, *N-person Game Theory.*

Session 15—Strategic Negotiation
- T.C. Schelling, *The Strategy of Conflict.*
- R. Jervis, *The Logic of Images in International Relations.*

Session 16—Intellectualization of War
- H. Kahn, *Thinking About the Unthinkable in the Eighties.*
- C.S. Gray, *Strategic Studies and Public Policy.*

IV. The Systemic Dimension

Session 17—The Systemic Outlook
- A. Rapoport, *General Systems Theory.*

Session 18—Arms Races
- P. Noel-Baker, *The Arms Race.*
- A. Myrdal, *The Game of Disarmament.*

Session 19—Global Trends
- Stockholm International Peace Research Institute (SIPRI) publications on arms expenditures and the arms trade.

Session 20—Perpetual War Economy
- S. Melman, *The Defence Economy.*

Session 21—The War System
- Q. Wright, *Study of War.*
- M. Small and J.D. Singer, *Resort to Arms: International Civil War 1816–1980.*

Part V. Quest for Peace

Session 22—Harbingers of Englightenment
- J. Schell, *The Fate of the Earth.*
- H. Caldicott, *Missile Envy.*
- R.J. Lifton, *Death in Life.*

Session 23—Personal Pacifism
- L.N. Tolstoy, selected writings.
- H. Thoreau, *Walden* and *Civil Disobedience.*

Session 24—Political Pacifism
- J. Brown, *Gandhi and Civil Disobedience.*
- G. Sharp, *The Politics of Nonviolent Action.*

Session 25—Creative Negotiation and Conciliation
- R. Fisher and W. Ury, *Getting to Yes: Negotiating Without Giving In.*
- C.E. Osgood, *An Alternative to War or Surrender.*
- M. Yarrow, *Quaker Experiences in International Conciliation.*

Session 26—Problems of Peace Research and Peace Education
Concluding remarks.

ADDITIONAL READINGS

H.C. Kelman, ed. *International Behavior.*
L. Festinger. *Conflict, Decision, and Dissonance.*
W. Eckhard. *Compassion.*
Craig and Jungerman. *Nuclear Arms Race.*
W.J. Broad. *Star Warriors.*
A. Ulam. *Expansionism and Coexistence.*
A. Rapoport, *Fights, Games and Debates.*
H. Kahn. *On Escalation! Metaphors and Scenarios.*
R. Malcolmson. *Nuclear Fallacies.*
A. Rapoport. *Conflict in Man-made Environment.*
S. Melman. *The Perpetual War Economy.*
F. Dyson. *Weapons and Hope.*

4. The Quest for Peace

Chadwick Alger   *Spring 1987*
Political Science Dept., Ohio State University,
Columbus OH 43201

Taking a comprehensive overview of approaches to peace in the twentieth century, this course assesses what we have learned. Twenty-three approaches are considered under eight headings: (1) Use and control of military power (balance of power, collective security, disarmament/arms control); (2) Third Party Roles (peace settlement, peacekeeping, non-alignment/neutrality, problem-solving workshops); (3) Centralized Political Power (world government, federalism, neo-functionalism); (4) Self-Determination for Peoples, Groups and Individuals (self-determination, anarchism, human rights); (5) Economic Well-being and Equity (functionalism, development, international economic equity, international communications equity); (6) Grassroots Movements (peace movements, basic human needs/conversion, feminist movement); (7) Non-violence (non-violent politics, non-military defense); and (8) Governance of the Commons (atmosphere, space and oceans). An additional topic, and of concern throughout the course, will be the twentieth century's global dialogue on the meaning of peace. This dialogue is now playing a critical role in the global quest for peace.

Mid-term Examination: May 6.

Term Paper
Due June 4. Will consist of two parts: (1) A comprehensive evaluative overview of approaches to peace covered in the course, and (2) a proposed peace strategy for the remainder of the twentieth century that is based on this appraisal.

Readings
It would not be prudent to pursue an understanding of the quest for peace within the boundaries of a single discipline, or a single country. The readings draw on scholarship from at least six disciplines and at least eleven countries. References in the course outline without complete bibliographic data generally refer to the following sources.

Bankyopadhuaya, Jayantanuja. *North Over South: A Non-Western Perspective of International Relations.* New Delhi: South Asian Publishers Pvt. Ltd., 1982.

Bennett, A. LeRoy. *International Organizations: Principles and Issues,* 3rd. ed. Englewood Cliffs: Prentice-Hall, 1984.

Birgit Brock-Utne. *Educating for Peace: A Feminist Perspective.* New York: Pergamon Press, 1985.

Brown, Seyom, Nina W. Cornell, Larry L. Fabian and Edith Brown Weiss. *Regimes for the Ocean, Outer Space and Weather.* Washington, D.C.: Brookings Institution, 1977.

Claude, Inis. *Swords into Plowshares.* New York: Random House, 1971.

———, *Power and International Relations.* New York: Random House, 1962.

Falk, Richard, and Samuel Kim. *The War System: An Interdisciplinary Approach.*

Fischer, Dietrich. *Preventing War in the Nuclear Age.* Totowa, NJ: Rowman and Allanheld, 1984.

Forsythe, David P. *Human Rights and World Politics.* Lincoln: University of Nebraska Press, 1983.

Galtung, Johan. *The True Worlds.* New York: The Free Press, 1980.

———, *There Are Alternatives!: Four Roads to Peace and Security.* Chester Springs, PA: Doufour Editions, 1984.

Nye, J.S. *Peace in Parts.* Boston: Little, Brown, 1977.

Ronen, Dov. *The Quest for Self-Determination.* New Haven: Yale University Press, 1979.

Sharp, Gene. *The Politics of Non-Violent Action.* Boston: Porter Sargent, 1973.

Taylor, Paul, and A.J.R. Groom. *International Organizations: A Conceptual Approach.* London: Frances Pinter, 1978.

COURSE OUTLINE

Introduction (Mar. 30)
Personal Inventory of Beliefs About Ways to Peace
- "Opinions on Ways to Peace," distributed in class.

Course Overview
- Chadwick F. Alger, "The Quest for Peace," *Quarterly Report*, Mershon Center, OSU, Vol. 11, No. 2, Autumn, 1986, distributed in class.

Historical Context (Apr. 1)
- Claude (1971), ch. 2, "The Development of International Organization in the Nineteenth Century," pp. 21–40; ch. 3, "The Establishment of the League of Nations," pp. 41–56; ch. 4, "The Origins of the United Nations System," pp. 57–80; "The Covenant of the League of Nations," pp. 453–462; "The Charter of the United Nations," pp. 463–489.

Use and Control of Military Power
Balance of Power (Apr. 6)
- Claude (1961), ch. 2, "Balance of Power: An Ambiguous Concept," pp. 11–39; ch. 3, "A Critique of the Balance of Power," pp. 40–93.

Collective Security (Apr. 6)
- Claude (1962), ch. 4, "Collective Security: An Alternative to Balance of Power?" pp. 94–149; ch. 5, "A Critique of Collective Security," pp. 150–204.

Disarmament/Arms Control (Apr. 8)
- Claude (1971), ch. 13, "Disarmament as an Approach to Peace," pp. 286–161.

Third Party Roles
Peaceful Settlement (April 13)
- Claude (1971), ch. 11, "Peaceful Settlement of Disputes," pp. 215–244; ch. 15, "The Grand Debate Approach to Peace," pp. 335–348.

Problem Solving Workshops
- John Burton, "The Facilitation of International Conflict Resolution," 1985.
- Herbert C. Kelman and Stephen P. Cohen, "The Problem-Solving Workshop," Harvard University, 1974.

Peacekeeping (Apr. 15)
- Bennett, ch. 7, "Peacekeeping Innovations," pp. 155–181.
- Gunther G. Greindl, "UN Peace-Keeping Operations: History and Operational Concepts with Special Reference to UNFICYP and UNDOF," United Nations University, 1985.

Non-Alignment
- Bandyopadhuaya, ch. 7, "Nonalignment and World Order," pp. 197–236.
- Galtung (1984), "Non-alignment: Gradual Decoupling from the Superpowers," pp. 184–192.

Centralized Political Power
World Government (Apr. 20)
- Claude (1962), ch. 6, "World Government: Monopoly of Power," pp. 205–242; ch. 7, "World Government: Law and Politics," pp. 243–285.

Federalism
- George Codding, "Federalism: The Conceptual Setting," in Taylor and Groom, pp. 326–341.

Neo-Functionalism (Apr. 22)
- R.J. Harrison, "Neo-Functionalism," in Taylor and Groom, pp. 253–269.
- Nye, ch. 2, "Regional Integration: Concept and Measurement," pp. 21–54; ch. 3, "A Political Model of Regional Economic Integration," pp. 55–107.

Global Dialog on the Meanings of Peace, Conflict, Violence, Development and Security (Apr. 27 & Apr. 29)
- Quincy Wright, "The Nature of Conflict," in Falk and Kim, ch. 13, pp. 317–333.
- Lewis A. Coser, "Some Social Functions of Violence," in Falk and Kim, ch. 14, pp. 334–346.
- Charles Chatfield, "Peace Theory," International Peace Academy, no date.
- Johan Galtung, "Peace Theory," International Peace Academy, no date.
- Kinhide Mushakoji, "Peace Research as an International Learning Process: A New Meta-Paradigm," *International Studies Quarterly*, Vol. 22, No. 2, June 1978, pp. 173–194.
- Robert Johansen, "Toward an Alternative Security System," *Alternatives*, Vol. VII, No. 3, Winter 1983, pp. 293–349.

Self-Determination for Peoples, Groups and Individuals
Self-Determination (May 4)
- Claude (1971), ch. 16, "Trusteeship as an Approach to Peace," pp. 349–377.
- Ronen, pp. 1–70; 90–120.

Anarchism

- Richard A. Falk, "Anarchism and World Order," in Falk and Kim, pp. 37–57.

Human Rights (May 6)

- Forsythe, ch. 1, "Promoting Human Rights: Human Rights as a Legal Ideal," pp. 1–40; ch. 2, "Protecting Human Rights: The Politics of Implementing Rights," pp. 41–87; ch. 5, "The Political Philosophy of Human Rights," 158–186; "The International Bill of Human Rights," pp. 261–301.

Economic Well-Being and Equity
Functionalism (May 11)

- Claude (1971), ch. 17, "The Functional Approach to Peace," pp. 378–410.
- Paul Taylor, "Functionalism: The Theory of David Mitrany," in Taylor and Groom, pp. 236–252.

Development

- Bjorn Hettne, *Approaches to the Study of Peace and Development: A State of the Art Report*, University of Gothenburg, 1984, pp. 1–18.
- Bjorn Hettne, "Peace and Development: Contradictions and Compatibilities," *Journal of Peace Research*, Vol. 20, No. 1, 1983, pp. 329–342.
- George Sorensen, "Peace and Development: Looking for the Right Track," *Journal of Peace Research*, Vol. 22, No. 1, 1985, pp. 69–77.

International Economic Equity (May 13)

- Bruce Russett, "Prosperity and Peace," *International Studies Quarterly*, Vol. 27, December 4, 1983, pp. 381–388.
- Bandyopadhuaya, ch. 5, "Strategy for the New International Economic Order," pp. 107–132.
- Johan Galtung, "Self-Reliance and Global Interdependence: Some Reflections on the 'New International Economic Order,'" University of Oslo.

International Communications Equity

- Bandyopadhuaya, ch. 6, "The Structure of International Communication," pp. 165–196.

Grassroots Movements
Peace Movements (May 18)

- Chadwick F. Alger, "Preparation of Societies for Life in Peace: A Grassroots Movements Perspective," Tokyo: UN University, 1986.
- Nigel Young, "The Peace Movement: Traditions and Innovation: A Comparative and Analytical Survey," Committee on a Just World Peace, January 1985.

- Chadwick F. Alger, "Creating Local Institutions for Sustained Participation in Peacebuilding," International Society of Political Psychology Annual Meeting, 1985.
- Chris Smith, "Disarmament, Peace Movements and the Third World," *Third World Quarterly,* Vol. 6, No. 4, October 1984, pp. 392–910.

Feminist Movement

- Betty Reardon, *Sexism and the War System.* New York: Teachers College Press, 1985, pp. 10–63.
- Brock-Utne, pp. 1–32; 143–150.

Basic Human Needs / Conversion

- Robin Luckham, "Armament Culture," *Alternatives,* Vol. X, No. 1, Summer 1984, pp. 1–44.
- David Elliott and Hilary Wainright, "The Lucas Plan: The Roots of the Movement," in Suzanne Gordon and Dave McFadden, eds., *Economic Conversion: Revitalizing America's Economy.* Cambridge, MA: Ballinger, 1984, pp. 89–107.
- Gordon Adams, "Undoing the Iran Triangle: Conversion and the 'Black Box' of Politics," in Gordon and McFadden, pp. 147–163.
- Gordon Adams, "Economic Conversion Misses the Point," *Bulletin of the Atomic Scientists,* February 1986, pp. 24–28.
- Lloyd J. Dumas, Suzanne Gordon, Kevin Bean and Gordon Adams, "Economic Conversion: An Exchange," *Bulletin of the Atomic Scientists,* June/July 1986, pp. 45–51.
- Robert De Grasse, Jr., "Shifting MX Expenditures to Energy Efficiency: Memo on the National Security Applications of Alternative Energy Development," Council on Economic Priorities, 1980.
- Grace Robinson, "Economic Conversion in the State of Ohio," Department of Economics, New York University.

Non-Violence

Non-Violent Politics (May 25)

- Margaret W. Fisher, "Contrasting Approaches to Conflict," in Falk and Kim, pp. 58–73.
- Glenn D. Paige, "Nonviolent Politics for Disarmament," *Alternatives,* 1980, pp. 287–305.
- Glenn D. Paige, "Nonviolent Political Science," *Social Alternatives,* Vol. I, No. 6/7, June 1980, pp. 104–12.

Nonmilitary Defense (May 27)

- Gene Sharp, *National Security Through Civilian Based Defense.* Omaha: Association for Transarmament Studies, 1985, pp. 13–55.
- Fischer, pp. 112–132.
- Galtung (1980), pp. 205–215.

Governance for the Commons

Overview of the Commons (June 1 & 3)

• Per Magnus Wijkman, "Managing the Global Commons," *International Organization*, Vol. 36, No. 3, Summer 1982, pp. 511–536.
• Brown, Cornell, Fabian and Weiss, "Regime Alternatives for the Ocean, Outer Space and the Weather," pp. 1–18; "Toward Effective International Management of the Oceans, Outer Space and Weather," pp. 239–250.

The Law of the Sea Treaty as a Quest for Peace

• Bernardo Zuleta (Under-Secretary General, Special Representative of UN Secretary for LOS), "Introduction to Law of the Sea Treaty."
• David L. Larson, "Security Issues and the Law of the Sea: A General Framework," International Studies Association Convention, 1984.
• A.O. Adede, "The Basic Structure of the Disputes Settlement Part of the Law of the Sea Convention," *Ocean Development and International Law Journal*, Vol. 11, No. 1/2, 1982.
• "The Law of the Sea: Official Text," Part XI, Section 5; Part XV; Annex V, Section 2; Annex VI.

SUGGESTED OUTLINE FOR EVALUATING EACH APPROACH TO PEACE

Your term paper will require careful evaluation of each approach as it is covered during the course. The outline below is suggested as a guide for your personal assessment of each approach.

    I.   Approach
   II.   Definition
  III.   Origins
  IV.   Experience
       1. Examples of successes
       2. Examples of failures
    V.   Evaluation
       1. My initial opinion in pre-course survey
       2. Strengths
       3. Weaknesses
       4. My revised opinion
       5. Reason for revised opinion
  VI.   Relevance for future peace strategy

OPINIONS ON WAYS TO PEACE

Listed below are 37 statements about ways for achieving peace. First, you are asked to respond to each statement by checking the appropriate box in one of the first four columns. Then, score your opinion about the relative usefulness of each approach for achieving peace on a scale that ranges from +5 (exceedingly useful) to −5 (exceedingly negative impact). A score of 0 would mean that you believe a particular approach would neither help nor hinder the achievement of peace.

1. People should become more religious all over the world.
2. One should start with the single individual everywhere and make him/her less aggressive.
3. One should create more peaceful relations in the family, at school, and at work.
4. Countries should be (politically, economically, socially) more similar to each other than they are today.
5. An economy based mainly on private ownership should be introduced all over the world.
6. An economy based mainly on public ownership should be introduced all over the world.
7. An economy based on a mixture of private and public ownership should be introduced all over the world.
8. Countries should keep national armies.
9. Countries should have less to do with each other and become self-sufficient.
10. Small countries all over the world should unite to have more influence on the affairs of the world.
11. We should improve the United Nations so as to make it more efficient than it is today.
12. A world language that can be understood in all countries should be adopted all over the world.
13. Countries should be members of military alliances so that no country or group of countries dares to attack others.
14. UN collective security should be strengthened by eliminating the Security Council veto.
15. We should have general and complete disarmament as soon as possible.
16. Procedures for peaceful settlement of disputes should be strengthened.
17. We should have a strong international peacekeeping force that can stop aggression from any country or group of countries.
18. Countries should withdraw from military alliances.
19. We should have a world state with disappearance of national borders and an efficient world government.
20. Regimes should integrate into single states.
21. The colonial system should be abolished all over the world.
22. All countries should completely stop intervening in the internal affairs of other countries.
23. The world should be organized into smaller countries, thereby eliminating the problems created by big powers.

24. The rights embodied in the Universal Declaration of Human Rights should be guaranteed to all people.
25. It should be possible for people to choose their governments freely all over the world.
26. We should have increased trade, exchange and cooperation between countries that are not on friendly terms.
27. Developed countries should give more technical assistance and aid to developing countries than they do today.
28. Hunger and poverty should be abolished all over the world.
29. The gap between poor and rich countries should disappear.
30. Poor countries all over the world should unite to obtain a bigger share of the wealth of the world.
31. Communications among countries and regions should be more balanced and reciprocal.
32. Stronger grassroots peace movements are needed.
33. Stronger feminist movements are needed.
34. Arms industries should be converted to production of goods that fulfill basic needs.
35. We should expand the use of nonviolent methods for achieving societal change.
36. We should employ nonmilitary methods for national defense.
37. We should establish international governance for the commons (oceans and space).

5. War, Revolution, and Peace

Michael T. Klare and Daniel C. Thomas Fall 1987
School of Social Science, Hampshire College,
Amherst, MA 01002

War, in all of its myriad forms, is one of the most momentous of all human experiences. It is interwoven into our culture, our political and economic system and, in many cases, our family histories. Revolution, the overthrow of an existing social order, has played a major role in shaping the current world system. Peace, as the nonviolent resolution of conflicts, is a process practiced by millions of people on a daily basis and a goal aspired to by almost all societies. It is not hard to see how these social processes are closely linked.

Though the United States is not currently engaged in a major war, the shadow of nuclear holocaust hangs over us from birth. Moreover, as we look abroad, we can see a proliferation of regional conflicts, guerrilla wars, terrorist incidents, and other forms of "low-intensity conflict." Many of these, of course, have come to play a part in the confrontation between the superpowers, the United States, and the USSR. Clearly, if we are to have any understanding of contemporary international affairs, we must know something about the origins, nature, and consequences of war and revolution. Similarly, if we are ever to succeed in replacing the "war system," we must become familiar with the theories and methods of war-prevention and peace-making.

This course, designed to serve as an introduction to peace and world security studies, examines the major forms of contemporary international conflict and some approaches to peace and peace-making. In particular, we will analyze the evolution of armed conflict in the 20th century by examining its three most prominent forms: large-scale conventional war (World War I); nuclear war (strategies and actual); and revolutionary warfare (Vietnam). Our analysis is intended to enable us to gain a basic understanding of the dynamics of military conflict, and also to develop an awareness of the gap between the theories and the realities. In addition, we will examine various theories and methods for peace, including "alternative security," nonviolent social protest, arms control negotiations, and international mediation and conflict resolution.

Requirements

1. Attend all class meetings and discussion sessions having completed all assigned readings. Each class session will last two hours; the first hour will consist of small discussion groups. Attend at least two lectures or panels sponsored by the Five College Program in Peace and World Security Studies (PAWSS), and view the movie *All Quiet on the Western Front*.

2. *First Option:* Write three 5-10 page essays on topics assigned by the instructor during the semester. These essays are intended to test analytical and critical abilities, and to measure comprehension of assigned readings. *Second Option:* Write one short and one long essay. The short essay is identical to that assigned to all students at the beginning of the semester and is due on the same date; the long essay is due at the end of the semester and must include additional reading and research. An outline and preliminary bibliography for this long essay must be submitted at the same time as the second paper required of all other students. The long essay itself must be submitted at the same time as the third paper required of all other students.

Required Readings

Seyom Brown. *Causes and Prevention of War.* St. Martin's Press, 1987.
Barbara Tuchman. *Guns of August.* Bantam Books, 1962.

John Keegan. *The Face of Battle.* Penguin/Viking, 1976.
John Hersey. *Hiroshima.* Bantam Books, 1946.
Jonathan Schell. *The Fate of the Earth.* Avon Books, 1982.
Bruce Russett. *Prisoners of Insecurity.* W.H. Freeman, 1983.
Frances Fitzgerald. *Fire in the Lake.* Random House/Vintage, 1972.
Michael Herr. *Dispatches.* Avon Books, 1968.
Robert Johansen. *Toward a Dependable Peace.* Booklet. New York: World
    Policy Institute, 1983.
Gene Sharp. *Making the Abolition of War a Realistic Goal.* Booklet. World
    Policy Institute. New York, 1983.
Other brief handouts as assigned.

CLASS SCHEDULE

Part I: Introduction

Sept. 11—Introduction

Sept. 14—Introduction to Peace and World Security Studies
 • Ronald J. Glassop, "The Nature of the War Problem," in *Confronting
    War,* 2nd ed., McFarland & Co, 1987.

Sept. 16—Aggression and War: Biological or Social?
Film on boot camp: "Anybody's Son Will Do" from *War* series on PBS.
 • Brown, pp. 1–54.
 • Margaret Mead, "Warfare Is Only an Invention, Not a Biological
    Necessity," handout.

Sept. 21—Causes of War: Various Theories
PAWSS movie: All Quiet on the Western Front.
 • Brown, pp. 55–109.

Sept. 23—War, Society, and Technology Through History
 • Keegan, pp. 117–206.

Part II: The First World War

Sept. 28—Origins of WWI: Politics, Plans, and Strategy
 • Tuchman, pp. 15–30 (skim) & 33–87.

Sept. 30—Follies of WWI: Everything Goes Wrong
 • Tuchman, pp. 91–157.

Oct. 5—WWI from the Trenches: What It Was Really Like
 • Keegan, pp. 207–290.
 • Tuchman, pp. 347–362.

Oct. 7—Large-Scale Conventional War: WWI, WWII, and Now
- Tuchman, pp. 440–489.

Part III: The Nuclear Age

Oct. 12—Origins of the Nuclear Age: From the Manhatten Project to Hiroshima
Paper #1 due.
- Hersey, entire.

Oct. 14—The Theory of Nuclear Deterrence
Guest lecturer: Allan Krass, Natural Sciences.
- Russett, pp. 1–44, 69–98.

Oct. 14—PAWSS Lecture
Jonathan Dean, "Threshold of Negotiation: US-Soviet Arms Control Negotiations."

Oct. 19—No class

Oct. 21—The Arms Race: Weapons and Strategy
Film: Hiroshima/Nagasaki—August 1945.
- Russett, pp. 153–192.

Oct. 22—PAWSS Lecture
Martin Sherwin, "Lessons of the Cuban Missile Crisis, 25 Years Later."

Oct. 26—Escalation and the Nuclear Firebreak
- Schell, pp. 3–96.

Oct. 28—No class

Oct. 28—PAWSS Lecture
Robert Johansen and Archie Singham, "Peace Through International Cooperation: Prospects for the United Nations and the Non-Aligned Movement."

Part IV: Vietnam War

Nov. 2—Limited War: Fighting Below the Firebreak
- Fitzgerald, pp. 3–95.

Nov. 4—Revolution & Counter-revolution
- Fitzgerald, pp. 185–283.

Nov. 9: War in Vietnam
- Fitzgerald, pp. 283–313, 352–367, 452–480.

Nov. 11—Film: *Hearts and Minds*
Paper #2 due.
- Fitzgerald, pp. 481–535.

Nov. 16—Consequences of Vietnam War for U.S. Foreign Policy
- Fitzgerald, pp. 537–590.

Part V: Movements and Strategies for Peace

Nov. 18—The Anti-Vietnam War Movement in the U.S
- Herr, as much as possible.

Nov. 23—Civil Rights Movement
Film: "Bridge to Freedom" from PBS' *Eyes on the Prize* series.
- Sharp, entire.

Nov. 25—No class
- Johansen, entire.

Nov. 30—Arms Control and Verification
Guest lecturer: Allan Krass, Natural Sciences.
- Brown, pp. 211–260.

Dec. 2—Conflict Resolution Techniques
- Hand-out T.B.A.

Dec. 7—Today's Peace Movement
- "Contending for Power, 1969–1983," and "Conclusion: The Political Relevance of the Peace Movement," pp. 276–306, in Lawrence S. Wittner, *Rebels Against War: The American Peace Movement, 1933–1983* (Temple University Press, 1984).

Dec. 9—Wrap-up
Paper #3 due Dec. 11.

6. Issues of War and Peace

Carolyn M. Stephenson   Fall 1987
Political Science Dept., University of Hawaii–Manoa,
Honolulu, HI 96822

War and peace have been generally thought of as the central issues of international politics. This course explores some of those issues, raising questions of whether war is an inevitable part of the international system, whether it is a desirable part of the system, and whether it can or should be abolished. Is war a question of morality, economics, psychology, and/ or politics? What alternatives are there to nuclear deterrence? What are the conditions of a peaceful world?

Required Readings

Daggett, Stephen, and Jo Husbands. *Achieving an Affordable Defense.* Washington, D.C.: Committee for National Security, 1987.

Sivard, Ruth Leger. *World Military and Social Expenditures 1986.* Washington, D.C.: World Priorities, 1986.

Stephenson, Carolyn, ed. *Alternative Methods for International Security.* Washington, D.C.: University Press of America, 1982. (Hereinafter identified as *AMIS.*)

Most of the readings are photocopied articles which will be on reserve at Sinclair library or available for purchase as a collection.

Requirements

A mid-term (30%), a final exam (30%), and a combination of paper requirements totalling 10–12 pages—Paper #1 due September 17 (20%), and Paper #2 due December 3 (20%): What is and should be the U.S. strategy for dealing with international conflict, and what does and should that cost amount to? See individual handouts for each paper. You are expected to have completed the readings *before* class. Effective participation in class discussion will improve a borderline grade.

SCHEDULE OF CLASSES

Aug. 25—Introduction and Administrivia

I. War as a Moral and Political Question

Is war moral? Are there certain circumstances when the use of armed force is justified, and others when it is not? How does an individual choose which war to support? Is there such a thing as a "just war" using modern means of warfare?

Aug. 27

Film: Hiroshima/Nagasaki—August 1945.
  • Potter, "The Moral Logic of War." (photocopy)

  Recommended
  • Bernstein, Barton, "The Dropping of the A-Bomb," *The Center Magazine,* March/April 1983.

Sept. 1—National Conference of Catholic Bishops
  • International Meeting of Latin American Bishops. (photocopies)

Recommended
- Horsburgh, "Critique of Armed Force as an Instrument of Justice."
- Tolstoy, "Advice to a Draftee."

II. Theories of Conflict, Violence and War

What are the causes of conflict, violence and war? Some believe that war is the result of innate human tendencies, while others believe that it is a social invention used to achieve certain ends. Is war implicit in the nation-state system, or can nation-states exist without war? Will there always be wars while oppression exists?

Sept. 3—The Nation-State
- Hobbes, "On the Natural Condition of Mankind."
- Niebuhr, "The Morality of Nations."
- Barne, "Farewell to the Nation-State."

Sept. 8—Human Aggression
Film: Obedience.
- Corning, "Human Violence: Some Causes and Implications."
- Mead, "Warfare Is Only an Invention—Not a Biological Necessity."

III. The Economy of War: Guns vs. Butter?

War preparation has become big business since World War II—so big that some say that it has led to the development of an economic and social system that is guided by military rather than civilian needs. How do our institutions influence our ways of thinking and vice versa? How have the vast sums of money spent on the military affected the economy? Can we convert from military to civilian production without hurting the economy? What are the trade-offs between military spending and social services? How do arms sales affect the developing nations?

Sept. 10
Please develop your own hypotheses from the data on pp. 32–35 of the reading assignment and be prepared to discuss these in class.
- Sivard, *World Military Expenditures*, all.

Sept. 15
- Eisenhower, "Farewell Address."
- Melman, "Ten Propositions on the War Economy."

Sept. 17
Paper #1 is due.
- Pilisuk and Hayden, "Is There a Military-Industrial Complex that Prevents Peace?"

Sept. 22
- Daggett, Stephen, and Jo Husbands, *Achieving an Affordable Defense.*

Recommended
- Morrison and Walker, "A New Strategy for Military Spending," *Scientific American*, Vol. 239, No. 4 (October 1978), pp. 1–19.

IV. Defense, Deterrence, the Arms Race and Nuclear War

Arising out of the Cold War, deterrence has guided much of superpower foreign policy over the last forty years. Does deterrence work? Is there really a "Russian threat" that justifies ever-larger American weapons systems? Can American weapons meet their supposed missions? What would a nuclear war mean to our allies and to the rest of the world?

Sept. 24
Videotape: The Road to Total War.
- Patterson, "A Historical View of American Security," in *AMIS.*

Recommended
- Morgenthau, "Origins of the Cold War."

Sept. 29
- Schelling, "The Diplomacy of Violence."
- McNamara, "Mutual Deterrence."

Oct. 1
Guest Lecturer: Colonel Ralph Wetterhahn, Assistant Deputy Chief of Staff for Plans, Headquarters Pacific Air Forces, Hickam Air Force Base.
- Ikle, "What It Means to Be Number Two."
- Kaldor, "Is there a Soviet Military Threat?"

Oct. 6
- U.S. Department of Defense, *Soviet Military Power*, chaps. I, II, and IV.

Recommended
- Center for Defense Information, "Soviet Geo-Political Momentum: Myth or Menace?" *Defense Monitor.*
- Arkin, "Nuclear War in Triplicate," *Bulletin of the Atomic Scientists* (December 1986), pp. 6–7.

Oct. 8—The Strategic Defense Initiative, or "Star Wars"
Videotape: The Real Star Wars.
- Reagan speech of March 23, 1983.

V. Arms Control and Disarmament

Disarmament has long been a goal of peace movements and often of governments as well. But nuclear weapons have changed the character of the debate. In the 1960s the concept of arms control came about and in many ways superseded the disarmament debate. What are the differences between arms control and disarmament? Is arms control central to a peaceful world? How are issues of nuclear proliferation addressed by different participants in the debate?

Oct. 13—Arms Control vs. Disarmament
- Sivard, p. 28.
- York, "A Little Arms Control Can Be a Dangerous Thing."
- Kennan, "A Proposal for International Disarmament."

Recommended
- Fry, "The South Pacific Nuclear-Free Zone."

Oct. 15—Vertical and Horizontal Proliferation
- Yergin, "The Terrifying Prospect: Atomic Bombs Everywhere."
- Myrdal, "The High Price of the Nuclear Arms Monopoly."

VI. Isolation and Intervention:
The Superpowers and the "Third World"

While there has not been a direct military confrontation between the superpowers, there have been over 130 wars with combined casualties of over 30 million since World War II. Many of these wars have occurred in the former colonies of major powers in the "third world." What is the relationship between these wars and the actions of the superpowers and major powers? Does deterrence work?

Oct. 20
Film: El Salvador, Another Vietnam?
- Singham and Hune, "Antecedents and Origins of the Non-aligned Movement," ch. 3 of *Non-alignment in an Age of Alignments.*

Oct. 22
- Center for Defense Information, "A World at War: Small Wars and Superpower Intervention," *Defense Monitor.*

Recommended
- Klare, "The Global Arms Market," ch. 1–12, *American Arms Supermarket.*

VII. Alternative International Security Systems

Are there viable alternatives to the use of violence in our global system, and, if so, how can these be institutionalized? Can the United Nations resolve conflicts and maintain peace in the world? Would a global legal system enforced by a world government bring security, or repression, or be too unwieldy to work at all? Can alternative security systems arise from smaller efforts at regional integration or conflict resolution?

Oct. 29
- Stephenson, "Alternative International Security Systems: An Introduction" and table, p. 209, in *AMIS*.

Recommended
- Mische, "Revisioning National Security: Toward a Viable World Security System," in *AMIS*.
- Keys, "The Abolition of War: Neglected Aspects," in *AMIS*.
- Johansen, "Building a New International Security Order," in *AMIS*.

Nov. 3—The United Nations
- U.N. Charter and U.N. Organization Chart.

Nov. 5—World Federation/World Government
- Clark, "Introduction to World Peace Through World Law."
- Claude, "World Government."

Nov. 12—Mid-term Exam

Nov. 10—Functionalism and Regionalism
- Mitrany, "The Functional Alternative."
- Russett, "Causes of Peace," in *AMIS*.

Nov. 17—Conflict Resolution
- Yarrow, "Unofficial Third Party Conciliation in International Conflicts," in *AMIS*.
- Kriesberg, "Noncoercive Inducements in International Conflict," in *AMIS*.

Recommended
- Prutzman, "Children's Creative Response to Conflict," in *AMIS*.
- Stephenson, "A Review of the Literature," pp. 214–221—on conflict resolution—in *AMIS*.

VIII. Nonviolence

Nonviolence is the most radical challenge to the perceived need for the use of violent force. As a political strategy, nonviolence has been used successfully throughout history. Proponents argue that it is the only way to bring about lasting change. Opponents argue that it is not feasible. Can nonviolence work? Is it an end or a means to an end?

Nov. 19
Film: Gandhi.
- (1) Gandhi, "On Nonviolence," (2) "Satyagraha or Passive Resistance," and (3) "Some Picketing Rules."
- Horburgh, "The Bases of Satyagraha."

Recommended
- Stephenson, "A Review of the Literature," pp. 210–212, in *AMIS*.

Nov. 24
- Sharp, "Making the Abolition of War a Realistic Goal," in *AMIS*.
- Sharp, "Disregarded History, The Power of Nonviolent Action."

Nov. 26—Holiday: Thanksgiving

Dec. 1
- Schelling, "Some Questions on Civilian Defense."
- Deming, "Nonviolence and Casualties."

Recommended
- Woodward, "Nonviolent Struggle, Defense and Peacemaking," in *AMIS*.

IX. Individual Action for Social Change

Society is always in flux. How do we act responsibly for the society we are in? How can we strengthen those aspects of society that we think are good and work to change those which need improvement? What are the best places to take action, and what are the methods? Is action for social change really an individual effort, or does it involve working in community with others?

Dec. 3
Paper #2 is due: "Toward a Strategy for Peace."
- Walzer, "Strategic Choices."
- Pickus and Woito, "What Can I Do? 23 Answers."

Recommended
- Beitz and Washburn, "On Choosing a Social Change Vocation."
- Washburn and Wehr, "Working for Peace and Justice."

Dec. 8
Dandelion: "Movement Action Plan."
- Beitz and Washburn, "Questions for Yourself and Others."

- Berrigan, "The Price of Peace."
- Thoreau, "On the Duty of Civil Disobedience."

Dec. 14–18—Final Exams

7. Introduction to Peace and Conflict Studies

Andrew Murray   *Fall 1987*
Peace and Conflict Studies Institute, Juniata College,
Huntingdon, PA 16652

This course is designed for students who will make Peace and Conflict Studies (PACS), Political Science, or International Relations a major part of their program. It also tries to develop a style of thinking which will enable the student in other areas to apply interdisciplinary methods to particular problems.

The Nature of Peace and Conflict Studies

The normative and positive nature of PACS puts it in the company of what are usually referred to as applied disciplines. Such disciplines (including education, social work, environmental studies, medicine, and public health) apply positive sets of theory and knowledge to particular problems and are guided by the advantage assumed to be inherent in moving toward a solution to those problems. PACS has a field of inquiry (conflict) which may be approached from the methodologies and knowledge banks of nearly every formal academic discipline (the liberal arts). The insights of such inquiry are applied to a specific human problem (war), and the whole enterprise is given impetus by the value of peace. (Abstracted from: *Peace and Conflict Studies as Applied Liberal Arts: A Theoretical Framework for Curriculum Development*, by M. Andrew Murray, 1981, 120 pages.)

Course Objectives

By the end of the term, students should be able to trace and articulate the conceptual development of his or her definition of peace, conflict, war, justice, and peace and conflict studies. They should be familiar with the more common sociological typologies of conflict, should develop their own typology for peace, and should be able to show the relationship between the two. They should have a speaking acquaintance with those persons who have been pivotal in developing the idea of peace studies, including Wright, Richardson, Boulding, and Galtung. Students should practice systemic thinking and develop an interdisciplinary methodology which will aid in applying the resources of the academic community to war as a human problem. Finally, the student should be able to identify several peacemaking paradigms and articulate a comparative and critical analysis.

Texts

Falk, Richard A., and Samuel S. Kim, eds. *The War System: An Interdisciplinary Approach.* Boulder, CO: Westview Press, 1980.

Boulding, Kenneth E. *Stable Peace.* Austin, TX: University of Texas Press, 1978.

Sharp, Gene. *The Politics of Non-Violent Action*, Part I. Boston: Porter Sargent, 1973.

Evaluation

The following assignments will not be graded, but must be satisfactorily completed for course credit:

Two Journal Reports. One page each. Due Aug. 28 and Sept. 4. Give author, title of article, journal, date, and page numbers. Give a brief summary of the article. Give a brief personal reaction. Your reaction may be critical or analytical, or it may describe some new thought stimulated by the article. (Any question about the appropriateness of an article should be cleared with the instructor before reporting.)

One Book Report. Two pages. Due Oct. 14. Choose a book from the Garland Library of War and Peace. Give author, title, publisher, and the pages read. Read at least 150 pages. State the problem or question that the book addresses, how the author approaches the problem, and your own critical reaction to the author's approach.

COURSE OUTLINE

Peace and Conflict: Theory and Policy

Aug. 24—Preview Syllabus and Requirements

Aug. 26—Peace: Issues of Definition
• Boulding, pp. 3–66.

Aug. 28—PACS and Other Disciplines
Journal report due.

Aug. 31—The Relationship of Peace and Justice
• Boulding, pp. 67–91.

Sept. 2—Peace and Policy
• Boulding, pp. 93–143.

Sept. 4—Discussion
Journal report due.

Sept. 7—Conflict: A Typology
- Falk and Kim, Introduction to Part 5, "Sociological Inquiries," pp. 311–316.
- Quincy Wright, "The Nature of Conflict," Falk and Kim, pp. 317–333.

Sept. 9—A Functional Approach to Conflict
- Lewis A. Coser, "Societal Approaches to the Study of War," Falk and Kim, pp. 334–346.

Sept. 11—Book Reports

The Roots of Aggression:
An Interdisciplinary Inquiry

Sept. 14—Introduction
- Falk and Kim, General Introduction, pp. 1–12.

Sept. 16—Ethological Inquiry
- Falk and Kim, Introduction to Part 2, "Ethological and Psychological Inquiries," pp. 77–81.
- Samuel S. Kim, "The Lorenzian Theory of Aggression and Peace Research: A Critique," Falk and Kim, pp. 82–115.

Sept. 18—Book Reports

Sept. 21—Film: *Obedience*

Sept. 23—Psychological Inquiry
- Albert Bandura, "The Social Learning Theory of Aggression," Falk and Kim, pp. 141–155.

Sept. 25—Sociopsychological Inquiry/Book Reports
- Ted Gurr, "Psychological Factors in Civil Violence," Falk and Kim, pp. 248–281.

Sept. 28—Anthropological Inquiry
- Falk and Kim, Introduction to Part 3, "Cultural and Anthropological Inquiries," pp. 159–162.
- Robert A. LeVine, "Anthropology and the Study of Conflict," Falk and Kim, pp. 163–179.
- David Fabbro, "Peaceful Societies," Falk and Kim, pp. 180–203.

Sept. 30—Sociological Inquiry
- Falk and Kim, Introduction to Part 5, "Sociological Inquiries," pp. 311–316.
- Quincy Wright, "The Nature of Conflict," Falk and Kim, pp. 317–333.
- Lewis A. Coser, "Some Social Functions of Violence," Falk and Kim, pp. 334–346.

Oct. 2—Book Reports

Oct. 5—Economic Inquiry
- Falk and Kim, Introduction to Part 6, "Socioeconomic Inquiries," pp. 371–376.
- David S. Landes, "Some Thoughts on the Nature of Economic Imperialism," Falk and Kim, pp. 377–384.

Oct. 7—Systemic Inquiry
- Falk and Kim, Introduction to Part 8, "International Systemic Inquiries," pp. 531–535.
- Boulding, Kenneth, "National Images and International Systems," Falk and Kim, pp. 536–550.

Oct. 14—Review and Discussion
Written book reports due.

Oct. 16–23
Mid-term test (Oct. 16). Review (Oct. 21). Prepare for field trip (Oct. 23).

Oct. 26–30
Field trip to Washington, D.C.

Paradigms for Peacemaking:
International Law and Organization

Nov. 2—The Control of Force
- Falk and Kim, Introduction to Part 9, "Normative Inquiries," pp. 585–587.
- Stanley Hoffmann, "International Law and the Control of Force," Falk and Kim, pp. 588–612.

Nov. 4—The Limits of Sovereignty
- Hedley Bull, "The Grotian Conception of International Society," Falk and Kim, pp. 613–634.

Nov. 6—Book Reports

Paradigms for Peacemaking:
Disarmament

Nov. 9—Film: *War Without Winners*

Nov. 11—Baker Lecture

Paradigms for Peacemaking:
Nonviolence and Civilian Defense

Nov. 13—Satyagraha and Praxeology
• Margaret W. Fisher, "Contrasting Approaches to Conflict," Falk and Kim, pp. 58–73.

Nov. 16 & 18—An Alternative Theory of Political Power
• Sharp, pp. 3–32.

Nov. 20—Strategy and Practice
• Sharp, pp. 63–101.

Nov. 23—Book Reports
Review and discussion.

Nov. 30—Simulation
Six hours: schedule to be announced.

Dec. 2-9—Paper Preparation and Exam
Discussion for paper (Dec. 2). Individual help with paper (Dec. 4). Final paper due Dec. 7. Review for exam (Dec. 9).

8. Self and Society in the 21st Century: Peace and War

Marilyn A. Davis   *Spring 1987*
and B. LaConyea Butler
Political Science Dept. (*Davis*) and Psychology Dept.
(*Butler*), Spelman College, Atlanta, GA 30314

This course is designed to delineate the causes and consequences of war, and to examine the conditions, concepts and definitions relative to peace and war. Students will be introduced to types of conflict and will examine ways of resolving conflict. Emphasis will be placed on nuclear war. A major focus will be on the role of the individual in times of war and peace, as well as on peaceful alternatives to war. Upon completion of the course, the student should be able:

- to define and explain relevant concepts and definitions and to make distinctions between the various concepts;
- to explain theories of the underlying causes of war and the conditions of peace, citing pertinent examples;
- to explain and illustrate psychological, social, economic, and political problems of nuclear war and to suggest preventive measures;
- to identify economic, psychological, political, and social factors and consequences underlying peace and war and to cite implications for a global society;
- to analyze the moral and ethical issues involved in nuclear war and in the struggle for peace;
- to explain the role of the individual in times of war and peace;
- to suggest alternatives for the development of world peace.

Required Text
Small, Melvin, and J. David Singer. *International War: An Anthology and Study Guide.* Homewood, N.J.: Dorsey Press, 1985.

Papers
Required papers for the course include a three-page summary and analysis of the two books listed below and a one-page summary for each of the six required video-cassettes used in the class. The summary and analysis of

the books must follow the guidelines distributed in class. The two books required are:

Reardon, Betty. *Sexism and the War System.* New York: Teachers College Press, 1985.
Fisher, Roger, and William Ury. *Getting to Yes: Negotiating Agreement Without Giving In.* New York: Penguin Books, 1983.

Examinations
Three hour-long examinations and a final examination will be administered. Each student is required to take all examinations.

Attendance
Attendance is required and punctuality is expected for all class sessions. At least two chapel periods will be devoted to speakers on topics relevant to the course. Attendance at these sessions is also required.

Grading Procedure
Grades will be computed according to the following formula: book summaries and analyses (2)—20%; videocassette summaries (6)—20%; examinations (3 one-hour + final)—60%. Points will be added to the final result for class discussion and attendance according to the subjective evaluation of the student and the faculty.

COURSE OUTLINE

Required readings and audio-visual materials are indicated by use of an asterisk (*). Others listed are recommended for additional enrichment. (Full bibliographic references follow this section.)

Introduction

Overview of Social Sciences and Methods
  • Perry and Perry, Chapter 1, "Through the Lens of Science."

Relevant Concepts and Definitions—Conditions of Peace and War
Peace (true peace); competition; conflict (intrapersonal, interpersonal, intragroup); aggression; violence; revolution; crisis; war (limited, just, cold, guerrilla, nuclear, civil).
  • *Small and Singer, pp. 1–4.
  • Davies, James C., "Aggression, Violence, Revolution, and War," ch. 9 in Knutson.
  • Howell, Richard W., "Wars Without Conflict," pp. 675–692 in Nettleship et al.
  • May, ch. 9, "Psychological Conditions of Peace," pp. 219–234.
  • Nettleship, Martin A., "Definitions," pp. 73–93 in Nettleship et al.

- Schelling, Thomas, "The Diplomacy of Violence," pp. 78–84 in Beitz and Herman.
- Schurmann, Franz, "Revolutionary Conflict," pp. 261–271 in Smith.
- von Clausewitz, "What Is War?" ch. 1, pp. 101–122.
- Zawodny, J.K., "Unconventional Warfare," pp. 393–397 in Smith.

Historical Perspectives

Pacifism; peace societies; militarism. *Videocassette: The Road to Total War.*
- *Small and Singer, ch. 2, pp. 5–36.
- York, Herbert, "A Little Arms Control Can Be a Dangerous Thing," pp. 257–264 in Beitz and Herman.

Selections from Weinberg and Weinberg (chronologically)
- Early pacifism: the Bible, pp. 461–462.
- Protestant pacifism: Immanuel Kant (1795), pp. 410–414.
- Era of peace societies: Jane Adams (1907), pp. 305–307.
- Cry for universal disarmament: Mahatma Ghandi (1930, 1940), pp. 211–214.
- Resistance to war: Harry Emerson Fosdick (19410, pp. 146–151.
- Nuclear pacifism: Martin Luther King, Jr. (1960), pp. 69–75.

The Psychology and Sociology of War

Psychology of Nuclear War

Conflict systems and resolution
Intrapersonal conflict; interpersonal conflict; intragroup conflict; intergroup conflict; conflict resolution. *Videocassettes: Anybody's Son Will Do,* and *The Profession of Arms.*
- *Small and Singer, ch. 3, pp. 37–94.
- Coser, Lewis A., "The Termination of Conflict," pp. 486–491 in Smith.
- Deutsch, Morton, "Conflict and Its Resolution," pp. 36–57 in Smith.
- *Fisher and Ury, *Getting to Yes.*
- Goldschmidt, Walter, "Personal Motivation and Institutionalized Conflict," in Foster and Rubinstein.
- Gurr, Ted, "Psychological Factors in Civil Violence," pp. 248–281 in Falk and Kim.
- Himes, Joseph S., "The Functions of Racial Conflict," pp. 170–179 in Smith.
- Katz, Daniel, "Nationalism and Strategies of International Conflict Resolution," pp. 416–444 in Smith.
- *Stagner, Ross, "Personality Dynamics and Social Conflict," pp. 98–109 in Smith and pp. 231–247 in Falk and Kim.

Socialization process
Nature of the socialization process: definition and characteristics, factors influencing socialization; *Principles of psychological control as related to*

the process of socialization: control through positive reinforcement, aversive techniques (use of fear), control and socialization of the individual; *Aggression*: learning of aggression and aggressive behavior, frustration and aggression, war and aggressiveness; *Sexism and the war system*: the patriarchal military system, sexism and feminism.

- Bandura, Albert, "The Social Learning Theory of Aggression," pp. 141–155 in Falk and Kim.
- Berkowitz, Leonard, "The Frustration-Aggression Hypothesis," pp. 116–137 in Falk and Kim.
- Kim, Samuel S., "The Lorenzian Theory of Aggression and Peace Research: A Critique," pp. 82–110 in Falk and Kim.
- *Reardon, chs. 1–3, pp. 1–63.
- *Sipes, Richard C., "War, Combative Sports, and Aggression: A Preliminary Causal Model of Cultural Patterning," pp. 749–765 in Nettleship et al.
- Skinner, B.F., *Beyond Freedom and Dignity*.

Personality characteristics of the policymakers—selected examples

National images, personality, and foreign policy: selected American leaders (Eisenhower, Kennedy, Johnson, Carter, Reagan); selected Russian leaders (Khrushchev, Brezhnev, Chernenko, Gorbachev); Interpersonal and international tensions.

- Boulding, Kenneth, "National Images and International Systems," pp. 536–550 in Falk and Kim.
- *Etheredge, Lloyd S., "Personality and Foreign Policy: Bullies in the State Department," *Psychology Today* (March 1975).
- Hermann, Margaret, "Effects of Personal Characteristics of Political Leaders on Foreign Policy," pp. 49–68 in East.
- Holsti, Ole, "Crisis, Stress, and Decisionmaking," pp. 491–508 in Falk and Kim.
- Kelman, Herbert C., "Societal, Attitudinal and Structural Factors in International Relations," pp. 445–455 in Smith.

Impact of war on family life

- *To be selected from *Marriage and Family Review* (special issue devoted to the family and the threat of nuclear war, edited by Marvin B. Sussman and Teresa Marciano).

The threat of war—psychological aspects

Slides/cassette: M.A.D. (Mutual Assured Destruction): The Psychology of Nuclear Armament.

- *Deutsch, Morton, "The Prevention of World War III: A Psychological Perspective," *Political Psychology* (March 1983), pp. 3–31.
- Escalona, S.K., "Growing Up with the Threat of Nuclear War: Some Indirect Effects on Personality Development," *American Journal of Orthopsychiatry*, Vol. 52, No. 4, 1982, pp. 600–607.

- Frank, J.D., "The Nuclear Arms Race: Sociopsychological Aspects," *American Journal of Public Health*, Vol. 70, No. 9, 1980, pp. 950–952.
- Frank, Jerome, "Sociopsychological Aspects of the Prevention of Nuclear War," in Foster and Rubinstein.
- Huppert, Peter, "The Psychology of Nuclear War," *Mental Health in Australia*, Vol. 1, No. 10, July 1983, pp. 1–13.
- Jervis, Robert, "Hypotheses on Misperception," pp. 465–490 in Falk and Kim.
- Milburn, T.W., "The Concept of Deterrence: Some Social and Psychological Considerations," *Journal of Social Issues*, Vol. 17, No. 3, 1961, pp. 3–11.
- Morawski, J.G., and Goldstein, Sharon E., "Psychology and Nuclear War: A Chapter in Our Legacy of Social Responsibility," *American Psychologist*, Vol. 40, No. 5, May 1985, pp. 549–556.
- Wagner, Richard V., "Psychology and the Threat of Nuclear War," *American Psychologist*, Vol. 40, No. 5, May 1985, pp. 531–535.

War as a Social Problem
The sociology of conflict
- *Small and Singer, ch. 3, pp. 37–94.
- Clard, M. Margaret, "The Cultural Patterning of Risk-Seeking Behavior: Implications for Armed Conflict," in Forster and Rubinstein.
- *Wilson, "Game Theory," pp. 58–59, ch. 10 (pp. 167–183).
- Wright, Quincy, "The Nature of Conflict," pp. 317–333 in Falk and Kim.

Sociocultural factors and war
Social functions of violence; characteristics of groups in combat; effects of war on selected groups in society (e.g., Blacks, women); war and cultural values.
- Coser, Lewis A., "Some Social Functions of Violence," pp. 34–346 in Falk and Kim.
- Smith, Estelle M., "Cultural Variability in the Structuring of Violence," pp. 599–618 in Nettleship et al.
- *Spretnak, Charlene, "Naming the Cultural Forces that Push the U.S. Toward War," *Journal of Humanistic Psychology*, Vol. 23, No. 3, 1983, pp. 104–114.

Sociological consequences of war
Disruption of social order; disruption of family; residential pattern changes.
- *Sanford, Nevitt, "Dehumanization and Collective Destructiveness," *International Journal of Group Tensions*, Vol. 1, No. 1, January 1971, pp. 26–41.
- *Selected readings from *Marriage and Family Review* (issue on family and the threat of nuclear war, edited by Sussman and Marciano).

Anthropological considerations
Structural levels of conflict; sources of conflict; conflict control and resolution.
- *LeVine, Robert A., "Anthropology and the Study of Conflict., pp. 163–178 in Falk and Kim.
- Mandelbaum, David G., "Anthropology for the Second Stage of the Nuclear Age," in Foster and Rubinstein.

Justifying War

Normative Criteria
Biblical interpretations; individual intentions; group intentions; superior-subordinate relationships; organic relationships; national values.

Protection of Peace
Protection of life; crusader mobilization; respect for law; dispute arbitration; collective security.
- *Small and Singer, ch. 4, pp. 95–140.
- *Brayton and Landwehr, ch. 3, pp. 60–113.

A Theoretical Study of War

Approaches to the Study of War
The biological approach; the psychological and socio-psychological approach; the anthropological approach; the ecological approach; the geopolitical approach; the legal approach; the moral approach; the military-technical approach; the sociological approach; the political approach; the politico-economic approach; multi-dimensional approaches.
- *Small and Singer, ch. 5, pp. 141–178.
- Haas, Michael, "Societal Approaches to the Study of War," pp. 347–367 in Falk and Kim.
- *Lider, "Approaches," pp. 5–47, ch. 2.

Causes and Effects of War
Primitive view of war; instinct theories of war; religious causes; war as a means to social evolution; war as a necessary social vitamin; war as a result of economic competition; war as a result of economic competition; war as a means of settling disputes; difference between causes of war and reasons for war; effects of war. *Videocassette: The Deadly Game of Nations.*
- Ansari, Chaus, "The Role of Anthropology in the World Crises," pp. 21–28 in Nettleship et al.
- *Atkinson, Henry, "Religious Causes of War," pp. 114–118 in Porritt.
- Carroll, Bernice A., and Fink, Clinton F., "Theories of War Causation: A Matrix for Analysis," pp. 55–71 in Nettleship et al.
- Esser, A.H., "War as Part of Social Pollution," pp. 417–437 in Nettleship et al.
- Foster, Mary, "Is War Necessary?" in Foster and Rubinstein.

- *Freud, Sigmund, "The Psychological Basis for War," pp. 37–41 in Brayton and Lendwehr.
- Gonzales, Nancie L., "Ethnic Targeting as a Defense Strategy," in Foster and Rubinstein.
- Hobbes, Thomas, "On the Natural Condition of Mankind," pp. 27–29 in Brayton and Landwehr.
- Jacobs, Ruth H., "Sociological Perspectives on the Etiology of War," pp. 29–41 in Nettleship et al.
- *Levi, Werner, "On the Causes of War and the Conditions of Peace," pp. 318–326 in Smith.
- MacDonald, Norman, "The Biological Factor in the Etiology of War: A Medical View," pp. 209–234 in Nettleship et al.
- Mead, Margaret, "Warfare Is Only an Invention—Not a Biological Necessity," pp. 112–118 in Beitz and Herman.
- Morganthau, Hans J., "Politics Among Nations," pp. 6–10 in Brook.
- *Salter, Arthur, "Economic Causes of War," pp. 1–25 in Porritt.
- Stark, J.G., "Conditions/Factors Unfavorable to Peace," ch. 3.
- *Steed, Wickham, "Political Causes of War," pp. 163–184 in Porritt.
- Stoessinger, ch. 8, "Why Nations Go to War," pp. 202–220.
- Young, Clarence W., "An Evolutionary Theory of the Causes of War," pp. 199–207 in Nettleship et al.
- *Zimmerman, Alfred, "Cultural Causes of War," pp. 131–144 in Porritt.

Political and Economic Perspectives on War

Political Perspectives
Explanations of war
Introduction—political interests and war; self-interested human nature.
- *Small and Singer, ch. 6, pp. 179–274.
- von Clausewitz, ch. 1.
- Waltz, *Man, The State and War.*
- *Hobbes, Thomas, "On the Natural Condition of Mankind," pp. 27–29 in Brayton and Landwehr.
- Morganthau, Hans, "Politics Among Nations," pp. 6–10 in Brook.

War, conflicts and crisis in the international system:
Structure and process
Building strategic alliances—the balance of power; military power and security.
- Wright, *A Study of War.*
- Bartholomay, Lucy, "Limits and Cuts: SALT and START," *The Boston Globe*, October 17, 1982.
- Boucher, Wayne, "Nuclear Weapons and Strategic Deterrence," *The Futurist*, December 1984.
- Craig and Jungerman, ch. 2, pp. 9–38.
- Feld, Bernard, "End Space Race Now," *Bulletin of the Atomic Scientists*, October 1984.

- *Fischer, ch. 12, pp. 142–153.
- Hoeber, *How Little Is Enough? Salt and Security in the Long Run.*
- Holzman, Franklyn, "Myths that Drive the Arms Race," *Challenge,* September/October 1984.
- Kaiser, Robert, "U.S.-Soviet Relations: Goodbye to Detente," *Foreign Affairs,* Special Issue 1980, pp. 500–521.
- Klare, Michael, "Learning the Firebreak," *The Progressive,* September 1983.
- The Stanley Foundation, "Space Weapons and Arms Control," pp. 27–37 in *Strategy for Peace,* U.S. Foreign Policy Conference Report, 1984.
- Wiesner, Jerome, "Russian and American Capabilities," *The Atlantic Monthly,* July 1982.
- York, Herbert, "A Little Arms Control Can Be a Dangerous Thing," in Beitz and Herman, pp. 257–264.

Political power and conflict management
- Beeman, William, "Conflict and Belief in American Foreign Policy," in Foster and Rubinstein.
- Brucan, Silvia, "Ideology and Institutions in Peace and War," in Foster and Rubinstein.
- Brucan, Silvia, "Global Policy and Revolution in Social Sciences," in Foster and Rubinstein.
- deMause, Lloyd, *Reagan's America.*
- Kennedy, Robert, *Thirteen Days: A Memoir of the Cuban Missile Crisis.*
- *Lider, "War as an Instrument of Policy," ch. 3, pp. 48–85.
- Markey, Edward, "The Politics of Arms Control," *American Psychologist,* May 1985, pp. 557–560.
- Melman, Seymour, "The War-Making Institutions," in Foster and Rubinstein.
- Paige, Glenn, "Comparative Case Analysis of Crisis Decisions: Korea and Cuba," in Falk and Kim, pp. 509–527.
- Rubinstein, Robert, "The Collapse of Strategy: Toward an Anthropological Understanding of Ideological Bias in Policy Decision," in Foster and Rubinstein.

Economic Perspectives on Nuclear Weapons/War
Explanations of war
Population and crisis/war possibilities:
- *Philip Hauser, "Demographic Dimensions of World Politics," pp. 339–348 in Smith.

Imperialism:
- Marxism-Leninism on War and Army, "The Economic Foundations of Wars: A Soviet View," pp. 377–384 in Falk and Kim.
- Landers, David, "Some Thoughts on the Nature of Economic Imperialism," pp. 385–401 in Falk and Kim.

- Galtung, Johan, "A Structural Theory of Imperialism," pp. 402–455 in Falk and Kim.

Military-industrial alliance:
- *Pilisuk, Marc, and Thomas Haydon, "Is There a Military-Industrial Complex Which Prevents Peace?" pp. 294–317 in Smith.

Military budgets and spending
Military expenditures compared to expenditures for peace; military defense spending and influence on domestic programs; the defense business–American vested interests in war; military waste. *Slides:* Defense budgets, expenditures, and comparison of military and social program spending.
- Ball, John, *An Atlas of Nuclear Energy.*
- Bartel, ch. 1, pp. 297–323.
- Clayton, James, *On the Brink: Defense, Deficits, and Welfare Spending,* New York: Ramapo Press, 1984.
- Craig and Jungerman, ch. 25, pp. 394–408.
- *Tobias, Sheila, "Toward a Feminist Analysis of Defense Spending," *Frontiers,* Vol. 8, No. 2, 1985, pp. 65–68.

Problems of employment in the nuclear age
Employment in wartime and in peacetime; shifts in employment relative to military expenditures; the nuclear power industry and employment.
- Council on Economic Priorities: *The Costs and Consequences of Reagan's Military Buildup. A report to the International Association of Machinists and Aerospace Workers, AFL-CIO,* New York, 1982.

Nuclear War

Power, Security, and Destruction
War scenarios; ecological destruction; first-use of nuclear weapons; 21st century strategic concepts; weapons technology; negotiation and arms reduction. *Cassettes: Nuclear Proliferation: Race to Extinction?; The Most Dangerous Game; The Role of Nuclear Weapons in the 1980s; The "Star Wars" Initiative of Ronald Reagan; Threat of Nuclear War; U.S. vs. U.S.S.R.: Who's Ahead?; War 1980s. Film: Hiroshima/Nagasaki—August 1945. Videocassette: Notes on Nuclear War.*
- *Small and Singer, ch. 8, pp. 333–393.
- *Craig and Jungerman, ch. 18, pp. 292–306.

The Search for Peace: The Prevention of War and the Resolution of Conflict

Arbitration and mediation systems; civilian-based defense policy; graduated reciprocation in tension-reduction; world federation. *Cassettes: Joanne Woodward on Women's Role in Preventing Nuclear War; Nuclear War; The Day After. Videocassette: Goodbye War.*

- *Small and Singer, ch. 7.
- Beer, Francis A., "American Major Peace, War, and Presidential Elections," *Peace and Change*, Vol. X, No. 1, Spring, 1984, pp. 23–39.
- *Boals, Kay, "Some Reflections on Women and Peace," *Peace and Change*, Vol. 1, No. 2, Spring, 1973, pp. 56–59.
- Bruyn and Rayman, ch. 12, pp. 254–266.
- Bull, Hedley, "The Grotian Conception of International Society," pp. 613–634, in Falk and Kim.
- Claude, Inis, "United Nations Use of Military Force," pp. 503–514 in Smith.
- Curle, Adam, and Dugan, Maire A., "Peace-making: Stages and Sequence," *Peace and Change*, Vol. VIII, Nos. 2, 3, Summer 1982, pp. 19–29.
- Glagolev, I., and M. Goryainov, "Some Problems of Disarmament Research," pp. 498–502 in Smith.
- Hoffman, Stanley, "International Law and the Control of Force," pp. 588–612 in Falk and Kim.
- Kimmel, Paul, "Learning About Peace," *American Psychologist*, May 1985, pp. 536–541.
- *Paine, Christopher, "Breakdown on the Build-Down," *Bulletin of the Atomic Scientists*, December 1983.
- *Reardon, chs. 4–5.
- Scoville, Janet, and Mark Pavelchak, "The Day After: The Impact of a Media Event," *American Psychologist*, May 1985, pp. 542–548.
- Wilson, Clifton, "The Use and Abuse of International Law," pp. 233–270, Houghton.

Bibliography

Ball, John. *An Atlas of Nuclear Energy.* Atlanta: Georgia State University, 1985.

Bartel, Richard D., ed. *Readings from Challenge.* Armonk, New York: M.E. Sharpe, Inc.

Beitz, Charles R., and Theodore Herman. *Peace and War.* San Francisco, CA: W.H. Freeman and Company, 1973.

Brayton, Abbott, and Stephani Landwehr, eds. *The Politics of War and Peace.* Washington: United Press of America, 1981.

Brook, David, ed. *Search for Peace: A Reader in International Relations.* New York: Dodd, Mead and Company, 1970.

Bruyn, Severyn, and Paula Rayman. *Nonviolent Action and Social Change.* New York: Irvington Press, 1979.

Cantril, Hadley. *Tensions that Cause Wars.* Urbana: University of Illinois Press, 1950.

Clayton, James. *On the Brink: Defense, Deficits, and Welfare Spending.* New York: Ramapo Press, 1984.

Craig, Paul P., and John A. Jungerman. *Nuclear Arms Race: Technology and Society.* New York: McGraw-Hill Book Company, 1986.

Dennis, Wayne, et al., eds. *Current Trends in Social Psychology.* Pittsburgh: University of Pittsburgh Press, 1948.

deMause, Lloyd. *Reagan's America.* New York: The Atlantis Institute, Atcom Publishing, 1985.

East, Maurice, et al., eds. *Why Nations Act: Theoretical Perspectives for Comparative Foreign Policy Studies.* Beverly Hills, California: Sage, 1978.

Falk, Richard A., and Samuel S. Kim. *The War System: An Interdisciplinary Approach.* Boulder, Colorado: Westview Press, 1980.

Fischer, Dietrich. *Preventing War in the Nuclear Age.* New Jersey: Rowman and Allanheld, 1984.

Fisher, Roger, and William Ury. *Getting to Yes: Negotiating Agreement Without Giving In.* New York: Penguin Books, 1983.

Foster, Mary LeCron, and Robert A. Rubinstein, eds. *Peace and War: Cross-Cultural Perspectives.* New Brunswick, New Jersey: Transaction Books, 1985.

Houghton, N.G., ed. *Struggle Against History.* New York: Simon and Schuster, 1968.

Kennedy, Robert. *Thirteen Days.* New York: W.W. Norton, 1971.

Knutson, Jeanne N., ed. *Handbook of Political Psychology.* San Francisco: Jossey-Bass, 1973.

Lider, Julian. *On the Nature of War.* Farnborough, Hants: Saxon House, 1977.

Nettleship, Martin A., Dale R. Givens, and Anderson Nettleship. *War: Its Causes and Correlates.* Paris: Mouton Publishers (distributed in the United States by Aldine, Chicago), 1975.

Perry, John A., and Erna K. Perry. *Contemporary Society: An Introduction to Social Science.* 4th ed. New York: Harper and Row Publishers, 1984.

Porritt, Arthur, ed. *Causes of War.* Libraries Press, 1969.

Reardon, Betty A. *Sexism and the War System.* New York: Teachers College Press, 1985.

Skinner, B.F. *Beyond Freedom and Dignity.* New York: Alfred A.Knopf, 1971.

Smith, Clagett G., ed. *Conflict Resolution: Contributions of the Behavioral Sciences.* Notre Dame, Indiana: University of Notre Dame Press.

The Stanley Foundation. *Strategy for Peace 1984.* U.S. Foreign Policy Conference Report, 1984.

Stoessinger, John G. *Why Nations Go to War.* 4th edition. New York: St. Martin's Press, 1985.

von Clausewitz, Carl. *On War* (edited by Anatol Rapoport). New York: Penguin Books, 1976. (reprint)

Waltz, Kenneth. *Man, the State and War.* New York: Columbia, 1959.

Wilson, Andrew. *The Bomb and the Computer.* New York: Delacorte Press, 1969.

Additional readings may be selected from the following periodicals:

Conflict Management Peace Science.
International Journal on World Peace.
Journal of Conflict Resolution.

Marriage and Family Review.
Peace and Change (Summer 1982, special isssue on conflict resolution).
Psychology Today.
Scientific America.
Time (July 29, 1985, special section, "The Atomic Age").

9. Politics of War and Peace

Glen Gersmehl   *Spring 1988*
Peace Studies Program, Clark University,
Worcester, MA 01610

This course is designed to provide students with an opportunity to examine some of the principal actors and policy-making processes concerning issues of war and peace. It will focus on the post–World War II period in the U.S.—especially the past decade—although comparisons will be made with other countries and historical periods. Traditionally, political science and history courses have viewed these issues from the standpoint of political leaders and generals, wars and conflicts. In this course the primary emphasis will be placed on the role of citizens and interest groups, and on the processes of peacemaking.

The course objectives are (1) to explore the principal philosophies of peacemaking; the goals, strategies, and problems of U.S. peace groups today; and the role those groups and philosophies play in the U.S. political arena; (2) to understand the key policy-making institutions and processes concerned with war and peace in the U.S. political system today, the roles of the various branches and agencies of government, and the social and political context of government and interest group activity; (3) to strengthen the skills of analysis, written expression, and public speaking; and (4) to provide a context for students to think about their own hopes, fears and involvement as citizens concerning the issues of war and peace.

Course Requirements
Regular attendance, participation in class discussion, completion of readings (readings average 60–90 pages per week; more when you are preparing a paper); 4–6 evening or weekend sessions to view films and hear outside speakers; and small-group participation (for discussion or to prepare for presentations)—10%.

Four papers, two on weekly topics, one in each half of the course (4–5 pages each), one biographical sketch and discussion of the ideas and activity of a figure involved in peacemaking (3–4 pages), and one wrap-up paper due at the end of the course in which you engage several key issues of the course in a thoughtful way (5–6 pages)—60%.

Two in-class presentations on the two papers on weekly topics (4–6 minutes each); one 3-column chronology of events: (1) in your own life and your family, (2) in the larger culture (an almanac is a good source), (3) regarding war and peace (see the 2-page chronology in "Arms Control and National Security"); the purpose is to help you think about the development of your understanding of war and peace issues. (See also the sheet on "papers and presentations.") Two to three quizzes (historical overview, policy context, philosophies of war and peace).—30%

You may negotiate with me to merge two of the papers into a longer paper or to substitute a project with a Worcester area peace group for one paper. I'll be available to assist by helping identify materials available in the library on course topics, by lending materials (please be responsible), by helping think through problems you encounter, and by helping with the writing mechanics.

Required Texts

DeBenedetti, Charles, ed. *The Peace Reform in American History.*
Jordon, Amos A., and William J. Taylor, Jr. *American National Security.*
Arms Control Association. *Arms Control and National Security.*
Alternative Defense Network. *Reading Packets* (IDDS).
Sweeney, Duane, ed. *The Peace Catalog.*
Gersmehl, Glen. *Tools of Peacemaking.*

COURSE OUTLINE OF TOPICS
AND READINGS

Required readings are marked with asterisks.

I. Historical Overview of Peace Movements in the United States

The purpose of this three-week session is to place contemporary government and interest group activity and philosophies in historical perspective.

Week 1

Introduction

The purpose of this session is to clarify the goals, structure, and content of the course, including the concepts of "peace," "politics," and violence in America.

- *Sheet of quotations on war and peace by Martin Luther King, Gandhi, Thoreau, etc.

- *Hofstadter and Wallace, eds., "Contents," *American Violence: A Documentary History.*

Colonial Period to the Civil War

1607–1763—Quakers, Mennonites, Native Americans, William Penn, John Woolman. *1763–1815*—Paine, Benezet, revolutionary war and war of 1812, Manifest Destiny, frontier. *1815–1865*—peace societies, abolitionists, William Lloyd Garrison, Alan Ladd, William Burritt. *Slide presentation* by Michael True on "American Tradition of Nonviolence."

- *Charles DeBenedetti, chs. 1–3.
- Cooney and Michalowski, "The Roots of American Nonviolence," in *the Power of the People.*
- Peter Mayer, *The Pacifist Conscience.*
- Weinberg, eds., *Instead of Violence* (see biographies of Penn, Woolman, Ballou, Burritt).
- Merle Eugene Curti, *The American Peace Crusade, 1850–1860* (on peace societies), and *Peace or War: The American Struggle, 1636–1936.*

Colonial Period to the Civil War (Cont'd)

1865–1900—internationalists, Red Cross, international law socieites, Anti-Imperialist League, Alfred Love, UPU, Spanish-American War, Mohonk Conferences, Tolstoy, Hague. *1900–1919*—progressive era, Carnegie, Addams, Debs, Root, WWI COs, FOR, WPP, AFSC. *1919–1941*—Kellogg-Briand, World Court, League of Nations, LEP, WILPF, WRL, NCPW.

- *DeBenedetti, chs. 4–5.
- Cooney and Michalowski, "The Anti-War Movement," in *The Power of the People.*
- Robert Beisner, *Twelve Against Empire: The Anti-Imperialists, 1898–1900.*
- Charles Chatfield, ed. *Peace Movements in America* (especially articles by Paterson, Cook, DeBenedetti, Chatfield, Peterson) and *For Peace and Justice: Pacifism in America 1914–1941, The Radical "No"* (on Evan Thomas, WWI resister).
- *Lake Monhonk Conference Report* (1895–1916).
- *American Friends' Peace Conference* (1901).
- Marie Louise Degen, *A History of the Women's Peace Party* (1915).
- Gertrude Bussey and Margaret Tims, *Pioneers for Peace: WILPF, 1915–1965* (see also biographies of Addams, Carnegie, Debs).

Week 2

World War II and the Beginning of the Nuclear Age

Bohr, Szilard, FAS, Cousins, World Federalists, test ban, Pauling, Russell, Einstein, Dellinger, Muste, SANE. *Video* segment on Hiroshima.

- *DeBenedetti, ch. 7.

- Cooney and Michalowski, "WWII and the Pacifist Community," "Direct Action for Disarmament," and "Towards Revolutionary Nonviolence,"in *The Power of the People.*
- Dave Dellinger, "Statement on Entering Prison," *Revolutionary Nonviolence.*
- Lawrence Witner, *Rebels Against War: The American Peace Movement, 1941–1960.*
- Nat Hentoff, *Cold War America.*
- *The Essays of A.J. Muste,* Peter Mayer, ed.
- Arthur and Lila Weinberg, eds., *Instead of Violence.*
- Milton S. Katz, "Nuclear Pacifism in Cold War America," in *Ban the Bomb.*
- Robert Gilpin, *American Scientists and Nuclear Weapons Policy.*
- Ackland and McGwire, eds., *Assessing the Nuclear Age* (articles from *Bulletin of the the Atomic Scientists*).

Week 3

The Sixties

SCLC, Parks, King, Montgomery, sit-ins, SNCC, Carmichael; CNVA, WRL, W.E.B. Dubois Clubs, WILPF, WSP, SANE, FOR, AFSC, SDS, Vietnam Day Committee, CALCAV, Spring Mobilization, BEM, VVAW, McCarthy, Columbia, Berrigans, MLK and RFK assassinations, Moratorium, March Against Death, Calley, Weathermen, Cambodia, Kent State, Jackson State, NPAC, Winter Soldier, Pentagon Papers, COINTELPRO, IPC. **Film:** *The War at Home,* and segments of the videotape *Eyes on the Prize.*

- *DeBenedetti, ch. 8.
- Cooney and Michalowski, "Civil Rights, Peace Movements," in *The Power of the People.*
- **The Civil Rights Movement**—*Eyes on the Prize: A Reader and Guide;* Raines, *My Soul is Rested* (oral histories of civil rights activists); Carson, *In Struggle;* Belfrage, *Freedom Summer;* Lewis, *King;* Stephen Oates, *Let the Trumpet Sound;* Lincoln, *MLK.*
- **Vietnam Protest**—Thomas Powers, *Vietnam: The War at Home;* Albert and Albert, *The Sixties Papers* (good overview); Morrison, *From Camelot to Kent State* (interviews with participants); Todd Gitlin, *The Sixties;* Zaroulis and Sullivan, *Who Spoke Up;* David Dellinger, *More Power Than We Know, Vietnam Revisited;* Gabriel Kolko, *Anatomy of a War* (good analysis of the war itself); Walt Anderson, ed., *The Age of Protest;* Alice Lynd, *We Won't Go* (profiles of war objectors); Milton S. Katz, *Ban the Bomb.*
- Browsing through bound volumes of magazines from the Sixties like *Life, Time,* and *Newsweek,* provides a wonderful way of getting a feel for the period.

II. The Policy Context

The purpose of this section is to examine the principal U.S. government institutions and processes involved in military and arms control policy today. This is a useful object of study both as a central component of the politics of war and peace, and as the policy context of the perceptions and activity of the public interest groups.

Week 4—The Military

Dept. of Defense, the services, Joint Chiefs, DIA, CIA. *Presentation* by Rob Leavitt, Alternative Defense Network of the Institute for Defense and Disarmament Studies on "A Critique of Current U.S. Military Strategy and Force Structure," "Alternative Defense," and "The INF Treaty and Beyond."

- *Jordon and Taylor, "Military Power and the Role of Force in the Nuclear Age," "The Role of the Military in the National Security Policy Process," "Intelligence and National Security" (skim one military journal).
- *Sweeney, "The View from the Brink."
- *Matthew Goodman, "Two Europes: Airland Battle vs. Alternative Defense," and "Alternative Defense: A Specter Is Haunting NATO," *Defense and Disarmament News.*
- *Howard Morland, "A Few Billion for Defense" (Coalition for a New Foreign Policy).
- *Richard Fieldhouse, "Nuclear Weapons at Sea," *Bulletin of the Atomic Scientists.*
- *Current Official U.S. Policy*—Joint Chiefs of Staff, *Annual Posture Statement,* "National Security Strategy of the U.S." (White House), "U.S. Strategy" (CBO).
- *Critiques of Current U.S. Military Policy*—"Briefing Book," Institute for Defense and Disarmament Studies (overall analysis); Harold Feiveson et al., "Reducing U.S. and Soviet Nuclear Arsenals" (*Bulletin of the Atomic Scientists,* August 1985); Michael Ferber, "Beneath the Stars: The Real Arms Race," *Tikkun* (strategic force structure); Jack Beatty, "In Harms Way," *Atlantic Monthly* (maritime strategy).
- *Strategic Theory*—Morton H. Halperin and Madalene O'Donnell, "The Nuclear Fallacy," *Bulletin of the Atomic Scientists* (Jan.-Feb. 1988); Desmond Ball, "U.S. Strategic Forces: How Would They Be Used?" and Bernard Brodie, "Development of Nuclear Strategy," in Steven E. Miller, ed., *Strategy and Nuclear Deterrence;* Fred Kaplan, *Wizards of Armageddon* (or: Lawrence Freedman, *Evolution of Nuclear Strategy;* Greg Herken, *Counsels of War).*
- *Blacks and Women in the Military*—"Blacks in the Military: The Myth of Equality of Opportunity" (CCCO); Daniel Buford, *Feet of Clay in Black America: Studies in Racism and Militarism;* Wendy Chapkis, *Loaded Questions: Women in the Military;* Cynthia Enloe, *Does Khaki Become You?;* "The War and Race," "Women and War" and "What Did You Do in the Class War, Daddy?" in Horne, *The Wounded*

Generation; Carol Cohn, "Nuclear Language," in *Bulletin of Atomic Scientists* (June 1987).
* **Intelligence (CIA, DIA, NSA)**—Freedman, *U.S. Intelligence and the Soviet Strategic Threat;* Thomas Powers, *The Man Who Kept the Secrets;* Marchetti and Marks, *CIA and the Cult of Intelligence;* John Prados, *The President's Secret Wars.*
* **Arms Sales and Covert Operations**—Michael T. Klare, *American Arms Supermarket;* Michael Klare and Cynthia Arnson, *Supplying Repression;* Edward S. Herman, *The Real Terror Network;* Michael Klare and Peter Kornbluh, *Low-Intensity Warfare;* Ruth Sivard, *World Military and Social Expenditure.*
* **Military Technology**—Frank Barnaby, "How the Next War Will Be Fought; *Just Defense Discussion Papers* (espeically on new technologies); Teena Meyers, *Understanding Nuclear Weapons and Arms Control;* James Dunnigan, *How to Make War* (how various weapons and strategies work).

Week 5—The Administration
National Security Council, White House Staff, OSD. See also Week 7.
* *Jordan and Taylor, "Presidential Leadership and the Executive Branch," and "The National Security Decision-Making Process: Putting the Pieces Together."
* *"U.S. Soviet Strategic Competition," and "Strategic Arsenals of the Superpowers," in *Arms Control and National Security.*
* **Case Study**—"What Happened to the CTB in the Carter Administration?" or "Lessons of Contragate," or "The INF Treaty: A Case Study in Arms Control."
* **The NSC and White House Staff**—Alexander George, "The President and Defense Policymaking," *American Defense Policy;* "The National Security Council," in *The Tower Commission Report;* John Endicott, "The National Security Council," in *American Defense Policy;* Jonathan Marshall et al., *The Iran Contra Connection.*
* **The State Department and the Arms Control and Disarmament Agency (ACDA)**—Duncan Clarke, *Politics of Arms Control* (on ACDA); Barry Rubin, *Secrets of State* (on the State Department).
* **Recent Secretaries of Defense**—Richard Stubbing, *The Defense Game* (profiles).
* **US-Soviet Relations and Current Arms Control Issues**—Robert S. McNamara, *Blundering into Disaster;* David Holloway, *The Soviet Union and the Arms Race;* Fred Kaplan, *Dubious Specter: A Skeptical Look at the Soviet Military Threat.*
* **The Cold War**—Fred Halliday, *The Origins of the Second Cold War;* Noam Chomsky, *Towards a New Cold War;* Lawrence Wittner, *Cold War America;* Walter LaFebre, *America, Russia and the Cold War, 1965–84;* Howard Zinn, *Postwar America, 1945–71.*

Week 6—Congress

Armed services, foreign affairs, budget and appropriations committees. *Talk* on "Hunger and U.S. Policy: A Legislative View," with Marlene Kiingati, staff member of Bread for the World, a respected Washington-based lobbying group on hunger and development issues.

- *Jordon and Taylor, "The Impact of Congress on National Security Policy."
- *Sweeney, "How to Influence Congress to Reverse the Arms Race."
- *Federal Defense Budget Process*—Common Cause, *Defense Dollars and Sense*.
- *Critiques*—Joshua M. Epstein, *The 1988 Defense Budget*; Center on Budget and Policy Priorities, "End Results" (effects of military budget on various programs).
- *Alternative Budgets*—Children's Defense Fund, "A Children's Defense Budget"; WILPF, "Womens' Budget"; Congressional Black Caucus, "Alternative Budget"; Marion Anderson, "Bombs or Bread: Blacks, Unemployment and the Military Budget," "Neither Jobs Nor Security: Women's Unemployment and the Military Budget."
- *Congress and Arms Control*—Douglas C. Waller, *Congress and the Nuclear Freeze*.
- *Legislative Program of Several Peace Groups.*
- *Procurement, Research and Development, Defense Contractors*—*Jordon and Taylor, "Research and Development"; Gordon Adams, "Controlling Weapons Costs" (CEP); James Fallows, *National Defense*; Mary Kaldor, *Baroque Arsenal*; Dina Rasor, *The Pentagon Underground*.
- *Economic Effect of Military Spending*—*Sweeney, "Military Sepnding and Its Effects"; Robert DeGrasse, *Military Expansion, Economic Decline*; Seymour Melman, *The Permanent War Economy*; Gordon and McFadden, *Economic Conversion*; Harold Willens, *The Trimtab Factor*; Gordon Adams, *Iron Triangle: The Politics of Defense Contracting*.

Week 7—The Policy Formation Process

The role of political parties, the media, interest groups, think tanks, schools, churches, community groups.

- *Polls and Public*—"The National Survey on Arms Control" (WAND, 1985); "A Survey of American Voters' Attitudes Concerning National Security Issues" (Americans Talk Security, 1987); Public Agenda Foundation, *Voter Options on Nuclear Arms Policy* (1984); Louis Harris, *Inside America* (1987), *The Anguish of Change* (1973).
- *Political Parties and Candidate Selection*—Defense policy statements of 1988 presidential candidates; selected articles on election process.
- *The Media*—Michael Parenti, *Inventing Reality: The Politics of the Mass Media*.
- *Selected articles from *Deadline* newsletter.
- *Policy Formation Process*—G. William Domhoff, "The Policy Formation Process," in *The Powers That Be*; Susan Shepard, "American

Foreign Policy Think Tanks: A Critical Guide," *Book Forum* (Vol. V, No. 4, 1981).
- *Interest Groups*—Randall Forsberg et al., "Peace Movement Strategies," in *Peace Resource Book* (will serve as transition to Part III).

III. Philosophies of War and Peace

The purpose of this section is to explore the principal ways war and peace have been understood and expressed by the wide spectrum of U.S. interest groups currently active. We will examine their goals and strategies as well as evaluate their effectiveness and impact.

Week 8
Containment
The beginnings of the Cold War.
- *Selections from NSC-68 and other official statements of U.S. policy.
- Eugene Carroll, "Nuclear Weapons and Deterrence," and Michael MccGwire, "Dilemmas and Delusions of Deterrence," in Gwyn Prins, ed., *The Nuclear Crisis Reader.*
- *Jerome Weisner, "A Militarized Society," *Bulletin of Atomic Scientists* (Aug. 1985).
- Richard Barnet, *Intervention and Revolution* and *Roots of War.*
- Joint Chiefs, *Posture Statement*; OSD, *Annual Report.*
- John Gaddis, *Strategies of Containment.*
- Alexander George and Richard Smoke, *Deterrence in American Foreign Policy.*
- Leon Wofsky, *Before the Point of No Return.*

Peace Through Strength
For example, American Security Council, Committee on the Present Danger, American Enterprise Institute, Heritage Foundation, High Frontier.
- *Colin Gray, "Nuclear Strategy: A Case for a Theory of Victory."
- Committee on the Present Danger, "Common Sense and the Common Danger."
- Jerry Sanders, *Peddlers of Crisis.*

Week 9
Arms Control
Arms Control Association (ACA), Center for Defense Information (CDI).
- *ACA, *Arms Control and National Security.*
- ACA, *Arms Control Today.*
- CDI, *Defense Monitor.*
- *Schwartz and Derber, "Arms Control: Misplaced Focus," *Bulletin of the Atomic Scientists.*
- Bundy et al., "Back from the Brink," *The Atlantic Monthly.*
- National Academy of Sciences, *Arms Control: Background and Issues.*

- Strobe Talbott, *Deadly Gambits.*
- Allison, Carnesale, and Nye, *Hawks, Doves and Owls.*

Disarmament
Mobilization for Survival, pacifist groups, nuclear free zone movement.
- "Disarmament 2000" (coalition conference report, 1987).
- Robert C. Johanson, "Toward a Dependable Peace."
- Jonathan Schell, *The Abolition.*
- Freeman Dyson, *Weapons and Hope.*
- Alva Myrdal, *The Game of Disarmament* (history).

Common Security
Palme Commission, Expro, IDDS, Disarmament 2000.
- Independent Commission, *Common Security.*
- Richard Barnet, *Real Security.*
- *Bruce Birchard and Rob Leavitt, "A New Agenda," *Nuclear Times* (Nov.-Dec. 1987).
- Lester Brown, "Redefining National Security," *State of the World, 1986.*

International Law, International Institutions
United Nations, UNA, NGOs.
- *Henry Wiseman, "Peacekeeping and the Management of International Conflict" (Background Paper, Canadian Institute for International Peace and Security, Sept. 1987).
- David Ziegler, "The United Nations," in *War, Peace and International Politics.*
- Richard Falk et al., *International Law: A Contemporary Perspective.*

World Order
World Federalists, World Policy Institute.
- Grenville Clark and Louis Sohn, *Introduction to World Peace Through World Law.*
- Falk, Kim, and Mendlovitz, eds., *Toward a Just World Order.*
- Robert C. Johanson, *The National Interest and the Human Interest.*
- Mische, *Toward a Human World Order.*

Forum
With Andrei Melville, researcher at the Institute of USA and Canada of the USSR Academy of Sciences and contributor to *Breakthrough,* the first book on the nuclear threat written jointly by U.S. and Soviet scholars and scientists.

Week 10—Citizen Initiatives
SANE-Freeze, American Friends Service Committee, Jobs with Peace, Physicians for Social Responsibility, Professionals Coalition, Peace Links.
- *Sweeney, "How You Personally Can Prevent Nuclear War."
- *Sweeney, "Converting to a Peacetime Economy"; review "Military Spending and Its Effects."

- *Randall Forsberg et al., "Peace Movement Strategies," in *Peace Resource Book* (review).
- *Gersmehl, *Tools of Peacemaking*.
- Don Carlson and Craig Comstock, eds., *Citizen Summitry*.
- Gordon C. Bennett, *The New Abolitionists* (on nuclear free zones).
- *The Cambridge Case for Diversification Planning*.
- Program materials from the Jobs With Peace campaign (on jobs and peace).
- Brugmann and Schulman, "Thinking Globally, Acting Locally."
- *Rob Leavitt, "Freezing the Arms Race: The Genesis of a Mass Movement" (case study on the Nuclear Weapons Freeze Campaign, supplements on Washington, public opinion).
- Gordon Feller and Mark Sommer, "Lessons of the Nuclear Freeze."
- Randall Forsberg, "A Step-by-Step Approach," in Craig and Comstock, eds., *Securing Our Planet*.
- Robert F. Drinan, "The Origin of the Nuclear Freeze Movement," and "Congress and the Nuclear Freeze in 1982," in *Beyond the Nuclear Freeze*.
- Edward M. Kennedy and Mark O. Hatfield, *Freeze*.
- Douglas C. Waller, *Congress and the Freeze*.
- American Academy of Arts and Sciences, *The Nuclear Weapons Freeze and Arms Control*.

Week 11—Nonviolence, Pacifism, Direct Action
War Resisters League, Mobilization for Survival, Pacifist Churches (Quakers, Mennonites, Brethren), Pax Christi, Fellowship of Reconciliation, American Friends Service Committee, Plowshares, war tax resistance and draft resistance groups, Peace Camps. *Talks* by Adolfo Perez Esquivel, director of Peace and Justice Service, winner of the 1980 Nobel Peace Prize for his work with Amazonian Indians, trade unions, "Mothers of the Disappeared," political prisoners, and the poor in Latin America.
- *Sweeney, "Nonviolent Action."
- *Martin Luther King, Jr., "Loving Your Enemies," "Letter from a Birmingham Jail," "Declaration of Independence from the War in Vietnam."
- Gene Sharp, *The Politics of Non-Violent Action* (especially pp. 63–101).
- *Joan Boudurant, *Conquest of Violence* (especially pp. 15–104).
- Cooney & Michalowski, *The Power of the People*.
- M.K. Gandhi, *Non-Violent Resistance*.
- Arthur J. Laffin and Anne Montgomery, eds., *Swords into Plowshares*.
- WRL, *Guide to War Tax Resistance* (especially pp. 5–38 and 62–107).
- Mulford Q. Sibley, *The Quiet Battle*.
- War Resisters League, *Organizer Manual*.

Week 12—Feminism
WILPF, Women's Strike, WAND, Women's Pentagon Action, Women for a Meaningful Summit, Grandmothers for Peace, Women's Peace Camps. *Talk*

and slideshow, "Report from Greenham Common," by Gwyn Kirk, co-author of "Greenham Women Everywhere" on the Greenham Common Women's Peace Camp.

- *Cynthia Enloe, *Does Khaki Become You?* (first chapter, plus one other chapter).
- Betty Reardon, *Sexism and the War System*.
- Wendy Chapkis, *Loaded Questions*.
- Dorothy Thompson, ed., *Over Our Dead Bodies: Women Against the Bomb*.
- Cambridge Women's Peace Collective, *My Country Is the Whole World*.
- Alice Cook and Gwyn Kirk, *Greenham Women Everywhere*.
- Caroline Blackwood, *On the Perimeter*.
- Leslie Cagan, "Feminism and Militarism," in Dellinger, ed., *Beyond Survival*.

Week 13
Involvement with Third World Issues
CISPES, Nicaragua Network, Washington Office on Latin America, Witness for Peace, sanctuary movement, TransAfrica, American Committee on Africa, Washington Office on Africa. Academy award winning *film*, *Witness to War*, and *talk* by Charlie Clements, former U.S. Air Force pilot in Vietnam who became a physician and spent a year in the war zones in El Salvador.

- *Fandall Forsberg, "The Case for a Nonintervention Regime," *Defense and Disarmament News* (Aug.–Sept. 1987).
- *Carl Conetta, "The New Dilemmas of Intervention," *Defense and Disarmament News* (Sept.–Oct. 86).
- *"Some Elements of a U.S.-Soviet Modus Vivendi," *FCNL* Washington newsletter (July 1985).
- *Lester Brown, "Redefining National Security," *Nuclear Times* (May–June 1986).
- *Richard Barnet, "The Costs and Perils of Intervention," in *Low-Intensity Conflict*, Michael Klare and Peter Kornbluh, eds.
- *Brochures from Central America and South African groups.
- Charlie Clements, *Witness to War*.
- Melissa Evert, *Building Bridges, Bearing Witness*.
- Richard Fagen, *Forging Peace: The Challenge of Central America* (PACCA).
- Gary MacEoin, *Sanctuary*.
- James McGinnis, *Solidarity with the People of Nicaragua*.
- *No Mandate for War: Pledge of Resistance Handbook* (Emergency Response Network).
- Joe Gerson, *The Deadly Connection*.
- "Militarization and Indigenous Peoples," *Cultural Survival Quarterly*, Vol. II, No. 3 (Americas & Pacific), No. 4 (Africa, Asia, Mideast).

Religious Group Activities
Moral and Ethical Perspectives. Fellowship of Reconciliation, Clergy and Laity Concerned, Shalom Center. *Talks* by Arthur Waskow, director

of the Shalom Center on "Preventing the Nuclear Holocaust: A Jewish Response."

- **The Challenge of Peace*, National Conference of Bishops (summary).
- Jim Wallis, *Waging Peace*; NISBCO, "Words of Conscience."
- Alan Geyer, *The Idea of Disarmament*.
- **"In Search of Shalom: Jewish Statements on the Nuclear Arms Race,"* Shalom Center.
- *Preventing the Nuclear Holocaust: A Jewish Response*, Union of American Hebrew Congregations.
- "Roots of Jewish Nonviolence," Jewish Peace Fellowship.

Week 14
Alternative Defense
Institute for Defense and Disarmament Studies (IDDS), Expro. *Talk* by Rob Leavitt (see Week 4).

- **"Briefing Book,"* IDDS.
- Rob Leavitt, "Vision Quest," *Defense and Disarmament News* (Aug.–Sept. 1987).
- **Dieter Senghaas, "Dismantle Offense, Strengthen Defense," *Bulletin of the Atomic Scientists* (Dec. 1987).
- Robert Neild and Anders Boserup, "Beyond INF," *World Policy Journal* (Fall 1987).
- Lester Brown, "Redefining National Security," *State of the World*.
- Independent Commission on Disarmament and Security Issues, *Common Security*.
- Mark Sommers, *Beyond the Bomb*.
- Gene Sharp, *National Security Through Civilian-Based Defense*.

Empowerment
Interhelp, the Nuclear Network, Waking Up in the Nuclear Age.

- **Sweeney, "Empowerment."*
- Joanna Rogers Macy, *Despair and Personal Power in the Nuclear Age* (selections).
- Fran Peavey, *Heart Politics*.
- Neil Wollman, *Working for Peace*.
- Ralph White, ed., *Psychology and the Prevention of Nuclear War*.

Week 15—Wrap-Up
The wrap-up is an opportunity to compare and contrast the various philosophies and approaches you've studied, to pull together what you've learned, and to examine how your perspective has changed or been confirmed.

BIOGRAPHICAL PAPER

This list of books available at the peace studies library aims to convey some of the breadth of what is possible. The point of the biographical paper is not to recount the events of the student's life, but to explore the key issues of war and peace dealt with by the student as a means of expanding his or her own knowledge, insight and values. I will consider requests to interview someone (e.g., a local peace group leader) rather than reading about a student.

Addams, Jane. *Newer Ideals of Peace.*
———, *Second Twenty Years at Hull House.*
Benjamin, Medea, ed. and transl. *Don't Be Afraid Gringo: A Honduran Woman Speaks from the Heart: The Story of Elvia Alvarado.*
Young-Bruehl, Elizabeth. *Hannah Arendt: For Love of the World.*
Berrigan, Dan. *Trial of the Catonsville Nine, No Bars to Manhood;* and John Deedy, *Apologies Good Friends: An Iterim Biography of Daniel Berrigan.*
———, *Widen the Prison Gates.*
Woods, Donald. *Biko.*
Clements, Charlie. *Witness to War.*
Day, Dorothy. *The Long Loneliness;* and Quigley and Garvey, *The Dorothy Day Book.*
Dellinger, David. *Revolutionary Nonviolence, More Power Than We Know: Vietnam Revisited.*
Nathan, Otto, and Heinz Norden. *Einstein on Peace.*
Gandhi, M.K. *Autobiography;* Eknath Easwaran, *Gandhi the Man;* Ved Mehta, *Mahatma Gandhi and His Apostles;* Gene Sharp, *Gandhi as Political Strategist;* Mark Shepard, *Gandhi Today: The Story of Mahatma's Successors.*
Easwaran, Eknath. *A Man to Match His Mountains* (Badshah Khan).
King, Martin Luther, Jr. *Why We Can't Wait;* and Stephen Oates, *The Trumpet Shall Sound.*
Kuzwayo, Ellen, *Call Me Woman.*
Benson, Mary. *Nelson Mandela: The Man and the Movement.*
Mandela, Winnie, *Part of My Soul Went with Him.*
Peace Pilgrim, *Peace Pilgrim: Her Life and Work in Her Own Words.*
Powelson, Jack. *Facing Social Revolution.*
(See also the autobiographies of Adin Balou and Elihu Burritt, and the biographies of Andrew Carnegie, William Penn, Leo Tolstoy, and John Woolman among others)

Collections

Select and discuss several biographies if you choose one of these.

Beisner, Robert. *Twelve Against the Empire: The Anti-Imperialists, 1898–1900.*
Bruyn, Severyn T., and Paula M. Rayman. *Nonviolent Action and Social Change.*
Cook, Alice, and Gwyn Kirk. *Greenham Women Everywhere.*
Evert, Melissa. *Building Bridges, Bearing Witness.*
Harford, Barbara, and Sarah Hopkins, eds. *Greenham Common: Women at the Wire.*
Herman, Sandra R. *Eleven Against the War.*
Hope, Marjorie, and James Young. *The Struggle for Humanity.*

Loeb, Paul. *Hope in Hard Times.*
Mayer, Peter, ed. *The Pacifist Conscience.*
Raines, Howell. *My Soul Is Rested.*
Randall, Margaret. *Sandino's Daughters: Testimonies of Nicaraguan Women.*
Totten, Sam, and Martha Wescoat Totten. *Facing the Danger.*
True, Michael. *Justice Seekers, Peace Makers.*
Wallis, Jim. *Peacemakers.*

10. International Politics

Lynn H. Miller   Fall 1985
Political Science Department, Temple University,
Philadelphia, PA 19122

This course is an introduction to the theory and problems of contemporary international politics. We will trace the logic of the Westphalian system of sovereign nation-states, its growth and development over the past three hundred years as the organizing mode for the entire world, and the threats to its continued ability to provide the kind of ordering framework needed today. We will examine the roles of power and values in state-craft, including the use and threat of force, the relativity of both anarchy and order in the international system, and the relationships between politics and law.

We will systematically explore the principal world order problems of international warfare and the nuclear threat, global economic inequality, human rights deprivations, and planetary resource scarcity and environmental degradation. We will also investigate the possibilities for implementing preferable alternatives and thus improving the human condition in all nations.

Requirements
There will be two written assignments, consisting of essays on topics to be assigned in class, in addition to a mid-term and final examination.

Readings
All reading assignments are from the following texts:

Annual Editions: World Politics 84–85. Dushkin Publishing Group.
Miller, Lynn H. *Global Order: Values and Power in International Politics.* Westview Press, 1985.

COURSE OUTLINE

Values and International Politics
- Miller, ch. 1, pp. 1–16.

The Growth of the Westphalian System
- Miller, ch. 2, pp. 17–38.

Early Twentieth Century Challenges to International Order
- Miller, ch. 3, pp. 39–51.

Current Challenges to International Order
- Miller, ch. 3, pp. 51–67.
- *Annual Editions*, sec. 5.

Statism, World Order, and International Government
- Miller, ch. 4, pp. 68–91.

The Superpowers
- *Annual Editions*, secs. 1–2.

The East-West Dimension
- *Annual Editions*, secs. 3–4.

The Challenge of Nuclear Politics
- Miller, ch. 5, pp. 92–110.
- *Annual Editions*, sec. 7.

Alternatives to International Violence
- Miller, ch. 5, pp. 110–124.

Economic Development in Historical Perspective
- Miller, ch. 6, pp. 125–137.

Contemporary Development Problems
- Miller, ch. 6, pp. 137–155.

Human Rights in International Politics
- Miller, ch. 7, pp. 156–184.

The Global Commons in International Politics
- Miller, ch. 8, pp. 185–204.

International Politics and the Future of World Order
- Miller, ch. 9, pp. 205–217.
- *Annual Editions*, sec. 9.

11. Global Disorders and Orders: A Peace Studies Perspective

Rajendra Dave   *Spring 1987*
Program in Non-Violent Conflict and Change,
Syracuse University, Syracuse, NY 13210

This seminar course attempts to provide an understanding of how the present global system works, an appreciation of the major problems (disorders) the world faces today, and an opportunity to explore peace-intensive remedies to solve the global puzzle. The course is divided into two parts. In the first part we will discuss the theories of peace and peace research. In the second part we will attempt to analyze the global disorders and explore their remedies. Your reading of the assigned materials before classes and your active class participation are essential if you are to maximize your learning experience.

Evaluation
Your performance will be evaluated along these lines: 25% for class participation; 25% for writing a summary of six articles on any topic from the course outline or a 10-15 page research paper on a selected topic; 25% for a mid-term paper (deadline 3rd March); 25% for a final paper (deadline 5th May).

Required Readings
Johan Galtung. *The True Worlds: A Transnational Perspective.* New York: The Free Press, 1980.
Kenneth Boulding. *Stable Peace.* Austin: University of Texas Press, 1978.

Additional books and readings will be announced in class.

COURSE SCHEDULE

Section I. Theories of Peace Research

Jan. 13—Introduction
- Burns H. Weston, "Peace and World Order Education: An Optimal Design, in *Peace and World Order Studies: A Curriculum Guide,* Institute for World Order, 1981, pp. 55–77.

- Andrew Mack, *Peace Research in the 1980s,* The Strategic and Defence Studies Centre, Canberra, 1985, pp. 3–15.

Jan. 20—Theories of Peace

- Kenneth Boulding, *Stable Peace,* pp. 1–91.
- Johan Galtung, "Violence, Peace, and Peace Research," in *Peace: Research, Education, Action,* Vol. 1, pp. 109–134.
- William Malley, "Peace, Needs and Utopia," in *Political Studies,* Vol. XXXIII, pp. 478–591.

Jan. 27—Theories of Peace Research

- Johan Galtung, "Peace Research: Science, or Politics in Disguise?" and "Peace Research: Past Experiences and Future Perspectives," in *Peace: Research, Education, Action,* Vol. I, pp. 224–262.
- Kenneth Boulding, *Stable Peace,* pp. 93–143.
- Marek Thee, "The Scope and Priorities in Peace Research," in *Trends and Approaches to Peace and Conflict Studies,* pp. 3–14.
- Peter Lawyer, "Peace Research and International Relations: From Divergence to Convergence, Millennium," *Journal of International Studies,* Vol. 15, No. 3, Winter 1985.

Section II. From Disorders to Orders

Feb. 3—The Nature of Global Disorder

- Johan Galtung, *The True Worlds,* pp. 1–79.
- Rajni Kothari, *Footsteps into the Future: Diagnosis of the Present World and a Design for an Alternative,* pp. 21–48.

Feb. 10—Nuclearization to Denuclearization

- Richard Falk, "Nuclear Policy and World Order: Why Denuclearization," Working Paper No. 2, WOMP.
- Burns Weston, ed., *Toward Nuclear Disarmament and Global Security: A Search for Alternatives* (part I includes articles by Harold Freeman and Jonathan Schell as well as a Report of the UN Secretary General), pp. 1–64.

Feb. 17—From Militarization to Demilitarization

Presentation by Professor Miles Wolpin, S.U.N.Y. Potsdam.

- Johan Galtung, *The True Worlds,* pp. 179–253.

Feb. 24—The Unequal World to Egalitarian World

- Johan Galtung, *The True Worlds,* pp. 255–303.
- Gernet Kohler, "The Global Apartheid," in Falk, Kim and Mendlowitz, eds., *Toward a Just World Order,* pp. 315–235.

Mar. 3—Eco-Crisis to Eco-Development

- Rajni Kothari, "Environment and Alternative Development," Working Paper No. 15, World Order Models Project.

- Ignacy Sachs, "Civilization Project and Ecological Prudence," *Alternatives*, Vol. III, No. 1, August 1977.
- E.F. Schumacher, "Alternatives in Technology," *Alternatives*, Vol. I, No. 1, March 1975.
- Dennis Pirages, "The Origins of Ecopolitics," in Falk, Kim and Mendlowitz, eds., *Toward a Just World Order*, pp. 442–455.

Mar. 17—From Maldevelopment to True Development
- Johan Galtung, *The True Worlds*, pp. 107–178.
- F.H. Cardoso, "Towards Another Development," in Falk, Kim and Mendlowitz, eds., *Toward a Just World Order*, pp. 343–356.
- Dieter Senghaas, "Introduction," *Journal of Peace Research*, Vol. XII, No. 4, 1975.

Mar. 24—Social Well-Being
- Fouad Ajami, "Human Rights and World Order Politics," in Falk, Kim and Mendlowitz, eds., *Toward a Just World Order*, pp. 371–399.
- Cheryl Christensen, "The Right to Food: How to Guarantee," World Order Models Project working paper.

Section III. Peace Studies Perspectives

Mar. 31—The Conflict Resolution Approach
Presentation by Professor Neil Katz.
- Johan Galtung, "Conflict as a Way of Life," and "Institutionalized Conflict Resolution: A Theoretical Paradigm," in *Peace and Social Structure*, Vol. III, pp. 434–507.
- Louis Kriesberg, "Social Conflict Theories and Conflict Resolution," *Peace and Change*, Vol. VIII, No. 2/3, Summer 1982.
- Jacob Bercovitch, "International Mediation: A Study of the Incidence, Strategies and Conditions of Successful Outcomes," *Cooperation and Conflict*, Vol. XXI, No. 3, 1985, pp. 155–158.

Apr. 7—The World Order Models Project
- Richard Falk and Samuel Kim, "An Approach to World Order Studies and the World System," Working Paper No. 22, WOMP.
- Harold Lasswell, "The Promise of the World Order Modelling Movement," *World Politics*, Vol. XXIX, No. 3, April 1977.
- R.J. Yalem, "Conflicting Approaches to World Order," *Alternatives*, Vol. V, No. 3, November 1979.

Apr. 14—Gandhi and the Contemporary World
- J.D. Sethi, "Gandhian Approach to a New World Order: Human Predicament in the Nuclear Era," in Mishra and Gangal, eds., *Gandhi and the Contemporary World*, pp. 111–128.
- Ignacy Sachs, *Gandhi and Development*, Seminar, 1977.

- Rajendra Dave, "Gandhi's Moral Concept of Development," a technical note prepared for class discussion.

Apr. 21—The Peace Movements Perspective
- Nigel Young, "The Peace Movements: A Comparative and Analytical Survey," *Alternatives*, Vol. XI, No. 2, April 1985.
- Saral Sarkar, "The Green Movement in Germany," *Alternatives*, Vol. XI, No. 2, April 1986.

Apr. 28—The Images of Preferred Worlds
- Johan Galtung, *The True Worlds*, pp. 81–105.
- Rajni Kothari, "Towards a Just World," Working Paper No. 11, World Order Models Project.

V

War and International Conflict

1. Studies in International Conflict

Deborah Gerner   *Winter 1986*
Northwestern University*

This course is designed to introduce students to a wide range of literature focused on the phenomenon of international conflict—primarily, but not exclusively, war. Although the principal focus will be on material from political science, evidence from anthropology, sociology, psychology, economics and biology will be examined where appropriate. The course will be run primarily as a seminar, with some lecturing to introduce the material. Ideally, class meetings should involve an exchange of ideas among all participants. A number of the issues we will be discussing (Are humans innately aggressive? Do alliances cause war?) have been debated for thousands of years, so it is doubtful that we will exhaust their potential in an hour and a half. Given the seminar/lecture format, you are expected to attend regularly and to complete the assigned readings by the day on which they are to be discussed.

Books
In addition to photocopied articles the following books are required.

---

*Deborah Gerner now teaches in the Political Science Department, University of Kansas, Lawrence, KS 66045.

Falk, Richard A., and Samuel S. Kim, eds. *The War System.* Westview Press, 1980.

Howard, Michael. *The Cases of War,* 2nd edition. Harvard University Press, 1983.

Johansen, Robert C. *Toward an Alternative Security System.* World Policy Institute, 1983.

Lebow, Richard Ned. *Between Peace and War: The Nature of International Crisis.* Johns Hopkins University Press, 1981.

Waltzer, Michael. *Just and Unjust Wars.* Basic Books, 1977.

Evaluation

Class participation (20%). Quality, including integration of the readings, is the key here, but quantity is also important. Two 6–9 page essays (20% each). Each essay should address the issues raised in the question and integrate the literature you have read. Two 1–2 page book or article summaries (5% each). These summaries should indicate the main topic or question, the research methodology, the results and interpretation, and some assessment of the usefulness of the piece. You can choose any book or article on the recommended reading list, but check with me first to make sure no one else has already picked it. These are due no later than January 31 and February 28, respectively. Ideally, you should complete these so that they are available to other students before the class at which the relevant topic is to be discussed. Take-home final exam or 15–20 page research paper (30%). If you choose the research paper option, it can involve either a "survey of the literature" discussing the major questions and research results on some issue, or a report on your own research on a topic relevant to this course.

COURSE SCHEDULE

Part I. Introduction

Jan. 6—Course Introduction

Jan. 8—Defining International Conflict
- Howard, "The Cases of War."
- Lebow, "Introduction."
- Waltzer, chs. 2, 3, 11.
- Wright, Quincy. 1964 (1942). *A Study of War* (abridged). University of Chicago Press, ch. 1, pp. 1–19.

Part II. Individual and Societal-Level Theories

Jan. 13—Instinctual Aggression Versus Learned Aggression
- Falk and Kim, eds., chs. by Bandura (6) and Fabbro (8); also the Intro. to Parts 2 and 3.

- Mead, Margaret. 1973 [1940]. "Warfare Is Only an Invention—Not a Biological Necessity," in Charles R. Beitz and Theodore Herman, eds., *Peace and War*, W.H. Freeman, pp. 112–118.
- Einstein, Albert, and Sigmund Freud. 1959 [1932]. "Why War? An Exchange of Letters Between Albert Einstein and Sigmund Freud," in Robert A. Goldwin, ed., *Readings in World Politics*, Oxford University Press.

Jan. 15—Psychological Factors
Frustration-Aggression, Groupthink.
- Falk and Kim, eds., chs. by Berkowitz (5), Gurr (11), and Feierabend and Feierabend (12).
- Janis, Irving L. 1982. *Groupthink*, Houghton Mifflin Co., chs. 1 and 10, pp. 1–13, 242–259.

Jan. 20—Problems of Imaging and Misperception
- Lebow, chs. 5 and 6.
- Levy, Jack S. 1983. "Misperception and the Causes of War," *World Politics* 36 (1), pp. 76–99.
- Falk and Kim, eds., ch. by Jervis (19).
- Howard, "Three People."

Jan. 22—Environmental Theories
Governmental Structure, Population, Natural Resources.
- Choucri, Nazli, and Robert C. North. 1975. *Nations in Conflict: National Growth and International Violence*, Freeman, ch. 1.
- Howard, "War and the Nation State" and "Social Change and the Defense of the West."
- Morgenthau, Hans. 1973. *Politics Among Nations*, 5th ed., Alfred A. Knopf, ch. 9, pp. 112–140.

Jan. 27 & 29—Economic Theories on War
- Baran, Paul, and Paul Sweezy. 1972 [1966]. "Notes on the Theory of Imperialism," in Kenneth E. Boulding and Tapan Mukerjee, eds., *Economic Imperialism*, University of Michigan Press, pp. 156–170.
- Barnet, Richard J. 1972. "Changing Patterns of Imperialism: Capitalism, Expansion, and War," in *Roots of War*, Pelican Books, pp. 206–238.
- Falk and Kim, eds., part 6, articles 16, 17 (Landes) and 18 (Galtung), plus Intro. to Part 6.
- Hobson, J.A. 1972 [1905]. "The Economic Taproot of Imperialism," in Boulding and Mukerjee, eds., pp. 1–17.

Part III. Systemic
and Macro-Level Theories

Feb. 3—Issues and Methodology in the Study of International Conflict
- Bueno de Mesquita, Bruce. 1980. "Theories of International Conflict: An Analysis and an Appraisal," in Ted Robert Gurr, ed., *Handbook of Political Conflict*, Free Press, ch. 9, pp. 361–398.

- Howard, "The Use and Abuse of Military History."
- Most, Benjamin, and Harvey Starr. 1982. "Case Selection, Conceptualizations and Basic Logic in the Study of War," *American Journal of Political Science* 26(4), pp. 834–856.
- Waltzer, chs. 1, 4, 14.
- Zinnes, Dina. 1980. "Why War? Evidence on the Outbreak of International Conflict," in Ted Robert Gurr, ed., *Handbook of Political Conflict*, Free Press, ch. 8, pp. 331–360.

Feb. 5—Patterns and Trends in International Conflict

- Faber, Jan, Henk W. Houweling and Jan G. Siccama. 1984. "Diffusion of War: Some Theoretical Considerations and Empirical Evidence," *Journal of Peace Research* 21(3), pp. 277–288.
- Thompson, William R. 1985. "Cycles of General, Hegemonic, and Global War," in Urs Luterbacher and Michael D. Ward, eds., *Dynamic Models of International Conflict*, Lynne Rienner Publishers, ch. 19, pp. 462–488.

Feb. 10—Balance of Power: Alliances

- Duncan, George T., and Randolph M. Siverson. 1982. "Flexibility of Alliance Partner Choice in a Multipolar System," *International Studies Quarterly* 26(4), pp. 511–538.
- Kegley, Charles W., and Gregory A. Raymond. 1982. "Alliance Norms and War," *International Studies Quarterly* 26(4), pp. 572–595.
- Levy, Jack S. 1981. "Alliance Formation and War Behavior," *Journal of Conflict Resolution* 25(4), pp. 581–613.
- Waltzer, chs. 5 and 6.

Feb. 12—Balance of Power: Systemic Polarity

- Bueno de Mesquita, Bruce. 1978. "Systemic Polarization and the Occurence and Duration of War," *Journal of Conflict Resolution* 22(2), pp. 241–267.
- Wayman, Frank Whelon. 1984. "Bipolarity and War: The Role of Capability Concentration and Alliance Patterns Among Major Powers, 1816–1965," *Journal of Peace Research* 21(1), pp. 61–78.

Feb. 17—Arms Races and War

- Diehl, Paul. 1983. "Arms Races and Escalation: A Closer Look," *Journal of Peace Research* 20(3), pp. 205–212.
- Howard, "Weapons and Peace," and "Surviving a Protest."
- Wallace, Michael D. 1982. "Armaments and Escalation: Two Competing Hypotheses," *International Studies Quarterly* 26(1), pp. 37–56.

Feb. 19—Internal-External Conflict Nexus

- Falk and Kim, eds., chs. by LeVine (7) and Coser (14).
- Stohl, Michael. 1980. "The Nexus of Civil and International Conflict," in Ted Robert Gurr, ed., *Handbook of Political Conflict*, Free Press, ch. 7, pp. 297–330.

Feb. 24—Arms Transfers, Military Expenditures and War

- Gerner, Deborah J. 1982. "Arms Transfers to the Third World," *International Interactions* 10(1), pp. 5–37.
- Klare, Michael T. 1984. *American Arms Supermarket*, University of Texas Press, ch. 1, pp. 1–25.

Part IV. Crisis Management and Conflict Resolution

Feb. 26—The Nature of International Crises

- Lebow, chs. to be assigned.
- Leng, Russell J., and Charles S. Gochman. 1982. "Dangerous Disputes: A Study of Conflict Behavior and War," *American Journal of Political Science* 26(4), pp. 664–687.

Mar. 3—Crisis Decision-Making

- Falk and Kim, eds., Intro. to part 7, chs. by Holsti (20) and Paigne (21).

Mar. 5—International Law and Non-Violent Conflict Resolution

- Falk and Kim, eds., Intro. to part 9, chs. by Hoffman (25), Bull (26) and Falk (27).
- Howard, "The Strategic Approach to International Relations."
- Johansen, all.
- Waltzer, "Afterward" on Non-Violence.

ESSAY QUESTIONS

Assignment #1

1. Are humans innately aggressive? If not, how would you explain the existing theories and literature which argue in the affirmative? If so, does this necessarily imply that (a) international conflict is inevitable; (b) international conflict expressed in fatal disputes is inevitable?

2. The argument has been made that human nature ensures the continuance of war, due to a mixture of factors, including original sin (e.g., Niebuhr), the instinctual drive toward death (e.g., Freud), the preservation of territory (e.g., Ardrey), the desire to dominate others (e.g., Lorenz), or to achieve power (e.g., Moregenthau), and greed (e.g., Plato). How would you respond to this position?

3. What is the linkage, if any, between the aggressive tendencies of a single individual in a position of national leadership (e.g., Hitler, Napolean, Attila the Hun) and the conflictual behavior of a nation-state as a whole? In other words, can national aggressiveness, as expressed in war, be explained by the aggressiveness of a single individual, or is it necessary that the entire society, or at least large parts of it, be aggressive? Be specific and cite historical examples, and try to anticipate counter-arguments.

4. Discuss the linkage, if any, between conflict and violent conflict. Do the two differ merely in degree, or are they separate phenomena? You may also want to link this discussion with the distinction between rational and arational conflict ("arational" means not involving considerations of rationality, as distinct from "irrational").

5. Social learning theorists have maintained that the existence of peaceful societies is proof that the use of violent expressions of conflict represents behavior which is taught rather than being an inherent part of human personality. What can be learned about international conflict and war from studying the examples of peaceful societies? Do these communities provide insights into how contemporary society could organize itself to minimize the likelihood of war, or are they anomalies with no modern-day relevance in a world of nuclear weapons, nation-states and powerful leaders?

6. What are the strengths and weaknesses of the frustration-aggression theory and its modifications in explaining *international* (as opposed to *domestic*) conflict? Can you propose a series of empirical tests which would allow us to more carefully assess its applicability to violent international conflict?

7. Design a research program that would provide evidence regarding the extent to which the expression of international conflict through physical violence is due to instinct or to learned behavior (the nature/nurture debate). This is not a simple question; people have been arguing about it for years. I'm looking for some concrete hypotheses and means of testing them which would distinguish between these two sets of theories.

Assignment #2

1. What is the importance of individual perception in explaining the actions taken by decision-makers in international relations? What models have international relations (IR) researchers used to investigate the role of perception in decision-making? What evidence, if any, is there that specific international conflicts might have resolved themselves differently had the perceptions of the decision-makers been other than what they were?

2. What are the theorized causes of misperception in international relations (specifically in terms of situations involving war)? Describe a research project designed to investigate the extent to which several of these potential sources of misperception actually existed in crucial situations of crisis. Be sure to make this project realistic—i.e., what can you actually study given the known problem of access to and quality of information about decision-making?

3. To what extent is so-called misperception due to a lack of complete information (which could conceivably be rectified by greater levels of communication, political and military intelligence, etc.)? Alternatively, misperception on key points may be primarily a psychological phenomenon which cannot be significantly affected by a greater quantity or quality of information. Defend one position or the other.

4. At least two approaches have been taken to explain persistent patterns of misperception (e.g., stereotyping) by foreign policy decision-makers. According to one approach, these misperceptions are due to early socialization

and acculturation and the patterns of misperception basically reflect the society as a whole. According to an alternative approach, patterns of misperception have their roots in an organizational milieu (e.g., the foreign policy bureaucracy, or smaller units within that bureaucracy), where certain patterns of thinking are required in order for individuals to be bureaucratically successful. If the first model is correct, changes in political leadership will have little effect on patterns of misperception (i.e., US foreign policy makers will always bring the United States' pattern of perception with them); if the second model is correct, changes in leadership may cause some changes in perception. Defend one position or the other; also determine whether it would be possible to design a study which could decide between the two models.

5. Assess the possibilities of international conflict being caused by each of the following resource constraints: food, energy, raw materials other than energy, and land (population question). Use historical examples when possible and applicable, and use the general literature when historical examples are not available.

6. Are geographical and environmental constraints on international political activities, particularly war, likely to become more important or less important in the future? Consider specifically those factors (e.g., specific technological innovations, specific resource constraints) which are likely to affect international relations in either way.

7. Assess the utility of military power in maintaining oil flow to industrialized states. Is military power likely to become an important variable in the near future in the distribution of oil resources? Extend your answer to include protection of transportation routes as well as production facilities.

8. Is imperialism a necessary stage of capitalism? Is capitalism a necessary condition for imperialism? Is imperialism either a necessary or a sufficient condition for war? Be sure to define your terms.

Empirical Studies of International Conflict

For each of the major statistical projects on international conflict (Correlates of War, Stanford 1914 Studies, Events Data Research, etc.), consider the following issues:

1. What are the major questions being addressed by the research? What are the implicit assumptions behind the hypotheses, in terms of how the "real world" operates? Is the research rooted in any of the traditional schools of thought about IR, and if so, which one(s)? Is research addressing questions that, for example, Hans Morgenthau or Lenin would find interesting? If not, why not?

2. What are the data sources? To what extent is the project or method determined by the data? What are the inherent weaknesses in the data being used, and how have the researchers attempted to get around these (if they have)? Is the quality of the data sufficiently high to give a meaningful answer to the questions being addressed? Are there alternative data sources which could have been used but were not?

3. What is the primary method of analysis? How is this related to the questions being asked; i.e., did the analysis arise from the questions, or were the questions determined by the availability of the analytical technique (e.g., factor analysis, multivariate regression, linear differential equations)? Are there any obvious improvements which could be made in the analytic methods? How aware are the researchers of the implicit assumptions and/ or weaknesses in their methods?

4. What are the major conclusions of the research? To what extent can one trust those results, particularly with respect to questions (1), (2), and (3) above? Have the studies been replicated in any war, or are there studies addressing similar questions with different techniques and data, and how do the results compare? Do any of the results add anything to what we know about IR that wasn't available in the traditional literature? Is there any evidence that these results are cumulative, or are we simply dealing with a large number of virtually independent research efforts?

5. How general are the methods that have been developed? In other words, is there evidence of cumulativeness in technique, and have we learned anything about how to study IR "scientifically" by pursuing these various techniques in depth?

6. What is the sociological structure of the research, and is there any evidence that this structure might have affected the results and/or the impact of the research on the profession? Is it better to spend a million dollars on one large project or on ten smaller ones? What are the trade-offs? In the current atmosphere of funding reductions, is this even a relevant question?

Assignment #3

There are many questions approaching from different angles the issue of whether it is possible to identify empirical regularities in international conflict and, if it is possible, how it is best accomplished.

1. Is the search for the origins of international conflict more productively done at the level of the individual or at aggregate levels (i.e., groups, classes, nation-states)? Take a position defending one approach or the other. You should mention the merits of both approaches, but make your final choice clear. If you are defending the individual approach, be sure to directly address the problem of deriving aggregate behavior from individual behavior. If you are defending the aggregate approach, be sure to directly address the problem of dealing with the "behavior" of entities which are in fact only aggregates of individuals.

2. How has the necessity of relying on uncontrolled historical data on war affected research on the subject? (For example, we can't produce "experimental wars." In contrast to elections, we don't even know when wars are going to occur, and in contrast to crimes of violence, we have a relatively small and culturally heterogeneous sample.) Does this reliance on "quasi-experimental data" affect the study of war more than the study of other international political phenomena?

3. Are patterns of human behavior sufficiently consistent throughout history that it makes sense to study them over, say, periods of centuries?

In other words, is it the case that the same "system," in some sense of the term, was operating in 1550 as is operating today and as will be operating in 2150? If so, what factors reveal that sort of consistency and why? If not, in what time frame is such consistency observable, and why?

4. Consider the following proposition: "Everything you need to know about international conflict can be learned by reading Thucydides' *History of the Pelopponesian Wars.* Agree or disagree. If you haven't read Thucydides, consider this statement: "The variety of actions/events in international conflict is sufficiently limited that studying in detail one or two important events (wars) will give you most of the insights you need to study a much larger class of events (wars)." Contrast this approach with the aggregate data analysis approach, if there is a contrast. Is this statement scientific?

5. The scientific approach is usually considered to consist of the search for empirical regularities in the world. (These are then organized into theory and so forth, but the regularities have to be there first.) What sort of regularities are we likely to find in the area of international conflict? A list might be appropriate here. What is the temporal framework? Should we confine ourselves to the present, or is the entire scope of history open to us? If the latter, how do we differ from historians (aside from reading less and computing more)?

6. What is the role of violent conflict (e.g., war, but also revolution/ civil war) within balance of power theories? Is war a central focus of balance of power, or is it just one of a number of possible consequences? Use specific citations from various discussions of balance of power and systemic polarity.

7. What evidence exists regarding the periodicity of international conflict? It is pursuasive? What are the implications of the evidence for policy makers?

8. What have we learned from empirical studies of alliances and war? In particular, have there been any insights with real-world practical implications, given that countries are unlikely to change their alliances based on a political scientist's assessment that alliances might lead to war?

9. Choose one to three hypotheses about war and present an argument that there is sufficient empirical regularity in the world that these hypotheses might be reasonable topics for study in an attempt to establish scientific "laws" about war behavior. You do not have to show that the laws hold; determine only that there is sufficient evidence that they might hold, and that an intelligent person might want to spend time on the subject. Existing empirical studies should be part of your argument. Alternatively, argue that no such hypotheses exist, again, on the basis of empirical evidence. (Blaney comes close to doing exactly this in his book *Causes of War.*) It may make sense to limit your hypotheses to certain time periods or economic conditions; they need not be truly universal.

10. What would an empirical "explanation" of war look like (i.e., what would it have to accurately predict on the basis of what information)? Would it have to predict outbreak, magnitude, involvement, length, issues, mode of resolution, or what? On what would it base these predictions on: systemic variables, national variables, personality? And what do you see as the likelihood of such an explanation?

Assignment #4

On Arms Races (Compliments of Philip Schrodt)

1. Discuss the arms race literature from the perspective of whether internal or external stimulants to military expenditures are more important. Look at this literature from both a quantitative and non-quantitative (i.e., bureaucratic decision-making) perspective.

2. Why has the phenomenon of the arms race attracted so much attention? Is it simply because it is one of the few areas where there is widely studied (if not accepted) models, or are there substantive reasons to focus on the topic? In preparing an answer to this question, look at some of the arms race model articles, including those assigned, and try to figure out what motivated the authors to study the subject in the first place. Have the results been worth the effort?

3. Discuss the "N-nation" problem in arms race models—the fact that states are probably influenced by a large number of other states in the international system and that any realistic arms race model would be so complex that its parameters could not be estimated. Is there any way around this problem and how important a problem is it? Is it important in all international arms race situations, or just some of them?

4. Consider the following statement: There don't appear to be any "magic" additional variables for the arms race model—i.e., variables that when added to the model consistently explain the variance. First, is this statement true? (Look through some of the recent literature—don't take my word for it.) If it is, then why? If not, what are some other variables which have not been looked at and might work? Be realistic.

5. On the basis of the empirical tests and your knowledge of the real world, discuss the necessary and/or sufficient conditions for an arms race in which a Richardson arms race model would be likely to work. For starters, you can consider the fact that the US/USSR arms race is not modeled very accurately, that the Israeli/Arab arms race is, and that the NATO/WTO arms race falls somewhere in between.

6. How should one measure "arms" in the Richardson model? Look at this question from both the perspective of what has been done in the literature and from the perspective of what you think should be done in terms of measurement. Assume that you have substantial, though not unlimited, research money available for data collection.

7. Discuss the role of rationality in the arms race literature. Richardson said his models described how arms races would occur "if people did not stop to think," and people have criticized the model on these grounds. At the same time, the model has been derived from assumptions involving rationality, and bureaucracies are not renowned for rational behavior. Comments?

On Arms Transfers

8. Based on your examination of the literature, do you detect any theory of arms transfers? Or anything remotely capable of being called a theory,

or proto-theory, or even a consensus for that matter? If so, what? If not, why not?

9. "Empirical studies of arms transfers are a waste of time and money because the data aren't good enough. More can be learned from case studies." (This view is held by almost everybody in the arms transfer study business except Ed Laurance, Ron Sherwin, Jo Husbands, Mike Mihalka, and Robert Harkavy, among others.) Agree or disagree? Basically, this question boils down to ascertaining how good/reliable data must be before we are likely to detect any patterns in it, and whether what we've got meets these criteria. Consider this issue in terms of arms transfers as a dependent variable, an independent variable, or both. Alternatively, or additionally, argue the value of case studies.

10. Assess the evidence for and against the "arms lead to political influence" question. If the evidence appears strong, design an empirical study to test the hypothesis (keeping in mind the possibility of control variables). If the hypothesis appears false, discuss why it seems to have so much support in Washington, Moscow, London and Paris.

11. Assess the arguments in favor of and against the notion that some arms transfers are necessary in order to "stabilize the balance of power" in a region (i.e., to prevent war by giving arms to one side in a conflict since the other side already has them). If possible, use specific examples of successes and failures of this policy.

12. As long as there are political, diplomatic, economic and security reasons for arms transfers, especially to the Third World, what is the likelihood of strict arms trade regulation by supplier states? Is it more feasible to place limitations on the sophistication of the arms transferred? If limitations could effectively be imposed, would there be any change in the number or the intensity of international conflicts?

13. Consider the following proposition: "Arms transfers are only the most modern variant on the general issue of 'power transfers'—i.e., the ability to augment the power of an ally without actually forming an alliance. What is now done with AK-47s, tanks and F-5e planes was once done with gold and mercenaries. Therefore, in terms of their political impact and their relationship to international conflict and war, arms transfers are nothing new. It should be possible to identify analogous phenomena with analogous impacts at earlier times in history, and from that to develop a general theory of the impact of power transfers on war" (an optimistic view of the possibilities of arms transfer research). Agree or disagree, and explain why.

14. Consider the following proposition: "Arms transfers, in and of themselves, have almost no political impact and therefore have little relationship to the likelihood of war or to the path that a war will take once it is begun. The patterns of arms sales are sporatic and determined mostly by the availability of surplus resources for purchasing those arms, while political events such as war are determined almost totally by factors other than arms availability or arms transfers" (a pessimistic assessment of the possibilities of arms transfer research). Agree or disagree, and explain why.

Assignment #5

1. Is war inevitable? If so, in what sense? If not, how might it be avoided? Relate your answer to the issue of what is to be gained by studying war. Be realistic, and don't assume any major changes in human nature unless you can come up with a reason for those changes. One way you might approach this assignment is to use Bernard Brodie's observation that in European society the institution of dueling used to be considered inevitable, but no longer is—disputes are either resolved peacefully or considered cases of assault or murder. Could the same *social* change occur vis-à-vis war?

2. General George S. Patton stated: "Compared to war, all other human activities are insignificant." Do you agree or disagree? Is war all that important? Should it be, as many have argued, the *central* focus of international relations study? In particular, is war more important than international economic activity? If so, or if not, on what grounds?

3. Discuss the role of "crisis" in foreign policy decision-making. Do foreign policy crises involve a different form of decision-making, or are they simply more interesting to study? Consider this issue from the perspective of both the organization and the individual decision-maker.

4. Are there patterns in a crisis ending in war that are different from those in a crisis ending peacefully? If yes, what are they and how can these be promoted? If no, how then can we predict the direction in which a crisis will evolve?

5. Is it possible to develop a covering law applicable across time and space on the internal-external conflict nexus? If so, why has this not been accomplished thus far? If not, design a research project that would enable us to determine which hypotheses on the relationship between internal and external conflict are true under what conditions and during which time periods.

6. Can there be a "universal" (i.e., global) international law to deal with international conflicts in the face of the legal and cultural diversity we observe on the planet? To what extent has recent (post-1960) international law been determined in the context of the entire international system as opposed to the legal traditions of Western Europe and North America? Consider both sides of this question—i.e., whether a truly global conceptualization of international law is even possible, and then the extent to which it exists.

7. "The Law of War is a contradiction of terms—in war there is no law." Discuss.

8. Is non-violent conflict resolution possible at the level of the international system? Under what conditions? For what types of issues?

9. Why are we still working with essentially the same concepts of international law as were set down around 1650? In particular, why has international law thus far survived despite substantial changes in technology and internal patterns of authority? Is this status likely to continue in the future (i.e., over the next 20–30 years), or will there be changes? If so, which changes? If not, why not? In your answer, feel free to disagree with

any part of the basic premise of this question and then develop the essay from there.

2. Issues in International Conflict

Louis Kriesberg *Spring 1988*

Program on the Analysis and Resolution of Conflicts,
Syracuse University, Syracuse, NY 13244

We will examine the concepts and theories needed for analyzing international conflicts: their bases, emergence, and particularly their de-escalation and termination. We will review the nature of the contemporary world system. Special attention will be given to the conflicts between the U.S. and Soviet governments, and among the governments and peoples of the Middle East. We will examine ways of managing world conflicts, considering non-coercive ways of waging struggles and methods of negotiation and mediation.

The course will focus on strategies of peacemaking. Among other cases, we will use the rise and fall of detente between the U.S. and Soviet governments and peace negotiations between the Egyptian and Israeli governments as examples.

Texts

Khouri, Fred J. *The Arab-Israeli Dilemma*, 3rd ed. Syracuse: Syracuse University Press, 1985.

Nogee, Joseph L., and Robert H. Donaldson. *Soviet Foreign Policy Since World War II*, 2nd ed. New York: Pergamon Press, 1984.

Weston, Burns, H., ed. *Toward Nuclear Disarmament and Global Security*. Boulder: Westview Press, 1984. Class handouts.

Recommended

Kriesberg, Louis. *Social Conflicts*, 2nd ed. Englewood Cliffs, NJ: Prentice-Hall, 1982.

Touval, Saadia. *Peace Brokers*. Princeton University Press, 1982.

George, Alexander L. *Managing U.S.-Soviet Rivalry*. Boulder: Westview Press, 1983.

Congressional Quarterly (CQ). *Middle East*, 5th ed., 1981.

Near East Report. *Myths and Facts*, 1985.

COURSE OUTLINE

I. Issues

Course Overview

World Actors
- Weston, selections 10, 26.

Peacemaking Ideas
- Weston, selections 22, 23, 25.
- Kriesberg, chs. 1, 6, 7.

War and Peace
- Weston, selections 2, 3, 8, Appendix A.

II. U.S.-Soviet Cases

Bases: 1945-1953
- Nogee & Donaldson, chs. 2, 4.
- Weston, selections 17, 18.

Pre-detente Efforts: 1953-1969
- Nogee & Donaldson, ch. 5.
- Kriesberg, "Noncoercive Inducements in U.S.-Soviet Conflict," *JPMS* (Spring 1981).

Rise of Detente: 1969-1972
- Nogee & Donaldson, ch. 6.

Conduct of Detente: 1972-1979
- Weston, selections 4, 6.
- George, chs. 2, 5.

Decline of Detente: 1975-1981
- Nogee & Donaldson, chs. 3, 7.
- Weston, Appendix B.
- George, chs. 9, 13.
- Kriesberg et. al., "Elites and Increased Support," *JPMS* (Fall 1982).

Current Reaction: 1981-1988
- Nogee & Donaldson, ch. 9.
- Weston, selection 21.
- Kriesberg and Quader, "Changing Public Views of Russia in the '70s."

III. Israeli-Arab Cases

Bases
- Khouri, chs. 1–4, Appendix A, #6.
- CQ, pp. 9–18.

Early Peace Efforts
- Khouri, chs. 7, 8, Appendix A, #7.
- CQ, pp. 22–29.

Additional Efforts Pre-1974
- Khouri, ch. 9, Appendix A, #16.
- Kriesberg, "Interlocking Conflicts."

1974–1976
- Khouri, ch. 10.

Sadat, Begin, Carter
- Khouri, ch. 11.

Post-Camp David
- Khouri, ch. 13.
- CQ, pp. 31–46.

IV. General Questions

Why Are Initiatives Made?
- Weston, selection 5 (variations, explanations).
- Weston, selections 19, 20 (background).

Why and When Do Negotiations Follow?
- Weston, selections 26, 27 (variations, explanation).
- Weston, selections 23, 24, 30 (inducements).

How Come Agree?
- Weston, selections 22, 25 (variations).
- Weston, selection 32 (negotiation).
- Weston, selection 25 (strategies).

How Come Endure?
- Weston, selections 14, 16; Kriesberg, "Consequences of Efforts at Deescalating American Soviet Conflict" (agreement).
- Weston, selections 6, 12 (context).

V. New Ideas, Policy

Reform
- Weston, selections 36, 37, 40.

Transformation
   • Weston, selections 39, 41, 44, 45.

Review

ASSIGNMENTS

1. Descriptive Account of De-escalating Efforts

Select four cases of de-escalating moves, two from the U.S.-Soviet and two from the Arab-Israeli conflicts. For each case, provide a brief account of its course and refer to each of the following:

Parties. Who are the major protagonists? Do not list just countries; cite the government (party and persons), non-governmental actors, and transnational actors if relevant.

Issues in Dispute. What is the conflict about, according to the primary adversaries and according to you?

Initiating Efforts. What inducements were made and who made them; did they contribute to the negotiations? (Give dates.)

Agreement. Did the negotiations lead to an agreement or not? (Give dates.) What was the agreement?

Write 1–2 pages for each case; the total length should not be more than 8 pages (a page totals 250 words—typed, double-spaced). Use and give complete citations of readings and course material. This constitutes 20 percent of course grade.

2. Analysis of Recent De-escalating Efforts

Select two cases of efforts to de-escalate the U.S.-Soviet and/or the Arab-Israeli conflicts; select cases which have happened since January 1983. Briefly describe the specific conflict: identify parties and issues in dispute. Describe the initiating efforts to de-escalate the dispute. Who did what? Then analyze and explain why the eforts did or did not succeed in de-escalating the conflict. Explain what you mean by succeed. To what extent do you attribute the success or the failure of the efforts to the means by which they were conducted and/or background conditions (domestic circumstances, adversary relations or international context)? The paper should be 6–9 pages in length. Give full citations of all sources. This constitutes 25 percent of your course grade.

3. Your De-escalating Effort

Write a letter to a member of Congress or another U.S. government official or to a non-governmental organization leader. In your letter, urge the reader(s) to do something you think will de-escalate an aspect of the conflict you have selected. (Focus on a conflict in U.S.-Soviet or Israeli-Arab relations.) Hand in your letter and a stamped, addressed envelope. (I will mail the letter.) Write a commentary on your letter. The commentary, not the letter's position, will be graded. In your commentary give your reasons for choosing the policy suggestion you did—what information from the course supports your choice, what values are you seeking to maximize, and what information are you putting aside? Explain, too, your choice of recipient for your letter and the choice of arguments used in the letter. The commentary should be 3–5 pages in length; it counts for 10 percent of the final grade.

Other Assignments

There will also be three brief in-class quizzes. Each quiz will contribute 5 percent of the course grade. No make-ups. Final exam constitutes 25 percent of course grade. Class participation contributes 5 percent of course grade.

3. International Conflicts in the Modern World

Joseph S. Nye, Jr.   *Spring 1987*
Government Dept., Harvard University,
Cambridge, MA 02138

Requirements

Lectures will be given Tuesday and Thursday. Sections will meet once a week for two hours. Attendance at sections is mandatory. The questions for the take-home midterm will be distributed on March 19th. It will be due on March 26th. There will also be a regularly scheduled three-hour final examination. Sectioning will take place on Thursday, February 5th, at lecture.

Readings

The books listed below are recommended for purchase. Most of the other readings will be included in a Historical Study A-12 sourcebook available for purchase. The sourcebook contains many essential readings, including most of the readings for the final third of the course. In previous years, students have found it difficult to obtain reserve readings due to the size of this course. Purchasing the sourcebook will enable you to avoid this problem. Because of copyright restrictions, some readings could not be included in the sourcebook. These readings will be available on reserve in the library.

Waltz, Kenneth. *Man, the State, and War.*
Thucydides. *The Pelopponesian War.* Penguin Edition.
Craig, Gordon, and Alexander George. *Force and Statecraft.*
Gulick, Edward V. *Europe's Classical Balance of Power.*
Wright, Harrison, ed. *The New Imperialism.*
Joll, James. *Europe Since 1870.*
Tuchman, Barbara. *The Guns of August.*
Gaddis, John Lewis. *Russia, the Soviet Union, and the United States.*
Kennedy, Robert F. *Thirteen Days.*
Herring, George. *America's Longest War.*
Nye, Joseph. *Nuclear Ethics.*

COURSE SCHEDULE

I. The Enduring Logic of Conflict

Feb. 5—Introduction
- Waltz, chs. 2, 4, 6 (pp. 16–41, 80–123, 159–186).
- Hans J. Morganthau, *Politics Among Nations*, ch. 1.

Feb. 10—Ethics and International Conflict
Feb. 12—Origins of the Pelopponesian War
Case: The Pelopponesian War.
- Thucydides, pp. 35–164; 212–223; 400–408 (Book I; Book II, paragraphs 1–65; Book III, paragraphs 36–50; Book V, paragraphs 85–116).
- Donald Kagan, *The Outbreak of the Pelopponesian War*, pp. 1–5; 31–56; 345–356.

II. The Origins of 20th Century Conflict

Feb. 17—International Systems of War
Feb. 19—The Balance of Power: Theory and Practice
Case: Germany and the 19th Century Balance of Power.
- Craig and George, chs. 1–3 (pp. 3–47).
- Gulick, pp. 1–34; 184–218; 280–296.
- Rene Albrecht-Carrie, *A Diplomatic History of Europe*, pp. 121–141; 162–206.

Feb. 24—Imperialism
Feb. 26—Domestic Politics and Foreign Policy
Case: Late 19th Century Imperialism.
- Wright, pp. 44–59; 69–88; 114–20.
- Joll, ch. 4 (pp. 78–112).
- Michael Doyle, "Metropole, Periphery, and System: Empire on the Niger and the Nile," in Peter Evans et al., eds., *States Versus Markets*, pp. 118–151.

III. The World Wars

Mar. 3—Origins of World War I
Mar. 5—Question and Answer Session
Case: World War I.
- Tuchman, pp. 15–157.
- Joll, chs. 7 and 8 (pp. 169–238).
- Arno Mayer, "Domestic Causes of the First World War," in Leonard Krieger and Fritz Stern, eds., *The Responsibility of Power*, pp. 286–300.

Mar. 10—The Rise and Fall of Collective Security
Mar. 12—Origins of World War II
Case: World War II.
- Craig and George, chs. 4–7 (pp. 49–100).
- DePorte, *Europe Between the Superpowers*, ch. 3 (pp. 21–41).
- Sagan, "The Origins of the Pacific War," entire (pp. 1–40).
- Wolfers, *Discord and Collaboration*, pp. 253–273.

IV. International Conflicts Since 1945

Mar. 17—The Cold War Debate
Mar. 19—Superpower Relations Today
Case: Origins of the Cold War.
- Craig and George, chs. 8–10 (pp. 101–145).
- Thomas G. Paterson, ed., *The Origins of the Cold War*, pp. 207–260.
- Gaddis, chs. 6–8 (pp. 147–240).

Mar. 24—Nuclear Weapons
Case: The Cuban Missile Crisis and Deterrence. (Hand mid-terms in on Mar. 26).
- Kennedy, entire.
- Harvard Nuclear Study Group, *Living with Nuclear Weapons*, chs. 3–5 (pp. 47–114).
- "Essay: The Cuban Missile Crisis," *Time*, September 27, 1982, pp. 85–86.
- George F. Will, "The Lessons of the Cuban Missile Crisis," *Newsweek*, October 11, 1982, p. 120.
- Scott Sagan, "Cuban Missile Crisis's Nuclear Lesson," *Boston Globe*, October 30, 1982, p. 20.
- Craig and George, ch. 15 (pp. 205–219).
- Marc Trachtenberg, "The Influence of Nuclear Weapons in the Cuban Missile Crisis," *International Security*, Vol. 10, No. 1 (Summer 1985), pp. 137–163.

Apr. 7—The Role of International Organizations
Apr. 9—Wars in the Middle East
Case: The Arab-Israeli Conflict.
- Stanley Hoffmann, "International Organization and the International System," *International Organization,* Vol. 24, No. 3 (Summer 1970), pp. 389–413.
- Ann Florini and Nina Tannenwald, *On the Front: The United Nations' Role in Preventing and Containing Conflict,* pp. 10–37.
- Congressional Quarterly Inc. *The Middle East,* 6th ed., chs. 1–3 (pp. 1–66).

Apr. 14—Economic Interdependence and Conflict
Apr. 16—The Transnational Politics of Oil
Case: The 1973 Oil Crisis.
- Raymond Vernon, ed., *The Oil Crisis,* essays by Knorr, Vernon (2), Girvan, and Stobaugh (pp. 1–14; 39–57; 145–158; 179–201; 229–257).
- Robert O. Keohane and Joseph S. Nye, Jr., *Power and Interdependence,* chs. 1, 2 (pp. 3–36).
- Robert W. Tucker, "Oil: The Issue of American Intervention," *Commentary,* January 1975, pp. 21–31.
- Stanley Hoffmann, "Response to Tucker," *Commentary,* April 1975, pp. 4–5.

Apr. 21—The United States in Vietnam
Apr. 23—The Question of Intervention
Case: The Vietnam War.
- Herring, entire.
- Norman Podhoretz, *Why We Were in Vietnam,* ch. 5 (pp. 174–211).
- Irving Howe and Michael Walzer, "Were We Wrong About Vietnam?" *The New Republic,* August 18, 1979, pp. 15–18.

V. Nuclear Deterrence and the Future of International Conflict

Apr. 28—Aternatives to Current International Conflict
Apr. 30—Question and Answer Session
- Nye, entire.
- Jonathan Schell, *The Fate of the Earth,* pp. 181–231.
- Robert Gilpin, *War and Change in World Politics,* pp. 211–244.

4. International Peace and Violence

Brian L. Job

Spring 1986

Political Science Dept., University of Minnesota,
Minneapolis, MN 55455

This course will explore a selected set of issues concerning the causes and occurrences of international violence. By and large the focus of our investigations will be on the "great powers," especially the US in the post-WWII environment—i.e., on their involvement in wars, their attitude towards revolution and change, and their forceful intervention in the affairs of smaller, Third World states. Certain topics will not be considered, such as conflict resolution, peaceful settlement, bargaining, nuclear war, and defense policy. Some of these are covered in other courses. Emphasis in this class will be placed upon thought and debate on issues rather than providing any "right" or final answers. In general terms the course will be divided into major topical sections for which there will be lectures on a number of topics and a major assigned reading, usually a case study of the type of violence under consideration.

The following topics will be considered, roughly in the order listed:

1. International violence: definitions, past and present incidences, cycles and trends.
2. The changing relationship between war, fighting, and society during modern history.
3. Major theories concerning the causes of wars among great powers— WWI as a case study.
4. Conflicts arising from great power intervention, especially the intervention of the US in Vietnam and Central America; justifications, strategies, and legacies.
5. Terrorism as a form of political violence; the response to terrorism by a liberal society.
6. The continuing relevance of certain moral and ethical questions concerning the justness of war and justice in war.

The course will proceed on the assumption that students have a background in political science and international relations.

There will be three graded assignments for the class: a midquarter exam, a final exam, and a 10–15 page paper. These will account for 20%, 40%, and 40% of the course grade, respectively. The final exam will be a take-home exam, with a strict page limit on length of answers. Topics and strategies concerning the assigned paper will be discussed in class.

Readings

The syllabus is organized around major subjects for which required readings are assigned. Recommended readings are not required of undergraduate students. The following paperback texts will be read for this course in the order listed.

Howard, Michael. *War in European History.*
Joll, James. *The Origins of the First World War.*
Herring, George. *America's Longest War.*
LaFebaer, Walter. *Inevitable Revolution.*
Wilkinson, Paul. *Terrorism and the Liberal State.*
Johnston, James. *Can Modern War Be Just?*

SCHEDULE OF TOPICS
AND READINGS

Mar 30—Introduction

Apr. 1–3—International Violence: Preliminary Considerations

Some issues of definition. The incidence of international violence since WWI, in the present international system. Trends or cycles in war.
- "War"—two article handouts, one from the Great Soviet Encyclopedia, one from the Encyclopedia of the Social Sciences.
- "A World at War."

Recommended reading
- P. Merkl, "Approaches to the Study of Political Violence."
- E. Cohen, "Distant Battles: Modern War in the Third World."
- M. Small and J.D. Singer, "Conflict in the International System, 1816–1977."
- J. Levy, *War in the Modern Great Power System.*
- J. Goldstein, "Kondratieff Cycles as War Cycles."
- W. Thompson, "Phases of the Business Cycle and the Outbreak of War."

Apr. 6–10—War, Technology, and Society: A Brief Historical Treatment

War and the Western European World. Technology and its impact on war and war making. War making and state making.
- Michael Howard, *War in European History.*
- Charles Tilly, "War and State Making as Organized Crime."

Recommended reading

Scholarship on war is currently undergoing a dramatic resurgence in all its aspects—history of war, conventional war fighting, nuclear strategy, etc. Concerning the books mentioned below: Keegan and McNeil are classics. Holmes is a recent book written from a psychologist's perspective. Paret is an update of a classic volume on military strategy that contains excellent long essays and a good bibliographic guide.

- J. Keegan, *The Face of Battle.*
- W. McNeil, *The Pursuit of Power.*
- R. Holmes, *Acts of War.*
- P. Paret, ed., *Makers of Modern Strategy.*

Apr. 13-22—War Among the Great Powers: Contending Explanations for World War I

Systemic explanations: alliances and the balance of power—the "realist" view; economics and imperialism—the liberal view and the Marxist-Leninist argument. Nation-state level explanations: cult of the offensive, and arms races and wars. Individual level/decision making explanations: crisis diplomacy, decision making under stress. (The readings below were chosen to illustrate particular approaches and arguments. Both Joll's book and Paret's edited volume contain excellent bibliographic guides to the historical literature on World War I.)

- James Joll, *The Origins of the First World War.*
- P. Kennedy, "The Fist World War and the International Power System."
- R. Lebow, "Decision Making in Crises."
- S. van Evera, "The Cult of the Offensive and the Origins of the First World War."
- M. Howard, "Strategic Aspects of the Anglo-German Naval Race" and "Arms Races and the Causes of War, 1850–1945."
- M. Kahler, "Rumors of War: The 1914 Analogy."

Recommended reading

- K. Nelson and S. Olin, *Why War? Ideology, Theory, and History*, pp. 1–132.
- B. Tuchman, *Guns of August*, pp. 1–157.
- O. Holsti, "Crisis, Stress, and Decisionmaking."
- J. Levy, "Misperception and the Causes of War."
- G. Craig, "Men Against Fire: The Doctrine of the Offensive in 1914," in P. Paret, ed., *Makers of Modern Strategy.*
- S. Sagan, "1914 Revisited: Allies, Offense, and Instability."
- "The Economic Foundations of War"—Introduction, A Soviet View, and a Liberal View (D. Landes).
- R. Owen and B. Sutcliffe, *Studies in the Theory of Imperialism*, pp. 15–60, 312–330.
- N. Choucri and R. North, "Dynamics of International Conflict."

- W. Thompson and C. Chase-Dunn, "An Exchange on the Interstate System and the Capitalist World Economy."

Apr. 24–May 4—Great Power Intervention, Part I: Vietnam

Social revolution: theories of social revolution, and the US as a status quo power. Guerrilla warfare and its role in revolutionary war fighting. The US intervenes in Vietnam: contending explanations. US military strategy in Vietnam: the failure of counter-insurgency. The US loses a war: the legacy of Vietnam. (Midquarter examination May 6.)

- T. Skocpol, "The Structural Approach to Revolutions."
- G. Chaliand, "National and Social Revolutions: The Case of North Vietnam."
- G. Herring, *America's Longest War.*
- L. Gelb and R. Betts, "Vietnam: The System Worked."
- G. Kolko, "America and Vietnam."

Recommended reading

A great deal has been written about wars of revolution and independence, especially regarding the experiences of Russia, China, and Cuba. The items noted below provide a sampling of these materials and tend to emphasize comparative and theoretical perspectives.

- J. Goldstone, ed., *Revolutions: Theoretical, Comparative and Historical Studies.*
- W. Laquer, *Guerrilla.*
- W. Laquer, *The Guerrilla Reader.*
- G. Chaliand, *Revolution in the Third World.*
- G. Chaliand, *Guerrilla Strategies.*

There is a huge and growing bibliography concerning the Vietnam war. Herring presents an excellent and even-handed guide at the end of his book.

- S. Karnow, *Vietnam: A History.*
- G. Kolko, *Anatomy of a War.*
- G. Herring, "American Strategy in Vietnam: The Postwar Debate."
- O. Holsti and J. Rosenau, "Consensus Lost. Consensus Regained? Foreign Policy Beliefs of American Leaders."

May 8–13—Intervention, Part II: The US in Central America

Central America: a history of US "management." The US and Nicaragua. US intervention: contemporary strategies and attitudes.

- E. LaFeber, *Inevitable Revolutions.*
- P. Waldmann, "Guerrilla Movements in Argentina, Guatemala, Nicaragua, and Uruguay."
- T. Walker, "The Nicaraguan Revolution."

Recommended reading

There is a lot (and in terms of volume and of lack of careful theorizing, perhaps even too much) being written today on this subject. The

items placed in the recommended list below were specifically chosen
to represent conservative and Reagan administration points of view.
- G. Fauriol, *Latin American Insurgencies.*
- US Dept of State, "President Reagan: US Interests in Central America,"
Current Policy, May 9, 1984.
- Report of the National Bipartisan Commission on Central America,
January 1984.

May 15–22—Terrorism

Terrorism as a form of political violence. The rationale of the adoption of
terrorist tactics. The response to terrorism.
- P. Wilkinson, *Terrorism and the Liberal State.*
- P. Merkl, "Collective Purposes and Individual Motives."

Recommended reading

In addition to the articles and bibliographic references in the books
edited by Merkl and Stohl, you might wish to look at P. Merkl, *The
Making of a Storm Trooper.*
- P. Merkl, *Political Violence and Terror.*
- D. Rapoport, "Fear and Trembling: Terrorism in Three Religious
Traditions."
- M. Stohl, ed., *The Politics of Terror.*
- R. Rubenstein, *Alchemists of Revolution.*
- F. Ford, *Political Murder.*
- W. Laquer, *The Terrorism Reader.*
- W. Laquer, *Terror.*

Much is written, on the basis of little evidence or thought, concerning
terrorism. A lot of this material follows the "your terrorist is my
freedom fighter" line of argument. One aspect of contemporary terrorism that we will not have time to explore is the employment of
terror by the state against its own people. This deeply troubling subject
has been eloquently treated by novelists and writers, often on the
basis of their own experience. Two examples of this genre, both
concerning Argentina, are A. Partnoy, *The Little School,* and J. Timmerman, *Prisoner Without a Name, Cell Without a Number.*

May 27–June 3—Moral and Ethical Issues Concerning International Violence

Jus ad bellum and *jus in bellum.* The troubling questions of guerrilla warfare
and terrorism. Individual responsibility.
- J. Johnston, *Can Modern War Be Just?* Read Intro. and chs. 1, 2, 7, 8,
and browse remainder.
- C. Krauthammer, "Moral Guide to Guerrilla War."

Recommended reading

Questions of "nuclear ethics" are beginning to receive some of the
attention they deserve. The Catholic Bishops' statement generated

much attention. Also worth a look are Joseph Nye, *Nuclear Ethics,* *"The Pastoral Letter of the US Bishops on Peace and War,"* and Susan Okin, *"Taking the Bishops Seriously," Journal of World Politics.*
- M. Walzer, *Just and Unjust Wars.*
- J. Johnston, *Just War Tradition and the Restraint of War.*

June 5—Conclusion
Take-home final examination: deadline May 12.

5. Third World Arms Race

Jean Stern   *Spring 1986*
Peace Studies Program, Siena College,
Loudonville, NY 12211

There has been much publicity surrounding the arms race between the two superpowers and its consequences for the United States and the Soviet Union as well as the rest of the world. Often overlooked is the growing arms race in the Third World. Since the early 1960s purchases of weapons by Third World governments have increased five-fold and account for nearly one-quarter of the world's military expenditures. This course will examine the internal and external causes of the arms race, assess the effects of the arms race and look at attempts to halt or contain the arms race.

Readings
Most of the assignments are found in the three required texts:

Klare, Michael T. *American Arms Supermarket.* University of Texas Press, 1984.
Spector, Leonard S. *The New Nuclear Nations.* Vintage, 1985.
Sivard, Ruth Leger. *World Military and Social Expenditures,* Washington, D.C.: World Priorities, Inc., latest annual edition.

Grades
The final grade is a result of the following: three class tests—45%; one 5–10 page paper—20%; class participation—10%; final examination—25%. The class test dates are included in the class schedule. The 5–10 page paper is a research paper which deals in greater depth with the arms acquisition policy and its consequences for one of the country case studies from class or for another country approved by the instructor.

CLASS SCHEDULE
AND READING ASSIGNMENTS

I. Introduction

Jan. 15—Overview

Jan. 17—History of Arms Races

II. Conventional Arms Transfers

Jan. 20—The Demand Side: Role of the Military in the Third World
- Claude E. Welch, Jr., "Civil-Military Relations: Perspectives from the Third World," *Armed Forces and Society*, Winter 1985, pp. 193–198.

Jan. 22—The Supply Side
Who and Why: the Primal Motives
- Klare, ch. 1, pp. 1–25, skim; ch. 2, pp. 26–38; ch. 10, pp. 204–233.

Jan. 24—Foreign Policy Link
- Klare, ch. 3, pp. 39–53; ch. 10, pp. 204–233.

Jan. 27—The Bureaucratic Link (U.S.)
- Klare, ch. 4, pp. 54–76.

Case Studies
Jan. 29—Latin America: Patterns
- Klare, ch. 5, pp. 77–107.

Jan. 31—Iran: Surrogate
- Klare, ch. 6, pp. 108–126.

Feb. 3 & 5—The Middle East: Saudi Arabia and Egypt-Israel
- Klare, ch. 7, pp. 127–162.

Proliferation
Feb. 7—Third World Suppliers
- "China's Arms Bazaar," *World Press Review*, May 1985, pp. 48–50.
- Brazil's Arms Export Bonanza," *World Press Review*, January 1986, pp. 48–50.

Feb. 10—Technology Transfer
- Klare, ch. 8, pp. 163–182.

Feb. 12—Test One

III. Nuclear Arms Transfer

Feb. 19—Development and Spread of Atomic Weapons and Technology
- Victor Gilinsky, "Nuclear Reactors and Nuclear Bombs," Washington, D.C.: Nuclear Regulatory Commission, 1980.

Feb. 21—Third World Demand
- K. Subrahmanyam, "Regional Conflicts and Nuclear Fears," *Bulletin of the Atomic Scientists* (May 1984), pp. 16–19.

Case Studies
Feb. 24—India/Pakistan
- Spector, ch. III, pp. 83–132.

Feb. 26 & 28—Middle East: Israel/Libya/Iraq
- Spector, ch. IV, pp. 133–176.

Mar. 3—Argentina/Brazil
- Spector, ch. V, pp. 177–212.

Mar. 12—South Africa
- Spector, ch. VI, pp. 213–230.

Mar. 14—Implications for the First and Second Worlds
- Lewis A. Dunn, "What Difference Will It Make?" in *Controlling the Bomb: Nuclear Proliferation in the 1980s*. New Haven: Yale University Press, 1982, pp. 69–94.

Mar. 17—Test Two

III. Attempts to Control Arms Races

Mar. 19—On the Elimination of War
- Gwynne Dyer, "Goodbye War," videotape.

Mar. 21—New Guidelines for Export Policies
Conventional Weapons
- Klare, ch. 11, pp. 234–250.

Mar. 24—Nuclear Weapons
- Spector, Appendix F, "Nuclear Supplier Organizations," pp. 340–346.

Mar. 26 & Apr. 7—Non-Proliferation Treaty
- Spector, Appendices D (Non-Proliferation Treaty) and E (International Atomic Energy Agency), ch. VII, pp. 231–252.
- Charles N. Van Doren, "Outlook Brightens for NPT Regime," *Arms Control Today*, October 1985, pp. 8–10.

Nuclear Free Zones

Latin America

- Spector, Appendix E, Treaty of Tlatelolco.
- Alfonso Garcia Robles, *The Latin American Nuclear-Weapon-Free Zone,* Occasional Paper 19, the Stanley Foundation, Muscatine, Iowa, May 1979.

Apr. 11—South Pacific

- David Lange, "New Zealand's Security Policy," *Foreign Affairs,* Summer 1985, pp. 1009–1019.

Apr. 14 & 16—Peace Movements

- Chris Smith, "Disarmament, Peace Movements and the Third World," *Third World Quarterly,* October 1984, pp. 892–910.
- Phil Esmonde, "Letter from Hawaii," *Peace Magazine,* February 1986.
- Anita Kronberg, "The Beginning of a Peace Movement in South Africa," *Disarmament Campaigns,* September/October 1985, p. 11.
- Kofi Ansong Owusu, "A Letter from Africa," *Disarmament Campaigns,* September/October 1985, p. 12.
- Augusto Varas interview, "Linking Peace and Democracy in Latin America," *Disarmament Campaigns,* November 1985, pp. 11–12.
- Sandra Ball, "Side-by-Side: Israel and Palestine," *Disarmament Campaigns,* September/October 1985, p. 16.

April 18—Test Three

IV. Domestic Effects of Arms Race and Arms Trade

Apr. 21 & 23—Human Rights

- Klare, ch. 9, pp. 183–203.

Apr. 25 & 28—Economic Development

- Sivard, entire.

Apr. 30—Summation

6. World War III

W. Warren Wager   *Spring 1986*
History Dept., State University of New York–Binghamton,
Binghamton, NY 13901

The objectives of this course are (1) to understand the function of warfare in human nature and history from earliest times to the present day; (2) to determine the likeliest causes and consequences of a third world war in the age of superpowers and superweapons; and (3) to survey the range of remedies against world war, the obstacles to their success, and the prospects for a peaceful world order.

Reading
Seven paperbound books are required for purchase. Melvin Small and J. David Singer, eds., *International War* (Dorsey Press, 1985), contains articles on military history and related topics that provide us with an introduction to the study of warfare. A second anthology, *The Nuclear Reader: Strategy, Weapons, War* (St. Martin's Press, 1985), edited by Charles W. Kegley, Jr., and Eugene R. Wittkopf, presents articles on the prospects for nuclear world war and arms control. The British science journalist Nigel Calder, in *Nuclear Nightmares: An Investigation into Possible Wars* (Penguin, 1980), sketches four scenarios of a future world war. William M. Arkin and Richard W. Fieldhouse inventory the world's nuclear arsenals in *Nuclear Battlefields* (Ballinger, 1985). Finally, we will read three novels about life during and after World War III: George Orwell, *Nineteen Eight-Four* (Signet, 1949); Pat Frank, *Alas, Babylon* (Bantam, 1959); and Whitley Strieber and James Kunetka, *Warday* (Warner, 1984).

Written Work
Midterm examination, and choice of (1) final examination, covering Topics 8–25; and (2) research paper on any topic germane to the themes of the course, of 20–25 average typewritten pages in length (6,000 to 7,500 words). Your topic must be cleared in advance with your discussion section leader and also with Mr. Wager.

Films
Five film programs are scheduled for selected Wednesday evenings. Attendance is optional, but highly recommended.

The Decision to Drop the Bomb. N.B.C. documentary, produced by Fred Freed (1965, 82 minutes).

Hiroshima/Nagasaki—August 1945. Documentary, directed by Akira Iwasaki (1970, 17 minutes).

Fail Safe. Directed by Sidney Lumet, with Henry Fonda, Walter Matthau, and Fritz Weaver, from the novel by Eugene Burdick and Harvey Wheeler (1964, 111 minutes).

Nuclear Nightmares. Screenplay by Nigel Calder, with Peter Ustinov (1980, 90 minutes).

Testament. Directed by Lynne Littman, with Jane Alexander and William Devane, from a short story by Carol Amen (1983, 90 minutes).

Red Dawn. Directed by John Milius, with C. Thomas Howell and Patrick Swayze (1984, 114 minutes).

Evaluation

35% of your grade will be based on the midterm examination, 15% on your participation in the discussion sections, and 50% on the final examination or research paper, whichever you select.

TOPICS

Introduction

Doomsday Plus One: Is There Life After Mega-Death?

Part I. The History and Causes of War

Six Thousand Years of Bloody Hell: An Overview

- Melvin Small and J. David Singer, eds., *International War*, chs. I–II, pp. 1–36 (Small & Singer, Levy, and Gochman & Moas).

Why Do We Do It? The Psychology and Social Science of Warfare

- Small and Singer, ch. III, pp. 47–55 (Gray) and 86–94 (Faris); ch. IV, pp. 95–114 (McKenna), 123–127 (Walzer), and 135–140 (Small); and ch. V, pp. 141–178 (Schellenberg, Freud, Soviet View, and Dougherty & Pfaltzgraff).

The Second Hundred Years War: From Louis XIV to Napoleon

- Small and Singer, ch. VI, pp. 182–195 (Deutsch & Singer).

The First World War: From World Peace to World Conflict

- Small and Singer, ch. VI, pp. 196–206 (Wallace) and 230–262 (White and Farrar).

The Second World War: Four Wars in One

Wars and Rumours of Wars: Visions of Armageddon in Literature
• Pat Frank, *Alas, Babylon.*

Part II: Third World Wars

The Third World Wars That Weren't: The Balance of Terror, 1945–1985
• Nigel Calder, *Nuclear Nightmares,* Author's Note and ch. 1.
• Small and Singer, ch. VI, pp. 207–229 (Leng) and 263–274 (Holsti et al.).

The Superpowers and Nuclear War: Strategic Thinking
• Calder, chs. 2 and 5.
• William M. Arkin and Richard W. Fieldhouse, *Nuclear Battlefields,* Introduction and ch. 5.
• Charles W. Kegley, Jr., and Eugene R. Wittkopf, eds., *The Nuclear Reader,* Introduction to Part I, pp. 9–20, and chs. 1–2, 6–7, 10, and 21–22 (Draper, Keny & Panofsky, Jervis, Dyson, Harvard Nuclear Study Group, Ball, and Schneider).

The Superpowers and Nuclear War: Wild Cards
• Calder, ch. 4.
• Arkin and Fieldhouse, chs. 1–4. Also scan Appendices A and B.

The Superbabies: Nuclear Proliferation
• Calder, ch. 3.
• Arkin and Fieldhouse. Review material on British, French, and Chinese nuclear arsenals scattered through ch. 3. Also scan Appendices C, D, and E.
• Kegley and Wittkopf, ch. 16 (Nye).

Flash Points: Europe
• Arkin and Fieldhouse, ch. 6.
• Kegley and Wittkopf, ch. 8 (Gallois & Train).

Flash Points: Asia, Africa, Latin America
• Arkin and Fieldhouse, chs. 7–8.

Bombs Away! The First Hours of World War Three
• Kegley and Wittkopf, Introduction to Part III, pp. 233–241, and chs. 19–20 (Harvard Nuclear Study Group and Schell).

Aftermaths: Who and What Will Be Left?
• Kegley and Wittkopf, chs. 23–24 (Weinstein and Sagan).
• Whitley Strieber and James Kunetka, *Warday.*

Non-Nuclear Nightmares: The Future of "Conventional" War
• Kegley and Wittkopf, chs. 13–14 (McNamara and Klare).

Space War: Warfare in the Next Century

Part III: The Alternatives

Peace Through Strength: Deterrence Reconsidered
- Kegley and Wittkopf, chs. 3–5, 9, and 17–18 (Catholic Bishops, Wohlstetter, Kattenburg, Ravenal, Payne & Gray, and Union of Concerned Scientists).
- Small and Singer, ch. IV, pp. 115–122 (Schneider).

Come Now, and Let Us Reason Together: The Diplomacy of Disarmament
- Calder, Postscript: "Looking for the Exit."
- Arkin and Fieldhouse, ch. 9.
- Kegley and Wittkopf, Introduction to Part II, pp. 111–120, and chs. 11–12 and 15 (Miller, Lewis, and Frye).

Barriers to Peace: The State System

Barriers to Peace: The World-Economy

When War Is Peace: The Managerial Solution
- George Orwell, *Nineteen Eighty-Four.*

Transforming the System: Values and World Order

Transforming the System: Rival Images of the Future
- Small and Singer, ch. VII, pp. 322–331 (Hudson).

Waging Peace: The Transition to Cosmopolis
- Small and Singer, ch. VII, pp. 291–304 (Sharp).

VI

The Nuclear Age

1. America in the Nuclear Age*

Martin Sherwin   *Fall 1987*
History Dept., Tufts University, Medford, MA 02155

This course examines the history of the nuclear arms race in the context of the politics, culture and diplomacy of the cold war. It is an interdisciplinary course that searches the insights of the humanities in order to understand better the influence of science and social sciences on the central problem of the present—the danger of nuclear war. Designed on the premise that current attitudes and assumptions about nuclear weapons and national security are imbedded in the American historical experience, the course analyzes the debates over these issues with careful attention to their origins and evolution. The "texts" for the course include works of history, social science, and literature, as well as films and contemporary documents.

Class meetings include two weekly lectures, a weekly section meeting, and a movie on Thursday evenings. You must be able to attend a section to take this course.

Requirements

In addition to attending two lectures and a discussion section per week, and keeping up with the assigned readings and movies, students will be responsible for two in-class midterm exams, one in-class final exam, and a take-home final essay.

---

*Martin Sherwin also teaches "The United States, the Soviet Union and the Nuclear Arms Race in Historical Perspective" (History 192A), which shares three class sessions per term via satellite link-up with a similar course at Moscow State University.

Assigned Readings
Carr, E.H. *What Is History?*
Clarefield and Wiecek. *Nuclear America.*
Doctorow, E.L. *The Book of Daniel.*
Hersey, John. *Hiroshima.*
Kaplan, Fred. *The Wizards of Armageddon.*
Kipphardt, Heinar. *In the Matter of J. Robert Oppenheimer.*
LaFeber, Walter. *America, Russia and the Cold War.*
Sherwin, Martin. *A World Destroyed.*
Vonnegut, Kurt. *Slaughterhouse Five,* or *Cat's Cradle.*
Williams and Cantelon. *The American Atom.*

SCHEDULE FOR LECTURES, READINGS, AND FILMS

Introduction and Film: *The Men Who Made the Bomb.*

The Origins of the Nuclear Arms Race
Film: *The World at War,* #24 (Hiroshima).
  • Sherwin, *A World Destroyed* (complete).

Hiroshima and America
Film: *Kistiakowsky.*
  • Kaplan, *Wizards of Armageddon,* chapters 1, 2.
  • Williams & Cantelon, *American Atom,* documents 1–22.
  • Clarefield & Wiecek, *Nuclear America,* chapters 1–4.

Hiroshima and History
Film: *The Day After Trinity.*
  • Carr, *What Is History?* chapters I, II, IV.
  • LaFeber, *America, Russia and the Cold War,* Introduction through ch. 3.
  • Hersey, *Hiroshima* (complete).

Bugs Trapped in Amber
Film: *Atomic Cafe.*
  • Vonnegut, *Slaughterhouse Five* or *Cat's Cradle.*

Cuban Missile Crisis, I
We will study the Cuban Missile Crisis (October 16–28, 1962) out of chronological order to take advantage of the publications and events surrounding the commemoration of the 25th anniversary of the event.
Film: Contemporary footage on Cuban Missile Crisis, I.
  • *America, Russia & Cold War,* pp. 224–235.
  • Kennedy, *Thirteen Days.*

Cuban Missile Crisis, II: Resolution & Aftermath

Film: Contemporary footage on Cuban Missile Crisis, II.
- *American Atom,* documents 44, 53–59.
- *Nuclear America,* pp. 262–272.

Science, Politics & Morality: The H-Bomb

Film: Foundations of Nuclear Strategy.
- *Nuclear America,* chapter 5.
- *American Atom,* documents 26–32.
- *America, Russia & Cold War,* chapter 4.
- *Wizards of Armageddon,* chapters 3–5.

Evolution of Nuclear Strategy

Film: Fail Safe.
- *America, Russia & Cold War,* chapters 5–8.
- *Wizards of Armageddon,* chapters 6–10.
- *Nuclear America,* chapters 6, 7, 8, 9.
- *American Atom,* documents 38–52.

The Rosenberg Case: McCarthyism & the Atom

Film: Seeing Reds.
- Doctorow, *Book of Daniel* (complete).

The Oppenheimer Case: Politics & Strategy

Film: On the Beach.
- Kipphardt, *In the Matter of J. Robert Oppenheimer.*
- *American Atom,* documents 33–37.

The Politics of Nuclear Culture

Film: Are We Winning, Mommy?
- *Wizards of Armageddon,* chapters 11–21.
- *Nuclear America,* chapter 12.

Nuclear Issues of the 1970s

Film: Dr. Strangelove.
- *American Atom,* documents 60–65, 72–73.
- *Wizards of Armageddon,* chapters 22–26.
- *Nuclear America,* chapters 9–11.
- *America, Russia & Cold War,* chapters 11, 12.

Nuclear Issues of the 1980s

- *American Atom,* documents 66–77, chapter X.
- *Nuclear America,* 13, epilogue.

2. The Nuclear Age

Allan Krass   *Spring 1987*
School of Natural Science, Hampshire College,
Amherst, MA 01002

This course is about nuclear weapons, their creation, their evolution and their future. There are presently about 50,000 nuclear weapons deployed over the face of the earth by at least 7 countries, and it is understood by everyone that the use of even a small fraction of these weapons would destroy most of what civilization has built for the past two hundred years and possibly create long-term or permanent changes in the earth's climate and ability to support life.

Where did these weapons come from? Why are they there? Why are even more of them being invented, produced and deployed all the time? Nuclear weapons are a technology, which the dictionary defines as "a method or process for handling a specific technical problem." What specific technical problems are being handled by 50,000 nuclear weapons? In short, what are nuclear weapons useful for? This is the question you will try to answer for yourself at the end of the course.

The plan of the course is to look first at the scientists who created the bombs that were dropped on Hiroshima and Nagasaki in August of 1945. Then we will look at the atomic bombings themselves and at their impact on the two destroyed cities and on American culture and politics. We follow this with a study of the political, strategic and technological developments which have created our era of "atomic diplomacy." Finally, we look for the roots of the nuclear dilemma in human psychology, scientific progress, and the behavior of nation states.

Readings

The following books will be required reading for the course. Our class discussions will rely heavily on the material in the readings, and you should come to class prepared to discuss what you've read.

Williams, R.C., and P.L. Cantelon, eds. *The American Atom: A Documentary History of Nuclear Policies from the Discovery of Fission to the Present, 1939–1984.* Philadelphia: University of Pennsylvania Press, 1984. (Designated "W&C" on reading assignments.)

Wyden, Peter. *Day One: Before Hiroshima and After.* New York: Simon & Schuster, 1984.

Boyer, Paul. *By the Bomb's Early Light: American Thought and Culture at the Dawn of the Atomic Age.* New York: Pantheon, 1985.

Stein, Jonathan B. *From H-Bomb to Star Wars: The Politics of Strategic Decision Making.* Lexington, MA: Lexington Books, 1984.

Dahl, Robert. *Controlling Nuclear Weapons: Democracy Versus Guardianship.* Syracuse, NY: Syracuse University Press, 1985.

Miller, Walter M., Jr. *A Canticle for Liebowitz.* New York: Bantam, 1961.

Holloway, David. *The Soviet Union and the Arms Race.* New Haven, CT: Yale University Press, 1983.

Blacker, Coit D. *Reluctant Warriors: The United States, the Soviet Union, and Arms Control.* New York: W.H. Freeman, 1987.

Dunn, Lewis A. *Controlling the Bomb: Nuclear Proliferation in the 1980's.* New Haven, CT: Yale University Press, 1982.

Frank, Jerome D. *Sanity and Survival in the Nuclear Age.* New York: Random House, 1982.

Articles and Excerpts

In addition to these books we will read five articles and excerpts from two other books. All of these will be photocopied and distributed in class.

Green, Harold P. "The Oppenheimer Case: A Study in the Abuse of Law." *Bulletin of the Atomic Scientists* (Sept. 1977), pp. 12–16, 56–61.

Joravsky, David. "Sin and the Scientist." *New York Review of Books* (July 17, 1980), pp. 7–10.

FitzGerald, Mary C. "The Strategic Revolution Behind Soviet Arms Control." *Arms Control Today* (June 1987), pp. 16–19.

Cohn, Carol Cohn. "Slick'ems, Glick'ems, Christmas Trees, and Cookie Cutters: Nuclear Language and How We Learned to Pat the Bomb." *Bulletin of Atomic Scientists* (June 1987), pp. 17–24.

Kull, Steven. "Nuclear Nonsense." *Foreign Policy,* No. 58 (Spring 1985), pp. 28–52.

Bernstein, Barton J. *The Atomic Bomb: The Critical Issues.* Boston: Little, Brown and Company, 1976 (excerpts).

Rhodes, Richard. *The Making of the Atomic Bomb.* New York: Simon & Schuster, 1986 (pp. 651–678).

Written Assignments

There will be three writing assignments in addition to the preparation of an annotated bibliography. The papers should be relatively short (5–10 pages) and should draw as much as possible on the readings and class discussion.

An annotated bibliography is a collection of brief summaries (one or two paragraphs each) of the books you read this semester. The summaries should not give your opinion of the book, but should describe as simply and directly as possible what its basic points are and how they are supported.

The ability to summarize books, chapters, or articles in this way is a valuable skill, and many students compile an annotated bibliography as part of their Division II work. Be sure that you write the summaries as soon as you finish the book. Don't wait until the end of the semester and try to write them all at once. If you would like advice on how to write a summary, hand in a draft of an early one and I will make some suggestions on how to improve it.

Paper Topics

1. The use of nuclear weapons against Hiroshima and Nagasaki has been both condemned and justified on military, political and moral grounds. In this paper you should summarize the pros and cons of *each* of these grounds and then describe the current state of your own thinking about the bombings. The point of the paper is not for you to pass judgment on the actions of people more than 40 years ago but to ask yourself what lessons the experiences of Hiroshima and Nagasaki have, or should have, taught us.

2. How is the "nuclear age" different from previous "ages"? Have nuclear weapons created a qualitatively new world, or is it really the same old world with international conflict and war simply raised to higher levels of technical sophistication and destructive potential? Just as in the first paper, try to organize your thinking into military, political and moral categories.

3. What are nuclear weapons useful for? By this point in the course you should have both strong feelings about nuclear weapons and a considerable body of knowledge with which to articulate and defend them. Feel free to structure this paper in the way you feel is most appropriate, but do try to come to grips with the question of why the nuclear arms race continues in the face of such mortal danger to civilization.

SCHEDULE OF CLASSES AND ASSIGNMENTS

- Sept. 14: Wyden, Part 1; W&C, pp. 1–23.
- Sept. 16: Wyden, Part 2; W&C, pp. 24–40.
- Sept. 21: Wyden, Parts 3–5; W&C, pp. 40–70, Rhodes excerpt.
- Sept. 30: No assignment; first paper due.
- Oct. 5: Boyer, Parts 1–4; W&C, pp. 71–97, 213–218.
- Oct. 7: Boyer, Parts 5–6 (Film: *Atomic Cafe*).
- Oct. 12: Boyer, Parts 7–8, Epilog.
- Oct. 14: W&C, pp. 141–175; Green and Joravsky articles.
- Oct. 19: Stein (whole book); W&C, pp. 114–140.
- Oct. 21: Dahl (whole book); W&C, pp. 292–320.
- Oct. 26: Miller (whole book); W&C, pp. 282–291.
- Oct. 28: Exam day—No class; second paper due.
- Nov. 2: Holloway, chs. 1–4.
- Nov. 4: Holloway, chs. 5, 8, 9; FitzGerald article.

- Nov. 9: Blacker, chs. 1–4; W&C, pp. 176–209.
- Nov. 11: Blacker, chs. 5–7; W&C, pp. 210–213, 218–254.
- Nov. 16: Dunn, chs. 1–2; W&C, pp. 97–113.
- Nov. 18: Dunn, chs. 3–5, W&C, pp. 254–260.
- Nov. 23: Dunn, chs. 6–8.
- Nov. 25: Thanksgiving break—No class.
- Nov. 30: Frank, chs. 1–6; Cohn article.
- Dec. 2: Frank, chs. 7-9; Kull article.
- Dec. 7: Frank, chs. 10–13.
- Dec. 9: No assignment; overview and evaluation.
- Dec. 14: Third paper, annotated bibliography and self-evaluation due.

3. Culture and Nuclear War

Greg Urban   *Autumn 1985*

Department of Anthropology, University of Texas–Austin, Austin, TX 78712

This course introduces students to the basic concepts and techniques of cultural anthropology through their application to a pressing modern-world problem—the threat of global thermonuclear war. The course explores the problem of war and aggression within a perspective of the evolution of culture. It also deals with the "semiotics" of nuclear war—i.e., with an analysis of the cultural representations (novels, films, music) through which the possibility of nuclear war is apprehended. Finally, the course explores the nature of the modern world and possible solutions to the problem of nuclear war through an examination of "world culture."

Texts
The Harvard Nuclear Study Group. *Living with Nuclear Weapons.*
Schell, Jonathan. *The Fate of the Earth.*
Chant and Hogg. *Nuclear War in the 1980s.*
Frank, Pat. *Alas, Babylon.*
Miller, Walter M., Jr. *A Canticle for Leibowitz.*

Requirements
Grades will be based on three in-class exams, each of which will count for a third of the final grade. Exams will be administered during the fifth, eleventh, and fifteenth weeks of the course. Students who fail to show up

for a given exam, without prior arrangements, will be given an automatic failing grade for that exam.

Topics

Social Order
- Cultural Evolution and Nuclear War
- Nuclear Tools and Tool Use
- Aggression, Conflict, and Nuclear War
- Power and Nuclear Force
- Value Internalization, Collective Interest, and Nuclear War

Semiotic Order
- Nuclear Religion: Individual and Collective Death
- Nuclear Novels as Myth, I: *Alas, Babylon*
- Nuclear Novels as Myth, II: *A Canticle for Leibowitz*
- Nuclear Film as Myth, I: *Fail-Safe*
- Nuclear Film as Myth, II: *Dr. Strangelove*
- Nuclear Music and Art

Cultural Order
- Nation-State and World System
- Cultural Relativity and Deterrence Theory
- The Russians and Global Culture
- Planet Earth

WEEK-BY-WEEK OUTLINE

Cultural Evolution and Nuclear War
- Ernst Mayr, "Evolution," in *Scientifc American*, vol. 239, No. 3, 1978, pp. 47–55.
- Sherwood Washburn, "The Evolution of Man," in *Scientific American*, vol. 239, No. 3, 1978, pp. 194–207.
- Jonathan Schell, "A Republic of Insects and Grass," in *The Fate of the Earth*, Part I, pp. 3–96.

Nuclear Tools and Tool Use
- Kenneth P. Oakley, *Man the Tool-Maker*, pp. 1–4 and 125–139.
- The Harvard Nuclear Study Group, "Weapons and Rivalry: How Did We Get Here?" (ch. 4), "Nuclear Lessons: What We Have Learned" (ch. 5), and "Nuclear Arsenals: What Is in the Balance" (ch. 6), in *Living with Nuclear Weapons*.
- Chant and Hogg, *Nuclear War in the 1980s*, pp. 68–115.

Aggression, Conflict, and Nuclear War
Films: The Aggressive Impulse, and *The Axe Fight.*
- N. Tinbergen, "On War and Peace in Animals and Man," *Science,* vol. 160, pp. 1411–1418.
- Ashley Montagu, "Introduction" to *Learning Non-Agression,* pp. 3–11.
- N. Chagnon, "Yanomamo Warfare," in *Yanomamo,* pp. 170–177.
- The Harvard Nuclear Study Group, "The Shattered Crystal Ball: How Might a Nuclear War Begin?" (ch. 3), in *Living with Nuclear Weapons.*
- Chant and Hogg, *Nuclear War in the 1980s,* pp. 44–47.

Power and Nuclear Force
Film: No First Use: Preventing Nuclear War.
- R.N. Adams, "Power in Human Societies," in R.D. Fogelson and R.N. Adams, eds., *The Anthropology of Power,* pp. 388-389.
- The Harvard Nuclear Study Group, "Military Power and Political Purpose: What Do We Want from Nuclear Weapons?" (ch. 7), in *Living with Nuclear Weapons.*

Value Internalization, Collective Interest, and Nuclear War
- E. Durkheim, *Moral Education,* pp. 80–94.

Nuclear Religion: Individual and Collective Death
- C. Geertz, "Religion as Cultural System," in *The Interpretation of Culture,* pp. 87–125.
- Jonathan Schell, "Collective Death," in *The Fate of the Earth,* Part II, pp. 56–180.

Nuclear Novels as Myth, I
- B. Malinowski, "The Role of Myth in Life," in *Magic, Science, and Religion,* pp. 96–111.
- Office of Technology Assessment, "A Nuclear Weapon over Detroit or Leningrad: A Tutorial on the Effects of Nuclear Weapons" (ch. 2), pp. 15–46, and "Case 4: A Large Soviet Attack on U.S. Military and Economic Targets," pp. 94–100, in *The Effects of Nuclear War.*
- Pat Frank, *Alas, Babylon.*

Nuclear Novels as Myth, II
- Sidney R. Drell, "The Scientist's Dilemma," in *Facing the Threat of Nuclear Weapons,* pp. 58–67.
- Walter M. Miller, Jr., *A Canticle for Leibowitz.*

Nuclear Film as Myth, I
Film: Fail-Safe.
- G. Urban, "Cultural Representations of Nuclear War."

Nuclear Film as Myth, II

Film: Dr. Strangelove.
- H. Kahn, *On Thermonuclear War*, pp. 144–161.
- Bob Greene, "Rash of Patriotism Afflicts Young Chicago Girl."

Nuclear Music and Art
- *Music:* "Talking World War III Blues" (Dylan); "99 Red Balloons" (Nena)

The Nation-State and World System

Film: Nuclear Strategy for Beginners.
- Robert Wotto, "The State-Centered Approach," in R. Wotto, *To End War*, pp. 7–21.
- Immanuel Wallerstein, *The Modern World System*, pp. 228–239.
- The Harvard Nuclear Study Group, "Arms Control and Disarmament: What Can and Can't Be Done"" (ch. 9), and "Nuclear Proliferation: Can the Spread of Nuclear Weapons Be Controlled?" (ch. 10), in *Living with Nuclear Weapons.*

Cultural Relativity and Deterrence Theory
- The Harvard Nuclear Study Group, "The Endless Balancing Act: What Is New about the Nuclear World?" (ch. 2), in *Living with Nuclear Weapons.*
- L. Wieseltier, "And So, Deterrence," in *Nuclear War, Nuclear Peace*, pp. 72–84.
- M.J. Herskovits, "On Cultural Values" and "Cultural Relativism and Cultural Values," in M.J. Herskovits, *Cultural Relativism*, pp. 1–34.

The Russians and Global Culture
- G.F. Kennan, "Soviet Strategic Objectives" and "Politics and the East-West Relationship," in George F. Kennan, *The Nuclear Delusion*, pp. 127–147.
- Ground Zero, "Rough and Smooth Spots on the Soviet Bear: Soviet National Character and Culture," and "From Cradle to Grave in the USSR: Probing the Everyday Life of the Soviet Citizen," pp. 43–63 in *What About the Russians and Nuclear War?*

Planet Earth
- Jonathan Schell, "The Choice," in *The Fate of the Earth*, Part III, pp. 181–231.
- The Harvard Nuclear Study Group, "Living with Nuclear Weapons: Is There a Choice?" (ch. 11), in *Living with Nuclear Weapons.*

4. International Security

Richard Ned Lebow   *Spring 1987*
Peace Studies Program, Cornell University,
Ithac ι, NY 14853

The superpowers have possessed nuclear weapons for almost forty years.
Even so, there is no consensus about the political utility of these weapons.
Some students of strategy argue that nuclear deterrence is the principal
reason why World War III has not broken out. Others insist that the
competition to acquire ever more sophisticated weapons and, with it, the
growing insecurity of both superpowers, is likely to be the primary cause
of World War III. Opinion also differs about the diverse causes of strategic
competition, the definition and meaning of the nuclear balance, the value
of nuclear deterrence as a means of protecting third parties, and the
relationship between different force structures, strategies, targeting doctrines,
and deterrence. We will take up these and other questions in the course
of a review of the history of the nuclear arms race and of the most important
theoretical literature written about it.

Requirements
No research paper is required. Students are expected instead to use their
time to familiarize themselves with the extensive literature on this subject.
In this connection, each student will write one critical review of the literature
in a selected area. Details of the assignment will be provided in class.
Grades will be based on class participation (15%), critical review (35%)
and final examination (50%).

COURSE OUTLINE AND READINGS

**Week I—Introduction and Overview: History and Politics of the Arms
Race**

Week II—The Evolution of U.S. Strategy and Nuclear Weapons Policy
  • David Alan Rosenberg, "The Origins of Overkill: Nuclear Weapons
    and American Strategy, 1945–1960," *International Security* 7 (Spring,
    1983), pp. 3–71.

- Desmond Ball, *Politics and Force Levels: The Strategic Missile Program of the Kennedy Administration.*
- Desmond Ball, "Targeting for Nuclear Deterrence," *Adelphi Paper,* No. 185 (London: International Institute of Strategic Studies, 1983).

Week III—The Evolution of Soviet Strategy and Nuclear Weapons Policy

- David Holloway, *The Soviet Union and the Arms Race* (New Haven: Yale University Press, 1983).
- Stephen A. Meyer, "Soviet Theater Forces," 2 Parts, *Adelphi Papers,* Nos. 187–88 (London: International Institute of Strategic Studies, 1983–84).

Week IV—U.S.-Soviet Perceptions of Each Other's Strategy and Objectives

- Franklyn Griffiths, "The Sources of American Conduct: Soviet Perspectives and Their Policy Implications, *International Security* (Fall 1984), pp. 3–50.
- Henry Trofimenko, "Counterforce: Delusion or Panacea?" *International Security* 5 (Spring 1981), pp. 23–48.
- Richard Pipes, "Why the Soviet Union Thinks It Could Fight and Win a Nuclear War," *Commentary* 64 (July 1977), pp. 21–34.
- Richard Ned Lebow, "'Evil' Versus 'Benign' Explanations of Soviet Strategy and Nuclear Weapons Policy," manuscript.

Weeks V & VI—Deterrence and Its Critics

- Thomas Schelling, *Arms and Influence* (New Haven: Yale University Press, 1966).
- Robert Jervis, "Deterrence Theory Revisited," *World Politics* (January 31, 1979), pp. 289–324.
- Robert Jervis, Ricahrd Ned Lebow, and Janice Gross Stein, *Psychology and Deterrence* (Baltimore: Johns Hopkins University Press, 1985).
- Paul Huth and Bruce Russett, "What Makes Deterrence Work? Cases from 1900–1980," *World Politics* 36 (July 1984), pp. 496–526.
- Bruce Russett, "Economic Decline, Electoral Pressure, and the Initiation of International Conflict," in Charles Gochman and Alan Ned Salrosky, eds., *The Prisoners of War,* 1987.

Week VII—Bureaucratic Models of the Arms Race

- Herbert York, "Military Technology and National Security," *Scientific American* 221 (August 1969), pp. 17–29.
- Richard K. Betts, "Innovation, Assessment and Decision," in Richard K. Betts, ed., *Cruise Missiles* (Washington D.C.: Brookings, 1981), pp. 1–28.
- Robert J. Art and Stephen E. Ockenden, "The Domestic Politics of Cruise Missile Development," in *Cruise Missiles,* pp. 359–414.

- Arthur J. Alexander, "Decision-Making in Soviet Weapons Procurement," *Adelphi Papers*, Nos. 147–48 (London: International Institute of Strategic Studies, 1978–79).

Week VIII—Game Theory and International Conflict
- Bruce Bueno de Mesquita, *The War Trap* (New Haven: Yale University Press, 1981).
- Robert Axelrod, *The Evolution of Cooperation* (New York: Basic Books, 1984.

Week IX—The Political Utility of Nuclear Weapons
- Colin Grey, "Nuclear Strategy: The Case for a Theory of Victors," *International Security* 4 (Summer 1979), pp. 54–87.
- Robert Jervis, *The Illogic of American Nuclear Strategy* (Ithaca: Cornell University Press, 1985).
- Richard Ned Lebow, "Windows of Opportunity: Do States Jump Through Them?" *International Security* 9 (Summer 1984), pp. 147–86.

Week X—The Concept of Extended Deterrence
- McGeorge Bundy, George F. Kennan, Robert S. McNamara, and Gerard C. Smith, "Nuclear Weapons and the Atlantic Alliance," *Foreign Affairs* 60 (Spring 1982), pp. 753–68.
- Samuel P. Huntington, "Conventional Deterrence and Conventional Retaliation in Europe," *International Security* 8 (Winter 1983–84), pp. 32–56.
- Fen Osler Hampson, "Groping for Technical Panaceas: The European Conventional Balance and Nuclear Stability," *International Security* 8 (Winter 1983–84), pp. 57–82.
- Richard Ned Lebow, "The Soviet Conventional Offensive in Europe: The Schlieffen Plan Revisited," *International Security* 9 (Spring 1985), pp. 44–78.

Week XI—SDI, ASAT, and The Militarization of Space
- Franklin A. Long, Donald Hafner and Jeffrey Boutwell, eds., *Weapons in Space* (New York: Norton, 1986).

Week XII—Command, Control, and Intelligence
- Desmond Ball, "Can Nuclear War Be Controlled?" *Adelphia Papers*, No. 169 (London: International Institute of Strategic Studies, 1981).
- Paul Bracken, *The Command and Control of Nuclear Forces* (New Haven: Yale University Press, 1983).

Weeks XIII & XIV—Crisis Prevention and Management
- Alexander L. George, *Managing U.S.–Soviet Rivalry: Problems of Crisis Prevention* (Boulder, Co.: Westview, 1983).
- Richard Ned Lebow, *Nuclear Crisis Management: A Dangerous Illusion* (Ithaca: Cornell University Press, 1987).

5. Science, Technology, and Arms Control

Lester G. Paldy   *Fall 1987*
Dept. of Technology and Society, College of Engineering,
State University of New York–Stony Brook, Stony Brook,
NY 11794

"Science, Technology and Arms Control" provides the knowledge and perspective needed to begin the study of technical aspects of arms control issues. It also explores the implications of research on new weapons systems and strategies for national security and international affairs. The course will enable you to acquire an overview of the evolution of important weapons technologies, an understanding of the relationships linking scientific research and development to national security and arms control issues, and a better understanding of the design, functions, effects and implications for arms control of modern weapons systems.

Specifically, this course explores the following themes and issues:

- Science, Politics and Power
- Human Creativity and the Origins of New Weapons
- Arms Control and Strategic Doctrine
- Technical Intelligence and Verification
- Issues in Nuclear Proliferation
- The Strategic Defense Initiative
- The Control of Chemical and Biological Weapons
- Arms Control and Human Imagination

Those who master the material in this course will be well prepared for internships in organizations such as the Arms Control and Disarmament Agency, Department of State, Department of Defense, Department of Commerce, and Department of Energy. Internships may also be sought with nongovernmental organizations such as the Center for Defense Information, World Policy Institute, Arms Control Association and Carnegie Endowment for International Peace.

Background

Science involves the exploration of natural phenomena and the development of a body of knowledge describing the universe. It is pursued for its own sake by those who are attracted to its challenges and appreciate the substantial amount of individual freedom, prestige and economic reward associated with it. But science also has another dimension. Francis Bacon wrote in the mid-17th century that "knowledge and human power are synonymous," foreshadowing the full development of the scientific and industrial revolutions that followed. Science is now a matter of the highest state concern; it is supported by governments which understand the relationships linking science to economic welfare, human well-being and, not least, national security and military power.

Technology, or the organization of knowledge and material resources to achieve specific goals, is an intrinsic part of human culture. Technology has contributed to human well-being, enabling most of us in developed countries to enjoy longer and healthier lives. It has also contributed to the unwise use of natural resources and environmental damage where it has not been adequately assessed and monitored. This course will explore the implications of modern technology for national security, arms control and the enormous world expenditure on armament.

The potential of technology for the improvement of weapons systems has been appreciated since ancient times. It is only a small step from the development of tools to the development of weapons. The main difference between ancient systems for the development of weapons and our own is that modern technological advances are based on the systematic development of the applied sciences, rather than on chance discoveries and purely trial and error methods. One consequence of this is that weapons have become increasingly powerful. The use of nuclear weapons has the potential to produce long-term climatic consequences which are not yet understood.

Technology and Arms Control

Arms control agreements attempt to lower the probability of war, reduce its destructiveness if it occurs, and control military expenditures by minimizing the acquisition of unnecessary weapons. The process of developing arms control agreements involves politics and diplomacy; science and technology also contribute to these efforts in important ways. For example, the existence of reconnaissance satellites capable of photographing military installations and monitoring the movements of troops, vehicles and naval vessels from space has made possible arms agreements that would not have been feasible before. The SALT II agreement signed by President Carter in 1979 was shaped by the power of satellite photography and electronic intelligence methods capable of monitoring the deployment of missile systems. Seismographic techniques which can distinguish between earthquakes and underground explosions figure prominently in the discussion of a ban on all nuclear weapons testing.

Technology and Weapons

"High technology" based upon the latest developments in applied science is warmly embraced and routinely applied for military purposes by advanced industrial nations. Virtually all new weapons systems incorporate microprocessors, composite materials, lasers and electro-optical devices. Technological sophistication in weaponry is now taken for granted. Even less developed countries seek to acquire such weapons through a lucrative international arms trade. All governments are aware of the existence of new classes of weapons capable of revolutionizing warfare; only the poorest and most isolated are uninterested in acquiring them.

What is less apparent is that a significant fraction of the world's scientific and technological resources are involved in military enterprises. It has been estimated that about 25% of the world's scientists and engineers are involved in military research and development (R&D). The fraction of physical scientists and engineers involved in military R&D may be twice as large. In the U.S., more than 70% of all federal R&D expenditures are allocated for military purposes. The U.S.S.R. does not publish comparable data, but most analysts have concluded that military R&D consumes an even larger fraction of Soviet national wealth.

Technological Resources

In both East and West, science and technology are assigned high priority by policy-makers. Advanced technology is perceived as critically important to national security. Basic science is considered to be the foundation on which advanced technology rests. Even many non-scientists share this understanding, although they may not have a clear conception of the distinctions between basic research, applied research and the process of development. That is not surprising, since the distinctions are often blurred.

Scientific and technological resources play an important part in national security planning in East and West. In the U.S., federal agencies such as the Departments of Defense, State, and Energy, and the National Science Foundation allocate significant resources to universities and industry in continuing efforts to strengthen the nation's scientific resource base. The advance of science is understood to be essential to the develoment of new technologies. The recent discovery of superconducting materials that work at relatively high temperatures has the potential to revolutionize industry. It will also expedite the development of new technologies that have military potential. It is because of the implications of advanced technologies for military purposes that intelligence agencies in the East and West are engaged in efforts to assess how far the other side's technological developments have progressed. Assessments by the Department of Defense have revealed, for example, that the U.S. is superior to the Soviet Union in most, but not all, militarily significant technologies. It is more difficult to assess the costs to basic research—"civilian science"—of the diversion of such a large part of the nation's scientific and technological resources to defense research. Some consider the drain posed by large expenditures on defense R&D as a major factor in the deteriorating trade position of the U.S.

At the other end of the research and development pipeline, the Departments of Commerce, State, Defense and Energy and the Central Intelligence Agency are involved in efforts to restrict the transport of information about new technologies to potential adversaries. These efforts are particularly sensitive.

How does a democracy find an appropriate balance between the need for information exchanges among scientists and engineers, the constitutional rights of citizens and the legitimate interest of government in national security? If we must engage in technical espionage, how does the American system provide oversight and accountability controls for the intelligence agencies charged with the responsibility for operations when they are necessarily conducted in secrecy? These are not simple issues. As we have seen in recent congressional hearings, covert action serving secret purposes can threaten constitutional government while purporting to serve democracy elsewhere.

Questions and Issues

Despite our extensive experience with the application of science and technology for military purposes, many policy questions and issues are still debated. Analysts argue over the extent to which advances in science and technology drive weapons developments whose end results may reduce national security if they stimulate aggressive reactions by adversaries. Do the influential leaders of weapons laboratories in East and West assume policy-making roles by default? Has President Eisenhower's warning of the formation of a new scientific-technological elite been transformed into reality?

How can we assess the impact of technology? Few foresaw that the ability to place communications satellites in orbit would lead to multiple warhead missiles. How do we handle dual-use technologies? Bioengineering research on a vaccine for anthrax is easily diverted to the development of biological weapons. Reconnaissance satellites support the verification of arms control agreements, but they also pose a threat to the U.S. Navy's carrier groups and stimulate interest in antisatellite weapons.

What are the implications of all this for individuals? Students of science and engineering are not always aware of the probability that they will be employed in military enterprises. Most engineers and scientists who work in defense industries firmly believe that they are contributing to national security and helping to preserve the peace. Most codes of ethics for scientists and engineers—where they exist at all—make no mention of responsibility for end-use applications. There is no agreement on whether scientists and engineers can or should be in any sense "responsible" for the final applications of their work. These matters are rarely discussed in the context of national security and arms control. Should they be?

Most persons interpret the term "arms race" as implying that more weapons are being added to arsenals. While numbers are important, the arms race is also a scientific and technological competition for more powerful and accurate weapons. This course will concentrate on what is known about the technical dimensions of that competition and will treat only peripherally the political, economic and ethical issues associated with it. Those issues are worthy of disciplined analysis in political science, philosophy, sociology, economics and history courses.

Opinions abound, as you have observed if you have been reading newspaper editorials and articles. You can and should form and hold your own views. The course requires only that you support opinions with a chain of argument and evidence. The skills and knowledge that you acquire in this process may be applied in many ways. One of our former students is now a Ph.D. candidate in the arms control program at the Center for International Studies at MIT. After graduation from Stony Brook, he spent a year working with an activist group opposing the installation of cruise missiles in Italy. Another former student is now a staff member of the Senate Select Committee on Intelligence. Another graduate uses her knowledge of Russian as an analyst in the National Security Agency. Others are engineers, graduate students, or in business. Their views on these matters are undoubtedly diverse, but they all have a common core of knowlege in this critical area of human affairs.

The university has contacts with both governmental and non-governmental agencies that can be used to explore possibilities for internships and employment. I am always available to discuss career opportunities in this field.

Field Trips

We will arrange a field trip to Brookhaven National Laboratory to meet with groups involved in SDI and nuclear safeguard research. We will also try to plan a trip to Washington to meet officials and analysts concerned with arms control issues in the Departments of State, Defense, and Energy, as well as in the Arms Control and Disarmament Agency, the Central Intelligence Agency, the Arms Control Association, and the Institute for Policy Studies.

Readings and Course Requirements

The readings for each theme should be completed during the assigned time period to serve as the basis for class discussion. A short option paper associated with each theme is due on the assigned date. The class will be divided into working groups assigned to selected themes and issue areas associated with them. The working groups will be expected to take the lead in class discussions of the theme. There will be six short issue papers (2–3 typewritten pages each), to be submitted at two-week intervals, and a final examination.

McNeill, William. *The Pursuit of Power.* University of Chicago Press.
Dyson, Freeman. *Weapons and Hope.* Harper-Colophon.
Deitchman, Seymour. *Military Power and the Advance of Technology.* Westview Press.
Haley, P.E., and J. Merrit. *Strategic Defense Initiative.* Westview Press.

The following journal abbreviations are used: *Scientific American* (SA), *Foreign Affairs* (FA), *Bulletin of the Atomic Scientists* (BAS). References will also be made to articles in current issues of the *New York Times, Washington Post, Wall Street Journal, Times of London,* and *Pravda.*

SCHEDULE AND
READING ASSIGNMENTS

Sept. 3–10—Science, Technology and Power
- McNeill, pp. 1–184.
- McNeill, pp. 185–387.

Sept. 15–22—Human Creativity and the Origins of New Weapons
- Foley, George, and Werner Soedel. "The Crossbow," SA, Jan. 1985, p. 104.
- Florman, Samuel. *The Existential Pleasures of Engineering*, St. Martin's Press (recommended, particularly pp. 99–152).
- Pacey, Arnold. *The Culture of Technology*, MIT Press (recommended).
- Dyson, pp. 181–313.
- Taylor, Theodore. "Endless Generations of Nuclear Weapons," BAS, Nov. 1986, pp. 12–15.
- Kahn, James. "University Management of Weapons Laboratories?— Yes." BAS, Jan. 1986, pp. 39–40.
- Archer, Dave. "University Management of Weapons Laboratories?— No." BAS, Jan. 1986, pp. 41–44.
- Long, Franklin. "Government Dollars for University Research," BAS, March 1986, pp. 45–49.
- Eisenhower, Dwight D. "Farewell Address to the American People," 1961.
- Chalk, Rosemary. "The Continuing Debate Over Science and Secrecy," BAS, March 1986, pp. 14–16.
- Smith, B. "Priorities in a Military Culture," BAS, June 1987, pp. 25–29.

Sept. 29—Arms Control, Technology and Strategic Doctrine
- Sakharov, Andrei. "The Danger of Nuclear War," FA, Summer 1983, pp. 1001–1017.
- McNamara, Robert. "The Military Role of Nuclear Weapons," FA, Fall 1983, pp. 59–80.
- Steinbrunner, J. "Launch Under Attack," SA, Jan. 84.
- Garwin, Richard. "Antisubmarine Warfare and National Security," SA, July 1972.
- Deitchman, all.
- Bunn, M. "Uncertainties of Preemptive Nuclear Attack," SA, Vol. 249, Nos. 38–47, Nov. 1983.
- York, Herbert. "Bilateral Negotiations and the Arms Race," SA, Oct. 1983.
- Forsberg, Randall. "A Bilateral Nuclear Weapons Freeze," SA, Vol. 247, Nos. 52–61, Nov. 1982.
- Nye, Joseph. "Farewell to Arms Control," FA, Fall 1986, pp. 1–20.

- Schelling, Thomas. "What Went Wrong with Arms Control?" FA, Winter 1985–86, pp. 219–233.
- Carter, Ashton. "The Command and Control of Nuclear Weapons," SA, Jan. 1985, p. 32.
- Carter, Ashton, et al. *Managing Nuclear Operations*, Brookings Institution (recommended).

Oct. 29—Technical Intelligence and Verification

- Aspin, Les. "The Verification of SALT II," SA, Vol. 240, Feb. 1979, pp. 38–45.
- Timerbaev, Roland M. "A Soviet Official Looks at Verification," BAS, Jan. 1987, pp. 6–7.
- Scovile, Herbert. "Is Espionage Necessary?" FA, April 1976, pp. 482–495.
- Richelson, Jeffrey. "Old Surveillance, New Interpretations," BAS, Feb. 1986, pp. 18–23.
- Heckrotte, Warren. "A Soviet View of Verification," BAS, Oct. 1986, pp. 12–15.
- Arkin, William. "Long on Data, Short on Analysis," BAS, June 1987, pp. 5–6.
- Hafemeister, David, et al. "The Verification of Compliance with Arms Control Agreements," SA, March 1985, p. 38.
- Krepon, Michael. "CIA-DIA at Odds over Soviet Threat," BAS, May 1987, pp. 6–7.
- Tsipis, K., David Hafemeister and Penny Janeway, eds. *Arms Control Verification*, Pergamon-Brassey's, 1986 (recommended).

Nov. 3–12—Issues in Nuclear Proliferation

- Nye, Joseph. "Nonproliferation," FA, April 1978, pp. 601–623.
- Gilinsky, Victor. "Plutonium and Proliferation," Winter 1978–79, pp. 374–386.
- Smith, Gerard, et al. "Reassessing Nuclear Proliferation," FA, Spring 1981, pp. 875–894.
- Fischer, David. "The Challenge of Nuclear Safeguards," BAS, June 1986, pp. 29–33.
- Spector, Michael. "Nuclear Proliferation," BAS, May 1987, pp. 17–20.
- Albright, David. "Pakistan's Bombmaking," BAS, June 1987, pp. 30–33.
- Cohen, Avner, and Benjamin Frankel. "Israel's Nuclear Ambiguity," BAS, March 1987, pp. 15–19.
- Seaborg, Glenn. "Make the Partial Test Ban Complete," BAS, June 1987, p. 3.
- Doty, Paul. "A Nuclear Test Ban," FA, Spring 1987, pp. 750–769.
- von Hippel, Frank, and David Albright, et al. "Stopping the Production of Fissile Material for Weapons," SA, Sept. 1985, p. 40.
- Epstein, William. "A Critical Time for Nuclear Proliferation," SA, Aug. 1985, p. 33.

Nov. 17–24—The Strategic Defense Initiative
- Haley, all.
- Gollon, Peter, "SDI Funds Costly for Scientists," BAS, Jan. 1986, pp. 24–27.
- Payne, K., and Colin Gray. "Nuclear Policy and the Defensive Transition," FA, Spring 1984, pp. 820–842.
- Brown, Harold. "Is SDI Technically Feasible?," FA, 1985, pp. 435–454.
- Garwin, Richard, and Hans Bethe et al. "Space-Based Ballistic Missile Defense," SA, Oct. 1984.
- Lin, Herbert. "The Development of Software for Ballistic Missile Defense," SA, Dec. 1985, p. 46.

Dec. 1–3—Chemical and Biological Weapons
- Weickhardt, G.C. "New Push for Chemical Weapons," BAS, Nov. 1986, pp. 28–33.
- Meselson, Matthew. "Chemical Weapons and Chemical Disarmament," SA, April 1980.
- Bernstein, Barton. "The Birth of the U.S. Biological Weapons Program," SA, June 1987, pp. 116–121.
- Bartley et al. "Yellow Rain and the Future of Arms Control," FA, Spring 1983, pp. 805–826.
- Wright, Susan. "New Designs for Biological Weapons," BAS, Jan. 1987, pp. 43–46.
- Rosenberg, Barbara. "Updating the Biological Weapons Ban," BAS, Jan. 1987, pp. 40–43.
- Meselson, Matthew, et al., "Yellow Rain," SA, Sept. 1985, p. 28.

Dec. 8–15—Arms Control and the Human Imagination
Student presentations.

6. Nuclear War and Its Prevention

R. R. Holt   *Fall 1986*

Peace and Global Policy Studies Program,
New York University, New York, NY 10003

This course was developed at a faculty seminar in which a diverse group of colleagues wrestled with the dire current predicament of humankind—

the threat of extinction, how it arose, and what can be done about it. As citizens, all students will be called upon to make decisions about national leaders and policies that can affect the survival of our species and perhaps of all life, decisions which should be based on an informed and sophisticated grasp of issues relating to nuclear war. This course aims to fill that need. Because many different kinds of special knowledge are involved, the organizers sought the participation of colleagues from several other departments; the course is therefore truly interdisciplinary.

General Requirements

There will be a single weekly session usually consisting of a short lecture followed by discussion, and a weekly reading assignment. You will be examined on your grasp of the material presented in the required reading and the lectures in a final exam. Half of your course grade will be based on the final examination, the rest on the midterm exam and class participation. Be sure to sign the attendance sheet passed around each week.

Books

Students are expected to purchase and read the following three paperback books and one reprinted article. In addition, for those who are interested in digging into various subjects in more detail, recommended readings are also listed.

Ground Zero [Roger Molander]. *Nuclear War—What's in It for You?* New York: Pocket Books, 1982.

Weston, Burns H., ed. *Toward Nuclear Disarmament and Global Security.* Boulder, Colo.: Westview Press, 1984.

Sagan, Carl. "Nuclear War and Climatic Catastrophe: Some Policy Implications," *Foreign Affairs*, Vol. 62, No. 2. 1983 Reprint.

Sommer, Mark. *Beyond the Bomb: Living Without Nuclear Weapons.* New York: Talman Co., 1985.

WEEK-BY-WEEK OUTLINE

Sept. 24—Introduction and Overview
Lecturers: Holt and Michael Lutzker (History).

Oct. 1—Facing the Issues: Living in the Nuclear Age
Film: Hiroshima/Nagasaki—August 1945.
- Weston, pp. 1–15, 21–29, 56–64.
- Ground Zero, pp. 1–16; ch. 6.

Recommended
- Hersey, John. *Hiroshima.* New York: Bantam Books.
- PSR/NYC. *Preparing for Nuclear War: The Psychological Effects.* New York: Physicians for Social Responsibility, 1982, pp 19–76. (Also in *American Journal of Orthopsychiatry*, 1982.)

- Lifton, R.J., & Falk, R. *Indefensible Weapons.* New York: Basic Books, 1982, pp. 80–100, 274–278.
- Carnesale, A., Doty, P., Hoffman, S., Huntington, S.P., Nye, J.S., & Sagan, S.D. *Living with Nuclear Weapons.* New York: Bantam, 1983 (paperback), ch. 1 (hereafter cited as LWNW).

Oct. 8—The Nature of Nuclear Weapons and Their Direct Effects
Lecturer: Daniel Zwanziger (Physics).
- Ground Zero, chs. 1–3, 15.

Recommended
- Admas, R., & Cullen, S. (eds.). *The Final Epidemic.* Chicago: University of Chicago Press, 1982, chs. 7–11.
- Weston, pp. 29–55.
- Chivian, E., Chivian, S., Lifton, R.J., & Mack, J.E. (eds.). *Last Aid.* San Francisco: W.H. Freeman, 1982, chs. 3–17.

Oct. 15—Effects of Nuclear War on Climate and Environment
Lecturer: Evelyn Mauss (Physiology).
- Sagan.
- Ground Zero, chs. 9 & 10.

Recommended
- Abrams, Herbert, L., & von Kaenel, William E. "Medical Problems of Survivors of Nuclear War: Infection and the Spread of Communicable Disease," *New England Journal of Medicine,* 1981, No. 305, pp. 1226–1232.
- Adams, R., & Cullen, R. *The Final Epidemic,* Section IV (pp. 169–218).
- Ehrlich, Paul R., et al. "Long-term Biological Consequences of Nuclear War," *Science,* 1983, No. 222, pp. 1293–1300.
- Harwell, M.A. *Nuclear War: The Human and Environmental Consequences.* New York: Springer Verlag, 1984.
- National Academy of Sciences/National Research Council. *The Effects on the Atmosphere of a Major Nuclear Exchange.* Washington, D.C.: National Academy Press, 1985.
- Institute of Medicine. *The Medical Implications of Nuclear War.* Washington, D.C.: National Academy Press 1986.
- Scientific Committee on Problems of the Environment (SCOPE), International Council of Scientific Unions. *Report No. 28.* Chichester, UK: Wiley, 1985.
- Turco, R.P., et al. "Nuclear Winter: Global Consequences of Multiple Nuclear Explosions," *Science,* 1983, No. 222, pp. 1283–1292.
- Turco, R.P., et al. "The Climatic Effects of Nuclear War," *Scientific American,* August, 1984, No. 251, pp. 33–43.

Oct. 22—History of the Nuclear Arms Race
Lecturer: Michael Lutzker (History).
- Ground Zero, chs. 4, 5, 7.
- Weston, pp. 94–105.

Recommended

- Barnet, R.J. *Real Security.* New York: Simon & Schuster, 1981.
- Mandelbaum, M. *The Nuclear Question.* New York: Cambridge University Press, 1979.
- Boston Study Group. *Winding Down: The Price of Defense.* New York: Freeman, 1982, chs. 1 & 2.
- LWNW, ch. 4.

Oct. 29—Strategies of Deterrence and Nuclear Warfare
Lecturer: Seven Brams (Politics).
- Weston, pp. 67–94.

Recommended

- Brams, S. *Superpower Games: Applying Game Theory to Superpowere Conflict.* New Haven, Conn.: Yale University Press, 1985.
- Boston Study Group. *Winding Down.* chs. 6, 7, 8.
- LWNW, chs. 5 & 7.
- Weston, ch. 5.

Nov. 5—History of Disarmament and Arms Control
Lecturer: McGeorge Bundy (History).
- Ground Zero, chs. 11–13.

Recommended

- Greb, G.A., & Johnson, G.W. "A History of Strategic Arms Limitation," *Bulletin of the Atomic Scientists,* 1984, Vol. 40, No. 10, pp. 30–37.
- Keenan, G. *The Nuclear Delusion: Soviet-American Relations in the Atomic Age.* New York: Pantheon, 1983.
- LWNW, chs. 8 & 9.
- Bundy, M., Kennan, G.F., McNamara, R.S., & Smith, G. "The President's Choice: Star Wars or Arms Control," *Foreign Affairs,* 1984, Vol. 63, No. 2, pp. 264–278.
- Pipes, R. *U.S.-Soviet Relations in the Era of Detente.* Boulder, Colo.: Westview Press.
- Russett, B., & Blair, B. *Progress in Arms Control?* San Francisco: Freeman, 1979.

Nov. 12—Political and Economic Aspects of the Military-Industrial Complex
Lecturer: James T. Crown (Politics).
- Weston, pp. 157–172, 194–204.

Recommended

- Barnet, R., & Mueller, R. *Global Reach.* New York: Simon & Schuster, 1974.
- Crown, J.R. "The Military Establishment: High Water Mark?" *Journal of International Affairs,* 1972, Vol. 26, pp. 102–105.

- Gansler, J., & Melman, S. "The Military-Industrial Complex: A Debate," *Defense Management Journal*, March-April, 1979, Vol. 15, pp. 2–13.
- Sklar, H. (ed.). *Trilateralism*. Boston: South End Press, 1980.
- Sivard, R.L. *World Military and Social Expenditures, 1985*. New York: World Priorities, Inc., 1985.

Nov. 19—The Soviet Threat: How Great? How Real? How Inescapable?
Lecturer: Miroslav Nincic (Politics).
- Weston, pp. 278–317.
- Kull, S. "Nuclear Nonsense," *Foreign Policy*, Spring, 1985, pp. 28–52.

Recommended
- Weston, pp. 267–278.
- Ground Zero. *What About the Russians—And Nuclear War?* New York: Pocket Books, 1983.
- LWNW, ch. 2.

Nov. 26—Nuclear Weapons and Nuclear Power: The Problem of Proliferation
Lecturer: Warren Liebold (consulting engineer; member, National Energy Committee).
- Weston, pp. 429–454.
- Ground Zero, ch. 17.

Recommended
- Weston, pp. 463–479.
- LWNW, ch. 10.
- Lovins, E., & Lovins, H. *Energy/War: Breaking the Nuclear Link*. San Francisco: Friends of the Earth, 1981.
- Kaku, M., & Trainer, J. *Nuclear Power: Both Sides*. New York: Norton, 1982.

Dec. 3—Empowerment: What You Can Do to Impact National Policy
Lecturer: Andrea Ayvazian (Director of Training, Peace Development Fund).
- Weston, pp. 495–496.
- Sommer, pp. 3–48.

Recommended
- Weston, pp. 416–428, 481–488, 504–562.
- LWNW, ch. 11.

Dec. 10—Moral and Ethical Issues Concerning Nuclear War
Lecturer: William Ruddick (Philosophy).
- Weston, pp. 123–151.

Recommended
- Thompson, E.P., & Smith, D. (eds.). *Protest and Survive*. New York: Monthly Review Press, 1981, ch. 7.
- Schell, J. *The Fate of the Earth*. New York: Avon, chs 2 & 3.

Dec. 17—Alternative Security Systems

Lecturer: Dietrich Fischer (Economics/Politics, Princeton).
* Sommer, pp. 49–86.
* Weston, pp. 504–527.

Recommended
* Fischer, D. *Preventing War in the Nuclear Age.* Totowa, N.J.: Rowman & Allanheld, 1984.
* Galtung, J. *There Are Alternatives!* Nottingham & Spokesman, 1984. (Distributed in the U.S. by Dufour Editions, Chester Springs, Penn. 19425. Paperback, $10.95.)
* Weston, pp. 569–627.

Jan. 7—Alternatives to War: Short-term Possibilities

* Sommer, pp. 87–104, 108–124.

Recommended
* Galtung, J. *The True Worlds: A Transnational Perspective.* Boulder, Colo.: Westview Press.
* Johansen, R.C. *Toward a Dependable Peace: A Proposal for an Appropriate Security System.* New York: World Policy Institute, 1978. (Working Paper no. 8, World Order Models Project.)
* Weston, pp. 416–428, 481–488, 504–562.
* LWNW, ch. 11.

Jan. 14—Alternatives to War: Long-term Possibilities

Lecturer: Robert R. Holt (Psychology).
* Sommer, pp. 124–168.

Recommended
* Falk, R., Kim, S.S., & Mendlovitz, S.H. (eds.). *Toward a Just World Order.* Boulder, Colo.: Westview Press, 1982.
* Deutsch, M. "Preventing World War III: A Psychological Perspective," *Political Psychology,* 1983, Vol. 4, pp. 3–32.
* Forsberg, R. "The Freeze and Beyond: Confining the Military to Defense as a Route to Disarmament, *World Policy Journal,* Winter, 1984, pp. 285–318.
* Weston, pp. 631–700.
* Holt, R.R. "Can Psychology Meet Einstein's Challenge?" *Political Psychology,* 1984, Vol. 5, pp. 199–225.

VII

Global Security, Arms Control, and Disarmament

1. U.S. Security Policy in Global Perspective: Problems and Prospects

Robert C. Johansen

Fall 1987

Institute for International Peace Studies,
University of Notre Dame, Notre Dame, IN 46556

Our purpose in this course is to conduct a comprehensive examination of efforts to increase national security since the end of World War II. We will begin by asking: What are the sources of insecurity and war? Following Kenneth Waltz's analytic framework, students will be encouraged to evaluate evidence that the origins of war lie in human nature, in the nature of the state, or in the nature of the international system. U.S. security needs will then be more concretely identified by examining diverse views of specific threats.

After identifying challenges to U.S. security, we will, in the major part of our study, focus on efforts to meet those challenges and to enhance security. Readings and class discussions will include an evaluation of the nature and effects of nuclear weapons, the security impact of extended nuclear deterrence and of competition in the weaponization of space, and the evolution of U.S. and Soviet attitudes toward the use of nuclear weapons.

Conventional arms, of course, consume the largest portion of the military budget, and conventional military activities constitute the most vexing, day-to-day security problems. The utility of overt and covert military power and other instruments of security will be examined in brief case studies of conflict in Europe, Central America, Lebanon, southern Africa, Afghanistan, the Persian Gulf, Libya, and Grenada. Students will also consider optimal means for managing terrorism. The political economy of the arms buildup and of arms exports and military assistance will also be examined.

Arms control, although viewed by many as the main instrument of constraint on the arms buildup, has been discredited in both theory and practice in recent years. It has regained prominence in the treaty on intermediate-range nuclear forces. Students will study the reasons for the demise of arms control and look at the prospects for maintaining existing arms agreements and for achieving additional arms control. This discussion will include recommendations for making nuclear non-proliferation policies more effective.

In the final section students will consider the future of global security and examine recent proposals to reduce the risk of war. Topics include the Strategic Defense Initiative, the Arms Control Association's recommendations for extending the life of the SALT treaties, Gorbachev's proposal for nuclear disarmament, the Alternative Defense Commission's recommendations for non-nuclear defense in Europe, the future of NATO, New Zealand's non-nuclear alignment, United Nations peace-keeping and international satellite monitoring, and proposals for global demilitarization and an alternative security system.

Finally, my purpose in offering this course is to encourage you to form independent, informal judgments about what does and does not add to the security of people in this and other lands. We will succeed in this class if during the coming weeks you increase your ability to analyze current policy debates, to evaluate political candidates, to imagine more humane ways of handling international relations, and to commit yourself to implementing them.

Course Requirements

Because we will discuss contemporary and controversial security questions, we must draw upon a wide variety of recent sources. Many will be articles rather than books. In the interests of productive and efficient class dialogues, students must complete all required readings before the class session in which they are scheduled for discussion.

In addition to the items listed on this syllabus, students should regularly read international news stories and analysis from either *The New York Times*, *The Washington Post*, or *The Christian Science Monitor*. Because any realistic security policy must take into account other political cultures, students able to do so are also encouraged to read foreign language periodicals and to report the perspectives found there to the class. In this way we can enrich each other's knowledge far beyond what one of us could accomplish alone.

In addition to mid-term and final examinations, students will write a research paper of moderate length in which they either (1) evaluate the utility of a U.S. threat or use of force in a concrete case, or (2) describe what would constitute a prudent U.S. security policy in a specific area for the next 3 to 5 years. To illustrate the two approaches, a student might write an essay answering one of these questions: (1) What has been the utility of the U.S. use of force against Libya in April 1986? (2) What is a wise and prudent U.S. security policy toward Nicaragua over the next three years?

The paper should be typed and follow a standard style manual. It should be written as if for publication in a journal like *Foreign Affairs* or *World Policy* (but with more footnotes) and as if your purpose in publication is to advise the U.S. government on how to increase the wisdom of its policies, either by commenting on the strengths and weaknesses of a past policy or by carefully laying out an optimal path in the foreseeable future.

Students should retain all notes, outlines, and rough drafts of written work until two weeks after final grades are reported to the Registrar.

COURSE OUTLINE

An asterisk (*) indicates required readings; all others are recommended.

Identifying the Problem

Sources of Insecurity
Human Nature
- Freshbach, S. and J.J. White. "Individual Differences in Attitudes Toward Nuclear Arms Policies: Some Psychological and Social Policy Considerations," *Journal of Peace Research*, Vol. 23, No. 2 (June 1986).
- *Waltz, Kenneth. *Man, the State, and War* (New York: Columbia University Press, 1959), pp. 1–79.

The Nature of the State
- *Waltz, pp. 80–158.

The Nature of the International System
- Hardin, Garrett. "The Tragedy of the Commons," *Science*, Vol. 1627 (December 13, 1968), pp. 1243–1248.
- *Johansen, Robert C., *The National Interest and the Human Interest* (Princeton: Princeton University Press, 1980), pp. 3–37.
- *Waltz, pp. 159–238.
- *Russett, Bruce, "Why Do Arms Races Occur?" in Burns H. Weston (ed.), *Toward Nuclear Disarmament and Global Security: A Search for Alternatives* (Boulder, CO: Westview Press, 1984), pp. 69–89.

- *Goldman, Ralph M. "Political Distrust as Generator of the Arms Race: Prisoners' and Security Dilemmas," in Weston (ed.), pp. 90–93.

Defining the Threat Concretely
- *Barnet, Richard J., "The Illusion of Security," in Weston (ed.), pp. 161–71.
- *Boston Study Group. *Winding Down: The Price of Defense* (San Francisco: Freeman, 1982), pp. 3–60.
- Carnesale, Albert, et al. (Harvard Nuclear Study Group). *Living with Nuclear Weapons* (New York: Bantam, 1983).
- *Committee on the Present Danger, *Can America Catch Up? The U.S.-Soviet Military Balance* (Washington, D.C.: Committee on the Present Danger, 1984), pp. i–v; 1–4.
- *Committee on the Present Danger. *Countering the Soviet Threat: U.S. Defense Strategy for the 1980s* (Washington, D.C.: Committee on the Present Danger, 1980).
- Gaddis, John Lewis. *Strategies of Containment* (New York: Oxford University Press, 1983).
- Gray, Colin S., and Keith Payne. "Victory is Possible," *Foreign Policy*, No. 39 (Summer 1980), pp. 14–27.
- *Independent Commission on Disarmament and Security Issues. *Common Security: A Blueprint for Survival* (New York: Simon and Shuster, 1982), pp. 1–48.
- *Kaplan, Fred, "Dubious Specter: A Skeptical Look at the Soviet Threat," in Weston (ed.), pp. 303–316.
- *Kennan, George F. *The Nuclear Delusion: Soviet-American Relations in the Atomic Age* (New York: Pantheon, 1982), pp. ix–xxx; 13–47; 54–101.
- *Luckham, Robin, "Myths and Realities of Security," in Weston (ed.), pp. 159–160.
- *Ravenal, Earl C. "The Case for a Withdrawal of Our Forces," *New York Times Magazine*, March 6, 1983.
- *Schwenninger, Sherle R., and Jerry W. Sanders. "The Democrats and a New Grand Strategy," *World Policy*, Vol. 3 (Summer 1986), pp. 369–418.
- *White, Ralph K. *Fearful Warriors: A Psychological Profile of U.S.-Soviet Relations* (New York: Free Press, 1984), pp. 109–188.

Past Efforts to Enhance Security

Nuclear Deterrence
The Nature & Effects of Nuclear Weapons
- Adams, Ruth, and Susan Cullen (eds.). *The Final Epidemic: Physicians and Scientists on Nuclear War* (Chicago: The Educational Foundation for Nuclear Science, 1982).

- *Caldicott, Helen. *Missile Envy: The Arms Race and Nuclear War* (New York: Bantam, 1986).
- *Falk, Richard. "Nuclear Weapons and the End of Democracy," in Weston (ed.), pp. 194–203.
- *Freeman, Harold. "Imagine One Nuclear Bomb," in Weston (ed.), pp. 22–28.
- George, Alexander, and Richard Smoke. *Deterrence in American Foreign Policy* (New York: Columbia University Press, 1974).
- *Group of Experts. "Effects of the Use of Nuclear Weapons," in Weston (ed.), pp. 29–55.
- *Independent Commission on Disarmament and Security Issues, pp. 49–70.
- *Lifton, Robert J. "Beyond Psychic Numbing: A Call to Awareness," in Weston (ed.), pp. 111–222.
- *Schell, Jonathan. "A Republic of Insects and Grass," in Weston (ed.), pp. 26–63.

Evolution of U.S. Nuclear Strategy & Arsenals
- *Beres, Louis Rene. "Nuclear Strategy and World Order: The United States Imperative," in Weston (ed.), pp. 215–251.
- *Bull, Hedley. "The Prospects for Deterrence," in Weston (ed.), pp. 252–62.
- Caldicott, pp. 74–110; 167–210.
- *Krass, Allan. "Deterrence and Its Contradictions," in Weston (ed.), pp. 209–214.
- *Mrydal, Alva. *The Game of Disarmament: How the United States and Russia Run the Arms Race* (New York: Pantheon, 1976), pp. 1–61.

Evolution of Soviet Nuclear Policy
- *Evangelista, Matthew. "The New Soviet Approach to Security," in *World Policy*, Vol. 3 (Fall 1986), pp. 561–600.
- *McGwire, Michael. "Soviet Military Objectives," *World Policy*, Vol. 3 (Fall 1986), pp. 667–696.
- *U.S. International Communications Agency, "Soviet Perceptions of the U.S.—Results of a Surrogate Interview Project," in Weston (ed.), pp. 269–277.
- *Arbatov, Georgi A. "Relations Between the United States and the Soviet Union—Accuracy of U.S. Perceptions," in Weston (ed.), pp. 283–289.
- *Donaldson, Robert H. "Soviet Conceptions of Security," in Weston (ed.), pp. 290–301.

U.S.-Soviet Military Rivalry
Detente:
- Garthoff, Raymond. *Detente and Confrontation: American-Soviet Relations from Nixon to Reagan* (Washington, D.C.: Brookings, 1985), pp. 24–68; 1009–1067.

The Strategic Balance:
- **Arms Control Association. *Countdown on SALT II* (Washington, D.C., 1985).
- Caldicott, pp. 11–66.
- Committee on the Present Danger. *Can America Catch Up?* (Washington, D.C.: Committee on the Present Danger, 1984).
- Garthoff, pp. 785–800.
- Gervasi, Tom. *The Myth of Soviet Military Supremacy* (New York: Harper and Row, 1986).
- International Institute for Strategic Studies. *The Military Balance 1985–86* (London: International Institute for Strategic Studies, 1985).
- International Institute for Strategic Studies. *Strategy Survey 1985-86* (London: International Institute for Strategic Studies, 1985).
- *Kennan, pp. 127–133.

The Failure of Detente:
- *Frank, Jerome D. "Psychological Aspects of Disarmament and International Negotiations," in Weston (ed.), pp. 324–336.
- *Osgood, Charles E. "Disarmament Demands GRIT," in Weston (ed.), pp. 337–343.
- *Clemens, Walter C. "National Security and U.S.-Soviet Relations," in Weston (ed.), pp. 344–357.
- *Fischer, Roger. "Getting to 'Yes' in the Nuclear Age," in Weston (ed.), pp. 358–370.
- *Garthoff, pp. 1068–1126.
- *Kennan, pp. 134–150.

Conventional Military Preparedness and Action

- Caldicott, pp. 202–228.
- Chomsky, Noam. *Turning the Tide: U.S. Intervention in Central America and the Struggle for Peace* (Boston: South End Press).
- Dorman, William A. "Peripheral Vision: U.S. Journalism an the Third World," *World Policy*, Vol. 3 (Summer 1986), pp. 419–460.
- *Feinberg, Richard D., and Kenneth A. Oye. "After the Fall: U.S. Policy Toward Radical Regimes," *World Policy*, Vol. 1 (Fall 1983), pp. 201–216.
- *Feinberg, Richard E. *The Intemperate Zone: The Third World Challenge to U.S. Foreign Policy* (New York: Norton, 1983), pp. 13–82; 130–257.
- Hough, Jerry. *The Struggle for the Third World: Soviet Debates and American Options* (Washington, D.C.: Brookings, 1986).
- Johansen, Robert C., and Michael G. Renner. "Limiting Conflict in the Gulf," *Third World Quarterly*, Vol. 7 (October 1985), pp. 803–38.
- *Kennan, pp. 161–167.
- *Kenworthy, Eldon. "Grenada as Theatre, *World Policy*, Vol. 1 (Spring 1984), pp. 635–652.
- Kirkpatrick, Jeane. "Dictatorships and Double Standards," *Commentary*, November 1979.

- Krasner, Steven. *Structural Conflict: The Third World Against Global Liberalism* (Los Angeles: University of California Press, 1985).
- Sewell, John, Richard E. Feinberg and Valeriana Kallab (eds.). *United States Foreign Policy and the Third World Agenda 1985–86* (New Brunswick, N.J.: Transaction Books, 1985).
- Solarz, Stephen J. "When to Intervene," *Foreign Policy*, pp. 20–39.

Alliances
- *Alterman, Eric R. "Central Europe: Misperceived Threats and Unforeseen Dangers," *World Policy*, Vol. 2 (Fall 1985), pp. 681–710.
- Alternative Defense Commission. *Defense Without the Bomb* (New York: Taylor & Francis, 1983).
- *Bundy, McGeorge, George F. Kennan, Robert S. McNamara, and Gerard Smith. "Nuclear Weapons and the Atlantic Alliance," in Weston (ed.), pp. 374–383.
- *Kaldor, Mary. "Beyond the Blocs: Defending Europe the Political Way," *World Policy*, Vol. 1 (Fall 1983), pp. 1–22.
- *Sloan, Stanley R. *NATO's Future: Toward a New Transatlantic Bargain* (Washington, D.C.: National Defense University Press, 1985), pp. 127–194.

Arms Transfers
- Pierre, Andrew J. *The Global Politics of Arms Sales* (Princeton: Princeton University Press, 1982).

Arms Control and Disarmament
- *Kaldor, Mary. "Disarmament: The Armament Process in Reverse," in Weston (ed.), pp. 654–556.
- *National Academy of Sciences. *Nuclear Arms Control*, pp. 1–23.

Early Efforts
- *Myrdal, pp. 62–334.

SALT
- *Garthoff, pp. 801–827.
- Johansen. *The National Interest and the Human Interest*, pp. 38–125.

START
- *Johansen. "How to START Ending the Arms Race," *World Policy*, Vol. I (Fall 1983), pp. 71–100.

Nuclear Non-Proliferation
The NPT Regime
- *Falk, Richard. "Nuclear Policy and World Order: Why Denuclearization?" in Weston (ed.), pp. 463–480.
- *Goldblat, Jozef. "The Third Review Conference of the Nuclear Non-Proliferation Treaty," *Bulletin of Peace Proposals*, Vol. 17, No. 1 (1986), pp. 13–28.

- *Potter, William C. "Strategies for Control," in Weston (ed.), pp. 429–462.

The New Zealand Precedent and Allied Nuclear Protest
- *Mack, Andrew. "Crisis in the Other Alliance: ANZUS in the 1980s," *World Policy*, Vol. 3 (Summer 1986), pp. 447–472.

The Future of Global Security and the International System

Economic and Technological Dimensions of Military Competition
The Military-Industrial Complex
- Adams, Gordon. *The Iron Triangle* (New York: Council on Economic Priorities, 1981).
- Caldicott, pp. 31–73.

Technological Momentum
- Thee, Marek. *Military Technology, Military Strategy, and the Arms Race* (London: Croom Helm, 1986).
- *Thee, Marek. "Halting the Nuclear Arms Race: The Role of Science and Technology," *Bulletin of Peace Proposals*, Vol. 17, No. 1 (1986), pp. 41–46.

Economic Costs of the Arms Buildup
- *Dumas, Lloyd J. "Military Spending and Economic Decay," in Weston (ed.), pp. 172–193.
- *Independent Commission on Disarmament and Security Issues, pp. 71–99.
- Melman, Seymour. *The Permament War Economy* (New York: Simon & Schuster, 1985).
- *Sivard, Ruth L. *World Military and Social Expenditures 1985* (Washington, D.C.: World Priorities, 1985), pp. 5–52.

Recent Proposals to Reduce the Risk of War
The Strategic Defense Initiative
- *Bundy, McGeorge, George F. Kennan, Robert S. McNamara, and Gerard Smith. "The President's Choice: Star Wars or Arms Control," *Foreign Affairs*, Vol. 63 (Winter 1984), pp. 264–278.
- *Clausen, Peter. "SDI in Search of a Mission," *World Policy*, Vol. 2 (Spring 1985), pp. 249–270.
- Jasani, Bhupendra. "Outer Space Being Turned into a Battlefield," *Bulletin of Peace Proposals*, Vol. 17, No. 1 (1986), pp. 29–40.
- Union of Concern Scientists. *The Fallacy of Star Wars* (New York: Vintage, 1984).

Limited Nuclear Deterrence
- *Independent Commission on Disarmament and Security Issues, pp. 100–126.
- Mendelsohn, Jack. "Balanced Nuclear Deterrence," mimeographed.

A Minimum Nuclear Deterrent and General Nuclear Settlement
- *Gayler, Noel. "How to Break the Momentum of the Nuclear Arms Race," in Weston (ed.), pp. 396–403.
- *Kennan, George. "A Modest Proposal," in Weston (ed.), pp. 390–395.
- *White, pp. 273–349.

Defensive Defense: A Nuclear Freeze, Nuclear Free Zones, and Reduction of Foreign Bases
- Fischer, Dietrich. *Preventing War in the Nuclear Age* (Totowa, N.J.: Rowan & Allanheld, 1984).
- *Fischer, Dietrich. "Invulnerability Without Threat: The Swiss Concept of General Defense," in Weston (ed.), pp. 504–531.
- *Forsberg, Randall. "Call to Halt the Nuclear Arms Race—Proposal for a Mutual U.S.-Soviet Nuclear Weapon Freeze," in Weston (ed.), pp. 384–389.

Civilian-Based Defense
- *Alternative Defense Commission. "Defense by Civil Resistance," in Weston (ed.), pp. 532–550.
- *Kriesberg, Louis. "Noncoercive Inducements in International Conflict," in Weston (ed.), pp. 551–563.
- Sharp, Gene. *Making Europe Unconquerable: The Potential of Civilian-based Deterrence and Defense* (Cambridge, Mass.: Ballinger, 1985).
- *Sharp, Gene. *Making the Abolition of War a Realistic Goal* (New York: World Policy Institute, 1980), pp. 3–14.

Toward an Alternative Security System
- *Alger, Chadwick. "Reconstructing Human Polities: Collective Security in the Nuclear Age," in Weston (ed.), pp. 666–686.
- Clark, Michael. "The Alternative Defense Debate," *ADIU*, 1985.
- Galtung, Johan. *There Are Alternatives* (Chester Springs, PA: Dufour Editions, 1984).
- Stephenson, Carolyn (ed.). *Alternative Methods for International Security.* (Washington, D.C.: University Press of America, 1983).

The Utility of Violence and Military Competition:
- *Johansen, Robert C. "The Future of Arms Control," *World Policy*, Vol. 2 (Spring 1985), pp. 193–228.

Unilateralism and Internationalism in Peacekeeping:
- Florini, Ann, and Nina Tannewald. *On the Front Lines: The United Nations' Role in Preventing and Containing Conflict* (New York: United Nations Association of the United States of America, 1984).

- Garrity, Patrick J. "The United Nations and Peacekeeping," in Burton Yale Pines (ed.), *A World Without a U.N.* (Washington, D.C.: The Heritage Foundation, 1984), pp. 137–156.
- *Independent Commission on Disarmament and Security Issues, pp. 126–181.
- *Johansen, Robert C. "The Reagan Administration and the U.N.: The Costs of Unilateralism," *World Policy*, Vol. 3 (Fall 1986), pp. 601–642.

Transforming the Code of Conduct

- *Brucan, Silviu. "The Establishment of a World Authority: Working Hypotheses," in Weston (ed.), pp. 615–627, or *The Dialect of World Politics* (New York: Free Press, 1978), pp. 137–156.
- *Caldicott, pp. 229–265.
- *Dean, Jonathan. "Beyond the First Use," in Weston (ed.), pp. 496–503.
- *Deudney, Daniel, "Forging Missiles into Spaceships," *World Policy*, Vol. 2 (Spring 1985), pp. 271–304.
- Falk, Richard A. "Beyond Deterrence: The Essential Political Challenge," in Peter C. Sederberg (ed.), *Nuclear Winter, Deterrence and the Prevention of Nuclear War* (New York: Praeger, 1986), pp. 116–138.
- *Johansen, Robert C. "Toward an Alternative Security System," in Weston (ed.), pp. 569–603.
- Kennan, pp. 183–207.
- Raskin, Marcus. "Draft Treaty for a Comprehensive Program for Common Security and General Disarmament" (Washington, D.C.: Institute for Policy Studies, 1986).

2. Alternative International Security Systems

Carolyn M. Stephenson Spring 1988
Political Science Dept., University of Hawaii–Manoa,
Honolulu, HI 96822

The alternative international security systems approach is a new approach to international relations which questions many of the assumptions of traditional international relations. Neither neo-realist, neo-Marxist, nor idealist, it draws on elements of both conflict theory and consensus theory to address questions of security ranging from the individual to the global level. Following in the peace research tradition, it is explicit about values and goals; its goal is to improve both the theory and practice of conflicting and resolving conflict while reducing the amount of violence in the system. It takes seriously the question of whether there are methods which can maximize security and reduce violence, asking under what conditions various methods work.

Requirements

Reading is fairly heavy for this course, so there will be only one major writing requirement, that of a term paper on any part of this subject which interests you—for example, historical case studies of the use of particular methods, theoretical attention to how particular methods might be integrated, examination of the application of a group of methods to a particular conflict context, etc. You should also develop lists, from your writing and research, of the conditions under which violence, nonviolent sanctions, third-party conflict resolution, and alternative defense succeed. Please come to each class able to address the questions asked of you as well as prepared with questions you have asked the material or it has asked you.

SCHEDULE

Jan. 19—Introduction

A history of the field and its relationship to international relations and peace research. The need for alternative security systems. Defining alternative defense and alternative security.

- Margaret Mead, "War Is only an Invention—Not a Biological Necessity," *Asia*, Vol. 40, No. 8 (August 1940), pp. 402–405.
- Carolyn Stephenson, "The Need for Alternative Forms of Security: Crises and Opportunities," *Alternatives*, Vol. XIII, No. 1 (Jan. 1988).
- C. Stephenson, "Introduction" and "Review of the Literature" in Stephenson (ed.), *Alternative Methods for International Security* (Washington, D.C.: University Press of America, 1982) (hereafter: *AMIS*).

Jan. 26—Power, Violence and Nonviolence, Coercion and Force

What is power? Does violence represent power or, as Hannah Arendt has said, its absence? What is the relationship of obedience to power?

- Gene Sharp, in C. Stephenson, *AMIS*.
- Gene Sharp, *The Politics of Nonviolent Action*, Vol. I.

Feb. 2—Nonviolence, Nonviolent Action, and Nonviolent Civilian-based Defense

What kinds of nonviolence are there? For what are they used, or useful?

- Gene Sharp, *The Politics of Nonviolent Action*, Vol. III, Ch. 1–3.

Feb. 9—Nonviolent Political Action and Repression
What is the impact of repression on nonviolent action?
- Gene Sharp, *The Politics of Nonviolent Action*, Vol. III, Ch. 4–6.
- "Nonviolent Protestor Hit by Train," *New York Times*, Sept. 2, 1987.

Feb. 16—Nonviolence and Liberation
Was Fanon right: can liberation be accomplished only by violence?
- Walter H. Conser, Jr., Ronald M. McCarthy, David Toscano, and Gene Sharp (eds.), *Resistance, Politics, and the American Struggle for Independence, 1765–1775* (Boulder, Colo.: Lynne Rienner Publishers, 1985), Chapters 1, 9, 12.

Feb. 23—Pragmatic Nonviolence: The Compatibility of Violence and Nonviolence?
Are integrative and disintegrative, positive and negative, coercive and consensual, violent and nonviolent methods of conflict compatible? What specific methods are and are not? Why?
- Anders Boserup and Andrew Mack, *War Without Weapons* (New York: Schocken, 1975). Pay particular attention to Ch. 1.

March 1—Alternative Defense, Non-offensive Defense, Defensive Defense
Can offense be distinguished from defense? Does movement away from offense and toward defense provide more security?
- Dietrich Fischer, *Preventing War in the Nuclear Age* (Totowa, N.J.: Rowman and Allanheld, 1984). See also various issues of *NOD* (Non-Offensive Defense) *Newsletter*, available free from the Centre for Peace and Conflict Research in Copenhagen.

March 8—Alternative Defense Versus Alternative Security
What are the differences in approach?
- Johan Galtung, *There Are Alternatives!* (Chester Springs, Pa.: Dufour Editions, 1984).
- Stephenson (Conclusions), Johansen, and Mische, in Stephenson, *AMIS*.

March 15—De-escalation of Conflict
What are some ways in which those locked into an escalating conflict can turn that around? GRIT. Self-encapsulating conflicts. The Robber's Cave experiment. Principled negotiation.
- Charles Osgood, *An Alternative to War or Surrender* (Urbana, Ill.: Univ. of Illinois Press, 1962).
- Louis Kriesberg, in Stephenson, *AMIS*.
- Roger Risher and Bill Ury, *Getting to Yes* (New York: Penguin Books, 1983).

March 29—Conflict Resolution and the Role of the "Third Party"

Under what conditions can a "third party" be helpful? Can a third party actually be harmful? Can and should a third party be "neutral"? Does conflict resolution hurt the weaker party?

- Jacob Bercovitch, *Social Conflicts and Third Parties* (Boulder, Colo.: Westview Press, 1984).
- Yarrow, Prutzman, and Stephenson (Literature) in Stephenson, *AMIS.*
- Chris Mitchell, *Peacemaking and the Consultant's Role* (New York: Nichols Publishing Co., 1981).
- Adam Curle, *Peacemaking.* (out of print)
- If you are not familiar with the conflict resolution work of John Burton, see references in Stephenson (*AMIS* and *Alternatives*).

April 5—Collective Security and the Enforcement of Sanctions

The League of Nations, the United Nations and certain regional organizations have made attempts to develop "collective security," based on the collective ability to enforce sanctions. What kinds of sanctions are there, and under what conditions can they be successful? U.N. peacekeeping. Nonviolent peace forces. Economic sanctions. The utility of carrots and sticks. Threatened sanctions as deterrents.

- U.N. Charter.
- Lindsay, James M., "Trade Sanctions as Policy Instruments," *International Studies Quarterly*, Vol. 30, No. 2 (June 1986).
- David Baldwin, "The Power of Positive Sanctions, *Foreign Affairs.*
- Lall and Woodward in Stephenson, *AMIS.*
- Gene Sharp, *Making Europe Unconquerable* (Cambridge: Ballinger, 1985).

April 12—Alliances and De-alignment

How do alliances differ from collective security? Why is there movement toward de-alignment from alliances? What are the advantages and disadvantages of self-reliant defense? How does self-reliance differ from self-help and from self-sufficiency?

- Alternative Defence Commission, *Defence Without the Bomb* (London: Taylor and Francis, 1983).

April 19—Non-intervention and the Restructuring of Military Infrastructures

Some argue that a non-intervention pledge and/or the conversion of parts of the military infrastructure must be the first step. How do non-intervention and economic conversion thinking relate to thinking on an alternative international security system?

- Randy Forsberg, "Confining the Military to Defense."
- P. Morrison and P. Walker, "A New Strategy for Military Spending," in *Scientific American* (Oct. 1978). (Or see Boston Study Group, *The Price of Defense* (New York: Times Books, 1979).
- See also Gordon Adams on economic conversion.

April 26—Centralization and Decentralization: Alternative Approaches to Collective Action
Generations of political theorists have debated over the role of government, cooperation, coercion and force, hegemony, leadership, revolution and evolution and over the difference between them. If the goals include a broader definition of security, encompassing maximum peace, justice and freedom, then are there any guidelines as to the paths to steer between associative and dissociative politics?

- Hobbes, *On the Natural Condition of Mankind.*
- Garrett Hardin, "The Tragedy of the Commons," in William Daly, *Toward a Steady-State Economy* (San Francisco: W.H. Freeman, 1973).
- See also Michel Foucault, *Power and Knowledge.*
- William Ophuls, *Ecology and the Politics of Scarcity* (San Francisco: W.H. Freeman, 1977).

May 3—Beyond Security: The Politics of Agreement
Below and above national security lie individual human security and the security of the human race. What is the possibility, in the longer term, of developing a less coercive politics of agreement? Discussion.

Special Events and Speakers in Class

- Jan. 26: Arms Control? The INF Treaty with Michael Stafford, Assistant to Nitze on INF negotiations.
- Feb. 9: The U.S./U.S.S.R. Relationship? Security Issues in the Pacific, with Alexandr Vorontsov (Institute of Oriental Studies) and Artemy Saguirian (Institute of World Politics and Economics), U.S.S.R. Academy of Sciences.
- March 29: Nuclear Weapons and Arms Control in the Pacific, with Andrew Mack, Director, Peace Research Centre, Australian National University.
- Apr. 8: China, New Zealand, and the Nuclear-Free Pacific Issue, with Peter Van Ness, Department of International Relations, Research School of Pacific Studies, Australian National University.

3. Beyond the Arms Race: Alternative Defense and Security

Rob Leavitt and Alaina Smith   *Spring 1988*

Institute for Defense and Disarmament Studies,
2001 Beacon Street, Brookline, MA 02146

Editors' Note: Because of the importance of the new theories and policies currently being developed under the rubric of "alternative security," and because this literature is mostly too new to have yet been integrated into college curricula, we have asked the leading American research institute in this field, the Institute for Defense and Disarmament Studies (IDDS), to construct a reading list. Relevant topics that are covered elsewhere in this volume, such as civilian-based defense, international organization, non-violence, and peace movements, have not been included in this list. The readings were selected for use by advanced students already familiar with the history of the arms race and strategic theory, or in conjunction with other background materials. Those readings that are generally difficult to find are marked with an asterisk (*) and are available from IDDS.

I. New Thinking on Security in the United States

Richard Barnet, "Reflections: The Four Pillars," *The New Yorker*, March 9, 1987.

―――― , "Reflections: Rethinking National Strategy," *The New Yorker*, March 21, 1988.

David Calleo, *Beyond American Hegemony* (New York: Basic Books, 1987).

Richard Falk, "Openings for Peace and Justice in a World of Danger and Struggle," *Alternatives* XIII, 1988.

Archibald Gillies et al., *Post-Reagan America* (New York: World Policy Institute, 1987).

R. C. Johansen and S. H. Mendlovitz, "Why a Discussion of Security Alternatives," in Johansen and Mendlovitz, *The Future of National Security: Contending Options* (Boulder, CO: Lynne Rienner Publishers, 1989).

Paul Kennedy, "The (Relative) Decline of America," *The Atlantic Monthly*, August 1987.

Irving Kristol, "US Foreign Policy has Outlived Its Time," *Wall Street Journal*, January 21, 1988.

*Gwyn Prins, "Implications of the Changing Consensus on Nuclear Deterrence," Paper for the International Symposium "Dimensions of Security and Prospects for Defence After 2000," organised by the Federal Armed Forces Office for Studies and Exercises, Schloss Elmau, Bavaria, Federal Republic of Germany, April 26-28, 1988.

Carolyn Stephenson, "The Need for Alternative Forms of Security," *Alternatives* XIII, 1988.

II. New Thinking on Security in the Soviet Union

*Carl Conetta, "Perestroika in Soviet Security Policy," *Defense and Disarmament Alternatives*, April 1988.

Mikhail Gorbachev, *Perestroika: New Thinking for Our Country and the World* (New York: Harper and Row, 1987).

Jerry Hough, "The End of Russia's 'Khomeini' Period: Dilemmas for U.S. Foreign Policy," *World Policy Journal*, Fall 1987.

Paul Kennedy, "What Gorbachev Is Up Against," *The Atlantic Monthly*, June 1987.

Allen Lynch, "The Restructuring of Soviet Foreign Policy," *Bulletin of the Atomic Scientists*, March 1988.

Michael MccGwire, "New Directions in Soviet Arms Control Policy," *Washington Quarterly* 11:3, Summer 1988.

Thomas Powers, "What Is It About?" *The Atlantic Monthly*, January 1984.

Dimitri K. Simes and Keith B. Bickel, "For Fresh Diplomacy Toward Moscow," *New York Times*, April 1, 1988.

Jack Snyder, "The Gorbachev Revolution: A Waning of Soviet Expansionism," *International Security* 12:3, Winter 1987-88.

Bernard Trainor, "Soviet Arms Doctrine in Flux: An Emphasis on the Defense," *New York Times*, March 7, 1988.

III. New Long-Term Visions: Alternative Defense and Alternative Security

Daniel Deudney, "Whole Earth Security: A Geopolitics of Peace," *Worldwatch Paper 55* (Worldwatch Institute), July 1983.

*Disarmament 2000/Common Security Coalition, "Statement," 1988.

Dietrich Fischer, "Invulnerability Without Threat: The Swiss Concept of General Defense," *Journal of Peace Research* 19, 1982.

———, *Preventing War in the Nuclear Age* (Totowa, NJ: Rowman and Allenheld, 1984).

*Randall Forsberg, "Confining the Military to Defense as a Route to Disarmament," *World Policy Journal*, Winter 1984.

*———, "A Global Approach to Nonprovocative Defense," *Alternative Defense Working Paper No. 1* (Brookline, MA.: Institute for Defense and Disarmament Studies), 1988.

Johan Galtung, *There Are Alternatives!* (Chester Springs, PA: Dufour Editions, Inc., 1984).

Harry B. Hollins et al., *The Conquest of War: Alternative Strategies for Global Security* (Boulder, CO: Westview Press, 1989).

Independent Commission on Disarmament and Security Issues, *Common Security: A Blueprint for Survival* (New York: Simon and Schuster, 1982).

Robert Johansen, "Global Security Without Nuclear Deterrence," *Alternatives* XII, 1987.

Betty Goetz Lall, "Dismantling the War System," in Johansen and Mendlovitz, *The Future of National Security: Contending Options* (Boulder, CO: Lynne Reinner Publishers, 1988).

*Mark Sommer, "An Emerging Consensus: Common Security Through Qualitative Disarmament," *Pamphlet #1* (New York: Fund for Peace/ Alternative Defense Project, 1988).

IV. Denuclearization: Negotiated Solutions

McGeorge Bundy, et al., "The President's Choice: Star Wars or Arms Control," *Foreign Affairs*, Winter 1984–85.

Peter Clausen, "SDI in Search of a Mission," *World Policy Journal*, Spring 1985.

Daniel Deudney, "Forging Missiles into Spaceships," *World Policy Journal*, Spring 1985.

Harold A. Feiveson, Richard H. Ullman, and Frank von Hippel, "Reducing U.S. and Soviet Nuclear Arsenals," *Bulletin of the Atomic Scientists*, August 1985.

Richard Garwin, "A Blueprint for Radical Weapons Cuts," *Bulletin of the Atomic Scientists*, March 1988.

Noel Gayler, "The Way Out: A General Nuclear Settlement," *Yale Law & Policy Review*, V:1, Fall/Winter 1987.

Noel Gayler, "General Nuclear Settlement," in Johansen and Mendlovitz, *The Future of National Security: Contending Options* (Boulder, CO: Lynne Reinner Publishers, 1988).

George Kennan, *The Nuclear Delusion* (New York: Pantheon Books, 1983).

Andrei A. Kokoshin, "A Soviet View on Radical Weapons Cuts," *Bulletin of the Atomic Scientists*, March 1988.

Paul Rogers, "The Nuclear Connection," *Bulletin of the Atomic Scientists*, September 1988.

Thomas Powers, "Nuclear Winter and Nuclear Strategy," *The Atlantic Monthly*, November 1984.

Arthur Waskow, "Transarmament 2000: The Spirit and the Strategy," *Tikkun* I:1, 1986.

V. Denuclearization: Independent Solutions

*Ken Booth, "Nonnuclear Defense for Britain," *Alternative Defense Working Paper No. 2* (Brookline, MA.: Institute for Defense and Disarmament Studies, 1988).

McGeorge Bundy et al., "Back from the Brink," *The Atlantic Monthly,* August 1986.

"Facing Up to First Use of Nuclear Weapons," *F.A.S. Public Interest Report* 39:5, May 1986.

Kennedy Graham, "New Zealand's Non-Nuclear Policy: Towards a Global Security," *Alternatives* XII:2, April 1987.

Morton Halperin, *Nuclear Fallacy* (Cambridge, MA: Ballinger, March 1987).

Morton Halperin, "Nuclear Fallacy," *Bulletin of the Atomic Scientists,* January 1988.

*Andrew Mack, "'Nuclear Allergy': New Zealand's Anti-Nuclear Stance and the South Pacific Nuclear-Free Zone," *Working Paper No. 26* (Peace Research Centre, Research School of Pacific Studies, Australian National University).

*Robert E. White, "The New Zealand Nuclear Ship Ban: Is Compromise Possible?" *Working Paper No. 30* (Peace Research Centre, Research School of Pacific Studies, Australian National University).

VI: Alternative Defense in Europe: Military Solutions

"Arms Control: New Approaches in Europe," *F.A.S. Public Interest Report* 41:2, February 1988.

*Hans Gunter Brauch, "Ten Hypotheses on Confidence and Security Building and Risk Reduction Measures," Manuscript, April 1988.

Jonathan Dean, "Will Negotiated Force Reductions Build Down the NATO-Warsaw Pact Confrontation?" *Washington Quarterly,* Spring 1988.

*Randall Forsberg, "Toward A Non-Aggressive World," *Bulletin of the Atomic Scientists,* September 1988.

John Grin and Lutz Unterseher, "The Spiderweb Defense," *Bulletin of the Atomic Scientists,* September 1988.

Gunilla Herolf, "New Technology Favors Defense," *Bulletin of the Atomic Scientists,* September 1988.

Andrzej Karkoszka, "Merits of the Jaruzelski Plan," *Bulletin of the Atomic Scientists,* September 1988.

Andrei A. Kokoshin, "Restructure Forces, Enhance Security," *Bulletin of the Atomic Scientists,* September 1988.

Michael MccGwire, "Rethinking War: The Soviets and European Security," *Brookings Review,* Spring 1988.

Robert Nield and Anders Boserup, "Beyond INF: A New Approach to Nonnuclear Forces," *World Policy Journal,* Fall 1987.

George Perkovich, *Defending Europe Without Nuclear Weapons,* Council for a Livable World Education Fund, 1987.

"Reducing the Risk of Conventional War in Europe," Report of a Forum at the United Nations, May 8, 1987.

Jack Snyder, "Limiting Offensive Conventional Forces: Soviet Proposals and Western Options," *International Security,* Spring 1988.

*Lutz Unterseher, "Defending Europe: Toward a Stable Conventional Deterrent," University of Maryland Working Paper, 1987.

*Albrecht von Muller and Andrzej Karkoszka, "A Modified Approach to Conventional Arms Control," *Defense and Disarmament Alternatives,* May 1988.

*Albrecht von Muller, "Conventional Stability in Europe: Outlines of the Military Hardware for a Second Detente," Manuscript, 1987.

Albrecht von Muller and Andrzej Karkoszka, "An East-West Negotiating Proposal," *Bulletin of the Atomic Scientists,* September 1988.

Dmitri Yazov, "The Soviet Proposal for European Security," *Bulletin of the Atomic Scientists,* September 1988.

VII. Alternative Defense in Europe: Political Solutions

Ulrich Albrecht, "European Security and the German Question," *World Policy Journal,* Spring 1984.

Ulrich Albrecht, Burkhard Auffermann, and Pertii Joenniemi, "Neutrality: The Need for Conceptual Revision," Manuscript, April 1988.

*"The Helsinki Memorandum," *Across Frontiers,* Spring 1987.

Jolyon Howarth, "The Third Way," *Foreign Policy,* No. 65, Winter 1986-87.

Mary Kaldor, "Beyond the Blocs: Defending Europe the Political Way," *World Policy Journal,* Fall 1983.

Jerry Sanders and Scherle Schwenninger, "A New Grand Strategy: U.S. Policy Toward the Alliance," in Gillies et al., *Post-Reagan America* (New York: World Policy Institute, 1987).

E. P. Thompson and Dan Smith, *Prospectus for a Habitable Planet* (London: Penguin Books, 1987).

VIII. Alternative Defense and Naval Forces

William Arkin and David Chappell, "Forward Offensive Strategy: Raising the Stakes in the Pacific," *World Policy Journal* 11:3, Summer 1985.

Jack Beatty, "In Harm's Way," *The Atlantic Monthly,* May 1987.

*Anders Boserup, "Maritime Defence Without Naval Threat: The Case of the Baltic," Paper presented at the Fifth Workshop of the Pugwash Study Group on Conventional Forces in Europe, October 9–12, 1986.

*Andrew Mack, "Arms Control in the North Pacific: Problems and Prospects," Manuscript, March 1988.

John J. Mearsheimer, "A Strategic Misstep," *International Security*, Fall 1986.

*Bjorn Moller, "A Non-Offensive Maritime Strategy for the Nordic Area," *Alternative Defence Working Paper No. 3* (Institute for Defense and Disarmament Studies), 1988.

*Gwyn Prins, "Potential Naval Requirements Within a Reformed NATO Strategy," Paper presented at the Fifth Workshop of the Pugwash Study Group on Conventional Forces in Europe, October 9–12, 1986.

Lyuba Zarsky, Peter Hayes, and Walden Bello, "Brinksmanship in the Pacific," *Nuclear Times*, May/June 1987.

IX. Ending Superpower Intervention in the Third World

Walden Bello, "U.S.-Sponsored Low-Intensity Conflict in the Philippines," *Food First Development Report No. 2* (Institute for Food and Development Policy), December 1987.

Richard Fagen, *Forging Peace: The Challenge of Central America* (New York: Basil Blackwell, 1987).

*Randall Forsberg, "The Case for a Third World Nonintervention Regime," *Alternative Defense Working Paper No. 6* (Institute for Defense and Disarmament Studies), 1988.

Robert H. Johnson, "Exaggerating America's Stakes in Third World Conflicts," *International Security*, Winter 1985-86.

Michael T. Klare and Peter Kornbluh (eds.), *Low Intensity Warfare* (New York: Pantheon Books, 1988).

Jonathan Kwitny, *Endless Enemies* (New York: Penguin Books, 1986).

*Howard Morland, "Superpower Battlefields," Coalition for a New Foreign Policy, 1986.

Earl Ravenal, *Defining Defense: The 1985 Military Budget* (Washington, DC: Cato Institute, 1984).

Earl Ravenal, "An Alternative to Containment," Policy Analysis No. 94 (Cato Institute), November 1987.

Jerry Sanders and Sherle Schwenninger, "A New Grand Strategy: U.S. Policy Toward the Third World," Gillies et al., *Post-Reagan America* (New York: World Policy Institute, 1987).

Jerome Slater, "Dominoes in Central America: Will They Fall? Does It Matter?" *International Security*, Fall 1987.

Ramesh Thakur, "International Peacekeeping, UN Authority and US Power," *Alternatives* XII:4, October 1987.

Henry Wiseman, "Peacekeeping and the Management of International Conflict," Background Paper No. 15 (Canadian Institute for International Peace and Security), September 1987.

Henry Wiseman (ed.), *Peacekeeping: Appraisals and Proposals* (New York: Pergamon Press, 1983).

X. Nonmilitary Security

Morris J. Blachman, William M. LeoGrande, and Kenneth E. Sharpe (eds.), *Confronting Revolution: Security Through Diplomacy in Central America* (New York: Pantheon, 1986).

Elisabeth Mann Borgese, "Towards a World Space Organization," *Points of View Number 5* (Canadian Institute for International Peace and Security), November 1987.

Lester R. Brown and Edward C. Wolf, "Reclaiming the Future," Brown et al., *State of the World 1988* (New York: W.W. Norton, 1988).

Kevin Danaher, Phillip Berryman, and Medea Benjamin, "Help or Hindrance?: United States Economic Aid in Central America," *Food First Development Report No. 1* (Institute for Food and Development Policy), September 1987.

Disarmament and Development, Joint Declaration by the Panel of Eminent Personalities, United Nations, April 16–18, 1986.

Richard Hudson, "The Case for the Binding Triad," *Special Study No. 7* (Center for War/Peace Studies), Summer 1983.

Robert C. Johansen, "The Reagan Administration and the U.N.: The Costs of Unilateralism," *World Policy Journal*, Fall 1986 (pp. 601–641).

Francis Moore Lappe, Rachel Shurman, and Kevin Danaher, *Betraying the National Interest* (New York: Grove Press, 1987).

Lester Edwin J. Ruiz, "Quest for Authentic Polity: The Philippine Case," in Mendlovitz and Walker (eds.), *Towards a Just World Peace: Perspectives from Social Movements* (Boston: Butterworths, 1987).

D. L. Sheth, "Alternative Development as Political Practice," Mendlovitz and Walker (eds.), *Towards a Just World Peace: Perspectives from Social Movements* (Boston: Butterworths, 1987).

Lloyd Timberlake and Jon Tinker, "The Environmental Origins of Political Conflict," *Socialist Review* 84, November-December 1985.

Case Studies on Smaller Powers
Britain
Switzerland
New Zealand
Canada
Sweden
Finland
Austria

4. Scientific Cooperation and Superpower Security

Daniel Deudney   *Spring 1986*
Woodrow Wilson School, Princeton University,
Princeton, NJ 08544

Imagine that the largest and most dangerous military crisis since the end of the Second World War has just ended. Large-scale violence occurred and there were substantial casualties in third countries, but a full-scale nuclear exchange was avoided, and a fragile truce arranged. Throughout the world there is a tremendous sense of relief combined with a sense that a fundamentally new approach to the superpower relationship must be devised. The advocates of a hard line in both countries are in a temporary political eclipse. Despite the crisis—or perhaps because of it—many hard-liners in both countries feel that their view of the adversary has been proven true. Once things have returned to normal they expect to pursue their agendas with renewed vigor.

In short, the world is at one of those critical turning points that occur once every generation or so. The General Secretary of the CPSU has approached the President of the United States through diplomatic channels, urging that a bold new approach be forged while "the ruins are still hot." The shaken leaders have agreed to meet in three months. To prepare for this important meeting, three task forces, composed of key government officials and leading citizens, have been set up. One panel will look at ways to make deep reductions in existing nuclear forces and a second will propose changes in the political relationship and solutions to regional conflicts. In the United States, at the urging of the Director of the Office of Technology Assessment, a close personal advisor of the President, a third panel—this Policy Task Force—has been established to devise proposals for cooperative scientific and technological ventures between the superpowers. To be responsive to the opportunities and risks of this policy context, members of the Task Force will have to think about policy in non-incremental terms.

The Task Force will have a basic choice: whether to recommend very ambitious cooperative activities that could significantly constrain the U.S.-Soviet qualitative arms race, or to recommend cooperative activities in areas without military significance in an attempt to change attitudes and enmesh the two countries in a network of mutually beneficial activities. The risks of either course are high: should a major derailment of the arms race be attempted, and then fail, a last hope for reconciliation could be lost and relations could be further damaged. But should indirect methods be attempted, they might not be strong enough to overcome the established patterns of hostility. The President is willing to take risks, but he will accept only those proposals that are likely to make a real difference and become at least in part politically self-sustaining.

Issues at Stake

To gain a common background on the issues at stake, the Task Force will begin by examining theories that purport to explain how cooperation can alter international politics and the general role of science and technology in the U.S.-Soviet military competition. Then the Task Force will examine three important and very different case studies of the relationships between militarily significant innovations and politics: the Manhattan Project, the post-war proposals for international development of atomic power, and the International Geophysical Year. Next the Task Force will seek a more general understanding of the relationship among secrecy, innovation, and the arms race, and the different ways in which the United States and the Soviet Union harness science and technology for military uses. The Task Force will complete its initial orientation by examining the current policy debates over scientific exchange and communication, and more intensely examine specific proposals for space cooperation.

In formulating its policy recommendations, the Task Force will wrestle with the following questions:

1. How does functionalist theory maintain that cooperative problem solving alters political relationships? What are the limitations and possible extensions of this approach?

2. Why did the most important proposal for international scientific and technological development, the Acheson-Lillienthal-Baruch Plan, fail? If implemented could the plan have achieved its goals?

3. What policy lessons can be drawn from the most successful example of international cooperation, the International Geophysical Year?

4. Is an "Open Labs" agreement a means to stem the technological arms race? Is it a substitute for or a vital part of cooperative science?

5. How have disputes over Soviet dissidents, restive minority groups, and potential defectors affected previous U.S.-Soviet interactions in the field of science and technology? Will these problems plague large-scale ventures, or are there solutions for them?

6. What policies exist to encourage or impede the flow of scientific information, and how effective have these policies been in achieving their stated goals?

7. How will efforts either to constrain or expand the flow of scientific information internationally affect the quality of the scientific enterprise?

8. Are there definable "big science" projects (for instance, in space exploration, particle physics, oceanography, or energy production) with enough scientific merit and political visibility to warrant undertaking?

9. Should programs of international scientific cooperation be altogether avoided with the Soviet Union, conducted only in areas with negligible military importance, or pursued in areas most likely to be militarized if kept secret?

10. Given that the United States is generally ahead of the Soviet Union in most, but not all, areas of research, would programs of U.S.-Soviet scientific collaboration work to the general disadvantage of the United States, or are there compensating advantages, either scientific or political, to be gained from insight into the activities of the Soviet scientific establishment?

11. What role should the scientific community have in determining constraints on the exchange of scientific information or the direction of cooperative endeavors?

12. Should the rate of scientific exchange between the United States and the Soviet Union be linked to, or isolated from, short-term "ups and downs" in the two countries' relationship?

13. Can the United States impose constraints on the flow of scientific information to the Soviet Union and maintain extensive scientific contact with the rest of the world?

14. Should cooperation between the superpowers be given priority over cooperation with other countries so as to maximize the political "fallout," or should broad international participation be pursued so as to give the efforts extra staying power?

TIMETABLE

Weeks 1–3

Introductory lectures. Background readings. Bibliographical searches. Individual consultations on paper topics. One-page paper proposals due Feb. 26.

Weeks 4–6

Guest lecturers. Individual reading and writing. Advanced outlines due Mar. 22.

Recess:

Possible trip to Washington, D.C. (two days).

Weeks 7–8

Completion of individual papers, which are due Apr. 4.

Weeks 9–10

Oral presentation of papers. Group work on task force report.

Week 11

Revision of papers. Group work on task force report.

Week 12
Completion of final papers and task force report. Papers and report due
May 2.

LECTURE TOPICS WITH READINGS

Can Cooperation Alter International Relations? An Introduction to Functionalism
Main Sources
- David Mitrany, *A Working Peace System* (Chicago: Quadrangle, revised edition, original 1943). Selections.

Additional Sources
- David Mitrany, *The Functionalist Theory of Politics* (New York: St. Martin's Press, 1975).
- Ernst Haas, *Beyond the Nation-State* (Stanford, CA: Stanford University Press, 1964), pp. 3–126.
- A.J.R. Groom and Paul Taylor, *Functionalism: Theory and Practice in International Relations* (London: University of London Press, 1975).

The Role of Science and Technology in Modern Warfare
- William McNeill, chapter 9, "World Wars of the Twentieth Century," and chapter 10, "The Arms Race and Command Economies Since 1945," in *The Pursuit of Power: Technology, Armed Force, and Society Since A.D. 1000*, pp. 307–389.
- Harold Sapolsky, "Science, Technology, and Military Policy," in Ina Spiegel-Rosing and Derek de Solla Price, eds., *Science, Technology and Society* (London: Sage Publications), pp. 443–473.
- Merritt Roe Smith, "Introduction," *Military Enterprise and Technological Change* (Cambridge, MA: MIT Press, 1985), pp. 1–37. (Summarizes the vast literature on the complex interaction between the military and technology.)
- Herman Kahn and Anthony Weiner, "Technological Innovation and the Future of Strategic Weapons," *Astronautics and Aeronautics*, December 1967, pp. 29–48.

Secret Science and Its Consequences: The Manhattan Project and the Nuclear Arms Race
Main Sources
- Alice Kimball Smith, "The War Years," chapter 1, *A Peril and a Hope: The Scientist Movement in America, 1945–47* (Cambridge, MA: MIT Press, 1965) pp. 3–75.

Additional Sources
- The definitive and official history of the Manhattan Project is Richard Hewlett and Oscar Anderson, Jr., *A New World, 1939/1946*, Vol. I of

A History of the United States Atomic Energy Commission (University Park, PA: 1962).

- For an account of the political setting and consequences of the Manhattan Project, see Martin Sherwin, *A World Destroyed: The Atomic Bomb and the Grand Alliance* (New York, 1975).

The Failure of Nuclear Cooperation: The Acheson-Lillienthal-Baruch Plan

Main Sources

- Lenice Wu, "The Baruch Plan: U.S. Diplomacy Enters the Nuclear Age," in Vol. I, Congressional Research Service, *Science, Technology, and American Diplomacy*, pp. 53–123.
- James Franck et al., "A Report to the Secretary of War,"; Leo Szilard, "A Petition to the President of the United States,"; J. Robert Oppenheimer, "International Control of Atomic Energy," and "The Failure of International Control," in M. Grodzins and E. Rabinowitch, eds., *The Atomic Age* (New York: Basic Books, 1963), pp. 19–28, pp. 28–30, pp. 53–76.

Additional Sources

- Walter Lippmann, "International Control of Atomic Energy," in Dexter Masters and Katherine Ways, eds., *One World or None?* (London: Latimer House, 1947).
- Joseph Nogee, *Soviet Policy Toward International Control of Atomic Energy* (Notre Dame, Indiana: University of Notre Dame Press, 1961).

Cooperative Science and Its Consequences: The International Geophysical Year

Main Sources

- Harold Bullis, "The Political Legacy of the International Geophysical Year," in *Science, Technology, and American Diplomacy*, pp. 293–361.
- Y.K. Federov, "Antarctica: Experimental Proving Ground for Peaceful Co-Existence and International Collaboration," in Richard Lewis and Philip M. Smith, eds., *Frozen Future: A Prophetic Report from Antarctica* (New York: Quadrangle Books, 1973), pp. 64–86.

Additional Sources

- Lloyd Berkner, "International Scientific Action: The International Geophysical Year: 1957–1958," *Science*, April 30, 1954 (the original plan for IGY).
- Sidney Chapman, "Earth and Beyond: The International Geophysical Year in Retrospect: Was It a Turning Point in History?" *Science*, July 7, 1961.
- Sidney Chapman, *IGY: Year of Discovery* (Ann Arbor: University of Michigan Press, 1959).
- Walter Sullivan, "The IGY—Scientific Alliance in a Divided World," *Bulletin of the Atomic Scientists*, February 1958.

- Walter Sullivan, *Assault on the Unknown: The International Geophysical Year* (New York: McGraw Hill, 1961).
- J. Tuzo Wilson, *IGY: The Year of the New Moons* (New York: Alfred A. Knopf, 1961).

Secrecy, Innovation, and the Arms Race
Main Sources
- A. DeVolpi et al., "Government Secrecy," chapter VII, and "Misuses of Secrecy," chapter VIII, in *Born Secret: The H-Bomb, the Progressive Case and National Security* (New York: Pergamon, 1981), pp. 131–179.
- Edward Teller, "The Feasibility of Arms Control and the Principle of Openness," in Donald Brennan, ed., *Arms Control, Disarmament, and National Security* (New York: George Braziller, 1961), pp. 122–138.
- Sissela Bok, "Secrecy and Competition in Science," "Secrets of State," "Military Secrecy," in *Secrets: On the Ethics of Concealment and Revelation* (New York: Pantheon, 1982), pp. 153–210.
- Deborah Shapley, "Arms Control as a Regulator of Military Technology," *Daedalus*, Winter 1980, pp. 145–159.
- Owen Wilkes, "Military Research and Development Programs: Problems of Control," *Bulletin of Peace Proposals*, Vol. 9, No. 1, 1978, pp. 3–10.

Additional Sources
- Martin McGuire, *Secrecy and the Arms Race* (Cambridge, MA: Harvard University Press, 1965).

Contrasting Soviet and American Approaches to Strategic Science and Technology
Main Sources
- David Holloway, "The Defense Economy," chapter 6, and "Military Technology," chapter 7, *The Soviet Union and the Arms Race* (New Haven: Yale University Press, 1983), pp. 109–156.
- U.S. Department of Defense, *Soviet Military Power*, 1986 edition (selections).
- Herbert York and G. Allen Greb, "Military Research and Development: A Postwar History," *Bulletin of the Atomic Scientists*, January 1977, pp. 13–26.
- William Perry, "The Countervailing Strategy," *Technology Review*, 1979.

Additional Sources
- Kendall E. Bailes, *Technology and Society Under Stalin and Lenin* (Princeton University Press, 1978).
- Loren Graham, *The Soviet Academy of Sciences and the Communist Party*, 1967.
- Loren Graham, *Science and Philosophy in the Soviet Union* (New York: Knopf, 1972).
- D. Joravsky, *The Lysenko Affair* (Cambridge, MA: Harvard University Press, 1970).

- D. Joravsky, *Soviet Marxism and Natural Science* (New York: Columbia University Press, 1961).
- R.W. Judy, "The Case of Computer Technology," in M. Bornstein and D. Fusfeld, eds., *The Soviet Economy,* 4th edition (Homewood, IL: R.D. Irwin, 1974).
- Linda L. Lubrano and Susan G. Soloman, eds., *The Social Context of Soviet Science* (Boulder, CO: Westview Press, 1980).
- Zhores A. Medvedev, *The Rise and Fall of T.D. Lysenko* (Garden City, NY: Doubleday & Co., 1971).
- Mark Popovsky, *Manipulated Science: The Crisis of Science and Scientists in the Soviet Union Today* (Garden City, NY: Doubleday & Co. Inc., 1979).
- John R. Thomas and Ursala M. Krauss-Vaucienne, *Soviet Science and Technology: Domestic and Foreign Perspectives* (Washington, D.C.: The Program in Science and Technology Policy Studies, GWU, 1977).
- Alexander Vucinich, *Empire of Knowledge: The Academy of Sciences of the USSR (1917–1970)* (Berkeley, CA: University of California Press, 1984).
- E. Zaleski et al., *Science Policy in the USSR* (Paris: OECD, 1969).

An Overview of Recent U.S. Debates on East-West Trade in Technology and Controls on Scientific Communication

Main Sources

- Mary Cheh, "Government Control of Private Ideas," Stanford Unger, "National Security and the Free Flow of Technical Information," and Harold Relyea, "Shrouding the Endless Frontier: Scientific Communication" and "National Security: The Search for Balance," in Relyea, ed., *Striking a Balance: National Security and Scientific Freedom* (Washington, D.C.: AAAS, 1985), pp. 6–29, 29–47, 75–125.
- "Secrecy and University Research," special issue of *Science, Technology and Human Values*, Spring 1985 (selections to be announced).
- National Academy of Sciences, "Current Knowledge about Unwanted Technology Transfer and Its Military Significance," chapter 1, and "The Current Control System," chapter 3, in *Scientific Communication and National Security* (Washington, D.C.: National Academy Press, 1982), pp. 13–22, pp. 27–39.

Additional Sources

- Bruce Parrott, ed., *Trade, Technology, and Soviet-American Relations* (Bloomington, IN: Indiana University Press, 1985).
- Office of Technology Assessment, *Technology and East-West Trade* (Washington, D.C.: November 1979).
- Linda Lelvern et al., *Techno-Bandits: How the Soviets Are Stealing America's High-Tech Future* (New York: Houghton Mifflin Co., 1984).

The Record of U.S.-Soviet Cooperation
Main Sources

- Loren Graham, "How Valuable Are Scientific Exchanges with the Soviet Union?" *Science*, October 27, 1978.
- Linda Lubrano, "The Political Web of Scientific Cooperation Between the U.S.A. and U.S.S.R.," in Nish Jamgotch, Jr., *Sectors of Mutual Benefit in U.S.-Soviet Relations* (Durham, NC: Duke University Press, 1985), pp. 50–83. (Note: This book contains additional articles on specific areas of U.S.-Soviet cooperation as well as the texts of all major U.S.-Soviet cooperative agreements.)
- Loren Graham, "Scientific Exchanges with the Soviet Union," *Bulletin of the Atomic Scientists*, May 1983.

Additional Sources

- National Research Council, *Review of the U.S./U.S.S.R. Interacademy Exchanges and Relations* (Washington, D.C.: National Science Foundation, September 1977).
- National Research Council, *Review of the U.S./U.S.S.R. Agreement on Cooperation in the Fields of Science and Technology* (Washington, D.C.: National Science Foundation, 1977).

An Intensive Case Study: Competitive and Cooperative Alternatives in Space
Main Sources

- Office of Technology Assessment, *U.S.-Soviet Cooperation in Space: A Technical Memorandum* (Washington, D.C.: July 1985), pp. 1–97.
- Daniel Deudney, "Forging Missiles into Spaceships," *World Policy Journal*, Spring 1985, pp. 271–303.
- Soviet Space Cooperation and Arms Control," *Bulletin of the Atomic Scientists*, Vol. 41, No. 3, March 1985.
- Bruce Murray and Merton Davies, "Detente in Space," *Science*, Vol. 192, June 11, 1976.

Additional Sources

- James Oberg, "A Shuttle-Salyut Joint Mission," in *New Race for Space* (Harrisburg, PA: Stockpole Books, 1984).
- Edward Ezell and Linda Ezell, *The Partnership: A History of the Apollo-Soyuz Test Project* (Washington, D.C.: NASA, 1978).
- William Hayes, Jr., *Space: New Opportunities for International Ventures*, vol. 49 (San Diego: American Astronautical Society, 1980).

5. Arms Control and Disarmament

David Bernstein and Coit Blacker   *Winter 1988*
Political Science Dept., Stanford University,
Stanford, CA 94305

This course on arms control and disarmament deals with a wide spectrum of subjects and issues relating to efforts of the past, present, and future to control the spread of nuclear and conventional weapons.

Arms control and disarmament are often referred to by authorities and scholars as a complex field. In large part, this is because of the variety of technical, historical, political, military, and economic considerations involved in policy issues. The terminology of weapons systems, much of it of recent origin and yet frequently changing (e.g., Polaris, Poseidon, and Trident), also contributes to the problem of understanding the arms race and efforts to control it. But understanding the arms race and the issues involved is not difficult—with some study. Questions of judgment will remain, but judgments made on the basis of a clearer understanding of facts and of the real issues are more likely to be valid ones for students as well as specialists. One of the goals of this course is to help the student develop such a basis for judgment.

For the first time in history, a point has been reached where the world's superpowers can destroy each other's societies—and, perhaps, much of the globe. Stability of a kind exists between the United States and the Soviet Union, but competition between them in Europe, Asia, the Middle East, and Africa remains intense. And the arms competition continues. As this class begins, the United States and the Soviet Union have just signed a treaty to eliminate intermediate-range nuclear weapons, and negotiations on strategic nuclear weapons and space and defensive weapons are in progress.

How did we get to this point, and what can be done to change the situation? What role can arms control play in this effort, and what can we learn from the past successes and failures in this field? Related questions concerning the responsibility of scientists, the relationship between science and policy, and the relevance of war-making and expenditures on arms to the economic well-being of all societies will also be raised in this course. What role does (or can) the citizen-student play? Dealing with the control of weapons involves values, and it requires knowledge on matters of fact and some perspective. These and many more considerations have led us to offer this course.

The field of arms control and international security is still a relatively new area of study. It is in the process of development and refinement. This course reflects that fact. Previous teaching experience, including student critiques, has contributed to the content and design of the course outline. Several courses on arms control were offered earlier. Some of the faculty have offered courses in international politics, force and diplomacy, military history, peace studies, and legal problems of weapons control; this course has been offered in an interdisciplinary fashion since 1971. On the basis of past experience, some changes have been made in the course outline. This has been, in a sense, a pioneering effort, for until the past several years only a few universities offered any courses in the field. At the present time, this is one of the few fully interdisciplinary courses on arms control offered in the United States.

All of the faculty have had practical and/or research experience in dealing with matters of arms control, disarmament, and international security. Some have been involved in negotiations, and many have participated in the public debates on ABM, MIRV, chemical and biological warfare, and SALT and START. The staff for the course brings together political scientists, historians, physicists, medical doctors, lawyers, diplomats, and engineers. Although each field has its own language, intellectual traditions, and biases, we hope to present an integrated, multi-faceted understanding of the problems associated with arms control and disarmament. Coit Blacker and David Bernstein constitute "continuing staff" for the course. Students are also encouraged to see other faculty participants in the course, should they wish to do so.

In addition to the regular faculty who will be giving lectures in the course, the following individuals will join us as special lecturers: Gloria Duffy, a member of the Center for International Security and Arms Control (hereafter "the Center"); Philip Farley, a member of the Center; James E. Goodby, a member of the Center and former U.S. Ambassador to the CDE negotiations; Sidney Graybeal, a member of the Center and former Ambassador to the Standing Consultative Commission; Michael May, Associate Director of Lawrence Livermore National Laboratory; Dr. Alden Mullins, a Group Leader at the Lawrence Livermore National Laboratory and a former Fellow at the Center; Dr. William Perry, former Under Secretary of Defense for Research and Engineering in the Carter Administration; and Theodore Postol, Senior Research Associate at the Center.

Course Requirements

Considerable thought has gone into the selection of course readings. We have limited the number of books to be purchased to the following:

Blacker and Duffy, eds., *International Arms Control: Issues and Agreements*, second edition (Stanford: Stanford University Press, 1984); hereafter Blacker and Duffy.

National Academy of Sciences, *Nuclear Arms Control: Background and Issues* (Washington, D.C.: National Academy Press, 1985); hereafter NAS.

Richard A. Scribner, Theodore J. Ralston, and William D. Metz, *The Verification of Challenge* (Boston and Basel: Birkhauser, 1985).

The required readings for each unit are meant to complement the lectures; they are listed in the order that they should be read. All readings, other than those in the books to be purchased, are on reserve in Meyer Undergraduate Library. In making the selections, we have sought to combine more general writings with arms control documents of historical merit and selected material on specific topics. Students should complete the required readings along with the lectures in each unit and should seek clarification of any problems with respect to the readings in the discussion sections. Students seeking additional information on any lecture topic are encouraged to consult Coit Blacker or David Bernstein. The teaching assistants are also available for consultation and direction.

During the winter quarter, there will be four lectures a week. A weekly discussion section will be arranged (and attendance is strongly encouraged). Two exams will be given: a mid-term and a final. Attendance at exams is required. Make-up exams and incompletes will not be given, except in case of illness.

Although Political Science 138A has been offered in a similar manner before, we hope to improve the content and the manner of presentation of material. We welcome your suggestions and criticisms of the course. Interested students who complete this course may apply to take an advanced seminar simulating an actual treaty negotiation, Political Science 138B: "Arms Control Negotiation."

SCHEDULE OF LECTURES

I. Introduction

Jan. 5—Introduction [C. Blacker]

Readings for Section I
• Blacker and Duffy, Chapters 1–4.

II. The Role of Technology

Jan. 6—The Physics of Nuclear Weapons [S. Drell]

Jan. 7—The Technology and the State of Strategic Weapons Development [S. Drell]

Jan. 8—Consequences of Nuclear War [T. Postol]

Readings for Section II
- Blacker and Duffy, Chapter 9.
- Theodore Postol, "Nuclear War," *Encyclopedia Americana*, 1987, pp. 519–32.
- David Barash, *The Arms Race and Nuclear War*, Chapter 2.

III. Post-War Development of Nuclear Weapons and Arms Control

Jan. 11—The Benefits and Dangers of Nuclear Weapons—The Quest for Disarmament, 1943–1947 [B. Bernstein]

Jan. 12—The Benefits and Dangers of Nuclear Weapons—The Quest for Control, 1947–1957 [B. Bernstein]

Jan. 13—The Post-War Buildup of Strategic Weapons [C. Blacker]

Readings for Section III
- Blacker and Duffy, Chapters 5–7 and pp. 366–373.
- Barton Bernstein, "The Challenges and Dangers of Nuclear Weapons: American Foreign Policy and Strategy," *Foreign Service Journal*, September 1978, pp. 9–15 and 36.
- Dwight MacDonald, "The Bomb: The Decline to Barbarism," *The Atomic Bomb: The Critical Choices.*

IV. The Evolution of a Nuclear World: Political and Technical Considerations

Jan. 14—Technological Aspects of Nuclear Proliferation [D. Bernstein]

Jan. 14 & 15—Discussion Sections

Jan. 19—The NPT and the Politics of Non-Proliferation [P.J. Farley]

Jan. 20—Trends in a Proliferating World [A. Mullins]

Jan. 21—Nuclear Testing and Test Ban Negotiations [W.K.H. Panofsky]

Jan. 21 & 22—Discussion Sections

Readings for Section IV
- Blacker and Duffy, Chapter 8 and pp. 392–396, 434–437.
- Leonard Spector, *Going Nuclear*, Chapter 3 and pp. 130–146.
- NAS, Chapter 7.

V. Strategic Military Doctrines

Jan. 25—The Evolution of U.S. Strategic Doctrine I [C. Blacker]

Jan. 26—The Evolution of U.S. Strategic Doctrine II [C. Blacker]

Jan. 27—The Evolution of Soviet Strategic Doctrine I [D. Holloway]

Jan. 28—The Evolution of Soviet Strategic Doctrine II [D. Holloway]

Jan. 28 & 29—Discussion Sections

Feb. 1—British and French Approaches to Nuclear Weapons, Strategic Doctrine and Arms Control [C. Blacker]

Feb. 2—Chinese Approach to Nuclear Weapons, Strategic Doctrine and Arms Control [Lewis]

Readings for Section V
- Blacker and Duffy, Chapter 10.
- *Report of the President's Commission on Strategic Forces*, April 1983.
- Coit D. Blacker, *Reluctant Warriors: The United States, the Soviet Union, Arms Control*, Chapter 6.
- Caspar W. Weinberger, *Annual Report to Congress, FY 1988*, pp. 41–50.
- David Holloway, *The Soviet Union and the Arms Race*, pp. 15–64.
- Lawrence Freedman, *The Evolution of Nuclear Strategy*, Chapters 19–21.
- Chinese 1982 U.N. Statement.
- "China's Basic Position on Disarmament," *Beijing Review*, No. 12, March 24, 1986, pp. 14–15.

VI. U.S.-Soviet Strategic Arms Control Negotiations

Feb. 3—Strategic Defense and the Offense-Defense Relationship [W.K.H. Panofsky]

Feb. 4—SALT I [D. Bernstein]

Feb. 4 & 5—Discussion Sections

Feb. 8—SALT II [Duffy]

Feb. 9—Monitoring and Compliance [S. Graybeal]

Feb. 10—Assessing the U.S.-Soviet Balance [W. Perry]

Feb. 11—START and INF [C. Blacker]

Feb. 12—Midterm Examination

Feb. 16—SDI, Space Systems and ASAT [S. Drell]

Feb. 17—Future Arms Control Proposals [M. May]

Readings for Section VI
- W.K.H. Panofsky, Lecture notes PS138A, 1986, "Nuclear Offense and Defense: Current Policy Technology Interactions."
- NAS, Chapter 5.
- Blacker and Duffy, Chapters 11 and 12 and pp. 413–432, 446–477, 356 and 408–412.
- Richard A. Scribner, Theodore J. Ralston, and William D. Metz, *The Verification Challenge*, Chapters 1–3 and 8.
- Sidney Graybeal and Michael Krepon, *Bulletin of Atomic Scientists*, Dec. 1987, pp. 22–26.
- Ronald W. Reagan, *Department of State Bulletin*, April 1983, pp. 13–14.
- Sidney D. Drell, Philip J. Farley, and David Holloway, "Preserving the ABM Treaty: A Critique of the Reagan Strategic Defense Initiative," *International Security*, Fall 1984, pp. 51–92.
- Colin S. Gray, "A Case for Strategic Defense," *Strategic Defense Initiative: Folly or Future*, edited by P. Edward Haley and Jack Merritt, pp. 81–87.
- NAS, Chapter 6.

VII. Approaches to Conflict Prevention and Control

Feb. 18—Pathways to Nuclear War [S. Sagan]

Feb. 18 & 19—Discussion Sections

Feb. 22—Accidental and Inadvertent Nuclear War [Abrams]

Feb. 23—Crisis Management and Crisis Prevention [George]

Readings for Section VII
- Graham T. Allison, Albert Carnesale, and Joseph S. Nye, Jr., editors, *Hawks, Doves, and Owls*, Chapter 7.
- Scott D. Sagan, "Nuclear Alerts and Crisis Management," *International Security*, Spring 1985, pp. 99–139.
- Daniel Frei, *Risks of Unintentional Nuclear War*, pp. 1–22.
- Committee on International Security and Arms Control, National Academy of Sciences, *Crisis Management in the Nuclear Age*.
- Barry M. Blechman and Michael Krepon, *Nuclear Risk Reduction Centers*.

VIII. Regional Security Issues

Feb. 24—West European Approaches to Security [Blacker]

Feb. 25—East European Approaches to Security [Rice]

Feb. 26—Discussion Sections

Feb. 29—Conference on Security and Cooperation in Europe: The Helsinki Process, 1972–87 [Blacker]

Mar. 1—New Conventional Technologies and the Prevention of Nuclear War in Europe [W. Perry]

Mar. 2—Arms Sales and Arms Races in Critical Regions [A. Mullins]

Readings for Section VIII
- Blacker and Duffy, Chapter 13.
- Barry M. Blechman, editor, *Preventing Nuclear War*, Chapter 3.
- Andrew Pierre, "Arms Sales: The New Diplomacy," *Foreign Affairs*, Winter 1981–82, pp. 266–286.
- Alexander J. Bennett, "Arms Transfer as an Instrument of Soviet Policy in the Middle East," *Middle East Journal*, Autumn 1985, pp. 745–774.
- Pranay Gupte, "Russia: Arms Merchant to the World," *Forbes*, Nov. 2, 1987, pp. 168–171.

IX. Summary

Mar. 3—The Moral Implications of Nuclear Weapons and the Role of the Public [Hamerton-Kelly]

Mar. 3 & 4—Discussion Sections

Mar. 7—Outlook for Nuclear Arms Control [J. E. Goodby]

Mar. 8—Outlook for Conventional, Chemical and Biological Arms Control [J.E. Goodby]

Mar. 9—A Critique of Arms Control [Barton]

Mar. 10—Disarmament, Arms Control and the Future [Drell]

Mar. 10 & 11—Discussion Sections

Readings for Section IX
- National Conference of Catholic Bishops, *The Challenge of Peace: God's Promise and Our Reponse*, 1983, pp. 26–84.
- Reverend J. Bryan Hehir, "Ethical Considerations in the Nuclear Age," Keynote address in "Building a Safer 21st Century," Stanford, December 6, 1987, *Campus Report*, Dec. 9, 1987, pp. 14, 22–23.

- John Barton, _Politics of Peace_, pp. 200–232.
- Blacker and Duffy, Chapter 15.
- Joseph S. Nye, Jr. "Farewell to Arms Control?" _Foreign Affairs_, Fall 1986, pp. 1–20.
- Kenneth L. Adelman, "Arms Control With and Without Agreements," _Foreign Affairs_, Winter 1984, pp. 240–263.
- Sidney D. Drell, _Facing the Threat of Nuclear Weapons_, pp. 3–85.

Mar. 18—Final Examination

6. Arms Control Negotiations

John Lewis   _Spring 1987_
Political Science Dept., Stanford University,
Stanford, CA 94305

This seminar will build on and develop further the history, substance, and political-strategic consequences of arms control negotiations and agreements which were studied and assessed in Political Science 138A, "Arms Control and Disarmament."

It will analyze the policy-making and negotiating process in the field of arms control and will explore the ways in which political, military, technological and other factors combine to influence negotiations. One objective of the course is to study the nature of the U.S.-Soviet relationship in both its international and domestic settings by examining in depth how U.S. decision makers and negotiators have handled specific negotiating problems. Another objective is to analyze the theory and practice of negotiations. A third purpose of the course is to provide a basis for analyzing and forming judgments about national security issues.

The investigation of this process will begin with a discussion of the theory of negotiations and of U.S. and Soviet negotiating styles. An essential part of the negotiating process is the national decision-making process that precedes and accompanies international negotiations. Therefore, the seminar will review policy formulation in the U.S. Government. This will be followed by discussions of some case studies of actual experiences in U.S.-Soviet arms control negotiations. The case studies will provide the means of discerning the roles played by negotiators and policymakers in the policy and diplomatic process. It will highlight the types of problems they have confronted and analyze the approaches they adopted to policy and negotiating problems. The final phase of the seminar will consist of a simulation of a U.S.-Soviet negotiation on strategic nuclear arms control in which the students will form two delegations and engage in an effort to negotiate an agreement.

The attached schedule shows the sequence of topics to be taken up in the seminar. During the first meeting of the seminar we will discuss in detail the plans for the course and will begin the process of organizing teams for the simulation. When the simulation begins, participants will be expected to be informed about the issues and to have at their disposal adequate technical and other background information. Students also should be prepared to discuss and analyze each of the case studies during the sessions indicated on the attached schedule.

Contributions to the quality of the analysis through careful preparation and regular participation are essential both for the individual student and for the class as a whole. The students' grades will be based upon class participation in the discussions and the simulation.

The reading for each session is shown in the attached schedule. A bibliography of readings for the course is attached. All of the readings are on reserve in Meyer. All materials listed for each class should be read before the class since most of the discussion will focus on them.

The course will be taught by John Lewis, James Goodby, Coit Blacker, David Bernstein, and George Bunn, of Stanford's Center for Arms Control and International Security. These five will constitute the "control group" for the simulation.

SCHEDULE

Mar. 31—Introduction to the Course and Organization of the Simulation [Bernstein]

Apr. 2—Approaches to the Study of Negotiations [Lewis]
- Robert Jervis, "Cooperation Under the Security Dilemma," *World Politics*, Vol. 30, 1978, pp. 167–214.
- Fred C. Ikle, *How Nations Negotiate*, Chapters 1, 2, 4, and 11.
- Franklin A. Long and George W. Rathjens, eds. *Arms, Defense Policy, and Arms Control*, chapter by Schelling.

Apr. 7—Soviet Decision-Making and Negotiating Style—I [Blacker]
- David Holloway, *The Soviet Union and the Arms Race*, Chapters 6 and 7.
- William Potter and Jiri Valenta, eds. *Soviet Decisionmaking for National Security*, Ch. 1 and 11.
- Michael MccGuire, *Military Objectives in Soviet Foreign Policy*, Chapters 2 and 3.

Apr. 9—Soviet Decision-Making and Negotiating Style—II [Blacker]
- Robert J. Einhorn, *Negotiating from Strength: Leverage in U.S.-Soviet Arms Control Negotiations*, Chapter 3.

- Leon Sloss and M. Scott Davis, *A Game for High Stakes*, Chapters 3, 4, and 7.
- David Holloway, *The Soviet Union and the Arms Race*, Chapters 2, 3, and 5.

Apr. 14—The U.S. National Security/Arms Control Decision Making [Goodby]

- Morton H. Halperin, *Bureaucratic Politics and Foreign Policy*, Chapters 2, 7, 8.
- Gilbert R. Winham, "Practitioners' Views of Negotiations," *World Politics*, Vol. 32, No. 1, Oct. 1979, pp. 111–135.
- Henry A. Kissinger, *White House Years*, pp. 38–48.
- Leon Sloss and M. Scott Davis, *A Game for High Stakes*, pp. 88-90.
- Alexander L. George, *Presidential Decisionmaking in Foreign Policy*, pp. 145–166.

Apr. 16—U.S. Negotiating Style and Decision Making [Lewis]

- George F. Kennan, *American Diplomacy*, Chapter VI.
- Henry A. Kissinger, *The Necessity for Choice*, Chapter V.
- Henry A. Kissinger, *Years of Upheaval*, pp. 442–446.
- Ikle, pp. 235–253.
- Raymond L. Garthoff, "Negotiating SALT," *Wilson Quarterly*, Autumn 1977, pp. 76–85.
- Raymond L. Garthoff, "Negotiating with the Russians: Some Lessons from SALT," *International Security*, Vol. 1, No. 4, Spring 1977, pp. 3–24.

Apr. 21—Case Study: Arms Control Is Politics, I—President Johnson's ABM Decision [Bunn]

(1) To what extent was President Johnson's ABM decision based upon forces from within the administration and to what extent from outside? (2) Did the supporters of deployment have a single agreed reason? Was the decision rational in the sense that Halperin uses the word? Did McNamara present Johnson with the argument that whether the Soviets had an ABM system was irrelevant?

- Halperin, Chapters 1 and 16.

Apr. 21—Case Study: Arms Control Is Politics, II—President Reagan's MX Decision [Bernstein]

(1) Can Congress influence the progress of arms control negotiations? (2) Do arms control considerations influence weapons procurement plans, and vice versa?

- Herbert Scoville, Jr., *MX: Prescription for Disaster*, pp. 7–17.
- *Les Aspin and the MX.*
- *Report of the President's Commission on Strategic Forces*, April 6, 1983 (Scowcroft Commission report).
- Elizabeth Drew, "Letter from Washington," *New Yorker*, May 20, 1983, pp. 39–75.

Apr. 23—Case Study: Exploratory Openings: Back Channels and Bargaining Chips—Negotiation of the SALT I Framework Agreement of May 1971 [Bunn]

(1) How do Fisher and Ury's ideas for ending "positional bargaining" compare with the requirement that arms control negotiators make proposals on instructions from the President? Were the opening or subsequent sessions of SALT I consistent with Fisher and Ury? (2) Evaluate Kissinger's institutional arrangements for resolving bureaucratic disputes. Should they have been used by Kissinger for his own negotiations? Was Kissinger's back channel useful? Was it necessary? (3) Were U.S. ABM plans useful as bargaining chips in getting the Soviets to negotiate seriously? Were the negotiations useful bargaining chips in getting Congress to enact defense appropriations?

- Raymond L. Garthoff, *Detente and Confrontation*, pp. 133–155 and 182–183.
- Henry A. Kissinger, *White House Years*, pp. 534–551, 810–823.
- Gerard C. Smith, *Doubletalk*, pp. 75–90.
- Roger Fisher and William Ury, *Getting to Yes*, pp. 1–14.

Apr. 28—Case Study: Messenger or Mover—Paul Nitze's "Walk in the Woods" [Bunn]

(1) When are uninstructed negotiations permissible? How do you reconcile Nitze's walk in the woods with Ikle's description of the requirement of instructions from the President? (2) If U.S. negotiators cannot get their instructions changed, and if negotiations are stalemated because the Soviets also won't move, what can a U.S. negotiator legitimately do?

- Paul H. Nitze, "Negotiating with the Soviets," *State Department Bulletin*, Vol. 84, No. 2089, pp. 34–37 (August 1984).
- Strobe Talbott, *Deadly Gambits*, pp. 116–151 and 185–195.
- Fred Ikle, *How Nations Negotiate*, pp. 123–125.

Apr. 30—Case Study: Arms Control, Politics, and Leadership—The Last Phase of the Negotiations on the Limited Test Ban Treaty, August 1962–July 1963 [Goodby]

(1) How can a president deal with congressional opposition to his arms control policies? (2) How can a president guide an arms control negotiation?

- Harold Jacobson and Eric Stein, *Diplomats, Scientists, and Politicians*, pp. 397–416, 425–435, 444-464.
- Glenn T. Seaborg, *Kennedy, Khrushchev, and the Test Ban*, pp. 168–253.
- Selected documents from the Kennedy Library archives.

May 5—Case Study: The Impossible Takes a Little Longer—The Attempt to Negotiate Reductions in Strategic Offensive Forces in March 1977 [Goodby]

(1) How do presidential transitions affect arms control negotiations? (2) How can changes in positions be managed most effectively?

- Richard Neustadt and Ernest May, *Thinking in Time*, Chapter 7.

- Garthoff, *Detente and Confrontation*, pp. 801–810.
- Strobe Talbott, *Endgame*, Chapters 3 and 4.
- Zbigniew Brzezinski, *Power and Principle*, pp. 156–164.

May 7—Simulation: U.S.-Soviet Negotiation on Strategic Offensive and Defensive Forces After Reykjavik, Session 1 [Control Group]

May 12, 14, 19, 21, 28, June 2—Simulations [Control Group]

THE SIMULATION

The simulation will involve an attempted negotiation of an agreement dealing with strategic offensive and defensive forces using the situation as it stood at the end of the Reagan-Gorbachev meeting in Reykjavik (October 11 and 12, 1986) as the point of departure. The simulation will begin on May 7 and will conclude after eight sessions on June 2. The class will be divided into U.S. and Soviet teams during the first week of the seminar so that students may begin their own preparation for the simulation well before it begins. The course faculty and staff will be present throughout the course to assist the teams with technical and other factual information. Before the simulation, students should familiarize themselves with the nuclear and space talks up to and including the Reykjavik meeting. Background materials will be provided to each team when it is formed; these will include post-Reykjavik information. Other references available at the Center include *U.S. Nuclear Forces and Capabilities*, by Cochran, Arkin, and Hoenig; *U.S.-Soviet Military Balance 1980–1985*, by John M. Collins; Department of Defense Annual Posture Statements; *Strategic Survey*, published by the IISS; *Soviet Military Power*, prepared by the Department of Defense; *Arms Control and Disarmament Agreements*, prepared by ACDA; and *Nuclear Arms Control: Background and Issues*, published by the National Academy of Sciences.

During the weeks preceding the simulation, the teams will meet separately to draft options for their position papers, which should include a statement of each side's general objectives in the negotiations, an assessment of the other side's objectives, optional proposals which each is prepared to make, and any relevant foreign and domestic considerations. The draft of these options are to be handed in to the Control Group by April 30. The final versions should be completed before the first simulation session on May 7. Each side should also draft a statement describing its public relations strategy and a separate statement describing points to be made in consultation with allies. Teams also should consider whether a letter should be sent to the other side's head of government and what public relations strategy to follow. The teams should maintain strict security.

VIII

Militarism and Society

1. The War Economy

Seymour Melman   *Fall 1987*
Dept. of Industrial Engineering, Columbia University,
New York, NY 10027

Required Readings
S. Melman. *The Permanent War Economy.* Simon & Schuster, 1985 (paper).
_____ , *Pentagon Capitalism.* McGraw-Hill, 1970.
_____ , ed. *The War Economy of the U.S.* St. Martin's Press, 1971 (out of print).
_____ , *Profits Without Production.* Alfred A. Knopf, 1983.

TOPICS AND SELECTED READINGS

In the readings listed below, Melman books are identified by acronyms and chapter numbers (as in *PWE* 5, *PC* 2, *WEUS* 10, *PWP* 129, etc.). An asterisk (*) denotes required reading.

War Economy and the Development of State Capitalism: The Great Depression and After
- **PWE* 1.
- **WEUS* 2, 3, 6, 7.
- **J.R. Fox, *Arming America*, chs. 3, 4.
- **B. Mitchell, *Depression Decade*, chs. 1, 2, 9; pp. 404–7.
- **L.P. Ayres, *The Chief Cause of This and Other Depressions*.

- *S. Turkel, *Hard Times: An Oral History of the Great Depression*, pp. 129–55, 247–71, 285–324.
- L.V. Chandler, *America's Great Depression, 1929–1941*.
- W.E. Leuchtenberg, *Franklin D. Roosevelt and the New Deal*.
- D.A. Shannon (ed.), *The Great Depression*.
- P. Baran, P. Sweezy, *Monopoly Capital*.

The Arms Race

- *P. Noel-Baker, *The Arms Race*, chs. 1, 2, 6, 7, 45.
- *C. Gray, "The Arms Race Phenomenon," *World Politics* (Oct. 1971); also in R. Head, E. Rokke (eds.), *American Defense Policy*.
- *A. Waskow, "The Evolution of American Military Doctrine," in S. Melman (ed.), *Disarmament, Its Politics and Economics*.
- *H. York, *Race to Oblivion*, Prologue, chs. 3, 4, 12.
- *H. Kahn, *The Nature and Feasibility of War and Deterrence*, U.S. Senate, 86th Congress, 2nd Session, Doc. No. 101, Jan. 20, 1960.
- *R. Jung, *Brighter Than 1,000 Suns*, App. B, "The Franck Report," pp. 334–46.
- H. York, *Arms Control*, Readings from *Scientific American*, Part 1.
- U.S. Arms Control and Disarmament Agency, *World Military Expenditures and Arms Trade, 1963–1973*.
- R. Head, E. Rokke, *American Defense Policy*, ch. 2.
- SIPRI Yearbooks, Stockholm International Peace Research Institute.
- *World Military and Social Expenditures* (annual report from World Priorities, Box 25140, Washington, D.C., 20007).
- "U.S. Military Assistance and Sales," *The Defense Monitor* (May 1974).

Microeconomics of War Economy

- *PWE* 2.
- *PC* 2.
- *WEUS* 8, 10, 11, 12, 13.
- *A.E. Fitzgerald, *The High Priests of Waste*, chs. 1, 2, 3.
- *M. Weidenbaum, *The Economics of Peacetime Defense*, chs. 4, 5.
- *L. Rodberg, E. Shearer (eds.), *The Pentagon Watchers*, Part III.
- *J.R. Fox, *Arming America*, chs. 2, 5, 13; chs. 9–11, 20–23 optional.
- W.M. Proxmire, *Report from Wasteland*.
- C. Merton Tyrell, *Pentagon Partners: The New Nobility*.
- M. Peck, F. Scherer, *The Weapons Acquisition Process*.
- R. Kaufman, *The War Profiteers*.
- J. Gorgol, *The Military-Industrial Firm*.
- J. Gansler, *The Defense Economy*.

Macroeconomics of War Economy

- *PWE* 3.
- *PWP* 5, 8.
- *WEUS* 14, 17, 19.
- M. Weidenbaum, *The Economics of Peacetime Defense*, chs. 1–3.

- W. Adams, "The Military Industrial Complex and the New Industrial State," *American Economic Review* (May 1968).
- J. Wm. Fulbright, "Total Federal Budget Outlays by Functions," in *The Military Budget and National Economic Priorities.* Hearings before the Subcommittee on Economy in Government of the Joint Economic Committee, 91st Congress, 1st session, June 1969, Part I, pp. 100–103.
- G. Burck, "The Guns, Butter and Then Some Economy," *Fortune,* Oct. 1965.
- B. Russett, *What Price Vigilance?*
- J. Gansler, *The Defense Economy.*

Consequences of War Economy for Civilian Industry

- *PWE* 4.
- *PWP* 9, 10.
- *WEUS* 9, 15.
- *J. Holloman, A. Harger, "America's Technological Dilemma," *Technology Review* (Jul.–Aug. 1971).
- *PC* 3, 4.
- *W.N. Leonard, "Research and Development in Industrial Growth," *The Journal of Political Economy* (Mar.-Apr. 1971).
- D. Price, *The Scientific Estate.*
- M. Weidenbaum, *The Economics of Peacetime Defense,* ch. 10.
- N. Boretsky, *U.S. Technology: Trends and Policy Issues,* chs. 2, 3.

Consequences of War Economy for Civilian Economy and Society

- *PWE* 5.
- *PWP* 12.
- *PC* 8.
- *WEUS* 16, 22, 24.
- *"Federal Spending: The North's Loss Is the Sunbelt's Gain," *National Journal,* June 26, 1976.
- United Nations, Department of Political and Security Council Affairs, *Economic and Social Consequences of the Arms Race and of Military Expenditures.* Updated report of the Secretary-General (1978).
- K. Nelson (ed.), *The Impact of War on American Life.*
- E. Benoit, "The Monetary and Real Costs of Defense," *American Economic Review* (May 1968).
- K.E. Boulding, *The War Industry as a Sector of the Economy.*
- U.S. Dept. of Defense (controller), *The Economics of Defense Spending* (July 1972).
- A. Yarmolinsky, *The Military Establishment,* chs. 24, 25.
- See various Hearings and Reports of the U.S. Joint Economic Committee, Subcommittee on Economy in Government, 1965–1972.
- Y. Peri, A. Newbach, *The Military-Industrial Complex in Israel,* 1985.

Does Industrial Capitalism Require a War Economy?

- *PWE 10.
- *R. Barnet, Roots of War, chs. 6–8.
- *H. Magdoff, The Age of Imperialism, ch. 5.
- *M. Reich, "Does the U.S. Economy Require Military Spending?" American Economic Review (May 1972).
- *R.P. Smith, "Military Expenditure and Capitalism," Cambridge Journal of Economics (March 1977).
- *A. Szymanski, "Military Spending and Economic Stagnation," American Journal of Sociology (July 1973); and Comments (July 1974).
- P. Baran, P. Sweezy, Monopoly Capital.

Limits of Military Power

- *PWE 7.
- *PWP 11.
- *E.L. King, The Death of the Army, Part II.
- *PC 5.
- *L. Bohn, "Is Nuclear Deterrence Necessary?" War/Peace Report (Nov./Dec. 1972).
- U.S. Arms Control and Disarmament Agency, SALT Lexicon, 1974.
- "30,000 U.S. Nuclear Weapons," The Defense Monitor (Feb. 1975).
- See annual reports by the Secretary of Defense to the House Armed Service Committee on the military posture of the U.S.
- A. Waskow, The Limits of Defense.
- J. Fallows, National Defense.

The Vietnam War as a Model for the Dynamics of War Economy and Its Economic Consequences

- *PC 6.
- *WEUS 20, 21, 23.
- *Pentagon Papers (New York Times edition). Read the chapters comprising the articles prepared by The New York Times staff on the Pentagon Papers documents.
- *D. Hunt, "Villagers at War: The National Liberation Front in My Tho Province 1965–1967," Radical America, Vol. 8, Nos. 1–2 (Jan.–April, 1974).
- *N. Chomsky, For Reasons of State, ch. 1.
- *N. Chomsky, American Power and the New Mandarins, pp. 323–66.
- M. Raskin, B. Fall (eds.), The Vietnam Reader.
- M. Gettlemen (ed.), Vietnam: History, Documents and Opinions on a Major World Crisis. (Note: The Raskin/Fall and Gettleman books are probably the best collections of background materials and bibliography on the war in Vietnam.)
- S. Melman (ed.), In the Name of America.
- The Economist Intelligence Unit, The Economic Effects of the Vietnamese War on East and Southeast Asia, Nov. 1968.

- U.S. Senate, *The Impact of the War in Southeast Asia on the U.S. Economy*, April 1970.
- M. Weidenbaum, *The Economic Impact of the Vietnam War*, Special Report 5, Center for Strategic Studies, Georgetown University, June 1967.
- Stanford Biology Study Group, *The Destruction of Indochina*.

Arms Control or Disarmament: Alternatives for Security Policies, Military Forces and Budgets

- *S. Melman (ed.), *Disarmament: Its Politics and Economics*, chs. by Feld, Cavers, Fisher and Ritvo.
- *Members of Congress for Peace Through Law, *The Economics of Defense*.
- PC, Appendix C.
- R. Barnet, *The Economy of Death*, ch. 1.
- *Deterrence and Survival in the Nuclear Age* (the "Gaither Report" of 1957).
- *S. Melman, *Inspection for Disarmament*, the General Report.
- *D.G. Brennan (ed.), *Arms Control, Disarmament and National Security*, ch. 1.
- *J.H. Barton, L.D. Weiler, *International Arms Control*, chs. 5, 6, 9, 10.
- *P. Noel-Baker, *The Arms Race*, Parts 3, 4.
- H. York, *Race to Oblivion*.
- H. York, "Military Technology and National Security," *Scientific American* (August 1969).
- R. Lapp, *The Weapons Culture*.
- R. McNamara, *The Essence of Security*.
- M.T. Klare, *War Without End*.
- L. Bloomfield, A. Liess, *Controlling Small Wars*.

Options for Economic Reconstruction

- *PWE 8.
- *PWP 14.
- *WEUS 29, 30.
- *Cabinet Coordinating Committee on Economic Planning for the End of Vietnam Hostilities, Report to the President, in the *Economic Report of the President*, Jan. 1969, pp. 181–211.
- *J. Bergsman, *Economic Adjustment to New National Priorities*, the Urban Institute, July 1971.
- C.L. Schultze, *Setting National Priorities: The 1973 Budget*.
- E. Benoit, K. Boulding (eds.), *Disarmament and the Economy*.
- W. Leontief, "The Economic Impact of an Arms Cut," *Review of Economics and Statistics* (August 1965).
- V. Papanek, *Design for the Real World*.
- Engineers Joint Council, *The Nation's Engineering Research Needs, 1965–85*.

Convertibility of War Economy
- **PWE* 8.
- **PWP* 13.
- **WEUS* 26, 27, 32.
- *S. Melman, "Problems of Conversion from Military to Civilian Economy: An Agenda of Topics, Questions and Hypotheses," *Bulletin of Peace Proposals,* Vol. 16:1, 1985.
- *B. Udis (ed.), *Adjustments of the U.S. Economy to Reductions in Military Spending,* ch. 12 (from the U.S. Arms Control and Disarmament Agency).
- *S. Melman (ed.), *The Defense Economy,* chs. 10–12.
- *J.R. Cambern, D.A. Newton, "Skill Transfers: Can Defense Workers Adapt to Civilian Occupations?" *Monthly Labor Review* (June 1969), pp. 21–25.
- S. Melman (ed.), *Conversion of Industry from a Military to Civilian Economy* (a series of books published by Praeger).
- S. Melman, *Planning for Conversion of Military Industry and Military Base Facilities* (ms.).
- U.S. Arms Control and Disarmament Agency, *The Economic Impact of Reductions in Defense Spending.*
- R. Arousan, "Effect of Federal Spending on Scientists and Engineers," *Monthly Labor Review* (October 1970).

BOOKS FOR EVALUATION

Select one book from the following list. Write a 20-page typed critique or evaluation, not a summary of content.

The Boston Study Group. *The Price of Defense.*
Gorgol, J. *The Military-Industrial Firm.*
Yarmolinsky, A. *The Military Establishment.*
Kaufmann, R. *The War Profiteers.*
McNamara, R. *The Essence of Security.*
Barnet, R. *Intervention and Revolution.*
York, H. *Race to Oblivion.*
Magdoff, H. *The Age of Imperialism.*
Horowitz, D. (ed.). *Corporations and the Cold War.*
Russett, B. *What Price Vigilance?*
Gansler, J. *The Defense Economy.*
Klare, M.T. *War Without End.*
Enthoven, A.C., and K.W. Smith. *How Much Is Enough?*
Fitzgerald, A.E. *The HIgh Priests of Waste.*
Waskow, A. *The Limits of Defense.*
Schurmann, F. *The Logic of World Power.*
Chomsky, N. *For Reasons of State.*
The Pentagon Papers (Sen Gravel Edition; Beacon Press), Vol. 5.
Weidenbaum, M. *The Economics of Peacetime Defense.*

Fox, J.R. *Arming America.*
Barnet, R. *The Roots of War.*
Mitchell, B. *Depression Decade.*
Chomsky, N., and E.S. Herman. *The Political Economy of Human Rights,* Vol. 1 (the Washington Connection and Third World Facism).
Snepp, F. *Decent Interval.*
Stevens, R.W. *Vain Hopes, Grim Realities.*
Fallows, J. *National Defense.*
Ball, N., and M. Leitenberg. *The Structure of the Defense Industry.*

MAJOR BIBLIOGRAPHIES

Disarmament, A Selected Bibliography, 1967–72, E-73, I, 14 (United Nations).
Leitenberg, M. *Materials Prepared in Analysis and in Support of the Proposal— Disarmament and Development,* 1977.
Williams, S.P. *Disarmament and Conversion, A Selected Bibliography,* 1964.
Wong, C. *Economic Consequences of Armament and Disarmament (A Bibliography),* Center for the Study of Armament and Disarmament, California State University, Los Angeles, CA 90032.

2. The Economics of Defense

Tom Riddell   *Fall 1987*

Economics Dept., Smith College, Northampton, MA 01060

The objectives of this course are to help develop in the student a familiarity with and an understanding of the history, institutions and operation of the defense economy in the United States. This will include an examination of the defense budget, military contracting, the defense industry, the economic rationales of American foreign and military policy, and a variety of perspectives on these issues. We will also examine the current military build-up, its justifications and its likely economic effects.

There are three major questions that we will focus on in the course: (1) Why is military spending as large as it is? (2) What are the economic effects of military spending? and (3) What are the different possible/likely foreign and military policies, and what effects would they have on the U.S. economy?

Expectations

I expect everyone to do the assigned reading and to come to class prepared to discuss it. I would also recommend that you read a daily newspaper to keep up with emerging foreign and military policy, as well as with the status of the military budget.

There will be a mid-term exam, in class. This exam will count for 30% of your grade in the course. There will be a final, take-home exam, due on the last day of finals week. The questions for the exam are the three listed in the section above. As you develop your exposure to and understanding of the U.S. defense economy during the semester, you should keep these questions in mind. At the end of the course, for your final exercise, I would like you to do a ten-page essay that both addresses these questions and indicates the development of your own thinking on and analysis of these issues. Later in the course I will also provide some additional, more directed and specific questions as an alternative. This exam also counts for 30% of your grade.

Everyone is required to do a research project that will count for 40% of his/her grade. There will be a handout with more precise instructions and expectations about this assignment.

Texts

DeGrasse, Robert W., Jr. *Military Expansion, Economic Decline: Consequences of Reagan's Military Buildup*. M.E. Sharpe, 1983.
Gansler, Jacques. *The Defense Industry*. MIT Press, 1981.
Kaufmann, William W. *A Reasonable Defense*. Brookings, 1986.
Melman, Seymour. *The Permanent War Economy*. Simon & Schuster, 1985.
Smith, Dan, and Ron Smith. *The Economics of Militarism*. Pluto Press, 1983.
Snow, Donald M. *National Security*. St. Martin's Press, 1987.

COURSE OUTLINE

A General Introduction to Defense Issues

- Secretary of Defense Caspar W. Weinberger's *Annual Report to the Congress*, FY1988, pp. 3–5, 11–50, 51–81 (skim), 32–119, 281–287 (skim).

Recommended

- Congressional Quarterly. *U.S. Defense Policy*, 1983.

The Economics of Defense

- Neil M. Singer, "Defense Expenditures," from *Public Microeconomics*, 2nd ed. (Little, Brown, 1976).
- Charles J. Hitch and Roland N. McKean, *The Economics of Defense in the Nuclear Age* (Harvard, 1960), chs. 1 and 2 ("Defense as an Economic Problem" and "The Background: Defense Against What?").

Recommended

- Richard E. Wagner, "The Protective State," in *Public Finance* (Little, Brown, 1983).

The Current Military Buildup and Defense Budgets

- William W. Kaufman, *A Reasonable Defense,* all.
- Defense Budget Project, "The FY 1988 Defense Budget: Preliminary Analysis."
- Howard Morland, "A Few Billion for Defense."
- Franklyn D. Holzman, "Are the Soviets Really Outspending the U.S. on Defense?" *International Security* (Spring, 1980).

Recommended

- Joshua Epstein, *The FY1987 Defense Budget* (Brookings Institution, 1986).
- William W. Kaufmann, *The 1986 Defense Budget* (Brookings Institution, 1985).

The Historical Roots of the Modern Defense Establishment

- Robert Borosage, "The Making of the National Security State," from Leonard S. Rodberg and Derek Shearer (eds.), *The Pentagon Watchers* (Doubleday Anchor, 1970).
- Appendices A and B from Seymour Melman, *Pentagon Capitalism* (McGraw-Hill, 1970). (1946 Eisenhower memo and 1961 Eisenhower Farewell Address.)
- Charles J. Hitch, *Decision-Making for Defense* (University of California Press, 1965), ch. I ("1789–1960").

Recommended

- H.L. Nieburg, *In the Name of Science* (Quadrangle, 1970).

The Defense Establishment and the Defense Economy: Descriptions and Analyses

- Jacques Gansler, *The Defense Industry,* Introduction, chs. 1–9.
- Seymour Melman, The Permanent War Economy, skim Preface and chs. 1–5.
- Donald M. Snow, *National Security,* chs. 1–10.
- Daniel Ellsberg, "Introduction: A Call to Mutiny," in E.P. Thompson and Dan Smith (eds.), *Protest and Survive* (Monthly Review Press, 1981).

Recommended

- Gordon Adams and Geoffrey Quinn, "The Iron Triangle: The Politics of Defense Contracting," Council on Economic Priorities, *Newsletter* (June 1981). See also the book version: Gordon Adams, *The Iron Triangle,* Council on Economic Priorities, 1981.
- James Fallows, *National Defense* (Vintage, 1981).
- Christopher Paine, "On the Beach: The Rapid Development Force and the Nuclear Arms Race," *MERIP Reports* (January 1983).

- Boston Study Group, *Winding Down: The Price of Defense*, Foreword, Preface, Parts I–IV.

The Economics of Military Spending
- Department of Defense, *The Economics of Defense Spending: A Look at the Realities*, DOD, 1972. Read Introduction; skim chs. 1 and 2; read chs. 5–7, 17, 19, 20, and Conclusions.
- Dan Smith and Ron Smith, *The Economics of Militarism*, Introduction, chs. 1–4.
- Herb Gintis, "American Keynesianism and the War Machine," from David Mermelstein (ed.), *Economics: Mainstream Readings and Radical Critiques*, 1st edition (Random House).
- Michael Reich, "Military Spending and Production for Profit," from Edwards, Reich, and Weisskopf (eds.), *The Capitalist System* (2nd ed.) (Prentice-Hall, 1978).
- James Cypher, "Capitalist Planning and Military Expenditures," *The Review of Radical Political Economics* (Fall 1974).
- R.P. Smith, "Military Expenditures and Capitalism," *The Cambridge Journal of Economics* (March 1977).
- Tom Riddell, "Militarism: The Other Side of Supply," *Economic Forum* (Summer 1982).
- Teresa Amott and Tom Riddell, "The Freeze, Militarism, and the American Economy," *Socialist Review* (March/April 1984).

Recommended
- Michael Kidron and Dan Smith, *The War Atlas* (Simon and Schuster, 1983).
- Carl Oglesby, "Vietnamese Crucible: An Essay on the Meaning of the Cold War," skim chs. 1–3 and read chs. 4, 5, and 7, in Oglesby and Richard Shaull, *Containment and Change* (Macmillan, 1967).
- Robert A. Pollard and Samuel F. Wells, Jr., "1945–1960: The Era of American Economic Hegemony," and David P. Calleo, "Since 1961: American Power in the New World Economy," in William H. Becker and Samuel F. Wells, Jr. (eds.), *Economics and World Power: An Assessment of American Diplomacy Since 1789* (Columbia University Press, 1984).
- Gabriel Kolko, *The Roots of American Foreign Policy*, ch. 3, "The United States and World Economic Power" (Beacon Press, 1969).
- Richard J. Barnet, *The Roots of War*, part II, "The Political Economy of Expansionism" (Penguin, 1971).
- Harry Magdoff, *The Age of Imperialism*, chs. 2 and 5 (Monthly Review Press, 1969).

The Economic Effects of Military Spending and the Current Military Buildup
- Robert DeGrasse, *Military Expansion, Economic Decline*, Introduction and chs. 1–4.
- Congressional Budget Office, *Defense Spending and the Economy*, all.

- Tom Riddell, "The Employment Effects of Military Spending" (unpublished).
- Ann Markusen, "The Militarized Economy," *World Policy Journal* (Summer 1986).
- Lloyd J. Dumas, "The Military Burden on the Economy," *The Bulletin of the Atomic Scientists* (October 1985).
- Gordon Adams and David Gold, "Recasting the Military Spending Debate," *The Bulletin of the Atomic Scientists* (October 1986).

Recommended

- "The New Cold War Economy," *Business Week,* January 21, 1980.
- James M. Cypher, "The Basic Economics of Rearming America," *Monthly Review* (November 1981).
- Charles L. Schultze, "Economic Effects of the Defense Budget," *Brookings Bulletin* (Fall 1981).
- James M. Capra, "The National Defense Budget and Its Economic Effects," *FRBNY Quarterly Review* (Summer 1981).

Conclusion: The Future of the Defense Economy

- Snow, *National Security,* Conclusion.
- Melman, *Permanent War Economy,* chs. 8–10.
- Gansler, *The Defense Industry,* chs. 10–12.
- "Peace Conversion," WIN Magazine, Special Issue, October 1977.
- Smith and Smith, *The Economics of Militarism,* ch. 5.
- Tom Riddell, "Concentration and Inefficiency in the Defense Sector: Policy Options," *Journal of Economic Issues* (June 1985).
- Jerry Sanders, "Forty Years of Pax Americana: What Comes Next?" *World Policy Journal* (Summer 1984).
- Howard Morland, "Superpower Battlefields."
- *Recommended:* Earl Ravenal, "Defining Defense," The Cato Institute, 1984.

RESEARCH PROJECTS

The Process

Doing research is an important skill—finding out how to find out about something, deciding what to find out about, and finding out something. But there's more to it. Another step involves communicating what you found out to others. One powerful way to do this is through writing. This assignment is intended to give you practice (and to sharpen your skills) in doing research and in writing effectively.

I'd like you to do a research project on some aspect of the economics of defense. It should be about fifteen pages long. (You may work in groups if you'd like, and you may do something other than a paper. In either case, you should check with me.)

Possible Research Topics

The following topics are suggestions only. Some are overly broad and need to be narrowed. Remember to focus on economics. I also have a list of papers from previous years, as well as the papers themselves; you are welcome to examine these.

- energy and defense
- economic conversion
- U.S./Soviet military balance
- strategic concerns in Central America/Middle East/Africa/other areas
- women in the military
- weapons procurement
- the MX system
- the RDF and intervention
- Allies' defense budgets (e.g., Japan, West Germany)
- New England defense industry and effects
- military research on campuses
- Vietnam war
- arms exports and sales
- Trident sub program
- electronic warfare
- research and development
- a defense contractor
- the history of a weapon system—its R&D and production
- international economic policy and defense policy
- corruption in defense contracting
- battleships (their resurrection)
- strategic metals
- B-1 bomber
- Kollmorgen (defense contractor in Northampton)
- the economics of a nuclear freeze
- the militarization of space (Star Wars)
- the nuclear weapons industry
- NATO policy and budgets
- data collection
- econometric hypothesis testing using Econ 290 class account
- military contractor advertising
- selected literature reviews

You could also select one or two books at my suggestion and do a critical review (see me).

Research Guides and Bibliographies

The following will be very helpful for bibliographic references. They will also provide some guidance in doing research on military economics.

Defense Economics: A Preliminary Bibliography, by the Conversion Information Center, Council on Economic Priorities, 1979.

Arkin, William M. *Research Guide to Current Military and Strategic Affairs,* IPS, 1981. An excellent research guide!

Rosenberg, Douglas H., and Major Raoul H. Alcala, "The New Politics of National Security: A Selected and Annotated Research Bibliography," in Bruce Russell and Alfred Stepan (eds.), *Military Force and American Security* (Harper & Row, 1973). Lots of references, organized by topics.

Rodberg, Leonard S., and Derek Shearer (eds.), "How to Research the Military," appendix to *The Pentagon Watchers* (Doubleday Anchor, 1970). A good research guide.

3. Structural Violence

Richard E. Stryker Spring 1987

Political Science Dept., Indiana University,
Bloomington, IN 47405

We live in times of pervasive and frightful violence. It provides the major content of the daily "news" from Delhi, Beirut, the rural jungles of Central America and the urban jungles of North America. Reported violence, of course, constitutes only a fraction of the day-to-day, especially domestic, violence wreaked upon the relatively powerless in all societies. But direct or personal violence of all kinds is still not the half of it. Indeed, it may be more like 1/15th of the total violence suffered by human beings at any given time. We usually understand violence as the inflicting of direct harm by identifiable agents, with intent (or out of passion or insanity) and with some identifiable physical or psychological means (from fists and threats to guns and bombs). Yet, far more people are killed, harmed, damaged, and diminished by another kind of violence which may be termed "structural."

This concept derives from the observation that we live in a world of dramatically unequal life chances. Most of these inequalities—in life expectancy and life quality—result not from the direct actions or intentions of persons; rather, they are the outcome of (avoidable) social conditions and (unjust) social institutions. Violence is built into the very structure of some social arrangements, irrespective of the intentions or even the wishes of any individuals. Structural violence "just happens"; no one can be identified as directly responsible, and it is not "news" because it is so utterly ordinary.

For example, something like 35,000 human beings die every day from hunger-related causes, three-fourths of them children, the remainder largely women. These are all avoidable or "unnecessary" deaths in the sense that there is more than enough food available, globally and within virtually all countries, to prevent starvation anywhere. Moreover, the victims of hunger-related deaths come almost entirely from the most deprived and powerless segments of any society; there is a predictable sorting out of "candidates." If this were not so, if suffering and death were random, and if there were an absolute shortage of food, then the violence would have to be understood as natural rather than structural. In fact, even most "natural" disasters (droughts, floods, earthquakes) are quite selective, in that their victims are concentrated in poor countries and are among the poorest and most vulnerable groups and categories.

The consequences of structural violence include many forms of stunting or impeding human potential short of immediate death, though reduced life expectancy is the ultimate measure. Other indicators might be ill health, illiteracy, involuntary un- or under-employment for adults (involuntary employment for children), female seclusion, and racial, caste, or religious discriminatory segregation. Indeed, all forms of poverty and many forms of inequality are relevant.

The purposes of this course are to explore the concept and major types of structural violence in the world today; to research case studies of leading types of victims (landless peasants, women, children, untouchables, and other disadvantaged "minorities"); and to evaluate strategies for combatting structural violence (including those of Gandhi, Galtung, Freire, and others). The theoretical perspective promises a comprehensive and interdisciplinary approach to comparative and international human deprivation. It derives from the work of the Norwegian social scientist and peace research pioneer, Johan Galtung, and will be presented primarily in lecture. Given the small size and nature of the class, we will be engaged in extensive discussion.

Course Assignments

1. A critical-reflective essay (about 5 typed pages), described below (15% of the grade: due March 3).
2. A research paper (about 10 typed pages) and class presentation on victims of structural violence (35% of the grade: due April 7).
3. Participation in a debate and submission of a written evaluation (about 5 typed pages) comparing leading strategies for combatting structural violence (25% of the grade: due May 7).
4. Outstanding work on any of these efforts will benefit from an additional 5–10% of credit. The remaining 20% or so of the course grade will be based upon regular class participation.

Books

George, Susan. *Food for Beginners.*
Harrington, Michael. *The Vast Majority.*
Markandaya, Kamala. *Nectar in a Sieve.*
Wijkman, Anders, and Lloyd Timberlake. *Natural Disasters.*
Reprints collected for this course.

TOPICS, READINGS AND ASSIGNMENTS

I. Structural Violence: Concepts and Dynamics

Introduction
- Markandaya, all.
- Harrington, chs. 3 & 7.
- Denis Goulet, "Shock of Underdevelopment," *The Cruel Choice* (Atheneum, 1971), ch. 1.
- Jan Bremen, "Bottom of the Urban Order," *Development and Change*, Vol. 14 (1983), pp. 153–63 only.
- James Fenton, "Notes from the Drought," *N.Y. Review of Books*, Oct. 24, 1985, 4 pp.
- Johan Galtung, "Violence, Peace and Peace Research," *Journal of Peace Research*, Vol. 6, No. 3 (1969), pp. 167–86.
- Norman Alcock, "Magnitude of Structural Violence," in Gary Olson, ed., *How the World Works* (Scott, Foresman, 1984).

Imperialism: Structural Violence as a Global System
- D. Goulet, "Vulnerability," ch. 2 in *The Cruel Choice*.
- Harrington, chs. 1–2, 4–5, 9.

Hunger and Population
- Harrington, ch. 6.
- George, all.
- Roger Lewin, "Starved Brains," in Gary Olson, ed., *How the World Works* (Scott, Foresman, 1984).
- Barry Commoner, "Poverty Breeds Overpopulation," in Gary Olson, ed., *How the World Works* (Scott, Foresman, 1984).

Environmental Vulnerability
- Wijkman & Timberlake, all.

Critical Essay
"Structural violence is a simile: poverty, deprivation, low life expectancy, etc., are like a thug beating up a victim." Do you agree or disagree with the implications of that simile? Why? Is it illuminating or misleading? Explain. How "objective" can we be in identifying structural violence? Is it merely "anything we don't like"? As "outsiders," how can we understand the victims of structural violence? Draw upon the insights of Goulet, Harrington, Markandaya, Wijkman/Timberlake, and others, in addition to Galtung, in thinking about these issues (5 typed pages, due Mar. 3.).

II. Structural Violence: Victims

Four weeks of class presentations of criteria by instructor and case studies by students.

"Class"

Workers lacking access to productive resources (e.g., landless and near-landless peasants, animal-less pastoralists, migrant laborers, casual or "informal sector" workers, the un- and under-employed).

"Communal"

Disadvantaged culturally defined groups based on race, ethnicity, religion, caste, language or region (e.g., Indian "Untouchables" and Tribals"; South African Blacks and Coloreds; Amazonian, Andean and Central American Indians; Black, Hispanic and Native Americans, Iranian Bahais; Tibetans; West Bank Palestinians; Jews in Muslim Arab countries; Gypsies; and many, many others).

"Gender": Women

"Age": Children or the Elderly

Other Criteria (e.g., the handicapped)

Research Papers on Case Studies

Choose one major criterion with an in-depth description of victims of structural violence; explain the origins and causes of their repressed or exploited status, the character of the structural and direct violence to which they are subjected, changes over time, and political-economic-cultural responses (10 typed pages). See instructor for suggested sources. Due April 7.

III. Strategies Against Structural Violence

Three weeks of class presentations and debates. Leading relevant thinkers and activists include Mahatma Gandhi, Johan Galtung, Danilo Dolci, Faulo Freire, Denis Goulet, Richard Falk, Frantz Fanon, Communist revolutionaries (Marx, Lenin, Mao), and others. Written, comparative evaluations of strategies (5 typed pages) due at final exam time (May 7).

4. War, State, and Society

Nigel Young *Spring 1987*
Peace Studies Program, Colgate University,
Hamilton, NY 13346

This course examines the main theories of the origins and development of the state and explores the relationship between the state and war. Particular emphasis is placed on those dynamics operating in warfare which are mutually reinforcing to both war and the cohesion of the state (e.g., territorial integrity, national sovereignty, circumscription, patriarchy, imperialist expansion, and conscription). Moreover, the course investigates the evolution of warfare and statehood in its relation to society.

Purpose and Focus of the Course

Starting from Max Weber's famous definition of the state, emphasizing both its *legitimation* and its *monopoly of violence* and territoriality, this course will examine social and political theories of the origins and development of the state, particularly in relationship to war, conquest, human rights, colonialism and slavery, and the role of nationalist ideologies. The role of patriarchy and the division of labour and the destruction of local community will be related to the growth of conscription and modern warfare and to imperial expansion.

In the first and final sections, the tension between the concept of a global society and the system of nation states will be examined in relation to the literature on transnationalism, centralisation, the emergence of local and global relations, and linkages. The problem of the modern (nation) state will be examined as to whether it constitutes a major obstacle to a more peaceful, just, and less violent world community—or whether, if reformed, it can be a stepping stone through international organizations and disarmament and alternative security arrangements, to a globally organized society.

The distinction between state and society will be examined and developed from the sociological literature as relevant to the central themes of the course.

The State as a Focus of Peace Research and Social Science

The state is viewed both as a stepping stone to a more peaceful world and as a major obstacle to it. To what extent is nationalism to be considered "progressive" or peaceful? Is the history of war and conquest inseparable from the development of the state? Can peace be achieved through the inter-state system? Should the state be a focus for peace research or peace strategy? Are there alternatives to the state as a key form of social and political organization? What social and global tendencies support the view that other alternatives and strategies are possible and necessary if peace is to be attained? The record of the state on human rights and social justice will be examined.

The State and the Monopoly of Violence

Much violence, physical and structural, is vested in the monopoly of the means of violence centered in the State and its ancillary institutions. Some of the major forms of modern violence (nuclear weapons, concentration camps) are mainly associated with the largest political organization, which uses coercive means. The origins and development of states and the rise of the so-called nation states (nationalism) will be discussed with specific reference to territoriality (the defense of boundaries), conscription (the duty of military service), and sovereignty (the legitimation of the State's "right" of violence in the last resort). The relation of conquest and war to the rise and development of the State, and the alternative social forms preceded and coexist with it, will be discussed.

The History and Study of War as an Institution

Why study war in peace research? In answering this question, we will consider the role of polemological studies in the development of peace theory; the study of warless or stateless societies; a brief history of popular involvement in war and an intellectual critique of war; some of the strategies to prevent or avoid war that have evolved since the 18th century; the role of militarism and nationalism in state development; and the role of social resistance at the community level. (The video series *War* will be used in conjunction with the texts.)

War Resistance and the State

The phenomenon of war resistance throws into relief the character and activity of States. The social conditions under which mobilization or counter mobilization takes place is analyzed, as is the ability of certain States to penetrate and other societies to resist. Local communities in the process of war and conscription are also examined.

Course Organization

All students will be expected to attend each of the twelve evening classes. Assessment will be based on a continuing system of monitored participation and written work. At least one short in-class presentation on readings will be required, along with textual examination and comment as part of both class and written participation. The mid-term exam will constitute 20% of the grade; the final exam 25%; the paper 25% (presentation 5%); and the in-class exercise 5%.

There will be set topics for two take-home exams or two short papers. The class presentation will be written up as one paper. Class participation and attendance will constitute about 25% of the assessment. Students will be expected to view parts of the PBS video series, *War*. Other films and speakers will also be presented. There will be additional review sessions on the readings in smaller groups. Attendance at some films and lecture presentations will be required.

Required Readings to Be Purchased

Manual of Readings, Vol. I (a selection of readings used this fall in UNST, "Introduction to Peace Studies").
Manual of Readings, Vol. II.
Dyer, Gwynne. *War*.
Taylor, A.J.P. *The First World War*.
Sharp, Gene. *Politics of Nonviolent Action*, Part 1, Vol. 1 ("Power and Struggle").
Oppenheimer, F. *The State*.
Shaw, M. *War, State and Society*.

Recommended

Sharp, Gene. *Social Power and Political Freedom*.
Tivey, L. *The Nation State*.
Carter, A. *Direct Action and Liberal Democracy*.
Lubasz, H. *Development of the Modern State*.
Bourne, R. *War and the Intellectuals*.
Hinsley, F. *Power and the Pursuit of Peace*.
Bramson, L., and G. Goethals. *War*.
Fried, M. *War*.
Joll, J. *The Second International*.
Galtung, J. *The True Worlds*.

SCHEDULE OF LECTURES
AND READINGS

Feb. 3—Introduction
Handout: Max Weber's Definition of the State.

Feb. 9—Defining and Relating War, State, and Society
Film: Dead Birds. Discussion of film.
- Dyer, ch. 1.
- Sharp, Vol. I, pt. 1, Introduction.
- Oppenheimer, Introduction.
- Shaw, Introduction.

Feb. 16—War and the Evolution of Political Society (Illustrated)
- Margaret Mead, "Warfare Is Only an Invention—Not a Biological Necessity," in *Peace and War*, C. Beitz and T. Herman, eds. (San Francisco: W.H. Freeman, 1973).
- Quincy Wright, "Analysis of the Causes of War."
- Gardiner and Heider, "Violence," *Gardens of War*, pp. 135–144.

- T.B. Bottomore, "Force in Social Life," *Sociology: A Guide to Problems and Literature* (London: George Allen and Unwin Ltd.), pp. 217–228.
- Robert. L. Carneiro, "A Theory of the Origin of the State," *Science*, Vol. 169, August 21, 1970, pp. 733–738.
- Charles Hamilton, "Introduction," *The State* (May 1975), pp. iii–xx.
- Robert E. Park, "The Social Function of War."
- Stanislav Andreski, "Ferocity and Convention," *Elements of Comparative Sociology*, pp. 108–128.
- Nigel J. Young, "Transnationalism," *World Encyclopedia of Peace*, Vol. 2, Linus Pauling, ed. (New York: Pergamon Press, 1986).
- Ekkehart Krippendorff, "The State as the Focus of Peace Research," *Peace Research Society*, Vol. XVI, The Rome Conference, 1970, pp. 47–59.
- Dyer, *War*, ch. 2.

Feb. 23—The Origins and Development of the State and the Monopoly of Violence

Presentation/discussion.
- W.G. Runciman, "The Emergence of Political Sociology."
- Otto Hintze, "The State in Historical Perspective."
- Heinz Lubasz, Introduction to *The Development of the Modern State*.
- Otto Hintze, "The Emergence of the Democratic Nation-State."
- Cornelia Navari, "The Origins of the Nation-State."
- Reinhard Bendix, "The Rise of National Feeling in Western Europe."
- G. Kitson Clark, "The Modern State and Modern Society."
- Ralph Miliband, "Marx and the State."
- Randolph S. Bourne, "The State."
- Sharp, Vol. I, ch. 1, pp. 7–48.
- Dyer, ch. 7.

Mar. 2—The Origins and Development of the Modern ("Nation") State: The Role of Conquest

Presentations.
- Oppenheimer, pp. 1–40.
- Shaw, entire.

Mar. 9—Analyzing the History of War as an Institution: The Organization of Armed Violence and the Role of Conscription

Film: The Road to Total War.
- Dyer, chs. 3–6.

Mar. 14–22

Review readings for weeks 1–5 for mid-term exam.

Mar. 23—War Resistance and Internationalism: A Case Study

Mid-term exam during first half of class.
- Henry David Thoreau, "Civil Disobedience" (Revised), *Pacifist Conscience*, Peter Mayer, ed. (Chicago: Henry Regnery Co., 1966).

- Geoffrey Ostergaard, "Resisting the Nation-State: The Pacifist and Anarchist Traditions," *The Nation State*, L. Tivey, ed., pp. 171–195.
- Martin Shaw, "Socialism Against War: Remaking a Tradition," *Socialism and Militarism*, pp. 1–33.
- Nigel J. Young, "On War, National Liberation, and the State."
- Kenneth E. Boulding, "Power in Society," *Ecodynamics: A New Theory of Societal Evolution* (Beverly Hills: Sage, 1978), pp. 240–252.
- V.G. Kiernan, "Conscription and Society in Europe Before the War of 1914–18."
- J. Joll, "Summer 1914," and Conclusion.
- Randolph S. Bourne, "Below the Battle."
- Shaw, ch. 4.
- Sharp, ch. 2, pp. 63–101.
- A.J.P. Taylor (References to "Opposition to War").

Mar. 30—Marxist Approaches to the State
- Shaw, chs. 1, 2, 5, 6.
- Mark Pilisuk and Tom Hayden, "Is There a Military-Industrial Complex that Prevents Peace?" *Peace and War*, C. Beitz and T. Herman, eds. (San Francisco: W.H. Freeman, 1973), pp. 288–315.
- Ralph Miliband, "Marx and the State."
- Ralph Miliband, "The State System and the State Elite."

Apr. 6—Critiques of the State (Liberal, Anarchist, Feminist, Conservative)
- Charlene Spretnak, "Naming the Cultural Forces that Push Us Toward War."
- Nigel J. Young, "Transnationalism and Communalism."
- Roy Preiswerk, "Could We Study International Relations as if People Mattered?"
- C. Wright Mills, "Political Sociology, Values, and the Classical Tradition."
- Sharp, ch. 1 (review).

Apr. 9—Film
White Rose (Resistance to Nazis).

Apr. 13—1914–1918 as a Case Study: Mobilization, War, and Nationalism
- Taylor, entire.

Apr. 20—Nationalism, the State and Totalism
- Reinhard Bendix, "The Rise of National Feeling in Western Europe."
- David Beetham, "End of the Nation State."
- Robert O. Matthews et al., "Introduction to the State."
- Donald J. Puchala, "Origins and Characteristics of the Modern State."
- John H. Herz, "Rise and Demise of the Territorial State."

- Robert H. Jackson and Carl G. Rosberg, "Why Africa's Weak States Persist: The Empirical and Juridical in Statehood."
- *Recommended:* F. Hinsley, *Power and the Pursuit of Peace* (especially parts 2 and 3).

April 27—Transnationalism: The Role of Society
- James N. Rosenau, "Capabilities and Control in an Interdependent World."
- Joseph S. Nye, Jr., and Robert O. Keohane, "Transnational Relations and World Politics."
- *Recommended:* J. Galtung, *The True Worlds.*

May 4—The Current Crisis and Alternatives
- Review Beetham and Preiswerk.
- Richard A. Falk, "Contending Approaches to World Order."
- Dyer, chs. 8–11.

MANUAL OF READINGS

Readings not listed in Schedule of Lectures and Readings:

Nigel J. Young, "War Resistance, State and Society."
Ernest Barker, "Conscription."
Hans J. Morgenthau, "The Paradoxes of Nationalism."
Barrington Moore, Jr., "Notes on the Process of Acquiring Power."
Donald J. Puchala, "Origins and Characteristics of the Modern State."
Fred W. Riggs, "The Nation-State and Other Actors."
J. David Singer and Michael Wallace, "Intergovernmental Organization and the Preservation of Peace, 1916–1964: Some Bivariate Relationships."
Kjell Skjelsbaek, "The Growth of International Nongovernmental Organizations in the Twentieth Century."
Eric R. Wolf, "Peasant Problems and Revolutionary Warfare."

5. The Psychology of Peace and War

Ofer Zur   *Spring 1987*
California Institute of Integral Studies, 765 Ashbury,
San Francisco, CA 94117

The twentieth century has been a century of war. In its first quarter, five million people died in the "war to end all wars," World War I. Twenty years later fifty million people died in World War II. Between 1960 and 1980 another ten million have died in combat. War continues to ravage Central America and the Middle East, while the possibility of a nuclear holocaust continues to dominate our future.

This course attempts to mark the territory covered by the too-long neglected and newly emerging field of the psychology of peace and war. The study of war has traditionally been carried on by the military, which has concentrated on developing modes of training and techniques of fighting what was clearly defined as an enemy. Political scientists are usually in charge of exploring and studying the relationship with these enemies and allied subjects in the international realm.

In the past, peace studies have been the realm of humanists, educators, leftists, and more recently, feminist-oriented scholars. By contrast, the psychology of war had been mostly limited to the areas of treating soldiers for shell shock, combat fatigue, or post-traumatic stress disorder symptoms, and to aiding the millitary with testing, screening and training highly specialized military groups.

Even though the UNESCO Charter acknowledged that "since wars are made in the minds of men, it is in the minds of men that the defense of peace must be constructed," the contribution of psychology to the study of peace and war has ranged from minimal to absent—to our loss and detriment. The alarming fact that psychologists, who are supposed to be the leading scientists on human behavior, have consistently neglected to explore the roots of war in human behavior and clearly calls for the development of a psychological based knowledge of peace and war dynamics. In the face of the unthinkable nuclear war, development of this field becomes crucial for world survival.

Indeed, in the last two decades we have witnessed the emergence of a new field of the psychology of peace and war. Psychologists were joined by political psychologists, social psychologists, psychohistorians, and others to evolve and create the field of the psychology of peace and war.

As the title of the first class ("Neither Doves nor Hawks") suggests, this course attempts to take a non-adversarial approach to the study of peace and war. While many contemporary psychologists attend to the dynamics which define and promote peace, war has been looked upon as a social malignancy or a disorder that should be extracted and eradicated. The newly developed field of the psychology of peace and war should not fall into that trap, and should not join "the troops of anti-war warriors," marching toward another "just" or "holy" war-to-end-all-wars. This course will present war as part and product of a culture, along with education, prisons, corporations and family systems. As such it should be studied only within its psychohistorical context. Sam Keen, the philosopher and author, looks at warfare as a Rorschach of the culture, a projective device to illuminate the unconscious of individuals and cultures.

It has become fashionable to argue that war is somehow an innate human propensity or instinct; others have linked it to aggressive male hormones; still others explain all wars as the result of economic pressures or as the outcome of leaders' madness. This course examines many commonly held beliefs about war, investigates their historical and theoretical roots, and explores the ways in which these beliefs affect individuals and societies. Above all, it attempts to shed light on attitude and behavior change.

Through presentations, class discussions, original slide shows, films, personal projects and experiential work, the course will try to capture the complexity of the war phenomenon. The many theories as to why people have been going to war will be critically reviewed. The course also explores the important concept of the enemy, including its role and function for individuals and for groups. Special attention will be given to the evolution of warfare, the relationship among war, peace, violence and conflict, and the different roles of men and women in the making of war.

Peace has been traditionally seen as an absence of war, a kind of "non-event." In this course peace will be explored as a process that takes place simultaneously on the personal, familial, cultural, national and ultimately global levels. The course will attempt to demonstrate the important link between process and content. A common theme will be that the process of teaching is as, or more, important than what is taught. Peace research, peace education and critical thinking will also be examined in this light.

It is hoped that the exploration of the roots of war in the individual and in society will provide us with a body of knowledge (power) essential to prevent future wars.

In addition to the syllabus, the required text, and class readings, an extensive bibliography according to subject will be distributed to each student.

Students will be evaluated according to (a) class participation; (b) the mini-projects assigned during the course; and (c) the final paper or project and its presentation in class. The final project can involve artistic, video, or audio production and should be approved by the instructor. Research projects are encouraged. Other assignments are described in the syllabus.

COURSE OUTLINE

Class 1—Neither Doves nor Hawks: Marking the Territory of the Psychology of Peace and War

The major psychological dimensions relevant to peace and war issues will be identified and the different psychological and theoretical approaches to the study of peace and war will be reviewed. Our own beliefs, images, and relationship to peace and war will be explored. The event of war and the process of peace will be defined and the relationship among war, violence and aggression will be explored.

- Frank, J.D., *Sanity and Survival in the Nuclear Age* (Random House, 1982), chs. 1–2.
- Tavris, C., "Anger Defused," *Psychology Today* (Nov. 1982), pp. 25–35.

- Zur, O., "Neither Doves nor Hawks: The Psychology of Peace and War." Paper presented at the Western Psychological Association Annual Convention, Long Beach (April 1987).

Class 2—The Evolution of Warfare
The evolution of warfare from primitive warfare to modern Star Wars will be reviewed from a psychohistorical perspective and as a reflection of the historical changes of the human psyche. As human beings developed, their organization and the economic structure has evolved. Wars and enemies have evolved simultaneously. The following seven cultures of warfare will be reviewed: (a) primitive/ritualistic warfare; (b) political (greedy) wars; (c) heroic wars; (d) holy wars; (e) defensive modern wars; (f) revolutionary wars; (g) wars on terrorism. The belief that there have always been wars and that war is part of human nature will be critically explored.
- Frank, J.D., *Sanity and Survival in the Nuclear Age* (Random House, 1982), ch. 4.
- Zur, O., "The Psychohistory of Warfare: On the Co-evolution of Culture Psyche and War," *Journal of Peace Research*, Vol. 24, No. 2, June 1987.

Class 3—The Dynamics of Making Enemies
This class will explore the process of making enemies on the personal, national and global levels. The role and function of the enemy for the individual and the group will be examined. The role of the media and its relationship to our own personal need for enemies will be studied. The concepts of mirror image and paradoxal perception of the enemy and the dynamics of change will be explored as we try to comprehend the process of creating enemies. As we analyze war propaganda from all around the world, we will explore our struggles with enemies and our inner battles between good and evil.
- Frank, D.J., *Sanity and Survival* (1982), chs. 6–7.
- Gault, W.B., "Some Remarks on Slaughter," *American Journal of Psychiatry*, Vol. 128, pp. 450–459.
- Keen, S., "Faces of the Enemy," *Esquire* (Feb. 1984), pp. 67–72.
- Zur, O., "The Concept of the Enemy," in O. Zur, *Psychological Foundation of War and Peace*, Teaching and Resource Guide, 1987.

Class 4—Propaganda and Social Paranoia
This class will explore different propaganda techniques and their relationship to the cultures that engage in propaganda. We will study the logic of social paranoia and document its cross-cultural elements. We will also examine the process of enmity as reflected in the media, in our own minds, and in our daily lives. Using the images of the enemy presented in the previous week, we will explore our own relationship to evil. Students will present in class their own battles with their enemies. The process of making enemies in everyday life will also be explored through media analysis of war, battle, and enemy images. Current political events will be explored for their mythical

and fantasy components. In the first part of the class we will share our mini-project of the media analysis. (See Project #2.)

Personal Mini-Projects

(1) Prepare a short presentation describing your process with your personal enemy. Try to apply the complex dynamics of enmity presented the previous week to your own relations with your enemy. Art work and music can also be part of the presentation. (If you take the course for a grade: submit 1–2 pages on the shared theme). (2) Develop a small project in which you analyze and document mythical and fantasy components in the media, including enemy, war, and battle dynamics. (Visual collages are encouraged. Bring them to class to be shared.)

- Corcoran, F., "The Bear in the Backyard: Myth, Ideology and Victimage Ritual in Soviet Funerals," *Communication Monographs* (1983), pp. 305–370.
- Frank, D.J., *Sanity and Survival* (1982), ch. 5.

Class 5—On Getting to Know One's Inner Enemy: Transformational Perspective on the Conflict of Good and Evil

Guest Lecturer: Ralph Metzner, Ph.D., Academic Dean, California Institute of Integral Studies. This lecture features an in-depth exploration of the concept of good and evil as presented in philosophy, religion, psychology, and spirituality. The roots of good/evil and good/bad judgment and the concept of the shadow are explored, and its relationship to war/peace are discussed. Nuclear weaponry and its potential destructive power will also be examined as a transformational image and as a metaphor for a world and psyche in transition.

- Metzner, R., "On Getting to Know One's Inner Enemy: Transformational Perspective on the Conflict of Good and Evil," *Re-Vision* (Fall 1985), pp. 41–51.
- Kull, S., "Nuclear Arms and the Desire for World Destruction," *Political Psychology*, Vol. 4 (1983), pp. 563–591.
- Zur, O., "War-Myths: Exploration of the Dominant Collective Beliefs About Warfare," 1987. (First myth: pp. 4–18).

Class 6—Why Men Love War, *or* Is Man the Maker of War or War the Maker of Man?

The complex relationship between men and war will be expored. The developmental role of war, battle and armies for men will be discussed, and the dynamics of recruitment will be studied. Movies such as *Patton*, *Rocky*, *Rambo*, *Platoon*, and many westerns will be analyzed as we explore the concept and image of the man-warrior here in our own culture. The special appeal of the military and battle for men will also be discussed. In light of this exploration and in the context of the nuclear age, the inevitable shift in the concept of man-hero will be examined. The concept of the spiritual warrior will also be introduced.

- Broyles, W. Jr., "Why Men Love War," *Esquire* (Nov. 1984), pp. 55–65.
- Hillman, J., "Wars, Rams, Arms, Wars: On the Love of War," in R. Rossinger and L. Hough (eds.), *Nuclear Strategy and the Code of the Warrior* (Berkeley, CA: North Atlantic, 1984).

Class 7—Gender and War: Men–Women, Militarism–Feminism, Peace–War

This class will explore the unacknowleged role of women in the making of war. Are women victims or co-contributors to war? Using a systems approach, the myth of the warrior and the beautiful soul will be explored. Carrying the systems approach to the cultural context, the relationship between militarism and sexism (pornography and rape) will be explored in addition to the dynamics of feminization of the enemy. The unique roles and tasks involved in bringing about world survival will be explored in light of the new analyses of gender and war.
  - Adcock, C., "Fear of the 'Other': The Common Root of Sexism and Militarism," in McAllister (ed.), *Reweaving the Web of Life: Feminism and Nonviolence* (Baltimore: New Society Publishers, 1982), pp. 209–219.
  - Warnock, D., "Patriarchy Is a Killer: What People Concerned About Peace and Justice Should Know," in McAllister (ed.), *Reweaving the Web of Life: Feminism and Nonviolence* (Baltimore: New Society Publishers, 1982), pp. 20–29.
  - Zur, O., and C. Glendinning, "Men/Women, War/Peace: A Systems Approach," in M. Macy (ed.), *Solutions for a Troubled World*, ch. 10 (Boulder, CO: Earthian Press, 1987).

Class 8—The Concept and Process of Peace: East and West Perspectives

The concept, images and definition of peace will be explored in this class. Despite the most common use of the word "peace" as the absence of war, we will explore the meaning of the concept and its relevance to our personal and political lives. Peace will be approached on different levels: personal, social, national, international, ecological. Peacemaking activities will be explored, and the main obstacle for peace will be reviewed. The unique contribution of Eastern philosophies and practices to our understanding of peace dynamics will be presented.

Assignment

Each student who takes the course for a grade will submit a typed description (not longer than one page) of his/her final project or paper. During the coming classes *all* students will share their project/paper (and/or their struggle with their topic) with the class in the form of a 10–15 minute presentation/discussion.
  - Campbell, V., "Towards a Theory of Non-Force: Identifying Emotional and Behavioral Dynamics of Peace" (unpublished manuscript).

- Dali Lama, *A Human Approach to World Peace* (Wisdom Publications, 1984).
- Frank, J., *Sanity and Survival*, chs. 10, 12.
- Macy, J., "Buddhist Approach to Social Action," *Journal of Humanistic Psychology*, Vol. 24 (1984), pp. 117–129.
- Nagler, M., "Peace as a Paradigm Shift," *The Bulletin of Atomic Scientists* (1981), pp. 49–52.

Class 9—The Process of Conflict Resolution

Guest Lecturer: Terry Olsen, M.A. In the first part of the class we will discuss our impression of Keen's PBS movie *Faces of the Enemy*. In the second part of the class Terry Olsen, a former research assistant for the environmental mediator group, RESOLVE, and ombudsman for six colleges in the Claremont University system, will explore the process of mediation and conflict resolution. Two case studies will be presented and students will be asked to design a procedure for a mediation in their home, neighborhood, or workplace. In the last part of the class, students may start presenting their projects.

- Allman, W.F., "Nice Guys Finish First," *Science* (October 1984), pp. 25–32.
- Rogers, C.R., "A Psychologist Looks at Nuclear War: Its Threat, Its Possible Prevention," *Journal of Humanistic Psychology*, Vol. 22 (1982), pp. 9–20.

Class 10—The Psychology of the Nuclear Age

Guest Lecturer: Joanna Macy, Ph.D. The complexity of living in a nuclear age will be explored and its psychological impact on adults, children, family lifestyle, and the culture at large will be discussed. Concepts such as "psychic numbing," "despair work and empowerment," and "uncertainty and ambiguity" will be critically examined in light of the nuclear reality. Students will continue to present their work in the second part of the class.

- Frank, D.J., *Sanity and Survival*, ch. 8.
- Glendinning, C., "The Awesome Task," *Therapy Now* (Summer 1984), pp. 10–13.
- Lifton, R.J., "Beyond Psychic Numbing: A Call for Awareness," *Journal of Orthospychiatry*, Vol. 52 (1984), pp. 619–629.
- Macy, J., "Despair Work," *Evolutionary Blues*, pp. 36–47.
- Melamed, E., "Reclaiming the Power to Act," *Therapy Now* (summer 1984), pp. 8–10.
- Zur, O., "War-Myths: Exploration of the Dominant Collective Beliefs About Warfare," 1987. (Fourth myth: pp. 40–46).

Class 11—Peace as a Process: Peace Research, Peace Education and Peace Activism

A systems approach which exphasizes the interconnectedness of the whole universe with all its life forms will be described. Peace research, peace education, and peace activism will be critically discussed on the content, structure and process levels. The importance of the consistency and congruency between goals and processes will be illuminated. It will be argued that the underlying structure, belief system and dynamics of operations are the most crucial elements in peace making. In this light, the military, corporate world, educational systems and peace organizations will be critically examined. Case studies will be presented. Students will continue to present their work in the second part of the class.

- Hurst, J., "A Pedagogy for Peace," in *World Encyclopedia of Peace* (Oxford, U.K.: Pergamon Press).
- Zur, O., "Peace Research and Peace Education," in O. Zur, *Neither Doves nor Hawks: The Psychology of Peace and War*, Section 10. Paper presented at the Western Psychological Association Annual Convention, Long Beach, April 1984.

Class 12—Can We Meet Einstein's Challenge and Change Our Mode of Thinking?

Shortly after World War II had ended, in May 1946, Albert Einstein wrote the following fund-raising letter for the Emergency Committee of Atomic Scientists:

> Our world faces a crisis as yet unperceived by those possessing the power to make great decisions for good or evil. The unleashed power of the atom has changed everything save our modes of thinking, and thus we drift toward unparalleled catastrophe. We scientists who unleashed this immense power have an overwhelming responsibility in this world life-and-death struggle to harness the atom for the benefit of mankind and not for humanity's destruction.

Einstein's statement calls for change in "our mode of thinking" if humanity is to survive. We will evaluate our learning experience (content and process) in the class in light of this statement.

- Herman, W., "Peace on Earth: The Impossible Becomes Possible," *Journal of Humanistic Psychology*, Vol. 29 (1984), pp. 77–92.
- James, W., "The Moral Equivalent of War," in W. James (ed.), *Memories and Studies* (Longman's Green, 1910), pp. 267–296.

IX

World Political Economy and Economic Justice

1. The Political Economy of Development

Thomas Biersteker   *Fall 1987*
School of International Relations, University of Southern
California, Los Angeles, CA 90089

This seminar will examine alternative theoretical perspectives on the most important contemporary issues in the international political economy of North-South relations. We will begin with a general discussion of five contemporary theoretical approaches to the subject, including those of neo-classical conservatives, liberal internationalists, structuralists, dependency writers, and classical Marxists. We will continue with a more detailed discussion of the major issues, policy controversies, and strategies available to the principal parties involved in North-South relations.

We will consider international trade controversies (the terms of trade debate, protectionism, the NIEO, and cartel formation), international aid agencies (with a special focus on the World Bank), transnational corporations (their global expansion, the consequences of their activities in developing countries, and host-country efforts to control their operations), and international finance (IMF conditionality, the privatization of debt, the debt crisis, and the political economy of structural adjustment).

We will conclude the semester with a discussion of the alternative futures open to developing countries in the late 1980s, ranging from association and reform to de-development, self-reliance, and socialist dissociation.

There are no basic textbooks for this course. Most of the readings take the form of journal articles, chapters out of selected books, and unpublished manuscripts. We will be using most or all of the following books:

Required Books

Bauer, Peter. *Equality, the Third World, and Economic Delusion.*
Biersteker, Thomas. *Multinationals, the State, and Control of the Nigerian Economy.*
Foxley, Alejandro. *Latin American Experiments in Neo-Conservative Economics.*
Helleiner, G.K. *International Economic Disorder.*
Krasner, Stephen. *Structural Conflict.*
Moran, Theodore. *Multinational Corporations and the Politics of Dependence.*
Newfarmer, Richard, ed. *Profits, Progress, and Poverty.*
Warren, Bill. *Imperialism: Pioneer of Capitalism.*
Wilber, Charles, ed. *Political Economy of Development and Underdevelopment.*
World Bank. *World Development Report, 1987.*
Yoffie, David. *Power and Protectionism.*

Recommended Books

Ayres, Robert. *Banking on the Poor.*
Bergsten, C. Fred, Thomas Horst, and Theodore H. Moran, eds. *American Multinationals and American Interests.*
Biersteker, Thomas. *Distortion or Development?*
Cardoso, Fernando H., and Enzo Faletto. *Dependency and Development in Latin America.*
Payer, Cheryl. *The World Bank: A Critical Analysis.*

The major requirement for students taking this course is to write a research paper. Students wishing to undertake original research should select a topic after consultation with the instructor sometime during the first five weeks of the semester. Students interested in writing a secondary literature review paper can choose to (1) evaluate one of the five theoretical perspectives (with a review of empirical studies examining some important aspect of trade, aid, transnational corporations, or international finance), or (2) examine one of the principal issues, controversies, or international strategies involving rich and poor countries (with a review of empirical studies examining topics such as the terms of trade, protectionist tendencies, the generalizability of NIC's experience, commodity agreements, resource cartels, the performance criteria of the World Bank, the consequences of international aid efforts, international negotiations, indigenization programs, the economic, political, social or cultural consequences of transnational corporations, the dependency implications of the debt crisis, or the effects of IMF conditionality, extended austerity, and structural adjustment).

COURSE SYLLABUS AND CLASS OUTLINE

Part I. Alternative Theoretical Perspectives

Sept. 9—Introduction

Sept. 16—Neo-Classical Conservative Perspectives
- Bauer, chs. 1, 4, 5, 8, 9 and 10.
- Foxley, ch. 5.
- Theodore Levitt, "The Globalization of Markets," *Harvard Business Review*, May–June 1983, pp. 92–102.
- Ayres, ch. 10.

Sept. 23—Liberal-Internationalist Views
- Bergsten, Horst and Moran, chs. 10 and 12.
- The World Bank, chs. 1, 9 and 10.
- Harry Johnson, *Economic Policies Toward Less Developed Countries*, ch. 2.
- Richard Cooper, "A New International Economic Order for Mutual Gain," *Foreign Policy*, No. 26, pp. 65–120.

Sept. 30—Structuralist Perspectives
- Helleiner, chs. 1, 2, 6 and 7.
- Dudley Seers, "The Meaning of Development," in Uphoff and Ilchman (eds.), *The Political Economy of Development*, pp. 123–129.
- Albert Hirschman, *A Bias for Hope*, ch. 13, pp. 225–252.
- Paul Streeten, "Development Dichotomies," postscript in Meier and Seers (eds.), *Pioneers of Development*, pp. 337–361.

Oct. 7—Dependency Approaches
- Wilber, chs. 6 and 7.
- Cardoso and Faletto, Preface to the English edition, Conclusion and Postscript.
- Peter Evans, *Dependent Development*, ch. 1.
- Gabriel Palma, "Dependency: A Formal Theory of Underdevelopment or a Methodology for the Analysis of Concrete Situations of Under-development?" *World Development*, Vol. 6, No. 7/8, 1978, pp. 881–924.

Oct. 14—Classical Marxist Assessments
- Warren, chs. 1, 5, 6, 7 and 8.
- Anthony Brewer, *Marxist Theories of Imperialism*, chs. 7, 11 and 12.
- Colin Leys, "Capital Accumulation, Class Formation and Dependency—The Significance of the Kenyan Case," *Socialist Register*, 1978.
- Wilber, ch. 3.
- Gavin Kitching, *Development and Underdevelopment in Historical Perspective*.

Part II. Important Issues,
Controversies, and Strategies in Development
and North-South Relations

Oct. 21—International Trade Issues, I

The terms of trade controversy, protectionism, and the NIEO reform proposals.
- H.W. Singer, "The Terms of Trade Controversy and the Evolution of Soft Financing," in Meier and Seers (eds.), *Pioneers of Development*, pp. 275–311.
- S. Smith and J. Toye, "Three Stories About Trade and Poor Economies," *Journal of Development Studies*, Vol. 15, No. 3, April 1979.
- Helleiner, ch. 3.
- Yoffie, chs. 1 and 6.
- The World Bank, ch. 8.
- Krasner, chs. 1–5 and 10.
- Wilber, ch. 9.

Oct. 28—International Trade Issues, II

Cartel formation and proposals for trade dissociation.
- Davis Bobrow and Robert Kudrle, "Theory, Policy and Resource Cartels," *Journal of Conflict Resolution*, Vol. 20, 1976, pp. 3–56.
- Bergsten, Horst and Moran, ch. 5, pp. 122–164.
- Wilber, ch. 13.
- Thomas Biersteker, "Self-reliance in Theory and Practice in Tanzanian Trade Relations," *International Organization*, Vol. 34, No. 2, 1980, pp. 229–264.

Nov. 4—International Aid Issues: The World Bank

- Ayres, chs. 1–4.
- Payer, chs. 1, 12 and Conclusion.
- Helleiner, ch. 8.
- Gunnar Myrdal, "International Inequality and Foreign Aid in Retrospect," in Meier and Seers (eds.), *Pioneers in Development*, pp. 151–172.

Nov. 11—Transnational Corporations, I

Their global expansion and the consequences of their activities.
- Bergsten, Horst and Moran, chs. 1–3, pp. 3–98.
- Biersteker, *Distortion or Development?*, chs. 1–3.
- Newfarmer, chs. 1–3, 6, 8, and 11.
- United Nations Economic and Social Council, "Aspects of the Social and Political Effects of the Activities of Transnational Corporations" (mimeo).

Nov. 18—Transnational Corporations, II

Host-country efforts to control their operations (nationalization and indigenization).

- Bergsten, Horst and Moran, selections from chs. 9 and 10, pp. 335–353 and 369–400.
- Moran, chs. 3–6.
- Biersteker, chs. 2–7.

Nov. 25—International Finance, I: The Debt Crisis
- William Eskridge, "Les Jeux Son Faits: Structural Origins of the International Debt Problem," *Virginia Journal of International Law*, Volume 25 (2), Winter 1985.
- Stefany Griffith-Jones, "The Growth of Multinational Banking, the Eurocurrency Market and their Effects on Developing Countries," *Journal of Development Studies*, January 1980.
- Foxley, chs. 1, 2, and 6–8.
- The World Bank, ch. 2.
- Anatol Kaletsky, "The Logic of Default," 20th Century Fund Report (details to be supplied).

Dec. 2—International Finance, II: IMF Conditionality and the Political Economy of Structural Adjustment
- John Williamson (ed.), *IMF Conditionality*, chs. 2, 3, 5, 10 and 24.
- Tony Killick et al., "The IMF: Case for a Change in Emphasis," in Feinberg and Kallab (eds.).
- *Adjustment Crisis in the Third World*, ch. 2.
- Stephan Haggard, "The Politics of Adjustment," *International Organization*, Vol. 39 (3), 1985.
- Thomas Biersteker, "Reaching Agreement with the IMF: The Nigerian Negotiations, April 1983–November 1986," Pew Project Case Study.

Part III. Alternative Futures
Open to Poor Countries in the Late 1980s

Dec. 9—From Association and Reform to De-development and Dissociation
- Wilber, ch. 22.
- Manfred Bienefeld, "The International Context for National Development Strategies: Constraints and Opportunities in a Changing World," in Bienefeld and Godfrey (eds.), *The Struggle for Development*, ch. 1, pp. 25–63.
- Alain Lipietz, "How Monetarism Has Choked Third World Industrialization," *New Left Review*, No. 145, 1984, pp. 71–87.

2. Development Problems of the Third World

Richard E. Stryker   Fall 1986
Political Science Dept., Indiana University,
Bloomington, IN 47405

The Third World marks off an area of social analysis and moral concern: the human drama of global poverty. Poverty cannot be separated from conditions of inequality and powerlessness, so our inquiry encompasses the whole of "underdevelopment" and the efforts of individuals, communities, social movements, governments, and international organizations to alter (or perpetuate) those conditions. Development is a dynamic process. It promises generalized, if never equal, gains; but it creates new differentiations among social groups, new stratifications among countries, and sometimes even immiserization of "the last and the least." It has both polarizing and integrative dimensions. Development is, above all, an evaluative concept, with both ends and means in dispute.

This is not an area studies course, but a broadly comparative investigation into the political economy of less developed countries. We will be concerned with diversities as well as similarities in development processes and goals across Asia, Africa, and Latin America. The objectives of the course are empathetic, analytical, and prescriptive. Students should become better enabled to evaluate controversies (empirical and ethical) over development alternatives, and to place "news" from and about the Third World into clearer perspective.

The course is designed for advanced undergraduates and graduate students in the social sciences, journalism, history and related fields. Coursework beyond the 200-level in social science is probably essential as a prerequisite. Lectures and readings presuppose familiarity with basic political-economic concepts and with world affairs.

Course Format and Procedures

We will meet twice weekly. Classes will be devoted mostly to lecture and discussion. Attendance is absolutely essential at all sessions. Examinations will draw extensively on materials from lecture, as well as from the required readings. It is not possible to neglect either and perform adequately in the course. Students are personally responsible for everything, including possible scheduling changes, that might be presented in class. Find or make a friend to rely on in need.

There will be two examinations, written in class, made up of short essays and identifications of key concepts. The first accounts for 20% of the course grade and the final for 30%. Three critical essays are also assigned, each worth 15% of the course grade. Class attendance/participation accounts for the remaining 5%. Topics and due dates are listed below. Graduate students do not have additional requirements, but they are expected to read more widely (among the recommended readings), and their work will be evaluated on the basis of more demanding criteria.

Required Readings

Achebe, Chinua. *Things Fall Apart*. Fawcett, 1959, novel.

Chambers, Robert. *Rural Deveopment: Putting the Last First*. Longman, 1983.

Harrison, Paul. *Inside the Third World*. Penguin, 1981, 2nd ed.

Markandaya, Kamala. *Nectar in a Sieve*. Signet, 1955, novel.

Randall, Vicky, and Robin Theobald. *Political Change and Underdevelopment: Critical Introduction to Third World Politics*. Duke, 1985.

Wilber, Charles, ed. *The Political Economy of Development and Underdevelopment*. Random House, 1984, 3rd. ed.

Reprints.

All students are expected to read the entire set of required readings on this syllabus. Graduate students and those undergraduates interested in pursuing further some or all of the issues in this course, now or later, are directed as well to the recommended readings.

Course Assignments

Essay #1: Critically evaluate two articles in the first section on the meaning of development. What are their major strengths and weaknesses (in terms of theoretical clarity, explanatory power, realism, ethical criteria)? Which do you find the more insightful and persuasive approach to "development" and why? (3–5 pages, typed, double-spaced; due no later than Sept. 16—15%.)

Essay #2: In a recent *World Development Report*, the World Bank argued that "over the past quarter-century, the international environment (one of increasing interdependence between developed and developing countries) has been largely supportive of development." Evaluate this claim in general and with respect to international capital transfers in particular. (Be clear as to your meaning of "development.") (3–5 pages, typed, double-spaced; due no later than November 11—15%.)

Essay #3: Write a comparative review of Achebe's *Things Fall Apart* and Markandaya's *Nectar in a Sieve* as "development novels." How can you judge the "authenticity" or representativeness of such works? What did you learn from them, above and beyond other course materials, that illuminated your understanding of major development problems? (3–5 pages, typed, double-spaced; due no later than December 11—15%.)

Examinations: October 14—20%; December 18—30%.

LECTURE AND READING SCHEDULE

I. Introduction: The Third World and the Meaning of Development

Sept 2—Introduction to Course. Sept. 4—The "Third World": Scope, Levels and Dimensions. Sept. 9—Meanings of and Approaches to "Development." Sept. 11—Discussion.

- Markandaya, all.
- Harrison, Introduction and ch. 1.
- Randall and Theobald, Introduction.
- Wilber and Jameson, "Paradigms of Economic Development," ch. 1 in Wilber.
- Warren, "Postwar Economic Experience of the Third World," ch. 8 in Wilber.
- Goulet, "Development or Liberation?" ch. 28 in Wilber.
- Falk, "Satisfying Human Needs," ch. 34 in Wilber.
- Nayar, "Political Mainsprings of Economic Planning." (reprint)
- Wiarda, "Toward a Nonethnocentric Theory of Development." (reprint)

II. Modernization Theory, Traditional Societies and the Colonial Impact

Sept. 16—Modernization and Political Development Theory. Sept. 18—Traditional Societies: Misplaced Polarities, Moral Economy. Sept. 23—The Colonial Impact: Creation of a Global System.

- Achebe, all.
- Harrison, ch. 2.
- Randall, chs. 1–3.
- Gusfield, "Tradition and Modernity." (reprint)
- Griffin, "Underdevelopment in Theory," and "Underdevelopment in History." (reprint)
- Scott, "Moral Economy of the Peasant." (reprint)

III. Dependency Theory, Social Classes and the State

Sept. 25—Imperialism and Dependency. Sept. 30—Dependency and Development. Oct. 2—Social Classes and Communal Cleavages. Oct. 7—The State, Dependency, Development and Democracy. Oct. 9—Conclusion and Discussion.

- Harrison, chs. 3 and 19.
- Randall, chs. 4–6.
- Baran, "Political Economy of Backwardness," ch. 6 in Wilber.
- Frank, "Development of Underdevelopment," ch. 7 in Wilber.
- Weaver and Berger, "Marxist Critique," ch. 3 in Wilber.
- Falk, "Militarisation and Human Rights," ch. 27 in Wilber.
- Sklar, "Nature of Class Domination in Africa." (reprint)
- Becker, "Development, Democracy and Dependency in Latin America." (reprint)

- Rubin, "Economic Liberalisation and the Indian State." (reprint)
- Review Nayar, "Political Mainsprings of Planning."

IV. International Political Economy

Oct. 16—International Stratification and Division of Labor. Oct. 21—Trade and Money. Oct. 23—Multinational Corporations. Oct. 28—Capital Transfers: Aid and Commerce. Oct. 30—No class. Nov. 4—Third World Debt Crisis and Discussion.

- Harrison, chs. 18, 21 and pp. 453, 455–58.
- Girvan, "Swallowing IMF Medicine," ch. 11 in Wilber.
- Newfarmer, "Multinationals and Marketplace Magic," ch. 12 in Wilber.
- Senghaas, "Case for Autarchy," ch. 13 in Wilber.
- Streeten, "Approaches to NIEO," ch. 29 in Wilber.
- Ruggie, "International Division of Labor." (reprint)
- Krueger, "Import Substitution vs. Export Promotion." (reprint)
- Bradford, "East Asian Models: Myths and Lessons." (reprint)
- Singh, "World Trading and Payments, Economic Growth, Strategic Change." (reprint)
- Colaco, "International Capital Flows." (reprint)
- Burki and Ayres, "Fresh Look at Development Aid." (reprint)
- Fishlow, "Debt Crisis: Round Two Ahead." (reprint)
- Bodganowicz-Bindert, "World Debt." (reprint)
- *New York Times:* "Latin Debtors," "Mexico," "Wings of Capital." (reprint)
- Dadzie, "Africa's Commodity Crunch." (reprint)
- Ndegwa, "Africa's Debt Dilemma." (reprint)

V. Poverty, Inequality and Development

Nov. 6—Economic Growth, Inequality and Poverty. Nov. 11—Poverty in Comparative Perspective. Nov. 13—Who Are "the Poor?"

- Harrison, chs. 4–6, 8–12, 20, 22 and p. 454.
- Chambers, chs. 1, 2 and 5.
- Griffin and Ghose, "Growth and Impoverishment, Asia," ch. 15 in Wilber.
- Bhagwati, "Growth and Poverty." (reprint)
- Donnelly, "Human Rights and Development." (reprint)
- Esman, "Landlessness in Developing Countries." (reprint)
- Jacquette, "Women and Modernization Theory." (reprint)
- Goddard and White, "Child Workers and Capitalist Development." (reprint)

VI. Population, Food, Social Issues

Nov. 18—Population and Poverty. Nov. 20—Food and Hunger.

- Harrison, chs. 7, 13–17, and pp. 449–52.
- Hardin, "Lifeboat Ethics." (reprint)
- Lamm, "Attach Strings." (reprint)
- Commoner, "How Poverty Breeds Overpopulation." (reprint)

- Birdsall, "Population Growth." (reprint)
- Mahar, "Population Distribution." (reprint)
- Ainsworth, "Population Policy." (reprint)
- Tierney, "Fanisi's Choice." (reprint)
- *New York Times*: "Natural Disasters" (2); "Green Revolution." (reprint)
- Reutlinger, "Food Security and Poverty." (reprint)

VII. Development Strategies

Dec. 2—Development Strategies—Goals, Policies and Actors. Dec. 4—Agrarian Reform and Rural Development. Dec. 9—The African Crisis and the Indian "Miracle." Dec. 11—Conclusion and Discussion.

- Chambers, chs. 6 and 8.
- Review Griffin and Ghose, "Growth and Impoverishment," in Wilber.
- *Economist*: "Peasants Rising"; "Green Revolution" (2); "Praise Peasants." (reprint)
- Adelman, "Poverty-Focused Approach to Development Policy." (reprint)
- Stryker, "World Bank and Agricultural Development." (reprint)
- Esman, "Landlessness in Developing Countries." (reprint)
- Lofchie, "Africa's Agrarian Malaise." (reprint)
- Hyden, "Urban Growth and Rural Development." (reprint)
- Stryker, "Discussion of Lofchie and Hyden." (reprint)
- Stryker, "Poverty, Inequality and Development: Africa." (reprint)
- Sen, "How is India Doing?" (reprint)

RECOMMENDED READINGS
AND RESEARCH RESOURCES

I. Introduction: The Third World and the Meaning of Development

Bratton, M. "Patterns of Development and Underdevelopment," *International Studies Quarterly*, Sept. 1982.

DeKadt, E. "Markets, Might and Mullahs," *World Development*, 4, 1985.

Galtung, Johan. "Violence, Peace and Peace Research," *Journal of Peace Research*, 6, 3, 1969.

Goulet, Denis. *The Cruel Choice* (1971).

Korten, David and R. Klauss (eds.). *People-Centered Development* (1984).

Phillips, Anne. "Concept of Development," *Review of African Political Economy*, Jan.–April 1977.

Schumacher, E.F. *Small Is Beautiful* (1973).

Smith, Tony. "Requiem or New Agenda for Third World Studies?" *World Politics*, July 1985.

Streeten, Paul. *First Things First: Basic Human Needs* (1981).

Wilber, Charles (ed.). *Political Economy of Development*: Nugent and Yoto-poulos, "Orthodox Development Economics," ch. 3; Wilber, "Human Costs," ch. 26; Freire, "Pedagogy of Oppressed," ch. 33.

II. Modernization Theory, Traditional Societies and the Colonial Impact

Avineri, Shlomo, ed. *Karl Marx on Colonialism and Modernization* (1968).

Barratt-Brown, Michael. *Economics of Imperialism* (1974).

Bates, Robert. "People in Villages" and "Conventional Orthodoxies in Study of Agrarian Change," *World Politics* (Oct. 1978; Jan. 1984).

Bendix, Reinhard, ed. *State and Society* (1968): classics by Roth, Eberhard, Almond, Collins, Fallers, Furnivall, Balandier, et al.

Dalton, George, ed. *Economic Development and Cultural Change, 1971*: see Dalton, Epstein, Fallers, Wolf, Geertz, Singer, Myrdal.

Finkle, Jason, and Richard Gable, eds. *Political Development and Social Change* (1971, 2nd ed.): classics by Black, Rostow, Shils, Kilson, Pye, Deutsch, Huntington, Lipset, Zolberg, Geertz, Wallerstein et al.

Higgott, Richard. *Political Development Theory* (1983).

Huntington, Samuel. *Political Order in Changing Societies* (1968).

———. "The Change to Change," *Comparative Politics*, 3, 3, 1971.

Polanyi, Karl. *The Great Transformation* (1944).

Worsley, Peter. *The Third World* (1967, 2nd ed.) Introduction, ch. 1.

III. Dependency Theory, Social Classes, and the State

Alavi, Hamza, and T. Shanin, eds. *Introduction to the Sociology of Developing Societies* (1982): see Wallerstein, Brenner, Cardoso, Alavi.

Booth, D. "Marxism and Development Sociology," *World Development*, 6, 1985.

Cardoso, F.H., and E. Faletto. *Dependency and Development in Latin America* (1979): see especially the Preface and Postscriptum.

Carnoy, Martin. *The State and Political Theory* (1984).

Collier, David, ed. *New Authoritarianism in Latin America* (1979).

Evans, Peter. *Dependent Development: Brazil* (1979): chs. 1 and 6.

Jackson, Robert, and Carl Rosberg. *Personal Rule in Black Africa* (1982).

Kitching, Gavin. "Kenyan Debate," in H. Bernstein and B. Campbell, eds., *Contradictions of Accumulation in Africa* (1985).

Leys, Colin. "African Economic Development in Theory and Practice," *Daedalus*, Spring 1982.

Seers, Dudley, ed. *Dependency Theory: Critical Reassessment* (1981): especially Palma, "Dependency and Development"; and Bienefeld, "NICs."

Wallerstein, Immanuel. *The Capitalist World-Economy* (1979).

Young, Crawford. *Politics of Cultural Pluralism* (1976).

———. "Patterns of Social Conflict: State, Class and Ethnicity," *Daedalus*, Spring, 1982.

IV. International Political Economy

Alavi, H., and T. Shanin, eds. *Introduction to the Sociology of Developing Societies*: see especially Hymer, Barratt Brown, Bernstein.

Blake, David, and Robert Walters. *Politics of Global Economic Relations* (1983, 2nd ed.).

Caporaso, James. "Industrialization in the Periphery," *International Studies Quarterly*, Sept. 1981.

International Organization: P. Gourevitch, "Second Image Reversed" (Autumn 1978); J. Frieden, "Third World Indebted Industrialization" (Summer 1981); C. Lipson, "International Organization of Third World Debt" (Autumn 1981).

Modelski, George, ed. *Transnational Corporations and World Order* (1979): especially Perlmutter, Gilpin, Vernon, Cos, Galtung, Sunkel, Hymer.

OECD. *25 Years of Development Cooperation: 1985 Report.*

Saunders, Christopher, ed. *Political Economy of New and Old Industrial Countries* (1981): excellent articles by Saunders, Hager et al.

Sewell, John, et al. *U.S. Foreign Policy and the Third World: Agenda 1985–86* (annual publication of Overseas Development Council).

Torrie, Jill, ed. *Banking on Poverty: IMF and World Bank* (1983).

Wilber, Charles, ed. *Political Economy of Development*: Dell, "Stabilization" (ch. 10); Cline, "East Asian Model" (ch. 22).

Wood, R. "Aid Regime and International Debt," *Development and Change*, 4, 1985.

World Bank, *World Development Reports* (annual, especially 1985 on International Capital Flows); and *Staff Working Papers* (numerous resources).

V. Poverty, Inequality, and Development

Ahluwalia, Montek. "Inequality, Poverty and Development"; "Growth and Poverty," *Journal of Development Economics*, 3, 1976, and 6, 1979.

Bromley, Ray, and Chris Gerry, eds. *Casual Work and Poverty in Third World Cities* (1979): excellent articles by eds., Birkbeck et al.

Charleton, Sue Ellen. *Women in Third World Development* (1984).

"Child Workers," special issue of *Development and Change* (Oct. 1982).

Fields, Gary. *Poverty, Inequality and Development* (1980).

International Labor Office. *Poverty and Landlessness in Rural Asia* (1977); *Poverty in Rural Asia* (1983); *Agrarian Policies and Rural Poverty in Africa* (1983); *Challenge of Rural Poverty* (1981).

Lipton, Michael. "Why Poor People Stay Poor" (and Critique by Corbridge), in John Harriss, ed., *Rural Development* (1982); "Urban Bias Revisited," *Journal of Development Studies*, April 1984.

Rodgers, G.B. "Conceptualiztion of Poverty in Rural India," *World Development*, April 1976.

Sen, Amartya. *Poverty and Famines* (1981); *Resources, Values and Development* (1984); "Poor, Relatively Speaking," *Oxford Economic Papers* (1983).

Srinivasan, T., and P. Bardhan, eds. *Poverty and Income Distribution, India* (1974).

Wood, Geoff. "Politics of Development Policy Labelling," *Development and Change*, 16, 3, 1985.

World Bank: Staff Working Papers (numerous resources): see especially *Poverty and Development of Human Resources: Regional Perspectives* (1980); series by Lipton on Poverty (1983–85); and country studies.

VI. Population, Food, Social Issues

Foreign Affairs: A. Biswas, "Water for Third World" (Fall 1981); N. Guppy, "Tropical Deforestation" (Spring 1984); R. McNamara, "Population Problem" (Summer 1984); B. Insel, "World Awash in Grain" (Spring 1985).

Hunger Project. *Ending Hunger* (1985).

Johnson, D. Gale, and G.E. Schuh, eds. *Role of Markets in World Food Economy* (1983); especially Johnson, Poleman, Srinivasan, de Janvry, Bates.

Lieberson, Jon. "Too Many People?" *New York Review of Books* (June 26 1986).

Mellor, John, and B. Johnston, "World Food Equation," *Journal of Economic Literature*, June 1984.

Murdoch, William. *The Poverty of Nations: Political Economy of Hunger and Population* (1980).

Timberlake, Lloyd. *Africa in Crisis* (1985); and A. Wijkman, *Natural Disasters* (1984).

Timmer, C. Peter, et al. *Food Policy Analysis* (1983).

World Bank, *World Development Report* (1984): special issue on population; and *Staff Working Papers* (numerous issues on population, education, food policy, etc.).

VII. Development Strategies: General, Comparative and Theoretical

Arjomand, S.A. "Iran's Islamic Revolution in Comparative Perspective," *World Politics*, April 1986.

Berger. P. *Pyramids of Sacrifice: Political Ethics and Social Change* (1974).

Bienefeld, Manfred, and M. Godfrey, eds. *Struggle for Development: National Strategies in International Context*: Introduction and country chapters on Kenya, Tanzania, North and South Korea, Brazil, PRC, Japan, and India.

Dernberger, Robert, ed. *China's Development Experience in Comparative Perspective* (1980).

Ghai, Dharam, et al., eds. *Agrarian Systems and Rural Development* (1979): see editor's Introduction and country chapters on Tanzania, China, India, South Korea, Guyana, Bangladesh, Cuba, Soviet Central Asia, and Egypt.

Ghose, Ajit, ed. *Agrarian Reform in Contemporary Developing Countries* (1983): see editor's Introduction and country chapters on Nicaragua, Chile, Peru, Ethiopia, Iran, India (Kerala, W. Bengal).

Griffin, Keith. *Political Economy of Agrarian Change* (1974); "Communal Land Tenure Systems" (unpub. ms., 1983); *Institutional Reform and Economic Development in Chinese Countryside* (1984); and with J. James, *Transition to Egalitarian Development* (1981).

Hewlett, Sylvia Ann, and R. Weinert, eds. *Brazil and Mexico* (1982).

Hirschman, Albert. *Strategy of Economic Development* (1958); *Bias for Hope* (1971); and *Essays in Trespassing* (1981).

Lee, Eddy. "Changing Approaches to Rural Development," *Internal Labor Review*, Jan.–Feb. 1980.

Maxwell, N., and B. McFarlane, eds. *China's Changed Road to Development* (1984).

Morawetz, David. "Economic Lessons from Small Socialist Developing Countries," *World Development*, May–June 1980.

Uphoff, Norman, et al. *Feasibility and Application of Rural Development Participation* (1979); *Rural Development and Local Organization in Asia* (1982), 3 vols.; and with M. Esman, *Local Organizations* (1984).

Wilber, Charles, ed. *Political Economy of Development*: de Janvry, "Land Reform" (ch. 17); Streeten, "Industrialization" (ch. 19); Foxley, "Chile," (ch. 23); Knight, "Brazil" (ch. 24); Stewart and Streeten, "New Strategies for Development" (ch. 27, 2nd ed.).

World Bank, *World Development Reports* (especially 1986 on agriculture); and *Staff Working Papers* (numerous resources: countries and issues).

VIII. Development Strategies: South Asia

Bardhan, P.K. *Political Economy of Development in India* (1984).

Bhatt, V.V. "Development Problem, Strategy and Technology Choice: India," *Economic Development and Cultural Change*, Oct. 1982.

Dandekar, V.M., and N. Rath. *Poverty in India* (1971).

Franda, Marcus. *India's Rural Development* (1979).

Frankel, Francine. "Compulsion and Social Change," *World Politics*, Jan. 1978; and *India's Political Economy* (1978).

Guhan, S. "Rural Poverty: Policy and Play Acting," *Economic and Political Weekly*, Nov. 22, 1980.

Gwin, Catherine, and Lawrence Veit, "The Indian Miracle," *Foreign Policy*, Spring 1985.

Herring, Ronald. *Land to the Tiller: Political Economy of Agrarian Reform in South Asia* (1983); and "Guaranteeing Employment to Rural Poor," *World Development*, July 1983.

International Labor Office: *Poverty and Landlessness in Rural Asia*, K.Griffin and A. Chan, eds. (1977): case studies of Pakistan, Bangladesh, Sri Lanka, India, etc.; and *Poverty in Rural Asia*, A. Khan and E. Clay, eds., *Food Policy Issues in Low-Income Countries* (1981); and "Conditions of Poverty Groups . . . India," *Development and Change*, Oct. 1984.

Mellor, John, and G. Desai, eds. *Agricultural Change and Rural Poverty* (1985); and Mellor, *The New Economics of Growth* (1976).

Morris-Jones, W. "India After Indira," *Third World Quarterly*, 4, 1985.

Ramachandran, G., et al. *Gandhi: His Relevance for Our Times* (1967).

IX. Development Strategies: Sub-Saharan Africa

Barkan, J., ed. *Politics and Public Policy in Kenya and Tanzania* (1984).

Bates, Robert. *Markets and States in Tropical Africa* (1981).

Berg, Robert, and J.S. Whitaker, eds. *Strategies for African Development* (1986): see especially Young, Hyden, Leonard, Guyer, Hardy.

Berry, Sara. "Food Crisis and Agrarian Change in Africa," *African Studies Review*, June 1984.

Glantz, M., ed. *Denying Famine or Future* (1986): especially R. Baker, "Linking and Sinking: External Factors, Drought and Destitution, Africa."

International Labor Office: *Agrarian Policies and Rural Poverty in Africa*, D. Ghai and S. Radwan, eds. (1983): case studies, Kenya, Ivory Coast, Malawi, Botswana, Zambia, Nigeria, Ghana, Mozambique, Somalia; and *Food Policy and Equity in Sub-Saharan Africa*, D. Ghai and L. Smith (1983).

Hyden, Goran. *Beyond Ujamaa in Tanzania* (1980); *No Shortcuts to Progress* (1983); and critique by N. Kasfir, "Are African Peasants Self-Sufficient?" *Development and Change*, 17, 1986.

Lele, Uma. "Food Security in Developing Countries," in C. Eicher and J. Staatz, eds., *Agricultural Development in the Third World* (1984); "Problems of Rural Development: Asia and Africa," in K. Nobe and R. Sampath, eds., *Issues in Third World Development* (1983); and "Rural Africa," *Science*, 2, 1981.

Rose, Tore, ed. *Crisis and Recovery in Sub-Saharan Africa* (1985).

Sandrook, Richard. "State and Economic Stagnation in Tropical Africa," *World Development*, 3, 1986; and *Politics of Basic Needs* (1982).

Wheeler, David. "Sources of Stagnation in Sub-Saharan Africa," *World Development*, Jan. 1984.

World Bank. *Accelerated Development in Sub-Saharan Africa* (1981); and *Toward Sustained Development in Sub-Saharan Africa* (1984).

Young, Crawford. *Ideology and Development in Africa* (1982).

3. The Experience and Legacy of Colonialism

Libby Rittenberg   Fall 1987

Economics Dept., Lafayette College, Easton, PA 18042

European colonialism was a force which totally transformed the way of life for the majority of the world's people. It was an alien force in the sense that it came about because of the needs and desires of the colonized powers rather than from events internal to the colonies. The purpose of this colloquium will be to examine the many facets of this transformation, to recognize the challenge which colonialism represented to the conquered peoples and to analyze the responses which arose in the colonized and colonizer countries. A major tenet of this course is that while formal colonialism had ended for most countries by 1960, it continues to affect the lives and thinking of both colonizer and colonized in the post-colonial era. An understanding of the impact and meaning of colonialism can aid significantly in understanding international relations and tensions in the world today.

Examples will be drawn from a variety of former colonies. Emphasis will be placed on the common elements of and reactions to the colonial experience. As such, this course will be cross-cultural, multi-disciplinary, integrative and value-oriented.

It is hoped that this colloquium will allow the student to momentarily escape from his or her own perspective in order to comprehend the experience and legacy of colonialism.

Course Requirements
Reaction Papers (33%)
Students will submit a 1–2 page typed statement of the major thesis/ theses of selected readings and a list of questions for discussion.

Term Project (33%)
The term project is an exploration of the relationship between a contemporary international problem and colonialism. We commonly approach international issues through our national press, which reflects our national political ideology and cultural perspective. The purpose of this assignment is to help us become aware of other perspectives, particularly those of former colonies. Listed below are some recent events and issues that involve the developed world and former colonies: you may think of others or narrow one of these. Select one such issue and analyze it in the following five-step process:

1. Review the American popular press accounts of the issue.
2. Seek out perspectives from the international press, including, if possible, that of any former colonies involved.
3. Define the problem: What issues does it raise? What theories in the experience of colonialism does it reflect?
4. Research and analyze the colonial background of your topic.
5. Return to the popular press and critically analyze its assumptions.

Timetable: Week 3: Select topic. Weeks 3–6: Library session and preliminary research. Week 6: Written proposal of topic, issues, and research plan. Week 7: Conference with instructors. Week 13: Submit 2 copies of finished paper, one for instructors, one for student discussion. Week 14: Oral presentation of topic in class conference.

Suggested Topics:
- Famine in Africa
- Nestle's boycott
- Bhopal gas explosion
- Biafran war
- Independence of Bangladesh
- UNESCO-U.S. withdrawal, Dec. 1983 & Dec. 1984
- Spanish-American War—T. Roosevelt
- U.S. invasion of Grenada, Oct. 1983
- Election/murder of Allende

- Katanga secession issue—Lamumba—U.N. peacekeeping mission
- U.S. Marines to Dominican Republic, 1964
- Brazil's or Mexico's debt payment problem
- U.S. import quotas on textiles, shoes, and other products produced in third world countries
- Assassination of Indira Gandhi
- Bilingual education in U.S.
- Contemporary movies(s): *King Solomon's Mines, Passage to India, Temple of Doom, Gandhi, Mission*
- Manley election in Jamaica
- Panama Canal—turning over to Panama (Carter administration)
- Nationalization, e.g., Suez Canal
- Release of Nelson Mandela
- Debate over liberation theology—role of church in colonialism

Class Participation (33%)
Students will submit a list of five discussion questions for each class.

COURSE OUTLINE

Introduction: Raising the Questions, Establishing the Issues, Relating to Contemporary Concerns

- U.N. General Assembly Resolutions 3201 (S-VI) and 3202 (S-VI), *Declaration and Action Programme on the Establishment of a New International Economic Order,* May 1, 1974, reproduced in Erb, Guy F., and Valerie Kallab, eds., *Beyond Dependency: The Developing World Speaks Out* (New York: Praeger, 1975), pp. 185–202.
- Current Events Readings.

The Origins of Colonialism

- Achebe, Chinua, *Things Fall Apart* (Portsmouth, NH: Heinemann Edition Books, 1962).
- Lenin, V.I, *Imperialism, the Highest State of Capitalism* (London: Martin Lawrence, 1933).
- Muir, Ramsay, "The Meaning and Motives of Imperialism," *The Expansion of Europe* (Boston: Houghton Mifflin, 1919), pp. 1–12.
- Kipling, Rudyard, "White Man's Burden."

The Impact of Colonialism
Changes in the Material World

- Silverblatt, Irene, "Andean Women Under Spanish Rule," in Leacock, Eleanor, ed., *Women and Colonization* (New York: Monthly Review Press, 1973).

Psychological Tensions
- Memmi, Albert, *The Colonizer and the Colonized* (Boston: Beacon, 1965).
- Fanon, Frantz, *The Wretched of the Earth* (New York: Grove, 1963), selected case studies.

Perspectives of the Colonizer
- Orwell, George, "Shooting an Elephant," in Lyons, Robert, ed., *Autobiography: A Reader for Writers* (New York: Oxford University Press, 1977).
- Williams, Gertrude Marvin, *Understanding India* (New York: Coward-McCann, 1928), pp. 13–17.
- Maugham, Somerset, "The Force of Circumstance," in *The Casuarina Tree* (New York: George H. Doran, 1926), pp. 151–189.
- Conrad, Joseph, "The Outpost."

Perspectives of the Colonized
- Soyinka, Wole, "Death and the King's Horseman," in *Six Plays* (London: Methuen, 1984).
- Readings on the Negritude Movement.
- Selections by Nehru.

The Struggle for Independence
Preconditions
- Sembene, Ousmane, *God's Bits of Wood* (Portsmouth, NH: Heinemann Edition Books, 1970).
- Wallerstein, Immanuel, *Africa: The Politics of Independence* (New York: Vintage, 1961), pp. 29–79.

Approaches to Revolution
- Fanon, Frantz, *The Wretched of the Earth* (New York: Grove, 1963), pp. 7–106.
- Selections by Gandhi.

Revolution
- Urdan, Stephanie, *Fighting Two Colonialisms: Women in Guinea-Bissau* (New York: Monthly Review, 1979), pp. 13–41, 57–74, 101–166, 237–314.
- Rowbotham, Sheila, "Colony Within a Colony," *Women, Resistance and Revolution* (London: Vintage Books, 1974), pp. 200-247.
- Emerson, Rupert, *From Empire to Nation* (Boston: Beacon, 1960), pp. 3–85.

The Legacy of Colonialism
Integration into the World Economy
- Bauer, P.T, "The Economics of Resentment: Colonialism and Underdevelopment," in *Dissent on Development*, revised edition (Cambridge, MA: Harvard University Press, 1976), pp. 147–163.

- Bauer, P.T, "Black Africa: The Living Legacy of Dying Colonialism," in *Reality and Rhetoric* (Cambridge: Harvard University Press, 1984).
- Hirschman, Albert O., "Ideologies of Economic Development in Latin America," in *A Bias for Hope: Essays on Development and Latin America* (New Haven: Yale University Press, 1971), pp. 270–311.
- Frank, Andre Gunder, "The Development of Underdevelopment," in Rhodes, Robert I., ed., *Imperialism and Underdevelopment: A Reader* (New York: W.W. Norton, 1983), pp. 14–38.

Problems of Modernization: Bridging the Technological Gap

- Clark, Wilson, "Intermediate Technology," in Burke, J.G., and M.D. Eakin, eds., *Technology and Change* (San Francisco: Boyd and Frazer, 1979), pp. 198–202.
- Erickson, Ronald E., "Environmental Consequences of the Development of the Amazon," in Barret, Richard M., ed., *International Dimensions of Environmental Crisis* (Boulder, CO: Westview Press, 1982), ch. 7, pp. 93–109.
- Kang, Darshan S., "Environmental Problems of the Green Revolution with a Focus on Punjab, India," in Barret, Richard M., ed. *International Dimensions of Environmental Crisis* (Boulder, CO: Westview Press, 1982), ch. 13, pp. 191–215.
- Koehn, Peter, "African Approaches to Environmental Stress: A Focus on Ethiopia and Nigeria," in Barret, Richard M., ed., *International Dimensions of Environmental Crisis* (Boulder, CO: Westview Press, 1982), ch. 17, pp. 253–298.
- Pool, Ithiel de Sola, "Technology and Human Communication," in Desai, A.R., *Modernization of Underdeveloped Societies* (New York: Humanities Press, 1972), ch. 31, pp. 514–522.

Post-Colonial Culture

- Achebe, Chinua, "Thoughts on the African Novel," in *Morning Yet on Creation Day: Essays* (Garden City: Anchor, 1976), pp. 65–84.
- Ngugi, Wa Thiong'o, "Towards a National Culture," in *Homecoming: Essays on African and Caribbean Literature, Culture, and Politics* (New York: Lawrence Hill, 1972), pp. 3–50.
- Opaku, Joseph, "Editor's Preface," and "Culture and Criticism: African Critical Standards for African Literature and the Arts," in Okpaku, Joseph, ed., *New African Literature and the Arts*, Vol. I (New York: Thomas Y. Crowell, 1970), pp. xi–xv and pp. 13–23.
- Mahood, Molly M., "Intentions," in *The Colonial Encounter: A Reading of Six Novels* (London: Rex Collings, 1977), pp. 1–3.
- JanMohamed, Abdul R., "Introduction," in *Manichean Aesthetics: The Politics of Literature in Colonial Africa* (Amherst: University of Massachusetts Press, 1983), pp. 1–13.

The Search for Political Stability

- Wallerstein, Immanuel, *Africa: The Politics of Independence* (New York: Vintage, 1961), chs. VI and IX, pp. 103–120 and 153–167.

- Caldwell, Malcolm, "Problems in Socialism in Southeast Asia," in Rhodes, Robert I., ed., *Imperialism and Underdevelopment: A Reader* (New York: Monthly Review, 1970), pp. 376–400.

Contemporary Concerns Revisited
Student reports and conference days.

4. The State and Third World Development

Frank Holmquist   *Spring 1988*
School of Social Science, Hampshire College,
Amherst, MA 01002

This course examines the state in Third World capitalist development. Both liberal and Marxist traditions of economic and political thought are based on similar conceptions of capitalism, which historically has been seen as relentlessly progressive in economic (material) terms and conducive to the creation of democracy in the political order. These expectations are often difficult to reconcile with the historical experiences of African, Asian, and Latin American nations, and scholars have made notable efforts to reformulate both traditions in an effort to account for the present and to understand the economic and political prospects of Third World nations. In order to do so it has been necessary to rediscover the state. It is evident that states in the Third World are both highly interventionist in their economies and authoritarian almost regardless of formal ideology.

In this class we will first attempt to explain the pervasive impact of states in Third World capitalist development. Second, we will try to explain why state activity brings certain results for popular welfare, modernization of forces of production (capital accumulation, technology, organization and skills), the wider social structure, and the strength of the state itself. Third, we will try to understand the multiple causes of the authoritarian state in the Third World and the possibility of its replacement by more democratic forms. We will address these general questions primarily through six books and some photocopies. We will get at the large issues by closely examining the questions posed, and conclusions found, in each of the readings. As a part of this exercise we will assess the adequacy of the concepts, theories, and research methodologies employed.

Active participation in seminar discussion is required, as is an extended research paper, plus an early outline of the paper a week before a brief class presentation of its main points. The research paper is due on May 9. No papers will be accepted after that date.

Required Books

Bates, Robert H. *Markets and States in Tropical Africa: The Political Basis of Agricultural Policies.* Berkeley: University of California Press, 1981.

Grindle, Merilee. *State and Countryside: Developoment Policy and Agrarian Politics in Latin America.* Baltimore: Johns Hopkins Press, 1986.

Harris, Nigel. *The End of the Third World: Newly Industrializing Countries and the Decline of an Ideology.* New York: Penguin Books, 1986.

Kitching, Gavin. *Development and Underdevelopment in Historical Perspective.* New York: Methuen Press, 1982.

Rudolph, Lloyd I., and Susanne Hoeber Rudolph. *In Pursuit of Lakshmi: The Political Economy of the Indian State.* Chicago: University of Chicago Press, 1987.

Sen, Gita, and Caren Grown. *Development, Crises, and Alternative Visions: Third World Women's Perspectives.* New York: Monthly Review Press, 1987.

There will be a small packet of photocopies that each student will be asked to purchase.

COURSE SCHEDULE

Jan. 27—Introduction: The State and the State of Development Theory

Feb. 3—Historical Perspective
• Kitching.

Feb. 10—Third World Women Today
• Sen & Grown.

Feb. 17—India
• Rudolph & Rudolph, Parts 1 & 2 (scan ch. 3).

Feb. 24—India
• Rudolph & Rudolph, Parts 3 & 4 (scan ch. 11).

Mar. 2—Latin American Agriculture
• Grindle, chs. 1–5.

Mar. 9—Latin American Agriculture
• Grindle, chs. 6–9.

Mar. 16—African Agriculture
• Bates.

Spring Break

Mar. 30—Asian and Latin American Industry
- Harris, chs. 1–4.

Apr. 6—Asian and Latin American Industry
Outlines of research papers are due.
- Harris, chs. 5–8.

Apr. 13—Student Presentations of the Major Findings of Their Papers

Apr. 20—Advising Day: No Class

Apr. 27—Authoritarianism, Democracy and Development
- TBA.

May 4—Authoritarianism, Democracy and Development
- TBA.

May 9—Research Paper Due

5. International Community Development

Galen R. Martin   Fall 1987
International Studies, University of Oregon,
Eugene, OR 97403

> *All I maintain is that on this earth there are pestilences and there are victims, and it's up to us, so far as possible, not to join forces with the pestilences. That may sound simple to the point of childishness; I can't judge if it's simple, but I know it's true.*
>
> —Albert Camus, *The Plague*

This course is meant to serve as an introduction to village communities and their development. We will attempt, via multiple methods, to gain an understanding of "universal" village culture, to explore a wide range of critical skills necessary for effective community development work, and to choose preferred courses of action from among the myriad techniques of village development being practiced today. This emphasis on appreciating values, investigating alternative development tactics, and making choices describes the basic pedagogic framework for our examination of village development.

As Jayne Millar-Wood of *DEVRES* has pointed out, development education can be many things to many people. For purposes of discussion and direction, I have defined my goals for this course, incorporating both process and content elements, to encompass the following:

- to transfer factual information about developing countries and people as well as about global, social economic, and political structures and problems;
- to foster understanding of development as a process that involves people, not objects;
- to promote values and attitudes which will encourage a feeling of responsibility to correct injustices;
- to create a consciousness of the problems shared by most people;
- and to encourage various actions and advocacy activities that will promote justice, equity, and dignity, and will lead to an improvement in the quality of life for all people, especially those in the Third World.

My satisfaction with this course will be determined by the extent to which we meet the above goals, as individuals and together as a group. I would urge you, as you wonder about the meaningfulness and fulfillment of your own life, to divest yourself of self-interest for our brief time together and consider the world's poor: Who are they? What are their dreams? Their disappointments? What kinds of development for the poor will be most appropriate? What are the barriers to this development? Can they be removed? How does development relate to the problem of equity among people? Do the aspirations of the poor conflict with, or complement, your own? These questions are a few among the many that have stimulated the development of this course. Together with those topics enunciated in the outline below, they suggest the broad parameters within which we will be working.

Readings

Critchfield, Richard. *Villages.* Garden City: Anchor Press/Doubleday, 1981. A packet of readings.

Course Requirements

Attendance and participation. Assigned readings. Village film critique/essay (30%). One short analytical examination (30%). Final examination, consisting of a critique of an assigned case study (40%).

COURSE OUTLINE

Overview of the Course

"Man will become better when you show him what he is like," runs an entry in *Anton Chekhov's notebooks. It follows that if we want to help ourselves become better, the place to start is to learn more about what we are like.*
—Richard Critchfield, "Revolution of the Village"

September 29
No readings.

Getting to Know the Rural Poor

One important conclusion . . . is that the first "must" for anyone desiring to help the rural poor is to get to know them—to appreciate not only their physical circumstances and needs, but their social and political environment: their beliefs, traditions, values, and psychological outlook; their life style and the daily demands upon their time and energies. This may seem self-evident, yet many well-intentioned schemes have foundered for lack of sufficient understanding of the people they were intended to benefit.

—Philip H. Coombs,
Meeting the Basic Needs of the Rural Poor

Oct. 1
Films: Potato Planters and *Afghan Village.*

Oct. 6
Film: Miao Year.
- Critchfield, Acknowledgments, Contents, People: chs. 1–14.

Oct. 8
Film: A Ghanian Fishing Village.
- Crtichfield, Ideas: chs. 15–18.

Oct. 13
- Critchfield, Ideas: chs. 19–23.

Oct. 15
- "Why Poor People Are Not Peasants," P. Hill, from *Development Economics on Trial.*

What Do We Mean by "Development"?

The crucial task of this decade, therefore, is to make the development effort appropriate and thereby more effective, so that it will reach down to the heartland of world poverty, to two million villages. If the disintegration of rural life continues, there is no way out—no matter how much money is being spent. But if the rural people of the developing countries are helped to help themselves, I have no doubt that a genuine development will ensue, without vast shanty towns and misery belts around every big city and without the cruel frustrations of bloody revolution. The task is formidable indeed, but the resources that are waiting to be mobilized are also formidable.

—E.F. Schumacher,
Small Is Beautiful: Economics as if People Mattered

Oct. 20
- "Redefining Development," C. Bryant and L.G. White, from *Managing Development in the Third World.*
- "Economic Development, Progress and Culture," Paul-Marc Henry.

Oct. 22

Film: Development Without Tears.
- "Development: Metaphor, Myth, Threat," Gustava Esteve.
- "Historical Fallacies," P. Hill, from *Development Economics on Trial.*

Meeting the Basic Needs of the Poor

Under capitalism, man exploits man; under socialism, it is the other way around.
　　　　　　　　　　　　　　　　　　　　　　　　　—Anonymous Pole

Oct. 27

Film: Kenya Boran.
- "It Won't Go Away," from *The Economist.*

Oct. 29

- "Conventional Development Strategies and Basic Needs Fulfillment," F. Lisk, from *The Struggle for Economic Development.*
- "For or Against Basic Needs?," J. Loup, from *Can the Third World Survive?*

The Difficulties of Reaching the Poorest People

Nov. 3

- "Why Things Go Wrong in Africa," P. Harrison, from *The Greening of Africa.*
- "Rural Poverty Unperceived: Problems and Remedies," R. Chambers, from *World Development*, Vol. 9, No. 1.
- "Indicators of Rural Inequality," A. Castro, N.T. Hakansson, and D. Brokensha, from *World Development*, Vol. 9, No. 5.

Nov. 5

Film: Andean Women.
- "The Development Set," R. Coggins, from *Adult Education and Development.*
- "The Foreign Advisor: Expert or Colleague?" G.W. Fry.

Nov. 10

- "Revolting Development," from *IDR Focus* and response from *Reports.*

Community Organization for Rural Development: The Rhetoric and Reality of Managing Participation

Nov. 12

- "By Their Own Bootstraps," R. Harrison, from *The Greening of Africa.*
- "Beyond the Rhetoric of Rural Development Participation: How Can It Be Done?," D. Gow and J. Vansant, from *World Development*, Vol. 11, No. 5.

Nov. 17

Films: Sarvodaya and *View from the Hills: Saemaul Undong.*
- "Development as Liberation," D. Goulet.

Nov. 19

Film: Health Care by People. Mid-term exam.

Implementing Participatory Development: Strategies for Project Design, Implementation, and Evaluation

Nov. 24

- "Empowering People to Develop," "Working from the Inside: Enhancing Participation in Project Design," "Working from the Inside: Enhancing Participation in Project Implementation," G. Gran, from *Developing by People.*

Dec. 1

Film: Chronicle.
- "The Secrets of Success," P. Harrison, from *The Greening of Africa.*
- "U.S. and Canadian PVOs as Transnational Development Institutions," Brian H. Smith.

Dec. 3

- "Measuring Success and Failure," John G. Sommer.
- "Evaluation as if People Mattered," G. Gran, from *Development By People.*

Managing Myself: Resolutions

We have a tremendous stake in all this, because we have a false picture of Afro-Asian villages as dreary collections of huts, flies, dust and grim fatalistic inhabitants. Whereas reality in the green and often idyllic pastoral world of the villages is completely different, with a truth and simplicity of its own. Once this world starts coming equipped with sanitation, pure water and adequate health care—and the day is not far off—our own overcomplex 20th-century existence may suffer from comparison. Then we will start learning from them how to find our way back to the simple society.

—Richard Critchfield, "Revolution of the Village"

Dec. 8

- "Living with Scarcity," R.L. Shinn, from *Small Comforts for Hard Times.*

Dec. 10

Film: Do You Speak Agriculture?

Dec. 14

Final examination. Development case study critique due.

> *Goodness is something so simple: always to live for others, never to seek one's own advantage.*
>
> —Dag Hammarskjold, *Markings*

X

Human Rights and Social Justice

1. Colloquium on International Human Rights

Louis Henkin and Michael Posner　　　　　*Fall 1987*
School of Law, Columbia University, New York, NY 10027

Session I—Introduction: The Contemporary Concern with Human Rights
Rights and human rights. The international human rights movement: (1) pre–World War II antecedents; (2) World War II, Nuremberg; (3) the United Nations Charter and its aftermath. National and international perspectives on human rights. *Discussion:* Rights and alternative visions of the Good Society, historically and now. The significance of "human" "rights." How and why did human rights enter the international political process in past centuries? Since World War II?

Universal Declaration of Human Rights.
Henkin, Louis. *The Rights of Man Today.* Boulder: Westview Press, 1978, chs. 1 and 3.
Robertson, Arthur H. *Human Rights in the World Today.* New York: Humanities Press, 1972.

Session II—The Western Rights Tradition
Rights in the Western liberal-democratic tradition: Locke and Rousseau, the American constitutional tradition, the primacy of civil and political rights,

and economic and social rights in the West. Alternative visions of the Good Society: (1) rights and "Western" religious traditions; (2) non-Western religious traditions—Islam, Hinduism, Buddhism, and Confucianism; (3) traditionalism and traditional societies; (4) Marx and socialism—rights in bourgeois societies, Marx and the Good Society, and communist states and human rights. *Discussion:* To what extent do international human rights reflect the Western rights tradition and the liberal view of the state? How do human rights fare in contemporary Western analytic and legal philosophy? Can the major non-liberal conceptions of the Good Society assimilate the idea of individual rights? How might human rights be modified or interpreted under these influences?

Locke, John. *Second Treatise of Government,* chs. 2, 5, 7, 9 and 11.
Rousseau, Jean-Jacques. *The Social Contract.* Book 1.
Virginia Bill of Rights.
The French Declaration of Rights of Man and the Citizen.
U.S. Declaration of Independence.
U.S. Constitution.
Shestack, Jerome J. "Jurisprudence of Human Rights," in *Human Rights in International Law.* Ed. Theodor Meron. Clarendon Press, 1984, ch. 3.
Henkin, Louis. "Judaism and Human Rights." *Judaism* 25:4 (Fall 1976).
Hollenback, David. "Global Human Rights: An Interpretation of the Contemporary Catholic Understanding." *Human Rights in the Americas: The Struggle for Consensus.* Eds. Alfred Hennelly and John Langan. Washington, D.C.: Georgetown University Press, 1982.
Stackhouse, Max. "A Protestant Perspective on the Woodstock Human Rights Project." *Human Rights in the Americas: The Struggle for Consensus.* Eds. Alfred Hennelly and John Langan.
Coulson, N.J. "The State and the Individual in Islamic Law." *International and Comparative Law Quarterly* 6:1 (1957): 49–60.
Said, Abdul Aziz. "Precept and Practice of Human Rights in Islam." *Universal Human Rights* 1 (1979): 63–79.
Donnelly, Jack. "Human Rights and Human Dignity: An Analytic Critique of Non-Western Conceptions of Human Rights." *American Political Science Review* 76 (1982): 303–316.
Marx, Karl. "On the Jewish Question." *Collected Works, Vol. 3, Karl Marx and Frederick Engels.* New York: International Publishers, 1975.
Przetacznik, Franciszek. "The Socialist Concept of Human Rights: Its Philosophical Background and Political Justification." *Revue Belge de Droit International* 13:1/2 (1977): 238–278.
Markovits, Inga. "Law or Order—Constitutionalism and Legality in Eastern Europe." *Stanford Law Review* 34 (1982): 513–613.

Session III—International Human Rights Standards: Rights and Limitations

International standards. History: U.N. Charter, Nuremberg, Universal Declaration and Covenants, European, American and African arrangements, adherence of various states. Content: political-civil, economic-social, other (self-determination, development, peace); limitations, derogation; interpretation of particular rights and by whom. New generations of rights: development, peace, environment. *Discussion:* Why are standards desirable? Are standards sufficiently concrete to be useful? What uses might they serve? Which philosophical traditions are the standards based upon? Were any rights omitted? Are some included that should not have been? Should new rights be developed? Are differences between universal and regional standards significant?

United Nations Charter. Preamble, Articles 2, 55, 56.
Universal Declaration.
Covenant on Civil and Political Rights.
Covenant on Economic, Social and Cultural Rights.
European Convention on Human Rights.
Inter-American Convention on Human Rights.
African Charter on Peoples' and Human Rights.
Luard, Evan. "The Origins of International Concern with Human Rights." *The International Protection of Human Rights.* Ed. Evan Luard. New York: Frederick A. Praeger, 1967.
Whitaker, Ben. "Minority Rights and Self-Determination." *Human Rights and American Foreign Policy.* Eds. Donald P. Kommers and Gilbert D. Loescher. Notre Dame University Press, 1979.
The International Bill of Rights. Introduction. Ed. Louis Henkin. New York: Columbia University Press, 1982.

Session IV—Implementing International Standards: Conventional Machinery

Implementation machinery under international agreements. The Genocide Convention. The covenant on Civil and Political Rights. The Optional Protocol. The Human Rights Committee. The Covenant on Economic and Social Rights: ECOSOC and the General Assembly; the Committee on Economic, Social and Cultural Rights. The Convention on Racial Discrimination. Enforcing Regional Conventions: the European Convention, the American Convention, the African Convention. The Helsinki Accord and its enforcement. *Discussion:* The special character of human rights enforcement. General political enforcement and special treaty machinery. Universal and regional conventional machinery; its effect on domestic protection. Is international protection effective?

The implementation sections of the Genocide Convention, the two principle covenants, the Convention on Racial Discrimination, the European Convention, the American Convention and the African Convention.
U.N. ECOSOC Resolution 1985/17, creating the Committee on Economic, Social and Cultural Rights.
Buergenthal, Thomas, ed. *Human Rights, International Law and the Helsinki Accord.* New York: Universe Books, 1977.
Yearbook of the Human Rights Committee 1977–78.

Session V—Implementing International Standards: International Political Machinery

The United Nations: the Human Rights purposes of the UN; non-intervention and Article 2(7). The General Assembly and Human Rights: the Assembly, ECOSOC, the Human Rights Commission, the Subcommission and its working group, ECOSOC and Economic-Social Rights, and proposals for High Commissioner. Politicization, double standard—selective targeting: South Africa, Chile, Israel. Evolution of UN human rights agenda: dominance of the Third World; collective rights, New International Economic Order. Other international Institutions: UNESCO, ILO, WHO. Regional political machinery: the OAS, the Inter-American Commission, the OAU. *Discussion:* Is depoliticization of human rights possible? UN politics and state interests. Are there alternatives to the UN?

Institutional chart of the United Nations System.

United Nations Action in the Field of Human Rights (1983). Read carefully the Table of Contents, pp. v–xiv; also pp. 271–350.

Sohn, L.B. "Human Rights: Their Implementation and Supervision by the United Nations." *Human Rights in International Law.* Ed. T. Meron. 1984, pp. 369–94.

Tolley, H. *The UN Commission on Human Rights.* 1987.

Haver, Peter. "The United Nations Sub-Commission on the Prevention of Discrimination and the Protection of Minorities." *Columbia Journal of Transnational Law* (1982): 103–134.

Americas Watch, Asia Watch, and Helsinki Watch Committees. *Four Failures: A Report on the U.N. Special Rapporteurs on Human Rights in Chile.* Guatemala, Iran and Poland, January 1986.

Donnelly, Jack. "Recent Trends in U.N. Human Rights Activity: Description and Polemic." *International Organization* 25:4 (1981): 633–655.

Liskofsky, Sidney. "The United Nations and Human Rights: 'Alternative Approaches.'" *Essays on Human Rights: Contemporary Issues and Jewish Perspectives.* Ed. David Sidorsky. 1979.

Valticos. "The Role of the ILO." *Human Rights: Thirty Years After the Universal Declaration.* Ed. B.G. Ramcharan. 1979.

Buergenthal, Thomas. "Interamerican System for the Protection of Human Rights." *Human Rights in International Law.* Ed. T. Meron. 1984.

Farer, Tom. "The Inter-American Commission on Human Rights: Operations and Doctrine." *International Journal of Law Libraries* 9 (1981): 251.

Session VI—National Implementation of International Standards

International obligation and national enforcement. International human rights in United States Law: customary human rights law. International human rights instruments and proposed reservations. Human rights as a guide for U.S. courts in Constitutional or statutory interpretation and in prison and mental hospital cases. U.S. courts and human rights abroad. *Discussion:* Extensions of the Filartiga principle to other violations, e.g., racial discrimination, prolonged detention and torture. Is *Filartiga* a good idea?

Schachter. "The Obligation to Implement the Covenant in Domestic Law." *The International Bill of Rights.* Ed. Louis Henkin. 1981, p. 311.
Four Treaties Pertaining to Human Rights. Message of President Carter. Executives C, D, E and F. 95 Cong. 2nd sess. 1978.
Sei Fujii v. California. 38 Cal. 2d 718, 242 P.2d 617 (1952).
Rodriguez-Fernandez v. Wilkinson. 654 F.2d 123 (1981).
Garcia-Mir v. Meese. 788 F.2d 1446 (11th Cir. 1986).
Sterling v. Cupp. 625 F.2d 123 (1981).
Lareau v. Manson. 507 F. Supp. 1177 (D.C. Conn. 1980).
Filartiga v. Pena-Irala. 630 F.2d 876 (2d Cir. 1980).
Tel-Oren v. Libyan Arab Republic (D.C. Cir. 1984).
Torture Victims Protection Act.
Claydon, John. "The Application of International Human Rights Law by Canadian Courts." *Buffalo Law Review* 35:4 (1981): 727–752.

Session VII—Refugees: International Standards and Procedures
The right to leave one's country. Asylum. International protection of refugees: the Refugee Convention and Protocol and the U.N. High Commissioner for Refugees. *Discussion:* Should there be a right to asylum? For whom? Causes of refugee flow; any cures? A viable international program.

Convention Relating to the Status of Refugees.
Protocol Relating to the Status of Refugees.
Teitelbaum, Michael. "Right vs. Right—Immigration and Refugee Policy." *Foreign Affairs* 59 (Fall 1980): 21.
Aleinikoff, T. Alexander. "Political Asylum in the Federal Republic of Germany and the Republic of France: Lessons for the United States." *University of Michigan Journal of Law Reform* 17:4 (1982): 182.

Session VIII—Refugees: U.S. Law and Practice
U.S. refugee policy and immigration policy. Refugees in U.S. courts: interdiction and detention. *Discussion:* A practicable U.S. policy. Refugee admission. Asylum policy. Detention. Other means of deterrence.

Martin, David. "The Refugee Act of 1980: Its Past and Future." Transnational Legal Problems of Refugees. *Michigan Yearbook of International Legal Studies* (1982).
Helton, Arthur. "Political Asylum Under the Refugee Act: An Unfulfilled Promise." *University of Michigan Journal of Law Reform* 17:2 (1984): 243.
Jean v. Nelson. 727 F.2d 957 (11th Cir. 1984), *aff'd,* 105 S. Ct. 2992 (1985).
Perliss, Deborah, and Hartman, Joan. "Temporary Refuge: Emergence of a Customary Norm." *Virginia Journal of International Law* 26:3 (1986): 551.
Plender, Richard. "Admission of Refugees: Draft Convention on Territorial Asylum." *San Diego Law Review* 15:1 (1977): 45.
Martin, David. "Due Process and Membership in the National Community: Political Asylum and Beyond." *University of Pittsburgh Law Review* 44:2 (1983): 165.

Anker, Deborah, and Posner, Michael. "The Forty-Year Crisis: A Legislative
History of the Refugee Act of 1980." *San Diego Law Review* 19:1 (1981):
9.

Session IX—The Politics of Human Rights in a World of States and Human Rights in East-West Relations: The Helsinki Accord

Human rights in international politics: antecedents. The post-war international
human rights movement: realism and idealism, statesmen and citizens,
domestic/international forces, the United Nations and other international
institutions. State sovereignty and non-intervention: "domestic jurisdiction,"
and international concern. Human Rights and national interest: national
interest and domestic human rights, and national interest and the rights of
other people. The politics of standards, adherence, and enforcement. The
Helsinki Accord. Human rights, détente, and *glasnost. Discussion:* The reality
of and limitations on international concern with human rights. The effect
of contemporary international politics on human rights. The effect of human
rights on international politics. The successes and limitations of the Helsinki
Accord. Human rights in U.S.-U.S.S.R. relations and other Eastern European
countries.

Walzer, Micahel. *Just and Unjust Wars: A Moral Argument.* New York: Basic
Books, 1977. Chapter 1.
Beitz, Charles, R. *Political Theory and International Relations,* pp. 67–123.
Hoffman, Stanley. *Duties Beyond Borders.* Chapter 3.
The Helsinki Accord.
Korey, William. "Human Rights and the Helsinki Accord: Focus on U.S.
Policy" (Foreign Policy Association, Headline Series No. 264, 1983).
Korey, William. "Helsinki, Human Rights and the Gorbachev Style." *Ethics
and International Affairs* 1(1987): pp. 113–33.

Session X—Human Rights in North-South Relations

Human rights, modernization, and development. Human Rights in North-
South relations: (1) controversies as to definition and priorities; (2) diverging
national politics as to which rights, which violators, which sanctions (South
Africa); (3) Human Rights in the United Nations; (4) freedom of the press,
and "cultural self-defense"; (5) "non-alignment" and human rights. New
international economic order. *Discussion:* In North-South relations, are human
rights text or pretext? The right of other states to intervene to protect civil-
political rights; the obligation of other states to promote economic-social
rights. Prospects for human rights in a diverse and divided world.

Brewin, Christopher. "Justice in International Relations." *The Reason of States.*
Ed. Michael Donelan. London: Allen and Unwin, 1979. Chapter 9.
Singer, Peter. "Famine, Affluence and Morality." *Philosophy, Politics and
Society* (Fifth Series). Eds. Peter Laslett and James Fishkin. Oxford: Basil
Blackwell, 1979, reprinted in *International Ethics,* C.R. Beitz et al., eds.,
1985.

Nyerere, Julius K. *Man and Development*. New York: Oxford University Press, 1974. Chapter 8.

Hewlett, Sylvia Ann. "Human Rights and Economic Realities: Tradeoffs in Historical Perspective." *Political Science Quarterly* 94:4 (1979): 453–73.

Emerson, Rupert. "Human Rights in the Third World." *World Politics* (January 1975).

Chichilnisky, Graciela, and H.S.D. Cole. "Human Rights and Basic Needs in a North-South Context." *The Politics of Human Rights*. Ed. Paula R. Newberg. New York: University Press, 1980.

Alston, Philip. "Human Rights and the New International Development Strategy." *Bulletin of Peace Proposals* 10:3 (1979): 281–90.

Donnelly, Jack. "The Right to Development." *Human Rights and Development in Africa*. Eds. Claude E. Welch, Jr., and Ronald I. Meltzer. 1984, pp. 261–83.

Zvobyo, Edison J.M. "A Third World View." *Human Rights and American Foreign Policy*. Eds. Donald P. Kommers and Gilburt D. Loescher.

Asante, S.K.B. "Nation Building and Human Rights in Emergent African Nations." *Cornell International Law Journal* 2 (1969): 72–108.

Session XI—Human Rights and Foreign Policy: U.S. Human Rights Policy

National interest and the promotion of human rights. Moralism vs. pragmatism in national foreign policy. "Sanctions" for human rights violations. Multilateral and bilateral measures for promoting human rights in other countries. The U.S. record on human rights in other countries: in multilateral and bilateral diplomacy; the United Nations covenants. Actors in forming U.S. foreign policy: executive branch, Congress, NGO, individuals, media, etc. Human rights and "linkages" to other United States interests. *Discussion:* Do governments care? Should governments care? Can international human rights actions be "apolitical"? Is foreign implementation of human rights desirable? Successful? Human rights and other U.S. interests. Sanctions, rhetoric, and "quiet diplomacy." Congress and the Executive.

Current U.S. Legislation on Human Rights in other countries.

Weissbrodt, David. "Human Rights Legislation and U.S. Foreign Policy." *Georgia Journal of International and Comparative Law* 1 (1977-supplement): 231–87.

National Policy Panel. *United States Foreign Policy and Human Rights: Principles, Priorities, Practices*. Washington, D.C.: United Nations Association of the U.S.A., 1979.

Henkin, Louis. "Human Rights and U.S. Foreign Policy." Publication pending.

Cohen, Stephen B. "Conditioning U.S. Security Assistance on Human Rights Practices." *American Journal of International Law* 76 (April 1982): 246–279.

Kirkpatrick, Jeanne. "Dictatorships and Double Standards." *Commentary* (November 1979).

Jacoby, Tamar. "The Reagan Turnaround on Human Rights." *Foreign Affairs* (Summer 1986).

Kirkpatrick, J. "New Revisonists." *Washington Post* (July 1986).

Jacoby, Tamar. Letter to the Editor. *Washington Post* (1986).

Hoffmann, Stanley. "Reaching for the Most Difficult: Human Rights as a Foreign Policy Goal." *Daedalus* (Fall 1983).

"A Summing Up: Some Basic Issues." *Human Rights and U.S. Foreign Policy.* International Commission of Jurists, 1984.

Session XII—Human Rights and Foreign Policy: Case Studies—South Africa

South Africa: pariah state, relations with other countries. South Africa–U.S. relations: constructive engagement, sanctions. U.S. domestic interests and constituencies. Prospects for change in South Africa. *Discussion:* Human rights and other U.S. interests in South Africa, in Southern Africa. South Africa and U.S. geo-political interests. Congress and the Executive.

Report on South Africa in 1985, *Country Reports.*

Comprehensive Anti-Apartheid Act of 1980, P.L. 99-440.

Chaskalson. "The South African Legal System: Possibilities and Limitations for Human Rights Protection." Unpublished.

Boulle. "Elements in the Crucible: Developing Public Law for the Future." *South African Law Journal* 104 (1987).

Davis, Donald M. "Legality and Struggle: Towards a View of a Bill of Rights for South Africa." Unpublished.

Special Session—The Role of Non-Governmental Organizations

The special role for NGOs in international human rights. National and international NGOs, varieties of NGOs. NGOs in national and international fora. NGOs, Congress, and the Department of State. NGOs and the courts. NGOs and the press. *Discussion:* Improving the effectiveness of NGOs. Relations between NGOs and governments. Competition and cooperation between NGOs.

Lawyer's Committee for International Human Rights. "Non-Governmental Organization (NGOs) Working on International Human Rights."

Shestack, Jerome J. "Sisyphus Endures: The International Human Rights NGO." *New York Law School Review* 24:1 (1978): 89–123.

Weissbordt, David. "The Role of International Nongovernmental Organizations in the Implementation of Human Rights." 12 *Texas International Law Review* 293 (Winter, 1977).

Plant, Roger. "Making Waves: The Emerging Activism." *Development: Seeds of Change* (1984): 3.

Session XIII—Human Rights and U.S. Foreign Policy Case Studies: Central America, the Philippines

El Salvador: repressive ally. Nicaragua: human rights as a foreign policy tool. Philippines: strategic ally. *Discussion:* "Consistency" in U.S. human rights policy. The forms and limits of linkage. Double standards.

Reports on El Salvador, Nicaragua, the Philippines, in *Country Reports on Human Rights Practices for 1986.* Department of State.

Schoultz, Lars. *Human Rights and United States Policy Towards Latin America.* 1981. Introduction, chapters 3 and 5, and conclusion.

Jacoby, Tamar. "The Reagan Turnaround on Human Rights." *Foreign Affairs* (Summer 1986).

Kirkpatrick, J. "New Revisonists." *Washington Post* (July 1986).

Jacoby, Tamar. Letter to the Editor. *Washington Post* (1986). "A Summing Up: Some Basic Issues." *Human Rights and U.S. Foreign Policy.* International Commission of Jurists, 1984.

Veutley, Michel. "Implementation and Enforcement of Humanitarian Law and Human Rights Law in Non-International Armed Conflicts: The Role of the International Committee of the Red Cross." 33 *American University Law Review* (Fall 1983).

Plant, Roger. "Making Waves: The Emerging Activism." *Development: Seeds of Change* (1984): 3.

2. Human Rights in the World Community

Richard P. Claude   Fall 1988
and Burns H. Weston

Claude: Government Dept., University of Maryland, College Park, MD 20742. *Weston:* School of Law, University of Iowa, Iowa City, IA 52242

This syllabus relies upon a one-semester college and law school course on international human rights designed to be taught in the Fall of 1988 by Richard P. Claude at the University of Maryland, and by Burns H. Weston at the University of Iowa. The syllabus draws upon and should be used in conjunction with the paperback edition of Claude and Weston, *Human Rights in the World Community: Issues and Action* (Philadelphia: University of Pennsylvania Press, 1989). This text is designed for pedagogically creative approaches to teaching international human rights inasmuch as every excerpt is followed by elaborate "Questions for Reflection and Discussion," and every section is followed by an "Annotated Bibliography" as well as an "Annotated Filmography," which the instructor may wish to draw upon so as to ensure that the student has an "eye witness" sense of human rights as a global issue.

This course, broadly divided between *issues* and *action*, is also subdivided into six sections. In Claude and Weston, *Human Rights in the World Community*, each section is preceded by a lengthy editors' introduction. The purpose of the six editors' introductions is to introduce the major thematic concerns associated with the issues and institutions discussed in the assigned excerpted essays. For example, in Introduction I, the history of human rights concepts, the development of international law, concepts of sovereignty, and changing theories of international relations are set out. These thematic concerns supply ample bases for the development of lectures, in combination with the fully annotated bibliography and filmography which accompany each section. In short, *Human Rights in the World Community* is designed to be a comprehensive, systematic, and sufficient set of materials and pedagogical tools to open up a course on global perspectives on human rights.

For research purposes, readers should be aware of the *Human Rights Quarterly*, edited by the Urban Morgan Human Rights Institute of the University of Cincinnati and published by the Johns Hopkins University Press (Richard Claude, Founding Editor). The *Quarterly* is a comparative and international journal of the social sciences, humanities, and law which presents wide-ranging research on public policy within the scope of the Universal Declaration of Human Rights. The Human Rights Internet (Harvard Law School) publishes the *HRI Reporter* four times a year. It supplies "clearinghouse" information on human rights developments from country to country and news on non-governmental organizations concerned with international human rights; in the Fall of 1988, Human Rights Internet will begin publication of a newsletter for college faculty on teaching about human rights. In 1983, the Center for the Study of Human Rights at Columbia University published a *Human Rights Bibliography* (Westview Press), organized topically and by author. See also Julian Freedman et al., eds., *International and Comparative Law of Human Rights: A Comprehensive Bibliography* (Paris: UNESCO, 1981), and Julian Freedman and Laurie Wiseburg, eds., "A Bibliography of Bibliographies in Human Rights" (Human Rights Internet, 1981).

COURSE OUTLINE

I. International Human Rights: Overviews

- Weston, Burns H. "Human Rights," in *Encyclopedia Britannica*, Vol. 20 (15th ed. 1985), pp. 713–721.
- Falk, Richard A. "Theoretical Foundations of Human Rights," in Richard A. Falk, *Human Rights and State Sovereignty* (New York & London: Holmes & Meier Publishers, Inc., 1981), pp. 33–63.

Issues

II. Basic Decencies and Participatory Rights

- Kuper, Leo. "The Sovereign Territorial State: The Right to Genocide," in Leo Kuper, *Genocide: Its Political Use in the Twentieth Century* (New Haven, CT: Yale University Press, 1981), pp. 161–185.
- Lippman, Matthew. "The Protection of Universal Human Rights: The Problem of Torture," in *Universal Human Rights*, Vol. 1, No. 4 (Oct.– Dec. 1979), pp. 25–55.
- Lillich, Richard B. "Civil Rights," in Theodor Meron, ed., *Human Rights in International Law: Legal and Policy Issues*, Vol. I (Oxford: Clarendon Press, 1984), pp. 115–169.
- Greenberg, Jack. "Race, Sex, and Religious Discrimination in International Law," in Theodor Meron, ed., *Human Rights in International Law: Legal and Policy Issues*, Vol. II (Oxford: Clarendon Press, 1984), pp. 307–339.
- Ghosal, Animesh, and Thomas M. Crowley. "Refugees and Immigrants: A Human Rights Dilemma," in *Human Rights Quarterly*, Vol. 5, No. 3 (August 1983), pp. 327–347.
- Bay, Christian. "Human Rights on the Periphery: No Room in the Ark for the Yanonami?" in *Development Dialogue*, Nos. 1–2 (1984), pp. 23–41.

III. Basic Human Needs, Security Rights, and Humane Governance

- Lane, David. "Human Rights Under State Socialism," in *Political Studies*, Vol. 32 (1984), pp. 349–368.
- Kothari, Fajni. "Human Rights as a North-South Issue," in *Bulletin of Peace Proposals*, Vol. 11, No. 4 (1980), pp. 331–338.
- Alston, Philip. "International Law and the Right to Food," in Eide, Asbjrn, et al., eds., *Food as a Human Right* (Tokyo: The United Nations University, 1984), pp. 162–174.
- Uibopuu, Henn-Juri. "The Internationally Guaranteed Right of an Individual to a Clean Environment," in *Comparative Law Yearbook*, Vol. 1 (1977), pp. 101–120.
- Dinstein, Yoram. "Self-Determination and the Middle East Conflict," in Yonah Alexander and Robert A. Friedlander, eds., *Self-Determination: National, Regional, and Global Dimensions* (Boulder, CO: Westview Press, 1980), pp. 243–257.
- Tomasevski, Katarina. "The Right to Peace," in *Current Research on Peace and Violence*, Vol. 5, No. 1 (Stockholm International Peace Research Institute, 1982), pp. 42–69.

Action

IV. International Approaches to Implementation

- Farer, Tom J. "The United Nations and Human Rights: More than a Whimper," in *Human Rights Quarterly*, Vol. 9 (1987), pp. 550–586.

- Weston, Burns H., Robin Ann Lukes, and Kelly M. Hnatt. "Regional Human Rights Regimes: A Comparison and Appraisal," in *Vanderbilt Journal of Transnational Law*, Vol. 20, No. 4 (1987).
- Robertson, A.H. "The Helsinki Agreement and Human Rights," in Donald P. Kommers and Gilburt D. Loescher, eds., *Human Rights and American Foreign Policy* (Notre Dame & London: University of Notre Dame Press, 1979), pp. 130–144.

V. National Approaches to Implementation

- Luard, Evan. *Human Rights and Foreign Policy* (Oxford, New York, Toronto, Sydney, Paris, Frankfurt: Pergamon Press, 1981), pp. 1–38.
- Donnelly, Jack. "Humanitarian Intervention and American Foreign Policy: Law, Morality and Politics," in *Journal of International Affairs*, Vol. 35 (1983), pp. 311–328.
- Forsythe, David P. "Congress and Human Rights in U.S. Foreign Policy: The Fate of General Legislation," in *Human Rights Quarterly*, Vol. 9 (1987), pp. 382–404.
- Claude, Richard P. "The Case of Joelita Filartiga and the Clinic of Hope," in *Human Rights Quarterly*, Vol. 5 (1983), pp. 275–295.

VI. NGO, Corporate and Individual Approaches to Implementation

- Dean, Richard N. "Non-Governmental Organizations: The Foundation of Western Support for the Human Rights Movement in the Soviet Union" (unpublished manuscript, 1987).
- Gosiger, Mary C. "Strategies for Divestment from United States Companies and Financial Institutions Doing Business with or in South Africa," in *Human Rights Quarterly*, Vol. 8 (1986), pp. 517–539.
- Paust, Jordan J. "Human Right to Participate in Armed Revolution and Related Forms of Social Violence: Testing the Limits of Permissibility," in *Emory Law Journal*, Vol. 32 (1983), pp. 545–581.

ADDITIONAL RECOMMENDED READINGS AND FILMS

I. International Human Rights: Overviews

Alston, Philip. "Conjuring up New Human Rights: A Proposal for Quality Control." *American Journal of International Law*, Vol. 78 (1984), p. 607. A listing and critique of some currently advocated human rights.

D'Amato, Anthony. "The Concept of Human Rights in International Law." *Columbia Law Review*, Vol. 83 (1982), p. 1110. A critical analysis of the sources of international human rights law with particular attention to custom.

Brownlee, Ian. *Basic Documents on Human Rights*. 2nd ed. New York: Oxford University Press, 1981. A large but accessible handbook of human rights documents containing most of the relevant international instruments on human rights to date.

Forsythe, David P. *Human Rights and World Politics.* Lincoln: University of Nebraska Press, 1983. A wide-ranging and highly readable introduction to the law and politics of international human rights.

Rosenbaum, Alan S., ed. *The Philosophy of Human Rights: International Perspectives.* London: Aldwych Press, 1980. Explores the foundations of contemporary human rights in Jewish, Catholic, Islamic and other ethical and cultural sources.

Sieghart, Paul. *The Lawful Rights of Mankind: An Introduction to the International Legal Code of Human Rights.* New York: Oxford University Press, 1985. The international law on human rights—what it says, how it was made and how it works; a guidebook for the non-specialist reader.

Filmography

Memory of Justice. Marcel Ophuls. France: FilmsInc, 1976. 278 minutes, color, French, English subtitles, 16 mm. Landmark documentary of the Nazi war crimes trials at Nuremburg. Filmmaker Ophuls traveled throughout Germany looking at the peoples' attitudes about the past, and about other atrocities of war, probing the questions of guilt and responsibility.

The Forgotten Genocide. Michael Hagopian. U.S.A.: Atlantic, 1976. 28 minutes, color, 16 mm. Story of the genocide of the Armenian people in 1915 told with the intent to show that such events do occur and threaten all humanity.

Prisoners of Conscience. Noel Fox. Great Britain: Facets/Cinema Guild, 1980. 30 minutes, color, 16 mm. The film illustrates the work of the human rights organization Amnesty International by tracing efforts to achieve the release of two prisoners, a Russian and an Argentine. Follows A.I.'s actions on behalf of each from the London research department to an adoption group working to obtain the prisoners' freedom.

II. Issues of Civil and Political Liberties

Henkin, Louis, ed. *The International Bill of Rights: The Covenant on Civil and Political Rights.* New York: Columbia University Press, 1981. An authoritative guide to the provisions of the Covenant. Topics include a description of the Covenant as well as an examination of its meaning and interpretation.

Stover, Eric, and Elena O. Nightengale, eds. *The Breaking of Bodies and Minds: Torture, Psychiatric Abuse and the Health Professions.* New York: W.H. Freeman and Co., 1985. An analysis of medical ethics and international human rights, with case studies from Chile, Paraguay, and the Soviet Union illustrating the use of psychiatry for political purposes and abuse of health professionals by repressive regimes.

Symposium. "Security of the Person and Security of the State: Human Rights and Claims of National Security." *Yale Journal of World Public Order,* Vol. 9 (Fall 1982). In this volume, authors analyze how "national security" is used to derogate basic personal rights. The U.S. Constitution and European human rights law serve as the backdrop for much of their analysis.

van Dyke, Vernon. *Human Rights, Ethnicity and Discrimination.* Greenwood Press, 1985. A highly readable introduction to global problems of racial, linguistic, and religious discrimination; also includes analysis of invidious treatment of indigeneous peoples.

Filmography

Prisoner With a Name, Cell Without a Number. Linda Yellin. U.S.A.: Yellin, 1983. 100 minutes, color, videotape. Dramatization of the story of Jacobo Timmerman, exiled Argentine newspaper editor, who was imprisoned and tortured by the military regime for being Jewish and for publishing editorials asking for an account of the "disappeared" in Argentina.

Your Neighbor's Son. J.F. Pederson, E. Stephensen. Denmark: Facets, 1976. 55 minutes, color, Greek, English subtitles, 16 mm. Documents the training of Greek torturers under the military junta of the early 1970s; dramatic re-enactments are combined with interviews with former torturers, who recall their transformation from innocent recruits into merciless torturers, as well as with the testimony of victims and their families.

Eyes of the Birds. Gabriel Auer. France: Facets, 1982. 80 minutes, color, French, English subtitles, 16 mm. Dramatization of an International Red Cross delegation visit to Libertad Prison, Uruguay, a so-called model prison in which they discover the effects of physical and psychological torture of prisoners.

III. Basic Human Needs and Third World Human Rights

Crahan, Margaret E., ed. *Human Rights and Basic Needs in the Americas.* Washington, D.C.: Georgetown University Press, 1982. Uses case studies drawn from Latin America to test claims about political, military and economic factors affecting basic needs and related U.S. policy.

Shepherd, George W., Jr., and Ved P. Nanda, eds. *Human Rights and Third World Development.* Westport, CT: Greenwood Press, 1985. A political science–oriented collection of essays, including several area studies, concerned with the view that human rights and development concerns are not competing but complimentary goals.

Welch, Claude E., and Ronald I. Meltzer, eds. *Human Rights and Development in Africa: Domestic, Regional and International Dilemmas.* Albany: State University of New York Press, 1984. Political science–oriented essays on the realistic prospects for economic and political development in Africa with attention to related human rights issues and problems.

Ziman, John, Paul Sieghart, and John Humphries. *The World of Science and the Rule of Law.* New York: Oxford University Press, 1986. Surveys the performance of 35 countries under the Helsinki Agreement in enforcing particular human rights crucial to the work of scientists.

Filmography

The Big Village. United Nations. Barr/UnivILFilms, 1979. 25 minutes, color, 16 mm. A view of the relations between the "rich" and the "poor" nations from a Third World perspective; the film asks why there are persistent inequities and how the resources and bounty of the earth can be shared.

South Africa Belongs to Us. C. Austin, P. Chappell, R. Weiss. U.S.A.: Icarus/ So. Africa Media/Ecufilm/Michigan Media, 1980. 57 minutes, color, 16 mm videotape. Portrait of five Black women in South Africa depicts their struggle for human dignity in the face of apartheid, for homes and food for their children, and for the liberation of the Black people; an in-depth focus on the economic and emotional burdens borne by Black women in South Africa.

IV. International Institutions

Joyce, J.A. *The New Politics of Human Rights.* London: Macmillan, 1978. Describes the new international law and international organizations which seek to impose limits on the treatment of individuals deprived of their liberty; focuses on international politics affecting specific cases (Chile under Pinochet, decolonization in North Africa) and issues (science and technology, the right to peace).

Robertson, A.H. *Human Rights in the World: An Introduction to the Study of the Internatioanl Protection fo Human Rights.* 2nd ed. Manchester: Manchester University Press, 1982. A beginner's introduction to international concern for human rights and the international and regional organizations which seek to protect them; by the former Director of Human Rights in the Council of Europe (1962–73).

Filmography

Human Rights. Thames Television. Great Britain: Media Guild, 1984. 120 minutes, color, videotape. British television documentary traces the development of human rights since the 1948 adoption of the UN Universal Declaration of Human Rights. Includes interviews with diplomats, human rights advocates, and victims of violations around the world who attempt to discuss the concept of universal and inalienable human rights.

Nambia: A Trust Betrayed. United Nations. UN IL Films, 1974. 27 minutes, color, 16 mm. Nambia, previously known as South West Africa, instead of progressing towards independence has been swallowed up into South Africa in defiance of the United Nations and the Internaitonal Court of Justice. Despite the termination of the mandate, South Africa refuses to relinquish the mineral-rich country. The South African race system, apartheid, has been applied in the territory, where ninety percent of the population is black.

V. National Implementation of Human Rights

Farer, Tom. J, ed. *Toward a Humanitarian Diplomacy: A Primer for Policy.* New York: New York University Press, 1980. Essays in "moral diplomacy" address the potential influence of the United States in global affairs due to its economic and technological power.

Fowler, Micahel Ross. *Thinking About Human Rights: Contending Approaches to Human Rights in U.S. Foreign Policy.* Lanham, MD: University Press of America, 1987. An analytic and critical assessment of the premises and underlying assumptions of four major schools of thought as they are brought to bear on human rights as a component of U.S. foreign policy.

Shue, Henry. *Basic Rights, Subsistence, Affluence, and U.S. Foreign Policy.* Princeton, NJ: Princeton University Press, 1980. A carefully argued brief for the universal human right to subsistence, combined with a systematic application of moral theory applied to United States foreign policy.

Vogelpesang, Sandy. *American Dream, Global Nightmare: The Dilemma of U.S. Human Rights Policy.* New York: Norton and Co., 1981. Explores the interconnections among diplomacy, U.S. domestic politics, and international economics as background for an analysis of human rights diplomacy, its limits, and possibilities from the vantage point of the Carter Administration.

Filmography

Unfinished Business. Steven Okazaki. U.S.A.: Couchette, 1984. 60 minutes, color, 16 mm. Documentary film tells the story of three men of Japanese ancestry who refused to go to internment camps in 1942 and were each convicted and imprisoned for violating the U.S. Executive Order 9066; their personal stories and their efforts through the courts to overturn the original convictions are interwoven with archival footage of the camps.

The Politics of Torture. ABC News. U.S.A.: Ecufilm. 50 minutes, color, 16 mm. With examples from Iran, Philippines, and Chile, this news documentary explores the foreign policy of the U.S. in fulfilling a highly publicized promise to promote human rights and raises questions regarding the role of the government and corporations in supporting such regimes.

VI. Private, Corporate and NGO Action

Larson, Egon. *The Flame in Barbed Wire: The Story of Amnesty International.* New York: Norton, 1979. A detailed and highly readable account of the origins (1961) of Amnesty International and the development of its policies on "prisoners of conscience" and avoidance of partisanship.

Nanda, Ved P., James R. Scaritt, and George W. Shepard, Jr. *Global Human Rights: Public Policies, Comparative Measures, and NGO Strategies.* Boulder: Westview Press, 1981. Brings political science perspectives to bear on efforts to develop human rights on a universal scale; includes significant analysis of NGOs.

Shestack, Jerome T. "Sisyphus Endures: The International Human Rights NGO," *New York Law School Review,* Vol. 24 (1978), pp. 89–123. A description of human rights action by private groups and an analysis of the multiple functions performed in international affairs by human rights NGOs.

Filmography

Sakharov. U.S.A.: Facets, 1984. 90 minutes, VHS videotape. Dramatization of the story of Russian physicist Andrei Sakharov and his wife Elena Bonner, who were restricted and imprisoned in the Soviet Union for speaking out against violations of human rights and for social and political change. Made-for-television film stars Jason Robards and Glenda Jackson.

Controlling Interest. California Newsreel. U.S.A.: SoAfMedia/Michigan Media/ UnivCaExtMedia, 1977. 45 minutes, color, 16 mm. Documentary indictment of the role of multi-national corporations and their efforts to oppress workers; focuses on the disastrous social and economic conditions of the Third World, where the corporations' presence is prevalent.

3. International Human Rights

Robert Elias   *Spring 1987*
Tufts University*

This course will emphasize process, as well as substance. Substantively, we will examine the role of human rights in international relations. Taking a broadly interdisciplinary approach, we will consider human rights philosophically, historically, comparatively, politically, economically, and legally, as outlined below. Most fundamentally, we will examine the victims of social injustice, the sources of oppression and global problems, and structural alternatives. As a process, the course encourages intellectual and personal development; ideally, it will promote "critical thinking" that integrates logic, imagination and vision, considers qualities, values, and feelings, examines processes and interrelationships, recognizes competing interests, questions conventional assumptions, and develops personal self-awareness. The course examines our social and individual responsibilities, and our personal or human relationship to oppression wherever it occurs. The course should provide a rigorous and challenging academic experience, with ample room for both intellectual growth and practical experience.

*Current address: Peace and Conflict Studies, University of California, Building T-5, Room 110, Berkeley, CA 94720

Requirements
Class participation—10%; Take-Home Midterm—35%; Take-Home Final—
35%; NGO Report—20%.

Periodicals
You owe it to yourself, at least for one semester, to break the habit of
relying on conventional American media for your understanding of the
world. Contrary to the commericals ("Read *Time*, and Understand."), if you
rely only on *Time* (or its counterparts, *Newsweek, U.S. News and World Report,
The Boston Globe, The New York Times,* etc.), you probably will not really
understand at all. For periodicals that regularly cover human rights, I
recommend *The New Internationalist, The Human Rights Internet Reporter*
(both international), and *The Nation, Radical America, In These Times,* and
The Progressive (both foreign and domestic). Others highly recommended
are *Alternatives, Human Rights Quarterly, Race and Class, Socialist Review,
Multinational Monitor, NACLA Report on the Americas, World Press Review,*
and *World Policy Journal.*

COURSE OUTLINE

Introduction: Literary, Historical and Philosophical Views
Literary and autobiographical examination of oppression and social injustice.
What are the barriers to understanding and thinking "critically" about
national policy, human rights and world problems? History of social, economic
and political victimization (or oppression), and the historical development
of countervailing protections (or rights). Philosophical development of the
concept of a just society, and of human rights. Documentary sources of
human rights: rights of governments, individuals or peoples. What are the
roots of oppression, and how can we eliminate structural sources?
 • Baraheni, *God's Shadow.*
 • Coetzee, *Waiting for the Barbarians* (optional).
 • Shor, "Interferences to Critical Thought."
 • Minogue, "The History of the Idea of Human Rights."
 • Forsythe, *Human Rights and World Politics,* pp. 1–25.
 • Lacquer and Rubin, *The Human Rights Reader,* pp. 193–263, 282–291.
 • "Universal Declaration of the Rights of Peoples."

The International Relations Context
International context of social justice and human rights, i.e., the impact of
international relations and organizations, and of national vs. supranational
sovereignty on violating or promoting rights and victimization. What is the
proper balance between order and justice? Does order inevitably violate
justice, or does it provide the basis for building justice? What change should
we seek in the global or international system to reduce oppression? Must
we accept the limited gains of "realism" or should we seek the more far-
reaching goals of world order "idealism"—can we promote "practical uto-

pias"? What represents the major source of international terrorism: protest groups? foreign governments? state terrorism generally?

- Preiswerk, "Could We Study International Relations as if People Mattered?"
- Hoffman, *Duties Beyond Borders*, ch. 1.
- Bull, "Order Versus Justice in World Politics."
- Beitz, *Political Theory and International Relations*, pt. 3.
- Falk and Kim, "An Approach to World Order Studies and World System."
- Ajami, "Human Rights and World Order Politics."

Comparative Perspectives: Ideological, Cultural, Religious

Comparative perspectives on social justice and human rights, emerging from cultural, historical, religious and ideological differences. The universality of human rights, or the effort to develop norms and priorities of rights, and to reconcile differing rights conceptions (i.e., the search for basic human rights). How do we define human rights? Should we limit ourselves to the Western notion of political and civil rights, or also embrace the Eastern and Third World concept of economic, social and cultural rights?

- Pollis, "Liberal, Socialist and Third World Perspectives."
- Desmond, *Persecution East and West*, chs. 1, 4–6.
- Amnesty International, "Political Killings by Governments."
- Shue, "Security and Subsistence."
- Bay, "Universal Human Rights Priorities."

Implementation: Strategies and Obstacles

Prevention of victimization and the enforcement of human rights—legal and other mechanisms to implement or protect, and the potential of structural transformation. Can we reduce victimization through reforms, or must we seek structural change? What is the impact of non-governmental, transnational actors such as multinational corporations on oppression; do they enhance or reduce it? What are the most effective methods of enforcing or implementing human rights? What is the role of international law? What is the role of nongovernmental human rights organizations, and how can they best work with international governmental organizations? What is the role of religion in human rights? How does traditional religious doctrine and practice compare to liberation theology? What is the impact of human rights information and education? How reliable or biased are the sources, including government and the media?

Governmental
- Forsythe, "Protecting Human Rights."

Multinational Corporations
- Sklar, "Trilateralism: Managing Development and Democracy."
- McGinnis, "The Impact of Multinational Corporations."
- Lernoux, *Cry of the People*, ch. 7.

- Christian Conference of Asia, "Asian People's Struggle for Economic Freedom—Impact of Transnational Corporations."

Nongovernmental Human Rights Organizations
- Schoultz, Human Rights and U.S. Policy Toward Latin America, ch. 2.
- Wiseberg and Scoble, "Monitoring Human Rights Violations: The Role of Nongovernmental Organizations."
- Lernoux, Cry of the People, ch. 2.

Human Rights Information
- Herman, The Real Terror Network, ch. 1, 4.
- Chomsky, Pirates and Emperors, preface, chs. 1, 3.

Development and Intervention: Global Perspectives
Impact of oppression or victimization: the social, economic and political effects, as well as the personal ones (e.g., psychological effects of rights violations). Relationship between development and victimization—social injustice emerging from underdevelopment and overdevelopment, and from the split between First and Third Worlds. International human rights violations as manifested in poverty, inequality, hunger, sexism, racism, cultural intervention, wage slavery and environmental degradation. What is the relationship between repression and terrorism? Can terrorism be justified? Do terrorists have rights? What are the new international economic order and the new international information order, and how would they alter international relations?
- Hayter, On the Creation of World Poverty, pp. 9–49, 82–96, 109–117.
- Lappe and Collins, World Hunger: Ten Myths.
- Barry, Female Sexual Slavery, chs. 4, 7.
- Leghorn and Parker, "The Personal Is Economic."
- Kohler, "Global Apartheid."
- Portes, "Why Illegal Migration: A Human Rights Perspective."
- Schiller, "Cultural Domination."
- Ophuls, "Ecological Scarcity and International Politics."
- "What Are the Causes of Terrorism?"
- Gerstein, "Do Terrorists Have Rights?"
- Eide, "Choosing the Path to Development."

Peace and Disarmament
Impact of war and conflict on victimization: the direct and indirect victimization produced by the failure to achieve "negative" peace, and the relationship between war and injustice. Can we devise alternatives to war, conflict and the arms race to reduce their negative impact on justice and development? How do we balance the desire for self-determination and the desire to pressure nations to respect rights and promote justice?
- Sakamoto and Falk, "World Demilitarized: A Basic Human Need."
- Russett, "Disarmament, Human Rights and Basic Human Needs."
- Thompson, "Human Rights and Disarmament."
- Sharp, "Civilian Self-Defense."

Superpower Foreign Policy

Impact of superpower foreign policy on social injustice, e.g., aid, arms trade, intervention. How does the human rights record in the American and Soviet spheres compare? What are the ideological and political uses and functions of victims and human rights rhetoric in foreign policy? What role should human rights play in foreign policy? What distinguishes overt vs. quiet diplomacy, and what results do they produce? Can we legitimately distinguish between authoritarian and totalitarian governments, in terms of their effects on human rights? Does superpower foreign policy export repression? Does it enhance national security? Do arms sales promote Third World security needs or domestic oppression?

American Foreign Policy

- Kirkpatrick, "Dictatorships and Double Standards."
- Kissinger, "Continuity and Change in American Foreign Policy."
- Abrams, "Human Rights and the Reagan Administration: Another View."
- Frappier, "Above the Law."
- Herman, *The Real Terror Network*, chs. 2, 3, 5.
- Brown, "Apartheid and Trilateralism."
- Brown, *With Friends Like These*, chs. 1, 2, 4.
- Klare and Arnson, *Supplying Repression*, chs. 1, 6.

Soviet Foreign Policy

- Chailand, *Report from Afghanistan*, chs. 3, 5, conclusion.
- Masterman, "Poland: Eyewitness to Terror."
- Lasota, "Poland."
- Vogelgesang, "Soviet Union: Exile for Political Protest."
- Riese, *Since the Prague Spring*, pp. 3–8, 11–14.

Domestic Policy

How well do the superpowers fulfill human rights standards at home? What is the relationship between domestic and foreign policy in superpower violations internally? What strategies and changes would significantly improve human rights in the U.S. and U.S.S.R?

American Domestic Policy

- Parenti, *Democracy for the Few*, chs. 7–9.
- Wolfe, *The Seamy Side of Democracy*, chs. 4–6.
- Cripps, *Human Rights in a U.S. Colony*, ch. 1.

Soviet Domestic Policy

- Sakharov, "Peace, Progress and Human Rights."
- Syzmanski, *Human Rights in the Soviet Union*, chs. 8, 9.
- Mowrer, "Human Rights in the Soviet Union."
- Handler, "Soviet Union."

Citizen Action for Human Rights

Public participation and responsibility: examining social and political movements for rights and justice, and developing models of social responsibility, public action and democracy. Individual responsibility, i.e., the individual's relationship to social justice, and the relationship between personal development and social, political and economic development (values clarification, etc.). Should we promote political change to cope with victimization? How can we learn from the history of social movements, and how can we devise modern strategies and transition paths? What kinds of alternative structures could better promote social justice, from the personal to the global? What is the social responsibility of education, research and scientific inquiry; what are their roles in reducing victimization and suffering? What modes of "consciousness" might provide alternative approaches to personal, national and world behavior?

- Alger, "Reconstituting Global Activism."
- Bay, *Strategies for Political Emancipation*, ch. 6.
- Galtung, "Self-Reliance."
- Johansen, "Building a Just World Order."
- Freire, "Pedagogy of the Oppressed."
- Biko, "Black Consciousness Quest for Humanity."
- Brandwein, "Feminist Thought Structures."
- Fromm, *To Have or To Be*, chs. 1, 9.
- Leonard, *The End of Sex*, chs. 8, 14.

4. Human Rights and Economic Development*

Oscar Schachter and Stephen Marks   Fall 1987
Center for the Study of Human Rights,
Columbia University, New York, NY 10027

This seminar considers the impact of economic development on human rights and the problems of achieving human rights in developing societies.

---

*This syllabus is excerpted with permission of the authors from a more comprehensive version that is available from the Center for the Study of Human Rights (see address under title). Oscar Schacter is Hamilton Fish Professor Emeritus of International Law and Diplomacy at Columbia University. Stephen Marks runs the International Human Rights Program at the Ford Foundation and is a lecturer at the Columbia Law School.

It ranges broadly over political-economic and social issues that bear on internationally recognized human rights. Discussion is largely focused on problems that occur in developing countries that are diverse in their structures, resources, history, and aspirations. Our aim is to acquire insights into and understanding of problems that affect various societies and take specific forms in each of them.

The unifying thread in the seminar is the set of rights defined in the international instruments. Much of our discussion involves analysis of the meaning and reality of these rights in the face of adverse conditions. We take account of ideas and practices manifested in United Nations bodies and other international institutions. The role of political forces and non-governmental groups is given a prominent place.

Part I explores the human rights implications of economic development in general and theoretical terms. Most approaches to development focus on a wide range of factors without explicit reference to human rights and yet, in practice, they have a profound impact on those rights. Inasmuch as certain human rights—those referred to as economic, social, and cultural and the recently formulated right to development—are particularly associated with development, we examine them closely.

Part II deals with six areas in which the realization of human rights encounters serious obstacles as a result of the development process. Each constitutes a large and complex aspect of social and economic development with specific human rights implications. We endeavor to consider problems in a rounded manner, taking account of the diverse factors and conditions that bear on human rights.

Part III deals with the relations between human rights and development assistance provided through multinational and bilateral aid. Conditions linking the granting of aid to human rights observance are considered along with measures designed to give effect to human rights in the implementation of development assistance.

COURSE OUTLINE AND READINGS

Part I. Conceptions and Strategies of Development and Their Human Rights Implications

Sessions 1 & 2—Strategies of Development and Their Relation to Human Rights

Development is a many-sided concept that defies simple definition. It is widely viewed as a historical process that takes place in almost all societies characterized by economic growth and increased production and consumption of goods and services. Development is also frequently used in a normative sense as a multi-valued social goal to which all societies aspire. The process and results of economic development have both positive and negative effects on human rights. We need only reflect on the impact of industrialization, wage labor, displacement of people, changes in family relations, and the emergence of new social classes to become aware of their dual impact. Awareness of human rights—both of the traditional Western-style freedoms and the newer economic and social rights—may also affect development policies and the expectations of people. Competing strategies, such as free market, interventionist, socialist-oriented policies have been supported on diverse human rights grounds. In recent years, there has been much discussion of popular participation, decentralization, egalitarian values, and self-reliance as development goals.

Discussion

1. Does experience show that recognition and observance of human rights, particularly civil and political rights, require a relatively high level of economic growth and well-being?
2. Does history indicate that human rights observance is related to the role of social classes? Has a strong middle class been an important factor in achieving human rights? Have labor and peasant movements substantially affected human rights in practice?
3. Is there a positive correlation, as many argue, between market-oriented economies and individual freedoms? Have "command" economies substantially curtailed individual rights to freedom of expression, freedom from arbitrary arrest, and rights of political participation?
4. Have economic controls over investments, land use, labor, etc., tended to lead to repressive state action? If so, what causes are operative? The opposition of some groups to economic control? Bureaucratic tendencies? Weaknesses of law and judicial authority?
5. Does long-range growth require economic sacrifices by the present generation? Do such sacrifices give rise to opposition and consequential coercion?
6. Do development strategies tend to include uneven distribution of benefits among territorial or ethnic groups, giving rise to opposition?
7. Are restraints on freedom morally and politically justified as trade-offs required for long-term growth and national welfare?

Readings

References to writings relevant to all seminar sessions may be found in: Center for the Study of Human Rights, *Human Rights: A Topical Bibliography*, (Westview Press, 1983).

Books

Crahan, M. (ed.), *Human Rights and Basic Needs in the Americas* (1982).
Falk, Richard, *Human Rights and State Sovereignty* (1981).
Henkin, Louis, *The Rights of Man Today.*
Meron, Theodor (ed.), *Human Rights in International Law*, 2 vols. (1984).
Schachter, Oscar, *International Law in Theory and Practice*, Ch. XV on International Human Rights (1985).

Shepard, George W., and Ved P. Nanda, *Human Rights and World Development* (1986).
Vasak, Karel, and Philip Alston, (eds.), *International Dimensions of Human Rights*, 2 vols. (1982).
Welch, Claude E., Jr., and Robert I. Meltzer, *Human Rights and Development in Africa* (1984).

Articles

Chichilnisky, Graciela, and H.S.D. Cole, "Human Rights and Basic Needs in a North-South Context," *Politics of Human Rights*, Paula R. Newberg (ed.) (1980).
Claude, Richard P., and C. Strouse Jones, "Human Rights in Development Theory," 1 *Research in Law and Sociology* 45–48 (1978).
de Kadt, Emanuel, "Some Questions on Human Rights and Development," 8:2 *World Development* 97–105 (1980).
Donnelly, J., "Human Rights and Development: Complementary or Competing Concerns," 36 *World Politics* 255–283 (Jan. 1984).
Galtung, Johan, and Anders Wirak, "Human Rights and Human Needs," 8 *Bulletin of Peace Proposals* No. 3, 251–260 (1977).
Goodin, Robert E., "The Development-Rights Trade-off: Some Unwarranted Economic and Political Assumptions," 1 *Universal Human Rights* 31–42 (1979).
Howard, Rhoda, "The Dilemma of Human Rights in Sub-Saharan Africa," 35 *International Journal* No. 4, 72–77 (Autumn 1980).
Marks, Stephen, "Development and Human Rights," 8:3 *Bulletin of Peace Proposals* 236–246 (1977).
Marks, Stephen, "Human Rights, Activities of Universal Organizations," 8 *Encyclopedia of Public International Law* 274–284 (1985).

Session 3 & 4—Economic, Social and Cultural Rights and the Right to Development

The objectives of economic development generally include the attainment of certain standards of individual well-being—notably, an adequate standard of living, health care, education, social security, worker protection, and the like. These are also the subjects of "economic, social, and cultural rights," and to some extent the realization of those rights can be taken as a criterion of the success of economic development. However, the process of development may involve policies that run counter to the full realization of such rights and, according to some views, development would be impeded by treating such rights as legal entitlements.

Discussion

1. What is the difference between rights and goals in the context of economic, social, and cultural rights? What relation is there between the realization of these rights and the various approaches and strategies of development?

2. If a state is not under an obligation to ensure the present realization of economic, social, or cultural rights but only to take some steps towards its future realization, what remains of the substance of the right? Does the text of the International Covenant on Economic, Social, and Cultural Rights of 1966 provide a standard by which the action of a state can be judged as meeting the obligation of progressive realization? If the Covenant itself provides no such standard, is the state alone the judge of whether its economic and social welfare policies meet the requirements of Article 2? Would the "Limburg Principles" give more specific meaning to the general obligation? Do the obligations in the Covenant require a state party to adopt development policies it would not otherwise have to follow?

3. Does the qualifying clause in Article 2 of the Covenant "to the maximum of its available resources" merely make the obvious point that a state cannot be required to provide what it does not have? Or does it mean that a state may determine that national security or industrial development require resources and therefore that few resources are "available" for such rights as those to health, education, or an adequate standard of living? What other meaning can this clause plausibly have?

4. Assuming that the Covenant on Economic, Social, and Cultural Rights has been incorporated into domestic law (as is the case in many countries), would an individual be entitled to relief in a domestic court if his rights to health care, education, etc., were not "realized" because available resources were used for other purposes? Would the issues be justifiable?

5. Considering the provisions in the Covenant and related arrangements for implementation by international action, how would measures taken by UN organs or the specialized agencies reduce the uncertainty and vagueness of the Covenant's obligations? For example, would a program of health care by the World Health Organization provide the basis for compliance by the parties with Article 12 of the Covenant? What means are available to international agencies to secure greater compliance by states with the Covenant's obligations? Could international measures legitimately require a state to abandon a free market development policy in its domestic economy?

6. Should the reference to "international assistance and cooperation" in Article 2 of the Covenant and in other Articles be construed to require developed states to assist the poorer countries in taking steps to realize the rights of the Covenant? Would an interpretation of that kind be possible against the will of the developed states? Would it be desirable?

7. Who is deemed to have the right to development and against whom is it enforceable? What effect would the recognition of the right have on development policies?

8. Would recognition of a collective right to development provide a justification for overriding individual rights? What kinds of conflicts would arise in developing countries?
9. What would be the principal legal and policy issues faced by a developing state in giving effect to a "right to property"? Would recognition of the right to property as a human right significantly affect development policies (e.g., land reforms, private enterprise)?

Readings

Alston, Philip, "Out of the Abyss: The Challenges Confronting the New UN Committee on Economic, Social and Cultural Rights," 9 *Human Rights Quarterly* 332 (1987).

———, "Conjuring Up New Human Rights: A Proposal for Control," 78 *American Journal of International Law* 607–621 (1984).

———, "The Right to Development at the International Level," in *Colloque de La Haye*, October 1979, R.J. Dupuy (ed.), 1980, pp. 99–114.

Development as an Emerging Human Right: A Symposium, Feb. 22–23, 1985, 15:3 *California Western International Law Journal* 429–639 (Summer 1985).

Fishkin, J., *The Limits of Obligation* (1982); see pp. 46–47.

Frankel, Charles, *Human Rights and Foreign Policy, Headline Series* 241 (1978).

Galtung, Johan, and Anders Wirak, "Human Rights and Human Needs," 8:3 *Bulletin of Peace Proposals* 251–260 (1977).

Ganji, Manovchehr, *The Realization of Economic, Social, and Cultural Rights: Problems, Policies, Progress,* UN Co. E/CN.4/Conf. 5/1108, Rev. 1, 1975.

Kartashkin, V., "Economic, Social, and Cultural Rights," in Vasak and Alston, (eds.), *International Dimensions of Human Rights,* 1982, pp. 111–133.

Shue, H., *Basic Rights* (1980).

Siegel, Richard L., "Socioeconomic Rights: Past and Future," 7 *Human Rights Quarterly* 255 (1985).

Streeten, Paul, et al., "Basic Human Needs and Human Rights," 8 *World Development* 107–111 (Feb. 1980).

Trubek, D.M., "Economic, Social, and Cultural Rights in the Third World: Human Rights and Human Needs Programs," in *Human Rights in International Law* I, Meron (ed.), pp. 205–231.

United Nations, General Assembly Res. 41/128 and Annex (Declaration on the Right to Development).

United Nations, Secretary-General's Report on Regional and National Dimensions of the Right to Development as a Human Right, UN Doc. E/CNY/1448 (1981).

Part II. Major Human Rights Problems Arising from Development

Session 5—Agriculture and Rural Development Planning: Impact on Peasants and Indigenous Peoples

Economic development has had profound human rights consequences for the peoples in rural areas. In most countries the main source of capital accumulation for industrialization has been the agricultural sector. Mechanization and other technical advances reduced the need for farm labor and led many to migrate and enter the wage labor market, creating a supply of labor for industrial development. It also resulted in the rapid growth of cities, shanty towns, unemployment, and social pathology. Increasing awareness of human rights in many countries was one of the factors stimulating political unrest and demands by rural peoples. Those demands focused on land reform, tenure, limits on displacement, health care and other social services, legal rights, and greater political participation.

Discussion

1. In what respects do development policies that favor industrialization infringe on the basic rights of rural peoples? What measures would afford protection against such infringements?
2. In what ways have efforts to increase agricultural production resulted in deprivation of the rural poor and landless? Consider the effect of policies such as mechanization, cash crops, and water development.
3. What measures have been taken or should be taken to protect rights of rural peoples injured by development projects? What kinds of special protection are required for indigenous groups traditionally attached to particular lands or waters? Is there a human rights interest in maintaining traditional land tenure systems even if they are detrimental to productivity and development?
4. In what ways do human rights considerations compete with development interests with respect to land reform?
5. What development projects typically have a negative impact on indigenous peoples? Are the traditional (cultural) interests of such peoples necessarily incompatible with the development goals of the larger society? Under what circumstances may the interests of indigenous peoples be compatible with those of the larger society?
6. Does the cultural survival of indigenous peoples require that they be insulated from modernizing influences of development? To what extent does assimilation constitute a threat to their existence as peoples? To what extent can assimilation help ensure economic survival?
7. What human rights are most important for indigenous peoples in the context of development? What does self-determination mean for them? What considerations are pertinent to a policy of respect for indigenous peoples' rights and promotion of national development?

Readings

Barsh, R., "Indigenous Peoples: An Emerging Object of International Law," 80 *American Journal of International Law* 369 (1986).

Fanon, F., *The Wretched of the Earth* (1965).

Forman, S., "Rural Masses and the Brazilian Political Process," in *The Brazilian Peasantry*, New York: Columbia University, 1975.

George, Susan, *How the Other Half Dies*, Montclair, NJ: Allanheld, Osman, 1977.

Guillet, David, *Agrarian Reform and Peasant Economy in Southern Peru*, Columbia, MO: University of Missouri Press, 1979.

Hague, W., N. Mehta, A. Rahman, P. Wignaiaja, "Towards a Theory of Rural Development," 1977:2 *Development Dialogue* 11–66 (1977).

Herring, R.J., *Land to the Tiller: Political Economy of Agrarian Reform in South Asia* (Report of Seminar in Penang, Dec. 1981).

Lea, David A.M., and D.P. Chaudri (eds.), *Rural Development and the State: Contradictions and Dilemmas in Developing Countries*, New York: Methuen Press, 1983.

Lehman, D., (ed.), *Agrarian Reform and Agrarian Reformism* (1973).

Lipton, Michael, *Why Poor People Stay Poor* (1976).

Myrdal, G., *The Asian Dilemma* (1968).

Vallianatos, Evan, *Fear in the Countryside*, Cambridge, MA: Belinguer Co., 1976.

World Bank, *Tribal Peoples and Economic Development: Human Ecologic Considerations* (1982).

Session 6—Urbanization and Labor Changes Affecting Human Rights

Migration into cities and into the wage-labor market is a conspicuous feature of economic development. Individual migrants may benefit in important respects. Access to information through mass media, to education, and often to political participation represent gains for many from poor rural areas. Freedom from restrictions of tradition-bound societies is also significant, especially for women and young people who as wage earners attain relative independence from family and community. On the other hand, the disruption of communal support systems, the wretched conditions in urban slums and the difficulty of finding jobs contribute to the misery of urban masses. Urban slum dwellers are commonly deprived of legal rights and social benefits. Labor unions tend to be under government control and are often corrupt. Crime and local "gang" rule are common in many of the large urban concentrations in the developing countries. Under these conditions, the rights contained in the international covenants and other legal instruments seem to be largely "paper" rights. However, in some countries they have been invoked to support political and social reform, and to provide legal grounds for new legislation and judicial action.

Discussion

1. What measures can be taken, consistent with human rights, to control the overcrowding of cities and their slums?
2. If the mass movements from rural to urban centers are generally beneficial to development by providing a large labor supply, should such migration be encouraged or at least not impeded?
3. Can the problem of mass unemployment that exists in most countries (developed and developing) be significantly met by invoking human rights, particularly the right to work and the right to an adequate

standard of living? What changes in economic and social arrangements would be required to ensure that everyone able and willing to work has an adequately remunerative job? Are the I.L.O. proposals in that regard desirable and feasible?

4. Can the social pathology and disorder of urban slums be alleviated by human rights advocacy and application? What means would be appropriate and practical?

5. In view of the subordination of trade unions to government control in most Third World states, what measures can be taken to give effect to the trade union rights expressed in the International Covenant on Economic, Social, and Cultural Rights and in some of the I.L.O. Conventions and Recommendations?

Readings

Abu-Lughod, Janet, and Richard Hay, Jr. (eds.), *Third World Urbanization,* New York: Methuen, 1977.

Gibson, Mary, *Worker's Rights,* Totowa, NJ: Rowman and Allanheld Publishers, 1983.

Gilbert, Alan, and Josef Gugler, *Cities, Poverty and Development: Urbanization in the Third World,* New York: Oxford, 1983.

International Labor Organization, *The Impact of International Labor Conventions and Recommendations,* Geneva, 1976.

Jakobson, L., and V. Prakash (eds.), *Urbanization and National Development,* Sage, 1971.

Jenks, C. Wilfred, "The International Protection of Trade Union Rights," in *The International Protection of Human Rights,* Evan Luard (ed.), New York: Frederick A. Praeger, 1967.

Lipton, M., *Why the Poor Stay Poor,* chs. 2, 3, 9 (1976).

MacPherson, Stewart, *Social Policy in the Third World: The Social Dilemmas of Underdevelopment,* Totowa, NJ: Towman and Allanheld, 1982.

Trubek, D.M., "Economic, Social and Cultural Rights in the Third World: Human Rights and Human Needs Programs," in *Human Rights in International Law,* Meron (ed.), vol. I, pp. 205–272. See particularly the discussion of I.L.O. proposals relating to the right to work, pp. 232–242.

Valticos, N., "The Role of the ILO: Present Action and Future Perspectives," in *Human Rights: Thirty Years After the Universal Declaration,* B.G. Ramcharan (ed.), 1979.

Session 7—Problems of Governance Resulting from Development and Consequential Militarist and Authoritarian Tendencies in Developing Societies

The problems of governance that developing societies must face are daunting. Allowing the "people" to decide on economic policies through democratic processes may be seen by some Third World leaders as contributing further to their inefficiency since democratic institutions have not had the time to develop and be consolidated. Traditional elites, especially oligarchies, are likely to resist change that would threaten their privileges, which they protect with violent means if necessary. Dislocated peasants, removed from their traditional environment, support mass organizations often through violence if it is thought necessary to stop the exploitation. Ethnic conflicts and territorial rivalries are exacerbated by uneven economic development. Inflation and economic decline have also been seen as factors leading to a demand by business interests for a "depoliticized" authoritarian regime. All of these factors create incentives to use authoritarian means to control economic development. A well-organized military force often seems to provide the only relatively efficient centralized authority. Military rule not only eliminates the democratic right of political participation; in many cases it represses the principal civil liberties, and has recourse to torture, executions and disappearances.

Discussion

1. What have been the main reasons for military rule in developing societies? Why is military rule sometimes welcomed by most of the people? Does it signify that order and discipline are seen as more important than political freedoms?
2. What aspects of military rule assist and impede economic development? Have large expenditures for the military tended to retard economic growth? Have they helped in some ways to support industry and technological development?
3. What action has brought about the restoration of civilian rule? Have human rights demands been significant in ending military regimes?

Readings

Deger, S., and S. Sen. "Military Expenditures, Spin-Off, and Economic Development," 13 *Journal of Development Economics* 67 (Aug. 1983).

Forman, S., "Civil-Military Relations in Latin-America."

Falk, Richard, "Militarization and Human Rights in the Third World," 8 *Bulletin of Peace Proposals* 220–232 (1977).

Henderson, Conway, "Military Regimes and Rights in Developing Countries: A Comparative Perspective," 4:1 *Human Rights Quarterly* 110–123 (1982).

Huntington, Samuel, *No Easy Choice: Political Participation in Developing Countries,* Cambridge, MA: Harvard University Press, 1976.

International Commission of Jurists, *Human Rights in a One-Party State,* London: Search Press, 1978.

Jimenez, M., "In the Middle of the Mess." Notes on the Social Origins of Authoritarianism in Late Twentieth Century Latin America (unpublished paper).

Luckhan, Robin, "Armaments, Underdevelopment, and Demilitarization in Africa," VI:2 *Alternatives* 179–245 (1980).

Olatunde, Theophilus, *Military Politics in Nigerian Economic Development and Political Stability,* New Brunswick: Transaction Book, 1978.

Scott, J., *Comparative Political Corruption,* Englewood Cliffs, NJ: Prentice-Hall, 1972.

Sheahan, Hohn, "Market Oriented Economic Policies and Political Repression in Latin America," 28 *Economic Development and Cultural Change*, 268 (January 1980).

Wiatr, Jerzy J., "The Military in Politics: Realities and Stereotypes," 37:1 *International Social Science Journal* 97–107 (1985).

Wolpin, Miles D., *Militarization, Internal Repression and Social Welfare in the Third World*, Croom Helm Ltd., 1986.

Session 8—Effect of Development on the Status and Rights of Women

The role of women in economic and social life has been better understood in recent decades than in earlier periods, when they were often the "underside of history," playing a major role in society while being described (usually by male analysts) essentially as homemakers and mothers.

In spite of the considerable progress made in the recognition of their rights and the improvement of their status, they continue to be given unequal treatment in law and in practice. Women's rate of unemployment is higher than that of men in Western and Third World countries, and their income-earning opportunities tend to lag behind their entry into the job market. The liberating effect of even low-wage jobs for women in factories may result in exploitation and alienation from family and clan.

The reproductive role of women raises important human rights and development issues. Control over reproduction is crucial to women's health and the chances of survival for children, as well as to the full range of related economic and social ramifications.

This session will focus on some of these complex relationshps between economic development and women's status. We will also examine problems relating to the application of international human rights standards in the field of women's rights and how the development process affects the implementation of those standards.

Discussion

1. In what ways have changes in land tenure and land reform related to development strategy (especially in Africa) affected the status and rights of women? What remedial steps can be taken?
2. Has the influx of women into factory jobs in newly industrialized countries given rise to problems that require special protective measures?
3. Has economic development had a significant impact on women's rights relating to reproduction and health? Have international human rights instruments (particularly the International Convention on the Elimination of All Forms of Discrimination Against Women) adequately dealt with such rights? Has the UN World Plan of Action done so?
4. Have developing countries which are parties to the Convention significantly changed discriminatory social and economic practices? What steps may be taken through development policies and programs to bring about greater observance of the Convention's principles?

5. Where religious precepts or traditional practices involve special conditions or limitations on women's rights, should the international community seek to eliminate those conditions and limitations even when the women concerned do not object?

Readings

The special issue on women of *Human Rights Quarterly* (3:2, 1981), includes:

Bennett, Lisa, "Women, Law and Property in the Developing World."
Rogers, Barbara, "Land Reform: The Solution to the Problem."
Moen, Elizabeth, "Women's Rights and Reproductive Freedom."
Jull, Valerie, "The Right to Health Care: Building on Traditional Self-Reliance in Village Jaza."
Holmes, H., and S. Peterson, "Rights Over One's Own Body."
Tinker, Catherine, "Human Rights for Women: The United Nations Convention on the Elimination of All Forms of Discrimination Against Women."
Reanda, Laura, "Human Rights and Women's Rights: Some Observaitons on the United Nations Approach."

Other Articles and Books

Boserup, Ester, *Women's Role in Economic Development*, New York: St. Martin's Press, 1970.
Cairns, Gail, *Laws and Status of Women in Latin America: A Survey.*
Greenhalgh, Susan, "Sexual Stratification: The Other Side of 'Growth with Equity' in East Asia," 11:2 *Population and Development Review* 265–314 (June 1985).
Howard, Rhoda, "Women's Rights in English-Speaking Sub-Saharan Africa," in *Human Rights and Development in Africa*, Welch and Meltzer (eds.), SUNY Press, 1984, pp. 48–74.
Isaacs, Stephen, and Rebecca Cook, *Laws Affecting Fertility: A Decade of Change.*
M'sodzi Mutukwa, Gladys, *Implementation of the Convention on the Elimination of Discrimination Against Women in Africa*, Hubert H. Humphrey Institute of Public Affairs, 1987, 90 pp.
Rogers, Margaret, *A Decade of Women and the Law in the Commonwealth*, the Commonwealth Secretariat and the Hubert Humphrey Institute, 1987, 350 pp.
Jahan, Rov Nag, (ed.), *Women . . . A World Survey* (1987).
Tinker, Irene, and Jane Jaquette, "UN Decade for Women, Its Impact and Legacy," 15:3 *World Development* 419–427, 1987.

Session 9—Transnational Migration

In earlier sessions, we considered the human rights issues raised by population movements within a country, such as the displacement of peoples by development projects and the general movement from rural to urban areas. Economic development also has an impact on migration across national boundaries, and this too raises human rights problems.

Discussion

1. Is it desirable and practical for international policy to encourage freedom of movement across national lines? What steps may realistically be taken toward that end?

2. Should the right of states to exclude and expel "economic refugees" be limited by international law or treaties?

3. In what respects does existing international law protect the rights of foreigners admitted illegally or on a temporary basis when those persons do not meet the test of a "well-founded fear of persecution" as set forth in the Convention on the Status of Refugees? Do such migrants have a right to employment on a non-discriminatory basis? (Consider Articles 2[2], 3, and 6 of the Covenant on Economic, Social, and Cultural Rights.)

4. Are states that impose restrictions on the brain drain for economic reasons in violation of the right to leave as expressed in the Universal Declaration and Article 12 of the Covenant on Civil and Political Rights? May they require renunciation of citizenship before allowing emigration? May they impose a time limit on the stay abroad? Can such restrictions be justified on the grounds that they are necessary to enable a people to utilize fully their natural wealth and resources, as mentioned in Article 25 of the Covenant on Economic and Social Rights? Should the state have a legal claim on the skills and talents of its nationals who choose to leave?

5. Should the state from which skilled personnel leave be compensated for its economic loss by the country to which the persons have migrated? Would this have the undesirable effect of depriving individuals of economic and professional opportunities?

Readings

Chukunta, Onvola, "Human Rights and the Brain Drain," 15 *International Migration* 281 (1977).

Glaser, W., *The Brain Drain: Emigration and Return* (1978).

Goodwin-Gill, F., *International Law and the Movement of Persons Between States* (1978).

Hannum, Hurst, *The Right to Leave and Return in International Law and Practice*, Nijhoff, 1987.

―――, "The Strasbourg Declaration on the Right to Leave and Return," 81 *American Journal of International Law* 432 (1987).

Hucker, "Migration and Resettlement Under International Law," in *The International Law of Human Welfare* 322, Macdonald, Johnston & Morris (eds.), 1978.

Nafziger, James A.R., "The General Admission of Aliens Under International Law," 77 *American Journal of International Law* (1983).

Plender, R., *International Migration Law* (1972).

United Nations, *International Migration Policies: A World Survey, 1982*. UN Sales No. E. 32 X1114.

Walzer, M., *Spheres of Justice* 32–45. 1983.

Session 10—Use of Mass Media and Information Channels for National Development Aims and Consequential Restrictions on Freedom of Information

From the perspective of economic development, communication is both a sector of technological and industrial progress and an important tool to advance development in other areas. Difficult choices need to be made in developing countries regarding reliance on industrialized countries for communications technology—thereby linking development of communications to foreign trade and aid relations—or more self-reliant postures that are often coupled with a high degree of state control. The context within which these choices are made is one of a highly unbalanced flow of information due to *de facto* domination of the "world information order" by industrialized, especially Western, countries and challenges to that order by proponents of a "new world information and communication order." The images that the local population receives through the mass media often portray a life-style that may not only conflict with traditional or national values but may also generate expectations of a consumer society that the national government, whatever its resources and whatever its development strategy, cannot meet for the entire population. Therefore, another issue on which we will focus is the balancing of the various interests in developing societies as they relate to the free flow of ideas and to mobilization of the population to participate in efforts to achieve development objectives.

Discussion

1. Are governments ever justified in imposing restraints on the media and on the free flow of information in the interests of "national development"? Should the general interest in allowing free criticism and popular participation override the negative effects of "special interest" media and the promotion of life-styles that are in conflict with the goals of development? Could you suggest principles and criteria that would help resolve these conflicting interests?
2. Are there good reasons to support all or some of the elements in the proposed "New World Information and Communication Order"? What aspects, if any, are inimical to freedom of information? What action should be taken by international bodies to meet the problems raised by developing countries in regard to the mass media and foreign influence?

Readings

American Civil Liberties Union and Fund for Free Expression, *Free Trade in Ideas: A Conference (September 17, 1984)*, the Center for National Security Studies, 1985.

Boyd-Barrett, J. Oliver, "Western News Agencies and the 'Media Imperialism' Debate: What Kind of Database?," 35:2 *Journal of International Affairs* 247–260 (1981/82).

Curry, Jane L., and Joan R. Dassin, *Press Control Around the World*, New York: Praeger Publishers, 1982.

"Communication Revolution in Politics," 34:4 *Proceedings of the Academy of Political Science* (1982).

Gauhar, Artaf, "Third World: An Alternative Press," 35:2 *Journal of International Affairs* 165–178 (1981/82).

Raman, K. Venketa, "Towards a New World Information and Communication Order: Problems of Access and Cultural Development," in R. St. J. Macdonald and Douglas M. Johnston (eds.), *The Structure and Process of International Law: Essays in Legal Philosophy, Doctrine and Theory*, The Hague: Martinus Nijhoff (1983).

Schwartz, John, *The New World Information*, Oxford University Press, 1980.

Smith, Anthony, *The Geopolitics of Information*, Oxford University Press, 1980.

"Symposium: New World Information Order," 4:1 *New York Law School Journal of International and Comparative Law* (1982).

UNESCO, *Many Voices, One World*. Report of the Commission for the Study of Communication Problems (McBride Commission), Kogan Page/Unipub/UNESCO, 1980.

Part III. International Development Assistance and Human Rights

Session 11—Conditioning Bilateral and Multilateral Aid on Human Rights Observance

Whether development aid should be given to countries with governments that violate basic human rights has been a subject of controversy in the United States and in some international development agencies. U.S. legislation adopted in the 1970s prohibited economic assistance (as well as military aid) to governments that engaged in a consistent pattern of gross violations of human rights unless such assistance directly benefited those in need. An analogous problem has arisen for international development aid bodies. The financial institutions in particular were pressed to deny loans and grants to governments with a pattern of human rights abuses. A somewhat different and more complicated issue was raised by requirements imposed by the International Monetary Fund as conditions on loans by them. Such conditions called for stabilization measures, budget cuts, and reduction of subsidies that often tended to have adverse effects on the poorer sections of the recipient state.

Discussion

1. Principles that govern development aid from international organizations generally provide that the sovereign rights of recipient states and their political independence must be respected. In view of those principles, are international organizations legally entitled to impose human rights requirements as a condition of aid when the recipient government does not accept that condition? Should they? Should distinctions be drawn among the human rights that may be made

conditions of aid; that is, would compliance with certain human rights be more appropriate than others as conditions of aid?

2. What arguments are used to justify conditioning foreign economic aid on human rights performance? What has been the impact of such linkages?

3. Under what circumstances should aid to the needy prevail over the negative human rights record of a government? What other considerations would justify foreign aid to countries with a negative human rights record?

4. What measures can be taken to ensure that the observance of human rights standards as a condition of aid is applied on an impartial and well-founded basis?

5. Should human rights be considered as a "non-economic" or political matter and therefore excluded as a factor in decisions of the World Bank and International Monetary Fund?

Readings

Avery, William P., and David P. Forsythe, "Human Rights, National Security, and the U.S. Senate: Who Votes for What, and Why?" 23 *International Studies Quarterly* 303–320 (1979).

Berg, Wilfred, and Thole, Gunther, "IMF Policies and the Adverse Consequences for Human Rights," 12:3 *GDR Committee for Human Rights Bulletin* (1986).

Brecher, Irving, "Foreign Aid and Human Rights," *International Perspectives: The Canadian Journal on World Affairs* 23–26 (September-October, 1985).

Carleton, David, and Stohl, Michael, "The Foreign Policy of Human Rights: Rhetoric and Reality from Jimmy Carter to Ronald Reagan," 7:2 *Human Rights Quarterly* 205–229 (1985).

Cassese, Antonio, "Foreign Economic Assistance and Respect for Civil and Political Rights: Chile—A Case Study," 14:2 *Texas International Law Journal* 251–263 (1979).

Cohen, Stephen B., "Conditioning U.S. Security Assistance on Human Rights Practices," 76 *American Journal of International Law* 246–279 (1982).

Harkin, Tom, "Human Rights and Foreign Aid: Forging an Unbreakable Link," in *Human Rights and Foreign Policy*, Peter G. Brown and Douglas MacLean (eds.), Lexington, MA: Lexington Books, 1979.

Martin, Edwin M., "Should Observance of Basic Human Rights Be a Prerequisite for Aid?" 16:2 *Atlantic Community Quarterly* 216–221 (1978).

Meyers, R.J. (ed.), *The Political Morality of the International Monetary Fund* (1987).

Moeller, James W., "Human Rights and United States Security Assistance: El Salvador and the Case for Country-Specific Legislation," 24 *Harvard International Law Journal* 75–101 (1983).

Muravchick, J., *The Uncertain Crusade: Jimmy Carter and the Dilemmas of Human Rights Policy* (1986).

Schachter, O., "International Law Implications of U.S. Human Rights Policies," 63 *New York Law School Law Review* 87 (1978).

Schoultz, Lars, *Human Rights and United States Policy Toward Latin America* (1981).

Stohl, Michael, et al., "Human Rights and U.S. Foreign Assistance from Nixon to Carter," 21 *Journal of Peace Research* 215–226 (1984).

Vance, Cyrus R., "The Human Rights Imperative," 63 *Foreign Policy* 3–19 (Summer 1986).

Vogelgesang, S., *American Dream—Global Nightmare: The Dilemma of U.S. Human Rights Policy* (1980).

Session 12—Furthering Human Rights Through Development Assistance

Distinct from the issue of conditionality discussed in the previous session is the question of how development aid may be used positively to further human rights in recipient countries. This question arises in respect to both multilateral aid through international organizations and bilateral aid by donor governments.

Discussion

1. In what respects may human rights be furthered in development projects concerned with industrial or agricultural development?
2. Would the injection of human rights into economic and technical projects involve politicizing aid? Would it be perceived as impinging on sovereign rights?
3. What measures should donor governments or international organizations take to obtain cooperation of the recipient government in furthering human rights? In that connection, consider, in particular, situations in which the government or local community would be opposed to the human rights measures.
4. Should development assistance include aid to police and military forces? Could such aid serve human rights?
5. In what ways could advisory services and technical assistance serve human rights directly? How could governments be persuaded that such technical assistance would be helpful and not intrusive? Have the UN programs of advisory services in human rights proven useful?

Readings

Klare, Michael T., and Cynthia Arnson, *Supplying Repression: U.S. Support for Authoritarian Regimes Abroad*, Washington, DC: Institute for Policy Studies, 1981.

Marks, Stephen P., "The Contribution of the United Nations Educational, Scientific, and Cultural Organization to the Interpretation and Implementation of the International Covenant on Economic, Social, and Cultural Rights," published by the ASIL and UNITAR, the *Interpretive Guide to the International Covenant on Economic and Cultural Rights*, Louis Sohn (ed.).

Nanda, Ved P., "Development and Human Rights: The Role of International Law and Organizations," in *Human Rights and Third World Development,* George Shephard and Ved Nanda (eds.) (1986), pp. 287–307.

Skalnes, Tor, and Egeland, Jan (eds.), *Human Rights in Developing Countries 1986,* a Yearbook of Countries Receiving Norwegian Aid, Norwegian University Press, 1987.

United Nations, *UN Action in the Field of Human Rights* (1983), especially pp. 357–362.

5. Human Rights, Human Dignity, and Human Needs

Arthur Blaser   *Fall 1987*

Government Dept., University of Notre Dame,
Notre Dame, IN 46556

> *The bloody massacre in Bangladesh quickly covered the memory of the Russian invasion of Czechoslovakia; the assassination of Allende drowned out the groans of Bangladesh; the war in the Sinai desert made people forget Allende; the Cambodian massacre made people forget the Sinai; and so forth, until ultimately everyone lets everything be forgotten.*
>
> —Milan Kundera, *The Book of Laughter and Forgetting*
> (This passage is also used by William Shawcross
> in *The Quality of Mercy* to introduce his analysis
> of relief efforts for the Cambodian genocide.)

This course focuses on organizations which strive to help us remember, and to make the world more humane. Amnesty International, the Red Cross, the World Council of Churches, and OXFAM are four of the many organizations we will study. We will consider the objectives of the organizations, the motivations of their members and contributors, and the degree to which the organizations have an impact on world politics.

Course Requirements

Regular participation in the seminar is mandatory. This will include discussion of all of the required and many of the recommended readings, as well as the preparation of written summaries of key points from selected sources (25 percent of grade).

Also required are two short (5-page) reports on humanitarian activity: one focusing on a region of the world (Africa, Asia, Latin America, Soviet Union and East Europe, Western Europe, U.S. and Canada), the other focusing on a specific type of humanitarian organization, e.g., trade union, women, lawyers, journalists, youths and students, indigenous peoples, refugee assistance, humanitarian assistance in armed conflict, famine relief, religion. The short reports should comment on the resources which were most useful in analyzing your topics (25% percent of grade).

A third requirement is a major research paper on humanitarian activity, dealing with a topic of your choice. A short (2–3 page) topic description with a bibliography should be submitted by the end of September. Presentations, including distribution of summaries of analyses, will be scheduled in December. Final papers are due on Human Rights Day, Thursday, December 10 (50 percent of grade).

Topics and Readings

As the reading list is extensive, it is not assumed that you will digest each reading thoroughly. Your object should be to gain a basic familiarity with a wide range of humanitarian activity, as well as expertise in one specific area. Readings which will be primary foci for our discussions are asterisked (*). Seminar participants will be asked to prepare short reports on several of the other readings.

Alexeyeva, Ludmilla. *Soviet Dissent: Contemporary Movements for National, Religious, and Human Rights.* Middletown, CT: Wesleyan University Press, 1987.

Asian Coalition of Human Rights Organizations. *Human Rights Activism in Asia: Some Perspectives, Problems and Approaches.* New York: Council on International and Public Affairs, 1984.

Scoble, Harry M., and Laurie S. Wiseberg, eds. *Access to Justice: The Struggle for Human Rights in South East Asia.* London: Zed Press, 1985.

Peter Willetts, ed. *Pressure Groups in the Global System: The Transnational Relations of Issue-Oriented Non-Governmental Organizations.* London: Francis Pinter, 1982.

Bulletin of Peace Proposals (BPP), Vol. 18, No. 2 (1987), special issue ["Humanitarian Organization-Building in the Third World"]. Note: All mentions of *BPP* below refer to this special issue.

COURSE OUTLINE

I. Background

You will want to acquaint yourself with examples of human rights violation, and with examples of meritorious human rights activity. Such examples can be found in scholarly analyses, summary reports, novels, poetry, memoirs and film.

Begin by familiarizing yourself with the *Amnesty International Report*. Look at at least one report from the 1970s and at the most recent report. Examine the descriptions of several countries in each report. Also look at two other Amnesty International publications, *Political Killings by Governments* and *Torture in the Eighties*.

Then read journalists' and survivors' accounts of human rights violation. I recommend Jeffrey Harmon, "His Majesty, the Emperor Bokhassa," in *Harpers*, and Elie Wiesel's *Night* (a gripping account of the Holocaust). Philip Hallie's *Lest Innocent Blood Be Shed: The Village of Le Chambon and How Goodness Happened There* (New York: Harper and Row, 1979) is highly recommended as an account of why and how two individuals chose to endure great costs in defending human rights during the Holocaust.

II. Perspectives on Government, Society, and Social Organization

Before considering specific humanitarian organizations, we must determine where they fit in the social and political order. The readings indicate that their place (and their nature) will vary by region, and that their efforts must be analyzed in the light of national and global social structures.

Overviews
- *C.B. Macpherson, *The Real Worlds of Democracy* (New York: Oxford University Press, 1966).
- *Willetts: introduction, chs. 1 ["Pressure Groups as Transnational Actors"] and 10 ["The Impact of Promotional Pressure Groups on World Politics"] and appendices.
- Vladimir Hercik, "International Communication Within International Nongovernmental Organizations," *Transnational Associations*, No. 1 (1985), pp. 6–16.

Incentive Theory
We will be distinguishing among a variety of humanitarian organizations. There are different dynamics at work in an unpopular dissident movement, an international trade union confederation, and Amnesty International. One approach which is useful in understanding those dynamics is to consider the range of incentives and disincentives which lead particular people (and some demographic groups) to participate in humanitarian activity.
- *Jeffrey Berry, *The Interest Group Society* (Boston: Little, Brown, 1984), ch. 4 ["Origins, Maintenance, and Marketing"].
- Peter B. Clark and James Q. Wilson, "Incentive Systems: A Theory of Organizations," *Administrative Science Quarterly*, Vol. 5 (September 1961), pp. 129–166.

Critical Perspectives
Karl Marx argued that the bourgeoisie reaped the benefits of many "humanitarian" efforts. Many of Johan Galtung's works argue that center

countries, and within them the individuals at the center, are the primary beneficiaries of international activity. The extent to which this can be verified empirically with respect to international organizations has been addressed by Chadwick Alger and David Hoovler.

- *Karl Marx, "On the Jewish Question," and "Critique of the Gotha Program" (available in most edited collections of Marx's work, including Robert Tucker's *Marx-Engels Reader* and Eugene Kamenka's *The Portable Marx*).
- Chadwick F. Alger and David Hoovler, "The Feudal Structure of International Organizations," Proceedings of the International Peace Research Association, Varanasi, India, January 4–8, 1974.

III. Evolving Standards of Human Rights and Human Dignity

Begin your study of humanitarian standards by considering some important documents. A useful compilation is Ian Brownlie's *Basic Documents in Human Rights*, 2nd ed. (London: Oxford University Press, 1982).

Carefully read the language of the U.S. Declaration of Independence and *Bill of Rights. Also consider the four Constitutions of the USSR, paying special attention to Lenin's "Declaration of the Rights of Toilers" in the 1918 Constitution. The texts and excellent commentary are in Aryeh L. Unger, *Constitutional Development in the USSR* (New York: Pica Press, 1981).

Examine regional and international human rights documents, including the *Universal Declaration of Human Rights, *United Nations Covenants on Civil and Political Rights and on Economic, Social, and Cultural Rights, the *European Convention on Human Rights, the *Conference on Security and Cooperation in Europe's Final Act of 1975 (the Helsinki Declaration), and the *Universal Declaration of the Rights of Peoples (Algiers Declaration).

Also consider scholarly analyses of the evolving standards of human rights and human dignity, of which the following are excellent examples:

- *Asbjorn Eide, "Human Rights: The Universal Platform and Third World Action," in *BPP*.
- Richard Falk, "The Universal Declaration of the Rights of Peoples," in *Human Rights and State Sovereignty* (New York: Holmes and Meier, 1981).
- Richard Biler, "The Right to Peace as a Human Right," International Symposium on the Morality and Legality of Nuclear Weapons, New York City, June 4–5, 1982.
- *Rhoda Howard and Jack Donnelly, "Human Dignity, Human Rights, and Political Regimes," *American Political Science Review*, Vol. 80, No. 3 (September 1986), pp. 801–817.
- Farooq Hassan, "Solidarity Rights: Progressive Evolution of International Human Rights Law?" *New York Law School Human Rights Annual*, Vol. 1 (1983), p. 51–74.

IV. Humanitarian Organization

Overlapping worlds of humanitarian organization are emerging. We will first consider activity within selected countries and regions, and then consider various types of humanitarian activity.

Activity Within Countries and Regions
Humanitarian activity takes different forms in different regions. The directories published by Human Rights Internet each contain descriptions of hundreds of organizations. Begin your study of activity within countries and regions by browsing through the *Internet directories (Latin America, Africa, Asia: 1981; North America, 3rd ed.: 1984; Western Europe: 1982; Eastern Europe and the USSR: 1987). Note the degree to which some organizations focus solely on internal human rights concerns, while others are associated with larger, international organizations. The readings below are designed to describe several kinds of humanitarian activity in selected regions. If you would like to read about humanitarian activity in a country or region which is omitted (e.g., the Middle East, China, Japan), I will gladly provide you with some citations with which to begin your search.

Soviet and East European Organizations
The Soviet and East European governments contend that they share a common and correct approach to the world's humanitarian problems. The governments encourage public participation in activities which bolster that approach. Competing approaches are considered harmful to humanitarian goals, and are therefore discouraged.

Encouraged humanitarian activity: Millions of citizens of the Soviet Union and Eastern Europe participate in humanitarian activity. This activity takes many forms, ranging from the writing of letters protesting repression by governments in the Americas to the donation of funds to striking unionists in Africa, to sponsorship of a public forum on world hunger. Several mass organizations are involved in this activity, including women's organizations, youth organizations, labor organizations, and peace organizations. Such organizations are described in a biannual Soviet publication, N.N. Inozemtsev, Chief Ed., *Peace and Disarmament* (Moscow: Progress Publishers, 1984, 1986). Also see XX *Century and Peace,* the official periodical of the Soviet Peace Committee.

Discouraged humanitarian activity: An excellent, detailed analysis by a Soviet human rights activist who has emigrated to the United States is Ludmilla Alexeyeva's *Soviet Dissent: Contemporary Movements for National, Religious, and Human Rights* (Middletown, CT: Wesleyan University Press, 1987). (*Read preface, introduction, ch. 10, parts V–VII, and conclusion; skim remainder.) Be sure to note Alexeyeva's careful distinctions among the wide range of dissent movements.

• *Rasma Karklins, "The Dissent/Coercion Nexus in the USSR," Soviet Interview Project Working Paper No. 36, University of Illinois at Urbana-Champaign, May 1987.

- Marshall S. Shatz, *Soviet Dissent in Historical Perspective* (Cambridge: Cambridge University Press, 1980), introduction, ch. 7 ["The Soviet Dissidents"], ch. 8 ["Programs and Prospects"].
- Janusz Bugajski, *Czechoslovakia: Charter 77's Decade of Dissent* (New York: Praeger Publishers, 1987).

U.S. and Western European Organizations

- Americas Watch, Asia Watch, Helsinki Watch, and the Lawyers Committee for Human Rights, "Critique: Review of the Department of State's Country Reports on Human Rights Practices for 1986," Washington, D.C., April 1987.
- *Olle Dahlen, "A Governmental Response to Pressure Groups—The Case of Sweden," ch. 8 in Willetts.
- *Abdul S. Minty, "The Anti-Apartheid Movement and Racism in Southern Africa," ch. 2 in Willetts.
- *Lars Schoultz, *Human Rights and United States Policy Toward Latin America* (Princeton: Princeton University Press, 1981), ch. 2 ["Interest Groups"].

Latin American Organizations

Latin American humanitarian organizations are often associated with the Catholic Church. The number and nature of the humanitarian organizations differ greatly by country. The readings below include general analyses of humanitarian activity in Latin America, organizations' (or their leaders') analyses of humanitarian issues, and reports of human rights violations.

- *Adolfo Perez Esquivel, *Christ in a Poncho: Testimonials of Nonviolent Struggle in Latin America* (Maryknoll, NY: Orbis Books, 1983), skim.
- Dom Helder Camara, *Revolution Through Peace* (New York: Harper and Row, 1971), ch. 3 ["The Church in the World"], ch. 7 ["The Christian Half of the Underdeveloped World"].
- *Marcos Arruda, "The Role of Latin American Non-Governmental Organizations in the Perspective of Participatory Democracy," *Transnational Associations*, No. 6 (1986), pp. 314–320.
- *Ecumenical Consultation on Pastoral Work with Indigenous Peoples in Latin America, "To Organize Hope," *LADOC*, Vol. 15, No. 1 (September/October 1984), pp. 1–14.
- Ivan Illich, "The Seamy Side of Charity," *America* (January 21, 1967), pp. 88–91.
- *Permanent Commission on Human Rights (Nicaragua), "Report for December, 1986," Managua: PCHR. The Permament Commission is staffed by political opponents of the Sandinista government. Its findings are much more critical of that government than are the findings of other Nicaraguan and international NGOs. Compare the reports of Amnesty International and Americas Watch with the PCHR report.
- Archdiocese of Sao Paulo, *Torture in Brazil* (New York: Vintage Books, 1986).

- Brian Smith, *The Church and Politics in Chile* (Princteon, NJ: Princeton University Press, 1982), especially chs. 2 ["The Church as a Complex Religious Organization"] and 9 ["The Church and the Chilean Military Regime, 1973–1980"].

African Organizations

- *Gunnar Hagman and Dan Kaseje, "Community-Based Development: Its Third World Perspectives," *BPP,* pp. 193–199.
- *Bard-Anders Andreassen, "Building a National Humanitarian Organization: A Case Study of the Kenya Red Cross," *BPP,* pp. 209–216.
- Wogu Ananoba, *The Trade Union Movement in Africa: Promise and Performance* (New York: St. Martins, 1979). (Ananoba was an International Confederation of Free Trade Unions regional director, and is now at the ICFTU headquarters. Part 2 of his book, "Promise and Performance," includes discussion of human rights.)
- Richard Kiwanuka, "On the Paucity of Human Rights NGOs in Africa," *Human Rights Internet Reporter,* Vol. 11, No. 4 (November 1986), pp. 10–12.
- Rob Davies, Dan O'Meara, and Sipho Dlamini, *The Struggle for South Africa: A Reference Guide to Movements, Organizations, and Institutions,* Vol. 2 (London: Zed Press, 1984).
- *Raymond J. Smyke, "Teacher Organizations as NGOs in African Development," *Transnational Associations,* No. 1, 1985, pp. 143–149.
- *James C.N. Paul and Clarence T. Dias, "Developing Human Rights for Human-Needs-Centered Development," *Hunger Notes,* Vol. XII, Nos. 5–6 (October–November 1986).

Asian Organizations

These two edited volumes offer information about the status of human rights in several Asian countries, among them India, Indonesia, and the Philippines. The activities of humanitarian organizations are analyzed with special attention to legal and economic dimensions of humanitarian activity.

- *Asian Coalition of Human Rights Organizations, *Human Rights Activism in Asia: Some Perspectives, Problems and Approaches* (New York: Council on International and Public Affairs, 1984).
- *Harry M. Scoble and Laurie S. Wiseberg, *Access to Justice: The Struggle for Human Rights in South East Asia* (London: Zed Books, 1985).

International Nongovernmental Organizations and Private Voluntary Organizations (INGOs and PVOs)

Extensive nongovernmental humanitarian activity takes place at the United Nations. The dynamics of this activity are described in Chiang's book. Other readings discuss the development of humanitarian organizations and the organizations' contribution to third world development. In researching humanitarian activity you will find the publications of the Union of International

Associations useful, especially the *Yearbook of International Organizations* and the periodical *Transnational Associations.*

- *Chiang Pei-Heng, *Nongovernmental Organizations at the United Nations* (New York: Praeger Publishers, 1979), skim.
- Robert G. Gorman, ed. *Private Voluntary Organizations as Agents of Development* (Boulder: Westview, 1984). *Read Gorman's introduction and chapter 3, "PVOs and Development Through Basic Human Needs."
- *Jan Egeland and Thomas Kerbs, eds., *Third World Organisational Development: A Comparison of NGO Strategies* (Geneva: Henry Dunant Institute, 1987), chs. 1 ["Building Humanitarian Action Where the Needs Are the Greatest"], 6 ["UNDP and WHO: IGO Support for NGOs"], and 7 ["Conclusion—Indigenous NGOs: Effective but Fragile"].
- *Jan Egeland, "Discovering a First Line of Defence: Indigenous Humanitarian Organizations"; Peter Macalister-Smith, "Humanitarian Action by NGOs: National and International Law Perspectives"; and Michel Veuthey, "The Humanitarian Network: Implementing Humanitarian Law through International Cooperation," in *BPP.*

Food, Relief, Refugees

- *S. Aga Khan, "Global Development Challenges," in *BPP.*
- *Elizabeth Stamp, "Oxfam and Development," *Pressure Groups in the Global System,* ch. 5 in Willetts.
- Jorgen Lissner, *The Politics of Altruism: A Study of the Political Behavior of Voluntary Development Agencies* (Geneva: Lutheran World Federation, 1977).
- William Shawcross, *The Quality of Mercy: Cambodia, Holocaust and Modern Conscience* (New York: Simon and Schuster, 1984).
- Ben Whitaker, *A Bridge of People: OXFAM's First Forty Years* (London: Heinemann, 1983).
- *Gilbert Jaeger, "Participation of Non-Governmental Organizations in the Activities of the United Nations High Commissioner for Refugees," ch. 9 in Willetts.
- *Gil Loescher, "Humanitarianism in Crisis in Central America," in Raana Gauhar, ed., *Third World Affairs 1987* (London: Third World Foundation, 1987), pp. 330–336.
- *H. Hoegh and Gunnar Hagman, "The Red Cross and Red Crescent: Turning to Self Reliant Development," *BPP,* pp. 155–163.
- *"The International Red Cross and Red Crescent Movement," Egeland and Kerbs, ch. 2.

Women

The first three readings describe the activities of women's organizations. The Shah and Clark article considers the role of women in development activity.

- *Georgina Ashworth, "The United Nations 'Women's Conference' and International Linkages in the Women's Movement," pp. 125–147 in Willetts.
- Diana E.H. Russell and Nicole Van de Ven, *Proceedings of the International Tribunal on Crimes Against Women* (Millbrae, CA: Les Femmes, 1976).
- Mary Jane Hogan, "Grassroots Women's Movements and the Crises in Central America," paper delivered at the 1987 Annual Meeting of the Western Political Science Association.
- Bindi Shah and Anne Clark, "The Role and Status of Women in Development NGOs," *Transnational Associations*, No. 2, 1986, pp. 87–94.

Law

Human Rights Tribunals:
- Marta Harasowska and Orest Olhovych, eds., *The International Sakharov Hearing* (Baltimore: Smoloskyp Publishers, 1979).
- International Commission of Enquiry, *Israel in Lebanon* (London: Ithaca Press, 1983).
- *International Lelio Basso Foundation, "For the Rights and Liberation of Peoples," pamphlet (Rome: Lelio Basso Foundation, 1984).

The International Commission of Jurists:
- *International Commission of Jurists, *Development, Human Rights, and the Rule of Law* (New York: Pergamon Press, 1981), skim.
- *The Review of the International Commission of Jurists* is a periodical that includes scholarly analyses of human rights topics and reports of human rights missions.

The International Association of Democratic Lawyers:
- International Association of Democratic Lawyers, *The Inquiry Committee of Free Jurists of West Berlin: A Documentary Study* (Brussels: IADL, April 1957).
- The *International Review of Contemporary Law*, previously the *Review of Contemporary Law*, analyzes international issues (among them human rights issues) from a socialist perspective.

Ethnic Groups
- *Ben Whitaker, ed., *Minorities: A Question of Human Rights?* (New York: Pergamon, 1984).
- Theodore Freedman, ed., *Anti-Semitism in the Soviet Union: Its Roots and Consequences* (New York: Anti-Defamation League of B'nai B'rith, 1984).
- Nahum Goldmann, *Community of Fate: Jews in the Modern World* (Jerusalem: Israeli University Press, 1977).
- Douglas E. Sanders, "The Formation of the World Council of Indigenous Peoples," International Work Group for Indigenous Affairs, Document No. 29, Copenhagen, 1977.

Christian Religious Communities
- *Levi Oracion, "Church Organizations and the Logic of the Poor," *BPP*, pp. 165–171.
- *"The World Council of Churches and the Lutheran World Federation," Egeland and Kerbs, ch. 4.
- Dale L. Bishop, "The Churches and the Middle East," *American-Arab Affairs*, No. 20 (Spring 1987), pp. 123–127.
- Hans Hebly, "Liberty or Liberation: The Dilemma of the World Council of Churches," *Religion in Communist Lands*, Vol. 13, No. 2, Summer 1985, pp. 131–151.
- Eric Hanson, *The Catholic Church in World Politics* (Princeton: Princeton University Press, 1987).

The Environment and Environmental Politics
- Tom Burke, "Friends of the Earth and the Conservation of Resources," ch. 6 in Willetts.
- Petra Kelly, *Fighting for Hope.*

The Journalistic, Literary, and Scientific Communities
Journalists, writers, and publishers are frequent targets of repression. They are gathered together into several organizations, some of which work to train and influence third world writers. With the exception of the International Organization of Journalists (IOJ), they have been critical of UNESCO's means of creating a New World Information and Communications Order.

The International Organization of Journalists, headquartered in Prague, is the largest organization. It has a sizable membership in the socialist bloc and many third world affiliates. The IOJ's activities are described in the *Democratic Journalist*, a periodical which includes analyses from journalists and scholars around the world. Its Western counterpart is the International Federation of Journalists. Publishers have been especially active in the World Press Freedom Committee, the International Press Institute, and the InterAmerican Press Association.

A London organization, Writers and Scholars International, publishes the bimonthly *Index on Censorship*, which offers excellent coverage of human rights issues, and the "Index Index," a regular catalogue of incidents of repression.

- *John Ziman, Paul Sieghart, and John Humphrey, *The World of Science and the Rule of Law: A Study of the Observance of the Human Rights of Scientists in the Participating States of the Helsinki Accords* (London: Oxford University Press, 1986), ch. 13, "Sustaining Human Rights."

Labor
There are several international trade secretariats (ITS) with extensive human rights activities, e.g., the International Union of Food and Allied Workers Association, discussed in Egeland and Kerbs. There

are also three international confederations of labor, the International Confederation of Trade Unions, the World Confederation of Labor, and the World Federation of Trade Unions. Begin your consideration of labor's human rights activities by skimming the confederations' publications. The World Federation of Trade Unions is especially strong in the socialist bloc and among Communist trade unions in the first and third worlds. The WFTU's *World Trade Union Movement* includes excerpts from human rights activities of the WFTU and its affiliates. The World Confederation of Labor is the smallest confederation. Its Christian trade unions have some strength in Europe and Latin America. Its publication, *Labor,* includes some attention to human rights issues.

- *"International Trade Secretariats: IFPAAW and IUF," Egeland and Kerbs, ch. 5.
- The International Confederation of Free Trade Unions is discussed extensively in Ananoba, above. See the *Report of the Twelfth World Congress, 1979.*
- *John Logue, "Toward a Theory of Trade Union Internationalism," University of Gothenburg Research Section on Post-War History, Publication No. 7 (1980).

Amnesty International

- *"Amnesty International," ch. 3 in Egeland and Kerbs.
- *Martin Ennals, "Amnesty International and Human Rights," ch. 4 in Willets.
- Egon Larson, *A Flame in Barbed Wire: The Story of Amnesty International* (New York: W.W. Norton, 1979).
- Samuel Zivs, *Anatomy of a Lie* (Moscow: Progress Publishers, 1984).
- *Cosmas Desmond, *Persecution East and West* (London: Penguin, 1983), skim.

Coalitions, Leagues, and Clearinghouses

There are several channels through which humanitarian organizations cooperate. Among these channels are the Committees of Nongovernmental Organizations in consultative status with the U.N.'s Economic and Social Council and specialized agencies. Human Rights Internet, at Harvard Law School, acts as a clearinghouse for human rights information. Become familiar with its *Human Rights Internet Reporter.* National human rights groups have formed an International League of Human Rights, headquartered in New York, and an International Federation of Human Rights, headquartered in Paris. The Secretariats of the League and Federation carry out extensive human rights activities, including investigatory missions. The International Council of Voluntary Agencies is an avenue for the coordination of development activities.

V. Two Key Themes Interwoven with the Study of Humanitarian Organization

Nongovernmental organizations' assessments of human rights and human needs are frequently used by scholars and governmental policymakers. You should become familiar with several of these, and with how they compare with the assessments of United Nations bodies and of the U.S. Department of State.

Governments have great resources with which they can encourage or inhibit humanitarian activity. We will consider U.S. and Soviet government approaches toward nongovernmental activity in analyzing several types of government-organization interaction.

Assessing Human Rights, Human Dignity, and Human Needs

- *Hans Thoolen and Berth Verstappen, *Human Rights Missions: A Study of the Fact-Finding Practices of Non-Governmental Organizations* (Boston: Martinus Nijhoff, 1987).
- Raymond Gastil, ed., *Freedom in the World* (Westport, CT: Greenwood Press, annual).
- *Kumar Rupesinghe, "The Quest for a Disaster Early Warning System: Giving a Voice to the Vulnerable," in *BPP*, pp. 217–227.
- Laurie S. Wiseberg, "Human Rights Reporting," *Human Rights Internet Reporter*, Vol. 11, No. 4 (November 1986), pp. 3–6.
- *Morris David Morris, *Measuring the Condition of the World's Poor: The Physical Quality of Life Index* (New York: Praeger Publishers [Overseas Development Council], 1979).
- Bjorn Stormorken, *HURIDOCS: Standard Formats for the Recording and Exchange of Information on Human Rights* (Norwell, MA: Kluwer, 1985).
- *Human Rights Quarterly*, Vol. 8, No. 4 (November 1986), is a special issue dealing with human rights measurement. Especially recommended are Gloria Valencia-Weber and Robert S. Weber, "El Salvador: Methods Used to Document Human Rights Violations" (pp. 628–653): a comparison of methods used by the U.S. State Department with methods used by the Salvadorean NGO, Tutela Legal; Randy B. Reiter, M.V. Zunzunegui, and Jose Quiroga, "Guidelines for Field Reporting of Basic Human Rights Violations" (pp. 628–653): based in part on personal communications with leaders of human rights NGOs; and Michael Stohl, David Carleton, George Lopez, and Stephen Samuels, "State Violation of Human Rights: Issues and Problems of Measurement" (pp. 592–606).

The Governments Behind the NGOs and PVOs

- *International Council of Voluntary Agencies, "Suggested Guidelines on the Acceptance of Government Funds for NGO Programmes," *Transnational Associations*, No. 5, 1985, pp. 282–284.

- James T. Bennett and Thomas Di Lorenzo, "Tax Funded Unionism II: The Facade of Culture and Democracy," *Journal of Labor Research*, Vol. 8 (Winter 1987), pp. 31–46.
- Carl Gershman, "Fostering Democracy Abroad: The Role of the National Endowment for Democracy," paper delivered to the American Political Science Association Annual Meeting, August 29, 1986.
- Elizabeth Schmidt, Jane Blewett, and Peter Henriot, *Religious Private Voluntary Organizations and the Question of Government Funding* (Maryknoll, NY: Orbis Books, 1981).
- *Wallace Spalding, "Communist Fronts in 1986," *Problems of Communism*, Vol. 36, No. 2 (March–April 1987), pp. 57–68.

6. Human Rights and Basic Needs in the Americas

Margaret E. Crahan   Fall 1986

History Dept., Occidental College, Los Angeles, CA 90041

The purpose of this course is to develop your capacity to think analytically and to express yourselves coherently and convincingly, both orally and in writing. The course has the additional objective of demonstrating how history is made, reconstructed and interpreted. To accomplish all these goals, the course will focus on one of the major problems afflicting the modern world—the widespread violation of human rights. To give the course focus, we will analyze the underlying causes of such violations in Latin America, and some of the local, national and international responses to them.

The course will begin with an exploration of the nature and extent of human rights violations in Latin America as reported by the U.S. Department of State, the Interamerican Commission on Human Rights of the Organization of American States, Amnesty International, the International Commission of Jurists, the World Council of Churches, as well as other "experts" on the situation there. The underlying reasons for the observance or non-observance of human rights will be examined by analyzing normative values, cultural traditions, ideological developments, and sociopolitical and economic factors of the societies being studied. Variations of interpretations will be highlighted and students will be expected to critique them, as well as to develop their own explanations of violations that are well-rooted in factual data. This will involve study of such major institutions as the state, military, churches, labor organizations and political parties. The degree to which these have modified or expanded their traditional roles in recent years in Latin America will be explored in detail.

Course Requirements

Each student will select, by October 8, a Latin American country that he or she will become an "expert" on. Students will be expected to do the assigned reading prior to the date it will be discussed in class. Heavy emphasis will be placed on participation in these discussions, and one-fourth of the final grade can be determined by the quality of the students' contributions.

Short written assignments by each student are due on October 8, 14, 28, and November 18. An exam will be given November 4, on material covered in the course up to that date. There will be no exemptions. A ten to fifteen page analytical paper will be due December 2. There will be no extensions or incompletes given.

The final grade will be based on the November 4 exam (25%), on the October 8, 14, 28 and November 18 short papers (25%), on the December 2 term paper (25%), and on the quality of each student's contributions to class discussions (25%).

Required Reading

Crahan, Margaret E., ed. *Human Rights and Basic Needs in the Americas.* Washington, D.C.: Georgetown University Press, 1982.

Schoultz, Lars. *Human Rights and United States Policy Toward Latin America.* Princeton: Princeton University Press, 1981.

Timerman, Jacobo. *Prisoner Without a Name: Cell Without a Number.* New York: Vintage, 1981.

Wirarda, Howard J. *Human Rights and U.S. Human Rights Policy.* Washington, D.C.: American Enterprise Institute, 1982.

COURSE SCHEDULE

Sept. 30—Introduction to Course and to Topic
Films: Missing and *Choices of the Heart.*

Oct. 8—What Are Human Rights and What Is the Relationship of Civil/Political Rights to Social/Economic Rights?

Write a definition of human rights in your own words (not more than one paragraph). Write a description of how you believe civil/political rights and social/economic rights are related (not more than one page). On a 3 x 5 index card put your name and the name of the country you will become an expert on.

• UN Universal Declaration of Human Rights.
• UN Covenants.
• American Declaration of Rights and Duties of Man.

- Timerman, all.
- Wiarda, ch. 4.

Oct. 14—The Reality of Human Rights Observance in Latin America

Write a description of the basic geographic, demographic, political, economic and social characteristics of the country you are studying (not more than two pages). Read about your country in:
- Amnesty International, *Reports.*
- Organization of American States, Interamerican Commission on Human Rights, *Country Reports, 1977–1986.*
- U.S. Congress, *Human Rights Conditions in Selected Countries and U.S. Responses.*
- U.S. Congress, *Human Rights and U.S. Foreign Policy,* 1979.
- U.S. Congress, *Country Reports on Human Rights Practices for 1979–1986.*

Oct. 21—How Does a Country's Historical Heritage and Dominant Ideology Influence Human Rights Observance?

- Crahan, chs. 1, 2, 3.

Oct. 28—Factors Influencing Human Rights Observance: Evolution of the Military as an Institution

Write a description of the role of the military in a specific Latin American country (not more than two pages).

Nov. 4—Written Exam in Class

Study questions: (1) Describe the human rights situation in a specific Latin American country, explaining the reasons for observance or non-observance of rights. (2) Explain how the historical heritage of Latin America affects the observance of human rights in a specific Latin American country. (3) Describe the role of the military in a specific Latin American country and explain its impact on the observance or non-observance of human rights.

Nov. 11—Factors Influencing Human Rights Observance: U.S. Military Aid

Film: The Official Story.
- Schoultz, ch. 6.
- Crahan, ch. 9.

Nov. 18—Current Level of Fulfillment of Socioeconomic Rights in Latin America

Write a description of the current economic situation and level of fulfillment of basic needs in a specific Latin American country. (Some sources: *Interamerican Development Bank Country Indicators, World Bank Annual Report, Latin American Economic Report.*)
- Crahan, chs. 4-8.

Nov. 25—U.S. Human Rights Policy
- Crahan, ch. 10.
- Schoultz, chs. 1-5, 7, 8.

Dec. 2—Human Rights: Contrary to U.S. Interests?
Write a ten to fifteen page analytical paper covering the following points: (1) What is the current human rights situation in country X? (2) What are the reasons for the observance or non-observance of human rights in country X? (3) If you were called by the Department of State to recommend policy steps to promote human rights in country X, what would they be? Be specific.
- Wiarda, chs. 1-3, 5-7.

XI

Regional Conflicts

1. Southern Africa: Race, Class, and Political Change

David Abernethy
Political Science Dept., Stanford University,
Stanford, CA 94305

Spring 1986

This class meets on Mondays, Tuesdays, and Thursdays, with occasional meetings on Wednesdays for films and group discussions. The course requirements are: map assignment, due April 7; one-hour examination, May 5—20%; research paper or 12–15 pages, due May 30—40%; and final examination, June 6—40%.

Books to Purchase

Carter, Gwendolen, and Patrick O'Meara, eds. *Southern Africa: The Continuing Crisis.* 2nd edition. 1982.

Denoon, Donald, and Balam Nyeko. *Southern Africa Since 1800.* New edition. 1984.

Mphahlele, Ezekiel. *Down Second Avenue.* 1971.

Rotberg, Robert, et al. *South Africa and Its Neighbors: Regional Security and Self-Interest.* 1985.

Study Commission on U.S. Policy Toward Southern Africa. *South Africa: Time Running Out.* 1981.

READING LIST AND COURSE OUTLINE

The Politics of Individual Territories
Political History up to c. 1950

- Denoon and Nyeko, pp. 1–192.
- Leonard Thompson, *The Political Mythology of Apartheid* (1985), chs. 3 ("Unassimilable Races"), and 5 ("The Covenant"), pp. 69–104; 144–88.
- Martin Legassick, "Gold, Agriculture, and Secondary Industry in South Africa, 1885–1970," in Robin Palmer and Neil Parsons, eds., *The Roots of Rural Poverty in Central and Southern Africa* (1977), pp. 175–97.
- Mphahlele, chs. 1–19.
- Allen Isaacman and Barbara Isaacman, *Mozambique from Colonialism to Revolution, 1900–1982* (1983), chs. 2–4, pp. 11–78.
- Robin Palmer, "The Agricultural History of Rhodesia," in Palmer and Parsons, pp. 221–45.

Political History Since 1950: South Africa

- Mphahlele, ch. 20 to end.
- Study Commission, "South Africans Talking," pp. 1–22; 255–83; 367–85.
- Study Commission, chs. 2–10, pp. 42–232.
- South Africa, Information Service, "The Integration Model," in *Multinational Development in South Africa: The Reality* (1974), pp. 75–85.
- Laurine Platzky and Cherryl Walker et al., *The Surplus People: Forced Removals in South Africa* (1985), pp. 3–60; 238–66.
- Joseph Lelyveld, *Move Your Shadow* (1985), ch. 5 ("Forced Busing"), pp. 119–54.
- Tom Lodge, *Black Politics in South Africa Since 1945* (1983), chs. 2, 9, 12, 13, pp. 33–62; 201–30; 295–356.
- Documents from the 1950s: Defiance Campaign, Freedom Charter. From Thomas Karis and Gwendolen Careter, eds., *From Protest to Challenge*, Vol. 2 (1973), pp. 476–85, and Vol. 3, pp. 205–08.
- Nelson Mandela, "Statements in Court, 1962," in Karis and Carter, eds., *From Protest to Challenge*, Vol. 3, pp. 725–46.
- Steve Biko, *Black Consciousness in South Africa*, Millard Arnold, ed. (1979), Introduction, pp. 1–37; 140–63; 331–60.
- M. Gatsha Buthelezi, "White and Black Nationalism, Ethnicity, and the Future of the Homelands," Lucas Mangope, "The Political Future of the Homelands," in Hendrik van der Merwe et al., *African Perspectives on South Africa* (1978), pp. 51–68.
- Gavin Relly, "Influx Control and Economic Growth," in Hermann Giliomee and Lawrence Schlemmer, eds., *Up Against the Fences: Poverty, Passes, and Privilege in South Africa* (1985), pp. 296–303
- P.W. Botha, "Manifesto for the Future" (August 15, 1985).

- Selections from *Leadership*, Vol. 4, No. 3 (1985), on September 1985 meeting in Zambia between ANC leaders and South African Business leaders.
- Oliver Tambo, "Attack, Advance, Give the Enemy No Quarter!" (1986).
- Arend Lijphart, *Power-Sharing in South Africa* (1985), chs. 2 and 3, pp. 16–82.
- Xan Smiley, "A Black South Africa?" *Economist* (February 1, 1986), pp. 33–40.

Political History Since 1950: Other Countries in the Region
- Carter and O'Meara, chs. 2, 3, 5–8, pp. 18–92; 141–248 (Zimbabwe, Mozambique, Namibia, Angola, Zambia, and Botswana).

Southern Africa as a Region: Links and Conflicts Among the Territories
- Kenneth Grundy, "Economic Patterns in the New Southern African Balance," in Carter and O'Meara, pp. 291–312.
- Rotberg, chs. 1–7, pp. 1–150.

Southern Africa and the International System
- Colin Legum, "International Rivalries in the Southern African Conflict," in Carter and O'Meara, pp. 3–17
- Study Commission, chs. 13–15, pp. 301–39.
- Thomas Karis, "United States Policy Toward South Africa," in Carter and O'Meara, pp. 313–62.
- Kevin Danaher, *The Political Economy of U.S. Policy Toward South Africa* (1985), chs. 4–6 (Ford, Carter, Reagan policies), pp. 109–218.
- Peter Duignan and L.H. Gann, *The United States and Africa: A History* (1984), pp. 284–304; 309–313; 349–53.
- Gerald Bender, "American Policy Toward Angola: A History of Linkage," in Gerald Bender et al., *African Crisis Areas and U.S. Foreign Policy* (1985), pp. 110–28.
- Communications Task Group, "Meeting the Mandate for Change: Progress Report on Application of the Sullivan Principles" (1984).
- Jennifer Davis et al., Economic Disengagement and South Africa: The Effectiveness and Feasibility of Implementing Sanctions and Divestment," *Law and Policy in International Business*, Vol. 15, No. 2 (1983), pp. 529–63.

2. Palestine and the Arab-Israeli Conflict

Joel Beinin   *Fall 1986*
History Dept., Stanford University, Stanford, CA 94305

Course Requirements

Each participant in the colloquium is required to read all the assignments carefully and thoughtfully and to participate actively in the weekly discussions (20% of grade).

On November 3, a 6–7 page paper characterizing and analyzing the arguments of the four positions examined in the first five weeks of the course will be due (30% of grade).

Each student will be responsible for one oral class presentation initiating a discussion of the readings. This presentation will be based on a 3–4 page written analysis and critique of the readings to be handed in on the day the oral presentation is made. Neither the oral presentation nor the written analysis should simply summarize the material in a narrative fashion. Try to analyze the underlying structure of the arguments, why they are made in the way they are, and what their strengths and weaknesses are. Feel free to criticize the readings or to make any other remarks which will stimulate discussion (20% of grade).

A final paper is due December 17. This will be a 7–8 page review essay based on Book Two of *Israel: The Embattled Ally* and the sections of *Decade of Decisions, Camp David, Israel and the Arabs* and *The Fateful Triangle* which you will have read for weekly assignments during the second half of the course. This should be a comparative and analytical essay in which you point out the different approaches of the authors toward American policy in the Arab-Israeli conflict and argue their relative merits. Feel free to include material you have learned from other readings (with approriate references). If you are not clear about how to write this kind of essay, look at some of the reviews in *The New York Review of Books* and/or discuss the assignment with the instructor. Do not simply recapitulate the arguments of the authors. This assignment is different from the first essay. It is designed to let you show that you can think about what the authors you have read say and support your thinking with what you have learned in the course (30% of grade).

Texts for Purchase

Aruri, Naseer, ed. *Occupation: Israel over Palestine.*

Begin, Menachem. *The Revolt.*

Chomsky, Noam. *The Fateful Triangle: The United States, Israel and the Palestinians.*

Cobban, Helena. *The Palestinian Liberation Organization.*

Elon, Amos. *The Israelis: Founders and Sons.*

Graham-Brown, Sarah. *Palestinians and Their Society, 1880–1946.*

Quandt, William, Fuad Jabber and Ann Mosely Lesch. *The Politics of Palestinian Nationalism.*

Quandt, William. *Decade of Decisions: American Policy Toward the Arab-Israeli Conflict, 1967–1976.*

Rodinson, Maxime. *Israel: A Colonial Settler State?*

———— , *Israel and the Arabs.*

Said, Edward. *The Question of Palestine.*

Safran, Nadav. *Israel: The Embattled Ally.*

Sykes, Christopher. *Crossroads to Israel: 1917–1948.*

COURSE SCHEDULE

Oct. 1—Introduction to the Course

What images of Palestine and Palestinians do you receive from the photos? How are these different from or similar to images you (or others) may already have had about Palestine? To what extent are the photos an "objective" rendering of the realities of Palestinian society? Does the fact that they record what actually was in front of the camera necessarily make them "objective"? What does it mean to be "objective"?

• Graham-Brown, pp. 1–30, and browse through the photos.

Oct. 8—Political and Labor Zionism

What are the basic assumptions of Zionist thinking about the Jews and their status in the world? What are the differences between Herzl and the labor Zionists? What were the goals and accomplishments of the labor Zionist movement during the second and third *aliyot* (waves of immigration)? How did these Zionists see themselves? How did they see the Palestinans? How does Elon, as a native-born Israeli, view the Zionist founders and their activity?

• Elon, pp. 33–186.
• Arthur Hertzberg, ed., *The Zionist Idea*, pp. 201–26; 331–50; 353–54; 360–66.

Oct. 15—A British View

Who is Christopher Sykes? (Look him up in *Contemporary Authors* if you don't know.) What are the Husayn-McMahon correspondence, the Sykes-Picot Treaty, and the Balfour Declaration? Why did the British make these commitments? Are they consistent? What can you learn about the "official mind" of the British administration from Sykes' account of the mandate? What is Sykes' view of Weizmann, Ben Gurion, Begin and the Palestinian Arab political leaders? How does Sykes view the American and Soviet roles towards the end of the mandate?

- Sykes, all.

Oct. 22—Revisionist Zionism

What are Begin's views on the Soviet Union, armed struggle, the Jewish religion, Arabs, the British? What were the relations between the Irgun and the Haganah in the King David Hotel, Dir Yasin and Altalena incidents? How important was the Irgun to achieving Zionist aims in Palestine? Was the Irgun a terrorist organization? the Haganah? By now you should have some idea of the map of political forces within the *yishuv* (Jewish community in Palestine). Come prepared to talk about it.

- Begin, all.

Oct. 29—Palestinian Perspectives

Why did the Palestinians fail to attain their objectives during the Mandate period? How does Said explain why we have not heard his version of the story very often? What are his basic premises? What is the role of intellectuals in society according to Said? Is Israel a colonial settler state?

- Quandt, Jabber and Lesch, pp. 7–42.
- Said, pp. ix–114.
- Rodinson, *Israel: A Colonial Settler State?* pp. 27–96.

Nov. 5—Regionalization of the Conflict, 1948–1967

Who is Nadav Safran? Who is Maxime Rodinson? What is the status of Palestinians who are citizens of Israel? How did Israel regard and respond to Arab violations of the 1949 truce agreements? Compare the discussion of the "Lavon affair" by Safran and Rodinson and the significance each attributes to it. How did the U.S. view the Arab-Israeli conflict in the 1950s? What are the reasons for the outbreak of the 1956 and 1967 wars?

- Rodinson, *Israel and the Arabs*, chs. 3–5, 7–8.
- Safran, pp. 334–413.

Nov. 12—The Palestinian Arab National Movement

How did the PLO originate? How did it change after the 1967 war? What are the component elements of the PLO? What does the PLO want? Is the PLO a terrorist organization?

- Cobban, pp. 1–192.
- Yehoshafat Harkabi, "The Palestinian National Covenant" and "The Weakness of the Fedayeen?" from *Palestinians and Israel*, pp. 49–69, 107–114.

Nov. 17—Movie: *Stranger at Home*

Nov. 19—Israel and the Occupied Territories

What are Israel's objectives in the occupied territories? How have they changed over time? What are the differences between Labor and the Likud on this issue? How have different forces in Israel pursued their objectives? What has happened to the lands of these territories? Who represents politically the Palestinians of the occupied territories?

- Chomsky, pp. 54–63, 103–146.
- Aruri, chs. by Ibrahim Matar, Sheila Ryan and Salim Tamari.
- Yigal Allon, "Israel: The Case for Defensible Borders," *Foreign Affairs*, 55: 1 (Oct. 1976), pp. 38–53.
- Menachem Milson, "How to Make Peace with the Palestinians," *Commentary*, May 1981, pp. 25–35.
- Cobban, pp. 168–84.

Nov. 26—The American Decade

What were the policy objectives of Israel, Egypt, Syria, the U.S. and the U.S.S.R. from 1967 to 1973? Why did Egypt attack Israel in 1973, and what were the results of the war? How can the Kissinger and Rogers approaches to Israel be characterized? Which has been the dominant one in U.S. policy towards Israel? Why? How was this manifested in the diplomatic activities of the 1970s?

- Quandt, pp. 105–27, 287–300.
- Safran, pp. 414–598.
- Chomsky, pp. 9–54, 64–80.
- Rodinson, *Israel and the Arabs*, pp. 243–276. (Recommended: read to p. 300 if you have time.)

Dec. 3—Camp David

To what extent does U.S. domestic policy influence Middle East policy? What are the provisions of the Camp David Agreements, and why did they or did they not fail?

- Safran, pp. 599–622.
- Rodinson, *Israel and the Arabs*, pp. 300–13.
- William Quandt, *Camp David: Peacemaking and Politics*, pp. 6–29, 168–205, 320–39, 376–87.
- Joel Beinin, "The Cold Peace," *MERIP Reports*, No. 129, pp. 3–9.

Dec. 10—Israel's Lebanon War, 1982

How did the Palestinians get to Lebanon, and what were they doing there? Why did Israel invade Lebanon in 1982? Who wins the exchange between Martin Peretz and Noam Chomsky? Did the Israeli invasion achieve its objectives?

- Robert Tucker, "The Case for the War," *Commentary*, October 1982, pp. 19–30.
- Martin Peretz, "Lebanon Eyewitness," *The New Republic*, August 2, 1982, pp. 15–23.
- Chomsky, pp. 181–409.

3. The Middle East Since 1914

Zachary Lochman   *Spring 1988*
History Dept., Harvard University, Cambridge, MA 02138

This course is a survey of the history of the Middle East from the First World War until the present, with a geographical focus on the eastern half of the Arab world (the *Mashriq*). The first segment of the course looks at the broad sweep of social, economic and political change in the region from the beginning of the twentieth century through the 1960s. In the middle of this segment we will pause to look at various ways in which policy-makers, the media, "experts" and Americans in general have looked at the Middle East, at how power and knowledge (or what passes for knowledge) interact with regard to perceptions of—and policies toward—the Middle East. The second segment examines more closely the roots and development of three contemporary problems—the conflict over Palestine, the Lebanese civil war, and the Iranian revolution—and concludes with a look at the political uses of Islam in the contemporary Middle East and at the challenges and prospects facing the region.

There will be two lectures each week as well as a discussion section; participation in the section is required. Students are responsible for all the material presented in the lectures and in the required readings. All the readings in this syllabus are required. All readings are on reserve. In addition, the following books are available for purchase:

Elon, Amos. *The Israelis: Founders and Sons.*
Ibrahim, Saad Eddin. *The New Arab Social Order.*
Keddie, Nikki. *Roots of Revolution.*
Khomeini, Ruhollah. *Islam and Revolution.*
Mansfield, Peter. *The Arabs.*
Mortimer, Edward. *Faith and Power.*
Said, Edward. *Covering Islam.*
Shaarawi, Huda. *Harem Years.*

Note

Readings marked with an asterisk (*) should be read most carefully and thoughtfully, because they will be the focus of discussion in sections. Unmarked items are intended more for background and can be read more quickly, but they should be read.

Course requirements

A take-home map assignment (due Feb. 23); two short essays (3–5 pages each, due Mar. 24 and Apr. 28); a 10–15 page paper on a topic of your choice (subject to approval of the instructor, with a proposal and short bibliography due by Apr. 21, and the final paper due May 13); and a final exam (May 20).

LECTURES AND READINGS

Week 1
Feb. 4—Introduction to the Course

Week 2
Feb. 9—The Middle East in the Nineteenth Century
Feb. 11—The Ottoman Empire Before 1914

- Mansfield, chs. 5–7 (pp. 65–160).
- *Hourani, *Arabic Thought in the Liberal Age*, chs. 3–4.
- Issawi, "Middle East Economic Development, 1815–1914," in M.A. Cook, ed., *Studies in the Economic History of the Middle East*, pp. 395–411.

Week 3
Feb. 16—Arab Nationalism and the "Arab Revolt"
Feb. 18—The Imperialist Powers and the Postwar Settlement

- *Haim, ed. *Arab Nationalism*, pp. 75–96.
- Sachar, *The Emergence of the Modern Middle East*, chs. 4 (pp. 87–115), 7 (pp. 187–222).
- Stork, *Middle East Oil and the Energy Crisis*, pp. 5–28.
- *Hurewitz, *Diplomacy in the Near and Middle East*, Vol. II, documents 4, 8, 10, 13, 15.

Week 4
Feb. 23—The Turkish Republic: Egypt's Struggle for Independence
Feb. 25—Colonial Rule and the Struggle for Independence in Syria, Lebanon and Iraq

- *Shaarawi, all.
- Mansfield, ch. 10 (pp. 195–235).
- Mortimer, ch. 5 (pp. 226–158).
- Hurewitz, *Diplomacy*, documents 25, 36.

Week 5
Mar. 1 & 3—Knowledge and Power

- *Said, Introduction (pp. ix-xxxi), chs. 1 and 3 (pp. 2–64, 127–164).
- *Bernard Lewis, "Communism and Islam" (all).

Week 6

Mar. 8—The Postwar Arab East: The Crisis of the Old Order
Mar. 10—Challenges to the Old Order

- Hopwood, *Egypt: Politics and Society,* pp. 17–33.
- *Charles Wendell, ed. and trans., *Five Tracts of Hasan al-Banna,* "Between Yesterday and Today" and "Toward the Light."
- *Karpat, ed., *Political and Social Thought in the Contemporary Middle East,* pp. 138–153.
- *Gamal Abdul Nasser, *Philosophy of the Revolution* or *Egypt's Liberation* (same book, different titles), pages to be assigned.

Week 7

Mar. 15 & 17—The Middle East in World Politics

- Mansfield, ch. 12 (pp. 242–269).
- Polk, *The United States and the Arab World,* chs. 21–22.
- *Stork, *Middle East Oil,* pp. 29–71.
- *Hurewitz, *Diplomacy,* documents 85, 92, 97, 107, 111.

Week 8

Mar. 22—"Arab Socialism" in Egypt
Mar. 24—Arab Unity and the Defeat of June 1967

- *Karpat, *Political and Social Thought,* pp. 116–122, 157–182.
- *Malcolm Kerr, *The Arab Cold War,* ch. 3.
- Hopwood, *Egypt,* pp. 34–104.
- Mansfield, ch. 13 (pp. 270–299).

Week 9

Apr. 5 & 7—The Struggle for Palestine and the Arab-Israeli Conflict

- Elon, pp. 3–81, 256–289.
- *Ghassan Kanafani, "Men in the Sun" (entire story).
- *MERIP Middle East Report,* No. 146 (May–June 1987), pp. 3–22.
- *Amos Oz, *In the Land of Israel,* pp. 27–73.
- Abu Iyad (with Eric Rouleau), *My Home, My Land,* preface, chs. 1–3 (pp. vii–xiv, 3–49).
- Walter Lacqueur and Barry Rubins, eds., *The Israel-Arab Reader,* documents 15, 18, 19, 22, and pp. 504–518, 591–601, 663–664.

Week 10

Apr. 12 & 14—The Civil War in Lebanon

- *Owen, ed., *Esssays on the Crisis in Lebanon,* pp. 23–31.
- Khalidi, *Conflict and Violence in Lebanon,* pp. 33–45, 67–92.
- Farsoun and Caroll, "The Civil War in Lebanon: Sect, Class and Imperialism," *Monthly Review,* No. 98, pp. 12–37.
- *Randall, *Going All the Way,* pp. 1–60, 243–303.
- *MERIP Reports,* No. 133 (June 1985), pp. 3–7, 10–19, 23–29.

Week 11

Apr. 19 & 21—The Iranian Revolution

- Keddie, pp. 142–182, 231–276.
- Mark Gasiorowski, "The 1953 Coup d'Etat in Iran," *International Journal of Middle East Studies*, Vol. 19, No. 3 (August 1987), pp. 261–286.
- Mortimer, pp. pp. 39–55, 296–353.
- *Khomeini, "Islamic Government," in *Islam and Revolution*, trans. Hamid Algar, pp. 13–21, 55–83.
- *Said, ch. 2 (pp. 75–103).

Week 12

Apr. 26—Islam and Politics in the Middle East
Apr. 28—The Middle East Today and Tomorrow

- Mortimer, pp. 60–64, 159–185.
- *Gilles Kepel, *Muslim Extremism in Egypt: The Prophet and Pharaoh*, chs. 2–4.
- *Valerie Hoffman, "An Islamic Activist . . . ," in Elizabeth W. Fernes, ed., *Women and the Family in the Middle East*, pp. 233–254.
- Ibrahim, pp. 1–25, 63–122, 154–174.

4. Latin American Politics: Actors, Issues, and Models

Charles Gillespie   *Fall 1987*
Political Science Dept., Amherst College,
Amherst, MA 01002

This course is an introduction to politics in Latin America based on a thematic approach rather than country-by-country case studies. The subtitle suggests three ways in which it is possible to approach the comparative politics of the region: by focusing on social groups and institutions such as the Church, peasants, labor, the military or guerrillas; by analyzing processes such as revolution, development or underdevelopment, and problems such as dependency, transnational corporations, and U.S. foreign policy; or by testing theories, such as Corporatism, Populism, and Bureaucratic-Authoritarianism.

It is nowadays a cliche to point out that Latin America is an immensely diverse region, more a linguistic convenience than a concrete reality. One of the aims of this course will be to make students realize just how different its component polities are, ranging as they do from liberal democracies to patrimonial dictatorships, and from one-party socialist systems to authoritarian military regimes. Emphasis will also be placed on Latin America's *Western* social, cultural and political forms—in contrast to those who stress the region's "distinct Latin tradition."

Course Materials

Students are expected to be familiar with all the required readings for each class. Included are suggested further readings which will be especially useful when you write the term paper. A packet ("multilith") of articles and chapters from books is available for purchase at the Political Science Department office. Eight required books have been ordered, and there are two further books which are recommended. All readings are also on reserve at the library.

Books Required for Purchase

Wynia, Gary. *The Politics of Latin American Development*, 2nd edition.
Stepan, Alfred. *The State and Society.*
Hewlett, Sylvia, and Richard Weinert, eds. *Brazil and Mexico.*
O'Donnell, Guillermo. *Modernization and Bureaucratic Authoritarianism.*
Levine, Daniel, ed. *Religion and Political Conflict in Latin America.*
Vilas, Carlos. *The Sandinista Revolution.*
Lafeber, Walter. *Inevitable Revolutions.*
Blachman, Morris, et al. *Confronting Revolution.*

Books Recommended for Purchase

Rossi, E., and J. Plano, eds. *The Latin American Politics Dictionary.* (Provides explanations of key terms and debates.)
Skidmore, T., and P. Smith. *Modern Latin America.* (A compact history for filling in the background on each country.)

Course Requirements

Students must write a short paper early in the course to practice expressing themselves clearly, organizing an argument, and evaluating readings critically (3 pages). There will be a take-home midterm with a choice of questions designed to test the student's breadth of understanding (5 pages). Students will then write a term paper on a topic to be approved in advance. This must go beyond the required readings and should focus either on a theoretical problem, a detailed case-study, or a comparative analysis (10 pages). The final examination will include a broad choice of questions (in-class, Dec. 16).

COURSE OUTLINE AND READINGS

Week 1—Dependency Theory: Uses and Limitations for Understanding Development and Underdevelopment

During the 1960s, a school of thought rose to prominence among radical historians, sociologists, and economists which emphasized the distorting and debilitating effects of Latin American (and other third world) nations' links with developed countries, many of which had once colonized them. The fact that their economies had been organized for the benefit of trade with the developed nations was seen as the principal cause of their underdevelopment, poverty and domestic inequality. Galenao did much to popularize the theory in an explosive book which was banned when the military came to power in his country (Uruguay) in 1973. It soon became an international best-seller. Nevertheless, dependency analyses came under heavy criticism after a while. What does the theory assume? What does it imply? What does it ignore?

- *Definitions:* Rossi & Plano, pp. 169–190, 177–178.
- Eduardo Galenao, *Open Veins of Latin America*, chs. 1, 3.
- Arturo & Samuel Valenzuela, "Modernization and Dependency."
- Rodolfo Stavenhagen, "Seven Erroneous Theses About Latin America."

Suggested

- Fernando Henrique Cardoso & Enzo Falletto, *Dependency and Development in Latin America*.

Week 2—Peasant Revolutions: Mexico Versus Cuba

Too often the word *revolution* is used loosely to describe any sudden change of government achieved by illegal means. We are interested, however, in revolutions as periods of extensive and intensive mass-mobilization accompanied by violence against the State and existing elites producing major changes in the distribution of political power (political revolutions) or property ownership (social revolutions). As such, revolutions are rare events which typically begin as revolts by a social class which is usually considered conservative and apathetic: the peasantry. Peasants were clearly the driving force behind the Mexican Revolution, and they played an important role in that of Cuba as well.

- *Definitions:* Rossi & Plano, pp. 8–13, 15–17, 112–113, 118–119, 186.
- Wynia, ch. 9.
- Eric Wolf, *Peasant Wars of the Twentieth Century*, chs. 1, 6, Conclusion.
- Alan Knight, "The Mexican Revolution."

Suggested

- Thomas Carroll, "The Land Reform Issue in Latin America," in Thomasek, ed., *Latin American Politics*.
- Christopher Mitchell, *Bolivia: The Uncompleted Revolution*.

Week 3—The Corporatism Debate: Are State-Society Relations Different in Latin America?

Latin America is sometimes held to exhibit non-pluralistic interest groups and social institutions imbued with Catholic and organicist ideals rather than Lockean Liberalism. Those who disagree are accused of ethnocentrism. But just *who* is being ethnocentric? Are state-society relations so easily dichotomized in Latin America, the United States, or other nations? There has been a resurgence of interest in studies of "political culture," though the corporatist school is an even broader phenomenon. What is left of the corporatist model if we take out the stress on history and culture? (Clue: Think about Stepan's analysis of the way the State coopts and controls different social groups "from above.")

- *Definitions:* Rossi & Plano, pp. 27–28, 31–32, 60–63, 65, 75–76, 153.
- Stepan, part one.

Suggested

- Howard Wiarda, ed., *Politics and Social Change in Latin America.*
- James Malloy, ed., *Authoritarianism and Corporatism in Latin America.*
- Philippe Schmitter, "Still the Century of Corporatism?" in P. Schmitter and G. Lehmbruch, *Trends Towards Corporatist Intermediation.*

Week 4—Populism: The Political Incorporation of the Urban Masses

As the middle classes grew, urbanization and industrialization accelerated, and oligarchic politics began to decay, a new form of political mobilization gripped Argentina and Brazil. Charismatic dictators deliberately set the masses against traditional elites, promoting industrialization and welfare policies, but not necessarily liberal democracy. In the wake of the Great Depression, these and other countries industrialized by protecting their infant industries behind high tariff walls. However, the alliances of industrial workers and businessmen were unstable, and both great populist dictators, Peron and Bargas, were overthrown. Populism, however, had transformed the nature of politics in every country in which it occurred—above all, by bringing the masses onto the political stage for the first time in Latin America's history.

- *Definitions:* Rossi & Plano, pp. 72–74, 121–122, 128–130, 147–148, 170–171.
- Wynia, ch. 6.
- Hewlett & Weinert, ch. 3.
- Marysa Navarro, "Evita's Charismatic Leadership," ch. 3 of Conniff, *Latin American Populism.*

Suggested

- Skidmore and Smith, chs. 3, 5.
- Torcuato di Tella, "Populism and Reform in Latin America," in Claudio Véliz, ed., *Obstacles to Change in Latin America.*
- Thomas Skidmore, "A Case Study in Comparative Public Policy," Wilson Center Working Paper No. 3

- Eldon Kenworthy, "The Function of the Little-Known Case Study in Comparative Politics: Or What Peronism Wasn't," *Comparative Politics*, October 1973.

Week 5—Labor and the Popular Sectors: Urban Politics

Latin America has urbanized extremely rapidly over the past half-century. But its cities are unlike their European or North American equivalents. Industry is not developed enough to employ more than a small proportion of the urban population, so recent migrants cram into the peripheral shanty-town and seek a living in the so-called informal sector (crafts, peddling, recycling garbage, crime) or as service workers (including domestic service). This means that blue collar unionism has not been as strong as in Europe, for example. We shall compare Bergquist's history of the Chilean miners to Stepan's study of the Peruvian shanty-dwellers, and to the essay on the "corporatized" unions in Brazil and Mexico. Chile's export mines historically required a large number of workers; thus it is one country that has a long tradition of labor organization and militancy.

- *Definitions:* Rossi & Plano, pp. 20–22, 117–118.
- Charles Bergquist, *Labor in Latin America*, ch. 2.
- Hewlett & Weinert, ch. 6.
- Stepan, ch. 5.

Suggested

- Hobart Spalding, *Organized Labor in Latin America*.
- Charles Bergquist, *Labor in America*.

Week 6—Bureaucratic-Authoritarianism: Developmental Versus Neoliberal Exclusionary Military Rule

During the early 1960s optimism reigned in Latin American comparative politics: economic development was held to produce more equal societies, with larger middle classes, greater social statisfaction, and better resources for improving education, health, communications, etc. All of these were thought to mean better prospects for democracy. But O'Donnell pointed out that this optimistic scenario was apparently wrong: the most developed countries of the "Southern Cone" hit economic bottlenecks and experienced political crises. These ended in the creation of a new kind of modern military dictatorship in which politics was replaced by technology. For a time it seemed as though economic development required the abolition of democratic rights and freedoms, and the exclusion of the masses. Read O'Donnell's classic text carefully, and concentrate on identifying the causal relations he is suggesting existed. What kind of argument(s) is he making?

- *Definitions:* Rossi & Plano, pp. 138–140, 154–155, 161–162, 169–170, 185–186.
- O'Donnell, chs. 1, 2, 3
- Guillermo O'Donnell, "Reflections on the Pattern of Change in the Bureaucratic-Authoritarian State," in *Latin American Research Review*, 1978.

Suggested
- David Collier, ed., *The New Authoritarianism in Latin America*.
- Paul Cammack & Phil O'Brien, eds., *Generals in Retreat*.
- William Canak, "The Peripheral State Debate," *Latin American Research Review*, 1986.

Week 7—The Military: Varieties of Professionalism and Intervention

Military coups have been endemic in Latin America, but they began to change in nature during the 1960s. Alfred Stepan's landmark study of the Brazilian military (*The Military in Politics*) showed how they had come to concern themselves more with internal security and development than with external warfare. We shall compare the two variants of what he called the "New Professionalism": military populism in Peru and the "National Security Doctrines" in the Southern Cone and Brazil. What determines the political attitudes and actions of the military? To what extent is its actions internally or externally influenced? (The midterm exam will be given at the end of class Wednesday and is due by 4 P.M. on Friday.)
- *Definitions*: Rossi & Plano, pp. 127–140.
- Alfred Stepan, "The New Professionalism of Military Intervention and Role Expansion."
- Stepan, ch. 4.
- Loveman and Davies, *The Politics of Antipolitics* (selection).
- George Philip, *The Military in South America*.

Suggested
- Alfred Stepan, *The Military in Politics*.
- Eric Nordlinger, *Soldiers in Politics*.
- Abraham Lowenthal, ed., *Armies and Politics in Latin America*.

Week 8—Multinational Corporations: The Search for Resources, Labor and Markets

Multi- or transnational corporations have a variety of different goals in entering Latin American markets. Analyses of their effects have become increasingly sophisticated since the "modernization" or "developmentalist" views of the 1960s and their counterpart, the simple "plunder" thesis (think of Galeano's book, which we read in the first week). The impact of international economic integration is pervasive and has enormous significance for politics in the United States as well as in Latin America.
- *Definitions*: Rossi & Plano, pp. 187–189.
- Hewlett and Weinert, ch. 4.
- Theodore Moran, *Multinational Corporations and the Politics of Dependency*, chs. 5, 7.

Suggested
- Richard Fagen, ed., *Capitalism and the State in U.S.-Latin American Relations*.
- Peter Evans, *Dependent Development*.

- Douglas Bennet and Kenneth Sharpe, *Transnational Corporations Versus the State.*

Week 9—The Church: Conservative Social Control Versus Liberation Theology?

During the 1960s the Latin American Church adopted a new activist social role, particularly under the impetus of Pope John XXIII and the Second Vatican Council. These had their echo in the general meetings of the Latin American Catholic Bishops in Medelin, Colombia (1968), and Puebla, Mexico (1979). However, Liberation Theology, the most radical expression of this movement, has now come under attack from the Vatican, and Pope John Paul II is trying to prevent Church officials from entering politics. This has led to bitter struggles and even schisms, as in Nicaragua.
- *Definitions:* Rossi & Plano, pp. 102–103.
- Levine, chs. 1, 4, 5, 5, 8, 11.

Suggested
- Levine, entire.
- Brian Smith, *The Church and Politics in Chile.*
- Tomas Bruneau, *The Political Transformation of the Brazilian Catholic Church.*

Week 10—Guerrillas: Foquismo and Its Critics

The Cuban Revolution led to a whole new theory among revolutionaries about how they might be able to seize power in the third world. This theory—known as "Foquismo"—was highly controversial, and came under especially heavy criticism from the Communists. In fact, Castroism has had far more defeats than victories. We will discuss the conditions under which different kinds of guerrillas, urban and rural, may win popular support. (Papers are due in class when we get back from Thanksgiving break.)
- *Definitions:* Rossi & Plano, pp. 86–88, 83–84, 58–59, 61–62.
- Régis Debray, "Latin America: Some Problems of Revolutionary Strategy."
- Irving Louis Horowitz, "Military Origins and Outcomes of the Cuban Revolution."
- Richard Gillespie, "Urban Guerrillas in Latin America."
- Cynthia McClintock, "Sendero Luminoso."

Suggested
- Omar Cabezas, *Fire from the Mountain.*
- Richard Gillespie, *Soldiers of Peron.*
- Alain Labrousse, *The Tupamaros.*

Week 11—Contemporary Revolutions: Cuba Versus Nicaragua

What causes different social groups to violently reject the existing social and political order? What determines whether that order will be destroyed? What determines the new system that will replace it? In answer to the first question, we will be concerned with issues such as the political economy of deprivation and expectations, the role of intellectuals, and religion. In answer to the second question we will focus on the resources of the state and its coercive and cooptive apparatuses, as well as on the role of foreign intervention by outside powers. Regarding the question of the systems to which revolutions give rise, we will ask the question of whether bureaucratic degeneration is inevitable.

- *Definitions:* Rossi & Plano, pp. 92–96, 78–79, 58–59, 105–106, 148–150, 166–169, 174–176.
- Wynia, ch. 10.
- Irving Louis Horowitz, *Cuban Communism*, chs. 1, 9.
- Vilas, chs. 1, 2, 3, 7.

Suggested

- Hugh Thomas, *The Cuban Revolution.*
- John Booth, *The End of the Beginning.*
- Samuel Huntington, *Political Order in Changing Societies*, ch. 5.
- Ted Robert Gurr, *Why Men Rebel.*

Week 12—United States Foreign Policy in Central America: Historical Origins of Intervention

The United States has become increasingly preoccupied with a small region of Latin America that has little inherent importance save for its proximity to the United States and the Panama canal. The United States has intervened more or less covertly in all of Latin America, South and Central, but only in Central America has it been regularly involved in military actions. If there is any region of the hemisphere in which U.S. policy has come close to the caricature of imperialism, this is it. Ask yourself, as you read the sorry history of invasions and interference, whether the United States was pursuing strategic, political, or economic goals.

- *Definitions:* Rossi & Plano, pp. 193–244.
- LaFeber, pp. 5–39, 49–74, 78–83, 106–111, 148–164, 172–176, 209–213, 242–256.

Suggested

- Ralph Lee Woodward, *Central America*, 2nd ed.

Week 13—Central America: The Present Debate

Controversy continues to rage over a foreign policy area in which the Reagan Administration promised big changes from the Carter era. Seven years later it seems as though the United States is heading toward a replay if not of Vietnam, at least of Watergate. We shall read the enormously influential essay by Jeane Kirkpatrick, and then study in detail the Nicaraguan and Salvadorean imbroglios. For more on this huge topic, see recent issues of *Foreign Affairs.*

- Blachman, part 3.
- Jeane Kirkpatrick, "Dictatorship and Double Standards."

- Reports of the Bipartisan Commission on Central America and the Tower Commission (selections).
- Jefferson Morley, "Prisoner of Success."

Suggested
- Lars Schoultz, *Human Rights in US Foreign Policy.*

Finals Week—In-Class Final Examination

5. The United States and Vietnam: A Study of the Vietnam War and Its Impact on America and Indochina

Charles Chatfield   *Spring 1988*
History Dept., Wittenberg University,
Springfield, OH 45501

In the spring of 1970 a Catholic priest wrote from hiding, "America is Hard to Find." The Vietnam War was a period of enormous confusion in the United States: it raised questions about our very national identity, tied as it was to the issue of Vietnamese identity. For Americans, Vietnam was hard to find.

In this course of study, we will relate many perspectives and facets of the Vietnam War in an effort to assess its impact on the United States and Vietnam. What considerations, what decisions led the U.S. into Indochina? What was the Vietnamese struggle that involved America so much? What kind of war was it—how was it fought, and how shall we assess its strategy and tactics? Why and how did the U.S. withdraw from the war? What was the significance of the war for American society, U.S. international relations, and the people of Indochina?

In this course of study the student should expect: (1) to become familiar with the basic history of the Vietnam War; (2) to consider changes in American and Vietnamese society and in their relationships as they interacted with one another; (3) to weigh alternative perspectives on the war—pro- and antiwar views; (4) to read several forms of writing on the period and weigh them critically; and (5) to participate in a group learning process.

Required Texts
These are all relatively inexpensive and brief paperbacks.

Herring, George. *America's Longest War* (1979). Historical text.
Halberstam, David. *Ho* (1987). Biography of Ho Chi Minh.
Summers, Harry S., Jr. *On Strategy: The Vietnam War in Context* (1981).
    Interpretation of the war's strategy in a military and political context.
Herr, Michael. *Dispatches* (1978). Personal recollection of the war.
Anisfield, Nancy, ed. *Vietnam Anthology: American War Literature* (1987). An
    anthology of writing, mostly by veterans.

Audiovisual
I will incorporate extensively selections from the PBS series, *Vietnam,* in
order to give you as much of the first-hand view as possible.

Other resources
Maps in Herring, handouts, popular music of the period, this syllabus,
members of the class, and—for those interested in pursuing the subject
further—library holdings.

Course Requirements
Evaluation of reading and class presentations: There will be three in-class
tests, which will cover reading, lectures, and audio-visual resources.
    Essays: You will prepare a paper of about 6 pages in which you deal
carefully with three study questions of your choice from Anisfield, *Vietnam
Anthology.* You will also write an open-book, in-class essay in a half-hour's
time, on two questions which I will choose from the study questions.

CALENDAR OF STUDY

I. Perspectives on a Course of Study

This section of our study will introduce the American and Vietnamese
societies as they became involved with one another, up to about 1965 when
the U.S. government became involved in a full-scale war with North Vietnam.
How did this happen? What did each society bring to that involvement?
How did the Cold War context of U.S. policy contribute to its understanding
of its role and goals in Indochina? What decisions led the U.S. into war?
How did the Cold War affect Vietnam?

Mar. 28—Introduction
To the course and to one another. In-class pre-test. Vietnam on the map.
Alternative perspectives on the war.

**Mar. 30—U.S. Perspectives: Cold War Context of U.S. Policy in Asia,
1945–54**
   • Herring, pp. 1–42.

Apr. 4—U.S. Perspectives: U.S. & Nation-Building, 1955–63
- Herring, pp. 43–107.

Apr. 6—U.S. Perspectives: U.S. & War by the Back Door, 1964–65
- Herring, pp. 108–44.

Apr. 11—Vietnamese Perspectives: Vietnam Prior to 1945
- Halberstam, pp. 1–78.

Apr. 13—Vietnamese Perspectives: Vietnam, 1945–55
- Halberstam, pp. 78–104.

Apr. 18—Vietnamese Perspectives: Vietnam, 1955–65
- Halberstam, pp. 105–118.

Apr. 20—Test & Review
Covers reading, lectures, and audio-visual.
- Herring, pp. 1–144.
- Halberstam.

II. War in Vietnam:
Policy, Strategy and Tactics

By this point we should have a pretty good command of the overall and developing military situation, and of the different perspectives of the belligerents. Now we introduce a military analysis and assess U.S. policy to this point. For this purpose we will work with Herring's historical account, Summers' analysis, and Herr's recollections, and we will bring the story up to the turning point of 1968, when the U.S. formally limited its military options. To what extent were U.S. policy, strategy, and tactics congruent with one another and appropriate to one another?

Apr. 25—Policy and Strategy, 1966–69: The Air War—"Rolling Thunder"
- Herring, pp. 145–82.
- Summers, pp. 1–4, 51–109.

Apr. 27—Policy and Strategy, 1966–69: The Ground War—Enclave, Attrition, Tet
- Herring, pp. 183–216.

May 2—The Tactical Level
- Herr, *Dispatches.*

III. The War in America:
The Government and the Antiwar Movement

The assessment of strategy and tactics will have led us to two other large factors: the war as it was experienced in the field, and as it impacted on U.S. (and Vietnamese) society. In this section of our study we will assess the controversy over the war which took place in American society and in the antiwar movement.

May 4—The Origins, Character, and Dynamics of the Antiwar Movement, 1955–63; 1961–65

- Summers, pp. 5–50.

May 9—War and the Antiwar Movement, 1966–68

- Selections from *Who Spoke Up?* by Nancy Zaroulis and Gerald Sullivan.

IV. Widening the War in Withdrawal:
The Nixon War

In some respects national policy changed after 1968; in some respects it did not. We will consider Nixon's "Vietnamization" and negotiation against the background of the war as it widened in Indochina and of the politics of crisis in the U.S.

May 11—Widening the War in Withdrawal, 1969–73

- Herring, pp. 217–51.

May 16—War After Peace: Closing the Circle, 1973–75

- Herring, pp. 252–72.

May 18—Test and Review

Test covers reading, audio-visual, and lectures; multiple-choice and half-hour essay.

- Herring, pp. 145–272.
- Summers.
- Herr.

V. Assessment: The Meaning of It All

We are ready to assess the meaning of the war, tentatively, for all the parties on various levels. This is necessarily a subjective exercise, and it will test our ability to make critical distinctions about the various aspects of the war and its implications. How we understand the Vietnam experience will largely shape our approach to the challenges of our own time.

May 23—Assessment: Indochina, America, and the Vietnam Generation

- Begin reading Anisfield.

May 25—Assessment: Meaning as Experience
Test (in-class essay) and discussion. Anisfield papers due.

Jun. 1—Assessment: Historians' Retrospective

Jun. 6—Final Examination
Designed as a one-hour in-class essay.

6. Low-Intensity Conflict and the Lessons of Vietnam

Timothy J. Lomperis   *Fall 1986*
Political Science Dept., Duke University,
Durham, NC 27706

Vietnam lies at the root of the malaise that continues to afflict American society. It is hardly an exaggeration to note that the debacle in Indochina dealt telling blows to the bipartisan foreign policy of containment, turned our former arrogance of power to near impotence, and undermined our national self-confidence and even the legitimacy of our political institutions. For the Vietnamese, the war brought a national liberation triumph, a global revolutionary failure, and a regime which is currently as economically inept as it had previously been militarily adroit. Even if these assertions are only half-true, deriving some lessons from Vietnam are crucial to shaking this malaise, learning something from this long agony, and "getting on with it." This is at least the basic proposition and purpose of this course.

A secondary purpose, and really quite an important one, is to familiarize students with various approaches of comparative and international politics as they apply to a specific "laboratory" setting. These international approaches will be woven into the seminars and will form a part of the research papers. Generally speaking, approaches relevant to revolution, development, and group theory will be introduced. Specifically, revolution will be examined first from Chalmer Johnson's integration of structural-functionalism and political culture, then from T. Robert Gurr's perspective of relative deprivation, and lastly from Frances FitzGerald's application of Fanon to Vietnam. The examination of development will contrast the participation and bureaucratic schools of thought. The "macro paradigms" in comparative politics of Political Economy (Dependencia) and Rational Choice will be analyzed at the village level through the debate between James Scott's moral economy approach versus Samuel Popkin's political economy. Group theories of cumulative versus cross-cutting cleavages will also be discussed at this level.

Texts

Gelb, Leslie. *The Irony of Vietman.* (1979) A view of the U.S. decision-making establishment which argues that it did what it could.

FitzGerald, Frances. *Fire in the Lake.* (1972) A Pulitzer Prize winning account that remains the most widely read book on the war.

Karnow, Stanley. *Vietnam: A History.* (1984) Coming to rival FitzGerald in popularity. A better focus on the personalities, both Vietnamese and Americans, than on the history.

Lewy, Guenter. *Americans in Vietnam.* (1978) One of the first works to be called revisionist. Account of the war itself is quite straightforward.

Lomperis, Tim. *The War Everyone Lost—And Won.* (1984) Argues a thesis that is labelled revisionist and has been both acclaimed and widely criticized.

Race, Jeffrey. *War Comes to Long An.* (1972) Still the most insightful book on the war.

Woodside, Alexander. *Community and Revolution in Modern Vietnam.* (1976) A more scholarly analysis than that of FitzGerald.

Recommended Texts

Burns and Leitenberg. *The Wars in Vietnam, Cambodia and Laos, 1945–1982.* (1984) An excellent bibliographic guide.

Caputo. *A Rumor of War.* (1977) The moral impact of the war on the G.I.

Greene. *The Quiet American.* (1958) A classic novel.

Halberstam. *The Best and the Brightest.* (1969) Insightful gossip on Vietnam foreign policy.

Lomperis. *Reading the Wind.* (1986) A political critique of the novels and poetry of the war.

Summers. *Almanac on the Vietnam War.* (1985) A lot of basic information.

――――, *On Strategy.* (1982) What Clausewitz would have said about Vietnam; a major revisionist work.

Thies. *When Governments Collide.* (1980) An important but turgid examination of the utility of academic theories in understanding Vietnam.

CLASS SCHEDULE

I. Historical Antecedents

Sept. 1—Introduction: Scope and Nature of the Course

"Method" of deriving lessons. Discussion of *Heart of Darkness* and *The Quiet American.* Question of Judaic vs. Hellenic view of evil.

• Karnow, pp. 1–46.

Recommended
- Conrad, *Heart of Darkness.*

Sept. 8—Global Strategies
Containment vs. the revolutionary strategy of people's war.
- Karnow, ch. 5 (pp. 169–181).
- Gelb, Introduction, chs. 1, 2, 6.
- Kattenberg, *The Vietnam Trauma,* ch. 3.
- Lenin, "Theses on the Nationalist and Colonialist Question," entire 6 pages.
- Lin Piao, "Long Live the Victory of People's War," entire.

Recommended
For a quick list of the principal revisionist works on the Cold War, see Spanier, *Games Nations Play,* 5th ed., pp. 336–337. A review of postrevisionism is contained in Dennis Wrong, "The Cold War: Post-revisionism," *Dissent* (Fall 1982), pp. 490–495.
- "x" [George Kennan], "Sources of Soviet Conduct," *Soviet Affairs* (July 1987).
- Akira Iriye, *The Cold War in Asia* (1974).
- Robert Tucker, *The Radical Left and American Foreign Policy.*

Sept. 15—Crucible of Vietnamese Nationalism (and Legitimacy)
The political significance of dragons, fairies, Genghis Kahn, and Confucianism.
- Lomperis, pp. 1–31.
- Karnow, chs. 2, 3.
- FitzGerald, pp. 1–95.
- Woodside, chs. 1, 2, 4.
- Eqbal Ahmad, "Revolutionary War and Counterinsurgency," *International Affairs* (1971), pp. 1–15.

Recommended
For the communist perspective on Vietnamese history, see Le Than Khoi, *Le Viet-Ham: Historie et Civilization;* "Traditional Vietnam: Some Historical Stages," *Vietnamese Studies,* No. 21; and Nguyen Khac Vien, *Tradition and Revolution in Viet Nam,* pp. 15–75.
- John T. McAlister and Paul Mus, *The Vietnamese and Their Revolution,* chs. 1–3, 7.
- David Marr, *Vietnamese Anticolonialism.*
- Truong Buu Lam, "Patterns of Vietnamese Response to Foreign Intervention, 1858–1900," *Southeast Asia Studies* (1967), pp. 1–159.

Sept. 22—War Against the French
The August Revolution, Dienhbienphu, Geneva "Accords," Vietnamization, and communization.
- Lomperis, pp. 32–54.
- Woodside, chs. 5, 6 (study thoroughly).
- Karnow, chs. 4, 5.

Recommended

For a comparison of the French with the subsequent American style of campaigning, read a sample of the works of S.L.A. Marshall.
- Buttinger, *Vietnam: A Political History*, pp. 101–384.
- McAlister, *The Origins of Revolution*.
- Hammer, *The Struggle for Indochina, 1940–1955*.
- Devillers and Lacouture, *End of a War*.
- Fall, *Hell in a Very Small Place*.
- Fall, *Street Without Joy*.
- Truong Chinh, *Premier for Revolt*.
- Vo Nguyen Giap, *People's War, People's Army*.

II. Theoretical Explanations

Sept. 29—Revolution as a Strategy of Development

The socioeconomic angst out of which insurgencies originate.
- Chalmers Johnson, *Revolutionary Change*: study chs. 1, 5, 7, 8; read generally chs. 2 3, 4, 6.
- Mao Tse-tung, *The Hunan Report*.
- Woodside, ch. 7.

Supplemental

- Crane Brinton, *Anatomy of Revolution*.
- Hannah Arendt, *On Revolution*.
- T.R. Gurr, *Why Men Rebel*.
- Skocpol, *States and Revolution*.
- Lenin, *What's to Be Done*.
- Truong Chinh and Vo Nguyen Giap, "The Peasant Question."

Oct. 6—Nation-Building and Counterinsurgency

"Orthodox" evolutionary theories of development, "WHAM" vs. "cost push" theories of counterinsurgency, land reform, "contingent incentives" (Race), and the economics of insurgency (Sansom).
- Leonard Binder et al., *Cries and Sequences in Political Development*, ch. 1.
- Woodside, ch. 8.
- Robert L. Sansom, *The Economics of Insurgency*: skim chs. 2, 3; read ch. 12.
- Race, chs. 1, 4, 5, 6.

Recommended

- "Revolutionary War: Western Response," *International Affairs*, Vol. 25, No. 1 (1971): entire issue.
- Robert Packenham, *Liberal America and the Third World*.
- Harry Eckstein, *Internal War*.

- O'Neill and Alberts, eds., *Insurgency in the Modern World*, introductory chapter.
- FitzGerald, Part II, especially "Prospero & Caliban."

Oct. 12—The Viet Cong

"Micro" look at the Viet Cong: organization, motivation, group theory, and moral economy vs. political economy.

- FitzGerald, skim pp. 185–306, read pp. 122–135, 263–284, and 389–404.
- Andrews, *The Village War*, pp. 49–141.
- Paige, "One, Two or Many Vietnams?" pp. 1–11.
- Wolf, *Peasant Wars of the 20th Century*, Preface, ch. 4 (except for pp. 179–180 and 189–91, just skim), Conclusion.
- Popkin, *The Rational Peasant*, chs. 1, 6.
- Fanon, *The Wretched of the Earth*, pp. 35–106, pp. 139–147.

Recommended

On the subject of Viet Cong motivation and morale, the Rand Corp. has published numerous monographs based on its extensive interviews of Viet Cong prisoners and "Chieu Hois." See especially Bill Henderson, *Why the Vietcong Fought.*

- Douglas Pike, *The Viet Cong.*
- Stuart Herrington, *Silence Was a Weapon.*
- James Scott, *Moral Economy of the Peasantry.*
- Pierre Gouru, *The Peasants of the Tonkin Delta.*
- Gerald Chaliand, *The Peasant of North Vietnam.*
- Paul Mus, *Socialogie d'une Guerre.*
- John Womack, *Zapata and the Mexican Revolution.*
- Ronald Ragowski, *Rational Legitimacy.*
- Jeffrey Race, *War Comes to Long An.*
- Robert Sansom, *The Economics of Insurgency.*
- Barrington Moore, *The Social Origins of Dictatorship and Democracy.*
- Harry Eckstein, ed., *Internal War.*
- Nathan Leites and Charles Wolf, *Rebellion and Authority.*

III. Tale of Two Cities:
Competing Strategies

Oct. 27—From Washington: The Irony of Vietnam

Grand strategy and track record of the war from the perspective of Washington and Saigon. Kennedy "Study Teams," escalation decisions, Westmoreland's Three Phases, Big Unit War vs. Marine C.A.P. teams, Phoenix and Pacification, and evaluating the "Best and the Brightest."

- Lomperis, pp. 55–104.
- Lewy, chs. 2–6.
- Gelb, chs. 3–5.

- Karnow, chs. 6–12, 14–16 (*Suggestion:* Read only ch. 14 carefully; as for the rest, skim for flavor and insights on personalities and only those events not covered by other readings.)

Recommended

The literature dissecting the U.S. decision-making establishment is voluminous. The list here includes some of the prominent works.
- FitzGerald, Parts II & III.
- Halberstam.
- Neil Sheehan et al., *The Pentagon Papers.*
- Kahin and Lewis, *The United States in Vietnam.*
- Cooper, *The Lost Crusade.*
- Goodman, *The Lost Peace.*
- Summers, *On Strategy.*
- Kahin, *Intervention* (1964–65 decisions).
- Berman, *The Americanization of the War* (1964–65 decisions).
- Thies (the Johnson Years).
- Oberdorffer, *Tet!*
- Porter, *A Peace Denied* (Paris Peace Agreement).
- Snepp, *Decent Interval* (Fall of Saigon).
- Dillard, *60 Days to Defeat* (Implementation of Agreement).

Nov. 3—From Hanoi: Visions of Victory

Grand strategy and track record of the war from the perspective of Hanoi and the NLF. Themes of reinfiltration, Tet Mau Than, Nguyen Hue, Paris "Agreement," and The Great Spring Victory.
- Race, chs. 2, 3 (history), and 4 (review of concepts).
- Lomperis, pp. 107–176.

Recommended

- Truong Nhu Tang, *Viet Cong Memoir.*
- Nguyen Khac Vien, *The Long Resistance,* chs. 8, 9.
- Turner, *Vietnamese Communism,* chs. 7–11.
- Van Tien Dung, *Our Great Spring Victory.*

IV. Lessons

Nov. 10—How It Played in Peoria: Turmoil and Morality

The unravelling of containment, dissent in the streets, the 1960s and Watergate, the war as a "mistake" or "crime."
- Gelb, ch. 7.
- Karnow, ch. 13.
- Pohoretz, *Why We Were in Vietnam,* chs. 1, 6.
- Caputo, entire, but read quickly.

Recommended
- Haley, *Congress and the Fall of South Vietnam and Cambodia.*
- Fulbright, *The Arrogance of Power.*
- Vogelgesang, *Long Dark Night of the Soul.*
- Mailer, *Armies of the Night.*
- Ellsberg, *Papers on the War.*
- Barnet, *Roots of War.*
- Lewy, chs. 7–11.

Nov. 17—Through a Prism: Comparative Cases
Generalizing from the unique through the filter of other Western interventions in Marxist, people's wars: China, Greece, Philippines, Maylaya Laos.
- Lomperis, Ph.D. dissertation, ch. 7.
- Green, *Comparative Revolutionary Movements.*
- Vonder Mehden, *Comparative Political Violence.*
- Martic, *Insurrection: Five Schools of Revolutionary Thought.*

Nov. 24 & Dec. 1—Student Paper Presentations

Dec. 8—Conclusion: The Lessons of Vietnam
Class roundtable discussion.
- May, *"Lessons" of the Past*, chs. 4, 7.
- Race, chs. 5, 6.
- Gelb, ch. 13.
- Lewy, Epilogue.
- Woodside, Epilogue.

Recommended
- Butterfield, *The New Vietnam Scholarship.*
- Holsti and Rosenau, *Vietnam, Consensus, and the Beliefs of American Leaders.*
- Ravenal, *Never Again.*
- Galucci, *Neither Peace nor Honor.*
- "Cincinnatus," *Self-Destruction.*
- Sharp, *Strategy for Defeat.*
- Summers, *On Strategy.*

Week of Dec. 15—Final Exam

XII

International Law and Organization

1. International Law and a Just World Order

Saul Mendlovitz Fall 1988

Rutgers University Law School, Newark, NJ 07102

This course will address the role of legal processes, institutions and organizations in the evolving world community. Its focus is the study of four interrelated problems: war, poverty, oppression and social injustice, ecological imbalance; the manner in which law can contribute to defining and promoting the values of peace, economic well-being, social justice and ecological balance; and the role of law in contributing to positive human species identity. We will compare the function of law from the perspectives of system maintenance, system reform, and system transformation.

Required Texts

Weston, Burns H., Richard Falk, and Anthony A. D'Amato. *International Law and World Order.* St. Paul, MN.: West Publishing Co., 1980.
————, *Basic Documents, International Law and World Order.* St. Paul, MN.: West Publishing Co., 1980.

Supplementary Texts

Falk, Richard, Frederich Kratochwil, and Saul Mendlovitz. *International Law: A Contemporary Perspective.* Boulder, CO: Westview Press, 1985.
Mendlovitz, Saul H. ed., *On The Creation of a Just World Order.* Free Press, 1975.

Journals
Alternatives: A Journal of Global Transformation and Humane Governance.
American Journal of International Law.

COURSE OUTLINE

Part I—The Nuremberg Judgment and the International Legal Process
The reality of international law; sources of international law; wars of aggression; the individual in international law; jurisdiction; criminal responsibility and crimes against humanities.
- *International Law and World Order*, pp. 1–256.
- Designated materials in *Basic Documents*.
- London Agreement Establishing Nuremberg Tribunal.
- Introduction to Grenville Clark and Louis B. Sohn, *World Peace Through World Law*. Cambridge: Harvard University Press, 1966.
- Definitions and Matrices for Study of Just World Order.

Supplemental Reading
- Introduction to Saul H. Mendlovitz, ed., *On the Creation of a Just World Order*. New York: Free Press, 1975.
- Richard Falk, "Keeping Nuremburg Alive," pp. 494–500 in *International Law: A Contemporary Perspective*.

Part II—Preventing War and Violence; Achieving a Peace System
Civil war; belligerency; neutrality; recognition of states and governments; intervention by states and by the United Nations.
- *International Law and World Order*, pp. 259–409.
- Designated materials in *Basic Documents*.
- *World Peace Through World Law*, pp. xxix–xxxiii.
- "The Role of Enforcement of Just Law in the Establishment of New International Order: A Proposal for a Transnational Police Force," by Robert C. Johansen and Saul H. Mendlovitz, in *International Law: A Contemporary Perspective*, pp. 346–364.

Part III—Problems in Socio-Political Justice; Promoting Human Rights and Social Justice
Definition and sources of human rights; regional enforcement, especially in the European system; the individual in international law; terrorism and extradition; self-determination and minority rights.
- *International Law and World Order*, pp. 466–494.
- Designated materials in *Basic Documents*.

Supplemental Reading
- "Tensions Between the Individual and the State," four essays in *International Law: A Contemporary Perspective*.

Part IV—Problems of Development and Abolishing Poverty; Establishing a Basic Needs System for Humanity
Foreign investment and economic development; state responsibility; expropriation and nationalization; economic retortions and reprisals; right to food.
- *International Law and World Order,* pp. 652–767.
- Designated materials in *Basic Documents.*
- Right to Food: The Draft Charter for a World Food Authority.

Supplemental Reading
- Oscar Shacter, "Sharing the World's Resources," pp. 525–545 in *International Law: A Contemporary Perspective.*

Part V—Problems in Environmental Protection: Promoting a Sustainable, Equitable Environmental Regime for the Globe
Law of the Sea; maritime jurisdiction; marine pollution; military retortion and reprisals; executive agreements and termination of treaties.
- *International Law and World Order,* pp. 835–954.
- Designated materials in *Basic Documents.*

Supplemental Reading
- Per Magnus Wijkman, "UNCLOS and the Redistribution of Ocean Wealth," pp. 589–601 in *International Law: A Contemporary Perspective.*
- Jan Schneider, "State Responsibility for Environmental Protection," pp. 602–633 in *International Law: A Contemporary Perspective.*

Part VI—The Future of International Law and Promoting a Just World Order
- *International Law and World Order,* pp. 1026–1174.
- *On the Creation of a Just World Order,* chapters 1, 2, 4, 5, 7.
- Sylvia Brucan, "Establishment of a World Authority: Working Hypotheses," *Alternatives* (1982), pp. viii, 209–223.

2. Public International Law

Christopher C. Joyner   *Fall 1987*
Political Science Dept., The George Washington University,
Washington, DC 20052

The chief purpose of this course is to survey the field of international law, focusing especially on world order issues of legal importance. Since the legitimacy of international law *qua law* has sometimes been called into question, it will be necessary first to examine carefully the major principles and concepts of international law as gleaned from multilateral conventions, court decisions, and the writings of publicists. Having done this, we will then direct attention to specific legal problems found in contemporary international relations, particularly the law relating to ocean space, outer space, human rights, transnational terrorism, and economic development, as well as the evolving status of law in a multicultural world.

Required Reading
Booth, Ken. *Law, Force and Diplomacy at Sea.* London: George Allen & Unwin, 1985.

Boyle, Francis. *World Politics and International Law.* Durham: Duke University Press, 1985.

Falk, Richard, et al. *International Law: A Contemporary Perspective.* Boulder: Westview Press, 1985.

Miller, Lynn H. *Global Order: Values and Power in International Politics.* Boulder: Westview, 1985.

Shaw, M.N. *International Law.* Cambridge: Grotius, 2nd edition, 1986.

"Polar Politics in the 1980s," International Studies Association *Notes,* Vol. 11 (Summer 1985) (available from the professor).

Recommended
Akehurst, Michael. *A Modern Introduction to International Law,* 6th ed. London: George Allen, 1986.

Sohn, Louis. *The Law of the Sea in a Nutshell.* West Publishers, 1985.

Several selected readings will also be placed on reserve, and daily reading of *The New York Times* or *The Washington Post* is strongly encouraged.

Course Requirements
- A final examination, essay in format and comprehensive in coverage, to determine the student's understanding and mastery of lecture materials and assigned readings. (50%)
- A scholarly research paper, approximately 25 pages in length, dealing with a topic related to this course. It is strongly sugggested that you discuss your topic preference with the professor prior to commencing the research. (50%)
- Regular attendance and meaningfully active class participation.

COURSE OUTLINE AND READING ASSIGNMENTS

Part I. International Law as Law

Week 1—Introduction
- Shaw, chs. 1, 2.
- Falk, ch. 1.

- Boyle, chs. 1, 2, 3, 4, and 5.
- Akehurst, chs. 1 and 2.

Week 2—Sources and Sanctions of International Law

- Shaw, chs. 3, 4.
- Miller, ch. 1.
- Falk, ch. 2.
- C. Joyner, "U.N. General Assembly Resolution and International Law: Rethinking the Contemporary Dynamics of Norm Creation," *California Western International Law Journal*, Vol. 11 (Summer 1981), pp. 445–478.

Weeks 3–4—Subjects of International Law

- Shaw, chs. 5, 6.
- Miller, ch. 2.
- Falk, ch. 3.
- M.J. Peterson, "Recognition of Governments Should Not Be Abolished," *American Journal of International Law*, Vol. 77 (January 1983), pp. 31–50.
- Akehurst, chs. 5, 6.

Week 5—International Law and the Individual

- Shaw, ch. 6.
- Falk, ch. 7.
- Miller, ch. 7.
- Louis B. Sohn, "The New International Law: Protection of the Rights of Individuals Rather than States," *American University Law Review*, Vol. 32 (Fall 1982), pp. 1–63.
- Akehurst, chs. 6, 7.

Week 6—Territorial Questions

- Shaw, ch. 8, 11, 12, 13.
- Akehurst, chs. 8, 9, 11, 12.

Week 7—International Agreements

- Shaw, ch. 15.
- Falk, ch. 4.
- Boyle, pp. 77-170.
- Akehurst, ch. 10.

Week 8—Use of Force

- Shaw, chs. 16, 17.
- Boyle, pp. 171–290.
- Falk, ch. 5.
- Miller, chs. 3 and 4.
- C. Joyner, "Grenada and the United States' Invasion: Reflections on the Lawfulness of Action," *American Journal of International Law*, Vol. 78 (January 1984).

- C. Joyner and M. Grimaldi, "The United Staes and Nicaragua: Reflections on the Lawfulness of Contemporary Intervention," *Virginia Journal of International Law*, Vol. 25 (Spring 1985), pp. 621–689.
- O. Schachter, "The Right of States to Use Armed Force," *Michigan Law Review*, Vol. 82 (1984), pp. 16–20.

Also Recommended

- C. Joyner, "The Transnational Boycott as Economic Coercion in International Law: Policy, Place and Practice," *Vanderbilt Journal of Transnational Law*, Vol. 17 (Spring 1984), pp. 205–286.
- Akehurst, chs. 13, 14.

Week 9—War
- Miller, ch. 5.
- Falk, ch. 6.
- G. Aldrich, "New Life for the Laws of War," *American Journal of International Law*, Vol. 75 (October 1, 1981), pp. 764–783.
- Akehurst, chs. 15, 16, 7.

Part II. Contemporary Issues in International Law

Week 10—National Attitudes and International Law
- F.V. Garcia-Amador, "Current Attempts to Revise International Law—A Comparative Analysis," *American Journal of International Law*, Vol. 77 (April 1983), pp. 286–296.
- Kazimierz Grybowski, "Soviet Theory of International Law for the Seventies," *American Journal of International Law*, Vol. 77 (October 1983), pp. 862–871.
- R. Dean, "Beyond Helsinki: The Soviet View of Human Rights in International Law," *Virginia Journal of International Law*, Vol. 21 (Fall 1980), pp. 55–96.
- W. Levi, ch. 7, "Inequality," and ch. 8, "Cultural Heterogeneity and International Law," in *Law and Politics in the International Society* (1970), pp. 121–150.
- S. Kim, "The People's Republic of China and the Charter-Based International Legal Order," *American Journal of International Law*, Vol. 72 (April 1978), pp. 317–334.
- C. Osakwe, "Contemporary Soviet Doctrine on the Sources of General International Law," *American Society of International Law Proceedings*, Vol. 73 (1979), pp. 310–323.

Week 11—Common Space Resource Regimes: The Oceans
- Shaw, ch. 10.
- Miller, ch. 8.
- Falk, ch. 8.
- Booth, entire volume.

- Akehurst, ch. 18.
- Sohn, entire volume.

Week 12—Common Space Resource Regimes: Air, Outer Space, and Polar Spaces

- Shaw, ch. 9.
- C. Christol, "The Common Heritage of Mankind Provision in the 1979 Agreement Governing the Activities of States on the Moon and Other Celestial Bodies," *International Lawyer*, Vol. 14 (Spring 1980), pp. 429–465.
- C. Joyner and D. Miller, "Selling Satellites: The Commercialization of LANDSAT," *Harvard International Law Journal*, Vol. 17 (Winter 1985), pp. 63–102.
- Akehurst, ch. 19.
- ISA Notes, "Polar Politics in the 1980s," entire volume.
- R. Bilder, "The Present Legal and Political Situation in Antarctica," in J. Charney, editor, *The New Nationalism and the Use of Common Space* (1981), pp. 167–205.
- C. Joyner and P. Lipperman, "Conflicting Jurisdictions in the Southern Ocean: The Case of an Antarctic Minerals Regime," *Virginia Journal of International Law*, Vol. 27, No. 1 (Fall 1986), pp. 1–38.
- C. Joyner, "The Southern Ocean and Marine Pollution: Problems & Prospects," *Case Western Reserve Journal of International Law*, Vol. 17 (Spring 1985), pp. 165–194.
- C. Joyner, "Oceanic Pollution and the Southern Ocean: Rethinking the International Legal Implications for Antarctica," *Natural Resources Journal*, Vol. 24 (January 1984), pp. 1–40. (recommended)

Week 13—International Law and Economic Development

- Miller, ch. 7.
- B. Weston, "The Charter of Economic Rights and Duties of States and the Deprivation of Foreign-Owned Wealth," *American Journal of International Law*, Vol. 75 (July 1981), pp. 437–475.

Week 14—Crimes in International Law

- R. Finnegan, "Nuremberg and Tokyo: Uncertain Mandate in the Realm of International Legal Sanctions," *Towson State Journal of International Affairs*, Vol. 17 (Spring 1983), pp. 63–80.
- R. Friedlander, "The Enforcement of International Criminal Law: Fact or Fiction?," *Case Western Reserve Journal of International Law*, Vol. 17 (Winter 1985), pp. 79–90.
- Akehurst, pp. 237–239.

Conclusion

- Shaw, ch. 10.
- Miller, ch. 9.
- Boyle, pp. 293–296.
- Falk, ch. 9.

- J. Fried, "International Law—Neither Orphan Nor Harlot, Neither Jailer Nor Never-Never Land," in K. Deutsch and S. Hoffman, eds., *The Relevance of International Law* (1971), pp. 124–176.

3. International Organization

Saadallah Hallaba   *Fall 1987*
Political Science Dept., University of
South Carolina–Sumter, Sumter, SC 29150

This is an introductory course on the nature and functioning of international organization. It will explore different approaches to the study of international organization, and evaluate the performance of international organization in carrying out tasks and attaining goals. Specific activities of international organizations and their influence in shaping policy outcomes will be considered in a number of issues areas: peacekeeping and security; international trade, finance, and economic development; natural resource development and allocation; human rights; and population and environmental concerns. The course will also stress and assess the future trends and prospects for international organization as an element of world politics. Special emphasis will be raised as to the present role the U.S. is playing vis-à-vis the United Nations.

Required Texts
Claude, Inis L., Jr. *Swords into Plowshares*, Fourth Edition, New York: Random House, 1984.
UN Association of the USA. *Issues Before the 42nd General Assembly of the United Nations, 1986–1987*, 1987.
Department of Public Information, United Nations, N.Y., *Basic Facts About The United Nations*, 1984.
Saadallah Hallaba. *The Politics of Culture: The U.S. and UNESCO*, 1986.
————. *The U.S. and the U.N. Financial Crisis*, 1987.

Course Requirements
Midterm exam—20%; research paper—20% (see below); oral presentation—30%; final exam—30%.

COURSE CONTENT AND READING
ASSIGNMENTS

Introduction to the Course
* *Swords into Plowshares*, ch. 1.

The Emergence of International Organization and the League of Nations
* Claude, ch. 2.
* A. Leroy Bennett, *International Organizations*, 2nd edition, Prentice Hall, 1980, chs. 1 and 2.
* Plano & Riggs, *Forging World Order*, pp. 3–37.
* "Covenant of the League" in Claude, pp. 453–462.

Recommended reading
* Gerhart Niemayer, "The Balance Sheet of the League Experiment," in *International Organization*, Vol. 27:1, Winter 1973.
* G. Mangone, *A Short History of International Organization*.

The Creation of the United Nations
* Claude, ch. 4.
* *Basic Facts About the United Nations*, pp. 1–12.
* Bennett, chs. 3 and 14.
* Thomas M. Campbell, "Nationalism in America's U.N. Policy 1944–1945," in *International Organization*, Vol. 27:1, Winter.

Recommended reading
* Leland M. Goodrich, "From League of Nations to United Nations," *International Organization*, Vol. 1:1, 1947.

Structure of the United Nations
* Bennett, chs. 5, 8, and 13.
* *Basic Facts About the United Nations*, pp. 3–12.
* Plano and Riggs, pp. 53–105.
* "The U.N. Charter," in Claude, pp. 463–489.

U.N. Politics and Processes
* Claude, chs. 5–10.
* Hollis W. Barber, "The U.S. vs. the U.N.," in *International Organization*, Vol. 27:2, Spring 1973.

Recommended reading
* Bennett, chs. 5 and 6.
* David Kay, *The New Nations in the United Nations*.

Approaches to Peacekeeping Through International Organization
- Claude, chs. 11–17.
- Bennett, chs. 7 and 9.
- Plano and Riggs, pp. 207–380.

Recommended reading
- Lincoln Bloomfield, *International Military Force.*

The Future of the United Nations
- Claude, chs. 18 and 19.
- Bennett, ch. 17.
- *Issues Before the 42nd General Assembly of the UN, 1987.*
- *The Future of the United Nations* (tape). A roundtable sponsored by the American Enterprise Institute (AEI), Washington, D.C., 1977.

RESEARCH PAPER

Detailed reviews of the work of the United Nations, the Specialized Agencies and other International Institutions may be found in the annual editions of the *United Nations Yearbook*, the quarterly periodical *International Organization*, and the U.N.'s own monthly, *United Nations Chronicle*, which became a quarterly magazine starting with Issue No. 3, April 1986.

A number of useful texts and other studies have been published. Students are urged to take note of the following:

Leland M. Goodrich and Edward Hambro, *Charter of the United Nations, Commentary and Documents.* A classic and a must.

Stephen S. Goodspeed, *The Nature and Function of International Organization*, 2nd Ed. Oxford University Press. A classic.

Leland Goodrich, *The United Nations.* A valuable tool.

Études Internationales, Numéro Spécial: L'ONU: Quarante ans aprés, Centre Quebecois de Relations Internationales, Institut Canadien des Affairs Internationales, Université Laval, Quebec, Canada (*UNO—Forty Years After—A Special Issue*, Vol. XVI, No. 4, Dec. 1985).

Ruth B. Russel and Jeannette B. Muther, *A History of the United Nations Charter—The Role of the US, 1940–1945.* A must.

Norman J. Padelford and L. Goodrich, *The United Nations: Accomplishments and Prospects.*

Clyde Eagleton, *International Government.*

Inis L. Claude, *The Changing United Nations.*

Lincoln P. Bloomfield, *The UN and US Foreign Policy*, Rev. ed.

Additional bibliographies, which allow for study in greater depth of each of the topics we will consider, are to be found at the end of every chapter in *Swords into Plowshares*. *International Organization* also lists books and articles relevant to our study in its "Selected Bibliography." Readings are specifically cited for each topic.

Paper Topics and Some Selected Readings to Get You Started

The "VETO" as a Problem for International Organization

Sydney Bailey, "Veto in the Security Council," *International Conciliation,* January 1968.

Dwight E. Lee, "The Genesis of the Veto," *International Organization,* February 1947.

John Stoessinger, *The United Nations and the Superpowers,* Chapter 1, 1973.

Norman Padeldord, "The Use of the Veto," *International Organization,* June 1948.

Mona Gagnon, "Peace Forces and the Veto: The Relevance of Consent," *International Organization,* Autumn 1967.

The Role of the General Assembly in the United Nations System

H.G. Nicholas, *The United Nations as a Political Institution,* Fifth Edition, 1975.

Richard Falk, "On the Quasi-Legislative Competence of the General Assembly," *American Journal of International Law,* October 1966, Vol. 60, No. 4.

Alker, H.R., Jr., "Dimensions of Conflict in the General Assembly," *American Political Science Review,* Vol. 58, September 1964.

G.L. Lande, "The Effect of the Resolutions of the U.N. General Assembly," *World Politics,* October 1966.

Claude, I.L., Jr., *Power and International Relations,* Random House, 1962.

Financing as a Problem for International Organization

John G. Stoessinger et al., *Financing the UN System.*

U.N. General Assembly, Official Records: 21st Session, *Analysis of the Finances of the United Nations* (A/AC.124/1, 24 January 1966).

———, Official Records: 21st Session, *Report of the Ad Hoc Committee of Experts to Examine the Finances of the UN and the Specialized Agencies* (A/6289, March 28, 1966, and ADD. 1, March 31, 1966).

U.S. Congress, House of Representatives, Committee of Foreign Affairs, *UN Financial Situation,* Committee Print, 89th Congress, 2nd Session (1966).

The Political Role of the Secretary-General

Trygve Lie, *In the Cause of Peace.*

Andrew Dordier et al., *Public Papers of the Secretaries-General of the UN,* Vol. I. Trygve Lie, 1946–1953; Vol. II, Dag Hammarskjold, 1953–1956; Vol. III, Dag Hammarskjold, 1956–1957. (Five remaining volumes have been published by Columbia University Press.

Stephen Schwabel, *The Secretary-General of the U.N.*

June Bingham, *U Thant.*

Regionalism: Theory and Practice

This is not a paper topic, but the general readings here should be consulted by those working on specific regional organizations.

Ruth Lawson, *International Regional Organizations.*
Ronald Yalem, *Regionalism and World Order.*
Linda Miller, *World Order and Local Disorder.*

Regionalism: The Arab League
Robert MacDonald, *The League of Arab States.*
John C. Campbell, *Defense of the Middle East.*
Fayez Sayegh, *Arab Unity: Hope and Fulfillment.*

Regionalism: Organization of African Unity (OAU)
Ali Mazrui, *Towards a Pax Africana.*
Joseph Nye, *Pan-Africanism and East African Integration.*
I. William Zartman, "Africa as a Subordinate State System in International
Relations," *International Organization*, Summer 1977, Vol. 21.

Regionalism: The Organization of American States
John Drier, *The Organization of American States.*
Jerome Slater, *The OAS and U.S. Foreign Policy.*
_____ , *Reevaluation of Collective Security: The OAS in Action.*
Norman Bailey, *Latin America in World Politics* (Bibliography on pp. 157–
158).

Regionalism: Europe
Ernst Haas, *The Uniting of Europe.*
George Lichteim, *The New Europe.*
U.W. Kitzinger, *The Politics and Economics of European Integration.*
International Organizations Series, Department of State, *The European Com-
munities.*
_____ , The Organization for Economic Cooperation and Development
(OCED).

Conflict Resolution and International Organizations
This is a general topic, and the materials listed should be consulted by all
those writing on specific case studies.

Joel Larus, *From Collective Security to Preventive Diplomacy.*
Ruth Russell, *U.N. Experience with Military Forces.*
David Wainhouse, *International Peace Observations.*
Arthur Cox, *Prospects for Peacekeeping.*

Conflict Resolution: Suez, 1957
William Frye, *A U.N. Peace Force.*
Gabriella Rosner, *The United Nations Emergency Force.*
Carl Von Horn, *Soldiering for Peace.*
Robert O. Mathews, "The Suez Canal Dispute: A Case Study in Peaceful
Settlement," *International Organization* (Winter 1977).

Conflict Resolution: The October War, 1973

UN Monthly Chronicle, Vol. X, No. 10, November 1973.
UN Monthly Chronicle, Vol. XI, No. 2, February 1974.

Conflict Resolution: Cyprus

Stephen G. Xydis, *Cyprus: Conflict and Conciliation.*
James Boyd, "Cyprus: Episode in Peacekeeping," *International Organization,* Winter 1966.
J.K. Gordon, "The UN in Cyprus," *International Journal,* Vol. 19, Summer 1964.

Conflict Resolution: Congo

Ernest Lefever, *Uncertain Mandate.*
Carl Von Horn, *Soldiering for Peace.*
Connor Cruise O'Brien, *To Katanga and Back.*
Ernest Lefever, *Crisis in the Congo.*
Georges Abi-Saab, "The United Nations Operations in the Congo," OUP, 1978, paper.

Functionalism: UNCTAD

Kamal Nagras, *United Nations Conference on Trade and Development.*
Paul Prebish, *Towards a New Trade Policy for Development,* UN Publication Sales, No. 64 II.B.4.
Robert L. Rothstein, *Global Bargaining: UNCTAD and the Quest for a New International Economic Order,* Princeton University, 1979.

The Nations and International Organization

The following questions are guidelines for papers on Nations and International Organization:

1. Is the nation's voting behavior in a bloc?
2. Compare its behavior in the U.N. with its foreign policy outside the U.N. Does the U.N. affect its foreign policy?
3. What does it use the U.N. for? What does it want from the U.N.?
4. How does its foreign policy affect the U.N.?
5. What changes does it want in the U.N.? Why?
6. What is its overall attitude toward U.N. activities in the areas of: (a) Peacekeeping? (b) Economic Development? (c) Human Rights?
7. What other International Organizations does it belong to? Compare its relationship to them with its relationship to the U.N.

The USSR and International Organization

Alexander Ballin, *The Soviet Union at the United Nations.*
Harold K. Jacobson, *The USSR and the U.N.'s Economic and Social Activities.*
Alvin Z. Rubenstein, *The Soviets in International Organizations.*
John G. Stoessinger, *The UN and the Superpowers: U.S.-Soviet Interaction at the U.N.* (Third Ed., August 1973).

France and International Organization
James Combs, "France and UN Peacekeeping," *International Organization,* (Spring 1967).
Edgar Furniss, *France: Troubled Ally.*
Alred Crosser, *French Foreign Policy.*
W.W. Kulski, *De Gaulle and the World.*

The United States and International Organization
Richard Gardner, *In Pursuit of World Order.*
Lincoln Bloomfield, *The UN and U.S. Foreign Policy* (Rev. ed.).
Donald Bishop, *The Administration of U.S. Foreign Policy Through the U.N.*
Alfred Hero, "The American Public and the U.N., 1954–1966," *Journal of Conflict Resolution,* Vol. X, No. 4.

Africa and International Organization
"Africa Speaks to the U.N." Special issue of *International Organization,* Vol. 16 (Spring 1962).
Vernon McJay, *African Diplomacy.*
Ali A. Mazrui, "The U.N. and Some African Political Attitudes," *International Organization,* Vol. 18 (Summer 1964).

Private International Organization: A Study of the Petroleum Industry
Robert Engler, *The Politics of Oil.*
P.H. Frankel, *Mattei: Oil and Power Politics.*
J.E. Hartshorn, *Politics and World Oil Economics* (Rev. ed.).
George Lenczowski, *Oil and the State in the Middle East.*
William Bundy (ed.), *The World Economic Crisis,* 1975.
Oysten Noreng, *Oil Politics in the 1980s: Patterns of International Cooperation,* McGraw-Hill, 1979, paper.

---

4. International Organization

Lynn H. Miller   *Spring 1988*
Political Science Dept., Temple University,
Philadelphia, PA 19122

This course examines the process of international organization as a phenomenon in the contemporary world system. We begin with international organizational efforts prior to the twentieth century, then examine this century's global institutions, the League of Nations and the United Nations, and a number of its limited member arrangements, as well as non-governmental organizations. Throughout the course, we attempt to determine both how the international organizational process is transforming the global system and how it is preserving it. We consider the role(s) of various organizations in treating military conflict, human rights problems, economic development, global resource management, and other challenges of interdependence. We conclude with an effort to see how this process might assist in global problem solving in future years.

Readings

Claude, Inis L., Jr. *Swords into Plowshares*, 4th ed. New York: Random House, 1984.

Falk, Richard A. "On the Quasi-Legislative Competence of the General Assembly," *American Journal of International Law*, Vol. 60, No. 4 (October 1966), pp. 732–791.

Keohane, Robert O., and J.S. Nye. *Power and Interdependence*.

Mendlovitz, Saul. *On the Creation of a Just World Order*.

Miller, Lynn H. *Global Order*. Boulder, CO: Westview Press, 1985.

———. *Organizing Mankind*.

Nicholas, H.G. *The United Nations as a Political Institution*.

Riggs, Robert E., and Jack C. Plano. *The United Nations*. Dorsey Press, 1987.

Van Dyke, Vernon. *Human Rights, the United States, and the World Community*.

TOPIC OUTLINE AND
READING ASSIGNMENTS

International Organization in the State System

- Claude, ch. 1.
- Miller, *Global Order*, ch. 2.
- Miller, *Organizing Mankind*, ch. 1.

From the League of Nations to the United Nations

- Claude, chs. 2–3.
- Riggs and Plano, ch.1.

Overview of the U.N. System

- Nicholas, chs. 1–7.
- Riggs and Plano, ch. 2.

Actors and Politics in the U.N.

- Claude, chs. 7–9.
- Falk.
- Riggs and Plano, chs. 3–4.

Conflict Management: Collective Security
- Claude, chs. 11–12.
- Miller, *Organizing Mankind,* chs. 2–3.
- Riggs and Plano, ch. 5.

Conflict Management: Peacekeeping
- Claude, ch. 14.
- Miller, *Organizing Mankind,* ch. 4.
- Riggs and Plano, chs. 5 (review), 7.

Disarmament and Arms Control
- Claude, ch. 13.
- Miller, *Global Order,* ch. 5.
- Riggs and Plano, ch. 6.

Human Rights and Self Determination
- Miller, *Global Order,* ch. 7.
- Miller, *Organizing Mankind,* ch. 6.
- Riggs and Plano, ch. 8.
- Van Dyke, pp. 3–102.

Functionalism and Social Cooperation
- Miller, *Global Order,* ch. 4.
- Miller, *Organizing Mankind,* ch. 5.
- Riggs and Plano, ch. 9.

International Trade and Financial System
- Riggs and Plano, ch. 10.

World Economic Development
- Miller, *Global Order,* ch. 6.
- Riggs and Plano, ch. 11.

Regionalism and Neo-Functionalism
- Keohane and Nye, chs. 1–3.
- Miller, *Global Order,* ch. 4 (review).
- Riggs and Plano, ch. 9.

International Organization and "Spaceship Earth"
- Miller, *Global Order,* ch. 8.
- Miller, *Organizing Mankind,* ch. 7.

The Future of International Organization
- Mendlovitz, entire.
- Miller, *Global Order,* ch. 9.
- Riggs and Plano, ch. 12.

XIII

Nonviolence Theory and Action

1. Techniques, Strategies, and Politics of Nonviolent Struggle

Gene Sharp   *Spring 1986*
St. Thomas University*

Despite uncertainties, dangers, and great violence, people have for centuries improvised types of nonviolent struggle that have relied on social, economic, psychological, moral, and political action as weapons in confronting aggression, domination, dictatorships, oppression, and even genocide. In other comparable situations, the weapons used have been those of violence and war.

These nonviolent weapons were almost always improvised by people with little or no experience in their use. Mostly, they had little or no experience in previous attempts by others in different situations to apply similar types of action. Remarkably, although defeats occurred (as they do in war), in some of these cases people were able by these nonviolent means to gain their objectives, fully or in part.

It is possible to learn more about how this technique operates in efforts to gain objectives. In fact, nonviolent struggle in recent years has become

---

*This course was taught while Gene Sharp was a visiting professor at St. Thomas University. His permanent address is: Program on Nonviolent Sanctions in Conflict and Defense, Center for International Affairs, Harvard University, Cambridge, MA 02138.

the object of scholarly investigation and also of improvisation and deliberate organization in new settings.

Moreover, proposals have been made to refine the technique by deliberate efforts and to adapt it consciously with advance planning and preparations to future conflicts for use in place of violence and war.

Course Questions

What is the possible relevance of this technique? Does nonviolent struggle rest, as some have assumed, on the rejection of power, or instead on a more fundamental and significant application of power? What role has this technique played in history? What are its methods of action, or "weapons"? How does it operate against a hostile opponent willing and able to apply violent repression? What are the mechanisms by which this technique can achieve change? What factors contribute to failure or to success? What are the long-term consequences for a society of the increased use of the technique—positive or negative?

Does this technique have any relevance for the major conflicts of today and tomorrow? Does it have any role to play in the quest for human freedom, social justice, and world peace? Can it be a realistic way to deal with international aggression, internal take-overs, ruthless dictators, attempted genocide, and oppressive systems? Could a society responsibly and consciously choose to confront future threats and to wage serious conflicts by use of these nonviolent sanctions? How could such a shift occur?

How does this technique's existence, and our conclusions as to whether it is practical, affect our perception of the range of means of action among which we must choose?

Course Objectives

The primary aim of this course is to increase our understanding of, and ability to think about, the socio-political technique of nonviolent struggle as a substitute for violent sanctions. The goal is increased knowledge, independent thinking, and careful analysis—not to reach a particular viewpoint, much less to accept a particular belief, movement, or way of life. Critical responses are welcomed.

Videotapes

Five programs, two of 30 minutes and three of 60 minutes in length. Funded by the Fund for the Improvement of Post-Secondary Education, U.S. Department of Education. A project of the University City Science Center of Philadelphia. Available from W.T.L. Productions, Box 351 (D), Primos, Pennsylvania 19018.

Audiotapes

"A Modern Alternative to War?" and "More on Civilian-based Defense— Gene Sharp." Two 30-minute interviews in the *Common Ground* series from the Stanley Foundation, 420 East Third Street, Muscatine, Iowa 52761. $5.00 each.

"Making Europe Unconquerable," a 30-minute version of a talk by Gene Sharp, with questions and answers. Cambridge Forum, 3 Church Street, Cambridge, MA 02138. $7.00 per copy.

Required Textbooks and Other Readings

Alternative Defence Commission. *Defence Without the Bomb.* London and New York (now Philadelphia): Taylor & Francis, 1983. $9.00.

Atkeson, Brigadier General Edward B. "The Relevance of Civilian-Based Defense to U.S. Security Interests," *Military Review* (Fort Leavenworth, Kansas), vol. 56, no. 5 (May 1976), pp. 24–32, and no. 6 (June 1976), pp. 45–55. (photocopy)

Bondurant, Joan V. *Conquest of Violence: The Gandhian Philosophy of Conflict.* Berkeley and Los Angeles: University of California Press, 1965. $7.95.

Kruegler, Christopher, and Patricia Parkman. "Identifying Alternatives to Political Violence: An Educational Imperative" (9 pp.), in *Harvard Educational Review,* February 1985. (photocopy)

Roberts, Adam. "Civil Resistance to Military Coups," *Journal of Peace Research* (Oslo), vol. XII, no. 1 (1975), pp. 19–36. (photocopy)

Sharp, Gene. "Making the Abolition of War a Realistic Goal." Pamphlet (16 pp.). New York: World Policy Institute, 1983. $1.50.

————. *Social Power and Political Freedom.* Porter Sargent Publishers, 1980, $8.95. (Also available on audiotape from: Recording for the Blind, 20 Roszel Road, Princeton, NJ 08540.)

————. *The Politics of Nonviolent Action,* in three volumes: I, *Power and Struggle;* II, *The Methods of Nonviolent Action;* and III, *The Dynamics of Nonviolent Action.* Porter Sargent Publisher, 1973. $3.95, $4.95, $5.95. (Also available from Recording for the Blind.)

————. *Gandhi as a Political Strategist, with Essays on Ethics and Politics.* Porter Sargent Publishers, 1979. $7.95.

————. *Making Europe Unconquerable: The Potential of Civilian-based Deterrence and Defense.* Cambridge: Ballinger, 1985. $14.95.

————. *National Security Through Civilian-based Defense.* Omaha: Association for Transarmament Studies, 1985. $4.95.

————. Investigating New Options in Conflict and Defense," in *Education for Peace and Disarmament.* New York and London: Teachers College Press, 1983. (photocopy)

(Total printed text cost: $70.10.)

Optional Readings

Boserup, Anders, and Andrew Mack. *War Without Weapons: Non-Violence in National Defence.* (Denmark, 1971; London: Francis Pinter, 1974; New York: Schocken, 1975). Out of print.

Irwin, Robert. *U.S. Defense Policy: Mainstream Views and Nonviolent Alternatives: A Macro-Analysis Seminar Manual* (57 pages). Waltham, Mass.: International Seminars on Training for Nonviolent Action, 1982.

Lakey, George. *Strategy for a Living Revolution.* Philadelphia: New Society Publishers, 1986.

Roberts, Adam, ed. *Civilian Resistance as a National Defense.* Harrisburg: Stackpole Books, 1968. Out of print.

COURSE OUTLINE

The Relevance and Nature of Nonviolent Struggle

The Problems We Face and the Relevance of Nonviolent Sanctions
Session One

In light of the major unsolved political problems of this century, dictatorship, genocide, oppression, and war, why should we examine the technique of nonviolent action? What is the possible relevance of this technique?

- Christopher Kruegler and Patricia Parkman, "Identifying Alternatives to Political Violence."
- Gene Sharp, "Making the Abolition of War a Realistic Goal."

More advanced readings
- Gene Sharp, "Rethinking Politics," "Seeking a Solution to the Problem of War," and "The Societal Imperative," in *Social Power and Political Freedom.*

The Nature and Relevance of Power
Session Two

Does the choice of nonviolent means require the rejection of power, or is nonviolent struggle based instead on a more fundamental and significant application of power? What is the nature of power in politics? From where is it derived, and what determines its capacity? Under what conditions is it restricted or dissolved? What determines whether a society is relatively free or oppressed? What is the power basis of nonviolent action?

- Gene Sharp, "The Nature and Control of Political Power," in *Power and Struggle.*
- Gene Sharp, "Social Power and Political Freedom," in *Social Power and Political Freedom.*

The Nature of Nonviolent Struggle
Session Three

What role has this technique played in history? What are the main characteristics of this technique? How does it differ from simple abstention from violence, from violent forms of conflict, from negotiations, constitutional democratic procedures, and verbal persuasion?

- Gene Sharp, "Nonviolent Action: An Active Technique of Struggle," in *Power and Struggle.*

- Gene Sharp, "Gandhi's Political Significance," in *Gandhi as a Political Strategist*.

Session Four

What are its general and specific methods of action, or weapons?
- Gene Sharp, *The Methods of Nonviolent Action*. (*Note to Readers:* For this volume on methods only, you should read carefully all the introductory material for the volume and each chapter, and for each class and sub-class of methods, as well as at least the first paragraph (sometimes more) of each specific method. You can then skim the further detailed discussion of individual methods or the historical examples. The point is to get the general picture, the types of pressures exerted by these classes of methods, and something of their specific nature and past use, not to attempt to remember all the minute details—you can go back to look up details if you later need them.)

Sessions Five and Six

How does nonviolent struggle operate against a hostile opponent willing and able to apply violent repression? What are the mechanisms by which this technique can achieve change? What factors contribute to failure or to success? What are the long-term consequences for a society of the increased use of the technique—are they positive or negative?
- Gene Sharp, *The Dynamics of Nonviolent Action*. (*Note to Readers:* In contrast to the advice on reading about the methods, this volume does need to be read in full with care. Grasping how this technique "works" is essential for evaluating its potential and significance.)

Exploring the Policy Relevance of Nonviolent Struggle

Does this technique have any relevance for the major conflicts of today and tomorrow?

Approaches to Nonviolent Social Change
Session Seven

Does nonviolent action have any role to play in the quest for human freedom and social justice? Can it play any useful roles in extending political freedom and improving its qualities and in achieving domestic social changes? What potential exists for nonviolent social change programs or specific reforms and for more systemic changes, including popular empowerment?
- Joan Bondurant, "The Gandhian Dialectic and Political Theory," in *Conquest of Violence*.
- Gene Sharp, "Civil Disobedience in a Democracy," in *Social Power and Political Freedom*.

- Gene Sharp, "The Problem of Political Technique in Radical Politics," in *Social Power and Political Freedom*.
- Gene Sharp, "The Theory of Gandhi's Constructive Program," in *Gandhi as a Political Strategist*.
- Gene Sharp, "Popular Empowerment," in *Social Power and Political Freedom*.
- Gene Sharp, "Facing Dictatorships with Confidence," in *Social Power and Political Freedom*.

Civilian-based Defense
Sessions Eight and Nine

Can nonviolent struggle be a realistic way to deal with international aggression, internal take-overs, ruthless dictators, attempts at genocide, and oppressive systems? Could a society consciously choose to confront future threats and to wage serious conflicts by use of these nonviolent sanctions? How could such a shift occur?

- Gene Sharp, "The Political Equivalent of War—Civilian-based Defense," in *Social Power and Political Freedom*.
- Gene Sharp, *National Security Through Civilian-based Freedom*.
- Gene Sharp, "Gandhi's Defense Policy" and Gandhi as a National Defense Strategist," in *Gandhi as a Political Strategist*.
- The audiotapes "A Modern Alternative to War?" and "More on Civilian-based Defense."

More advanced readings
- Adam Roberts, "Civil Resistance to Military Coups."
- Bridgadier General Edward B. Atkeson, "The Relevance of Civilian-Based Defense to U.S. Security Interests."
- Gene Sharp, "The Lesson of Eichmann," in *Social Power and Political Freedom*.
- Alternative Defence Commission, "Strategies Against Occupation: 2. Defence by Civil Resistance," in *Defence Without the Bomb*.
- The audiotape "Making Europe Unconquerable."
- Gene Sharp, *Making Europe Unconquerable*.

Optional readings
- Dietrich Fischer, *Preventing War in the Nuclear Age*. Totowa, NJ: Rowman & Allanheld. $9.95.

Expanding the Range of Choices in Political Ethics
Session Ten

How do this technique's existence, and our conclusions as to whether it is practical, affect our perception of the range of political and ethical options among which we must choose?

- Gene Sharp, "Morality, Politics, and Political Technique," "Moral Principle or Political Technique?" and "Ethics and Responsibility in Politics," in *Gandhi as a Political Strategist*.

- Possible lecture or reproduced manuscript, "Neither Just War nor Pacifism."
- Excerpts from the Roman Catholic Bishops' Pastoral Letter on War and Peace, *The Challenge of Peace*, pp. 69–71. Washington, D.C.: United States Catholic Conference, 1983. (photocopy)
- Gene Sharp, "In Order to Speak to the Present Condition," a statement to the Council of Bishops, United Methodist Church, July 16, 1985. (photocopy)

Education, Public Information, and Research on Nonviolent Alternatives
Session Eleven

What is the relevance of the phenomenon of nonviolent action, and what are its policy implications for the development of education and public information? How can the misconceptions and lack of knowledge about nonviolent forms of struggle best be corrected? What approaches should be avoided in that effort? What are the various roles of formal courses, study groups, distribution of literature, public meetings, and similar methods? How can the wider consideration of nonviolent sanctions as an alternative to political violence be advanced in American society?

What is the role of research and policy studies? Why are these important? This is not the task for everyone—other important tasks exist—but for those with appropriate academic training, it is a possibility. What kinds of new or increased knowledge are needed? What kinds of problems merit investigation? What contribution can policy and feasibility studies make toward consideration of nonviolent options? What role can non-researchers play in making research possible? What role do research and policy studies play in the general advancement of consideration of nonviolent alternatives?

- Gene Sharp, "Investigating New Options in Conflict and Defense."
- Gene Sharp, "Research Areas and Policy Studies on Civilian-based Defense," and "Steps in Consideration of Civilian-based Defense," in *National Security Through Civilian-based Defense*.

Reassessment and Reflections
Session Twelve

We will survey where we have been and where we have come, and assess remaining and new points of discussion. How do these perspectives cause us to modify or confirm our views of the world, our perceptions of the choices before us, and our own roles?

2. Nonviolent Social Change

Harry G. Lefever   *Fall 1987*

Sociology Dept., Spelman College, Atlanta, GA 30314

This course is a study of how nonviolence was used as a method of social change in the past and how it is an option for social change today. The course focuses on the men and women who promoted nonviolence as a method of social change and the social movements they led or inspired. The examples examined are from many countries, both Third World and Western, and from a time span of several centuries. It is hoped that as a result of this course we (students and instructor) will be able to live more peaceful lives and to better promote nonviolent rather than violent methods of social change.

Course Objectives

To study the important principles and theories of nonviolence. To study the men and women who promoted nonviolence as a method of social change, and to consider the social movements they led or inspired. To investigate the relationship between socialization patterns and violent and nonviolent behavior. To encourage students to find nonviolent, rather than violent, means of social change.

Readings

Required

Cooney, Robert, and Helen Michalowski, eds. *The Power of the People: Active Nonviolence in the United States*, 1987.

Recommended

Bruyn, S.T., and P.M. Rayman, *Nonviolent Action and Social Change*, 1981.
Gregg, R. *The Power of Nonviolence*, 1959.
Sharp, G. *the Politics of Nonviolent Action* (3 vols.), 1973.
Fellowship, magazine published by the Fellowship of Reconciliation.

Course Requirements

Class attendance and participation in class discussions; three exams; two reports (oral and written)—(a) a report on some theoretical aspect of nonviolence (Pt. III), and (b) a report on one nonviolent social movement (Pt. V).

Grading

Three exams—50%; Report on nonviolent theory—20%; Report on non-violent social movement—20%; Class attendance and participation—10%.

COURSE OUTLINE

(*) signifies recommended readings.

Introduction to the Study of Nonviolence

- "Introduction to Nonviolence" (Statement by the Fellowship for Reconciliation and Resource Center for Nonviolence).
- G. Sharp, "Nonviolent Action: An Active Technique of Struggle," in *The Politics of Nonviolent Struggle*, Pt. I, ch. 2.

Origins of Violence and Nonviolence

Violence: Innate or Learned?

- A. Montagu, "The New Litany of 'Innate Depravity,' or Original Sin Revisited," *Man and Aggression* (1968); reprinted in R. Buckout et al., *Toward Social Change* (1971): pp. 139–143.
- Audiotape: "Ashley Montagu: On the Origins of Human Aggression."

The Psychology of Nonviolence

- Richard Gregg, "Moral Jiu-Jitsu," *The Power of Nonviolence*.

Socialization for Violence and Nonviolence in American Society

- A. Schlesinger, Jr., "The Dark Heart of American History," *Violence: America in the Sixties* (1968); reprinted in R. Buckout et al., *Toward Social Change* (1971): pp. 135–139.
- M. Gilula and D. Daniels, "Violence and Man's Struggle to Adapt," *Science*, 164 (April 25, 1969): pp. 396–405; reprinted in R. Buckout et al., *Toward Social Change* (1971): pp. 144–147.

Theory and Principles of Nonviolence

Overview: Ancient Times to the Present

- Matthew 5, 6, 7 (Jesus' "Sermon on the Mount").
- Chief Seattle, in Cooney & Michalowski, pp. 6–7.

Henry David Thoreau (1817–1862)

- "Civil Disobedience."

Leo Tolstoy (1828–1910)

- Excerpt from "The Kingdom of God," in *Tolstoy's Writings on Civil Disobedience and Non-Violence* (1967): pp. 285–307.

Mohandas K. Gandhi (1869–1948)
- Joan V. Bondurant, "Satyagraha: Its Basic Precepts," *Conquest of Violence,* ch. II.

Martin Luther King, Jr. (1929–1968)
- Martin Luther King, Jr., "Pilgrimage to Nonviolence," *Stride Toward Freedom,* ch. 6.
- Martin Luther King, Jr., "Letter from Birmingham Jail."

Civil Disobedience
- "Civil Disobedience," *International Encyclopedia of the Social Sciences* (*IESS*).
- Additional readings to be assigned.

Social Science Theories of Nonviolence
- S.T. Bruyn, "Social Theory of Nonviolent Action: A Framework for Research in Creative Conflict," in Bruyn & Rayman, ch. 1.
- G. Lakey, "Sociological Mechanisms of Nonviolence: How it Works," in Bruyn & Rayman.

Peace Organizations and Activities

Nonviolent Social Movements in the 19th and Early 20th Centuries
- Cooney & Michalowski, chs. 1 and 2.

The Abolition Movement in the United States
- Audiotapes: "Sojourner Truth"; "Harriet Tubman."

The Women's Rights Movement in the United States
- Audiotape: "Women to Women: Susan B. Anthony and Elizabeth Cady Stanton."
- *M. Roodkowsky, "Feminism, Peace, and Power," in Bruyn & Rayman.

Nonviolent Social Movements in the 20th Century
- *Richard Gregg, "Modern Examples of Nonviolent Resistance," *The Power of Nonviolence.*
- *P. Wehr, "Nonviolent Resistance to Occupation: Norway and Czechoslovakia," in Bruyn & Rayman.

Movements for Political, Civil and Human Rights—India (Gandhi)
- Reading to be assigned.
- Videotape: *Gandhi.*

Movements for Political, Civil and Human Rights—The Civil Rights Movement in the United States
- Cooney & Michalowski, ch. 8.
- Videotape: *Eyes on the Prize.*
- Videotape: *Memories: Dr. Martin Luther King, Jr.*

- Audiotape: "Rosa Parks."
- Audiotape: "Martin Luther King, Jr.: I Have a Dream."

Movements for Political, Civil and Human Rights—South African Movement (1950s to Present)

- C.C. Walker, "Nonviolence in Africa," in Bruyn & Rayman.

Movements for Economic Justice—The Labor Movement in the United States

- Cooney & Michalowski, ch. 3.

Movements for Economic Justice—United Farm Workers

- Cooney & Michalowski, ch. 9.
- Film: *Migrant.*
- Videotape: *Wrath of Grapes.*
- *S. Abrams, "The United Farm Workers Union," in Bruyn & Rayman.
- *M. Hope and J. Young, "The Third World in the United States: Cesar Chavez," *The Struggle for Humanity.*

Movements for Economic Justice—Poor People's Movements

- *F.F. Piven and R.A. Cloward, *Poor People's Movements.*

Anti-War and Peace Movements—WWI, WWII and the 1950s

- Cooney & Michalowski, chs. 1, 4, 5.

Anti-War and Peace Movements—The Viet Nam War to the Present

- Cooney & Michalowski, ch. 6, 7, 10.

Anti-War and Peace Movements—Latin America Since the 1960s

- "Declaration of the International Meeting of Latin American Bishops on 'Nonviolence: A Power for Liberation,'" in Adolfo Perez Esquivel, *Christ in a Poncho*, pp. 118–134.

Movements for Disarmament, Equality and a Healthy Environment

- Cooney & Michalowski, ch. 11.
- *H. Wasserman, "The Nonviolent Movement Versus Nuclear Power," in Bruyn & Rayman.

3. The Politics of Nonviolent Resistance

Stephen Zunes   *Spring 1987*
Government Dept., Cornell University, Ithaca, NY 14853

The goals of this freshman seminar are twofold: to teach the theoretical and historical bases of nonviolent action and, in the process, to help develop the basic writing composition skills expected of students at the college level.

Attendance is required for every class meeting. Unexcused absences will hurt your final grade. Students are expected to complete the assigned readings by classtime and to be prepared to comment or write about the readings, including both their content and the authors' style. There will be two feature-length movies shown during the semester at times to be announced later. Students will be expected to attend both films.

As with all freshmen seminars, there is an emphasis on writing in this course. There will be five writing assignments of 4–6 typewritten pages each and a final paper of 10–15 pages. Some of these essays will be shared in the class for peer critiques. Students dissatisfied with their performance on any of the first five papers can, after consultation with the instructor, present a re-written paper for a possible higher grade. There will be no final exam.

In addition to the specific reading assignments for each class meeting, students are expected to familiarize themselves with the Strunk & White book during the first few weeks of class, and to use it as a reference throughout the semester.

Readings

Awad, Mubarak, and Scott Kennedy. *Nonviolent Struggle and the Middle East.*
Bondurant, Joan. *Conquest of Violence: The Gandhian Philosophy of Conflict.*
Cooney, Robert, and Helen Michalowski. *The Power of the People: Active Nonviolence in the United States.*
Lakey, George. *Powerful Peacemaking: A Strategy for a Nonviolent Revolution.*
McAllister, Pam, ed. *Reweaving the Web of Life: Feminism and Nonviolence.*
Sharp, Gene. *The Politics of Nonviolent Action,* Vol. I: *Power and Struggle;* Vol. II: *The Methods of Nonviolent Struggle;* Vol. III: *The Dynamics of Nonviolent Action.*
Strunk, William, and E.B. White. *The Elements of Style.*
Wasserman, Harvey. *Energy Wars: Reports from the Front.*

COURSE OUTLINE

Jan. 27—Introduction

Jan. 29—Defining Nonviolence
Writing Assignment #1.

Feb. 3—Theory of Nonviolent Action
- Gene Sharp, *The Politics of Nonviolent Action, Vol. I: Power and Struggle*, entire.

Feb. 5—Ethical and Religious Bases of Nonviolence
- Scott Kennedy and Patrick Lacefield, "An Introduction to Nonviolence," pp. 5–12 in Therese de Connick, *Essays in Violence.*
- Adolfo Perez Esquivel, "Nonviolence: The Weapon of the Poor," pp. 29–31 in Therese de Connick, *Essays on Nonviolence.*

Feb. 10—Ethical and Religious Bases of Nonviolence (Cont'd)
- Jewish Peace Fellowship, *Roots of Jewish Nonviolence*, entire.
- William Barclay, *On Peace*, entire.
- Joseph J. Paley, *Peace, War and Christian Conscience*, entire.
- Richard Baggett Deats, "The Historic Peace Churches," entire.

Feb. 12—Nonviolence and Personal Ethics
Writing Assignment #2.

Feb. 17—Nonviolence and Sex Roles
- Cooney & Michalowski, pp. 56–61 and 213–219.
- McAllister, pp. i–viii, 20–29, 78–86, 156–161, 195–199, 231–240, 326–335, 347–351, 376–394.

Feb. 19—Nonviolence and Sex Roles (Cont'd)
Wrting Assignment #3.

Feb. 24—Gandhian Nonviolence
- Bondurant, pp. 3–104.

Feb. 26—Methods of Nonviolent Action
- Sharp, Vol. II, entire (skim).

Mar. 3—Dynamics of Nonviolent Action
- Sharp, Vol. III, pp. 451–481, 521–565, 657–697, 705–768.

Mar. 5—The Strategy of Nonviolent Action Campaigns
- Bill Moyer, "Movement Action Plan," entire.

Mar. 10—Personal Testimonies
- Hugo Adam Bedau, "Introduction," and Henry David Thoreau, "Civil Disobedience," pp. 15–48 in Bedau, ed., *Civil Disobedience.*

- Martin Luther King, Jr., "Pilgrimage to Nonviolence," pp. 379–396 in Lynd, ed., *Nonviolence in America.*
- Yvonne Dilling and Mary Jo Bowman, "Revolutionary Violence: A Dialogue on Central America."

Mar. 12—Nonviolent Action in the Labor Movement
- Cooney & Michalowski, pp. 52–71 and 176–181.

Mar. 17—Nonviolence in U.S. History: Pre-1960
- Cooney & Michalowski, pp. 14–55.
- Staughton Lynd, "Introduction," pp. xv–xiv in Lynd, ed., *Nonviolence in America.*

Mar. 19—Anti-War Movements: Personal Resistance
- Donald Benedict et al., "Why We Refuse to Register," pp. 296–299 in Staughton Lynd, ed., *Nonviolence in America.*
- Dale E. Noyd, "Particular War Objector," pp. 257–266 in Alice Lynd, ed., *We Won't Go.*
- Bob Seeley, "Three Hundred Years: The Struggle for Conscience in America."

Mar. 31—Anti-War Movements: Direct Action
- Cooney & Michalowski, pp. 182–209 and 228–245.
- Hugo Adam Bedau, "Introduction" to anti-war section, pp. 119–125 in Bedau, *Civil Disobedience.*
- "A Call to Resist Illegitimate Authority," pp. 162–164 in Bedau, ed., *Civil Disobedience.*
- Martin Luther King, Jr., "Declaration of Independence from the War in Vietnam."
- Richard Taylor, "Blockading for Bangladesh," in *The Progressive*, Feb. 1971 (for a detailed account, see Taylor, *Blockade*, pp. 3–101).
- Renny Golden, "Sanctuary: Churches Take Part in New Underground Railroad," *Sojourners*, Dec. 1982.
- Sanctuary Media Packet, "Emphases Within the Sanctuary Movement."
- Richard Baggett Deats, "Nonviolent Witness in Nicaragua," *The Christian Century*, March 7, 1984.

Apr. 2—The Civil Rights Struggle
- Cooney & Michalowski, pp. 150–175.

Apr. 7—The Civil Rights Struggle (Cont'd)
- Hugo Adam Bedau, Introduction to "Against Racism" section, pp. 51–58 in Bedau, ed., *Civil Disobedience.*
- Martin Luther King, Jr., "Letter from Birmingham City Jail," pp. 72–89 in Bedau, ed., *Civil Disobedience* (also pp. 461–481 in Lynd, ed., *Nonviolence in America*).
- Thomas Gaither, "Jailed-In," pp. 399–415 in Lynd, ed., *Nonviolence in America.*

- William Mahoney, "In Pursuit of Freedom," pp. 415–428 in Lynd, ed., *Nonviolence in America.*
- Louis Waldman, "Civil Rights—Yes; Civil Disobedience—No (A Reply to Dr. Martin Luther King)," pp. 106–118 in Bedau, ed., *Civil Disobedience.*
- Susan Kling, "Fannie Lou Hamer: Baptism by Fire," pp. 106–111 in McAllister.
- April Carter, "From Civil Rights to Black Power," pp. 57–74 in *Direct Action and Liberal Democracy.*
- Julius Lester, "The Angry Children of Malcolm X," pp. 346–380 in Meier, Rudwick, & Broderick, eds., *Black Protest Thought in the Twentieth Century.*
- Dave Dellinger, "The Future of Nonviolence," pp. 520–530 in Lynd, ed., *Nonviolence in America* (also in Dellinger, *Revolutionary Nonviolence,* pp. 293–301).

Apr. 9—Civil Rights Struggle (Cont'd)
Writing Assignment #4.

Apr. 14—Nonviolent Action on Energy and the Environment
- Harvey Wasserman, *Energy Wars: Reports from the Front,* pp. ix–xii, 1–23, 49–55, 69–85, 101–115, 127–129, 219–240 and 248–253.
- Stephen Zunes, "Seabrook: A Turning Point," *The Progressive,* Sept. 1978.
- Pamela Haines and William Moyer, "No Nukes Is Not Enough: Toward a People's Energy Movement." *The Progressive,* March 1981.
- Cooney & Michalowski, pp. 220–227.

Apr. 16—Nonviolent Action on Energy and the Environment (Cont'd)
Writing Assignment #4.

Apr. 21—Nonviolence in the Middle East
- Awad & Kennedy, entire (also in *Journal of Palestine Studies,* Winter 1984 and Summer 1984).
- Nat Hentoff, "Saying No to Illegitimate Authority in the West Bank," *Village Voice,* July 3, 1983.
- Frank Collins, "Nonviolent Struggle in the Middle East," *The Progressive,* July 1985.
- Lynne Shivers, "Inside the Iranian Revolution," pp. 56–78 in David Albert, ed., *Tell the American People: Perspectives on the Iranian Revolution.*

Apr. 23—Nonviolence in South Africa
- Stephen Zunes, "Revolution and Change in South Africa: The Case for Nonviolence."

Apr. 28—Nonviolence in the Phillippines
- Monina Allarey Mercado, ed., *People Power: An Eyewitness History,* entire.
- Stephen Zunes, "Active Nonviolence in the Phillippines: Its History and Triumph."

Apr. 30—Nonviolent Defense
- Gene Sharp, *Making Europe Unconquerable,* pp. 1–38, 67–74, 82–88, 90–108, 164–193.

May 5—Nonviolent Revolution
- Lakey, pp. TBA.

May 7—Summary

May 15
Final paper due.

4. Peace and Nonviolence*

Ross A. Klein   *Spring 1987*
Sociology Dept., Skidmore College,
Saratoga Springs, NY 12866

> *There is no such thing as a neutral educational process. Education either functions as an instrument which is used to facilitate the integration of the younger generation into the logic of the present system and bring about conformity to it, or it becomes "the practice of freedom," the means by which men and women deal critically and creatively with reality and discover how to participate in the transformation of their world.*
>
> —Richard Shaull

This course will focus on the issue of social change and how change can be facilitated through nonviolent action. Focusing on the nineteenth and twentieth centuries, the course will examine the concepts of peace and non-violence, survey the proponents and practitioners of nonviolent activism and of peaceful existence, and study the socio-historical context within

---

*Ross Klein also teaches a slightly amended version of this course at the Washington Correctional Facility, a medium-security prison 50 miles from Skidmore College.

which these ideas and movements emerged. The course will survey the concepts and theory underlying such things as active and passive resistance, noncooperation, civil disobedience, nonviolent activism, nonviolent national defense, pacifism, and activism for peace. The practical and the theoretical side of each concept will be considered, as will the implications of adhering to ideals associated with them. A concrete understanding of the concept and practice of nonviolent activism and of activism for peace will be gained from the consideration of specific activists and thinkers representing a variety of fields. The historical development of ideas supporting nonviolent activism and peaceful change will be studied, interrelationships of thinkers and ideas traced, and socio-historical forces impacting on non-violent thought and practice explored. The student will focus on nonviolent means for creating social change, as well as on socio-historical forces in time and space that have impacted and shaped these ideas across the nineteenth and twentieth centuries.

A number of proponents and practitioners of nonviolent activism and peaceful existence will be carefully considered in the course. These include: Henry David Thoreau, Jane Addams, Mohandas Gandhi, and Martin Luther King. Others who will be given attention include Leo Tolstoy, Rosa Luxembourg, Emma Goldman, Bertha von Suttner, and A.J. Muste. The course will also consider present-day organizations and individuals working for the cause of peace and nonviolent change.

The course overall has six objectives. By the end of the semester, the student should be able to:

1. Define and distinguish among active resistance, passive resistance, noncooperation, civil disobedience, pacifism, and nonviolent national defense.
2. Compare and contrast the nonviolent activism of Mohandas Gandhi and Martin Luther King, Jr.
3. Trace the development of nonviolent action theory from the early nineteenth century to the present day.
4. Identify and describe the positions taken by major practitioners and proponents of nonviolent change/peace.
5. Behave and communicate in ways free of violence.
6. Articulate and defend his or her own position with regard to nonviolence as a means for creating change and peaceful coexistence.

Class Structure

Class time will be a relatively even mix of lectures and discussion. Students are expected to have read the pages assigned for each class session and to engage in discussion about what they have read. Class sessions will range from being loosely structured (so as to allow students the opportunity to discuss those issues and ideas that are salient from their reading) to more formally structured (i.e., lectures) so as to allow dissemination of material that will supplement student understanding of the required readings and issues raised in readings and in class. In engaging in discussion of ideas, students are expected to respect the views and positions expressed by others. While a student may choose to disagree with and critique another's views, criticizing another for holding the views or beliefs he or she professes will not be tolerated.

Grading for the course will be based on five criteria. They are: (1) 10% for class attendance and participation. (2) 30% for weekly essays based on questions given out each Friday. Essays are due the following Monday and should be approximately 500 words in length. (3) 15% for essay defining peace and nonviolence. Specifically, provide a definition and discussion of your conception of nonviolence and of peace. Treating each concept separately, describe how you conceive of each, what each means to you individually and to your social relations with others, and discuss the role each has in your life. Finally, discuss the role you see nonviolence having in creating social change, if any, and discuss the prospects for peace on a national and an international scale. This paper should be eight to ten pages long and is due Jan. 26. (4) 30% for a formal research paper. Choose a peace activist or advocate of nonviolent change. In developing the paper, you should discuss the person's social and political background, the substance of his or her ideas and where his or her ideas were drawn from, the nature of his or her activism and the success of his or her action, and the impact he or she has had on creating lasting change. The paper should be both a presentation of what the person advocated and a critique/analysis of his or her thought. Those activists covered in class (i.e., Thoreau, Gandhi, King) cannot be used for this paper. If help is needed in identifying an activist, you should feel free to consult the instructor. This paper should be comprehensive and complete; its length will depend on your writing style and the person you have chosen to discuss. It is due April 13th. (5) 15% for a final in-class essay given during exam week. The essay will ask you to assume you have been asked to teach a course on peace and nonviolence. It will ask you how you would structure the course and what organizing concepts you would use to hold the course together and to provide continuity. Further, what would be important to cover and who would be necessary to cover, and to what extent? This essay is a thought essay and is intended as a means for pulling the course material together in some coherent and structured way.

Required Readings

Borman, William. *Gandhi and Nonviolence.* Albany: State University of New York Press, 1986.

Brock-Utne, Birgit. *Educating for Peace: A Feminist Perspective.* New York: Pergamon Press, 1985.

Ferencz, Benjamin B. *A Common Sense Guide to World Peace.* New York: Oceana Publications, 1985.

Gregg, Richard B. *The Power of Nonviolence.* Weare, NH: Greenleaf Books, 1960.

Hendrick, George. "The Influence of Thoreau's 'Civil Disobedience' on Gandhi's Satyagraha," *The New England Quarterly,* 29:462–71, 1956.

King, Martin Luther, Jr. *Why We Can't Wait.* New York: Harper and Row, 1963, pp. 15–38, 77–100.

————. *The Trumpet of Conscience.* New York: Harper and Row, 1967 (excerpts).

Nye, Joseph S. *Nuclear Ethics.* New York: Free Press, 1986.

Sharp, Gene. *Gandhi as a Political Strategist: With Essays on Ethics and Politics.*

Thoreau, Henry David. *Civil Disobedience.*

COURSE SCHEDULE

Jan. 19—Introduction

Jan. 21 & 23—Social Power: Its Bases and Uses

Jan. 26—Examples of Nonviolence
- Gregg, pp. 15–42.

Jan. 28 & 30—What Is Peace?
- Brock-Utne, pp. 1–32.

Feb. 2 & 4—Socialization for Violence/War
- Brock-Utne, pp. 70–110.

Feb. 6—Civil Disobedience
- Thoreau.
- Hendrick.

Feb. 9—The Power of Nonviolence
- Gregg, pp. 43–112.

Feb. 11—Peer Critique of Feb. 9th Essay

Feb. 13—The Power of Nonviolence
- Gregg, pp. 113–175.

Feb. 16—Film: *Gandhi's India*

Feb. 18—Film: *Gandhi**

Feb. 20—Satyagraha: The Practical Application of Nonviolence
- Borman, pp. 19–94.

Feb. 23—Types of Nonviolence
- Borman, pp. 95–115.
- Sharp, pp. 201–234; 273–309.

---

*Not the feature-length version.

Feb. 25 & 27—Critical Analysis of Gandhi's Thought
- Borman, pp. 119–198; 199–253.

Mar. 2—Martin Luther King: An Introduction
- King, *Why We Can't Wait.*

Mar. 4 & 6—Film: *Martin Luther King: The Man and the March*

Mar. 9—Film: *Martin Luther King: From Montgomery to Memphis.*

Mar. 11—Peer Critique Meetings

Mar. 13—Discussion: *The Trumpet of Conscience*

Mar. 23—Peace Activists on the Political Left

Mar. 25 & 27—Peace Activists: Women and Feminism
- Brock-Utne, pp. 33–69.

Mar. 30—Science, Higher Education and Peace Research
- Brock-Utne, pp. 11–149.

Apr. 1—The Structure of a Science Oriented Toward Peace and Nonviolence

Apr. 3—Peer Critique of Essays Due March 30

Apr. 6–10—Prospects for World Peace
- Ferencz, pp. vii–xvi; 1–98.

Apr. 13—Discussion of Papers

Apr. 15 & 17—Peer Critique Meetings

Apr. 20–24—Student Presentations

Apr. 27–May 1—The Nuclear Arms Race
- Nye, pp. 1–132.

5. Nonviolent Political Alternatives

Glenn Paige   *Fall 1988*
Political Science Dept., University of Hawaii–Manoa,
Honolulu, HI 96822

Conventional thought in the United States and many other societies—but not all—holds that the best way to solve domestic and international problems is to "get tough." This means arming ourselves to kill, making threats to kill, and demonstrating credibility by actual killing. Thus we fight crime by arming ourselves, demand capital punishment, threaten nuclear and "conventional" war, and extend our military power throughout the land, sea, and airspace of the earth as well as into outer space. Other societies have variations on the same theme, although a few have no armies, no capital punishment, unarmed police, unarmed citizens, and no intention of seeking global or regional military dominance.

One objective of a liberal arts education is to expand awareness of the cultural heritage of humankind as well as to develop a capacity for independent judgment. A university at its best seeks to nurture greater wisdom in oncoming generations than that which produced the problems bequeathed by predecessors.

This course challenges the assumption that what is wrong with contemporary civilization is that it has been too "weak" and "pacifistic." It advances the thesis that one root of the present difficulties facing humankind is that we have been too militaristic and too accepting of violence. It introduces past and present voices that cry out for the development of knowledge and wisdom to find alternatives to violence—not just threats of greater killing and destruction. The perspective is global, not just that of the United States.

There will be one lecture and one workshop discussion each week. Each participant will select a problem such as family violence, gender violence, school violence, homicide, armed robbery and assault, police violence, prison violence, the death penalty, media violence, sports violence, cultural violence, economic violence, ethnic violence, genocide, torture and repression, assassination, terrorism, armed revolution and counterrevolution, civil war, international war, and other forms of actual, threatened or commended killing. Together we will seek to explore and share worthwhile nonviolent alternatives.

A mid-term examination will have two parts: one to examine understanding of the basic ideas presented in the readings and lectures; another to measure capacity to argue for or against them from alternative points of view. A term paper will present the results of workshop projects and will be judged by capacity to identify and appraise alternatives. A final examination will provide an opportunity to review and reflect upon the course experience.

Participants should find the course a profoundly meaningful intellectual challenge, with significance reverberating far beyond the college years.

Basis of Grading
Mid-term examination—25%. Workshop participation—25%. Independent essay—25%. Final examination—25%.

Independent Essay
Please submit a 5–10 page paper on or before May 5. Late penalty 10%.

Final Examination
Tuesday, May 10.

Reading
Cooney, Robert, and Helen Michalowski. *Power of the People: Active Nonviolence in the United States.*
Gandhi, Mohandas K. *The Science of Satyagraha.*
Paige, Glenn D., ed. *Roots of Nonviolent Politics.*
Ross, David F., and Mahendra S. Kanthi. *Gandhian Economics.*
Sharp, Gene. *The Politics of Nonviolent Action* (Parts I, II, and III).
Shepard, Mark. *Gandhi Today.*
Sivard, Ruth Leger. *World Military and Social Expenditures, 1987.*

AGENDA

Jan. 14—Discussion
Is a nonkilling society possible?

Jan. 19—Lecture: The Logic of Nonviolent Political Analysis
• Konrad, "Violence and the Philosopher," in Paige.

Jan. 21—Discussion
Can you share any personal experience with violence? How might the logic of nonviolent analysis be applied?

Jan. 26—Lecture: Principles of Nonviolent Political Action
• Sharp, pp. 1–108.

Jan. 28—Discussion
How might the principles of nonviolent action be applied in a case of violence with which you are familiar?

Feb. 2—Lecture: Roots of Violence and Nonviolent Alternatives
- Tsai, "Peace and Cooperation Among Natural Enemies," in Paige.
- Eibl-Eibesfeldt, "Biological Roots of a Nonkilling Ethic," in Paige.
- Restak, "Nonviolent Self-Control of a Violent Brain," in Paige.

Feb. 4—Discussion
What do you think will be the subject of your workshop project and subsequent independent essay?

Feb. 9—Lecture: Nonviolent Alternatives in Language and Culture
- Gandhi, the first half.
- Cooley, "Beating Swords into Plowshares," in Paige.

Feb. 11—Discussion
Select an example of violence-prone language or imagery from everyday life and suggest a viable alternative.

Feb. 16—Lecture: Global Resources for Nonviolent Thought and Action
- Sivard, *World Military and Social Expenditures, 1987.*
- Gandhi, the second half.

Feb. 18—Discussion
What is the world configuration of violence-accepting forces? What countervailing configuration of nonviolent forces is possible and desirable?

Feb. 23—Lecture: Is Nonviolent Revolution Possible?
- Aristotle, "Changes in Constitution Without Violence," in Paige.
- Machiavelli, "From Liberty to Servitude and from Servitude to Liberty—Without Bloodshed," in Paige.
- Zhang, "We Should Positively Affirm Nonviolence," in Paige.
- Plimak and Karyakin, "Lenin on Peaceful and Nonpeaceful Forms of Revolutionary Transition to Socialism," in Paige.

Feb. 25—Discussion
What special obstacles to nonviolent revolution are posed by different types of regimes? What priority actions are appropriate for each?

Mar. 1—Discussion
Review. Bring outstanding questions needful of clarification in preparation for mid-term examination.

Mar. 3—Mid-term Examination
What basic ideas have been presented in lectures, readings, and discussions? With which do you agree or disagree? Why?

Mar. 8—Lecture: Can Nonviolent Politics Cope with a Mad Dictator?
- Sharp, Parts I, II, and III.

Mar. 10—Discussion
Select a case of dictatorship and suggest countervailing nonviolent actions that reasonably might be considered.

Mar. 15—Lecture: Nonviolent Common Security and the Shanti Sea
- Gene Keyes, "Force Without Firepower," in Paige.
- M. Aram and N. Radhakrishnan, *Training Youth to Nonviolence*. (To be provided.)

Mar. 17—Discussion
Field exercise to demonstrate some nonviolent action principles. Please wear comfortable outside clothing that can stand some scuffing.

Mar. 29—Lecture: Nonviolent Political Economy
- Ross and Kanthi.

Mar. 31—Discussion
What forms of nonviolent economy seem reasonable? Can you think of a new nonviolent economic service or enterprise? One to assist transition? What possibilities and priorities of transition from present violence-based capitalist or socialist economics do you suggest for consideration?

Apr. 5—Lecture: Nonviolent Community Transformation—Hawaii
- Shepard.

Apr. 7—Discussion
Suggest at least one innovation that would make Hawaii a more nonviolent society and a greater contributor to nonviolent national, regional, or global transformation.

Apr. 12—Lecture: Nonviolent Global Transformation
- *Universal Declaration of Human Rights*, in Paige.
- *Final Document of Assembly Session on Disarmament—1982*, in Paige.
- Inga Thorsson, "Environment, Development, Disarmament—Towards a Global Tomorrow," in Paige.
- Nobel Prize Recipients, "Manifesto on the Holocaust of Hunger and Political Deprivation," in Paige.

Apr. 14—Discussion
What are the three most important things you think should be done to improve nonviolent processes of problem-solving in each of the areas of (1) security and disarmament, (2) economic equity, (3) human rights, (4) environmental vitality, and (5) global problem-solving cooperation?

Apr. 19 & 21—Reports: Shared Explorations of Alternatives
- Cooney and Michalowski, pp. 1–150.

Apr. 26 & 28—Reports: Shared Exploration of Alternatives
- Cooney and Michalowski, pp. 151–270.

May 3—Reports: Shared Explorations of Alternatives
- Burgess, "Battlefield Vow," in Paige.
- Paige, "Nonviolent Political Science," in Paige.

May 5—Lecture & Discussion: Nonviolence and the 21st Century

XIV

Social Movements and Revolution

1. War and Peace Movements in Twentieth-Century America

Roger Burbach   *Spring 1987*
Peace and Conflict Studies Program, University of
California–Berkeley, Berkeley, CA 94305

Required Texts for Course
DeBenedetti, Charles. *The Peace Reform in American History.* Bloomington:
    Indiana University Press, 1980.
Wittner, Lawrence S. *Rebels Against War: The American Peace Movement, 1933–
    1983.* Philadelphia: Temple University Press, 1984.

Recommended Books for Course
DeBenedetti, Charles. *Peace Heroes in Twentieth Century America.* Bloom-
    ington: Indiana Univ. Press, 1986.
Eagan, Eileen. *Class, Culture and the Classroom: The Student Peace Movement
    of the 1930s.* Philadelphia: Temple Univ. Press, 1981.

Reference
Howlett, Charles F., and Glen Zeitzer. 1985. *The American Peace Movement:
    History and Historiography.* Washington, D.C.: American Historical As-
    sociation.

LECTURES AND
READING ASSIGNMENTS

January 19 & 21—War or Peace: America's Dilemma

- "Peace in the Classroom," *Newsweek* (Oct. 1987).
- DeBenedetti, 1986: Introduction and Afterword by Merle Curti, pp. 1–27, 255–270.

January 26 & 28—War and Peace Movements from the Colonies to 1898

- DeBenedetti, 1980: Preface & pp. 3–78.

February 2 & 4—Rise of the Anti-Imperialist Movement, 1898–1901

- Gatewood, Willard B., Jr. 1975. *Black Americans and the White Man's Burden, 1898–1903.* Urbana, IL: University of Chicago Press, chs. 1, 8 & 9, pp. 1–21, 180–260.
- Welch, Richard E. 1972. *Response to Imperialism: The United states and the Philippine-American War, 1899–1902.* Chapel Hill: University of North Carolina Press, chs. 3 & 8, pp. 43–57, 117–131.
- Tompkins, E. Berkeley. 1970. *Anti-Imperialism in the United States: The Great Debate, 1898–1920.* Philadelphia: University of Pennsylavania Press, ch. 15, pp. 236–256.
- Twain, Mark. "To a Person Sitting in Darkness."

February 9 & 11—Disarmament, Pacifism, Social Reform and Opposition to World War I

Guest Lecturer: David Landes, Foothill College.

- DeBenedetti, 1980: ch. 5, pp. 79–107.
- Marchand, C. Roland. 1972. *The American Peace Movement and Social Reform, 1898–1918.* Princeton: Princeton University Press, chs. 5, 6 & 8, pp. 144–223, 266–322.
- DeBenedetti, 1986: chs. 1 & 2, pp. 28–84.

February 16 & 18—The Pacifist and Anti-War Movements in the 1920s

- Curti, Merle. 1936. *Peace or War: The American Struggle, 1636–1936,* chs. 9 & 10, pp. 262-210.
- DeBenedetti, 1980: ch. 6, pp. 108–137.
- Hentoff, Nat, ed. 1967. *The Essays of A.J. Muste.* New York: The Bobbs-Merrill Company, Inc. Read "Pacifism and Class War," pp. 179–186.
- Lewis, John. 1973. *The Case Against Pacifism.* London: George Allen & Unwin Ltd. Preface & ch. 11, pp. 5–12, 233–238.

February 23 & 25—Opposition to U.S. Intervention in Nicaragua and the Caribbean in the 1920s and 1930s

- Nearing, Scott, and Joseph Freeman. 1925. *Dollar Diplomacy: A Study in American Imperialism.* New York: Viking Press, ch. 9 (partial), pp. 258–280 .

- Selser, Gregorio. 1981. *Sandino, General of the Free*, Monthly Review Press, chs. 5, 6, & 8; pp. 62–87, 102–116.
- Collected readings on U.S. Opposition to Intervention.

March 1—Examination

March 3—Guest Lecturers
Hazel Grossman & Dick Riley (student peace activists in the 1930s).

March 8 & 10—Pacifism, Isolationism and the Anti-Fascist Movement in the 1930s
- Wittner, 1984: ch. 1, pp. 1–33.
- Eagan, 1981: chs. 4 & 5, pp. 97–150.

March 15 & 17—Opposition to World War II
- Wittner, 1984: ch. 1, pp. 1–33.
- Eagan, 1981: ch. 1, pp. 3–10, pp. 19–29, pp. 57–182.
- DeBenedetti, 1986: ch. on A.J. Muste, pp. 147–167.
- Westbrook, Robert. 1986. "Horrors—Their War and Ours: The Politics Circle and the Good War," *Radical History Review*, No. 36, pp. 9–15.
- MacDonald, Dwight. 1957. *Memoirs of a Revolutionist: Essays in Political Criticism*. New York: Farrar, Straus and Cudahy, pp. 159–179.

March 22 & 24—The Crisis of the Peace Movement: The Korean War and the Cold War
Guest participant in discussion section: Leon Wofsy, U.C. Professor, radical activist in the 1950s.
- Wittner, 1984: chs. 6, 7 & 8, pp. 151–239.
- Eagan, 1981: ch. 11, pp. 233–263.
- Cumings, Bruce. 1986. "Reckoning with the Korean War," *The Nation*, Oct. 25, pp. 393, 406–409.

April 5—The Cold War: Peace Through Military Preparedness?
Guest Lecturer: Captain Lee McClain, Assistant Instructor in R.O.T.C. program, U.C. Berkeley.

April 7—Examination
Guest participant in discussion: Madeline Duckles (peace activist in the 1950s and 1960s).
- Wittner, 1984: chs. 9 & 10, pp. 240–275.
- Swerdlow, Amy. "Ladies' Day at the Capitol: Women Strike for Peace Versus HUAC," *Feminist Studies*, vol. 8, no. 3 (Fall 1982), pp. 493-520.
- Grooms, Mary. 1962. "The Turn Toward Politics: Peace Takes to the Hustings," *The Nation*, July 28: pp. 27–29.
- Martinson, Robert. 1962. "A City Chose Peace." *The Nation*, Feb. 10: pp. 117–119.

April 14 & 19—the Rise of Anti-War Movements & Vietnam in the 1960s

Guest participant in discussion: Elizabeth Farnsworth, KQED (media and research activist).

- Zaroulis, Nancy, and Gerald Sullivan. 1984. *Who Spoke Up? American Protest Against the War in Vietnam 1963–1975*, pp. 1–68.
- Albert, Judith Clavir, and Stewart Edward Albert. 1984. *The Sixties Papers: Documents of a Rebellious Decade*, pp. 2–63.
- Breines, Wini. 1982. *Community and Organization in the New Left, 1962–68*, pp. xi–xv, 1–45.

April 19—Vietnam's Aftermath: The 1970s and 1980s

Theme for term papers: The Lessons of the Past for the Present.

- Joseph, Paul. 1981. *Cracks in the Empire*. Boston: South End Press, pp. 153–179, 287–305.
- Burbach, Roger. "The War at Home and Abroad," in *Transition and Development*, eds: Richard Fagen, Carmen Diana Deere and Jose Luis Coraggio.
- Klare, Michael, and Peter Kornbluh, eds. 1987. *Low Intensity Warfare*. Chs. to be assigned.
- Guest participation in discussion: Peter Camejo (anti-war activist and presidential candidate in 1976).

April 26—Non-Intervention Movements and Central America

Student presentations of papers on this topic.

May 3—The Anti-Nuclear Movement in the 1980s

Student presentations of papers on this topic.

May 5—The Anti-Apartheid Movement

Student presentations of papers on this topic.

May 12—Final Examination

2. Draft Resistance in U.S. History

Dave List   *Spring 1987*

Program on Nonviolent Conflict and Change,
Syracuse University, Syracuse, NY 13244

This course will examine the history of noncooperation with compulsory military service in the United States. We will consider religious and political resisters, pacifists and selective objectors, socialists and libertarian capitalists. Some intellectual figures who have had a key impact on the thinking of peace activists will also be read, including Thoreau, A.J. Muste, and Martin Luther King, Jr. The antidraft activity studied will range from revolts to hunger strikes in prison and from Congressional debates to GI antiwar organizing. The role of antidraft issues in the 1930s student peace movement, the labor movement, the contemporary feminist movement, and the struggle for Afro-American rights will also be noted.

Course requirements include a twelve page-research paper and six written questions on each week's readings. There are no exams or tests. There will be at least one guest speaker who has direct experience in the antidraft movement.

Required Readings

Graham, John R. *The Draft: By What Authority? A Constitutional History of the Military Draft.* Minneapolis, MN: Ross and Haines, 1971.

Kohn, Stephen M. *Jailed for Peace: The History of American Draft Law Violators, 1658–1985.* Westport, CT: Greenwood, 1985.

O'Sullivan, John, and Alan M. Meckler, eds. *The Draft and Its Enemies: A Documentary History.* Chicago, IL: University of Illinois, 1974.

Eichel, Julius. *The Judge Said "20 Years": The Story of a Conscientious Objector in World War I.* Yonkers, NY: A M P & R, 1981.

Kniss, Lloyd A. *I Couldn't Fight: Experiences of a Conscientious Objector in World War I.* Scottsdale, PA: Herald, 1974.

Goldman, Emma. *Preparedness: The Road to Universal Slaughter and the Individual, Society and the State,* pamphlet published as Essay No. 5 of A.J. Muste Memorial Insitute's *Essay Series.* New York, NY: A.J. Muste Memorial Institute, n.d.

Reserved Readings

Ameringer, Oscar. *If You Don't Weaken.* Chicago, IL: Charles Kerr, 1986 (autobiography of socialist organizer; excerpt is account of WWI revolt).

Anderson, Jervis. *A. Philip Randolph: A Biographical Portrait.* New York, NY: Harcourt Brace Jovanovich, 1973 (excerpt on how threat of draft resistance helped desegregate U.S. military).

Bedau, Hugo A., ed. *Civil Disobedience: Theory and Practice.* New York, NY: Pegasus, 1969 (excerpt is Thoreau's "Civil Disobedience").

Cook, Blanche Wiesen, ed. *Crystal Eastman on War and Revolution.* New York, NY: Oxford University, 1978 (excerpt on efforts to aid conscientious objectors).

Cooney, Robert, and Helen Michalowski. *The Power of the People: Active Nonviolence in America.* Culver City, CA: Peace Press, 1977 (excerpt on religious pacifism in 1600s).

Ekirch, Arthur A., Jr. *The Civilian and the Military: A History of the American Anti-Militarist Tradition.* New York, NY: R. Myles, 1972.

Ferber, Michael, and Staughton Lynd. *The Resistance.* Boston, MA: Beacon, 1970 (excerpts on precedents for Viet Nam resistance and on draft card protests, etc.).

Flynn, John T. *As We Go Marching.* New York, NY: Free Life Editions, 1973 (excerpt critiques draft as liberal-fascist "public works" program).

Gara, Larry. *War Resistance in Historical Perspective.* Lebanon, PA: Pendle Hill/Sowers Printing, 1970 (reprint by War Resisters League, 1981).

Hurwitz, Deena, and Craig Simpson, eds. *Against the Tide: Pacifist Resistance in the Second World War—An Oral History.* New York, NY: War Resisters League, 1983 (this is the 1984 War Resisters League desk calendar).

Jacobs, Paul, and Saul Landau, eds. *The New Radicals: A Report with Documents.* New York, NY: Vintage, 1969 (excerpts are documents of black students' antidraft declarations and an appeal to GIs).

Kittrie, Nicholas N., and Eldon D. Wedlock. *The Tree of Liberty: A Documentary History of Rebellion and Political Crime in America.* Baltimore, MD: Johns Hopkins University, 1986 (excerpts are accounts of 1982 Selective Service sit-in and Supreme Court's 1985 ruling on selective prosecution in *U.S. v. Wayte*).

Kohlman, W. "Our Missing Link." *Newsweek* 100 (July 1982), p. 13 (essay on connection between draft and nuclear disarmament).

Lynd, Staughton, ed. *Nonviolence in America: A Documentary History.* Indianapolis, IN: Bobbs-Merrill, 1966 (excerpt is M.L. King's "Letter from a Birmingham Jail").

McAllister, Pam, ed. *Reweaving the Web of Life: Feminism and Nonviolence* (excerpts on feminism's impact on peace movement, women and draft, male roles and the military).

Muste, Abraham J. *The Essays of A.J. Muste* (Nat Hentoff, editor). New York, NY: Simon and Shuster, 1970 (excerpt is "Of Holy Disobedience").

O'Brien, James. "Wobblies and Draftees: The IWW's Wartime Dilemma, 1917–1918." *Radical America* 1 (Sept. 1967), pp. 6–18 (excerpt on radical union and draft).

Peck, James. *Underdogs Versus Upperdogs.* New York, NY: A M P & R, 1980 (excerpt is account of prison desegregation strike from autobiography).

Schlissel, Lillian, ed. *Conscience in America: A Documentary History, 1757–1967.* New York, NY: Dutton, 1968.

Sibley, Mulford Q., ed. *The Quiet Battle.* Boston, MA: Beacon, 1963 (excerpt is trial transcript of a Christian resister, A.D. 295).

Stapp, Andy. *Up Against the Brass.* New York, NY: Simon & Schuster, 1970 (excerpt is Stapp's account of work as GI antiwar organizer).

Thomas, Norman. "'Hire Learning' at Ohio State." *Nation,* June 1931 (article is account of professor fired for part in anti-ROTC protests).

Wallis, Jim, ed. *Peacemakers: Christian Voices from the New Abolitionist Movement.* San Francisco, CA: Harper & Row, 1983 (selection is an interview with activist Mennonite nonregistrant from 1982 *Sojourners* magazine).

Wittner, Lawrence. *Rebels Against War: The American Peace Movement, 1933–1983.* New York, NY: Columbia University, 1982.

COURSE OUTLINE
AND READING ASSIGNMENTS

Week 1—Religious Background and Colonial Era
- Graham, pp. 1–44.
- Kohn, pp. 3–24.
- Gara, pp. 1–21.
- Cooney & Michalowski, pp. 14–22.
- Sibley, p. 17.

Week 2—Revolutionary War Era Through the 1850s
- Graham, pp. 45–92.
- O'Sullivan, pp. 40–50.
- Bedau, pp. 27-48.

Week 3—Civil War
- Graham, pp. 93–114.
- O'Sullivan, pp. 53–61, 67–72, & 93–101.
- Ekirch, pp. 90–116.
- Schlissel, pp. 102–127.

Week 4—World War I
- Kohn, pp. 25–44.
- O'Sullivan, pp. 103–107, 111–115, 129–139, 149–151.
- Kniss, pp. 1–47.
- Goldman, pp. 1–27.
- O'Brien, pp. 6–18.

Week 5—World War I, cont'd.
- Eichel, pp. 1–90.
- Cook, pp. 252–265.
- Ameringer, pp. 347–358.

Week 6—The 1930s and World War II
- Kohn, pp. 45–62.
- O'Sullivan, pp. 156–163, 173–176.
- Peck, pp. 35–86.
- Thomas, pp. 654–656.
- Wittner, pp. 1–33.

Week 7—World War II, cont'd.
- O'Sullivan, pp. 186–191, 196–202, 213–219.
- Wittner, pp. 62–97.
- Hurwitz, all (no pagination, about 25 pages).
- Flynn, pp. 213–212.

Week 8

No readings. Term paper due. Guest speaker(s).

Week 9—Between World War II and Vietnam: 1946–1963
- Kohn, pp. 63–72.
- Muste, pp. 355–377.
- Lynd, pp. 461–481.
- Wittner, pp. 151–164.
- Ekirch, pp. 271–290.
- Anderson, pp. 274–282.

Week 10—The Vietnam War
- O'Sullivan, pp. 220–229.
- Ferbery & Lynd, pp. 1–44.
- Schlissel, pp. 271–312.
- Jacobs & Landau, pp. 249–257.

Week 11—The Vietnam War, cont'd.
- Kohn, pp. 73–100.
- Stapp, pp. 11–17, 28–54, 83–91.
- Schlissel, pp. 316–320.
- Ferber & Lynd, pp. 149–184.
- McAllister, pp. 135–142.

Week 12—The Carter/Reagan Era: Draft Registration and Resistance
- Kohn, pp. 101–110.
- McAllister, pp. 322–335.
- Kittrie & Wedlock, pp. 620–623, 637–639.
- Wallis, pp. 135–143.
- Kohlman, p. 13.
- *New York Times* articles on Andy Mager's case: 5 Jan. 1985, sec. 1, p. 21.; 6 Jan. 1985, sec. 11, p. 1; 9 Jan. 1985, sec. 2, p. 24; 11 Jan. 1985, sec. 2, p. 2; 5 Feb. 1985, sec. 2, p. 5.

3. Movements for Peace and Social Change: Violence and Nonviolence

Nigel Young   *Spring 1987*
Peace Studies Program, Colgate University,
Hamilton, NY 13346

This course is intended for those students with a general interest in social movements, political change and issues of peace and justice. The course focuses on two main themes: a theoretical examination of social change movements from a sociological and transdisciplinary peace studies perspective, and an applied analysis of particular movements using a historical and empirical approach (about ten case studies) on movements for peace, social change and social justice. The course is concerned with basic issues in the relationship between the concept of peace and the desire to change society: Does the first entail the second? How do societies change? When do they change peacefully and when violently? How far is social change humanly controlled? To what extent can societies move toward peace, insofar as it involves changing violent structures and confronting social injustice, and still avoid intended or unintended violence? What kinds of examples of peaceful change and peaceful structures can one find historically and in contemporary society? Are they relevant to all situations?

A particular focus of this course is on the political sociology and history of social and political movements concerned with international peace, social revolution or radical reform, and the abolition of social injustice or inequality. The problem of "revolution" and the character of such movements will be examined in specific case studies of violent and nonviolent movements and events; how do such movements relate to the modern (national) state and to nationalism? Most of the case studies are Western and are drawn from the historical and sociological literature on twentieth-century movements, but earlier experiences and non-Western experiences are also relevant to the debate and will be touched on.

In analyzing the rise of modern movements in the course, we will note the parallels and differences between change as it occurs in advanced or industrial societies and in pre-industrial societies, and the relationships between levels of change: individual, communal, structural (national) and global. The ideas of Gandhi and Marx and also of the psychoanalytic tradition are relevant to analyzing problems of social change. Other ideologies—

Fascism, Anarchism, Utopian Socialism, Liberalism, religious traditions and Nationalism—will be illustrated for the relationship of their theory to practice (or actuality).

Finally, some assessment of the success and failure of such human efforts might be attempted and the issue of peace studies raised. Can peace education be a form of social education for change? Should it be? What is the place of peace and disarmament *movements* in this process? What are the characteristics of these contemporary movements? Can they succeed? How and in what ways?

Main Movements Covered

- Millennial movements and religious sects: Anabaptism, Utopia and Revolt.
- The Nazi movement in Germany (1920–1945) and resistance to it: Nationalism and Militarism.
- The labour movement in early industrial Britain (1780–1848) and in the United States (19th/20th centuries).
- The Quakers (1650–). Communitarianism and oppositional politics.
- War resistance as a social movement (focus on WWI opposition in Europe and USA): Socialist, Internationalist/Anti-Militarist Movements, 1889–1919.
- The Women's Peace Movement (1900–1920) and the Suffrage Movement.
- Gandhi's Indian National Congress (1917–1947): Nonviolence in change.
- The Civil Rights Movement in the USA (M.L. King, 1955–1968).
- Opposition to the Indochina wars (1965–1972): USA and Europe, and the "New Left."
- The anti-nuclear weapons movements (1957–1963; 1979–1985); USA and Europe.
- The contemporary peace movement (including the women's peace movement).

Course Requirements

Main course requirements will be attendance at all sessions, a mid-term and final, and a 15–20 page analytical case study of a particular social movement. Assessment will also be based on attendance and participation in class, or discussions, and at evening movie film series, and other events and speakers. (Case study—20%; Proposal—5%; Review—5% Mid-term—20%; Final—20%; Class attendance and participation—20%; Quizzes—10%).

Required Texts to Be Purchased

Manual of Readings, Volume I (a selection of readings previously used last fall in UNST 211: Introduction to Peace Studies).

Manual of Readings, Volume II: Readings on Social Movements (selected for this course).

Overy, R. "How Effective Are Peace Movements?"

Bondurant, Joan. *Conquest of Violence.*
Sharp, Gene. *The Methods of Nonviolent Action* (Vol. 2 of *The Politics of Nonviolent Action*).
Cooney, Robert, and Helen Michalowski. *The Power of the People: Active Nonviolence in the United States.*

Recommended Texts
Cantril, Hadley. *Psychology of Social Movements.*
Brock, Peter. *Twentieth-Century Pacifism.*
Wood, J., and M. Jackson. *Social Movements: Development, Participation, Dynamics.*
Carter, April. *Direct Action and Liberal Democracy.*
Sharp, Gene. *Social Power and Political Freedom,* and Vol. I of *Politics of Nonviolent Action.*
Woito, Robert. *To End War.*
Young, Nigel J. *An Infantile Disorder? The Crisis and Decline of the New Left.*
Heberle, R. *Social Movements.*
New Society Publishers. *Off Their Backs . . . and On Our Own Two Feet* (a 23-page pamphlet).

Bibliographies will be distributed for your own information and as possible sources for papers.

SCHEDULE OF LECTURES, READINGS, ASSIGNMENTS, MOVIES, AND DUE DATES

Feb 4—Introductory Session: Defining Social Movements—Movements and Change
- R. Heberle, from *Social Movements,* pp. 6–19, 23–37.
- *Handout:* "Political Movements."

Feb. 6—Movements for Peace and Social Change: An Historical Overview
- Peter Mayer, Introduction from *The Pacifist Conscience* (Chicago: Gateway Edition).
- Cooney and Michalowski, Introduction and ch. 1.
- *Handout:* Brock, Mayer and Thoreau.

Feb. 10—Violence and Nonviolence as a Focus for Studying Political Movements
- Gene Sharp, "Examples of Nonviolent Resistance," *Politics of Nonviolent Action: Part One, Power and Struggle* (Boston, 1973), pp. 86–90.
- Pat Lacefield and Scott Kennedy, "An Introduction to Nonviolence," *Fellowship* (Mar./Apr. 1980), pp. 3–6.
- Sue Carroll et al., "Organizing for Social Transformation," *Peace and War,* Charles Beitz and Theodore Herman, eds. (San Francisco: W.H. Freeman, 1973), pp. 415–424.

- Sharp, Vol. 2: Contents (xi–xviii), Introduction (109–115), and Introduction to ch. 3 (117–119).

Feb. 11—Analyzing and Explaining Social Movements
- Rudolph Heberle, "General Principles and Survey of Social Movements: An Introduction to Political Sociology," in *Social Movements.*
- James Wood and Maurice Jackson, "Social Movements: An Overview," in *Social Movements: Development, Participation, Dynamics*, pp. 3–13.
- Lewis M. Killian, "Social Movements," *Handbook of Modern Sociology*, Robert E.L. Faris, ed., pp. 426–455.
- James Wood and Maurice Jackson, excerpts from *Social Movements.*
- Hans Gerth, "The Nazi Party: Its Leadership and Composition," *American Journal of Sociology*, Vol. XLV, No. 4 (Jan. 1940), pp. 517–541.
- Cantril, chs. 8 & 9, pp. 210–270.

Feb. 12—Movie: *Huelga!*

Feb. 13—Discussion Groups

Feb 17—Movements of Transition: Millennialism and Revitalization
- Anthony F.C. Wallace, "Revitalization Movements," *American Anthropologist*, Vol. LVIII (1956), pp. 421–429.
- Peter Worsley, "Conclusions," *The Trumpet Shall Sound*, pp. 221–256.
- Norman Cohn, Introduction and Conclusion, *The Pursuit of the Millennium* (New York: Harper & Row Books), pp. 21–32, 307–319.
- E.J. Hobsbawn, "Millenarianism II: The Andalusian Anarchists," *Primitive Rebels*, ch. V, pp. 74–92.
- Cooney & Michalowski, "Chief Seattle's Message," pp. 6–7.

Feb. 18—The Early Labour Movement and Industrialization
- E.J. Hobsbawn, "The Labour Sects," *Primitive Rebels*, ch. VIII, pp. 126–149.
- George Rude, "Luddism," *The Crowd in History*, pp. 79–91.
- E.J. Hobsbawn, "The Machine Breakers," *Essays in Labor History*, pp. 5–22.
- E.P. Thompson, *The Making of the English Working Class*, excerpts.
- Nigel Young, "The English Working Class in Capitalist Society," *Problems of Modern Society*, Peter Worsley, ed. (Penguin Books), pp. 193–200.
- Sharp, ch. 6.

Feb. 19—Video: "Union Maids"

Feb. 24—Movements Compared: The Nazis, Their Appeal and Their Opponents
Proposal (2-3 pp.) for case study due in class (see note below).
- Review Gerth and Cantril readings for Feb. 11.

Feb. 25—Movements for Suffrage and Civil Rights: Women, Labour and Black Movements
- Review Thompson reading for Feb. 18.
- Cooney & Michalowski, "Woman's Suffrage," ch. 2.

Feb. 26—Video: "Seeing Red"

Feb. 27—Discussion Groups and Short Quiz
Short quiz covers readings and lectures for weeks 1–4 (in class). Sign up for appointments to review proposals Mar. 2–12.
- Sharp, Introduction, pp. 109–115.

Mar. 3—Social Movements and Revolutionary Change
- Nigel Young, "On War, National Liberation and the State," pp. 1–16.
- Barbara Deming, "On Revolution and Equilibrium," *Revolution: Violent and Nonviolent*, pp. 2–13.
- Frantz Fanon, "The Wretched of the Earth," *Reader in Political Sociology*, Frank Lindenfeld, ed. (New York: Funk and Wagnalls, 1968), pp. 486–505.
- Bondurant, chs. 1 and 2.
- Sharp, ch. 8, pp. 390–398.

Mar. 4—The Gandhian Movement in India: Liberation and Nonviolence
- Bondurant, chs. 3 and 4.
- Krishnalal Shridharani, "War Without Violence," *Reader in Political Sociology*, Frank Lindenfeld, ed. (New York: Funk and Wagnalls, 1968), pp. 444–456.
- H.J.N. Horsburgh, "The Bases of Satyagraha," *Nonviolence and Aggression* (Oxford, 1968), pp. 27–40.
- Joan Bondurant, "The Salt Satyagraha," *Conquest of Violence: The Gandhian Philosophy of Conflict* (Princeton University Press, 1958), pp. 88–102.
- Mohandas K. Gandhi, "On Nonviolence," *Peace and War*, Charles Beitz and Theodore Herman, eds. (San Francisco: W.H. Freeman, 1973), pp. 345–348.
- *Recommended*: Sharp, Vol. I, p. 82–86.

Mar. 5—Video: "Gandhi"

Mar. 6—Discussion Groups
- Bondurant, ch. 5.
- Kenneth E. Boulding, "Power in Society," *Ecodynamics: A New Theory of Societal Evolution* (Beverly Hills: Sage, 1978), pp. 240–252.

Mar 10—Violent and Nonviolent Methods in Social Movements
- Sharp, ch. 3.
- Complete Bondurant.

- Cooney & Michalowski, "Direct Action for Disarmament," ch. 7.
- Review Lacefield & Kennedy, Carroll (readings for Feb. 10).

Mar. 11—(Illustrated) The U.S. Civil Rights Movement
- Martin Luther King, Jr., "New Day in Birmingham, Alabama."
- Nigel Young, "Turn Towards Violence," *The Crisis and Decline of the New Left*," pp. 223–237.
- Sharp, ch. 5.
- Cooney & Michalowski, "The Civil Rights Movement," ch. 8.

Mar. 12—Movie: *Martin Luther King: An Amazing Grace*
Followed by discussion.
- *Recommended:* Sharp, Vol. I, pp. 95–96.

Mar. 13—Midterm
In class (no discussion groups): take-home section distributed.

Mar. 17-22—Recess

Mar. 24—The Peace Movement: An Overview
Take-home section of midterm due in class.
- Nigel J. Young, "The Peace Movement: A Comparative and Analytical Survey."
- Nigel J. Young, "The Contemporary European Anti-Nuclear Movement: Experiments in the Mobilization of Public Power."
- Elise Boulding, "New Developments in the U.S. Peace Movement: Challenges and Obstacles in Historical Context."
- Cooney & Michalowski, Review Introduction, chs. 1 & 4.

Mar. 25—Analyzing Peace Movements
- Overy, *How Effective Are Peace Movements?* (whole book).

Mar. 26—Movie: *Eyes on the Prize: America's Civil Rights Years*

Mar. 27—Discussion Groups
- Complete Overy, and review.

Mar. 31—War Resistance: Quakers, Socialists, Internationalists
- Geoffrey Ostergaard, "Resisting the Nation-State: The Pacifist and Anarchist Traditions," *The Nation State*, L. Tivey, ed., pp. 171–195.
- James Joll, "The Stuttgart Resolution," *The Second International: 1889–1914*, pp. 196–198.
- Cooney & Michalowski, "World War I and the Pacifist Community," ch. 5, and "Towards Revolutionary Nonviolence," ch. 6.

April 1—The Women's Movement and Peace Issues
- Josephine Eglin, "Women and Peace: From the Suffragists to the Greenham Women."
- Review Cooney & Michalowski, ch. 2.

- *Recommended:* Lakey and Kokopeli, *Off Their Backs and On Our Own Two Feet.*

April 2—Movie: *7 Days to Remember*
Czech resistance.

April 3—Feminism and Nonviolent Action
Group will meet as as a whole for lecture and discussion.
Book review due in class (related to case study).

April 7—Nonviolence and Resistance
- Sharp, Vol. 2, ch. 7.
- Cooney and Michalowski, "Direct Action for Disarmament."

April 8—Socialist Movements, War and Violence
- Readings to be announced.
- Review Ostergaard on Stuttgart Resolution (Mar. 31).
- *Recommended:* Shaw, *Socialism and Anti-Militarism.*

April 9—Movie: *White Rose*
On resistance to Nazis.

April 10—Discussion Groups
- Sharp (complete readings in Vol. II, chs. 3–8).
- *Recommended:* Sharp, Vol. I, pp. 87–90.

April 14—The New Left as Movement: Violence and Nonviolence
- Nigel Young, Chronology and Introduction, *The Crisis and Decline of the New Left*, pp. xi–7.
- Nigel Young, "The New Left: A Core Identity," *The Crisis and Decline of the New Left*, pp. 24–50.
- James L. Wood and Maurice Jackson, "A Social Movement Illustrated: The New Left," *Social Movements*, pp. 15–25.
- Nigel Young, "Turn Towards Violence," *The Crisis and Decline of the New Left*, pp. 223–237.

April 15—(Illustrated) Vietnam: Oppositional Movements at Home and Abroad
- Cooney & Michalowski, "The Peace Movement," ch. 10.
- Norma Wikler, "Vietnam and the Veterans' Consciousness," *Social Movements*, James L. Wood and Maurice Jackson, eds., pp. 159–170.

April 16—Video: "Homefront USA"
Part II of *Vietnam, a Television History.*

April 17—Good Friday; Discussion Groups
- Readings to be announced.

April 21
Short in-class quiz on readings from weeks 5–9. Discussion.

April 22—(Illustrated) The Movements Against Nuclear Weapons
- Readings to be announced.
- Review *Manuals* and Overy.

April 23—Video: "The War at Home"
Madison, Wisconsin, 1960s.

April 24—Discussion Groups
Case study due.

April 28—(Illustrated) Nationalism, Globalism, and Community: The Orientations of Social Movements
- Reading to be announced.

April 29—The Concept of "New Social Movements"
- Peter Kivisto, "Contemporary Social Movements in Advanced Industrial Societies and Sociological Intervention: An Appraisal of Alain Touraine's *Practique*," *ACTA Sociologica 1984*, Vol. 27, No. 4, pp. 355–366.
- Review Wood and Jackson, excerpts from *Social Movements*.
- Cooney & Michalowski, conclusion.

April 30—Movies: *Gods of Metal, World Peace Is a Local Issue,* and *Louder Than Our Words*
Three short films on the peace movement.

May 1—Discussion Groups
Take-home section of final distributed.
- Review Boulding (Mar. 24).

May 5—The New Women's Peace Movement
- Review Eglin (Apr. 1), and Overy.

May 6—Contemporary Movements for Peace and Change: An Overview
- European Nuclear Disarmament (END) Campaign Appeal.
- Nigel J. Young, "The Contemporary European Anti-Nuclear Movement: Experiments in the Mobilization of Public Power."
- Cooney & Michalowski: Afterword.

May 11
Take-home section of the final due in Peace Studies Office. One-hour final in allotted period.

4. Explaining Revolutions in the Modern World

Theda Skocpol   *Spring 1988*
Sociology Dept., Harvard University,
Cambridge, MA 02138

This course surveys major theoretical perspectives that have been used by social scientists since the nineteenth century to interpret and explain revolutions. With the aid of the best available theories, we will examine a series of historical instances, ranging from the English Revolution of the seventeenth century, through the French, Russian, and Chinese Revolutions, to more recent revolutions in Vietnam, Iran, and Nicaragua.

Certain basic questions and themes will recur throughout the course, including the following:

- Why have major revolutions occurred relatively infrequently, and why at some times and places but not others?
- What sorts of social changes and political conditions have brought about revolutionary outbreaks?
- What have revolutions actually changed, and have the changes been for better or for worse?
- What roles have been played—in causing revolutions or shaping their outcomes—by organized, self-conscious revolutionaries, and by popular revolts and political participation?
- What, if anything, can the study of past revolutions tell us about present and possible future revolutions?

Required Books

Adelman, Jonathan. *Revolution, Armies, and War* (Boulder, Colorado: Lynne Rienner Publishers, 1985).

Goldstone, Jack. *Revolutions: Theoretical, Comparative, and Historical Studies* (New York: Harcourt, Brace, & Jovanovich, 1986).

Skocpol, Theda. *States and Social Revolutions* (Cambridge: Cambridge Univ. Press, 1979).

Stone, Lawrence. *The Causes of the English Revolution* (New York: Harper and Row, 1972).

Rudé, George. *The Crowd in the French Revolution* (New York: Oxford Univ. Press, 1967).

Kaiser, Daniel H., ed. *The Worker's Revolution in Russia, 1917: The View from Below* (Cambridge: Cambridge Univ. Press, 1987).

Wolf, Eric. *Peasant Wars of the Twentieth Century.*

Paige, Jeffrey. *Agrarian Revolution* (New York: Free Press, 1975).

Dunn, John. *Modern Revolutions* (Cambridge: Cambridge Univ. Press, 1972).

Bakhash, Shaul. *The Reign of the Ayatollahs* (New York: Basic Books, 1984).

Recommended

Hinton, William. *Fanshen* (New York: Vintage Books, 1968).

Course Organization and Requirements

All students are expected to keep up with the readings and to attend lectures every Tuesday and Thursday. By the second week of class, sections will be organized (including a special graduate student section, if needed). Regular, informed participation in the weekly section meetings will count for 20% of the final grade. There will be three five-page essays assigned during the semester, the first due on March 1, the second due on March 22, and the third due on April 19. Together, these short essays will count for 40% of the final grade. The final examination, which will count for 40% of the grade, will be based on six questions handed out in advance, of which three will actually appear on the exam. Students may prepare notes and outlines and bring them to the exam. Graduate students have the option of arranging to substitute a research paper for the short essays and the final examination.

COURSE OUTLINE AND READING LIST

Week 1—Introduction to the Course

I. Theoretical Perspectives on Revolutions

Week 2—What Causes Revolutions?
Theories of Societal Change and Revolutions
Political Conflicts and Revolutionary Outbreaks

- Goldstone, "The Comparative and Historical Study of Revolutions," pp. 1–17.
- Karl Marx and Frederick Engels, "Manifesto of the Communist Party," in Goldstone, pp. 20–29.
- Samuel P. Huntington, "Revolution and Political Order," in Goldstone, pp. 39–47.
- Charles Tilly, "Does Modernization Breed Revolution?" excerpted in Goldstone, pp. 47–57.
- Skocpol, ch. 1.

Week 3—What Do Revolutions Change, and Why?
Classes and Vanguards in Revolutions
Transformations of the State and Politics

- Michael Walzer, "A Theory of Revolutions," pp. 201–23 in his *Radical Principles* (New York: Basic Books, 1980).
- Nikolai Lenin, *The State and Revolution.*
- Alexis de Tocqueville, "The French Revolution and the Growth of the State," in Goldstone, pp. 30–31.
- Max Weber, "Bureaucracy and Revolution," in Goldstone, pp. 31–37.
- Adelman, chs. 1 and 12.

II. Analyzing Political and Social Revolutions: The Classic Cases

Week 4—Political Revolution in Early Modern England
Causes of the English Revolution
The English Revolution and Parliamentary Politics

- Stone.
- Goldstone, "The English Revolution: A Structural-Demographic Approach,"pp. 88–104.
- E.W. Ives, editor, *The English Revolution, 1600–1660* (New York: Harper and Row, 1971), chs. 2, 3, 4 and 10.
- Adelman, ch. 2.

Week 5—Revolutions from Above and Social Revolutions
Bureaucratic Monarchies and Agrarian Classes in a Modernizing World

- Skocpol, chs. 2, 3, and 4.
- Ellen Kay Trimberger, "A Theory of Elite Revolutions," in Goldstone, pp. 159–72.

Week 6—Political Conflicts and Revolutionary Outcomes in France
Popular Revolts and Conflicts Among Elites
Analyzing the Revolutions' Transformations

- Rudé, chs. 7–9.
- T.J.A. LeGoff and D.M.G. Sutherland, "The Revolution and the Rural Community in Eighteenth-Century Brittany," *Past and Present,* no. 62 (1974): 96–119.
- Skocpol, ch. 5.
- William Sewell, Jr., "Ideologies and Social Revolutions: Reflections on the French Case," *The Journal of Modern History* 57 (1985): 57–85.
- Skocpol, "Cultural Idioms and Political Ideologies in the Revolutionary Reconstruction of State Power: A Rejoinder to Sewell," *The Journal of Modern History* 57 (1985): 86–96.
- Adelman, ch. 3.

Week 7—Political Conflicts and Revolutionary Outcomes in Russia and China
Communists, Workers, and Peasants
Stalinism, Maoism, and Afterwards
- Kaiser, chs. 1, 3, and 5.
- Wolf, ch. 3.
- Thomas Bernstein, "Leadership and Mass Mobilisation in the Soviet and Chinese Collectivisation Campaigns of 1929–30 and 1955–56: A Comparison," *The China Quarterly*, no. 31 (1967): 1–47.
- Alvin Gouldner, "Stalinism: A Study of Internal Colonialism," *Political Power and Social Theory*, volume 1 (1980): 209–259.
- Sheila Fitzpatrick, "The Russian Revolution and Social Mobility," *Politics and Society* 13 (1984): 119–41.
- Martin King Whyte, "Inequality and Stratification in China," in Goldstone, pp. 248–68.
- Adelman, chs. 4–11.
- Optional: Skocpol, chapters 6 and 7.
- Recommended: Hinton.

III. Social Revolutions in Emerging Nations

Week 8—The Politics of Revolution in Dependent Countries
An Overview of the Issues
The Mexican Revolution as an Example
- Elbaki Hermassi, "Toward a Comparative Study of Revolutions," *Comparative Studies in Society and History* 28 (1976): 211–35.
- Jack Goldstone, "Revolutions and Superpowers," in *Superpowers and Revolutions*, edited by Jonathan Adelman (New York: Praeger Publishers, 1986), pp. 38–48.
- Josef Gugler, "The Urban Character of Contemporary Revolutions," *Studies in Comparative International Development* 27 (1982): 60–73.
- Paige, ch. 1.
- Wolf, ch. 1 and Conclusion.
- Walter L. Goldfrank, "The Mexican Revolution," in Goldstone, pp. 104–17.

Week 9—Spring Break

Week 10—Southeast Asia and the Vietnamese Revolution
Colonialism, War, and Regional Conflicts
Dynamics of the Vietnamese Revolution
- Jeff Goodwin, "War and Revolution in Southeast Asia, 1940–54: A Comparative Analysis." (Typescript).
- Dunn, ch. 5.
- Wolf, ch. 4.
- Paige, ch. 5.

- David Hunt, "Village Culture and the Vietnamese Revolution," *Past and Present*, no. 94 (1982): 131–57.

Week 11—Central America and the Nicaraguan Revolution
Patterns of Revolt in Central America
The Nicaraguan Revolution

- *The Nicaraguan Revolution:* Thomas W. Walker on "The Economic and Political Background" and Ricardo E. Chavarria on "The Revolutionary Insurrection," in Goldstone, pp. 140–59.
- Lisa North, "Bitter Grounds: Roots of Revolt in El Salvador," in Goldstone, pp. 195–206.
- Robert H. Dix, "Why Revolutions Succeed and Fail," *Polity* 16 (1984): 423–46.
- Manus I. Midlarsky and Kenneth Roberts, "Class, State, and Revolution in Central America" *Journal of Conflict Resolution* 29 (1985): 163–93.

Week 12—The Iranian Revolution in World-Historical Perspective
Roots of the Iranian Revolution
Statebuilding and War Since 1979

- Theda Skocpol, "Rentier State and Shi'a Islam in the Iranian Revolution," *Theory and Society* 11 (1982): 265–83.
- Bakhash.

Week 13—Looking Ahead in Theory and History
Settled Issues and Open Questions
Where Might Revolutions Happen—And Where Are They Unlikely?

5. Third World Revolutions

Anthony Lake   Fall 1986
International Relations Program, Mount Holyoke College,
South Hadley, MA 01075

This seminar will speculate on the purposes, causes and results of revolutions in the Third World.

Each participant will prepare an analytical research paper (c. 20 pages, due December 3) on one of the case studies to be examined, and summarize its findings, in fifteen minutes, for class discussion. A system of cunning encouragement for undertaking the earlier cases will be devised. There will also be a brief, final, take-home examination, due for the last class on December 10.

Participants will be expected to read the assigned materials on the cases and to comment on the others' presentations. The theoretical readings in the first few weeks are particularly important in establishing the questions to be addressed in subsequent writing and discussion.

OUTLINE

I. Visions of Revolution
Film: The Battle of Algiers.
* Andre Malraux, *Man's Fate.*

II. Anatomies of Revolution—Pt. 1
* Hannah Arendt, *On Revolution* (Viking/Compass), pp. 1–68.
* Crane Brinton, *The Anatomy of Revolution* (Vintage), pp. 237-264.
* Gerard Chaliand, *Revolution in the Third World* (Viking), pp. 1–32.
* Frantz Fanon, *The Wretched of the Earth* (Grove), pp. 7–31, 35–106, 311–316.
* Jack A. Goldstone (ed.), *Revolutions: Theoretical, Comparative and Historical Studies* (Harcourt, Brace, Javanovich), pp. 1–17.

III. Anatomies of Revolution—Pt. 2
* Claude E. Welch, *Political Modernization: A Reader in Comparative Political Change* (Duxbury), pp. 1–16.
* Samuel Huntington, "Political Development and Decay," in Welch, *Political Modernization,* pp. 238–277.
* Charles Tilly, "Does Modernization Breed Revolution?" in Goldstone, *Revolutions,* pp. 47–57.
* Mancur Olson, Jr., "Rapid Growth as a Destabilizing Force," in Jason L. Finkle and R.W. Gable, eds., *Political Development and Social Change* (Wiley), pp. 557–568.
* Ted Gurr, *Why Men Rebel* (Princeton), pp. 3–15.
* Eric R. Wolf, "Peasant Rebellion and Revolution," in Goldstone, *Revolutions,* pp. 173–182.

IV. China, 1949
* Lucien Bianco, *Origins of the Chinese Revolution, 1915–1949* (Stanford), pp. 1–208.
* Judith Stacey, "Peasant Families and People's War in the Chinese Revolution," in Goldstone, *Revolutions,* pp. 182–194.

V. Vietnam, 1945
* Frances Fitzgerald, *Fire in the Lake* (Vintage), pp. 3–95.
* John T. McAlister, *Vietnam: The Origins of Revolution,* pp. 3–106, 325–347.

- Ho Chi Minh, "The Path Which Led Me to Leninism," in Bernard Fall, *Ho Chi Minh on Revolution* (Signet), p. 507.

VI. Cuba, 1958

- George Dominguez, *Cuba: Order and Revolution* (Harvard), pp. 1–133.
- George Dominguez, *Cuba: The Making of a Revolution* (U. Mass.), pp. 141–169.

VII. Nicaragua, 1979

- Thomas Walker, Ricardo Chavarria and Harry Vanden in Walker, ed., *Nicaragua in Revolution* (Praeger), pp. 1–62.
- John Booth, *The End and the Beginning: The Nicaraguan Revolution* (Westview), pp. 1–181, 215–222.

VIII. Iran, 1978–1979

- Jerold D. Green, "Counter Mobilization in the Iranian Revolution," in Goldstone, *Revolutions*, pp. 127–138.
- Nikki Keddie, *Roots of Revolution: An Interpretive History of Modern Iran*, pp. 142–258, 273–276.

Or

- Ervand Abrahamian, *Iran Between Two Revolutions*, pp. 419–537.
- Shaul Bakhash, *The Reign of the Ayatollahs*, pp. 3–51.
- J.C. Miklas, *The Iranian Revolution and Modernization*, pp. 15–65.

IX. The Revolution in Power: China and Vietnam

- Goldstone, *Revolutions*, pp. 319–322.
- Jonathan Kelly and Herbert S. Klein, "Revolution and the Rebirth of Inequality: Stratification in Post-Revolutionary Society," in Goldstone, *Revolutions*, pp. 209–218.
- Chaliand, *Revolution in the Third World*, pp. 184–195.
- M.K. Whyte, "Inequality and Stratification in China," in Goldstone, *Revolutions*, pp. 248–268.
- Further readings to be assigned.

X. The Revolution in Power: Cuba and Iran

- Susan Eckstein, "The Impact of Revolution on Social Welfare in Latin America," in Goldstone, *Revolutions*, pp. 280–307.
- Dominguez, *Cuba*, selections from pp. 134–330.
- William Leogrande, "Cuban Dependency: A Comparison of Pre-Revolutionary and Post-Revolutionary International Economic Relations," *Cuban Studies* (Vol. 9, No. 2, July, 1979), pp. 1–28.
- Robert A. Packenham, "Capitalist Dependency and Socialist Dependency: The Case of Cuba," paper delivered at the annual meeting of the APSA, 1985, pp. 1–39.
- Keddie, *Roots of Revolution: An Interpretive History of Iran*, pp. 258–272.
- Bakhash, *The Reign of the Ayatollahs*, pp. 52–250.

XI. The Revolution in Power: Nicaragua
- Shirley Christian, *Revolution in the Family* (Random House), pp. 119–311.
- Further readings to be assigned.

Revolutions to Come? El Salvador?
- Contemporary readings to be assigned.

XII. Revolutions to Come? The Philippines, South Africa and Zaire?
- Contemporary readings to be assigned.

XIII. Conclusions
Discussion of take-home examinations due.

Conflict Resolution

1. International Conflict and Conflict Resolution

P. Terrence Hopmann   *Spring 1986*

Political Science Dept., Brown University,
Providence, RI 02912

This seminar deals with one of the central problems of global civilization—namely, the causes of violent international conflict and methods for the resolution of such conflict by nonviolent means. The first part of the seminar will focus on the causes of international violence, exploring primarily three alternative levels of explanation: (1) individual human beings, (2) the nature of nation-states, and (3) the structure of the international system. No attempt will be made to identify a single cause, but rather the difficult dilemmas in explaining the sources of international violence will be explored. The second part of the course will then examine some of the methods through which international conflicts may be resolved and violence may be averted. There can be little doubt that in a world armed with nuclear weapons, violent resolution of conflicts, at least among the nuclear powers, can have only drastic consequences for human civilization. In spite of these terrible consequences, we really know very little about how to resolve conflicts and how to avoid such a catastrophe. This course will thus explore a number of techniques, especially those involving international bargaining and negotiation, that may enhance the possibility for the peaceful resolution of major international conflicts.

Evaluation

Students in the seminar will be evaluated on the basis of the following assignments:

(1) Five short critical essays of no more than 5 pages each will be required throughout the semester on topics which will be assigned in class. These essays will be worth a total of 50% of the final grade.

(2) Students will be expected to participate actively in seminar discussions, completing the reading assignments for each week prior to seminar sessions. In addition, all students will be expected to participate in a simulation exercise. Participation in these class activities will be worth 10% of the final grade.

(3) A final examination covering the entire course will be given during the usual examination period, May 9. This examination will give approximately equal weight to assigned readings and to seminar discussion.

Course Texts

Fisher, Roger, and William Ury. *Getting to Yes*. Penguin.

Rapoport, Anatol. *Fights, Games, and Debates*. University of Michigan Press.

Rubin, Jeffrey. *Dynamics of Third Party Intervention: Kissinger in the Middle East*. Praeger.

Snyder, Glenn, and Paul Diesing. *Conflict Among Nations*. Princeton University Press.

Stoesinger, John. *Why Nations Go to War*. St. Martin's Press.

Waltz, Kenneth. *Man, the State, and War*. Columbia University Press.

Zartman, I. William, and Maureen Berman. *The Practical Negotiator*. Yale University Press.

WEEKLY TOPICS AND
READING ASSIGNMENTS

Jan. 22—Introduction

Jan. 29—The Onset of War: Case Studies

- Stoesinger, entire.

Feb. 5—The First Image: The Individual and War

- Waltz, chs. I–III.
- Charles Hermann, *International Crises: Insights from Behavioral Research*, chs. 3 and 4.
- Ralph K. White, chs. 1, 8–10.
- Stephen D. Nelson, "Nature/Nurture Revisited II," *Journal of Conflict Resolution*, Vol. XIX, No. 4 (Dec. 1975), pp. 734–768.
- Charles R. Beitz and Theodore Herman, *Peace and War*, ch. 4, pp. 109–143.

Feb. 12—The Second Image: Nation-State Explanations
- Waltz, chs. IV and V.
- A.F.K. Organski and Jacek Kugler, *The War Ledger*, ch. 1.
- Ivo K. Feierabend et al. (eds.), *Anger, Violence, and Politics*, chs. 5 and 7.
- Charles R. Beitz and Theodore Herman (eds.), *Peace and War*, Section 7.

Feb. 19—The Third Image: International System Explanations
- Waltz, chs. VI, VII, and VIII.
- Nazli Choucri and Robert C. North, "Dynamics of International Conflict," *World Politics*, Vol. XXIV, Spring 1972 Special Supplement, pp. 80–122.
- David Edwards, *International Political Analysis: Readings*, pp. 318–376.
- Bruce M. Russett (ed.), *Peace, War, and Numbers*, chs. 1 and 2.

Feb. 26—International Crises and Bargaining
- Snyder and Diesing, chs. I, VI, and VII.
- Ole R. Holsti, *Crisis, Escalation, War*, chs. 7 and 8.

Mar. 5—Fights: Arms Races and Conflict
- Rapoport, Introduction and Part I.
- Colin S. Gray, "The Arms Race Phenomenon," *World Politics*, Vol. 24, No. 1 (Oct. 1971), pp. 39–79.

Mar. 12—Negotiations as Games
- Rapoport, Part II.
- Snyder and Diesing, ch. II.

Mar. 19—Negotiations as Strategy and Tactics
- Zartman and Berman, entire.
- Thomas Schelling, *The Strategy of Conflict*, chs. 1 and 2.
- Snyder and Diesing, ch. III.

Apr. 2—Negotiations as Debates
- Rapoport, Part III.
- Snyder and Diesing, ch. IV.
- Daniel Druckman (ed.), *Negotiations: Social Psychological Perspectives*, ch. 6.

Apr. 9—Simulation Exercise
Note: Do not read these articles until after the simulation exercises have been completed!
- Gilbert R. Winham and H. Eugene Bovis, "Agreement and Breakdown in Negotiations," *Journal of Peace Research*, Vol. XV, No. 4 (1978), pp. 285–297.
- P. Terrence Hopmann and Charles Walcott, "The Impact of International Conflict and Detente on Bargaining in Arms Control Negotiations: An

Experimental Analysis," *International Interactions*, Vol. 2, No. 4 (1976), pp. 189–206.

Apr. 16—The Nuclear Test Ban Negotiations: A Case Study

- Lloyd Jensen, "Approach-Avoidance Bargaining in the Test Ban Negotiations," *International Studies Quarterly*, Vol. 12 (1968), pp. 152–160.
- Daniel Druckman (ed.), *Negotiations: Social-Psychological Perspectives*, ch. 10.
- P. Terrence Hopmann and Timothy King, "Interactions and Perceptions in the Test Ban Negotiations," *International Studies Quarterly*, Vol. 20, No. 1 (1976), pp. 105–142.
- I. William Zartman (ed.), *The Negotiation Process*, ch. 8.

Apr. 23—Kissinger in the Middle East: A Case Study

- Rubin, entire.

Apr. 30—Reading Period

- Fisher and Ury, entire.

May 9—Final Examination

2. Nonviolent Conflict Intervention

Terrie Northrup   *Fall 1987*

Program on the Analysis and Resolution of Conflicts,
Syracuse University, Syracuse, NY 13210

This course is designed as a survey of the field of conflict resolution, a "movement" which has surfaced in many settings, from interpersonal to international relations. The first third of the course will address theoretical and philosophical positions and approaches to conflict. The second phase of the course will deal with the resolution and management of conflict, including an overview of specific conflict settings, for example, interpersonal relations. The final phase of the course will address special problems and issues related to conflict resolution, such as male-female relationships, the effect of race/ethnicity/culture on relationships, factors related to war and peace, and intractable conflicts. The learning process will be accomplished in several ways, through lectures, readings, class exercises, open discussions, homework exercises, and exams. Graduate students will also be required to write a paper.

Required Readings

Hocker, J.L., and W.W. Wilmont. *Interpersonal Conflict*, second edition. Wm. C. Brown, 1985.

Pruitt, D.G., and J.Z. Rubin. *Social Conflict: Escalation, Stalemate, and Settlement.* Random House, 1986.

Assigned articles, found in the class session descriptions.

Course Requirements

Class Participation: This is a relatively small class which will be run to a large extent as a seminar. The expectation is that all members will attend regularly. Class participation should provide some evidence that you are keeping up with the readings and continuing to think about the issues raised in the course.

Homework assignments: You are required to complete 3 of the 4 homework assignments which will occur periodically throughout the semester. You have the option of completing a fourth assignment for extra credit, if you are interested in raising your grade.

Exams: There will be three exams which will cover each of the three sections of the course. They will be a combination of objective questions, short-answer essays, definitions of terms and analytical questions. The third exam will be given during finals week, and will cover the last third of the course.

Paper (for graduate students only): The paper is due at the end of the semester. The length of the paper is dependent upon the nature of the project you choose to do, but it should be a major project. You should begin to think about the topic of your paper at the beginning of the semester and identify which faculty person you want to work with you on this project.

Grading: Undergraduates: class participation—10%; homework assignments—15%; exams—75%. Graduates: class participation—10%; homework assignments—15%; exams—45%; paper—30%.

CLASS SESSION SCHEDULE

Section I: Theories and Models of Conflict and Conflict Resolution

Sept. 9—Introduction: Overview of the Conflict Resolution Field and Definition of Terms

Sept. 16—Theory Concerning the Nature of Conflict: Sources of Conflict
- Pruitt, chs. 1 & 2.
- Hocker, ch. 1.
- Pneuman & Bruehl.

Sept. 23—Conflict Models and Processes
- Pruit, chs. 3, 6 & 7.
- Hocker, ch. 2.

Sept. 30—The Role of Power in Conflict
Homework #1 is due.
- Pruitt, ch. 5.
- Hocker, ch. 3.
- Doyle.

Oct. 7—Exam #1 (first half of class)
Grad students should meet with professor concerning paper topic.

Section II: Methods of Conflict Resolution

Oct. 7—Overview (second half of class)

Oct. 14—Interpersonal Relations
- Hocker, chs. 4 & 5.
- Pruitt, chs. 4 & 8.

Oct. 21—Interpersonal Relations: Conflict Resolution in Different Settings
- Hocker, ch. 7.
- Pruitt, ch. 9.
- *Getting to Yes* excerpts: Allman & Katz.

Oct. 28—Third Parties
Homework #2 is due.
- Hocker, ch. 8.
- Pruitt, ch. 10.
- Fogg.
- ADR packet.

Nov. 4—Exam #2 (first half of class)

Section III: Factors Affecting the Conduct and Resolution of Conflict

Nov. 4—The Alternative Dispute Resolution "Movement": Environmental Conflict, Workplace Conflict (second half of class)

Nov. 11—The Role of Gender in Conflict and Conflict Resolution: Gender as a Metaphor for Status and Power Differences

- *Patriarchy:* Gray, E.D. (1971). *Patriarchy as a Conceptual Trap* (Wellesley, MA: Roundtable Press).
- *Gender:* Doyle, James A. (1985). *Sex and Gender: The Human Experience* (Dubuque: Wm. C. Brown Publishers).
- *Race:* Pettigrew, T.F. (1977). "Racially Separate or Together?" in J.C. Brigham & L.S. Wrightsman, eds., *Contemporary Issues in Social Psychology.*
- *Culture:* Segall, M.H. (1979). "Cultural Differences in Motives, Beliefs, and Values," in *Cross-Cultural Psychology* (Monterey: Brooks-Cole), ch. 6 (pp. 136–175).
- *Culture:* Kidder, L.H. (1987). "There Is No Word for 'Fair': Notes from Japan," in *Internationally Speaking*, Vol. 12.
- *Ethnicity:* Cairns, E. (1982). "Intergroup Conflict in Northern Ireland," in Tajfel, H., ed., *Social Identity and Intergroup Relations* (Cambridge: Cambridge University Press), pp. 277–295.
- *Ethnicity:* Smith, A.D. (1983). "Ethnic Identity and World Order," in *Millennium*, Vol. 12, pp. 149–161.

Nov. 18—The Role of Race, Ethnicity, and Culture in Conflict and Conflict Resolution

- Couloumbis, T.A., & Wolfe, J.H. (1982). *Introduction to International Relations: Power and Justice* (Englewood Cliffs, New Jersey: Prentice-Hall), ch. 1.
- White, R.K. (1985). "Ten Psychological Contributions to the Prevention of Nuclear War," in *Applied Social Psychology Annual* 6.
- Zartman, I.W., & Touval, S. (1985). "International Mediation: Conflict Resolution and Power Politics," *Journal of Social Issues* 41, pp. 27–45.
- Davidson, W.D., & Montville, J.V. (1981–1982). "Foreign Policy According to Freud," *Foreign Policy* 45, pp. 145–157.
- Janis, I.J. (1985). "International Crisis Management in the Nuclear Age," in *Applied Social Psychology Annual* 6.
- Cordes, C. (1985). "Psychology and the Theory of Deterrence: The Gap Widens," *APA Monitor* (December), p. 7.
- Holsti, K.J. (1968). "Resolving International Conflicts: A Taxonomy of Behavior and Some Figures on Procedures," in Louis Kriesburg, ed., *Social Processes in International Relations* (New York: John Wiley & Sons).
- Mendlovitz, S.H. (1982). *The Struggle for a Just World Order.* World Policy Paper #20, World Policy Institute. (Optional)
- Johansen, R.C. (1983). *Toward an Alternative Security System.* World Policy Paper #24, World Policy Institute.

Dec. 2—International Relations

- Moyer, R.S. (1985). "The Enemy Within," *Psychology Today* 19 (1), pp. 30–37.

- Plous, S., & Zimbardo, P.G. (1984). "The Looking Glass War," *Psychology Today* 18 (11), pp. 48–59.
- Hocker & Wilmot, ch. 6 (pp. 129–133, 140–142, 149–156 optional).
- Segall, M.H. (1979). *Cross-Cultural Psychology* (Monterey: Brooks-Cole), ch. 8 (pp. 221–223, 228–234, rest of chapter optional).
- Kriesberg, L. (1980). "Interlocking Conflicts in the Middle East," in *Research in Social Movements: Conflicts and Change* 3, pp. 99–105 (rest of chapter optional).

Dec. 9—Creative Alternatives
Homework #3 is due.

Finals Week—Exam #3 and Papers Due

3. Conflict and Conflict Management: A Cross-Cultural Approach

Marc Ross   *Spring 1986*
Political Science Dept., Bryn Mawr College,
Bryn Mawr, PA 19010

Conflicts are found in all human societies. As Nader and Todd have written, "In all human societies there are persons who have problems of debt, of theft, of infidelity, of employment, of consumption, and of personal injury. Many of these people seek to do something about their problems, and in so doing resort to remedy agents that the society has previously developed to deal with them." When we look at who or what these remedy agents are, we find great variety. In some societies the original disputants settle the matter themselves, sometimes in a peaceful fashion, sometimes resorting to physical force. In other cases third parties are quickly brought into a dispute and the members of a community work towards achievement of a settlement. Some third parties are specialists in this area, while in other cases the third parties include all members of the community. We can also observe similar variation in how societies deal with conflicts involving members of other societies.

How can we understand such great variation in the conflict process? For the most part social scientists have been better at documenting human variation in conflict behavior than in understanding its underlying dynamics.

This course aims to (1) provide some familiarity with the broad range of human variation in the conflict and dispute settlement processes through an examination of small-scale, traditional societies typically studied by anthropoligists; (2) examine two major theoretical approaches to this field, one accounting for conflict behavior in terms of social or political structures found in a society, and the other focusing on variation arising from differences in personality dispositions across societies; (3) attempt to reconcile the differences in these perspectives, suggesting compatibilities and incompatibilities between them; and (4) consider ways in which the insights gained from these societies, quite different from our own, can provide insights into conflict and dispute settlement in our society. The first half of the course is organized around the concept of conflict, the second around conflict management. The integration of ideas from the two is a major goal for the semester.

The material covered in the course is wide ranging, and includes readings in social anthropology, psychoanalysis and political science. Students are expected to have had some introductory course work in at least one social science, but no specific knowledge is assumed. There is a good deal of reading assigned, and students are expected to complete it before the classes to benefit from questions and discussions. There will be a number of short writing assignments, a research project on a local conflict, and a midterm and final exam.

READING ASSIGNMENTS

Conflict

Week 1—Introduction: Some Cases of Conflict and Dispute Settlement in Small-Scale Societies

- Napoleon Chagnon, "Yanomamo Social Organization and Warfare," in Morton Fried et al. (eds.), *War: The Anthropology of Armed Conflict and Aggression.* Natural History Press, pp. 109–159.
- Colin Turnbull, "The Politics of Non-Aggression," in Ashley Montagu (ed.), *Learning Non-Aggression: The Experience of Non-Literate Societies.* Oxford Univ. Press, pp. 161–221.

Week 2—Conceptualizing the Conflict Process: Propositions from Social Psychology and Anthropology

- Morton Deutsch, *The Resolution of Conflict,* Yale Univ. Press, chs. 1, 13, pp. 3–19, 351–400.
- Laura Nader and Harry Todd, "Introduction: The Disputing Process," in *The Disputing Process—Law in Ten Societies,* Columbia Univ. Press, pp. 1–40.

Week 3—Psychodynamics of Conflict

- Patricia Draper, "The Learning Environment for Aggression and Anti-Social Behavior Among the !Kung," in Ashley Montagu (ed.), *Learning Non-Aggression.*
- Beatrice Whiting, "Sex Identity Conflict and Physical Violence: A Comparative Study," *American Anthropologist,* 1965, part 2, pp. 123–140.
- Franco Fornari, *Psychoanalysis of War,* Indiana Univ. Press, Introduction and ch. 1, pp. xii–xxxi, 3–38.

Week 4—Social Structure and Political Conflict: Theoretical Concerns

- James Coleman, *Community Conflict,* Free Press.
- Keith Otterbein, "Internal War: A Cross-Cultural Study," *American Anthropologist,* 1968, pp. 277–289.
- Robert Murphy, "Intergroup Hostility and Social Aggression," *American Anthropologist,* 1957, pp. 59, 1018–1035.
- Robert LeVine and Donald T. Campbell, *Ethnocentrism,* John Wiley Press, ch. 4, pp. 43–59.

Week 5—Social Structure and Political Conflict: A Case Study

- Victor Turner, *Schism and Continuity in an African Society,* Manchester Univ. Press, chs. 3–4 (pp. 61–130), chs. 5, 9, 10 (pp. 131–168, 258–317).

Week 6—Warfare and Alliances: A Social/Structural Explanation and a Psychological Puzzle

- Mervyn Meggitt, *Blood Is Their Argument,* Mayfield Press.
- Mervyn Meggitt, "Male-Female Relations in Highland New Guinea," *American Anthropologist.*

Week 7—Towards an Integrated Explanation for Conflict

- Robert LeVine, "Socialization, Social Structure and Inter-Societal Images," in Herbert Kelman (ed.), *International behavior,* Holt, Rinehart and Winston Press.
- Marc Howard Ross, "The Limits to Social Structure: Psychological and Social Structure Explanations for Conflict and Violence."

Conflict Management

Weeks 8 & 9—Third Parties and Dispute Settlement

- P.H. Gulliver, *Disputes and Negotiations: A Cross-Cultural Perspective,* Academic Press.

Week 10—Negotiations: What Is Managed and What Is Resolved?

- Mario Cuomo, *Forest Hills Diary.*

Week 11—The Failure of Negotiations: MOVE and Northern Ireland
- Ed Cairns, "Intergroup Conflict in Northern Ireland," in Henri Tajfel (ed.), *Social Identity and Intergroup Relations*, Cambridge Univ. Press, pp. 277–297.
- Liz McWhinter, "Northern Ireland: Growing Up with the Troubles," in Arnold P. Goldstein and Marshall H. Segall (eds.), *Aggression in Global Perspective*. Pergamon Press, pp. 367–400.

Week 12—Adjudication
Laura Nadar and Harry F. Todd, *The Disputing Process: Law in Ten Societies*, chs. 2, 3, 7, 8, 9, 10.

Weeks 13 & 14—Conflict Mangement in the International System
- Ralph K. White, *Fearful Warriors: A Psychological Profile of U.S.-Soviet Relations*, Free Press.

4. Dispute Resolution

Barbara Fick and George A. Lopez　　　Fall 1987

Institute for International Peace Studies, University of
Notre Dame, Notre Dame, IN 46556

This course examines the rationale for and execution of processes available for resolving serious social disputes. Specifically, the course aims to train participants in both the literature and the techniques of negotiation, mediation and arbitration. As detailed in the schedule below, the instructors have constructed a variety of exercises and assembled a diverse group of readings to facilitate the course objective.

The course emerges from the recognition in both the legal and policy fields that dispute resolution, or conflict management as it is called in some circles, has become a matter of national importance and an area demanding a high level of professionalism.

Partly out of concern for the overburdened court system, the American Bar Association became heavily involved during the early seventies with the development of alternative centers for resolving citizen and community conflicts. This development paralleled an information explosion generated by social scientists, lawyers, community organizers, negotiators and mediators regarding how and why various racial, communal and public policy disputes of the sixties and seventies were being (or had been) resolved.

By 1980 a national professional organization, the Society for Professionals in Dispute Resolution (SPIDR), had been formed, community dispute resolution centers existed in nearly every major American city, and the Alternative Dispute Resolution (ADR) movement among lawyers had changed the curriculum of various law schools and the issues to which the ABA would be attuned.

This course is designed to put students in touch with these developments as they affect the legal profession.

Course Texts

Riskin, Leonard L., and James E. Westbrook. *Dispute Resolution and Lawyers.* West Publishing Company, 1987.

Rogers, Nancy H., and Richard A. Salem. *A Student's Guide to Mediation and the Law.* Matthew Bender, 1987.

Readings for Dispute Resolution. Compiled reserve readings available for purchase.

Various background papers and other reading materials relevant to the assigned problems will be distributed throughout the semester.

Course Requirements

Class attendance and completion of assigned readings. Because this course combines theory, case knowledge and skilled practice, class participation is much more than a desiderata for the course.

Completion of two written problem assignments in mediation and negotiation. These will be distributed and discussed during class.

Completion of two simulation exercises in negotiation and mediation skills. This includes the preparation of planning and evaluation memoranda and the execution of the exercises themselves.

Writing an arbitration award based on material developed and submitted to the class by the instructors.

Writing a 12–15 page research paper on a topic of your choice in the field of dispute resolution. Possible topics include, but are certainly not limited to, the following:

- public sector negotiation (or mediation)
- mediation in small claims cases
- divorce mediation
- neighborhood justice centers
- victim-offender reconciliation projects
- arbitration (in salary disputes, border disputes, etc.)
- the establishment of court-annexed programs
- the mediation of prison riots
- mediation in domestic violence
- role of lawyers in: mediating racial disputes (Boston school desegregation); mediating school-community conflicts (textbooks); founding dispute resolution centers

- environmental mediation (including nuclear power issues; waste disposal–community conflicts; forestry conflicts, etc.)
- mediation of native American (or other ethnic group) land or resource claims
- ombuds structures (in public or private institutions)
- various topics on the training or ethics of dispute resolution
- various topics in international dispute resolution

The expectation of the instructors is that you will employ a full library (law and university) search strategy to uncover materials for your paper and that you will query (when applicable and appropriate) various persons and agencies regarding their practice and experience in the topic area.

CLASS SCHEDULE

Jan. 12—Course Introduction
- Riskin & Westbrook, pp. 1–70.
- Stephen B. Goldberg et al., "The Disputing Universe," ch. 1 of Goldberg et al., *Dispute Resolution* (Little, Brown and Company, 1985), pp. 3–16.
- Robert Coulson, "What Can One Person Do to Support Dispute Resolution?" *Negotiation Journal* (Oct. 1986), pp. 329–331.

Jan. 14—A Social Science View of Conflict and Its Resolution
- Louis Kriesberg, "The Bases of Social Conflicts," ch. 2 of Louis Kriesberg, *Social Conflicts* (Prentice Hall, 2nd edition), pp. 23–65.
- Riskin & Westbrook, pp. 403–436.

Jan. 19—A Lawyer's Approach to Conflict Analysis
- Riskin & Westbrook, pp. 71–110, 436–491.

Jan. 21—Synthesizing the Social Science and Law Views
- Richard Wendell Fogg, "Dealing with Conflict: A Repertoire of Creative, Peaceful Approaches," *Journal of Conflict Resolution*, vol. 29, no. 2 (June 1985), pp. 330–358.

Jan. 26—Negotiation Models
Receive Negotiation Problem #1. Selection of topic due.
- Riskin & Westbrook, pp. 112–145.
- John S. Murray, "Understanding Competing Theories of Negotiation," *Negotiation Journal*, vol. 2, no. 2 (April 1986), pp. 179–185.

Jan. 28—Negotiation Planning
In-class negotiation of Problem #1. Receive #2 (to be negotiated outside of class time).

Feb. 2—Negotiation Tactics
- Riskin & Westbrook, pp. 146–181.
- Dean G. Pruitt, "Strategic Choice in Negotiation," in Lawrence Susskind and Jeffrey Z. Rubin, eds., *Negotiation: Behavioral Perspectives*, a special issue of *American Behavioral Scientist*, vol. 27, no. 2 (Nov./Dec. 1983), pp. 167–194.

Feb. 4—View Negotiation Film
Negotiation Problem #2 due. Receive Negotiation Problem #3.

Feb. 9—Negotiation Ethics
Preparation memo for Problem #3 due.
- Riskin & Westbrook, pp. 181–195.
- David A. Lax and James K. Sebenius, "Three Ethical Issues in Negotiation," *Negotiation Journal*, vol. 2, no. 4 (Oct. 1986), pp. 363–370.

Feb. 11—In-Class Discussion of Negotiation Problem #3
Bibliography for paper due.

Feb. 16—In-Class Discussion of Negotiation Problem #3
Evaluation memo of Problem #3 due.

Feb. 18—Concluding Thoughts on Negotiation
- Roger Fisher, "Negotiating Power: Getting and Using Influence," in Lawrence Susskind and Jeffrey Z. Rubin, eds., *Negotiation: Behavioral Perspectives*, a special issue of *American Behavioral Scientist*, vol. 27, no. 2 (Nov./Dec. 1983), pp. 149–166.

Feb. 23—Mediation: An Extension of Negotiation and a Process in Its Own Right
- Riskin & Westbrook, pp. 69–78, 196–206.
- Rogers & Salem, pp. 1–61.
- Larry Ray, "The Alternative Dispute Resolution Movement," *Peace and Change: A Journal of Peace Research*, vol. VIII, nos. 2, 3 (Summer 1982), pp. 117–128.

Feb. 25—Who Are Mediators? What Makes for a Good Mediator?
- Rogers & Salem, pp. 107–136.
- Richard A. Salem, "Community Dispute Resolution Through Outside Intervention," *Peace and Change: A Journal of Peace Research*, vol. VIII, nos. 2, 3 (Summer 1982), pp. 91–104.
- Stephen B. Goldberg, "Meditations of a Mediator," *Negotiation Journal*, vol. 2, no. 4 (Oct. 1986), pp. 345–350.

Mar. 1—Mediation Styles and Process
Preparation memo for Problem #4 due. Outline for paper due.
- Rogers & Salem, pp. 223–244.
- Riskin & Westbrook, pp. 207–226.

- John M. Haynes, "Avoiding Traps Mediators Set for Themselves," *Negotiation Journal,* vol. 2, no. 2 (April 1986), pp. 187–194.

Mar. 3—In-Class Negotiation/Mediation of Problem #4

Mar. 8—In-Class Discussion of Problem #4
Evaluation memo of problem #4 due. Discussion on dealing with post-mediation issues.
- Rogers & Salem, pp. 171–186.

Mar. 10—Dispute Arenas of Mediation
- Riskin & Westbrook, pp. 227–249.
- Rogers & Salem, pp. 187–222; 255–263.

Mar. 22—An Analysis of the Legal and Social Conflict at SKOKIE
View film: *SKOKIE.*
- David Hamlin, *The Nazi/Skokie Conflict,* pp. 151–177.
- Richard A. Salem, "Mediating Political and Social Conflicts: The Nazi-Skokie Dispute," *Mediation Quarterly,* no. 5 (Sept. 1984), pp. 65–76.

Mar. 24—Ethical Issues in Mediation
- Rogers & Salem, pp. 61–106, 137–170, 255–268.
- James Laue, "Ethical Considerations in Choosing Intervention Roles," *Peace and Change: A Journal of Peace Research,* vol. VIII, nos. 2, 3 (Summer 1982), pp. 29–42.

Mar. 29—Introduction to Arbitration
Receive arbitration assignment.
- Riskin & Westbrook, pp. 250–296.

Mar. 31—Uses of Arbitration
View arbitration film.
- Riskin & Westbrook, pp. 296–323.

Apr. 5—Alternative Adjudication Methods
- Riskin & Westbrook, pp. 324–376.

Apr. 7—Concluding Thoughts on Arbitration
Arbitration assignment due.

Apr. 12—Emerging Trends in Dispute Resolution
- Riskin & Westbrook, pp. 377–402.

Apr. 14—New Techniques in Social Conflict
- Herbert Kelman, "The Reduction of International Conflict: An Inter-actional Approach," mimeo.

Apr. 19—The Social and Public Conflicts of the Next 30 Years
Paper due.
- Riskin & Westbrook, pp. 403–435.

Apr. 21—Applying Domestic Techniques to International Conflicts

- Daniel Druckman, "Four Cases of Conflict Mangagement: Lessons Learned," in *Perspectives on Negotiation*, eds., Diane B. Bendalmane and John W. McDonald, Jr., The Foreign Service Institute, 1986, pp. 263–288.

Apr. 26—New Ethical Challenges in ADR

- Marguerite Millhauser, "The Unspoken Resistance to Alternative Dispute Resolution," *Negotiation Journal* (Jan. 1987), pp. 29–35.

Apr. 28—Concluding Comments about ADR

Ecological Balance

1. Global Environmental Politics

Marvin S. Soroos   *Fall 1987*
Political Science Dept., North Carolina State
University, Raleigh, NC 27695

> *One rules Nature only by obeying it.*
>
> —Sir Francis Bacon

> *Earth provides enough to satisfy every man's need but not for every man's greed.*
>
> —Mahatma Gandhi

Global Environmental Politics explores the international politics of the ecological problems that confront humanity. Emphasis is placed upon the nature of global problems related to population, food, energy and non-fuel resources, pollution, and other forms of environmental degradation, as well as upon the responses of nations and international organizations to these problems. Conflicts over the use and management of the resources of international commons, in particular the ocean and other nonnational areas, will also be discussed.

Books to Purchase
Dahlberg, Kenneth, et al. *Environment and the Global Arena.* Duke University
    Press, 1985.
All non-Dahlberg reading assignments in this course syllabus can be found in a photocopy book to be purchased at Kinko's. See attached bibliography for additional readings.

Requirements

Each student will be required to write two papers. The first is a 4–6 page summary and application of Garrett Hardin's classical article, "The Tragedy of the Commons," which will be undertaken early in the semester. The second is a term paper of 8–12 pages that analyzes an international or foreign environmental problem. A more detailed description of this project will be circulated during the semester. There will be one midterm and a final examination. The course grades will be based on the two examinations (60%), the two papers (30%), and participation in class discussions (10%).

COURSE OUTLINE AND SCHEDULE

I. Overriding Issues and Problems

Considerable disagreement has arisen about the nature and severity of the ecological problems confronting humanity. Are we in the throes of a global "problematique" that jeopardizes the future quality of life? Or are those who predict ecological doom needlessly pessimistic, as their critics suggest? Hardin's "tragedy of the commons" will also be examined as a core theory for the study of environmental politics.

Session 1—Course Introduction
- Dahlberg, chs. 1 & 6.

Session 2—Overview of the Global Environment: Problematique or Cornucopia?
- Osterfeld, "Resources, People, and the Neomalthusian Fallacy," *Cato Journal* (Spring/Summer 1985), pp. 67–102.
- Burton, Review of "Our Common Future," in *Environment* (June 1987), pp. 25–29.

Session 3—The Tragedy of the Commons Game
- Myers and Myers, "From Duck Pond to the Global Commons: Increasing Awareness of the Supranational Nature of Emerging Environmental Issues," *Ambio*, Vol. 11, No. 4 (1982), pp. 195–201.

Session 4—Discussion of the Tragedy of the Commons
- Dahlberg, pp. 86–93.

Session 5—Environmental Values

Tragedy of the Commons paper is due.
- Dahlberg, ch. 3.
- Text of Environmental Principles—United Nations.
- Brown, "Principles for Resolving Conflicts Between Generations Over New Natural Resources," *Mazigira*, Vol. 7, No. 2 (1983), pp. 45–55.

II. Actors and Arenas

Understanding international responses to environmental problems requires some knowledge of the key types of international actors—nation-states and both governmental and nongovernmental types of international organizations. It is also important to know something about the arenas in which they interact, in particular permanent bodies and ad hoc world conferences.

Session 6—The Nation-State in Environmental Politics
* Dahlberg, ch. 2.

Session 7—International Organizations and the World Conference
* Perry, "Managing the World Environment," *Environment* (January/ February 1986), pp. 10, 15, 37.

III. Global Population Issues

Rapid rates of population growth are an underlying cause of many environmental problems. Numerous countries, most notably China, have adopted population policies to curb future growth. In 1984 a major world conference on population was held in Mexico City, at which the United States took a controversial stance on national and international population policies. Several other types of population problems are taken up, including migrations of people both within countries and between nations.

Session 8—World Population Trends
* Demeny, "The World Demographic Situation," pp. 27–66 in Menkin (ed.), *World Population & U.S. Policy* (1986).
* Tables, from the report of the World Resources Institute, *World Resources 1987.*

Session 9—The Family Planning Approach to Population Control
* Mosher, "Human Rights in the New China," *Society* (January/February 1986), pp. 27–35.
* Djerassi, "Abortion in the United States: Politics or Policy?" *Bulletin of the Atomic Scientists* (April 1986), pp. 38–41.

Session 10—International Population Programs
* Finkle and Crane, "Ideology and Politics at Mexico City: The United States at the 1984 International Conference on Population," *Population and Development Review* (March 1985), pp. 1–28.

Session 11—Migration and Urbanization
* Keely, "The Global Phenomenon of Immigration," *The World and I* (January 1987), pp. 97–105.
* Hardoy and Satterthwaite, "Third World Cities—The Environment of Poverty," World Resources Institute, *Journal 85,* pp. 45–57.

- Lamm, "The United States Cannot Be the Haven for All People," *Christian Science Monitor* (June 11, 1985), p. 16.
- "1985 World Refugee Statistics and Country Reports," pp. 36–40 in *World Refugee Survey*, U.S. Committee for Refugees.

IV. Global Food Issues

Can adequate food be provided for a mushrooming human population? Is widespread hunger caused by too many people or by political and economic processes? These questions are especially timely in view of the severe famine in Africa. Hardin's theory of "lifeboat ethics" will be discussed as a possible solution to the world's food/population problems. The dynamics of world food trade will also be examined.

Session 12—Global Food Trends
- Insel, "A World Awash in Grain," *Foreign Affairs* (Spring 1985), pp. 892–911.
- Population Crisis Committee, "Food and Population: Three Country Studies," *Population* (April 1987).

Session 13—Famine and Its Causes
- Dow, "Food and Security," *Bulletin of the Atomic Scientists* (September 1985), pp. 21–26.
- London and Lee, "Bread, Rice, and Freedom: The Peasantry and Agriculture in the USSR and China," *Freedom at Issue* (May/June 1987), pp. 3–8.

Session 14—The Lifeboat Debate
- Soroos, "Coping with Resource Scarcity: A Critique of Lifeboat Ethics," pp. 350–366 in Kegley and Wittkopf (eds.), *The Global Agenda* (1985).
- Madeley, "Does Economic Development Feed People?" *Ecologist*, Vol. 15, No. 1/2 (1985), pp. 36–41.
- Dogra, "Forcing the Starving to Export Their Food," *Ecologist*, Vol. 15, No. 1/2 (1985), pp. 42–43.

Session 15—Midterm Examination

V. Global Resource Issues

Resources are vital to modern industrial production. Periodically, concerns have been expressed about the adequacy of the remaining stocks of minerals to satisfy world demands and about the availability of "strategic" minerals from unreliable exporters, especially during times of war. The 1970s was the era of the world "energy crisis" as OPEC dominated international oil markets. In recent years, however, an oil glut resulted in lower prices. Should it be assumed that the crisis is over for the foreseeable future? A related issue is the potential for a proliferation of nuclear weapons, which is intractably related to the use of nuclear power throughout the world. Finally, consideration will be given to several dramatic industrial accidents with international ramifications.

Session 16—The Adequacy of Global Reserves and Minerals

- Trainer, "Potentially Recoverable Resources: How Recoverable?" pp. 396–412 in Glassner (ed.), *Global Resources* (1983).
- Center for Defense Information, "Resource Wars: The Myth of American Mineral Vulnerability," *Defense Monitor*, Vol. 14, No. 9 (1985).

Session 17—Oil and OPEC

- Kegley and Wittkopf, "Oil, Energy, and Resource Power," in *World Politics* (1985), pp. 310–342.
- Fri, "New Directions: Rethinking Energy Security," *Environment* (June 1987), pp. 16–42.

Session 18—Nuclear Energy and Proliferation

- Soroos, "Nuclear Proliferation: Preventing a Threat to World Peace," pp. 163–194 of Soroos, *Beyond Sovereignty* (1986).

Session 19—Environmental Accidents: Chernobyl, Bhopal, and Basil

- Shaikh, "The Dilemmas of Advanced Technology for the Third World," *Technology Review* (April 1986), pp. 57–66.
- Flavin, "Reassessing Nuclear Power," pp. 57–80 in Report of the Worldwatch Institute, *State of the World 1987*.

VI. Managing Global Commons

Many resources are located in global commons beyond the jurisdiction of individual states. Recently, the United Nations adopted a comprehensive ocean law treaty designed to manage the exploitation of most types of marine resources, including fisheries and seabed minerals. The treaty governing Antarctica has become a subject of increasing controversy as it comes up for review. Likewise, international policies are needed to regulate the rapidly growing use of outer space. Pollution of the global environment is an increasingly serious problem, especially in regard to the phenomena of acid rain, the greenhouse effect, depletion of the ozone layer, and oil substances in the oceans.

Session 20—The Law of the Sea Conference and the Seabed Regime

- Soroos, "Ocean Resource: Negotiating a New Law of the Sea," pp. 261–293 in Soroos, *Beyond Sovereignty* (1986).
- Pardo, "Ocean Space and Mankind," *Third World Quarterly* (July 1984), pp. 559–572.

Session 21—Preserving Living Resources of the Oceans

- Dahlberg, pp. 93–98.
- Carroz, "World Fisheries Face Change and Challenges," *Mazingira* (July 1984), pp. 17–23.

Session 22—Pollution of the Oceans and Atmosphere
- Dahlberg, pp. 103–115.
- LaBastille, "International Acid Test," *Sierra Club Bulletin* (May/June 1986), pp. 41–54.

Session 23—The Antarctic and Outer Space Regimes
- Kimball, "Antarctica: Testing the Great Experiment," *Environment* (September 1985), Vol. 27, No. 7, pp. 14–30.

VII. Miscellaneous Issues

Several other issues have arisen that deserve attention. Deserts are spreading. Tropical rainforests are being destroyed, and plant and animal species are becoming extinct at unprecedented rates. Much worse yet, the ultimate environmental catastrophe could occur in the form of what has been called a "nuclear winter," should large numbers of nuclear weapons be detonated in war. Finally, several contrasting designs for environmental futures will be examined.

Session 24—Desertification, Tropical Forests, and the Preservation of Species
- Dahlberg, pp. 98–103.
- Drengne, "Aridity and Land Degradation," *Environment* (October 1985), pp. 16–33.
- Myers, "The Global Heritage," pp. 333–346 in Myers, *The Ultimate Resource* (1984).

Session 25—"Nuclear Winter."
- Crutzen, "The Global Environment After Nuclear War," *Environment* (October 1985), pp. 6–37.

Session 26—Environmental Futures
- Dahlberg, ch. 5.

BIBLIOGRAPHY

General

Caldwell. *In Defense of Earth*, 1972.

Pirages. *The New Context for International Relations: Global Ecopolitics*, 1978.

Orr and Soroos. *The Global Predicament: Ecological Perspectives on World Order*, 1979.

Eckholm. *Down to Earth*, 1982.

UNEP. *The World Environment: 1972–1982*, 1982.

Kay and Jacobson. *Environmental Protection: The International Dimension*, 1983.

Caldwell. *International Environmental Policy: Emergence and Dimension*, 1984.

Myers. *GAIA: An Atlas of Planet Management*, 1984.

Dashmann. *Environmental Conservation,* 5th edition, 1984.
Southwick. *Global Ecology,* 1985.
Leonard. *Divesting Nature's Capital,* 1985.
Brown et al. *The State of the World,* 1984, 1985, 1986, 1987.

Doomsdayers and Cornucopians
Falk. *The Endangered Planet,* 1971.
Meadows et al. *The Limits of Growth,* 1972.
Mesarovic and Pestel. *Mankind at the Turning Point,* 1974.
Beckerman. *Two Cheers for the Affluent Society,* 1974.
Heilbroner. *An Inquiry into the Human Prospect,* 2nd edition, 1980.

The Tragedy of the Commons
Hardin. *Exploring the New Ethics for Survival,* 1972.
Hardin and Baden. *Managing the Commons,* 1977.
Hardin. *Filters Against Folly,* 1985.

Ethics
Ophuls. *Ecology and the Politics of Scarcity,* 1977.
Attfield. *The Ethics of Environmental Concern,* 1983.

Global Population Problems and Policies
Ehrlich. *The Population Bomb,* 1968.
Brown. *In the Human Interest,* 1972.
Policy Studies Journal, special issue entitled "Symposium on Population,"
    winter 1977.
Salas. *International Population Assistance: The First Decade,* 1979.
Salk and Salk. *World Population and Human Values,* 1981.
Marden et al. *Population in the Global Arena,* 1982.
Saidik. *Population: The UNFPA Experience,* 1984.
Salas. *Reflections on Population.* 1984.
Newman and Matzke. *Population: Patterns, Dynamics, and Prospects,* 1984.
Hartmann. *Reproductive Rights and Wrongs: The Global Politics of Population
    Control and Contraceptive Choice,* 1987.
Menden. *World Population & U.S. Policy: The Choices Ahead,* 1986.

Global Food Problems and Policies
Borgstrom. *The Hungry Planet,* 1972.
Eckholm. *Losing Ground,* 1976.
Bryson and Murray. *Climates of Hunger,* 1977.
George. *How the Other Half Dies,* 1977.
International Organization, special issue on "The Global Political Economy
    of Food," summer 1978.
Lappe and Collons. *Food First,* revised edition, 1979.
Alamgir. *Famine in South Asia: Political Economy of Mass Starvation,* 1979.
Dahlberg. *Beyond the Green Revolution,* 1979.
Robson. *Famine: Its Causes, Effects, and Management,* 1981.

Gilmore. *A Poor Harvest: The Clash of Policies and Interests in the Grain Trade,* 1982.
Byron. *The Causes of World Hunger,* 1982.
Cathie. *The Political Economy of Food Aid,* 1982.
Bayliss-Smith. *Understanding the Green Revolutions,* 1984.
Paarlberg. *Food Trade and Foreign Policy: India, the Soviet Union, and the United States,* 1985.
Berardi. *World Food, Population, and Development,* 1985.
Mann and Huddleston. *Food Policy: Frameworks for Analysis and Action,* 1985.

Lifeboat Ethics and Triage

Paddock and Paddock. *Time of Famines,* 1976.
Lucas and Ogletree. *Lifeboat Ethics: The Moral Dilemma,* 1976.
Brown. *Food Policy: The Responsibility of the United States in the Life and Death Choices,* 1976.
Brown and Shue. *Boundaries: National Autonomy and Its Limits,* 1981.
Rubinstein. *The Age of Triage: Fear and Hope in an Over Crowded World,* 1983.

Resources (General)

Tilton. *The Future of Nonfuel Minerals,* 1977.
Ridgeway. *Who Owns the Earth?* 1980.
Barnet. *The Lean Years,* 1980.
Rifkin. *Entropy: A New World View,* 1980.
Glassner. *Global Resources: Challenges of Interdependence,* 1983.
Hughes et al. *Energy in the Global Arena: Actors, Values, Policies, and Futures,* 1985.
World Resources Institute. *World Resources,* 1986, 1987.
Editorial Research Reports. *Earth's Threatened Resources,* 1986.
Repetto. *World Enough and Time: Successful Strategies for Resource Mangement,* 1986.

Resources and National Security

Choucri. *International Politics of Energy Interdependence,* 1976.
Garvey and Garvey. *International Resource Flows,* 1976.
Doran. *Myth, Oil, and Politics,* 1977.
Eckes. *The United States and the Global Struggle for Minerals,* 1979.
Orbis, special issue on "Oil Politics," winter 1980.
Deese. *Energy and Security,* 1980.
Clark and Page. *Energy, Vulnerability, and War,* 1981.
Yergen. *Global Insecurity,* 1982.
Castle and Price. *United States Interests and Global Natural Resources,* 1983.
Westermeyer and Shusterich. *United States and Artic Interests,* 1984.
Bullis and Mielke. *Strategic and Critical Materials,* 1985.
Van Rensburg. *Strategic Materials* (2 volumes), 1986.

Global Resources and International Conflict: Environmental Factors in Strategic Policy and Action, 1986.
Mikesell. *Nonfuel Minerals: Foreign Dependence and National Security*, 1987.

OPEC and the Petroleum Industry
Engler. *The Brotherhood of Oil*, 1977.
Odell. *Oil and World Power*, 1979.
Shafer. *International Oil Policy*, 1979.
El Mallakh. *OPEC: Twenty Years and Beyond*, 1982.
Kohl. *After the Second Oil Crisis: Energy Policies in Europe, Japan, and America*, 1982.
Peterson. *The Politics of Middle Eastern Oil*, 1983.
Ghosh. *OPEC, the Petroleum Industry and United States Energy Policy*, 1983.
Tetreault. *Revolution in the World Petroleum Market*, 1985.
Ahrari. *OPEC: The Failing Giant*, 1986.
Gever. *Beyond Oil*, 1986.
Karlsson. *Oil and World Order*, 1986.
Ali. *Oil, Turmoil, and Islam in the Middle East*, 1986.

Nuclear Power and Weapons Proliferation
Wonder. *Nuclear Fuel and American Foreign Policy*, 1977.
Wholstetter et al. *Nuclear Policies: Fuel Without the Bomb*, 1978.
Kapur. *International Nuclear Proliferation: Multilateral Diplomacy and Regional Aspects*, 1979.
Alexander and Ebinger. *Political Terrorism and Energy*, 1982.
Jones. *The Nuclear Suppliers and Non-Proliferation: Multilateral Diplomacy and Regional Aspects*, 1979.
Fischer and Szase. *Safeguarding the Atom: A Critical Appraisal*, 1985.
Goldblat. *Non-Proliferation: The Why and the Wherefore*, 1985.
Dewitt. *Nuclear Non-Proliferation and Global Security*, 1987.

Resource Problems of the Third World
Tinbergen. *Reshaping the International Order*, 1976.
Leontief et al. *The Future of the World Economy*, 1977.
Rothstein. *Global Bargaining: UNCTAD and the Request for a New International Economic Order*, 1979.
Brandt Commission. *North-South: A Program for Survival*, 1980.
Dolman. *Resources, Regimes, and World Order*, 1981.
Leonard. *Divesting Nature's Capital: The Political Economy of Environmental Abuse in the Third World*, 1985.
Pearson. *Multinational Corporations, Environment, and the Third World*, 1987.

Economics and Alternative Technologies
Schumacher. *Small Is Beautiful*, 1973.
Daly. *Toward a Steady-State Economy*, 1973.
Ophuls. *Ecology and the Politics of Scarcity*, 1977.
Pirages. *The Sustainable Society*, 1977.

Stokes. *Helping Ourselves: Local Solutions to Global Problems,* 1981.
Gever. *Beyond Oil: The Threat to Food and Fuel in the Coming Decades,* 1986.

Preserving Genetic Diversity

Myers. *The Sinking Ark,* 1979.
Ehrlich and Ehrlich. *Extinction: The Causes and Consequences of the Disappearance of Species,* 1981.
Bordman. *International Organization and the Conservation of Nature,* 1981.
Kaufman and Mallory. *The Last Extinction,* 1966.

The Law of the Sea and Ocean Resources

International Organization, special issue on "Restructuring Ocean Regimes," spring 1977.
Barkenbus. *Deep Seabed Resources,* 1979.
Eckert. *The Enclosure of Ocean Resources: Economics and the Law of the Sea,* 1979.
Columbia Journal of World Business, special issue on Law of the Sea Conference, winter 1980.
Hollick. *U.S. Foreign Policy and the Law of the Seas,* 1981.
Shearer. *The International Law of the Sea,* 1982.
Shusterich. *Resource Management and the Oceans,* 1982.
Charney. *The New Nationalism and the Use of Common Spaces,* 1982.
Rozakis and Stephanson. *The New Law of the Sea,* 1983.
Oxman. *The Law of the Sea: U.S. Policy Dilemma,* 1983.
Laursen. *Superpower at Sea: U.S. Ocean Policy,* 1983.
Churchill and Lowe. *The Law of the Sea,* 1983.
Cuyvers. *Ocean Uses and Their Regulation,* 1984.
Sohn and Gustafson. *The Law of the Sea in a Nutshell,* 1984.
Booth. *Law, Force and Diplomacy at Sea,* 1985.

Living Resources of the Ocean

Knight. *Managing the Sea's Living Resources,* 1977.
Schmidhauser and Totten. *The Whaling Issue in US-Japanese Relations,* 1978.
Allen. *Conservation and Management of Whales,* 1981.
McNally. *So Remorseless a Havoc: Of Dolphins, Whales, and Men,* 1981.
Rothchild. *Global Fisheries: Perspectives for the 1980s,* 1983.
Kent and Valencia. *Marine Policy in South East Asia,* 1985.

Resources of Antarctica and Outer Space

O'Neil. *The High Frontier,* 1977.
Smith. *Space Stations and International Law and Policy,* 1979.
Soroos. "The Commons in the Sky," *International Organization,* summer 1982.
Karnik. *Alternative Space Futures and the Human Condition,* 1982.
Christol. *The Modern International Law of Outer Space,* 1982.
Auburn. *Antarctic Law and Politics,* 1982.
Quigg. *A Pole Apart: The Emerging Issue of Antarctica,* 1983.
Westermeyer. *The Politics of Mineral Resource Development in Antarctica,* 1984.

Pollution of the Oceans

Mostert. *Supership*, 1974.

Schneider. *World Public Order of the Environment*, 1979.

M'Gonigle and Zacher. *Pollution, Politics, and International Law: Tankers at Sea*, 1979.

Silverstein. *Superships and Nation States*, 1979.

Cusine and Grant. *The Impact of Marine Pollution*, 1980.

Gold. *Maritime Transport: The Evolution of International Marine Policy and Shipping Law*, 1981, ch. 7.

Johnston. *The Environmental Law of the Sea*, 1981.

Pollution of the Atmosphere

Enloe. *The Politics of Pollution in a Comparative Perspective*, 1975.

Van Lier. *Acid Rain and International Law*, 1981.

Nanda. *World Climate Change: The Role of International Law and Institutions*, 1983.

Wetstone and Roencrance. *Acid Rain in Europe and North America*, 1983.

Luoma. *Troubled Skies, Troubled Waters: The Study of Acid Rain*, 1984.

Schmandt and Roderick. *Acid Rain and Friendly Neighbors*, 1985.

Yanarella. *The Acid Rain Debate: Scientific, Economic, and Political Dimensions*, 1985.

Tickell. *Climate Change and World Affairs*, 1986.

Toxic Substances

Eckholm. *The Picture of Health*, 1977.

Weir and Shapiro. *Circle of Poison: Pesticides and People in a Hungry World*, 1981.

Ives. *The Export of Hazard: Transnational Corporations and Environmental Control*, 1985.

War and the Environment

Ehrlich et al. *The Cold and the Dark: The World After Nuclear War*, 1984.

Westing. *Environmental Warfare: A Technical, Legal, and Policy Appraisal*, 1984.

Dotto. *Planet Earth in Jeopardy: Environmental Consequences of Nuclear War*, 1986.

2. International Environmental Policy and Development

Arpad Von Lazar and Joanne Kauffman   *Spring 1988*
Fletcher School of Law and Diplomacy, Tufts University,
Medford, MA 02155

The aim of this seminar is to introduce students to the arena of international environmental policy and its relationship to economic development. The course will present an overview of the roles of governments, international organizations, industry, and Non-Governmental Organizations (NGOs) in developing and implementing policies that affect the global environment. It examines relations between industrialized and developing nations and how policies and actions taken in one country impact both environmentally and economically on others. Particular emphasis will be placed on exploring global environmental issues that require international management.

The seminar meets on Tuesdays from 3 to 5 P.M. Class sessions will include presentations by guest specialists on the topic and discussions of readings. Active student participation is expected. The seminar is broadly organized into three main areas: global challenges (including discussions of major international environmental themes); the institutional response (describing and analyzing the roles of institutional players in determining international environmental policy); and global opportunities for addressing the issues.

Readings

One text has been ordered from the book store: the *Report of the World Commission on Environment and Development.* A selection of recommended readings in each of the three general areas will be on reserve at the Fletcher School Library. Other assigned readings will be made available in advance of presentations.

Requirements

A letter grade will be given based on class participation and completion of a paper of 20–30 pages.

COURSE OUTLINE AND READINGS

Global Challenges

Jan. 26—Introduction to the Seminar
Materials, expectations, historical background.
- The World Commission on Environment and Development, *Our Common Future*, Introduction.

Feb. 2—Population and Development
Speaker: Janet Bauer, Tufts University, Anthropology.
- Lester Brown et al., *State of the World 1984*, ch. 2, "Stablilizing Population."
- *Our Common Future*, ch. 4, "Population and Human Resources."

Feb. 9—International Management of Chemicals
Speaker: Dr. Rashid Shaikh.
- R. Shaikh, "The Dilemmas of Advanced Technology for the Third World," *Technology Review*, April 1986, pp. 57–64.
- R. Shaikh and J. Kauffman-Nichols, "The International Management of Chemicals," *Ambio*, Vol. XIII, No. 2, 1984.

Feb. 16—Sustainable Development
Economic and political issues. Dr. Francisco Szekeley, Harvard University.
- *Our Common Future*, "Part I: Common Concerns," chs. 1–3.

Feb. 23—Environmental Pollution in Newly Industrialized Countries: The Case of Taiwan
Dr. Shil Pyng Shiah and Mr. George Liu, NE/Far East Environmental Service Co., Boston/Taiwan.
- Readings to be announced.

Mar. 1—Role of the Private Sector: The Politics of Business/Community Relations
Case example: "The Killing of the Rhine." Presentors: Professor von Lazar and Andy Durrell.
- C.S. Pearson, *Down to Business: Multinational Corporations, the Environment and Development*, World Resources Institute, Washington, D.C., Study 2, Jan. 1985.
- *Our Common Future*, ch. 8, "Industry: Producing More with Less."

Mar. 8—National Governments
Speaker: Dr. Shiela Jassanoff, Cornell University.
- Ronald Brickman, Sheila Jasanoff, and Thomas Ilgen, *Controlling Chemicals: The Politics of Regulation in Europe and the United States* (Ithaca, NY: Cornell University Press, 1985), ch. 2, pp. 28–53.

- David Vogel, *National Styles of Regulation* (Ithaca, NY: Cornell University Press, 1986), "The Dynamics of Business-Government Relations in Great Britain and the U.S.," ch. 6, pp. 226–263.

Mar. 15 & 22—No Class

Mar. 29—NGOs: Their Role in Integrating Environmental Concerns with Economic Development Plans and Programs
Kishore Mandhyan.
- Readings to be announced.

Apr. 5—Biological Species Preservation
Speaker: Peter Ashton, Harvard University.
- *Our Common Future*, ch. 6, "Species and Ecosystems: Resources for Development."

Apr. 12—International Organizations
Speaker: Dr. Jeremy Warford, Acting Director, Environmental Division, World Bank.
- John Horberry, "The Accountability of Development Assistance Agencies: The Case of Environmental Policy," *Ecology Law Quarterly*, Vol. 12, No. 4.
- *Our Common Future*, ch. 12, "Towards Common Action: Proposals for Institutional and Legal Change."

Apr. 19—International Dispute Resolution
Speaker: Dr. Larry Susskind, MIT.
- Selections from *The Intermediaries*, Oran Young.

Apr. 26 & May 3—Presentation of Student Papers

3. Introduction to Appropriate Technology

Kenneth A. Dahlberg   *Winter 1988*
Environmental Studies, Western Michigan University,
Kalamazoo, MI 49008

This course is an academic inquiry into the environmental, ethical, technological and socio-political aspects of "appropriate technology." Such technologies are designed to fit local environments and to be consistent with the resources and values of respective cultures. Lectures will review the development of appropriate technology, its importance in today's world, and its role in creating a livable future.

This course in appropriate technology involves an inquiry into how different societies have organized themselves to provide for their basic physical needs. These include energy or fuel, shelter, food, materials, and transportation. It also examines how cultural assumptions and values interact with technologies and how they in turn impact upon both society and the natural environment.

It thus seeks to help students develop better ways to evaluate technologies and their impacts. By critically examining technologies and their underlying values, the course should help us to realize that, as Tom Bender said, "before we choose our tools and technologies we must choose our dreams and values, for some technologies serve them, while others make them unattainable."

Grading Procedures
Your grade will be determined as follows: class attendance and participation—10%; quizzes—30%; midterm—30%; final exam—30%. In addition, students can choose to do a special project for extra credit.

Required Textbooks
Bodley, John H. *Victims of Progress.*
Harris, Marvin. *America Now.*
Course Packet.
See bibliography for additional readings.

COURSE OUTLINE,
SCHEDULE, AND ASSIGNMENTS

I. Introduction [Jan. 5]

Jan. 7—Basic Concepts: Culture, Society, Personality, Technology, and Environment

II. The Growth of Industrial Society and Its Impacts on the Third World

Jan. 12 & 14—Basic Concepts: Transitions, Energy and Industrialism, Informal and Formal Sectors
 • Scott Burns.

Jan. 19 & 21—Colonialism and Its Impacts on Indigenous Peoples
 • Bodley, chs. 1–6 and 7–10.

III. Technology, Resources, and the Limits
of Industrial Society

Jan. 26—Basic Concepts: Resources, Population, and Environment
- The Global 2000 Report.
- Myers.
- Dahlberg.

Jan. 28—Social Limits to Growth

IV. Technology and Social Change
in Industrial Society

Feb. 2 & 4—Basic Concepts: The Non-Neutrality of Technologies, Hard and Soft Energy Paths
- Schumacher, "Technology. . . ."
- Lovins.

Feb. 9, 16, & 18—Cultural Changes
Hard and soft path approaches. Midterm exam Feb. 25.
- Harris, chs. 1–5.
- Harris, chs. 6–9.
- Robertson, "Five Scenarios."

Mar. 1 & 3—Energy and Environmental Changes
Hard and soft path approaches.
- Davis.
- Olkowski.

Mar. 15 & 17—Food and Agricultural Changes
Hard and soft path approaches.
- Lappe.
- Collins.
- Van der Ryn & Bunnell.

Mar 22—Economics and Employment Changes
Hard and soft path approaches.
- Illich.
- Stein.

V. Technology and Social Change
in the Third World

Mar. 24—Basic Concepts: Appropriate Technology, Conventional Development Strategies (CDS), and Alternative Development Strategies (ADS)
- Diwan & Livingston.

Mar. 29—Cultural Changes
CDS, ADS, and Appropriate Technologies.
 • Schumacher, "Social and Economic Problems. . . ."

Mar. 31—Energy and Environmental Changes; Food and Agricultural Changes
CDS—the Lakhra Coal Project in Pakistan. ADS and AT. CDS—the green revolution. ADS and AT—agroecology.

Apr. 5—Economic and Employment Changes
CDS and the export of jobs. ADS and AT—local self reliance.
 • Darrow.

VI. Alternative Futures

Apr. 7—Basic Concepts: The Five Futures of Robertson
 • Review Robertson's "Five Scenarios."

Apr. 12—Individual and Community Action
 • Robertson, "Pieces of Action."

Apr. 14—Summary and Conclusions

Apr. 22—Final Exam

APPROPRIATE TECHNOLOGY BIBLIOGRAPHY

Compiled by Kenneth Dahlberg, Dennis Darling, and Maynard Kaufman

I. General Reference Books on Appropriate Technology

Andree, Carolyn. *Appropriate Technology—A Selected Annotated Bibliography.* East Lansing, MI: Women in International Development, 1982.

Baldwin, J., and Stewart Brand. *Soft-Tech.* New York: Penguin, 1978.

Brand, Stewart, ed. *The Next Whole Earth Catalog.* Random House, 1980.

Carr, Marilyn, ed. *The AT Reader: The Theory and Practice of Appropriate Technology.* Croton on Hudson, New York: ITDG/NA, 1985.

Darrow, Ken, and Mike Saxenian. *Appropriate Technology Sourcebook.* Stanford, CA: Volunteers in Asia, 1986.

DeMoll, Land, et al., eds. *Rainbook: Resources for Appropriate Technology.* New York: Schocken Books, 1977.

John Lobell, *The Little Green Book.* Shambhala, 1981.

Robert J. Mitchell, ed. *Experiences in Appropriate Technology.* Ottawa, Canada: 1980 or 1981.

II. Conceptual Basis of Appropriate Technology

Boyle, Godfrey, and Peter Harper. *Radical Technology*. Pantheon, 1976.

Congdon, R.J., ed. *Introduction to Appropriate Technology: Toward a Simpler Lifestyle*. Rodale Press, 1977.

DeMoll, Land, and Gigi Coe, eds. *Stepping Stones: Appropriate Technology and Beyond*. Schocken, 1978.

Dorf, Richard, and Yvonne L. Hunter. *Appropriate Visions: Technology, the Environment and the Individual*. San Francisco: Boyd & Fraser, 1978.

Dunn, P.D. *Appropriate Technology, Technology with a Human Face*. New York: Schocken, 1978.

Ekins, Paul, ed. *The Living Economy: A New Economics in the Making*. Routledge & Kegan Paul, in association with Methuen, 1987.

Illich, Ivan. *Tools for Conviviality*. Harper & Row, 1973.

———. *Shadow Work*. Marion Boyars, 1981.

Satin, Mark. *New Age Politics: Healing Self and Society*. Whitecap Books, 2229 Jefferson Ave., West Vancouver, BC V7V2A9.

Schumacher, E.F. *Good Work*. Harper & Row, 1979.

———. *Small Is Beautiful*. Harper & Row, 1973.

III. Critiques of High Technology and Centralization

Bookchin, Murray. *The Ecology of Freedom: The Emergence and Dissolution of Hierarchy*. Cheshire Books, 1982.

Commoner, Barry. *The Closing Circle: Nature, Man and Technology*. Bantam Books, 1971.

Ellul, Jacques. *The Technological Society*. Vintage Books, 1964.

Kohr, Leopold. *Overdeveloped Nations: Diseconomies of Scale*. Schocken, 1977.

Mumford, Lewis. *The Myth of the Machine: Technics and Human Development*. Harcourt, Brace & World, 1967.

———. *The Myth of the Machine: The Pentagon of Power*. Harcourt, Brace, Jovanovich, 1970.

Pacey, Arnold. *The Culture of Technology*. Oxford: Basil Blackwell, 1983.

Rifkin, Jeremy. *Algeny*. Penguin, 1984.

Schell, Jonathan. *The Fate of the Earth*. Avon, 1982.

Toffler, Alvin. *The Third Wave*. Bantam Books, 1981.

IV. Appropriate Technology, Decentralization and a Sustainable Society

Cotgrove, Stephen. *Catastrophe or Cornucopia: The Environment, Politics and the Future*. John Wiley, 1982.

Davis, W. Jackson. *The Seventh Year: Industrial Civilization in Transition*. New York: W.W. Norton, 1979.

Dickson, David. *Alternative Technology and the Politics of Technical Change*. 1974.

Goldsmith, Edward. *Blueprint for Survival*. Signet, 1972.

Hayes, Denis. *Rays of Hope: The Transition to a Post-Petroleum World*.

Henderson, Hazel. *The Politics of the Solar Age: Alternative to Economics*. Anchor Books, 1981.

Hawken, Paul, James Ogilvy, and Peter Schwartz. *Seven Tomorrows.* Bantam Books, 1982.

Robertson, James. *The Sane Alternative: A Choice of Futures.* St. Paul: River Basin Publishing Co., 1979.

Sale, Kirkpatrick. *Dwellers in the Land: The Bioregional Vision.* San Francisco: Sierra Club Books, 1985.

Stavrianos, L.S. *The Promise of the Coming Dark Age.* San Francisco: W.H. Freeman & Co., 1976.

V. Appropriate Technology and the Global Environment

Brown, Lester. *The Twenty-Ninth Day.* Norton, 1978.

Council on Environmental Quality. *The Global 2000 Report to the President.*

Eckholm, Eric. *Losing Ground: Environmental Stress and World Food Prospects.* Norton, 1976.

Meadows, Donella, et al. *The Limits of Growth.* Universe Books, 1972.

VI. Appropriate Technology and "Development"

Dahlberg, Kenneth. *Beyond the Green Revolution: The Ecology and Politics of Global Agricultural Development.* Plenum Press, 1979.

Diwan, Romesh, and Dennis Livingston. *Alternative Development Strategies and Appropriate Technology: Science Policy for an Equitable World Order.* Pergamon Press, 1979.

Goulet, Denis. *The Uncertain Promise: Value Conflicts in Technology Transfer.* Washington: Overseas Development Council, 1977.

Jequier, Nicolas. *Appropriate Technology: Problems and Promises.* Paris: Organization for Economic Cooperation and Development, 1977.

Max-Neef, Manfred A. *From the Outside Looking In: Experiences in "Barefoot Economics."* Sweden: Dag Hammarskjold Foundation, 1982.

Stewart, Francis. *Macro Politics for Appropriate Technology in Developing Countries.* Westview Press, 1987.

VII. The Energy Problem and Alternative Sources of Energy

Carter, Joe, ed. *The Energy Saver's Handbook.* Emmaus, PA: Rodale Press, 1982.

Clark, Wilson. *Energy for Survival: The Alternative to Extinction.* Anchor Books, 1975.

Kranzberg, Melvin, ed. *Energy and the Way We Live.* San Francisco: Boyd and Fraser, 1980.

Lovins, Amory B. *Soft Energy Paths: Toward a Durable Peace.* San Francisco: Friends of the Earth, Inc., 1977.

Merrill, Richard, et al. *Energy Primer: Solar, Water, Wind, and Biofuels.* Delta Books, 1978.

Odum, Howard, and Elizabeth C. Odum. *Energy Basis for Man and Nature.* McGraw-Hill, 1976.

Rifken, Jeremy. *Entropy: A New World View.* Viking Press, 1980.

Seymour, John. *The Forgotten Crafts.* Knopf, 1984.

Stobaugh, Robert, and Daniel Yergin, eds. *Energy Future: Report of the Energy Project at the Harvard Business School.* Random House, 1979.

Weedall, Mike, ed. *Financing Energy Conservation.* Washington, D.C.: American Council for an Energy-Efficient Economy, 1986.

VIII. Appropriate Technology on the Household Level

Center for Science in the Public Interest, *99 Ways to a Simpler Lifestyle.* Anchor Books, 1977.

Kleeberg, Irene O. *The Home Energy Saver.* New York: Butterick Publishing, 1977.

Leckie, Jim, et al. *Other Homes and Garbage: Designs for Self-Sufficient Living.* San Francisco: Sierra Club, 1975.

Morris, David J. *Be Your Own Power Company.* Rodale Press, 1983.

Nash, June. *Implications of Technological Change for Household Level and Rural Development.* East Lansing, MI: Office of Women in International Development, 1983.

Olkowski, Helga, et al. *The Integral Urban House: Self-Reliant Living in the City.* San Francisco: Sierra Club Books, 1979.

Strasser, Susan. *Never Done.* Pantheon Books: Random House, 1982.

Tood, Nancy Todd, ed. *The Book of the New Alchemists.* E.P. Dutton, 1977.

IX. Appropriate Technology and Community

Brunner, Ronald D., ed. *Community Energy Options.* Ann Arbor, MI: University of Michigan Press, 1982.

Carter, Joe, ed. *The Energy Saver's Handbook: For Town and City People.* Emmus, PA: Rodale Press, 1982.

Chapel, Paige, ed. *The City Greenhouse Book.* Chicago, IL: Center for Neighborhood Technology, 1980.

Frewdenberg, Nicholas. *Not in Our Backyards: Community Action for Health and Environment.* New York: Monthly Review Press, 1984.

Mayer, Neil, and Jennifer Blake. *Keys to the Growth of Neighborhood Development Organizations.* Washington, D.C.: Urban Institute, 1981.

Morris, David. *New City States.* Washington, D.C.: Institute for Local Self-Reliance, 1982.

Ross, David P., and Peter J. Usher. *From the Roots Up: Economic Development as if Community Mattered.* The Bootstrap Press, 1986.

Vine, Edward L. *Solarizing America—The Davis Experience.* Washington, D.C.: Conference on Alternative State and Local Politics, 1981.

Vogler, Jon. *Work from Waste: Recycling Waste to Create Employment.* Croton on Hudson, NY: ITDG/NA, 1981.

X. Appropriate Technology, Food, and Agriculture

Berry, Wendell. *The Gift of Good Land.* North Point Press, 1981.

————. *The Unsettling of America.* Sierra Club Books, 1977.

Branch, Diana, ed. *Tools for Homesteaders, and Small-Scale Farmers.* Rodale Press, 1978.

Gliessman, Stephen R. "An Agroecological Approach to Sustainable Agriculture," in *Good Farming*, Wes Jackson and Bruce Colman, eds., 1984.

Jackson, Wes. *New Roots for Agriculture*. San Francisco, CA: Friends of the Earth, 1980.

Knorr, Dietrich. *Sustainable Food Systems*. Westport, CT: AVI Publishing Company, 1982.

Lockeretz, William, ed. *Environmentally Sound Agriculture*. New York: Praeger Special Studies, 1983.

Richard Merrill, ed. *Radical Agriculture*. Harper & Row, 1976.

Mollison, Bill. *Permaculture One* and *Permaculture Two*. Stanley, Australia: Togari Books, 1979 & 1981.

Oelhaf, R.C. *Organic Agriculture: Economic and Ecological Comparisons with Conventional Methods*. New York: Halsted Press, 1978.

XVII

Women
and World Order

1. Women, Peace, and Protest

Jennifer Schirmer   *Fall 1983*
Women's Studies Program, Wellesley College,
Wellesley, MA 02135

Women play an important part in the movements for peace and human rights. This course will examine the nature and history of these movements as well as their organizational and ideological structures. We will focus on understanding if, why, and under what circumstances gender becomes a central force in the development of these movements. Questions we will address are 1) Why and in what ways have women been central to the European peace movement? 2) How has the involvement of women helped to define the human rights movement in Latin America? and 3) Has feminist theory accounted for the nature of women's protest?

Course Requirements
Classes will consist of both lectures and student-led discussions. Therefore, both attendance and preparation are the most important requirements for this course. A takehome midterm and final exam, together with a 20-page paper on one group discussed, are the other requirements. Grading is based on an average of exams, paper, class participation and preparation. Students are encouraged to read the daily press (at least two newspapers) and listen to National Public Radio's daily news broadcasts at 5 P.M. to be informed about both nuclear and human rights issues.

Course Materials

Johnstone, Diana. *The Politics of Euromissiles.* Verso, 1985.

Thompson, Dorothy, ed. *Over Our Dead Bodies.* Virago, 1983.

"Women and Peace," *END Journal,* Issue 14 (Feb.-Mar. 1985) (*Journal of European Nuclear Disarmament*).

Traba, Marta. *Mothers and Shadows.* Readers International, 1985.

Simon, Jean-Marie. Group of Mutual Support Americas Watch, 1985.

Disappearances: A Workbook. London: Amnesty International, 1981.

Suggested Readings

McAllister, Pam, ed. *Re-Weaving the Web of Life: Feminism and Non-Violence.* New Society, 1985.

Zuckerman, Solly. *Nuclear Illusion and Reality.* Vintage Books, 1982.

Langguth, A.J. *Hidden Terrors.* Pantheon Books, 1978.

Dorfman, Ariel. *Widows.* Aventura Books, 1983.

Argueta, Manlio. *One Day of Life.* Aventura Books, 1983.

LECTURES AND DISCUSSIONS

September 3 & 10—Women's Protest

Are there uniformities common to female militancy? What is non-violent protest? Can we talk about "universals" (i.e., are women naturally peaceful)? What are the difficulties with cross-cultural comparison? What is the difference between female and feminist consciousness? Can a feminist theory be developed which incorporates these differences among women?

- Stack, Caulfield, et al., "Anthropology: Review Essay." *Signs,* Vol. 1(1) (Autumn 1975).
- Leacock, E., & Nash, J., "Ideologies of Sex Archetypes and Stereotypes," *Annals of the New York Academy,* No. 285, 1977.
- Wipper, A., "Riot and Rebellion Among African Women: Three Examples of Women's Political Clout," in *Perspectives on Power,* O'Barr (ed.), Duke University Press, 1982.
- MacKinnon, Catherine, "Feminism, Marxism, Method and the State: Toward Feminist Jurisprudence," *Signs,* Vol. 8, No. 4, 1983.

Background Reading on Feminist Theory

- Keohane, N., Gelpi, B., Rosaldo, M. (eds.), *Feminist Theory: A Critique of Ideology,* University of Chicago Press, 1982.
- Caplan, P., & Bujra, J. (eds.), *Women United, Women Divided,* Indiana University Press.
- Campus Showing of BBC video "Threads" regarding nuclear war in England.

September 17—Women and Nuclear Protest: Greenham Common Women

What are the conditions that gave rise to such protest? Who are these women and what are their demands? What is the response of the political elites? How are they and the issue of nonviolent/violent actions presented to the public by the media? *Speaker:* Gwyn Kirk of Greenham Women Against Cruise Missiles, Transatlantic Peace Connections Project: New York and London. *Video:* Greenham Women's Peace Camps. *Photo Exhibit:* "The Early Years of the Peace Camp" at the Women's Studies Program office, Founders Hall.

- Center for Constitutional Rights, "Greenham Women Against Cruise Missiles," Legal Action Pamphlet.
- Thompson, D., *Over Our Dead Bodies*, Chapters 5, 6, & 18.
- Glasgow University Media Group, "TV News Coverage of Greenham Common," *War and Peace News*, 1986.
- Snitow, Ann, "Holding the Line at Greenham," *Mother Jones* (Feb.-Mar. 1985) (photocopy).
- Meyerding, J., "Re-claiming Non-violence," in *Re-Weaving the Web of Life*, pp. 5–15.
- Kogan, D., & Regan, M., "Groups of the Outside Left," in *The Battle of the Labour Party*, London: St. Martin's Press, 1983.
- Photocopies from *The Observer* and *The New Statesman*.

Background Reading

- Collective, "Breaching the Peace: A Collection of Radical Feminist Papers," OnlyWomenPress: London, 1983.
- Blackwood, Caroline, *On The Perimeter*, Penguin Books, 1985.
- Cook, Alice, & Kirk, Gwyn, *Greenham Women Everywhere*, South End Press: Boston, 1983.

September 24—Women and Nuclear Protest: Italian Women's Peace Movement

Speaker: Elisabetta Addis from Rome

- Addis, Elisabetta, & Tiliacos, Nicoletta, "The 10 March Group: The Political Experience of Feminists Dealing with the Issue of Peace in Europe," *Memoria*, No. 13, 1986
- Spotts, F., *Italy—A Difficult Democracy*, Cambridge University Press: Cambridge, England, 1985, chs. TBA.

October 1 & 8—General Discussion and Review

Oct. 3, Take-home exam handed out: due Oct. 15.

- Myrdal, A., *Dynamics of European Disarmament*, Spokesman Press: Nottingham, England, 1981, pages TBA.
- Johnstone, D., *The Politics of Euromissiles*, Verso, 1985.
- Cambridge, MA, Civil Defense Department, "Cambridge and Nuclear Weapons. Is There a Place to Hide?" (1984) (class handout).
- Wartenberg, Th. E., "Beyond Babes and Banners," *New Political Science*, Winter 1985–1986, No. 14, pp. 157–171.
- Kaplan, T., "Female Consciousness and Collective Action: The Case of Barcelona 1910–1918," *Signs*, Vol. 7 (3), (Spring 1982), pp. 545–566.

General Reading
- Zuckerman, S., *Nuclear Illusion and Reality.*
- Scheer, R., *With Enough Shovels: Reagan, Bush and Nuclear War,* New York: Random House, 1982.
- Minnian, J. & Bolsover, P. (eds.)., *The CND Story,* London: Allison & Busby, 1983.

German Greens
- Kelly, Petra, *Fighting for Hope,* South End Press: Boston.
- Markovits, A., "The Greens," *New German Critique.*

Women's Role
- Cambridge Women's Peace Collective, *My Country Is the Whole World,* Pandora Press, 1984.
- Laska, Vera (ed)., *Women in the Resistance and in the Holocaust,* Greenwood Press, 1983.
- Enloe, Cynthia, *Does Khaki Become You?* Boston: South End Press, 1983.

Protest
- Marsh, Alan, *Protest and Political Consciousness,* Sage Publications, 1978.
- Offe, Claus, "New Social Movements and the Meta-Political Conflict of Political Paradigms." Paper for Goldthorpe Working Group, 1982.

October 15—Women and Human Rights Protest in Latin America
What are the conditions that gave rise to such protest? Who are these women and what are their demands? What is the response of the political elites? How are they and the issue of nonviolent/violent actions presented to the public by the media? *Slides:* On torture, from SERPAJ in Chile. *Campus showing of film: Your Neighbor's Son* (Danish), regarding the training of torturers in Greece.
- Amnesty International, *"Disappearance": A Workbook*
- Amnesty International, *Torture in the Eighties*
- Schirmer, J., "Human Rights Protest by Women in Latin America," section on National Security State.

Background Reading—Repression
- Rivabella, Omar, *Requiem for a Woman's Soul,* Random House, 1985.
- Langguth, A.J., *Hidden Terrors.*

Resistance
- Andreas, Carol, *When Women Rebel: The Rise of Popular Feminism in Peru,* Lawrence Hill & Co., Westport, CT, 1985.

October 22 & 29—Guatemalan Group of Mutual Support (GAM)
Video: 60 Minutes on GAM. *Film: When the Mountains Tremble.*
- Simon, Jean-Marie, "Group of Mutual Support."

- McClintock, M., *The American Connection: State Terror and Popular Resistance in Guatemala*, Vol. 2, Zed Press: London, 1985.
- Burgos-Debray, E., *I, Rigoberta Menchu.*

Background Reading

- Black, George, *Garrison Guatemala*, New York: Monthly Review Press, 1984.
- Washington Office on Latin America, "Security and Development in the Guatemalan Highlands," August 1985.

November 5 & 12—Argentinian Plaza de Mayo Mothers
Film: Las Madres.
- Traba, Marta, *Mothers and Shadows*, Readers International, 1981.
- Simpson, J., & Bennett, J., *The Disappeared and the Mothers of the Plaza*, New York: St. Martin's Press, 1985, chs. 1, 9, 10, and Appendix.
- Corradi, Juan, *The Fitful Republic*, Boulder, CO: Westview Press, 1985.

Background Reading

- Partnoy, Alicia, *The Little School: Tales of Disappearance and Survival in Argentina*, Pittsburgh, PA: Cleis Press, 1986.
- Argentinian Commission for the Investigation of Disappeared Persons (CONADEP), *Nunca Mas*, Buenos Aires: Editorial El Cid.
- Americas Watch, "The State Department Misinforms: A Study of Accounting for the Disappeared in Argentina" (October 1983).
- Dabat & Lorenzano, *The Malkvinas War.*

November 19 & 26—Chilean Agrupacion
Videos: By Reason or by Force? and *Somos Mas.*
- Schirmer, J., "Human Rights Protest by Women in Latin America," section on Chile.
- Schirmer, J., "Legalised Repression in Chile," *Dissent* (Summer 1983).
- WOLA, Report on Chile, 1986.

Background Reading

- Vidal, Hernan, "Dar la Vida Por la Vida," University of Minnesota, 1984.
- Dorfman, Ariel, *Widows* (novel).

December 3—Summation and Review
What are the similarities and differences among these groups? Take-home final handed out.

2. Women in the Non-Western World

Deborah Gerner   *Fall 1983*
Hamilton College*

The life chances of most women—their participation in the economic system, their citizenship in the nation, and their role and rights (or lack thereof)— are determined to some degree by the political system of the nation within which they live. Conversely, women's participation in economic production, in political movements, and in revolutions may help to determine the kind of society in which they live. This course is intended to stimulate thinking on the differences in women's status in various Non-Western societies (capitalist, socialist, developed, underdeveloped, revolutionary, conservative) and to ask what attributes may be universally shared by all women.

Political systems will be defined broadly to include economic, religious and cultural systems, and the connections between these and the more narrowly defined formal political sphere.

This course is designed for upper-class students with some previous background in cross-national political science, anthropology, economics, sociology or history. Interested others should see the instructor before enrolling.

Evaluation

Students will be evaluated based on a combination of two short essays, a major term project focusing either on a single country or on an issue affecting several nations, and a final exam or a longer, final essay. In addition, students may be expected to attend no more than two evening guest lectures and/or films.

Essays: Each student is expected to hand in two 6-page essays. Specific questions for each essay will be provided at least one week before the essay is due, and will reflect major themes of the course (e.g., the conceptualization of women and comparative politics, women and revolutionary political structures). Each essay is worth 15% of the grade, for a total of 30%.

*Deborah Gerner now teaches in the Political Science Department, University of Kansas, Lawrence, KS 66045.

Term project: Each student will complete a major term paper (15–18 pp.) or other project, worth 35% of the final grade. This project will be due the week of Nov. 28. Papers handed in earlier in the week will be graded first. After December 2, papers will be considered late and they will be dropped one full letter grade. Details about the paper/project will be forthcoming in a couple of weeks.

Final exam: Students have the option of taking an in-class exam or preparing a final essay on an assigned topic. The final exam will be comprehensive and will count for 20% of the final grade.

Class participation: Students are expected to attend all class meetings and should speak with the instructor if they must miss a class. In addition to regular attendance, students are expected to have read the assigned materials and to be prepared to discuss them intelligently—or at least to ask well-thought-out questions. Participation will count for 15% of the final grade.

Readings

Reading assignments will be drawn primarily from the books listed below:

Davies, Miranda, ed. 1983. *Third World, Second Sex.* London: Zed Press (distributed by Lawrence Hill).

Huston, Perida. 1979. *Third World Women Speak Out.* New York: Praeger Publishers (in cooperation with the Overseas Development Council).

Iglitzin, Lynne B., and Ruth Ross, eds. 1976. *Women in the World.* Santa Barbara: ABC Clio.

Rowbotham, Sheila. 1972. *Women, Resistance and Revolution.* New York: Vintage Books.

Women and National Development. 1977. Special Issue of *Signs* (**WND**).

Additional readings included in the daily assignments have been placed on reserve at the library. For your information, their full citations are included in the syllabus.

COURSE SCHEDULE
AND READING ASSIGNMENTS

Conceptualizing the Cross-National Study of Women as Political Actors

Sept. 9—Course Description

Sept. 13—What Is Politics?

- Iglitzin and Ross, pp. xv–24 (Foreward, Intro., ch. 1).
- Chaney, Elsa M. 1975. "The Mobilization of Women," in Ruby Rohrlich-Leavitt (ed.), *Women Cross-Culturally: Change and Challenge.* Mouton Publications, pp. 471–489.

Sept. 15—Political Socialization, Political Culture
- Merkl, Peter H. 1977. "Individuals in Politics," in *Modern Comparative Politics*, 2nd edition. Dryden Press, pp. 28–68.

Sept. 20—Conventional Versus Non-Traditional Political Participation
- Iglitzin and Ross, pp. 55–74 (ch. 3).
- Collier, Jane Fishburne. 1973. "Women in Politics," in Michaelle Zimbalist Rosaldo and Louse Lamphere (eds.), *Women, Culture and Society*. Stanford University Press, pp. 89–96.

Sept. 22—Private-Public Split: Status Versus Power
- Giele, Janet Zollinger. 1977. "Introduction: Comparative Perspectives on Women," in Janet Zollinger Giele and Audrey Chapman Smock (eds.), *Women: Roles and Status in Eight Countries*. John Wiley and Sons, pp. 1–31.

Sept. 27—Forms of Feminism—A Quick Survey of Feminist Political Theory
- Jagger, Alison M., and Paula Rothenberg Struhl. 1978. "The Roots of Oppression," in *Feminist Frameworks*. McGraw-Hill, pp. 80–85.

Formal Political Participation in the Third World

Sept. 29—Differences Between First and Third World Women
- Huston, pp. 31–61, 9–112 (chs. 3, 4, 7).

Oct. 4—Factors Affecting Women's Formal Political Participation
- Davies, pp. 19–29 (ch. 2).
- *WND*, pp. 193–209 (Pnina Lahov).
- Iglitzin and Ross, pp. 243–255 (ch. 15).

Oct. 6—Women and "Modernization": Effects on Participation
Essay 1 due.
- Iglitzin and Ross, pp. 24–54, 185–201 (chs. 2, 11).
- Huston, pp. 17–30.
- *WND*, pp. 1–13; 154–166 (Carolyn Elliot, Achola Pala, Martha Mueller).

Oct. 11—Importance of Traditional Institutions: Case Study—Islam
- Handout on Qur'anic suras pertaining to women.
- Iglitzin and Ross, pp. 203–228 (chs. 12 and 13).
- White, Elizabeth H. 1978. "Legal Reform as an Indicator of Women's Status in Muslim Nations," in Lois Beck and Nikki Keddie (eds.), *Women in the Muslim World*. Harvard University Press, pp. 52–68.

Oct. 13—Women at the Top: Third World Political Elites
- *WND*, pp. 229–240 (Marysa Navarro).
- Iglitzin and Ross, pp. 257–267 (ch. 16).

• Kelly, Rita Mae, and Mary Boutilier. 1978. "Types of Female Political Participation," in *The Making of Political Women*. Nelson-Hall, pp. 85–169.
• Read general descriptions of types, and skim specific examples.

Oct. 18—Mid-term Recess—No Class

Oct. 20—More on Political Elites
• *WND*, pp. 210–228 (Lenore Manderson).
• Jahan, Rounaq. 1980. "Women in Politics: A Case Study of Bangladesh," in Sylvia A. Chipp and Justin J. Green (eds.), *Asian Women in Transition*. Pennsylvania State University Press, pp. 227–250.

Non-Traditional Forms of Participation

Oct. 25—Feminism, Nationalism and Liberation Movements
Film: A Veiled Revolution.
• Iglitzin and Ross, pp. 229–241, 319–340 (chs. 14 and 20).
• Philipp, Thomas. 1978. "Feminism and Nationalist Politics in Egypt," in Lois Beck and Nikki Keddie (eds.), *Women in the Muslim World*. Harvard University Press, pp. 277–294.
• Ferdows, Adele K. 1983. "Women and the Islamic Revolution," *International Journal of Middle East Studies*, Vol. 15, pp. 283–298.

Oct. 27—Feminism, Nationalism, and Liberation Movements (Cont'd)
• Davies, pp. 30–39, 61–123 (chs. 3, 5–11).
• Cherpak, Evelyn. 1978. "The Participation of Women in the Independence Movement in Gran Columbia, 1780–1830," in Asuncion Lavrin (ed.), *Latin American Women*. Greenwood Press, pp. 219–234.

Nov. 1—Women and Development: Potential for Participation
• Huston, pp. 85–98 (ch. 6).
• Davies, pp. 3–19 (ch. 1).
• *WND*, pp. 142–153 (Yolanda T. Moses).
• Iglitzin and Ross, pp. 269–284 (ch. 17).

Nov. 8—Women's Movements, Women's Organizations
• Davies, pp. 173–193 (chs. 17–19).
• Randall, Margaret. 1981. "The Federation of Cuban Women: The Role of a Woman's Organization in the Revolutionary Process," in *Women in Cuba: Twenty Years Later*. Smyrna Press, pp. 123–135.
• Rein, Natalie. 1980. *Daughters of Rachel: Women in Israel*. Penguin Books, pp. 101–113.

Nov. 10—Other Non-Traditional Forms of Participation: Religion, Ritual, Dance, Negotiation
Essay 2 due.
• *WND*, pp. 57–73, 101–112 (Deniz Kandiyoti, Fatima Mernissi).

- Beck, Lois. 1978. "Women Among Qashqa'i Nomadic Pastoralists in Iran," in Lois Beck and Nikki Keddie (eds.), *Women in the Muslim World*. Harvard University Press, pp. 351–373.

Women In Revolutionary and Post-Revolutionary Societies

Nov. 15—The Theory: Marx and Engels
- Rowbotham, pp. 59–98 (chs. 3 and 4).

Nov. 17—The Soviet Union and Eastern Europe
- Rowbotham, pp. 134–169 (ch. 6).
- Iglitzin and Ross, pp. 287–317 (chs. 18 and 19).
- Wolchik, Sharon. 1981. "Eastern Europe," in Joni Lovenduski and Jill Hills (eds.), *The Politics of the Second Electorate*. Routledge and Kegan Paul, pp. 252–277.

Nov. 22—China
- Rowbotham, pp. 170–199 (ch. 7).
- Iglitzin and Ross, pp. 345–373 (chs. 21 and 22).

Nov. 24—Thanksgiving Break

Dec. 1—Comparison of Revolutionary and Non-Revolutionary Societies
- Davies, pp. 125–171 (chs. 12–16).

Dec. 2—Research Paper Due

Dec. 6—Catch-up Class
No reading assignment.

Dec. 8—Summary
No reading assignment.

Dec. 12—Final Exam or Essay 3 Due

RESEARCH PROJECT

The task of your research project is to analyze a contemporary situation, group, class, policy, or relationship involving women as political actors in one or more nations. Students who are interested in arranging some type of project other than a term paper (e.g., class presentation) should speak with me before October 7. The paper/project is due the week of November 28. Papers handed in earlier in the week will be graded first. Papers are due by Friday, December 2, at 10:00, without exception. After 10:00 P.M., papers will be considered late and will be dropped one letter grade.

Papers should be 15–18 pages, typed, double-spaced, with reasonable margins. I will read longer papers, but the additional length should be justified—within limits; quality is more important than quantity. Use any formal citation style (look in a journal or use Kate Turabian's *A Manual for Writers* if you are unsure how to do this), so long as it indicates the author, source, publisher, location, date and pages. Footnotes can go at the bottom of the page or at the end of the paper. Make sure to cite all your sources and to include a bibliography. My own preference is for "scientific citation style." In the body of the paper, you replace each footnote with (Rowbotham, 1970:14) or (Sharara, 1983:23). Using scientific citation style, a bibliography looks like this:

Rowbotham, Sheila. 1970. *Women, Resistance & Revolution.* New York: Vintage Books.
Sharara, Yolla Polity. 1983. "Women and Politics in Lebanon," in Miranda Davies (ed.), *Third World, Second Sex.* London: Zed Press, pp. 19–29.

Once one gets accustomed to this method, it is quite simple, allowing you to credit others' work properly without having to use footnotes.

There are any number of possibilities for topics. Here are a few ideas to get you thinking; they are by no means exhaustive.

- Women in electoral politics in one or more countries.
- Political socialization as it relates to political participation.
- Relationship between political participation and economic roles.
- Women in movements of national liberation.
- Comparison between legal political rights and actual political opportunities.
- Alternative forms of political power for women.
- Views of women as political actors as expressed in the popular culture, i.e., poetry, music, short stories, film.
- Implications of the public-private world split for women as political actors.
- Political participation of women before and after a revolutionary movement.

Suggestions and Guidelines on Papers

1. If you are writing about an historical event, the choice of the event is critical. If it appears that you cannot find sufficient information, it is probably wise to choose a different topic. In general, start work on the paper early enough so that if your first idea does not seem to be working out, you can choose a different one.

2. Your first source of information is the assigned readings—these have extensive bibliographies and can direct you to additional readings. Be sure to use the assigned readings, but go beyond them—use the library for further research.

3. Be skeptical of your evidence—just because an author writes something doesn't mean that it is true, and presenting one or two sources to back up some outrageous statement doesn't mean that you have proven it. Your

research should be thorough enough that you can sort out the agreed-upon interpretations of an event from those which are controversial. This is not to say that you can't use controversial evidence—just present it as such and have some material defending it.

4. The level of detail should be such that it could be understood by someone who has taken this course: don't spend a lot of space repeating material we have already covered, but do explain obscure concepts, events, and so forth.

5. Unless I'm otherwise instructed, papers to be returned can be picked up outside my office. This is convenient, but they can be stolen, read, and otherwise misused here. If you *do not* want your paper left outside, put a note to that effect on the paper. It is also a very good idea to make a copy of your paper before handing it in—it is cheap insurance.

6. Due to the unfortunate proliferation of so-called research services, I would advise doing the following to reassure me that you wrote the paper: (1) Save your rough draft and notes—I may ask to see them. Most likely I won't, but keep them around in case a question arises—they are your best proof that your paper is legitimate. This is a requirement for passing papers. (2) Make intelligent use of the assigned readings. Use of relatively recent sources is also reassuring. (3) Stick to the assignment. Papers which deviate significantly from the assignment will be viewed very suspiciously.

Essay 1—Due October 6

In the past, the concept of power has been defined in such a way as to ignore or discredit many of the methods used by women acting as political strategists. In particular, far greater attention is given to formal methods of political participation (voting, running for elected office, etc.) than to informal or non-traditional forms of activity (force issue recognition, working through family structures, gift-giving and so forth). Furthermore, powerful women, regardless of the form of expression that power takes, tend to be discounted. For example, in their introduction to *Women, Culture and Society*, Rosaldo and Lamphere write:

> Because men everywhere tend to have more prestige than women, and because men are usually associated with social roles of dominance and authority, most previous descriptions of social processes have treated women as being theoretically uninteresting. *Women who exercise power are seen as deviants, manipulators, or, at best, exceptions. And women's goals and ideologies are assumed to be those coordinate with those of men.* (emphasis added)

In 6-7 double-spaced typed pages, develop and defend a non-ethnocentric definition of political participation and of power appropriate for examining women as political actors. How should a political scientist analyze and interpret the actions women take to create and shape their public and private environments? Should women be examined separately, or can their actions be subsumed in the category "men and women"? Utilize the readings from the first 3 1/2 weeks of the semester (through October 4), as well as the lectures and class discussion, to support your arguments.

Essay 2—Due November 15

For the past month we have been discussing various types of political participation available to Third World women—everything from voting and holding political office to revolutionary fighting, a certain choice of clothing, economic strikes and religious activities. Which has been most important and valuable in changing women's status and women's political power—formal avenues of participation or non-traditional, informal forms of political activity? Are there situations when one or the other type of political activity is simply not an option? Use examples of at least 4 specific countries to support your position. Length: 6-7 double-spaced typed pages.

Essay 3—Due December 14

Based on your experiences this semester, develop a proposal for a course entitled "Women in the Non-Western World." The 8-10 page proposal should include the following items:

1. Intellectual justification for such a course as it fits into a women's studies and/or political science curriculum.
2. Specification of the principal theoretical issues which should be addressed in the course.
3. Description of the types of readings to be assigned, and a list of some specific examples (5–10 articles and/or books).
4. Indication of the types of graded assignments and their justification.
5. One-page course outline—by week—indicating topics to be discussed; for example, indicate whether you would take a country or regional studies approach or a general themes approach or some combination (and if so, how).

FINAL EXAM: IN-CLASS OPTION

The goal of this exam is to sample your knowledge on a wide range of topics covered this semester. You have two hours to write the exam. In this time, please briefly answer five of the questions below. Lists and sentence fragments are acceptable; but do provide sufficient detail to indicate a familiarity with both the lectures and the readings. Please indicate which questions you are answering—and write legibly!

1. What are some of the attributes of third world female political elites? How do these differ, if at all, from the characteristics of third world women in general?

2. What is the situation for women in Japan in terms of their political participation and power?

3. Describe the women's movement in China or the Soviet Union, plus a second revolutionary society. What is the relationship of the movement to the government? What has it accomplished? Are women better off now than they were before the revolution?

4. Answer Part a or Part b:

    a. Describe and evaluate four different types of informal political participation in which women engage. Include at least one example from three of the following areas of the world: Latin America, Sub-Saharan Africa, the Arab world and Israel, and Asia.

    b. List and describe (with specific examples) four types of women's voluntary organizations/associations. At least two should have an explicit political or social change orientation.

5. What is the private-public split? Is this an important concept, or one whose impact is over-exaggerated? How does this concept differ cross-culturally? To the extent that it exists, are there any advantages to "the split"?

6. What is the impact of strong religious traditions on the ability of women to participate in formal or informal political arenas? Use examples from several third world countries to defend your position.

7. What is the connection among feminism, nationalism and political participation? What kinds of questions would we want to ask about women's involvement in nationalist movements?

8. How is the legal status of women related to their actual position in society? Is this relevant to political participation? Why or why not?

3. Feminist Issues and World Peace

Harriet Hyman Alonso   *Spring 1986*
Brooklyn College*

The purpose of this course is to educate students about women's participation in peace movements from a historical perspective (the emphasis is on U.S. women, though not exclusively so), and to raise issues of concern to women about war and peace.

Required Books
Brock-Utne, Birgit. *Educating for Peace: A Feminist Perspective.* Pergamon Press, 1985.

*Harriet H. Alonso teaches women's studies and is director of the Women's Center, Jersey City State College, Jersey City, NJ 07305.

McAllister, Pam (ed.). *Reweaving the Web of Life: Feminism and Nonviolence.*
   New Society Publishers, 1982.
Additional readings.

Course Evaluation
Exam #1—25%; Exam #2—25%; Media Watch—25%; Oral Report—25%.

COURSE SCHEDULE AND READINGS

Session 1—Introduction to Course and Requirements

Session 2—Opening Discussion
Why do some women feel so strongly about peace? *Film: Women—For
America, For the World,* a 1986 Academy award winning short documentary.

Part I: A Historical Look at Women,
Peace and War

Session 3—Women in Peace Movements Pre-World War I
- Brock-Utne, pp. 33–45.
- McAllister, pp. 28–86, "Nonviolence and Women: The Pioneers," by
  Margaret Hope Bacon.

Session 4—Women in the World War I Peace Movement
- Brock-Utne, pp. 45–56.
- "The Woman Who Said No to War," *Ms,* March 1986.
- "The Woman's Peace Party of New York City," by Harriet Alonso
  (photocopy).

Session 5—Continuing World War I
With an oral history tape of Rebecca Shelley, World War I peace activist.

**Sessions 6 & 7—The Interwar Women's Peace Movement: 1920s and
1930s**
- "No More War! Women Against War in the Interwar Years," by Harriet
  Alonso (photocopy).

Session 8—Oral History
Tapes: Women in Peace Movements on College Campuses during the 1920s
and 1930s. *Film: The Life and Times of Rosie, the Riveter.*
- "What Did You Do in the War, Grandma?" *Ms.*

Session 10—Women in the 1950s and 1960s Peace Movements
- "Killing McCarthyism with Kindness," by Amy Swerdlow, *Ms,* March
  1983.
- McAllister, pp. 128–134, "Sailing into Test Waters," by Barbara Rey-
  nolds.

Session 11—Peace Songs of the 1960s

Session 12—Women in the 1970s and 1980s Peace Movements
- "Will the Circle Be Unbroken?" *Women: A Journal of Liberation*, Vol. 8, No. 1.
- "The Seneca Stories," by Grace Paley, *Ms* (Dec. 1983).
- "Petra Kelly," *Ms* (Oct. 1983); "The Women Who Went to the Summit," *Ms* (Feb. 1986).

Session 13—Women in the 1970s and 1980s Peace Movements (Cont'd)
Slides of the Seneca, NY Women's Peace Encampment.
- Brock-Utne, pp. 46–89.
- McAllister, pp. 289–299, "Reweaving the Web of Life," by Catherine Field.
- "Cop Tales," by Grace Paley; "Letter to the IRS," by Meg Bowman.

Session 14—Peace Songs of the 1970s and 1980s
- McAllister, pp. 286-288, "Foolish Notion" by Holly Near.

Session 15—Exam on Part I

Part II: Feminist Issues and World Peace

Session 16—What Do You Know About the Arms Race?
- "What do you know about the arms race?" Quiz by WILPF.
- "An Intelligent Woman's Guide to the Arms Race," Parts I and II, *Ms* (July/August 1982 and March 1983).
- "Understanding Star Wars," *Ms* (Feb. 1986).

Sessions 17 & 18—Is War Patriarchal? Is Peace Biologically Natural to Women?
- "Women and Men: Peace and War," by Naomi Goodman, IFOR Report (May 1985).
- McAllister, pp. 2–4, "I Am a Dangerous Woman," by Joan Cavanagh.
- McAllister, pp. 266–284, "The Future—If There Is One—Is Female," by Sally Miller Gearhart.
- Brock-Utne, pp. 70–110.

Sessions 19 & 20—The Connection Among the Military, Patriarchy and Violence Against Women
- Brock-Utne, pp. 1–32.
- McAllister, pp. 20–29, "Women, Peace and Power," by Jo Vellacott.
- McAllister, pp. 195–199, "The Economic Roots of the Violent Male Culture," by Lisa Leghorn.
- McAllister, pp. 209–219, "Fear of 'Other': The Common Root of Sexism and Militarism."
- McAllister, pp. 326–335, "The Army Will Make a 'Man' Out of You," by Helen Michaelowski.

Session 21—Women, the Military and the Draft
- "Making the Draft a Women's Issue," *Women: A Journal of Liberation*, Vol. 8, No. 11.
- "Vietnam Nurses," *Ms.*

Session 22—*Film: Soldier Girls*

Session 23 & 24—Is Racism a Peace Issue? Is It a Feminist Issue?
- "Day-by-Day Apartheid," *Ms* (Nov. 1982); "Winnie Mandela," *Ms* (Nov. 1985).
- Leaflet, "Military Spending and Black Women."
- McAllister, pp. 87–97, "Ida B. Wells," by Rosemarie Freeney-Harding.
- McAllister, pp. 97–100, "Jessie Daniel Ames," by Jacquelyn Dowd Hall.
- McAllister, pp. 112–127, "We Started from Opposite Ends of the Spectrum," by Cynthia Washington.
- "Women's Consciousness and the Southern Black Movement," by Sara Evan.
- McAllister, pp. 317–321, "Breaking the Racism Barrier," by Donna Landerman.
- McAllister, pp. 262–264, "Only Justice Can Stop a Curse," by Alice Walker.

Session 25—Does War Affect Our Health?
Oral reports and Media Watch due.
- "Suits Claim A-Tests," *In These Times*, October 16, 1982.
- "The Last Testament," *Ms* (Aug. 1981).
- "Hunger and Militarism," published by AFSC (March/April 1983).
- McAllister, pp. 63–77, "Our Stunning Harvest," by Ellen Bass.
- McAllister, pp. 396–399, "Abortion: A Woman's Right to Live," by Leah Fritz.

Session 26—Can Women Wage War for Peace?
Oral reports.
- *Fighting Two Colonialisms: Women in Guinea Bissau*, by Stephanie Urdang (Monthly Review Press, 1979).
- "Women and the Cuban Revolution," from *Cuba Times Magazine*.
- "Feminism and the Nicaraguan Revolution," *IKON*, Second Series, No. 3.

Session 27—The U.N. Decade of Women
Videotape: Nairobi Conference of 1985. Oral reports.
- "Perspective on UN Decade for Women," *UN Chronical* (July/August 1985).

Session 28—Where Do We Go from Here?
- Brock-Utne, pp. 111 to end.
- McAllister, pp. 162–164, "Feminism and Peace: The Issues We Work On," by Kathy Bickmore.
- McAllister, pp. 407–411, "The Passive Violence of Noninvolvement and Our Work of Accountability," by Sue Dove Gambill.
- McAllister, pp. 414–415, "Exerpts from the Unity Statement," by Women's Pentagon.

Session 29—Formulating Our Very Own Peace Plan

Session 30—Exam on Part II

MEDIA WATCH

For one month, I'd like you to keep a media watch on one of the world's hot spots, e.g., South Africa, Lebanon, Israel, Syria, Libya, Nicaragua, Cuba, the USSR or any other place that suits your fancy. Using as many forms of media as possible (including fictional and artistic representations as well as non-fiction), write a report, a diary or some similar paper on how the area is handled. For example, do the media try to manipulate the public towards peace or violence? Do you feel the media are truthful? How would you improve on the coverage? Is any special attention paid to women? The paper should be at least seven typed, double-spaced pages unless you are planning a different medium, like a scrapbook, in which case the form will be different; but analytical writing is still required. Remember to be analytical in your report!

ORAL REPORTS

Below is a list of organizations. Working individually or in small groups, get information on one of these organizations. (We will have sign-ups in class.) Find out their positions on peace and women's issues. Try to get a leaflet, newsletter or brochure to give to each student. By the end of the term, each member of the class should have a reference library of peace organizations. All groups should be listed in the phone book; if not, see me.

National Organization for Women (NOW)
Women's International League for Peace and Freedom (WILPF)
Women's Pentagon Action
Women Strike for Peace
Committee in Solidarity with the People of El Salvador (CISPES)
War Resisters League
International Women's Tribunal Center
Women's International Research Exchange Service

Women for Racial and Economic Equality (WREE)
MADRE
Feminist Peace Institute
Mobilization for Survival
Pledge of Resistance
Church Women United
Citizens Against Nuclear War
Grandmothers for Peace
Peace Links
Women's Action for Nuclear Disarmament (WAND)
Women for a Meaningful Summit
Women's Program: American Friends Service Committee
Women's Division: United Methodist Church
Catholic Peace Fellowship
Clergy & Laity Concerned
Jewish Peace Fellowship
Christic Institute
Physicians for Social Responsibility
Educators for Social Responsibility
SANE

XVIII

Alternative Futures

1. Imaging a Peaceful World

Robert C. Johansen   *Summer 1987*
Institute for International Peace Studies, University of
Notre Dame, Notre Dame, IN 46556

This course is a concentrated, three-week immersion into what it means to think, feel, and act as global citizens. We will address three questions, which in their abstract form sound deceptively simple.

1. What is the present state of global society? (Where are we now?) Why has the globe evolved to its present political and military structure? Why do we have the present (admittedly limted and varying) degree of respect globally for human rights and social justice? What is the state of the globe economically and environmentally? What cultural traditions and forces, represented by the diverse nationalities of participants in this class, shed special light on present problems and hopes for maximizing peace, social and economic justice, human rights, and respect for nature?

2. What kind of world would you like to see developed during your lifetime? (Where do we want to go?) What will be the forms of conflict resolution and security maintenance? What will be the extent of success in rooting out humanity's age-old scourges of violence, prejudice, disease, economic inequity, and spiritual emptiness? What might it mean, two or three decades from now, to be a good global citizen?

3. What beliefs, values, policies, and institutions will be conducive to achieving your preferred world? (How do we get to where we want to go?) As we work our way back from our image of a preferred world future, we will consider what must happen by the year 2005 to achieve our long-term goals—by 2000? by 1995? by 1990?

The course of study and required readings follow. Readings for each topic will be supplemented with articles from current periodicals from each of the countries represented in the class.

Books to Be Purchased

Kim, Samuel S. *The Quest for a Just World Order.* Boulder: Westview Press, 1984.

Falk, Richard, Samuel S. Kim, and Saul H. Mendlovitz (eds.). *Toward a Just World Order.* Boulder: Westview Press, 1982.

Brown, Lester R., et al. *State of the World 1987.* New York: Norton, 1987.

August 3—Pessimistic and Optimistic Visions of Human Capability

Human behavior and conflicting values. The reconciliation of conflicting values. Changing social values.

August 4—What Are the Origins and Recent Evolution of the Present System of Global Order?

The Medieval conception of order. The sovereignty of nation-states. The balance of power system.

- Kim, "Introduction," ch. 1.
- "Introduction to the Sovereign State and World System," Falk, Kim and Mendlovitz, pp. 55–59.
- Hedley Bull, "The State's Positive Role in World Affairs," ch. 7, in Falk, Kim and Mendlovitz.
- Eqbal Ahmad, "Neo-Fascist State: Notes on the Pathology of Power in the Third World," ch. 8, in Falk, Kim and Mendlovitz.

August 5—What Are Today's Challenges to the Westphalian System of World Order?

The declining utility of war. The growing interdependency of societies. The rise of demands for human dignity. The long cycle in international relations. Collective security as an effort to interrupt the cycle. Revival of the balance of power vs. internationalism.

- Kim, ch. 2, "The Transformation of World Politics."
- Tom Hughes, "Internationalism," *Foreign Policy.*

August 5—How Do Power and Values Interact in World Society?

Statism, the national interest, the human interest, and security.

- Robert C. Johansen, "The Elusiveness of a Human World Community," *The National Interest and the Human Interest* (Princeton: Princeton University Press, 1980), reprinted in Falk, Kim and Mendlovitz, ch. 14.
- "Introduction to Peace," Falk, Kim and Mendlovitz, pp. 219–223.
- Kim, ch. 3, "In Search of a World Order Theory."

August 7—What Is a Realistic and Comprehensive Definition of National Security in the Modern World?
- Brown, "Redefining National Security," ch. 11.
- Anne Hayner, "A New Voice for an Old Vision: Toward an Alternate Language of Security," *Bulletin of the Peace Studies Institute*, Vol. 16, No. 1–2 (1986), pp. 11–17.
- Kenneth Boulding, "The War Trap," ch. 15 in Falk, Kim and Mendlovitz.

August 10—How Can We Minimize Violence?
Nuclear arms and the permeable state. The crisis in arms control.
- Kim, ch. 4, "Global Violence."
- "Disarmament for a Just World: Declaration of Principles, Proposal for a Treaty, and Call for Action," ch. 19 in Falk, Kim and Mendlovitz.

August 11 Workshop—Imaging the Future: Can We Imagine a Substantially More Peaceful and Just World?
Led by Professor Elise Boulding.
- Boulding, Elise, "Image and Action in Peace-building," photocopy.

August 12 Workshop—Imaging the Future: How Can a Preferred Future Become a Probable Future?
Led by Professor Elise Boulding.

August 13—How Can We Maximize Economic Well-Being in a Sustainable Society?
The rising voice of the Third World. Poverty and indebtedness. Equity.
- Kim, ch. 5, "Global Inequities."
- Mahbub ul Haq, "Negotiating the Future," ch. 22 in Falk, Kim and Mendlovitz.
- Fernando Henrique Cardoso, "Towards Another Development," ch. 10 in Brown.

August 14—How Can We Enhance Human Dignity?
The development of international human rights standards. The impact of cultural diversity on human rights standards.
- Kim, ch. 6, "Global Human Rights."
- "Manifesto of the Alliance for Human Rights in China," ch. 26 in Falk, Kim and Mendlovitz.
- "The Universal Declaration of Human Rights," ch. 28 in Falk, Kim and Mendlovitz.

August 17—Why and to What Extent Do States Comply with Human Rights Standards?
The impact of human rights on great power interventionism. Protecting human rights through international institutions.

August 18—What Degree of Harmony with Nature Is Desirable and Feasible?

Planetary Limits. Examples of planetary cooperation: the law of the sea; the Antarctica regime; ozone protection.

- Kim, ch. 7, "Global Human Environment."
- Brown, ch. 1: "Thresholds of Change;" ch. 11: "Charting a Sustainable Course."
- "Introduction to Ecological Balance," in Falk, Kim and Mendlovitz, pp. 435-441.
- William Ophuls, "Ecological Scarcity and International Politics," ch. 30 in Falk, Kim and Mendlovitz.
- Norman Cousins, "Who Owns the Ozone?" ch. 31 in Falk, Kim and Mendlovitz.
- "The Dai Dong Declaration," ch. 33 in Falk, Kim and Mendlovitz.

August 19—What Are the Most Important Ingredients in the Effort to Create a More Humane World Community? How Do Diverse Cultural Traditions Inform and Contribute to These Ingredients?

- Kim, ch. 8, "Alternative Future Images and Transition Orientations."

August 20—The Task Ahead: Developing a Multinational Consensus on a Preferred Future for the Human Species

Problems and Possibilities. Substance and process. Attitudes and Institutions.

- "Introduction to Alternative Images of the Future," in Falk, Kim and Mendlovitz, pp. 499–504.
- Sam Cole, "The Global Futures Debate," ch. 34 in Falk, Kim and Mendlovitz.
- Richard Falk, "What New System of World Order?" ch. 35 in Falk, Kim and Mendlovitz.
- "Introduction to Orientations to Transition," in Falk, Kim and Mendlovitz, pp. 559–566.
- Rajni Kothari, "Toward a Just World," ch. 36 in Falk, Kim and Mendlovitz.
- Johan Galtung, "Self-Reliance: An Overriding Strategy for Transition," ch. 37 in Falk, Kim and Mendlovitz.
- Richard Falk, "Normative Initiatives," ch. 38 in Falk, Kim and Mendlovitz.
- George Lakey, "A Manifesto for Nonviolent Revolution," ch. 39 in Falk, Kim and Mendlovitz.

2. Utopias and Dystopias

Thomas Bulger   *Spring 1986*
English Dept., Siena College, Loudonville, NY 12211

All utopian literature is vitally concerned with the issue of peace. The utopian writer sets forth a communal vision that secures harmony for an entire society; the dystopian writer laments the conditions in human existence that thwart the establishment of such harmony. Therefore, both the utopian and dystopian visions are in agreement that violence and aggression (the most pronounced example of which is war) must be checked if not eliminated altogether. Instead, the goal of society should be cooperation, with equity and justice for all. This course will discuss how different authors and different ages define such concepts as justice and equity. And since one person's utopia is another person's nightmare, we will analyze the latent prejudices and biases that inform the utopias under consideration.

By taking a historical approach, and by including contrasting views of utopia within a specific period of time (e.g., the Renaissance), this course will provide students with a diversity of perspectives. Not all utopias are totally pacifistic; Plato's guardians are warriors, and More articulates in *Utopia* a rationale for a just war. The range of readings demands that the student consider a broad scope of opinions on such subjects as war, peace, justice, discrimination, and the military.

Since a number of the authors assigned are not literary artists but philosophers (Plato) and scientists (Bacon, Campanella), this course will by no means be confined to a purely aesthetic approach. The subject matter dictates that students delve into such disciplines as psychology, economics, political science, history, religious studies, and sociology. Utopias are presented as comprehensive portraits of society; so any analysis of a utopian piece of writing requires an interdisciplinary approach.

It is hoped by the instructor that the students will recognize the strengths and weaknesses of past utopias, will arrive at a clearer view of the kind of society they live in, and will work to bring about their own vision of a better society. Utopian works posit their central principles not as foolish dreams but as attainable realities. I hope the students who take this course turn their knowledge into action (as utopian literature insists we must), and strive to implement the central concepts of utopianism (justice, love, peace) within their own lives and their own society.

Each student will write two short papers (3–4) pages, which will be presented in class. A longer research project (12–20 pages) is due at the end of the semester. In addition, each student will write a one-page analysis for each class reading assignment, defining what the particular author under discussion considers "utopian."

CLASS SCHEDULE

Jan. 14—Introduction: "What Is Utopia?"

Jan. 21
Plato, *The Republic*, and Aristophanes, *Women in Parliament*.

Jan. 28
More, *Utopia*, and selections from Rabelais.

Feb. 4
Francis Bacon, *The New Atlantis*, and Campanella, *The City of the Sun*.

Feb. 11
Shakespeare, *The Tempest*, and Montaigne, "Of Cannibals."

Feb. 25
Samuel Johnson, *Rasselas*, and Swift, Book IV of *Gulliver's Travels*.

Mar. 4
Hawthorne, *The Blithedale Romance*, and selected articles on 19th century American utopian communities (Brooke Farm, the Oneida community, etc.).

Mar. 11
Mark Twain, *A Connecticut Yankee in King Arthur's Court*, and *The Curious Republic of Gondour*, and selections from *What is Man?*

Mar. 18
Edward Bellamy, *Looking Backward*, and William Morris, *News from Nowhere*.

Mar. 25
Aldous Huxley, *Brave New World*, and other Huxley selections.

Apr. 8
Eugene Zamiatin, *We*.

Apr. 15
Charlotte Gilman, *Herland*.

Apr. 22
George Orwell, *1984*.

Apr. 29
Ursula LeGuin, *The Dispossessed: An Ambiguous Utopia,* and Kurt Vonnegut, selections from *Welcome to the Monkeyhouse.* Final discussion of the meaning of utopia.

UTOPIA/DYSTOPIA EVALUATIONS

In your one-page summaries, consider the following four areas as portrayed in literature:

The Utopian Individual: Assumptions about human nature. Traits of the utopian individual.

The Utopian Family: Primary functions. Ideal type of family situation. Male-female relationships.

The Utopian Community: Organization of government. Job arrangements. Social institutions (educational, religious, etc.)

Utopian Culture: Values. Cultural areas emphasized (art, employment, etc.)

FINAL PAPER ASSIGNMENT

Fiction
Create your own utopia. Make sure to discuss the major social institutions that would be found in such a place: political system, economic system, educational system, religious system, family structure, community obligations, gender relationships. Try to give as specific a blueprint of your vision of utopia as possible. Watch out for ionconsistencies (e.g., advocating indiviudal freedom while at the same time imposing severe restrictions). Invent a character as your central figure or narrator.

Or

Imagine yourself in one of the utopias we have discussed this semester, and describe life as you would find it in this society. Describe as fully as possible the positives and negatives of such a community. Try to give it the kind of fictional format we have seen in such works as *Utopia* (travel to remote places) and *Looking Backward* (waking up in the future). Note well: avoid putting yourself in a dystopic fiction, which in itself is already a strong criticism of the so-called utopia it describes.

Non-Fiction
Create a utopia, using an analytic, non-fictional essay format. Address the issues listed under the Fiction section above in a logical, coherent fashion. Use an objective, discursive style.

Or

Do a research paper on a particular utopia or comparison of several utopias. Cite secondary literature (literary history and criticism) where applicable.

Your assessment may revolve around theme (e.g., freedom), symbol (e.g., the city), social issues, structure, genre, and so on. In other words, compose a basic literary research paper.

Other Possibilities

If none of these four options appeals to you, and you have an alternative in mind, let me know what you intend to do. I'd be more than happy to entertain other possibilities.

3. Toward a World Beyond War

Donald Lathrop   *Fall 1987*

Philosophy Dept., Berkshire Community College,
Pittsfield, MA 01201

Peace means World Order, Social Justice, Cooperation, Nonviolent Resolution of Conflict. Peace means change. Peace in our day requires some re-worked mythology, able to constellate the hopes and aspirations of a cynical age.

To reach for peace is to define it, recognize its absence, study its requirements, itemize the necessary changes for movement in its direction, research the requisites for bringing about these changes, and then to take action on all of the above.

It is no wonder that so little movement toward peace is achieved by a few meetings or even a few hundred hours' worth of dedicated effort, when the enormity of the project is clearly confronted and accepted. If an industry wants to bring about a change no more significant than the type of automobile consumers are buying, it is likely to spend many thousands of hours and hundreds of thousands of dollars, simply picking a name for a new vehicle, let alone all other aspects of promotion. As part of the process of marketing, studies are made of the existent wants, as well as the "create-able" desires, among the designated population. After understanding as much as possible about those targeted for change (of buying habits), time and money are little object as the goal is overall commercial success, measured by a significant margin of profit.

Contrast this with how little the peace movement researches its goals and its requirements for bringing about change, particularly in the minds of those who promote the status quo or who can alter the power balance in favor of the elimination of exploitation, fear tactics, demonology, weapon-worship, and so forth. Of countless meetings over the years by the peace community, few have addressed goal definition, and tactics relative to the goal, as a function of maximal influence in the right places, rather than just doing what "needs" to be done, what "feels right," etc.

This course is a small step. It assumes that 3 hours a week, for 10 weeks altogether, plus a number of hours on the outside, reading, researching, reflecting, and gathering thoughts, are an extremely worthwhile project for those who wish to be more effective in the process of peacemaking—whether in regard to Central America, South Africa, the arms race, social injustice, or whatever. In summary, the course is an effort to move away from "reactive" peace thinking, while creating a "proactive" peace agenda through imagining a more just and harmonious world and then designing steps thereto. In effect, it is an experimental version of a peace-related think tank.

On Grades

Attendance is vital to the success of the class. Three points from a total of 30 will be subtracted for each class missed. Missing more than two classes will require makeup work equivalent to either a summary of a relevant book or four relevant articles to compensate for missed classes.

Seventy points will be the maximum that it is possible to earn from submission of a final paper for the second half of the grade. The paper is due at the end of the course (last class). The paper (a minimum of 20 pages—typed, double-spaced, and with reasonable margins—for 2 credits) shall be your vision of a World Without Weapons, 30 years in the future, and the steps needed to get there in 10-year increments. Your discussion should touch on such topics as the arms race, education, health care, social justice, population size, transportation, religion, ethics, race, scarce resource management, care of the environment, etc. You will want to specialize in one or two aspects of the overall problem.

Specialist roles will be apportioned throughout the class so that the collected papers will form a broad composite of the issues and answers generated during class work sessions.

Hard-working auditors, who will do all but compile and type up their final paper for submission, are most welcome.

COURSE OUTLINE

Sept. 14—Introduction: Moving Toward a Definition of Peace—Beyond the Pollyana

Sept. 21—Stimulating Your Creative Capacity
- *Wake Up Your Creative Genius,* by Kurt Hanks & Jay Parry, 1983, pp. 1–65.

Sept. 28—Tools and More Stimulation for Creative Thinking
- *Wake Up Your Creative Genius,* pp. 66–132.

Oct. 5—Creating a Vision of a World Without Weapons: 30 Years Hence

- *Nonviolence and Global Transformation,* by Beverly Woodward, 1979, pp. 1–7.
- *Beyond the Bomb,* by Mark Sommer, 1985, pp. 111–168.

Oct. 19—Refining a Vision of a World Without Weapons: 30 Years Hence

- *The United Nations in Weakness and in Strength,* by Adam Daniel Corson-Finnerty, 1982.
- *Making the Abolition of War a Realistic Goal,* by Gene Sharp, 1980.

Oct. 26-Creating a Vision of a World in Transition to a Weaponless Reality: 20 Years Hence

- *Beyond the Bomb,* pp. 67–100.

Nov. 2—Creating a Vision of a World in Transition to a Weaponless Reality: 10 Years Hence

- *Beyond the Bomb,* pp. 3–66.

Nov. 9—Design of First Steps to a Weaponless World

- "The Choice: A 'Thought World' for the American Peace Movement," by Andrea Ayvazian and Michael Klare, *Fellowship Magazine,* 1986.
- *Nonviolence and Global Transformation,* by Beverly Woodward.

Nov. 16—Design of First Steps to a Weaponless World: Refining Images and Myths

- All previous references.

Nov. 23—Putting It All Together: Sharing of Term Papers

- All previous references.

XIX

Religious and Ethical Perspectives

1. Justice Among Nations

Drew Christiansen, S.J.   *Spring 1988*
Theology Dept., University of Notre Dame,
Notre Dame, IN 46556

This course examines the role of morality, and especially justice, in international relations. We will consider mainline, neo-conservative, progressive, and religious approaches. Special topics are economic development, human rights, and refugee and immigration issues. Background lectures will be offered to supply needed ideas on general ethics, theories of justice, political philosophy and theology. Background material and special topics may be re-shaped to fit students' interests.

The course will consider whether and how principles of morality may be applied to relations between nation-states; the meaning of international justice, especially for relations between developing and developed nations; human rights and basic rights, especially the right to subsistence; and special issues, particularly immigration and refugee policy.

Except for background lectures, the course will be conducted in seminar fashion. Each week, one or two students will be asked to present issues for discussion with a 4–5 page seminar paper and short oral presentation. Some weeks at the end of the semester, depending on class size, will be given over to review of student research and presentation of term papers.

Requirements

Class attendance and active participation; seminar presentations (number to be determined); end-term research paper; and possible mid-term oral. (Length of paper will depend on student's degree program.)

Final grade will be based on class participation, seminar papers and oral presentations, research presentation, and end-term research paper. Written work will be evaluated as follows: C, general comprehension of subject mater; B, accurate knowledge, well organized and interpreted and/or applied; A, same as B, plus notable insight, research, and/or clarity of expression.

Readings

Hoffman. *Duties Beyond Borders.*
Tucker. *Inequality of Nations.*
Beitz. *Political Theory and International Relations.*
Shue. *Basic Rights.*
Brown and MacLean, eds. *Human Rights and U.S. Foreign Policy.*
Lewis and Kallab, eds. *Development Strategies Reconsidered.*
Brown and Shue, eds. *Boundaries.*
Dowty. *Closed Borders.*

Recommended Background Reading

Feinberg. *Social Philosophy.* (Ethics)
Sterba, ed. *Justice: Alternative Political Perspectives.* (Justice)
O'Brien and Shannon, ed. *Renewing the Earth.* (Theology)
Gremillion, ed. *Gospel of Peace and Justice.* (Theology)

COURSE SCHEDULE

Introduction

Class 1—Overview and Introduction

Class 2—Ethics and International Affairs: The Mainline View
• Hoffmann, pp. 1–94, 189–232.

Class 3—National Autonomy: Its Purpose and Limits
• Brown and Shue, chs. 1 and 3.
• Pope John XXIII, *Peace on Earth* (*Pacem in terris*), nos. 80–145.

Political Perspectives

Class 4—Mainline View II: Human Rights and Justice
• Hoffman, pp. 95–188.

Class 5—Neo-Conservative View
* Tucker.

Class 6—Revisionist (Progressive) View
* Beitz, pp. 3–124.

Class 7—International Distributive Justice
* Beitz, pp. 125–169.
* Pope Paul VI, *Development of Peoples* (*Populorum progressio*).
* Brown and Shue, pp. 147–176.

Special Topics

Class 8—Human Rights I: Basic Rights and the Right to Subsistence
* Shue.

Class 9—Human Rights II: Philosophical Premises and Political Implications
* Brown and MacLean, pp. 27–196.

Class 10—Human Rights III: Practical Issues of Application
* Brown and MacLean, pp. 199–302.

Class 11—Development Lessons and Priorities
* Lewis and Kallab.

Class 12—Immigrants and Refugees
* Dowty, pp. 37–78.
* Christiansen, "Sacrament of Unity: Ethical Issues in the Pastoral Care of Migrants and Refugees."

Student Research Presentations

Presentations, weeks 13–15. Exam, week of May 2–6. Papers due May 2.

2. Social Ethics

Thomas Derr   *Spring 1987*
Religion Dept., Smith College, Northampton, MA 01060

This course focuses on ethical problems arising in corporate, collective relations, as in the actions of the state, the economic order, and international affairs. It concerns the comparative place of ethical norms and "practical realism" in the moral behavior of groups. Topics include: power, violence, and vengeance; revolution and order; civil disobedience; human rights; liberation theology and Marxism; pacifism and just war theory; environmental ethics; property and poverty; business ethics; and religious liberty. This class is a mixture of fairly informal lecture and discussion. Some subjects will be handled entirely by discussion.

Course Requirements

A final exam in May, plus, at your choice, either a mid-semester exam on 13 March, or a 10–12 page paper, due 4 May (for seniors) or 11 May (all others), on a topic related to the course, the subject to be checked first with the instructor.

Readings

The readings listed in the Course Outline and Schedule are usually given as a set of choices for the topic. The first class will help you to deal with the book list so you can choose what you want to read. All books are on reserve in the library.

It will increase your awareness of the subject matter of this course a great deal if you have the habit of reading regularly a good newspaper, e.g., *The New York Times* or *The Christian Science Monitor*. If you are preparing a paper, or even if you are not and simply want to keep up with the latest thought in these fields, for which your appetite has presumably been whetted, you will also find the following journals, among others, pertinent:

Journal of Religious Ethics
Philosophy and Public Affairs
Christianity and Crisis
The National Catholic Reporter
The Christian Century
Journal of Law and Religion
Ethics
Commentary
Judaism
The Commonweal
This World
Cross Currents

COURSE OUTLINE AND SCHEDULE

Introduction: Religious Ideology and Secularism

Week 1

No assigned readings.

The Nature of the State

Positive and negative roles; power and coercion. Civil disobedience. Revolution and order. Democracy.

Week 2

Read *either* John C. Bennett, *Christians and the State*, chs. 3–7 and 11, *or* Reinhold Niebuhr, *Moral Man and Immoral Society*, introduction and chs. 1–3, and 7–10.

Week 3

Read *either* H.A. Bedau, ed., *Civil Disobedience: Theory and Practice*, pp. 15–18, 72–89, 106–115, 162–177, 194–209, and 213–263, *or* Carl Cohen, *Civil Disobedience: Conscience, Tactics, and the Law.*

International Relations

Nationalism and internationalism as moral issues. Human rights. Liberation theology and Marxism. Colonialism, neo-colonialism, and development.

Week 4

Read *either* Charles Frankel, *Morality and U.S. Foreign Policy*, *or* Stanley Hoffman, *Duties Beyond Borders.*

Week 5

Read *either* Charles Frankel, *Human Rights and Foreign Policy*, *or* Maurice Cranston, *What Are Human Rights?*

Week 6

Read *either* Frantz Fanon, *The Wretched of the Earth*, pp. 29–163, *or* James McGinnis, *Bread and Justice: Toward a New International Economic Order.*

Environment and Social Justice

Humanity's place in nature. Limits to growth, survival ethics.

Week 7

Read *either* Garrett Hardin, *Exploring New Ethics for Survival*, *or* George Lucas and Thomas Ogletree, eds., *Lifeboat Ethics*, *or* Thomas S. Derr, *Ecology and Human Need.*

Violence and War

Violence. Pacifism. The doctrine of the just war. The nuclear dilemma. Conscription and conscientious objection.

Week 8

Read Michael Walzer, *Just and Unjust Wars*, chs. 1–7, 11, 12, and 17–19.

Week 9

Read *either* M.K. Gandhi, *Gandhi on Non-Violence,* Thomas Merton, ed., *or* R.B. Gregg, *The Power of Non-Violence,* or Leo Tolstoy, *The Law of Love and the Law of Violence.*

The Economic Order

Property, religion and capitalism, relgous socialism. Poverty and affluence. Vocation, the work ethic, leisure. Business ethics, investments, corporate social responsibility.

Week 10

Read *either* R.H. Tawney, *The Acquisitive Society,* or J. Philip Wogaman, *The Great Economic Debate,* chs. 1–7.

Week 11

Read *either* Edward Stevens, *Business Ethics,* chs. 1, 5, 7, 8, and 10, *or* Oliver F. Williams and John W. Houck, *Full Value,* pp. 83–217. Read *also* the Catholic Bishops' Pastoral Letter on the U.S. Economy.

Church and State

Religious liberty. Private and public education, state aid. Religion in political campaigns. Other church-state issues.

Week 12

Read *either* Leo Pfeffer, *Church, State, and Freedom,* chs. 5, 9, 12, 13, 14, and "ten theses" (pp. 604–605), *or* J. Tussman, *The Supreme Court on Church and State* (the Pierce, Cochran, Cantwell, Gobitis, Barnette, Everson, McCollum, and Zorach cases), *or* John Courtney Murray, *We Hold These Truths,* chs. 2, 6, 7, 9.

3. Contemporary Religious Ethics: War and Peace in a Nuclear Age

Barry Jay Seltser   *Spring 1986*
School of Religion, University of Southern California,
Los Angeles, CA 90089

The two goals of this course are (a) to provide the student with a systematic overview of some central issues and concerns of recent ethical thinking in the Jewish and Christian traditions, and (b) to apply these traditions to contemporary debates about war and peace. The first few weeks of the course provide some background to the religious traditions themselves; the remaining time will be spent focusing on the specific topic.

This is a seminar course. Although occasional lectures will be given, the class sessions should consist primarily of discussion and debate among the students. Please do the reading carefully each week, and come to class prepared to raise issues and questions which concern you.

Course Requirements
The final grade will be determined as follows: term paper (approximately 20–30 pages)—50%; class participation—25%; and midterm, optional final examination—25%. If the student chooses not to take the final examination, the midterm grade will count the full 25%.

Books to Be Purchased
Dyson, Freeman. *Weapons and Hope.*
Gandhi, Mohandas. *Autobiography.*
Greene, Graham. *The Power and the Glory.*
Kellner, Mordecai. *Contemporary Jewish Ethics.*
LeGuin, Ursula. *The Eye of the Heron.*
Niebuhr, H.R. *Christ and Culture.*
O'Brien, W., and T. Shannon. *Renewing the Earth.*
Shannon, T. *What They Are Saying About War and Peace.*
Wiesel, Elie. *Dawn.*
Yoder, J. Howard. *The Politics of Jesus Christ.*

In addition, occasional photocopies will be distributed.

SCHEDULE OF CLASSES

Jan. 14—Introduction to Ethical Theory and Religious Ethics

Jan. 21—Ethics and Religion
 • Wiesel, entire book.
 • Niebuhr, pp. 1–44.

Jan. 28—Judaism and Ethics
 • Kellner, pp. 1–183.

Feb. 4—Christianity and Ethics
 • Niebuhr, remainder of book.
 • O'Brien and Shannon, pp. 11–43, 171–177, 384–389, 411–426.

Feb. 11—Religion and Modernity
 • Greene, entire book.

Feb. 18—War and Violence in Modern Society
Statement of paper topic due.
• Dyson, entire book.

Feb. 25—Midterm Examination

Mar. 4—Judaism and War
• Kellner, pp. 187–245, 401–436.

Mar. 11—Roman Catholicism and War
• Shannon, entire book.
• O'Brien and Shannon, pp. 117–170.

Mar. 18—Roman Catholicism and Violence
Detailed outline of paper due.
• O'Brien and Shannon, pp. 543–579.
• Handouts on Liberation Theology.

Apr. 1—Idealism, Realism, and Violence
• LeGuin, entire book.

Apr. 8—The Protestant Center and War
• Karl Barth, *Church Dogmatics*, Vol. III, No. 4, pp. 397–470 (handout).

Apr. 15—Protestantism and Pacifism
• Reinhold Niebuhr (handouts).
• J. Howard Yoder, entire book.

Apr. 22—Religion and Pacifism: A Cross-Cultural View
Final draft of paper due on Apr. 25.
• Gandhi, selections to be assigned.

Apr. 29—Overview

May 6—Optional Final Examination

4. Ethics and National Security Policy

Robert Fullinwider and Frances Harbour   *Fall 1987*
School of Public Affairs, University of Maryland,
College Park, MD 20742

This fifteen-week course is divided into three main sections. It begins with
the controversy about nuclear deterrence and strategic planning. Can there

be a morally acceptable policy on the possession and use of nuclear weapons? If so, what should such a policy look like? Are nuclear weapons really different from conventional arms? Why? What does the recent U.S. Catholic bishops' letter contribute to the understanding of possession and use of nuclear weapons? Was President Truman right to authorize the atomic bombing of Hiroshima and Nagasaki? Are there ways out of problems presented by a policy of extended deterrence?

The second part of the class examines dilemmas faced by military officers and civilians who want to develop and implement national security policy in a responsible way. What are the constraints and pressures of their roles? How can they reconcile duties as national trustees with responsibilities to humanity at large? Is everything really fair in war? What happens when people overstep the boundaries of the roles they have accepted—or of accepted morality? This section of the course also raises issues related to military manpower policy. It examines the all-volunteer force and the relation of military service to citizenship and to social justice.

The final section of the course deals with the state system itself. Is intervention in another state's internal affairs ever right? Is this even a meaningful question? Does the anarchical nature of the system remove it from the moral sphere? Do moral concerns have any place in the design and execution of security policy? Should they? Is there a difference between morality and moralism? Are principles incompatible with national interest?

The point of a course on ethics and national security policy is that it takes moral reasoning seriously. It does not teach predetermined "right answers," however. By covering the substance of both sides of important ethical debates, it can show students the conclusions and reasoning of other people who have thought carefully about an issue. By examining logical strengths and weaknesses in these arguments, it provides a model of how one might *go about* developing a workable position. By asking students to make and to defend arguments orally and in writing, it can help them to develop their own positions. This whole process should not only help students avoid shoddy thinking in the ethical sphere but may well extend beyond to improve critical thinking in all of their work.

Requirements

Each participant must complete a major critical paper on a topic or set of topics raised in course discussion or readings. In addition, you will periodically be assigned very short position papers for class presentation. Because we will rely a good deal on classroom discussion, it is important that you keep current with assigned reading so that you can participate fully.

Texts

Walzer, Michael. *Just and Unjust Wars.*
Beitz, Charles, et al., eds. *International Ethics.*
National Conference of Catholic Bishops. *The Challenge of Peace: God's Promise and Our Response.*

COURSE OUTLINE AND READINGS

Section I: Ethics and Nuclear Deterrence

Sept. 3—Introduction

Sept. 10—The Bombing of Hiroshima
- Walzer, pp. 263–268.
- Adam Meyerson, "Atoms for Peace," *Policy Review* (Summer 1985), pp. 46–47.
- Andre Ryerson, "The Cult of Hiroshima," *Commentary* (Oct. 1985), pp. 36–40.
- Kai Erikson, "Of Accidental Judgments and Casual Slaughters," *The Nation* (Aug. 3/10, 1985), pp. 80–85.
- Rufus E. Miles, Jr., "Hiroshima: The Strange Myth of Half a Million American Lives Saved," *International Security* (Fall 1985), pp. 121–140.
- Robert Batchelder, *The Irreversible Decision 1939–1950*, chs. 5–9, 17, pp. 41–107, 211–222.

Sept. 17—The Just War Tradition
- Walzer, pp. 21–47, 109–159.
- *The Challenge of Peace*, pp. 26–34.
- Thomas Nagel, "War and Massacre," in Beitz, pp. 52–74.

Sept. 25—The Bishops' Letter
- *The Challenge of Peace*, pp. i–viii, 20–26, 34–62, 73–84.
- Susan Okin, "Taking the Bishops Seriously," *World Politics* (July 1984), pp. 527–554.
- Albert Wohlstetter, "Bishops, Statesmen, and Other Strategists on the Bombing of Innocents," *Commentary* (June 1983), pp. 15–35.

Oct. 1—A Way Out? Unilateral Disarmament, Strategic Disengagement, Strategic Defense
- Robert W. Tucker, "The Nuclear Debate," *Foreign Affairs* (Fall 1984), pp. 1–32.
- Earl C. Ravenal, *Strategic Disengagement and World Peace*, pp. 3–38.
- Douglas P. Lackey, "Missiles and Morals: A Utilitarian Look at Nuclear Deterrence," in Beitz, pp. 109–151.
- Gregory Kavka, "Doubts About Unilateral Nuclear Disarmament," in Beitz, pp. 152–157.
- Lewis Lehrman, "The Case for Strategic Defense," *Policy Review* (Winter 1985), pp. 42–46.

Section II: Individuals in the System—
Questions of Responsibility and Justice

Oct. 8—The Case of Lt. Calley

- Walzer, pp. 304–327.
- *United States v. Calley*, 46 C.M.R. 1131 (1973), in Joseph Goldstein, Burke Marshall, and Jack Schwartz, *The My Lai Massacre and Its Cover-up: Beyond the Reach of Law?* pp. 491–506.
- Arthur Everett, Kathryn Johnson, and Harry Rosenthal, *Calley*, pp. 142–163.
- "The Confessions of Lieutenant Calley," *Esquire*, Vol. 74 (Nov. 1970), Vol. 75 (Feb. 1971), Vol. 76 (Sept. 1971).
- Army Pamphlet, "Your Conduct in Combat Under the Law of War," pp. 2–5, 13–17, 24–27.
- Judgment of the International Military Tribunal at Nuremberg: The Charter Provisions, in Adam Roberts and Richard Guelff, eds., *Documents on the Laws of War*, pp. 155–156.
- Robert H. Jackson, Chief Prosecutor's Opening Speech at Nuremberg Trials, November 11, 1945, in Goldstein et al., *The My Lai Massacre*, pp. 411–412.

Oct. 15—Institutional Roles and Individual Responsibility

- Walzer, pp. 176–196, 287–303.
- Richard Wasserstrom, "Roles and Morality," in David Luban, ed., *The Good Lawyer*, pp. 25–37.
- Malham Wakin, "Ethics of Leadership," in M. Wakin, ed., *War, Morality and the Military Profession*, pp. 197–217.
- James Dubik, "Social Expectations, Moral Obligations, and Command Responsibility," *International Journal of Applied Philosophy* 2 (Spring 1984), pp. 39–47.

Oct. 22—The All-Volunteer Force

- Eliot A. Cohen, "The Advent of the All-Volunteer Force," ch. 8 of *Citizens and Soldiers* (Ithaca, New York: Cornell University Press, 1985), pp. 166–182.
- James Fallows, *National Defense*, ch. 5, pp. 122–138.
- John G. Kester, "The Reasons to Draft," in William Bowman, Roger Little and G. Thomas Sicilia, eds., *The All-Volunteer Force After a Decade*, pp. 286–315.

Oct. 29—Minorities, Women, and Military Service

- Sara Ruddick, "Drafting Women: Pieces of the Puzzle," Center Working Paper, pp. 1–48.
- Michael Levin, "Women as Soldiers—The Record So Far," *The Public Interest* (Summer 1984), pp. 31–44.
- Commander R.M. Hixson, "Equal Rights, Equal Risks," *Proceedings of the U.S. Naval Institute* (Sept. 1985), pp. 37–41.

- R. Fullinwider, "The All-Volunteer Force and Racial Balance," Center Working Paper, pp. 1–15.
- Francois-Albert Angers, "Why We Shall *Never* Accept Conscription for Overseas Service," in Ramsay Cook, ed., *French-Canadian Nationalism* (Toronto: Macmillan of Canada), pp. 228–236.

Nov. 5—Workshop on Assigned Major Paper

Section III: Morality and the International System

Nov. 12—Intervention: Principles and Cases
- Walzer, pp. 51–63, 86–101, 106–108, 339–42, or: in Beitz, pp. 165–194.
- Materials on Rhodesia, Bangladesh, and Entebbe.
- Louis René Beres, "Becoming an Outlaw: U.S. Foreign Policy and Central America," *International Journal* (Summer 1985), pp. 510–529.
- Robert Tucker and Charles Krauthammer, *Intervention and the Reagan Doctrine*, pp. 1–17, 19–24.

Nov. 19—Sovereignty and Morality
- David Luban, "Just War and Human Rights," in Beitz, pp. 195–216.
- Michael Walzer, "The Moral Standing of States: A Response to Four Critics," in Beitz, pp. 217–237.
- David Luban, "The Romance of the Nation-State," in Beitz, pp. 238–242.
- Robert Art and Robert Jervis, eds., *International Politics: Anarchy, Force, Imperialism*, pp. 10–20, 21, 28.
- William D. Coplin, "International Law and Assumptions About the State System," in James N. Rosenau, ed., *International Politics and Foreign Policy*, pp. 142–152.
- Herbert Butterfield, "Global Good and Evil," in Kenneth Thompson and Robert J. Myers, eds., *Truth and Tragedy*, pp. 199–202.

Nov. 26—Realism vs. Moralism
- Walzer, pp. 3–20.
- Alexander Hamilton, "Pacificus," III, IV, V, and "Americanus," I, in H. Morgenthau and K. Thompson, eds., *Principles and Problems in International Politics*.
- Woodrow Wilson, "Speeches," in Arnold Wolfers and Lawrence Martin, eds., *The Anglo-American Tradition in Foreign Affairs*.
- Hans J. Morgenthau, "The Mainsprings of American Foreign Policy," in *In Defense of the National Interest*, pp. 3–4, 13–39.
- Lynn H. Miller, "Power and Value in World Society," *Global Order*, pp. 68–91.

Dec. 3—Morality and National Interest

- Marshall Cohen, "Moral Skepticism and International Relations," in Beitz, pp. 3–50.
- Peter G. Brown, ". . . in the National Interest," in P. Brown and D. MacLean, eds., *Human Rights and U.S. Foreign Policy*, pp. 161–171.
- Arnold Wolfers, "National Security as an Ambiguous Symbol," in *Discord and Collaboration*, pp. 147–165.
- Fred A. Sonderman, "The Concept of the National Interest," in William C. Olson, David S. McLellan, and Fred Sonderman, eds., *The Theory and Practice of International Relations*, pp. 57–65.

Dec. 10—Summary and Conclusion

XX

Literary and Media Perspectives

1. Images of War and Peace in Twentieth-Century Film, Art, and Literature

Curtis M. Hinsley   *Fall 1986*
Colgate University*

We live in a world constantly at war, in a century that has seen two global conflicts and countless wars across and within state boundaries. Today there are at least forty wars occurring around our globe. What are the origins of wars? What is the nature of war, and the legacy? Are wars inevitable or avoidable, and which wars? Our positions on such critical questions depend heavily on our perceptions of specific war experiences and images of war in general.

Perceptions and images are not, however, our own. They arrive to us from many sources, and, particularly in this century, they have been subject to control and manipulation, not simply during wartime but as a constant influence on our consciousnesses. For example, the use of emotive symbols in 1914 as in 1986 may actually change the course of history. This course examines that process, looking at the sources of imagery (newspapers, films, individual authors, poets and artists, poster art), the substance and messages of war images in historical context, and the political language used.

---

*Curtis Hinsley now teaches in the History Department of Northern Arizona University, Flagstaff, AZ 86011.

The bulk of the course is taken up with portrayal of war since 1914. The special emphasis on the First World War is because this appears in retrospect to have been a cultural watershed in the shifting consciousness, public awareness, and emerging mass stereotypes of war at the public level. It can be argued that the shift had started earlier, and some attention should be given to the gradual de-glamourizing of war during the 19th century in particular—and even earlier imagery of war. But it is contemporary warfare, the Spanish civil war, the Second World War, Korea, Vietnam, Central America, and potentially nuclear war that present the dominant imageries in contemporary film and art and literature—the language and symbols— as well as promote alternative views in writing and art. The varying presentation of peace (disarmament or peace movement) and contemporary conflict (the Falklands war or Libya) in the media is an entry into an analysis of our day to day interpretation of events.

Our inquiry is framed by what appears to be a widening dichotomy: on the one hand, a growing revulsion against the horrors of war, ending in visions of total extinction; on the other hand, a concomitant glorification of war as not only necessary but noble. It is arguable that twentieth century war is less easy to glamorize and that new techniques are therefore necessary. This divergence in attitude has been accompanied by a search for expressive terms, resulting in increasingly extreme imagery in film and print: in the first case, in an effort to express what seems to be inexpressibly negative visions; in the second case, to alter older terms of courage, chivalry, and sacrifice to fit modern conditions of technological warfare and civilian suffering. Most recently, probably in reaction to these dynamics of extremity, we have seen new emphasis on images of peace, as a positive antidote to the bombardment of images of fear and conflict. We urge you to bear in mind these themes and dynamics as the course proceeds (after a brief historical overview) from the First World War to the present, and images of our future.

In summary, the inquiry sets out to chart the developments, continuities, and changes in the portrayal of war (and peace), the contradictory images, and the effects of the civilianisation or "totalisation" of war since the 19th century both on our imaginations and on the role of media art and propaganda. We look at the latter as a filter of such images and symbols in either developing—or inhibiting—a more critical perception of this pivotal human experience.

Course Organization

In addition to the scheduled lecture and discussion sections, there will be frequent film presentations and at least one evening speaker. Professors Nigel Young and Terence Des Pres will give occasional lectures during the semester. These are an integral part of the course, and students are expected to attend all classes and presentations. The mid-term exam takes place in class on October 17. There will be a two-hour final exam as well. In addition, each student will regularly keep a journal on war, peace, and the media throughout the semester. (A separate description of journal format and expectations will be distributed.) The mid-term exam constitutes 30% of the course grade; the final is also 30%; the journal and class participation are 20% each.

Books to Be Purchased

Manual of Readings for Peace Studies 314, one volume.
Didion, Joan. *Salvador.*
Dyer, Gwynne. *War.*
Fussell, Paul. *The Great War and Modern Memory.*
Glasgow University Media Group. *War and Peace News.*
Heller, Joseph. *Catch-22.*
Herr, Michael. *Dispatches.*
Hersey, John. *Hiroshima.*
Orwell, George. *Homage to Catalonia.*
Remarque, Erich Maria. *All Quiet on the Western Front.*
The Shoshin Society. *Images for Survival.*
Taylor, A.J.P. *First World War: An Illustrated History.*

Recommended Books

Graves, Robert. *Goodbye to All That.*
Mailer, Norman. *The Naked and the Dead.*
Noble, *War and Peace Book.*
Silkin, Jon. *First World War Poetry.*
Unforgettable Fire. (Drawings by survivors of the atomic bombings of Hiroshima and Nagasaki.)

Films to Be Shown in Class

- *Battle of Culloden* (Watkins)
- *Killing Fields*
- *Behind the Front*
- *Paths of Glory* (Kubrick)
- *War,* Part 1: "The Road to Total War" (Gwynne Dyer)
- *Oh, What a Lovely War* (Attenborough)
- *All Quiet on the Western Front*
- *Spanish Earth*
- *Dr. Strangelove*
- *The Battle of Russia*
- *War,* Parts 4 & 5: "Road to War"
- Newsreels: "Stalingrad" and "Toranawa"
- Victory at Sea: "Guadalcanal"
- *Hiroshima/Nagasaki—August 1945*
- *Hearts and Minds*
- Newsreels from the Vietnam war
- *War,* Parts 6 & 7: "Road to War"
- *Testament*
- Clips from "Threads"

- *War Game* (Watkins)
- *Dead Birds*

COURSE SCHEDULE

Sept. 8—Film: *War*, Part 1—"The Road to Total War"
Visit the Active Arts Gallery of Case Library to see the international exhibit of peace posters.
- Dyer, Intro., and chs. 1–4.

Sept. 10—Discussion

Sept. 11—Film: *War*, Part 2—"Anyone's Son Will Do"

Sept. 12—Images of War and Peace in History
- Fussell, pp. 1–74.

Sept. 15—Discussion
- Taylor, pp. 1–119.
- Trumbull White, *Our War with Spain for Cuba's Freedom* (1898), frontispiece and title page.
- Richard Harding Davis, *Notes of a War Correspondent* (1910), excerpts.
- Theodore Roosevelt, "Brotherhood and the Heroic Virtues" and "National Duties," from *The Strenuous Life* (1904).

Sept. 17—The Demise of Chivalry
- V.G. Kiernan, "Conscription and Society in Europe Before the War of 1914–18."
- James Joll, *The Second International, 1889–1914* (excerpts).

Sept. 19—Film: *The Battle of Culloden* (P. Watkins)

Sept. 22—Imagery of the First World War
- V.G. Kiernan, "Conscription and Society in Europe Before the War of 1914–18."
- James Joll, *The Second International, 1889–1914* (excerpts).
- Taylor, pp. 120–221.
- H.G. Wells, "The Last War," from *The World Set Free* (1914).

Sept. 24—Propaganda in the First World War
- George P. Creel, *How We Advertised America* (excerpts) (1920).
- Randolph Bourne, "The State," from *War and the Intellectuals: Collected Essays, 1915–1919* (1964).

Sept. 25—Films: *Behind the Front* **and** *Paths of Glory*

Sept. 26—Discussion

Sept. 29—Literary Responses to World War I
- Fussell, chs. 5, 6, 8.
- Poems.

Oct. 1—Discussion
- Remarque, entire.

Oct. 2—Film: *Oh, What a Lovely War*

Oct. 3—Responses to War: Women, Workers, War Resisters and Artists
With illustrations. Journals due for review.
- John Dos Passos, "Randolph Bourne" and "The Body of an American," from *USA: Nineteen Nineteen* (1933).
- Vera Brittain, *Testament of Youth: An Autobiographical Study of the Years 1900–1925* (1933), excerpts.
- Jaroslav Hasek, *The Good Soldier Svejk and His Fortunes in the World War* (1921–22), excerpts.

Oct. 6—Gwynne Dyer on Making the *War* **Series**
Evening lecture: "Nuclear War and the Media."

Oct. 8—The Interwar Years: Isolationism, Economic Depression, War in Spain
- *Homage to Catalonia.*

Oct. 9—Film: *Spanish Earth*

Oct. 10—Discussion and Film: *Dr. Strangelove*
- *Homage to Catalonia.*

Oct. 13—The Spanish Civil War as Metaphor and Memory
- Ernest Hemingway, "Old Man at the Bridge."
- Luigi Pirandello, "War."
- Stephen Spender, "Writers in Uniform," *New York Times*, June 8, 1986.

Oct. 15
Midterm examination in class. Midterm break, Oct. 17.

Oct. 20—Images of the Second World War (Posters, Art, Photography)
Evening lecture: "Nuclear Weapons and American Society, 1945–55."
- Paul Fussell, "The Cultural Form of the Second World War" (1984).
- George Roeder, "V-Photographs: What the American Public Saw of World War II" (1984).

Oct. 22—Films: *Battle of Russia* **and** *Stalingrad*
There will be a discussion following the films.
- Orwell, "War Is Peace," handout.
- Dyer, ch. 5.

Oct. 23—Film: *War,* **Parts 4 and 5**
Oct 24—Discussion
- Fussell, "My War," in *The Boy Scout Handbook.*

Oct. 27—World War II Newsreels: Guadalcanal, Tarawa
There will be a discussion following the newsreels.
- Kurt Vonnegut, *Slaughterhouse Five* (1969), excerpts.
- Begin Joseph Heller's *Catch 22.*

Oct. 29—Discussion
- Fussell, "Time-Life Goes to War," in *Boy Scout Handbook.*
- Dyer, ch. 8.

Oct. 31—Film: *Hiroshima/Nagasaki—August 1945*
There will be a discussion following the film.
- Hersey.
- *Images for Survival.*
- *Unforgettable Fire.*

Nov. 3—Film: Korea Newsreel
- George Orwell, "Politics and the English Language" (1948).
- Finish *Catch 22.*

Nov. 5—Background to the Vietnam War
- Herr, *Dispatches.*
- C.D.B. Bryan, "Barely Suppressed Screams: Getting a Bead on Vietnam War Literature" (1984).
- Anonymous, "Letter from Vietnam" (1970).

Nov. 6—Film: *Hearts and Minds*

Nov. 7—Discussion
- Edward T. Linenthal, "From Hero to Anti-Hero: The Transformation of the Warrior in Modern America" (1983).

Nov. 10—Film: Vietnam Newsreel (Cronkite)
There will be a discussion following the newsreel.

Nov. 12—The Imagery of the Vietnam War
- Dyer, p. 142 and 163–166.

Nov. 13—Film: *War,* **Parts 6 and 7**

Nov. 14—Conflict in Central America
- Didion, *Salvador.*
- Pictures: Salvador.

Nov. 17—Contemporary Reporting of War/Peace Issues in Central America
- *War and Peace News,* Introduction and ch. 1 (pp. 1–28), ch. 11 (pp. 277–298) ("The Current Affairs Prism" and Conclusion).

Nov. 19—News Coverage: The Falklands War, Libya, Central America
Discussion.
- *War and Peace News,* chs. 2 and 3 (pp. 29–143), and Conclusion (pp. 172–174); also "News Language," Appendix (pp. 316–347).

Nov. 20—Film: *Testament*

Nov. 21—Reporting Nuclear Issues
- Film: Clips from "Threads" and "Countdown to Looking Glass."
- *War and Peace News,* chs. 5–8 and pp. 177–245.

Nov. 24—Peace Movements and the Media
Lecture and slides.
- *War and Peace News,* ch. 10.
- Handout on Greenham Women.

Dec. 1
Lecture. Journals due.

Dec. 3—Imaging World War III: Clips from the *War Game*
Discussion of *War Game.*
- Peter Watkins and Catherine Bragee, "The Nuclear War Film" (1984).

Dec. 4—Film: *The War Game*
Discussion Dec. 5.

Dec. 8—Peace as Art—and Propaganda
View illustrations.
- Dyer, ch. 11.

Dec. 10—Film: Clips from *Dead Birds*
Conclusion and summary.

2. War and Peace in English and American Literature

Dick Ringler   Spring 1987
English and Scandinavian Studies Dept., University of
Wisconsin–Madison, Madison, WI 53706

Course Requirements
Three five-week exams and a term paper.

Course Texts
Beowulf, tr. Wright.
Crane. *The Red Badge of Courage.*
Erasmus. *The Complaint of Peace.*
Fussell. *The Great War and Modern Memory.*
Gardner. *Grendel.*
Golding. *Lord of the Flies.*
Hersey. *Hiroshima.*
More. *Utopia.*
Vonnegut. *Slaughter-House Five.*
An anthology of miscellaneous pieces of poetry and prose will be available
     in sections, during the semester.

Jan. 21—General Introduction

Jan. 23—The Nuclear Foreground

Jan. 25—The *Iliad,* I
* Excerpts from the *Iliad.*

Jan. 28—The *Iliad,* II
* Simone Weil, "The *Iliad,* Poem of Might."

Jan. 30—War and Anti-War Reaction in Athens in the Late Fifth Century B.C.
* Thucydides, "The Melian Dialogue."
* Euripides, *The Trojan Women.*

Feb. 1—War and Peace in the Pre-Christian Germanic World
* "The Lay of Hloth."

Feb. 4—War and Peace in Judaism and Christianity
- John Ferguson, "Judaism" and "Christianity."

Feb. 6—Cain and Abel
- The story of Cain and Abel (from Genesis 4).
- Henry Vaughan, "Abel's Blood."
- Siegfried Sassoon, "Ancient History."
- Demetrios Capetanakis, "Abel."

Feb. 8—War and Peace in the Dark Ages
- Aneirin, Extracts from *The Goddoddin* (North British, after 600 A.D).
- Angilbert, "On the Battle which was fought at Fontenoy" (Latin, 841 A.D)..
- Anonymous, "The Battle of Maldon" (Old English, 991 A.D)..

Feb. 11—*Beowulf*, I
- *Beowulf* (tr. Wright), pp. 9–79 (top 3 lines).

Feb. 13—*Beowulf*, II

Feb. 15—*Beowulf*, III
- *Beowulf*, pp. 79–end

Feb. 18—*Grendel*, I
- John Gardner, *Grendel*.

Feb. 20—*Grendel*, II

Feb. 22—First Five-Week Examination

Feb. 25—More's *Utopia*
- Sir Thomas More (1478–1535), *Utopia*. Read Book I (1516) in its entirety. If you have time, read all of Book II (1515) as well; if not, read especially pp. 28, 42–54, 61–70, and 79–83.

Feb. 27—Erasmus' *Complaint of Peace*
- Desiderius Erasmus (?1466–1536), *The Complaint of Peace* (1517).

Mar. 1—The Burghers of Calais
- Excerpts from the *Chronicles* of John Froissart (?1333–1400).
- Robert Francis Cook, "The Burghers of Calais in History" (and study the suggested questions).
- Norma Broude, "Rodin's *Burghers of Calais*: An Art Historical Analysis."
- Dewey D. Wallace, Jr., "The Religious Background for Rodin's *Burghers of Calais*" (and study the questions for discussion).
- Robert A. Draghi, "The Burghers of Calais: Some Reflections on the Ethics of Sacrifice" (and study the questions and exercises for group discussion).

Mar. 4—Francois Rabelais

- Francois Rabelais (?1494–1553), selections from the first book of *The Histories of Gargantua and Pantagruel* (1534), Chapters 25–58.

Mar. 6—Shakespeare's *Henry V*

- William Shakespeare (1564–1616), *Henry V* (1599); read this in any edition available to you.

Mar. 8—Montaigne's and Bacon's *Essays*

- Michel de Montaigne (1533–1592), "Of Cannibals" (1578–80) and "Of Evil Means Employed to a Good End" (1578–80).
- Sir Francis Bacon (1561–1626), "Of Seditions and Troubles" (1625), "Of Empire" (1612), and "Of the True Greatness of Kingdoms and Estates" (1612).

Mar. 11—The Seventeenth and Eighteenth Centuries in England

- George Herbert (1593–1633), "Peace" (1620s).
- John Milton (1608–1674), excerpt from "A Hymn on the Morning of Christ's Nativity" (1629).
- Martin Parker (?1600–1656), "The Maunding Soldier."
- Henry Vaughan (1622–1695), "Peace" and "The Men of War" (both published 1650).
- Richard Lovelace (1618–1658), "Song Set by Mr. John Laniere to Lucasta, Going to the Warres" (published 1649).
- James Shirley (1596–1666), "The Glories of Our Blood and State," from *The Contention of Ajax and Ulysses* (1659).
- William Collins (1721–1759), "Ode, Written in the Beginning of the Year 1746."
- Samuel Johnson (1709–1784), Extract from "The Vanity of Human Wishes" (1749).
- William Blake (1757–1827), "A War Song to Englishmen" (1770s).
- William Cowper (1731–1800), Excerpts from *The Task* (1785).

Mar. 13—The Era of the Napoleonic Wars

- Robert Southey (1774–1843), "The Battle of Blenheim" (1798).
- Samuel Taylor Coleridge (1772–1834), "Fears in Solitude" (1798).
- Thomas Campbell (1777–1844), "Hohenlinden" (1802).
- William Wordsworth (1770–1850), "1801" (1802), "Character of the Happy Warrior" (1805–1806), "November, 1806," "The French and the Spanish Guerrillas" (1810–1811), "1811," and "The French Army in Russia 1812–13" (1816).
- Charles Wolfe (1791–1823), "The Burial of Sir John Moore" (1814–1815).
- George Gordon, Lord Byron (1788–1824), "The Destruction of Semnacherib" (1815) and Excerpt from *Childe Harold's Pilgrimage*, Canto III (1816).

- William Wordsworth, "After Visiting the Field of Waterloo" (1820).
- Percy Bysshe Shelley (1792–1822), Chorus from *Hellas* (1821).

Mar. 15—Art and War Slide Lecture

Mar. 18, 20, 22—Spring Recess

Mar. 25—The Early Nineteenth Century in England
- Lord Byron, Excerpt from *Don Juan* (early 1820s).
- Thomas Love Peacock (1785–1866), Extract from *The Misfortunes of Elphin* (1829).
- Winthrop Mackworth Praed (1802–1829), "Waterloo" (1830).
- Walter Savage Landor (1775–1864), Extracts from *Pericles and Aspasia* (1836) and "A Foreign Ruler" (published 1863).
- John Clare (1793–1864), "The Soldier," "The Soldiers Grave," and "The Returned Soldier."
- Robert Browning (1812–1889), "Incident of the French Camp" (1842).
- Arthur Hugh Clough (1819–1861), "Extracts from *Amours de Voyage* (1849), "Say Not the Struggle Naught Availeth" (1849).
- Alfred, Lord Tennyson (1809–1892), "The Charge of the Light Brigade" and "The Defence of Lucknow" (1850s).

Mar. 27—Meanwhile in America
- Nathaniel Niles (1741–1828), "The American Hero: A Sapphic Ode" (written to celebrate the Battle of Bunker Hill, 1775).
- Francis Scott Key (1779–1843), "The Star-Spangled Banner" (September 14, 1814).
- Ralph Waldo Emerson (1803–1882), "Concord Hymn" (1836).
- William B. Tappan (1794–1849), "I Am for Peace" and "Christian Wars."
- Henry Wadsworth Longfellow (1807–1882), "The Arsenal at Springfield" (1843).
- James Russell Lowell (1819–1891), "A Letter" (1846) from *The Biglow Papers*, First Series.
- From Edmund Wilson, "The Battle Hymn of the Republic: The Union as Religious Mysticism."
- From Edmund Wilson, "The Myth of the Old South: Sidney Lanier."

Mar. 29—Poetry of the Civil War
- From Edmund Wilson, "Poetry of the War."
- Walt Whitman, Extracts from *Drum-Taps* (1865) and *Sequel to Drum-Taps* (1865–1866).
- George Henry Boker (1823–1890), "Dirge for a Soldier" (1864).
- Thomas Bailey Aldrich (1836–1907), "Fredericksburg" and "By the Potomac" (both published 1865).
- Herman Melville (1819–1891), extracts from *Battle-Pieces and Aspects of the War* (1866).

- Henry Wadsworth Longfellow, "Christmas Bells" and "Killed at the Ford" (both published 1867).
- John Greenlead Whittier (1807–1892), "Barbara Frietchie" (1863) and "Disarmament" (1871).
- Emily Dickinson (1830–1886), "My Triumph Lasted Till the Drums" (c1872) and "Success Is Counted Sweetest."
- Henry Wadsworth Longfellow, "A Nameless Grave" (1874), "The Revenge of Rain-in-the-Face" (1876), and "Decoration Day" (c1880).
- Thomas Bailey Aldrich, "Spring in New England" (published 1876).

Apr. 1—Prose About the Civil War
- Ambrose Bierce (1842–1913), "An Occurrence at Owl Creek Bridge" (1891).
- Edmund Wilson, "Ambrose Bierce on the Owl Creek Bridge."
- Hamlin Garland (1860–1940), "The Return of a Private" (1891).

Apr. 3—Second Five-Week Examination

Apr. 5—Good Friday Recess

Apr. 8—Stephen Crane and After
- Stephen Crane (1871–1900), *The Red Badge of Courage* (1893).

Apr. 10—Back to England: The Coming of the Great War
- Gerard Manley Hopkins (1844–1889), "The Soldier" (1885).
- Robert Louis Stevenson (1850–1894), "If This Were Faith" (1893).
- William Watson (1858–1935), "The World in Armour" (1894) and "A Trial of Orthodoxy" (1896).
- A.E. Housman (1859–1936), "The Day of Battle" (Mar. 1895) and "'The Street Sounds to the Soldiers' Tread'" (May/June 1895).
- Rudyard Kipling (1865–1936), "Hymn Before Battle" (1896) and "Recessional" (1897).
- Thomas Hardy (1840–1928), "Drummer Hodge" (1899), "The Man He Killed" (1902), "His Country" (1913), and "Channel Firing" (1913).
- Alice Meynell (1847–1922), "Summer in England 1914."
- Rupert Brooke (1887–1915), "Peace" (1914).
- A.E. Housman, "'Oh Is It the Jar of Nations.'"
- Hilaire Belloc (1870–1953), "The Pacifist."
- Thomas Hardy, "Men Who March Away" (1914).
- William Butler Yeats (1865–1939), "On Being Asked for a War Poem" and "An Irish Airman Forsees His Death" (both pub. 1919).
- Laurence Binyon (1869–1943), "For the Fallen."
- Thomas Hardy, "In Time of 'The Breaking of Nations'" (1915).
- John McCrae (1872–1918), "In Flanders Fields" (Apr./May 1915).

Apr. 12—The Great War, I: Siegried Sassoon

- Paul Fussell, *The Great War and Modern Memory*, pp. 3–105.
- Siegfried Sassoon (1886–1967), "The Kiss," "A Working Party," "At Carnoy," "The Hero," "Dreamers," "The General," "Does It Matter?" "Fight to a Finish," "Suicide in the Trenches," and "Song-Books of the War."
- G.K. Chesterton (1874–1936), "Elegy in a Country Churchyard."
- Rudyard Kipling, "The Verdicts."
- Walter De La Mare (1873–1956), "The Marionettes."
- Thomas Hardy, "I Looked Up from My Writing" (pub. 1917), "Outside the Casement" (pub. 1922), and "Horses Aboard" (pub. 1925).
- William Watson, "The Battlefields of the Future."

Apr. 15—The Great War, II: Trench Poets

- Paul Fussell, *The Great War and Modern Memory*, pp. 105–54.
- Richard Aldington (1892–1962), "Bombardment" and "At All Costs."
- H. D'A.B., "Givenchy Field."
- Wilfrid Wilson Gibson (1878–1962), "The Dancers," "The Question," "Mark Anderson," "Breakfast," and "In the Ambulance."
- Patrick MacGill (1890–), "Before the Charge."
- Herbert Read (1893–1968), "The Happy Warrior," "Leidholz," and "My Company."
- Edgell Rickword (1898–), "Trench Poets."
- Charles Sorley (1895–1915), "'All the Hills and Vales Along.'"
- Edward Thomas (1878–1917), "This Is No Case of Petty Wrong or Right" (26 December 1915), "February Afternoon" (7/8 February 1916), "'As the Team's Head-Brass'" (27 May 1916), "The Trumpet" (26/28 September 1916), and "Lights Out" (November 1916).
- Arthur Graeme West (1891–1917), "'God! How I Hate You.'"
- T.P. Cameron Wilson (1878–1918), "Magpies in Picardy."

Apr. 17—The Great War, III: Robert Graves and Ivor Gurney

- Paul Fussell, *The Great War and Modern Memory*, pp. 155–220
- Robert Graves (1895–), "The Last Day of Leave" (1916), "Escape," "Corporal Stare," "Dead Cow Farm," "Sargeant-Major Money" (1917), and "Two Fusiliers."
- Ivor Gurney (1890–1937), "To His Love" (Aug./Sept. 1916), "Song of Pain and Beauty" (Mar. 1917), "Brown Earth Look," "Behind the Line," "Poem," "Strange Hells," and "The Not-Returning" (all 1919–1922), "To God" (Barnwood Mental Hospital, Sept./Dec. 1922), "The Pleasance Window" (24/25 Sept. 1926), "Here, If Forlorn," and "The Wind" (1929 or later).

Apr. 19—The Great War, IV: Isaac Rosenberg and Edmund Blunden

- Paul Fussell, *The Great War and Modern Memory*, pp. 221–54.
- Isaac Rosenberg (1890–1918), "August 1914" (1916)), "Break of Day in the Trenches" (June 1916), "Returning, We Hear the Larks" (1917), "Louse Hunting" (1917), and "Dead Man's Dump" (1917).

- Paul Fussell, *The Great War and Modern Memory*, pp. 254–69.
- Edmund Blunden (1896–1974), "Festubert," "Thiepval Wood," "Zillebeke Brook," "Vlamertinghe," and "Les Halles d'Ypres."

Apr. 22—The Great War, V: Wilfred Owen

- Paul Fussell, *The Great War and Modern Memory*, pp. 270–99.
- Wilfred Owen (1893–1918), "Preface," "The Parable of the Old Man and the Young," "Greater Love," "The Send-Off," "Exposure," "Dulce et Decorum Est," "The Last Laugh," "Futility," "Insensibility," "Spring Offensive," "Strange Meeting," "Mental Cases."
- Paul Fussell, *The Great War and Modern Memory*, pp. 299–335.
- Two postscripts to the Great War: Ted Hughes (1930–), "Six Young Men," and Donald Hall (1928–), "The Old Pilot's Death" (1960).

Apr. 24—Between the Wars: "Is It Peace?"

- Thomas Hardy, "Jezreel" and "'And There Was a Great Calm.'"
- Siegfried Sassoon, "Everyone Sang," "Memorial Tablet," and "Aftermath" (Mar. 1919).
- G.K. Chesterton, "For a War Memorial."
- Osbert Sitwell (1892–1969), "The Next War" (pub. 1921).
- William Butler Yeats, "The Second Coming" (pub. 1921).
- Ezra Pound (1885–1972), Excerpt from "Hugh Selwyn Mauberly" (pub. 1920).
- Thomas Hardy, "Christmas 1924" and "We Are Getting to the End" (1928).
- T.S. Eliot (1888–1965), "Triumphas March" (1931).
- Siegfried Sassoon, "Thoughts in 1932" and "At the Cenotaph" (1933).
- Frantisek Halas (1901–1949), "Again" (1934).
- Edmund Blunden, "Some Talk of Peace—" (1930s).
- Edna St. Vincent Millay (1892–1950), "Conscientious Objector (pub. 1934).
- Edwin Muir (1887–1959), "The Town Betrayed."
- Robert Graves, "Recalling the War."
- Leonard Bacon (1887–1954), "Veteran."
- Siegfried Sassoon, "A Prayer from 1936."
- Edna St. Vincent Millay, "'And Then There Were None.'"
- William Butler Yeats, "Politics."
- Wiegfried Sassoon, "A Local Train of Thought."
- W.H. Auden (1907–73), "O What Is That Sound" and "'Say That This City Has Ten Million Souls.'"
- Jocelyn Brooke (1908–), "Song."
- Louis MacNeice (1907–1963), "Autumn Journal VII" (1938).
- W.H. Auden, "September 1, 1939."

Apr. 26—England in World War II: Civilians and Soldiers
Civilians
- A.P. Herbert (1890–1971), "'No Quarrel.'"
- Anne Ridler (1912–), "Now as Then."

- Herbert Read, "To a Conscript of 1940" and "Ode Written During the Battle of Dunkirk."
- Louis MacNeice, "Jegu" (August 1940).
- Keith Douglas (1920–44), "John Anderson" (1940).
- Geoffrey Grigson (1905–), "The Landscape of the Heart" (1941).
- Charles Norman (1904–), "Speech by Moonlight."
- Virginia Woolf (1882–1941), "Thoughts on Peace in an Air Raid" (August 1940).
- Edith Sitwell (1887–1964), "Still Falls the Rain" (1940).
- Louis MacNeice, "Homage to Wren (A Memory of 1941)" (1957–1960).
- H.D. (1886–1961), "'Not in Our Time, O Lord'" (1944) and "'An Incident Here and There'" (1942).
- Richard Church (1893–1972), extract from *Twentieth Century Psalter* (1943).
- Edwin Muir, "Reading in Wartime" (1944).

Soldiers

- Henry Treece (1911–), "To Certain Ladies, on Going to the Wars."
- Alun Lewis (1920–44), "Goodbye."
- John Manifold (1915–), "Fife Tune."
- Roy Fuller (1912–), "Royal Naval Air Station."
- John Pudney (1909–), "Nocturne: The Mess" and "Missing."
- Charles Causley (1917–), "Song of the Dying Gunner AA1" and "Convoy."
- Roy Fuller, "Spring 1942" and "What Is Terrible."
- Keith Douglas, "Vergissmeinicht" (1943).
- Alun Lewis, "The Run-In" and "The Peasants."
- Gavin Ewart (1916–), "When a Beau Goes In" (1944).
- Henry Treece, "War Poem."
- Alun Lewis, "Song."

Apr. 29—America in World War II: Soldiers and Civilians
The Beginnings

- Robinson Jeffers (1887–1962), "Contemplation of the Sword" and "Battle."
- Blake Clark, "Pearl Harbor."
- Robinson Jeffers, "Black-Out" and "Fourth Act."

Soldiers

- John Ciardi (1916–), "Song."
- Richard Eberhart (1904–), "The Fury of Aerial Bombardment."
- Randall Jarrell (1914–65), "The Death of the Ball Turret Gunner."
- Alfred Hayes (1911–), "The Death of the Crane-man" (Italy 1944).
- Karl Shapiro (1911–), "Elegy for a Dead Soldier" (New Guinea 1944).

- John Ciardi, "Elegy Just in Case."
- Anonymous, "'Soldiers Who Wish to Be a Hero.'"

Civilians
- Harry Brown (1917–   ), "The Drill."
- Edith Lovejoy Pierce, "Patterns" and "Music Room."
- Dorothy Parker (1893–1967), "War Song."
- E. E. Cummings (1894–1962), "In Distrust of Merits."

May—"Now the Cities Lie Broken": Dresden, February 13–15, 1945
- H. D. [Hilda Doolittle], "'It is no madness to say/you will fall, you great cities'" (1944).
- Randall Jarrell, "Losses."
- Photograph of Dresden after the bombings: a sandstone figure atop the town hall gestures toward the ruins of the old quarter
- Deiter Georgi, "The Bombings of Dresden."
- Charles S. Maier, "Why the Allies Did It."
- Photograph of Flying Fortresses of the U.S. Eighth Air Force over Dresden.
- Randall Jarrell, "Eighth Air Force."
- Kurt Vonnegut, Jr. (1922–   ), *Slaughterhouse-Five, or the Children's Crusade: A Duty-Dance with Death* (1966).
- Charles Causley, "On Being Asked to Write a School Hymn."

May 3—"Where the End of the World Began": Hiroshima, August 6, 1945
- Lousie McNeill, "Night at the Commodore" (1984).
- John Hersey (1914–   ), *Hiroshima* (1946).
- Oliver Evans (1915–   ), "Of Atom Age" (1946).
- Siegfried Sassoon, "Litany of the Lost" (1945).
- Bertolt Brecht (1898–1956), "Swansong" (1945).
- Alexander Hammond, "God's Nation Interprets the Bomb" (pub. 1984).
- "An Interview with John Hersey: After Hiroshima" (1948).

May 6—"Who Must Be Blamed . . . But the Whole Heart of Man?"
- William Golding (1911–   ), *Lord of the Flies* (1945).

May 8—Looking Back to World War II
- John Ciardi, "The Formalities."
- Alex Comfort (1920–   ), "Song for the Heroes" (1946).
- Kenneth Rexroth (1905–   ), "On a Military Graveyard."
- W. H. Auden, "Epitaph for the Unknown Soldier."
- Wallace Stevens (1879–1955), "The Soldier's Wound" (pub. 1947).
- Walter Benton (1907–   ), "There Are No Good Giants" (pub. 1948).
- Edwin Muir, "The Good Town" (pub. 1949).
- Roy Fuller, "Schwere Gustav" (pub. 1949).
- Keith Barnes "Prologue."
- Richard Wilbur (1921–   ), "Mined Country."

- Thomas McGrath (1916–   ), "Remembering that Island" (pub. 1955).
- Charles Causley, "Recruiting Drive" and "On the Thirteenth Day of Christmas" (both pub. 1953).
- W. H. Auden, "Fleet Visit," Extract from "Memorial for the City," and "The Shield of Achilles" (all 1948–1957).
- Edwin Muir, "Impersonal Calamity."
- Donald Hall (1928–   ), "An Airstrip in Essex, 1969."
- John Beecher (1904–1980), "A Veteran's Day of Recollection."
- Sylvia Plath (1932–1963), "Daddy" (1962).
- Gavin Ewart, extract from "Madame Tussaud's" (pub. 1964) and "June 1966."

May 10—Looking Ahead to World War III
Interlude in Vietnam
- Mary Hacker, "Achtung! Achtung!"
- Denise Levertov (1923)–   ), "What Were They Like?" (pub. 1966).
- Langston Hughes (1902–67), "Without Benefit of Declaration" (pub. 1967).
- John Beecher, "Report to Herod" and "Viaticum."
- George Starbuck (1931–   ), "Of Late."
- Wendell Berry (1934–   ), "To Think of the Life of a Man," "Against the War in Viet Nam," and "Dark with Power."
- Norman Rosten (1914–   ), "Vietnam."
- Galway Kinnell (1927–   ), "Vapor Trail Reflected in the Frog Pond."
- John Beecher, "Engagement at the Salt Fort."
- Dave Etter (1928–   ), "The Hometown Hero Comes Home" (pub. 1966).
- Thomas McGrath, "Gone Away Blues."

Strictly Nuclear
- William Stafford (1914–   ), "At the Bomb Testing Site" (1977).
- Lindley Williams Hubbell (1901–   ), "At Hiroshima."
- Norman Rosten, "Harry" (1965).
- Robinson Jeffers, "The Great Explosion," "Unnatural Powers," and "To Kill in War Is Not Murder" (all c1965).
- Wendell Berry, "To My Children, Fearing for Them" (1968).
- John Beecher, "Moloch."
- Marge Piercy (1936–   ), "The Long Death" (1980).
- Evangeline Paterson, "Armaments Race."
- Karol Wojtyla (Pope John Paul II) (1920–   ), "The Armaments Factory Worker."
- Peter Appleton (1925–   ), "The Responsibility."
- Gavin Ewart, "Sonnet: Malthusian" (1976).
- Edwin Brock, "Five Ways to Kill a Man" (1963).
- Robert Lowell (1917–1977), "Fall 1961."
- Philip Levine (1928–   ), "Above It All" (1968).
- W. S. Merwin (1927–   ), "Postcards from the Maginot Line" (1970).

- Wendell Berry, "A Discipline" (1968).
- Roy Fuller, "Winter Roundel" (1954).
- Peter Porter (1929–   ), "Your Attention Please."
- Edwin Muir, "The Horses," "The Last War" (1958), "I See the 'I See the Image,'" and "The Brother" (1957).
- Richard Wilbur, "Advice to a Prophet" (1962).
- Robinson Jeffers, "How Beautiful It Is" (c1960).
- John Hall Wheelock (1886–1978), "Earth" (1961).
- Wendell Berry, "The Peace of Wild Things" (pub. 1968).

May 12—Third Five-Week Examination

3. Literature of Protest and Hope

Sandi Albertson   *Spring 1986*
Middlesex Community College, Bedford, MA 01730

Introduction to Course
- William Buckley, "Why Don't We Complain?"

Topic One—Response to Personal Loss and Suffering
- Old Testament, *Book of Job*.
- Archibald MacLeish, *J.B.* (excerpts).
- Robert Frost, *Masque of Reason* (excerpts).
- William Blake, illustrations of *Book of Job*.
- Peanuts cartoon.
- *Psalms* 23, 126, 137.
- New Testament, *Romans* 8, *Revelations* 21.
- *Music:* Brahms, "German Requiem."
- *Matthew* 4, *Psalms* 39, 126, and *I Peter* 1.
- *Art:* Edvard Muench, "The Scream."
- Annie Dillard, "Heaven and Earth in Jest."
- William Sloane Coffin, "My Son Beat Me to the Grave."
- Denise Levertov, "Despair."
- Edna St. Vincent Millay, "Lament."
- Emily Dickinson, "It Was Not Death for I Stood Up"; "I Measure Every Grief I Meet"; "Hope Is the Thing with Feathers."

Topic Two—Holocaust
Journals due.
- Elie Wiesel, *Night.*
- Victor Frankl, *Man's Search for Meaning.*
- *Film:* "Night and Fog."

Topic Three—American Abolitionist and Civil Rights Movements
- Frederick Douglas, "Letter to His Master."
- Susan Griffin, "I Like to Think of Harriet Tubman."
- Langston Hughes, "A Dream Deferred."
- Maya Angelou, "Harlem Hopscotch"; *I Know Why the Caged Bird Sings* (excerpts).
- *Music:* Spirituals—"Which Side Are You On"; "We Shall Overcome"; "Thirsty Boots"; "If I Had a Hammer."
- *Photography: With Grief Acquainted.*
- *Film: I Have a Dream.*
- Lorraine Hansberry, *A Raisin in the Sun.*

Topic Four—Human Rights Struggles: South Africa
- Athol Fugard, *Master Harold and the Boys.*
- *Photography: House of Bondage* (Earnest Coles)

Topic Five—Human Rights Struggles: Soviet Union
- Alexander Solzhenitsyn, *One Day in the Life of Ivan Denisovich.*
- *Film:* Solzhenitsyn—Nobel Peace Prize—*One Word of Truth.*
- Mandelstram, *Hope Against Hope* and *Hope Abandoned* (excerpts).

Topic Six—Labor/Poverty/Economic Justice
Essay due.
- Lowell Textile Mill workers.
- Kathy Kahn, *Hillbilly Women* (exerpts).
- *Music/Photography: Voice from the Mountains*; Dorothea Lange.

Topic Seven—Human Rights Struggles: Latin America
Journals due.
- Carolina DeJesus, *Child of the Dark.*
- Jacobo Timerman, *Prisoner Without a Name, Cell Without a Number* (exerpts).
- *Drawings:* Dr. Filartiga (Paraguay).
- Garcia Marquez, *100 Years of Solitude,* and *The Gospel in Solentiname.*

Topic Eight—Anti-War/Pro-War/Disarmament
Creative expression projects due.
- Stephen Vincent Benet, "By the Waters of Babylon."
- Wilfred Owens, "Dulce et Decorum Est"; "Parable of Old Man and Young."
- *Art:* Posters (World War I and II).
- *Photography:* David Duncan.

- *Painting*: Picasso, "Guernica."
- *Music:* Verdi; Brittain; "War Requiem"; military marches; anti-war protest songs.
- *Slide Show:* "Art with a Message."
- Thoreau, "Civil Disobedience."
- Joanna Macy, "Despair-Work."

Conclusion/Review

Trip to Museum of Fine Arts, Boston.
- *Theater:* Live dramatic presentation, Underground Railway Theater; *The Crucible.*
- *Film: The Official Story.*

4. The Press and the Arms Race

David Rubin   *Fall 1987*

Center for War, Peace, and the News Media, Journalism Dept., New York University, New York, NY 10003

This course will acquaint you with the particular difficulties confronting American journalists and the American news media as they report on the superpower relationship and the nuclear arms race. We will examine the political, legal, procedural, historical, and ethical conditions which shape national security journalism and which place constraints on what journalists can accomplish in this most difficult field. Some of the cases we examine will be historic, others current. The goal is to make you, as consumers of national security information, more aware of what the news media can and do deliver. A second goal is to acquaint the next generation of national security journalists and editors with these issues so that coverage may improve.

Readings

Two paperback books are required reading:

Cohen, Stephen F. *Sovieticus.* New York: Norton, 1986.
Russett, Bruce. *The Prisoners of Insecurity.* New York: W.H. Freeman, 1983.

I was hoping to assign two other books, but bookstore officials tell me they are out of print. I have, however, seen these two books on the shelves of Barnes and Noble, so I think they can still be purchased. The readings in them are therefore recommended rather than required, but I hope you will all make an effort to obtain them. Both will be useful in preparing your papers.

Dallin, Alexander, and C. Rice. *The Gorbachev Era.* Stanford Alumni Association, Stanford University, 1986.

Powers, Thomas. *Thinking About the Next War.* New York: Mentor Book from New American Library, 1983.

In addition, students should purchase a packet of materials from the NYU Center for War, Peace, and the News Media which includes 9 issues of the bulletin *Deadline* and 3 Occasional Papers. The price of this packet is $15; please make checks payable to NYU.

Ten magazine articles and legal cases have been placed on reserve at Bobst Library and at the Center Library.

Finally, you are requested to read all stories relating to U.S.-Soviet relations and the arms race that appear in the *New York Times* and the *Wall Street Journal.* Both papers are readily available at newsstands. As events dictate, we may spend a portion of each class session discussing coverage of current developments, so it will be necessary for each of you to be up to date.

Written Assignments

There are three assignments: two papers and a take-home essay final, for which you will have 72 hours. Each written assignment counts as 1/3 of your grade. The paper assignments are as follows:

An Annotation. You are asked to select and then to annotate either a news story (print or broadcast), an unsigned newspaper editorial, or an opinion column that deals with some aspect of U.S.-Soviet relations, arms talks, the arms competition, or life in the Soviet Union. Two examples of the genre appear in *Deadline,* Vol. 1, No. 5 (by Tsipis), and Vol. 2, No. 1 (by Feinstein). The purpose of an annotation is to indicate where facts are incorrect or have been used by the writer in a misleading manner; where alternate viewpoints have been ignored or dealt with improperly or cavalierly; where boilerplate explanations are substituted for critical thinking; and the like. You should select an article that deals with a subject of interest to you. Then read up on the subject in alternate sources (beyond what is required in class). Try to pick fertile ground; that is, select a news article about a controversial issue, or a column or editorial that is strongly argumentative. Your annotation need be no longer than the examples from *Deadline.* It is *what* you say, not how much you say, that counts. I will be looking for factual, pointed, insightful criticisms. This paper is due on December 8.

An Analysis of Press Coverage of a Significant Event in the History of U.S.-Soviet Relations or the Arms Race. Often, with the passage of time and the accumulation of scholarship, events look much different today from the way they were protrayed in the news media when they were breaking stories.

You are asked to select a significant news event (either one that was significant at the time, or has since become significant, or both) and review a sample of the contemporary daily and weekly press coverage. Compare what you find in the press to recent scholarship about the event. Where did the press succeed, and why? Where did it go astray, and why? What can we learn about the process of daily journalism, and the relationship between press and government, through such an analysis? As a model for this paper, pay special attention to the assigned Occasional Papers by LeoGrande and Massing, particularly the former. The types of events you might select are any of the reported weapons gaps between the U.S. and the U.S.S.R. (such as the bomber gap, the missile gap, or the window of vulnerability); the shootdown of Korean Airlines flight 007; the release of PD-59, or any of the other key policy decrees of the executive branch that defined U.S. use of nuclear weapons; the Soviet explosion of its first A-bomb, or H-bomb; and the like. The media sample will depend on the topic you choose. Both the topic and the specific news coverage to be studied *must be approved by me*. The topic must be selected and the sample chosen by November 10. This paper is due on January 5. Length must be between 3000 and 5000 words, not a word more. Please double space the paper and leave large margins (the better to write in).

WEEKLY SCHEDULE

Sept. 22—Lecture
Course requirements. Discussion of the substantive issues facing the press in reporting on U.S.-Soviet relations and the arms race.
- Dallin, chs. 2, 3, 8, 10, 11, and 13.
- Cohen, Introduction, all of Section I, "The Crisis of Liberal Dissent" in Section III, and all of Section IV.
- Russett, chs. 1, 2, 7, and 8.
- Powers, chs. 7, 10, 11, 13, and 14.

Sept. 29—Lecture
More discussion of the substantive issues facing the press in reporting on U.S.-Soviet relations and the arms race.
- Same as 9/22.

Oct. 6—Lecture
Group discussion of newspaper clips handed out the previous week; directions on what to look for will be provided in class on 9/29.
- Same as 9/22.

Oct. 13—Lecture
The various roles of the press in reporting national security information within the democratic system.

- Kaiser, "SALT Talks: Leading Toward Armageddon?" in *MORE* (Feb. 1978).

Oct. 20—Lecture
Historical review of how the press has covered a variety of national security issues.
- Occasional Paper by William LeoGrande.
- Manoff, "The Silencer," in *Quill* (Feb. 1984).
- Mitchell, *Deadline*, Vol. 2, No. 2.

Oct. 27—Lecture
Continued historical review of how the press has covered a variety of national security issues.
- Same as 10/20.

Nov. 3—Election Day
No class held.

Nov. 10—Lecture
Who are the journalists who cover national security issues, and what problems of process do they face? Paper topic must be chosen by this date.
- Occasional Paper by Manoff.
- Kaye, *Deadline*, Vol. 1, No. 1.
- Rubin, *Deadline*, Vol. 1, No. 1.
- Rubin, *Deadline*, Vol. 2, No. 1.
- Perkovich, *Deadline*, Vol. 2, No. 2.
- Hallin, *Deadline*, Vol. 2, No. 3.
- Rosen, *Deadline*, Vol. 2, No. 3.

Nov. 17—Lecture
Legal problems in access to national security information, and in publishing or broadcasting such information.
- Reed, "Can Our Public Affairs Officer Help?" in *Washington Monthly* (Oct. 1984).
- *U.S. v. NY Times.*
- Rubin, *Deadline*, Vol. 1, No. 3.

Nov. 24—Lecture
Continuation of legal problems in access to national security information, and in publishing or broadcasting such information.
- Same as 11/17.

Dec. 1—Lecture
Case study of press coverage of the neutron bomb affair.
- Occasional Paper by Massing.

Dec. 8—Lecture
The American experience in reporting on developments in the Soviet Union. Annotation due.

- Lippmann and Merz, "A Test of the News," in *The New Republic*, Aug. 4, 1940.
- Epstein, "The Andropov File," in *The New Republic*, Feb. 7, 1983.
- Kaye, *Deadline*, Vol. 1, No. 2.
- Kirkhorn, *Deadline*, Vol. 1, No. 2.
- Kay and Manoff, *Deadline*, Vol. 1, No. 5.
- Rubin, *Deadline*, Vol. 2, No. 2.
- Cunningham, *Deadline*, Vol. 2, No. 2.

Dec. 15—Lecture

Press coverage of peace groups. Could a peace beat exist? What would it be?

- Pollak, "Covering the Unthinkable," in *The Nation*, May 1, 1982.
- Ricks, "Dr. Caldicott Goes to War," in *Washington Journalism Review* (Oct. 1982).
- Rubin, "War 10, Peace 3," in *NYU Magazine*, Vol. 1, No. 1.
- Spiegelman, "Media Manipulation of the Movement," in *Social Policy* (Summer 1982).
- Rubin, *Deadline*, Vol. 1, No. 2.
- Abrams, *Deadline*, Vol. 1, No. 4.
- Dorman, *Deadline*, Vol. 1, No. 5.

Dec. 22 & 29—Christmas Holiday

No class held.

Jan. 5—Lecture

Discussion of ethical cases in national security reporting (to be handed out in class on 12/13).

Jan. 12—Lecture

Continued discussion of ethical cases in national security reporting. Historical analysis paper due. The final exam will be distributed at the end of class on Jan. 12 and must be returned to my mailbox in the Center (or postmarked) by 5:30 on Friday, Jan. 15.

Research Seminars

XXI

1. Research and Analysis of Current Topics in Defense and Disarmament

Michael T. Klare   *Spring 1988*
School of Social Science, Hampshire College,
Amherst, MA 01002

This seminar will examine the wide range of defense and disarmament issues facing the United States in the late 1980s and early 1990s, with a view toward developing student skills in policy-focused research and analysis. The presidential campaign of 1988 and the imminent start of a new administration provide an exciting backdrop for this analysis, although the class will not be limited by the context of the contemporary debate.

At the beginning of the semester, we will examine three broad areas of current policy debate: (1) nuclear strategy, "Star Wars," and nuclear arms control; (2) conventional forces in Europe, NATO, and "alternative security" concepts; and (3) regional Third World conflicts, interventionism, and "low-intensity warfare." In each case, students will be required to read and comment upon a number of readings representing different points of view on these issues. At the end of this process, by the fifth meeting of the course, students will be required to choose a current defense/disarmament issue that they will research on their own for the remainder of the semester.

For the following six sessions, we will consider the three basic aspects of the literature in this field: (1) *research,* or the use of scholarly skills to acquire reliable information; (2) *analysis,* or the assessment of such data for the purpose of drawing salient conclusions about current trends and patterns; and (3) *policy formulation,* or the identification and assessment of the risks and benefits of possible options for governmental or non-governmental action on a particular issue. Students will read a variety of essays on current peace and conflict issues that illustrate these three aspects. At the same time, the instructor will discuss research methods in the field and acquaint students with basic research tools such as Arkin's *Research Guide to Current Military and Strategic Affairs*, the *SIPRI Yearbook*, and *The Military Balance*. During this period, students will be conducting their own research and consulting with the instructor periodically on research problems and methods.

During the final weeks of the semester, students will give oral reports in class on the results of their own research on a particular issue.

Course Requirements

(1) Attend all class meetings and complete all assigned readings. Several times during the semester, prepare short oral commentaries on one of the assigned readings. (2) Conduct an independent research project on a topic approved by the instructor, and provide an oral report on your findings at the end of the semester. These projects must focus on a current issue of defense and disarmament policy, and must be framed as a policy briefing/advocacy paper. For example, papers could examine questions such as:

- Will introduction of the Trident D-5 SLBM system enhance or undermine strategic stability?
- Does Western European security require a build-up of conventional forces in the aftermath of the INF Treaty?
- Could United Nations forces effectively replace the U.S. Navy in trying to protect free passage in the Persian Gulf?
- What has been the record of the US and the USSR in complying with the ABM Treaty of 1972?
- What are the prospects for and potential benefits of peaceful US-Soviet cooperation in space exploration?

Research for the paper must entail the use of primary materials such as Congressional hearings, ACDA and Defense Deptartment reports, U.N. documents, industry journals, and university and think-tank studies. A written report of approximately 25 double-spaced typed pages will be due on Monday, May 9, following the last scheduled meeting of the class. This term paper must follow standard scholarly style, incorporate ample footnotes, and provide all relevant tables or charts.

Assigned Texts

William Arkin. *Research Guide to Current Military and Strategic Affairs* (Institute for Policy Studies, 1981).

Michael Klare and Peter Kornbluh, eds. *Low-Intensity Warfare: Counter-Insurgency, Pro-Insurgency, and Anti-Terrorism in the 1980s* (Pantheon, 1988).

Steven E. Miller, ed. *Conventional Forces and American Defense Policy* (Princeton University Press, 1986).

Robert Travis Scott, ed. *The Race for Security: Arms and Arms Control in the Reagan Years* (Lexington Books, 1987).

W. Scott Thompson, ed. *National Security in the 1980s: From Weakness to Strength* (Institute for Contemporary Studies, 1980).

Selected articles from *Arms Control Today, Bulletin of the Atomic Scientists,* and *World Policy Journal.*

CLASS SCHEDULE
AND READING ASSIGNMENTS

Jan. 27—Introduction

Part One: Defense Issues 1988

Become familiar with the basic parameters of contemporary defense/disarmament issues and some of the important literature from varying political perspectives.

Feb. 3—An Overview of the Reagan Legacy
- "Rearming America: The Reagan Administration Defense Program" by Lawrence Korb and Linda Brady, pp. 3–18 in Miller.
- "Jousting with Unreality: Reagan's Military Strategy" by Jeffrey Record, pp. 63–78 in Miller.
- "The Reagan Strategic Program" by Ronald Tammen, pp. 10–14 in Scott.
- "The Second Reagan Term: Arms or Arms Control?" by Strobe Talbott, pp. 15–19 in Scott.
- "The Reagan Nuclear Strategy" by Robert Gray, pp. 103–109 in Scott.
- "Introduction" by Scott Thompson, pp. 3–16 in Thompson.
- "Defense Innovation and Geopolitics" by Geoffrey Kemp, pp. 69–88 in Thompson.

Feb. 10—Nuclear Arms, Arms Control and S.D.I.
- "The Uncertain Future of Arms Control" by Spurgeon Keeny, pp. 3–9 in Scott.
- "The Case for Arms Control and the Strategic Defense Initiative" by George Keyworth, pp. 41–43 in Scott.
- "Reviving the ABM Debate" by Albert Carnesale, pp. 47–51 in Scott.
- "Star Wars Versus the ABM Treaty" by Edward Kennedy, pp. 52–58 in Scott.
- "Final Report of the President's Commission on Strategic Forces" (abstract), pp. 110–114 in Scott.
- "Tilting Toward Warfighting: The Scowcroft Commission" by Leon Sigal, pp. 115–120 in Scott.
- "Cruise Missiles: The Arms Control Challenge" by Thomas Longstreth, pp. 131–137 in Scott.

- "Midgetman: Our Best Hope for Stability and Arms Control" by Albert Gore, pp. 147–149 in Scott.
- "Midgetman: Superhero or Problem Child" by Jonathan Rich, pp. 150–156 in Scott.
- "Reducing U.S. and Soviet Nuclear Arsenals" by Harold Feiveson, Richard Ullman, and Frank von Hippel, in *Bulletin of the Atomic Scientists*, August 1985.

Feb. 17—Conventional Arms and European Security

- "Maneuver, Mobile Defense, and the NATO Central Front" by John Mearsheimer, pp. 231–250 in Miller.
- "Conventional Deterrence and Conventional Retaliation in Europe" by Samuel Huntington, pp. 251–276 in Miller.
- "Washington and the Atlantic Alliance" by Richard Burt, pp. 109–122 in Thompson.
- "Revitalizing Alliances" by Kenneth Adelman, pp. 295–318 in Thompson.
- "Beyond an INF Agreement: A New Approach to Nonnuclear Forces" by Robert Neild and Anders Boserup, in *World Policy Journal*, Fall 1987.

Feb. 24—Intervention and Low-Intensity War

- "The New Interventionism: Low-intensity Warfare in the 1980s and Beyond" by Michael Klare, pp. 3–20 in Klare.
- "Counterinsurgency's Proving Ground: Low-Intensity Warfare in the Philippines" by Walden Bello, pp. 158–182 in Klare.
- "Constraints on America's Conduct of Small Wars" by Elliot Cohen, pp. 277–308 in Miller.
- "Conventional Forces Beyond NATO" by Francis West, pp. 319–336 in Thompson.

Part Two: Research Methods

Evaluate the means by which evidence is gathered and arrayed in support of an argument, the choice of sources, and the use of charts and footnotes.

Mar. 2—Research Methods and Strategies

- Arkin, entire, examine thoroughly.
- "Low-Intensity Warfare: The Warriors and Their Weapons" by Stephen Goose, pp. 80–111, in Klare.
- "Counterforce at Sea: The Trident II Missile" by Richard Norris, pp. 157–165 in Scott.
- "The State of the Arms Trade" by Michael Klare, in the *Journal of International Affairs*, Summer 1986.

Mar. 9—Research Methods and Strategies

Class will be held at the University of Massachusetts Library's Government Documents Room, where a librarian will introduce the documents collection and demonstrate how to use them for research.

- "Measuring the European Conventional Balance" by Barry Posen, pp. 79–120 in Miller.
- "Heritage of Weakness: An Assessment of the 1970s" by Elmo Zumwalt, pp. 17–54 in Thompson.

Part Three: Analysis

How does one identify trends and extract significant meaning from a mass of raw data? How have the authors reached their conclusions?

Mar. 16—Analysis

- "The Interventionist Impulse: U.S. Military Doctrine for Low-Intensity Warfare" by Michael Klare, pp. 49–79 in Klare.
- "The Reagan Strategic Defense Initiative: A Technical and Strategic Appraisal" by Sidney Drell, Philip Farley, and David Holloway, pp. 71–82 in Scott.
- "Is There an ABM Gap?" by John Pike, pp. 83–88 in Scott.
- "Half-Wars and Half-Policies in the Persian Gulf" by Albert Wohlstetter, pp. 123–172 in Thompson.

Mar. 30—Analysis

- "Afghanistan: Soviet Intervention, Afghan Resistance, and the American Role" by Selig Harrison, pp. 183–206 in Klare.
- "Why the Soviets Can't Win Quickly in Central Europe" by John Mearsheimer, pp. 121–158 in Miller.
- "Uncertainties for the Soviet War Planner" by Benjamin Lambeth, pp. 159–186 in Miller.

Part Four: Policy Options

Based on your knowledge of the issues, research methods, and analytical techniques, evaluate the following prescriptive writings. Compare them with other prescriptive essays read earlier in the semester. Are they convincing? Which do you think are preferable policies for the United States to pursue? What alternatives would you propose?

Apr. 6—Some Policy Options for Arms Control

- "Arms Control for Real Security" by Richard Barnet, pp. 224–231 in Scott.
- "Beyond the Hot-Line: Controlling Nuclear Crises" by Richard Smoke and William Ury, pp. 252–254 in Scott.

- "The Candidates' Positions on Nuclear Arms and Arms Control" in *Arms Control Today*, February 1988—Democrats, and March 1988—Republicans.
- "Parallel Cuts in Nuclear and Conventional Forces" by Randall Forsberg, in the *Bulletin of the Atomic Scientists*, August 1985.

Apr. 13—Some Options for Strategic Policy
- "The Costs and Perils of Intervention" by Richard Barnet, pp. 207–221 in Klare.
- "Quick Fixes to U.S. Strategic Nuclear Forces" by William Van Cleave, pp. 89–108 in Thompson.
- "A Post-Reagan Military Posture" by Paul Walker, pp. 155–164 in *Post-Reagan America* (World Policy Institute, 1987). See other chapters for background.

Part Five: Reports

Based on the issue you have been investigating all semester, present your research findings, conclusions, and policy prescriptions to the class.

Apr. 20, 27, and May 4—Student Reports

2. Research Seminar in Peace and World Order Studies

Louis René Beres   *Spring 1988*
Political Science Dept., Purdue University,
West Lafayette, IN 47907

This course is designed to acquaint students with the essential norms, institutions and dynamics of international law. Adopting a "world order" perspective, we will examine international law as a strategy for supporting peace and human rights in global affairs. Special attention will be directed toward the problems of terrorism, insurgency, justice and nuclear war. Each student will be expected, among other responsibilities, to prepare a major research paper dealing with an appropriate topic of the course.

Books

Beres, L.R. *America Outside the World: The Collapse of U.S. Foreign Policy.*
Brierly, J.L. *The Law of Nations.*
Harris, J., and E. Markusen. *Nuclear Weapons and the Threat of Nuclear War.*
Weston, B., et al. *Basic Documents in International Law and World Order.*
Camus, Albert. *The Rebel.*
Sartre, Jean-Paul. *Anti-Semite and Jew.*
Konrad, George. *Antipolitics.*
Wiesel, Elie. *Night.*

SCHEDULE OF TOPICS

First Day
Introduction to the course: organization and procedure.

Topic I—Legal Order in the State of Nations: The Distinctive Quality of International Law

Within the decentralized system of world politics that has been in existence since the Peace of Westphalia in 1648, international law has always displayed a distinctive character. Unlike systems of national or municipal law, which exist within political systems that have government, international law exists within an anarchic system of states. This does not suggest that states coexist in an entirely "Darwinian" situation, but that they do exist together without the "cementing" institutions and agencies of government. Hence, modern international law has always been regarded as distinctive, as horizontal rather than vertical, as law of coordination rather than of subordination and superordination.

- Brierly, *The Law of Nations,* pp. 1–25; 41–85.
- Weston, *Documents,* 1.5.

Topic II—Trends and Patterns in the Development of International Legal Thought

International law has its origins in natural law, a system of norms based upon certain principles of right and justice that expect compliance because of their own intrinsic merit. Eternal and immutable, they are external to all acts of human will and interpenetrate all human reason. During the seventeenth and eighteenth centuries, natural law doctrine was reaffirmed and strengthened by Grotius and Newton, and in the twentieth century this doctrine played an essential role in the post-war judgments at Nuremberg. The challenge to naturalism has come from positivism, which deduces "true law" from the precedents of state practice (e.g., Zouche, Hobbes, Austin) and identifies such law with the command of a sovereign.

- Beres, ch. 2.
- Brierly, pp. 25–40.

Plus any one of the following:
- Aristotle, *Ethics.*
- Cicero, *The Republic* or *The Laws.*
- Thomas Paine, *The Age of Reason* (Part I)
- A.P. d'Entreves, *Natural Law.*
- Louis Rene Beres, "Human Rights and World Order: The United States Imperative," *Humanities in Society.*
- _____ , "Nation Without a Soul, Policy Without a Purpose," *Chitty's Law Journal.*

Topic III—Subjects of International Law
Tradition holds that only states are subjects of international law, and that non-state actors lack legal personality. This tradition is problematic today because of the growth, in number and importance, of certain non-state actors, especially international organizations, multinational corporations, and insurgent forces. Moreover, the role of the *individual* as a subject of international law continues to gain support.
- Brierly, pp. 126–161.
- Weston, 1.2; 1.6; 1.7; 1.8; 1.10.

Topic IV—Treaties
Pursuant to Article 38 of the Statute of the International Court of Justice, treaties are the primary source of modern international law. The most authoritative current document on treaties is the Vienna Convention on the Law of Treaties (1969), which sets forth operative doctrine on meaning, termination (*rebus sic stantibus*) and compliance (*pacta sunt servanda*). Nevertheless, the prospect of effective treaty support for peace and justice is hampered by the decentralized quality of international law.
- Brierly, pp. 317–345.
- Weston, 1.1; 1.9; 1.11.

Topic V—The Legal Status of War (Justice *of* War)
According to long-standing international law, war must always be evaluated along two distinct, logically independent dimensions: (1) the reasons for fighting; and (2) the means used in the fighting. Medieval writers described this division by distinguishing between *jus ad bellum* (justice of war) from *jus in bello* (justice in war). Not until this century, however, did violations of the first dimension become a genuine crime (aggression) under international law. We find evidence of such criminalization in the Pact of Paris (1928), the judgments at Nuremberg, the UN Charter and the General Assembly's Definition of Aggression (1974).
- Brierly, pp. 409–432.
- Weston, 2.3; 2.24.

Topic VI—The Legal Status of Behavior in War (Justice *in* War)
The laws of war on international law that concern *jus in bello* are of ancient origin. They flow from the principle, perhaps as old as the history of

organized warfare, that the ravages of war must be mitigated as much as possible. Today these norms are codified primarily in the Hague and Geneva conventions, and in certain protocols (addenda) to these conventions.
* Weston, 2.1; 2.2; 2.7; 2.8; 2.9; 2.10.

Plus any one of the following:
* Burns H. Weston, "Nuclear Weapons Versus International Law: A Contextual Reassessment," *McGill Law Journal*, July 1983, pp. 543–590.
* _____ , "Israel's Choice: Nuclear Weapons or International Law," in L.R. Beres, ed., *Security or Armageddon: Israel's Nuclear Strategy*, pp. 159–172.
* "The Illegality of Nuclear Weapons: Statement of the Lawyer's Committee on Nuclear Policy," *Alternatives: A Journal of World Policy*, Fall 1982, pp. 291–296.
* Richard A. Falk, Lee Meyrowitz and Jack Sanderson, *Nuclear Weapons and International Law*, Occasional Paper No. 10, Center of International Studies, Princeton University, 1981.
* Louis Rene Beres, "Nuclear War and the Jewish Tradition."
* R.A. Falk, G. Kolko and R.J. Lifton, *Crimes of War.*
* Telford Taylor, *Nuremberg and Vietnam: An American Tragedy.*

Topic VII—International Law and the Prevention of Nuclear War
International law seeks to prevent nuclear war through a series of bilateral and multilateral agreements, statutes and safeguards. In this effort, however, it must contend with the presumed imperatives of *realpolitik*. The interplay between these contending claims has thus far made it difficult to claim success for international law as a strategy for avoiding nuclear war.
* John H. E. Fried, "The Nuclear Collision Course: Can International Law Be of Help?" *Denver Journal of International Law and Policy*, Spring/Summer 1985, pp. 97–120.
* J. Harris and E. Markusen, *Nuclear Weapons and the Threat of Nuclear War.*
* Weston, 2.13; 2.14; 2.16; 2.17; 2.18; 2.19; 2.20; 2.22; 2.23; 2.25.
* Beres, ch. 7.

Plus any one of the following:
* L.R. Beres, *Security or Armageddon: Israel's Nuclear Strategy.*
* _____ , *Reason and Realpolitik: U.S. Foreign Policy and World Order*, chs. 2, 3 and 4.
* _____ , *People, States and World Order*, pp. 32–42.
* _____ , *Apocalypse: Nuclear Catastrophe in World Politics.*

Topic VIII—International Law and Human Rights
Since the end of World War II, the protection of human rights has been coequal with the avoidance of war as the dominant objective of international legal reform. Jurisprudentially, Nuremberg created a revolution in world law, removing a state's treatment of its own nationals from the realm of

"domestic jurisdiction" whenever such treatment fails to conform to particular normative standards. At the same time, the effective results of such removal have been modest at best, reflecting the primacy (as in the case of nuclear war avoidance) of *realpolitik*.

- Weston, Section 3 ("Human Rights"), entire.
- Jean-Paul Sartre, *Anti-Semite and Jew*.
- L.R. Beres, *Reason and Realpolitik*, ch. 5.
- _____ , "Straight Talk on South Africa," *The Michigan Quarterly Review*, Fall 1986.
- U.S. Department of State, *Country Reports on Human Rights Practices* (latest).
- *Amnesty International Report 1987*.

Topic IX—International Law, Insurgency and Terrorism

According to international law, not every instance of insurgency is an act of terrorism. Rather, certain forms of insurgency that promote codified human rights are treated as law-enforcing. These forms issue from "just cause" and are conducted according to the previously discussed standards of *jus in bello*.

- Albert Camus, *The Rebel*.
- L.R. Beres, *America Outside the World: The End of U.S. Foreign Policy*, ch. 5.
- _____ , "Becoming an Outlaw: United States Foreign Policy and Central America," *International Journal*.

Or

- L.R. Beres, "Ignoring International Law: U.S. Policy on Insurgency and Intervention in Central America," *Denver Journal of International Law and Policy*.

Or

- L.R. Beres, "Human Rights vs. New Initiatives in the Control of Terrorism," *1985 Proceedings of the American Society of International Law*.

Plus

- C.C. Joyner and M. Grimaldi, "The United States and Nicaragua: Reflections on the Lawfulness of Contemporary Intervention," *Virginia Journal of International Law*, Spring 1985, pp. 621–689.
- Lloyd N. Cutler, "The Right to Intervene," *Foreign Affairs*, Fall 1985, pp. 96–112.
- Weston, 1.12; 2.24; 3.19; 3.21; 3.23.
- *The Declaration of Independence*.

Topic X—International Law and Genocide

Although legal scholars understand that genocide has always been prohibited by international law (in the words of the Genocide Convention: "Genocide is a modern word for an old crime"), the post–World War II criminalization of genocide has been especially explicit and far-reaching. Building upon the norms established by international custom, the general principles of law recognized by civilized nations, the writings of highly qualified publicists, various treaties and conventions and the overriding principles of natural law, this criminalization has taken place under allied and UN auspices, and has flowed largely from early reactions to the Holocaust. Today, however, genocide continues in several parts of the world, and the enforcement of anti-genocide norms has been impaired by persistent adherence to geopolitics.

- Elie Wiesel, *Night.*
- *Case Western Reserve Journal of International Law,* Vol. 18, No. 2, Spring 1986, Special Issue on "Nuremberg Forty Years After: An Overview."
- Beres, ch. 6.

Plus any one of the following:

- L.R. Beres, *Reason and Realpolitik,* ch. 6.
- _____ , "Genocide and the State," *Salmagundi,* Spring 1988.
- _____ , "Genocide and Power Politics," *Bulletin of Peace Proposals,* Spring 1987.
- _____ , "Genocide and Genocide-Like Crimes," in M. Cherif Bassiouni, *International Criminal Law,* Vol. 1, *Crimes,* 1986, pp. 271–279.
- Leo Kuper, *Genocide.*
- _____ , *The Prevention of Genocide.*
- William Shawcross, *Sideshow: Kissinger, Nixon and the Destruction of Cambodia.*
- *Holocaust: The Obligation to Remember.*
- "Jewish Themes, Dispersal, Holocaust, Preservation," *Salmagundi,* Winter/Spring 1985.
- "Philosophy and the Holocaust," *The Philosophical Forum,* Fall/Winter 1984-1985.
- J. Porter, *Genocide and Human Rights.*
- Robert Jay Lifton, *The Nazi Doctors.*

Topic XI—The United States, The Cold War and International Law
U.S. foreign policy continues to be dominated by the dualism of incessant rivalry with the Soviet Union. Animated by the "need" to succeed in this bipolar contest, U.S. leaders are increasingly insensitive to the expectations of international law. This insensitivity is especially apparent in the failure of arms control, in the operation of the "Reagan Doctrine" and in the official disregard for the compulsory jurisdiction of the International Court of Justice.

- L. R. Beres, *America Outside the World: The End of U.S. Foreign Policy* (remaining chs.).
- George Konrad, *Antipolitics.*
- Benjamin Netanyahu, *Terrorism: How the West Can Win.*
- L.R. Beres, "The End of American Foreign Policy," *Third World Quarterly.*

Topic XII—Self and World
- Ralph Waldo Emerson, "Self-Reliance."
- Elias Canetti, *Crowds and Power.*

- L.R. Beres, "Death, Will, and Immortality."
- Elaine Scarry, *The Body in Pain.*
- Albert Camus, *Resistance, Rebellion and Death.*
- Herman Hesse, *Demian* or *Steppenwolf.*

Topic XIII—Alternative Systems of International Law and World Order

The extant system of international law is grievously unsatisfactory. Faced with widening circles of terrorism and repression, and with the glowing portent of an omnicidal nuclear war, students of world order must seek alternative arrangements for world legal reform. How can we identify these alternatives? What are they? No readings, but the final research paper will be discussed.

3. Research Theory and Method in Peace and Conflict Studies

John Ratcliffe   *Spring 1987*

Peace and Conflict Studies Program, University of California–Berkeley, Berkeley, CA 94705

This is not a survey course in social science research methods. Instead, it is a course in critical thinking, taught from the research perspective. It is designed to prepare students to think critically on and to reach reasoned and independent judgments about the problem of research itself, as well as about every phase of the research process.

Although those who teach research methods commonly use the terms "method" and "methodology" interchangeably, the terms are *not* equivalent. The term "method" denotes a scientific procedure; it is the specification of steps to be taken in order to achieve a desired end (data collection or analysis). "Methodology," on the other hand, is a concept of the next highest order; it stands above (or "meta") to method because it is not a method but, instead, is *about* methods. Methodology refers to the system of theory, logical principles, and philosophical assumptions that provides the justification for the invention, selection, and application of particular methods to gather and analyze data. And, just as there are different *methods* available to the researcher, so are there different *methodologies* available to guide the process of inquiry from inception (problem identification and formulation) through research design (selection and application of methods) to completion (conclusions and policy recommendations).

At a fundamental level all approaches to scientific inquiry are based on assumptions (articles of faith) about how the world "works"; such assumptions are inevitable because not everything of importance can be known with complete assurance or perfect certainty before action must be taken. The approach to research that currently dominates the thinking and practice of the scientific community is based on several fundamental assumptions, one of which is that a universal, objective reality exists "out there" that can be apprehended in an equally objective fashion by faithful adherence to The Scientific Method. Consistent with this fundamental assumption is the view that the practice of science is or can be *value-free* or *value-neutral*. For example, Bierstadt states that "Ethical neutrality . . . means that the scientist, in his [sic] professional capacity, does not take sides on issues of moral or ethical significance. . . . As a scientist he [sic] is interested not in what is right or wrong or good or evil, but only in what is true or false."

But another, competing conceptualization of science is emerging, one that is making itself felt across all the disciplines. This emergent paradigm is based on very different fundamental assumptions, one of which is that all systems, including systems of scientific inquiry, are purposeful and, therefore, necessarily *value-laden* or *normative*. This approach to science assumes that researchers inevitably take sides (consciously or unconsciously) on issues of moral and ethical significance, and that they cannot but be interested in and influenced by what they feel is good or bad, right or wrong, and what *should* or *ought* to be in their quest for what is true or false. From this paradigmatic perspective, *all* science is qualitative at a fundamental level, for it recognizes that since all science is ultimately based on assumptions, or articles of faith, there are no "givens," but only "takens" (i.e., assumptions that are *taken* as given). Said another way, research problems cannot be separated meaningfully from their human components, and they are thus inherently matters of values and ideology. Hence even the point of view that there can be no point of view (i.e., objectivity) is still a point of view. It is this latter paradigmatic perspective on research that constitutes the subject matter of this course.

Since a fundamental assumption is that all research is inherently value-laden, including that undertaken within the framework of the allegedly value-neutral "Scientific Method," the course will stress the *ethical dimension* of scientific inquiry—how to identify value biases in the work of others, how to deal with it in one's own research, and what its implications are for the professional practitioner. However, the primary focus of the course is how to *think* about research—how we currently think about it, and how to think about it from the perspective of a very different paradigm from that which currently holds sway over the scientific community.

While some methods unique to this paradigmatic perspective will be considered and applied, this is not a "methods" course but, instead, a course on methodology. Its intent is to provide a framework for thinking about research that will allow one to match the various methods of scientific inquiry usefully to the classes of problems and contexts to which they are relevant and applicable. This introduction to research in peace and conflict studies is not designed to restrict the researcher to a narrow set of methods or approaches; nor does it require the researcher to reject "old" methods in favor of "new" methods. What it does require is a willingness to open oneself up to a new worldview, one that necessitates active involvement in a major reformulation of one's thinking about and approach to scientific research in general, and about the nature of the relationships among theory, method, data, purpose, values, and assumptions in particular.

Course Objectives

The primary objectives of the course are as follows:

1. To provide participants with both a theoretical understanding of and a practical grounding in policy research methodology by broadening their theoretical-methodological conceptual frames.

2. To demystify the various approaches to research by presenting both general and particular critiques of the theory, assumptions, and applications of different approaches to scientific inquiry.

3. To sharpen crucial research skills of the participant; here it is assumed that a broader understanding of the relationships among methodological paradigms is a skill that will prepare the researcher to make more informed decisions in the future about which of those paradigms and, therefore, methods at her/his disposal will provide the approach most appropriate to the problem under study and most relevant to the purpose(s) of the researcher.

Pedagogical Approach

In order to provide an educational setting congruent with the material under review, the seminar will be structured generally after the manner of a colloquium, where students and instructor will gather to discuss the material in depth and in a critical and systematic manner. The exact nature of this structure, however, will be dynamic and evolving, because it will be defined by the group as a whole.

Class Projects

Two class projects are required for successful completion of the course. First, each participant is required to submit at the end of the term a constructively critical assessment of the course. This evaluation may focus on any facet(s) of the course judged to be relevant and appropriate, including the spirit and quality of the course, how it compares with other PACS and non-PACS courses, how the objectives might be more fully attained, how the pedagogy might be improved, etc. This project will be due during the next-to-last class meeting.

The second class project can be selected from among the following possibilities:

a. Graduate students will apply policy research methodology to a major problem of their choice that is related to peace and/or conflict. This application should be presented in a five- to fifteen-page typed report that addresses the following issues: purpose; problem identification and definition; theory (selection and associated assumptions); methodology (selection and associated assumptions); methods; and operationalization of variables.

b. Undergraduates will undertake a review of the research literature in their particular area of interest in order to identify, formally evaluate (i.e., in a five- to eight-page typed report), and share one or more research articles that illustrate application of "new" paradigm thinking at either the conceptual or the concrete level (examples of this will be provided in reading assignments.)

Required Texts

Thomas Kuhn. *The Structure of Scientific Revolutions* (2nd ed.), Chicago: University of Chicago Press, 1970.

All other readings can be found in the course packet.

How to Read Articles
I have found that most students have never received any formal training and/or practice in how to obtain the most from reading assignments in the least amount of time. The most effective approach to this task, in my experience, has been to follow—and to practice—very particular guidelines. Hence the following guidelines are to be applied in reading the assignments for this course:

a. What is the author's *thesis*? The major point s/he is trying to make?
b. What are the major *assumptions* the author makes (and expects you to accept) in arguing that thesis?
c. What are the *implications for research practice* if the author's thesis and underlying assumptions are valid or true?
d. What are some *important or useful concepts* the author presents?
e. How does the reading *relate to previous readings*?
f. Critically reflect on and assess the article as a whole; what are its *strengths and weaknesses*?

Class participants will be responsible not only for reading all assigned articles but also for being able to discuss every article in terms of each of the above guidelines.

READING ASSIGNMENTS

Jan 28—Introduction to Course

Feb 4—Paradigm Shifts and Scientific Revolutions: An Historical Perspective
• T. Kuhn, entire (210 pages).

Feb 11—The Paradigm Shift We Are In

- P. Schwartz and J. Ogilvy, *The Emergent Paradigm: Changing Patterns of Thought and Belief,* Menlo Park: SRI International, 1979, 60 pp.
- M. Maruyama, "Hierarchists, Individualists and Mutualists: Three Paradigms Among Planners," *Futures* 6(2):103–113, April 1974.

Feb 18—The Thought Revolution We Are In

- R. Ackoff, "The Revolution We Are In," in *Redesigning the Future,* NY: Wiley, 1979, pp. 1–54.
- C.W. Churchman, "What Is a System?" in *The Systems Approach,* NY: Delta, 1979, pp. 1–48.

Feb 25—The Theoretical Revolution We Are In

- G. Wunsch, "Theories, Models, and Knowledge: The Logic of Scientific Discovery," Working Paper 121, Demography Dept, University of Louvain, Belgium, pp. 1–17.
- R. Nisbett and L. Ross, "Theory Maintenance and Theory Change," in *Human Inference,* Englewood Cliffs: Prentice-Hall, 1978, pp. 167–192.
- W. Ryan, "The Art of Savage Discovery," in *Blaming the Victim,* NY: Bantam, 1971, pp. 1–30.

Mar 4—The Scientific Revolution We Are In

- M. Patton, *Alternative Evaluation Research Paradigm,* University of South Dakota, 40 pp.
- B. Fischoff, "Cost Benefit Analysis and the Art of Motorcycle Maintenance," *Policy Studies,* 8:177–202, 1977.

Mar 11—The Evolution of Scientific Methodology

- I. Mitroff and F. Sagasti, "Epistemology as General Systems Theory: An Approach to the Design of Complex Decision-Making Experiments," *Philosophy of the Social Sciences,* 3:117–134, 1973.
- J. Ratcliffe, "Notions of Validity in Qualitative Research Methodology, *Knowledge: Creation, Diffusion, and Utilization,* 5(2):147–167, Dec. 1983.

Mar 18—Conscious and Unconscious Factors that Affect Research Outcomes

- F. Lynn, "The Interplay of Science and Values in Assessing Environmental Risk," Doctoral Dissertation, Dec. 1983, 37 pp.
- J. Ratcliffe, "Analyst Biases in KAP Surveys: A Cross-Cultural Comparison," *Studies in Family Planning,* 7(11):322–330, Nov. 1976.
- V. Riley, "Mouse Mammary Tumors: Alteration of Incidence as Apparent Function of Stress," *Science,* 189:465–467, Aug. 1975.

Mar 25—Toward a More Rigorous Scientific Practice

- J. Ratcliffe, "Rigor in Research: Toward an Expanded Conceptualization," manuscript currently under review, 31 pp.

- N. Freudenberg, "Science and Politics: The Limitations of Environmental Health Research," in *Not in Our Backyards*, NY: Monthly Review Press, 1984, pp. 42–59.
- C. Hohenemser et al., "The Nature of Technological Hazard," *Science*, 220:378–384, April 1983.

Apr 1—Applications: How to Surface Your Own Ethical and Value Assumptions

- E. Shelp, "Justice: A Moral Test for Health Care and Health Policy," in *Justice and Health Care*, NY: Reidel, 1981, pp. 213–229.
- I. Mitroff and R. Kilmann, "Methodological Approaches to Social Science," in P. Reason and J. Rowan, eds., *Human Inquiry: A Sourcebook of New Paradigm Research*, NY: Wiley, 1981, pp. 43–51.
- I. Mitroff, *The Subjective Side of Science*, reviewed in *Human Inquiry*, pp. 37–41.
- E. Kennedy, "America's Activist Bishops: Examining Capitalism," *New York Times Magazine*, Aug. 12, 1984, 8 pp.

Apr 8—Applications: How to Surface the Value Assumptions of Others

- I. Mitroff and J. Emshoff, "On Strategic Assumption-Making: A Dialectical Approach to Policy and Planning," *Academy of Management Review*, 4(1):1–12, 1979.
- I. Mitroff and R. Mason, "Structuring Ill-Structured Policy Issues: Further Explorations in a Methodology for Messy Problems," *Strategic Management*, 1980, 23 pp.
- K.S. Schrader-Frechette, *Nuclear Power and Public Policy: The Social and Ethical Problems of Fission Technology*, Boston: Reidel, 1980, pp. 135–167.
- M. Reed, "The Mythical Content of Economic Theory," in *The Dark Side of Science*, Washington, D.C.: AAAS, pp. 172–186.

Apr 15—Looking Critically at Global Problems: International Development

- H. Rittel and M. Webber, "Dilemmas in a General Theory of Planning," *Policy Sciences*, 4:155–169, 1973.
- D. C. Tipps, "Modernization Theory and the Comparative Study of Societies: A Critical Perspective," *Comparative Studies in Society and History*, 15(2):199–226, 1973.
- W. Saint and E. W. Coward, "Agriculture and Behavioral Science: Emerging Orientations," *Science*, 197:733–737, 1977.

Apr 22—Looking Critically at Global Problems: International Health

- J. Ratcliffe, "The Influence of Funding Agencies on International Health Policy, Research and Programs, *Mobius* 5(3):93–115, 1985.
- Mosley, W. H., "Will Primary Health Care Reduce Infant and Child Mortality? A Critique of Some Current Strategies, with Specific Ref-

erence to Africa and Asia." IUSSP Monograph, Institut National d'Etudes Demographiques, Paris, March 1983.
- Cereseto, M., and Waitzkin, H., "Economic Development, Political-Economic System, and the Physical Quality of Life Index," *American Journal of Public Health*, June 1986, pp. 661–666.

Apr 29—Looking Critically at Global Problems: Overpopulation
- D. Harvey, "Ideology and Population Theory," *Economic Geography*, 50(3):256–277, 1974.
- J. Ratcliffe, "China's One Child Family Policy: Solving the Wrong Problem?" 1987, 34 pp.

May 6—Looking Critically at Global Problems: Peace Research
- B. Hall, "Participatory Research: Expanding the Base of Analysis, *International Development Review* 4:23–26, 1977.
- J. Ratcliffe, "Institute for Applied Research and Education: A Proposal," submitted to the Academic Council of the University of California (Systemwide), Dec. 18, 1981, 33 pp.

4. Seminar on Peace Research and Education

Neil Katz and Jim Zwick   *Spring 1985*
Program on Nonviolent Conflict and Change,
Syracuse University, Syracuse, NY 13244

This seminar will concentrate on readings and discussion of some of the major writings in the field of peace research and peace education. Since this is an advanced seminar, all participants are expected to be prepared for class presentations and to be actively involved in class discussion. In addition, students will be expected to produce a major research paper as a significant part of the learning and work in this course.

Some of the questions the seminar readings and discussions will deal with are as follows: What is peace research and peace education? How is peace studies different from other academic fields? Has peace research and/or peace action made any difference in public policy or the ways in which individuals/groups behave? What are some of the major themes and controversies in peace research and peace education? How is peace research and peace action different in different countries? How does peace action relate to peace research and peace education? Who does peace research and peace education? Where do they do it? Does it have any impact? What are some of the major organizations and journals dealing with peace research and peace education? What kinds of career opportunities are available in peace research and peace education? What constitutes quality and relevant scholarly research in the peace studies field?

Required Readings

The following titles are required for purchase, and numerous journal articles will be assigned from reserve.

Falk, Richard A., and Samuel S. Kim (eds.). *The War System: An Interdisciplinary Approach.* Boulder, CO: Westview Press, 1980.

————. *An Approach to World Order Studies and the World System.* New York: World Policy Institute, 1982.

Mendlovitz, Saul H. *The Struggle for a Just World Order: An Agenda of Inquiry and Praxis for the 1980s.* New York: World Policy Institute, 1982.

Requirements

Scholarly research paper

A paper of about 20 typed pages for graduate students (about 15 typed pages for undergraduate students). The paper should deal with some major theme, controversy, organization, or person in peace research and/or peace education and should include at least 10 sources in the bibliography. The research paper effort will be dealt with at 5 different times during the seminar. Dates should be strictly adhered to: Topic due—Feb. 6; annotated bibliography due—Mar. 20; paper outline due—Apr. 3; paper due—Apr. 24; and brief oral report due—May 1.

Notecards on readings

For each article on the syllabus, students are expected to write on a 5x8 index card their responses to the following questions: (a) What are the major points to the article? (b) What is the peace research relevance of the article (what does it add to new theory and knowledge)? (c) What is the policy/ social change significance of the article (its peace relevance)? and (d) Who is the target audience for the article? These notecards should be turned in each week, on time, for every article on the syllabus.

Class presentations

Graduate students (and undergraduate students if they choose) will be required to do two class presentations, each based on the readings for those weeks.

Grading

Class attendance and active participation—25%; Notecards on readings— 35%; Research paper—50%.

COURSE OUTLINE AND READINGS

Jan. 16—Introduction
Course overview and images of peace research and education.

Jan. 23—Defining the Field
- Marek Thee, "The Scope and Priorities in Peace Research," in UNESCO, *UNESCO Yearbook on Peace and Conflict Studies* (Westport, CT: Greenwood Press, and Paris: UNESCO, 1982): 3–14.
- Juergen Dedring, "Toward Appropriate Peace Research," *Peace and Change* 7:3 (1981): 1–21.
- Richard Falk, *An Approach to World Order Studies and the World System*, Working Paper No. 22 (New York: World Policy Institute, 1982).
- International Peace Research Association, "Reports of the Commissions," *International Peace Research Newsletter* 4 (1983): 11–54.

Jan. 30—Organizations and Journals
- Charles Chatfield, "International Peace Research: The Field Defined by Dissemination," *Journal of Peace Research* 16:2 (1979): 163–179.
- Chadwick Alger and Elise Boulding, "From Vietnam to El Salvador: Eleven Years of COPRED," *Peace and Change* 7:3 (1981): 35–43.
- F. Hilary Conroy, "The Conference on Peace Research in History: A Memoir," *Journal of Peace Research*.
- Hanna Newcombe, *Survey of Peace Research* 7:6 (October 1984).

Feb. 6—Peace Research Data and Methods
Your research topic is due today. In addition, you should read and be prepared to present in class three or four articles on your topic that use different research methods and data (e.g., quantitative analysis, qualitative analysis, survey, public opinion, historical or content analysis).

Feb. 13—Disciplinary Approaches: Anthropology and Sociology
- David Fabbro, "Peaceful Societies," in Falk and Kim.
- Leonard Berkowitz, "The Frustration-Aggression Hypothesis," in Falk and Kim.
- Albert Bandura, "The Social Learning Theory of Aggression," in Falk and Kim.

Feb. 20—Disciplinary Approaches: Sociology and Psychology
- Lewis Coser, "Some Social Functions of Violence," in Falk and Kim.
- Michael Haas, "Societal Approaches to the Study of War," in Falk and Kim.
- Ted Gurr, "Psychological Factors in Civil Violence," in Falk and Kim.

Feb. 27—Disciplinary Approaches: Political Economy and International Relations
- Kenneth Boulding, "National Images and International Systems," in Falk and Kim.

- Melvin Small and J. David Singer, "Patterns in International Warfare, 1816–1965," in Falk and Kim.
- Ole Holsti, "Crisis, Stress and Decision Making," in Falk and Kim.
- Marxism-Leninism on War and Army, "The Economic Foundations of Wars: A Soviet View," in Falk and Kim.
- David S. Landes, "Some Thoughts on the Nature of Economic Imperialism," in Falk and Kim.

Mar. 6—Controversies: Negative and Positive Peace

- Johan Galtung, "Violence, Peace and Peace Research," *Journal of Peace Research* 6:3 (1969): 167–191.
- Johan Galtung, "A Structural Theory of Imperialism," Richard Falk and Samuel S. Kim (eds.), *The War System: An Interdisciplinary Approach* (Boulder, CO: Westview Press, 1980), pp. 402–455.
- Kenneth E. Boulding, "Twelve Friendly Quarrels with Johan Galtung," *Journal of Peace Research* 14:1 (1977): 75–86.

Mar. 20—Controversies: Development and Peace

Bibliographies due.

- Emile Benoit, "Growth and Defense in Developing Countries," *Economic Development and Cultural Change* 26:2 (1978): 271–280.
- Nicole Ball and Milton Leitenberg, "Disarmament and Development: Their Inter-relationship," *Bulletin of Peace Proposals* 10:3 (1979): 274–259.
- U.N. Centre for Disarmament, *The Relationship Between Disarmament and Development: A Summary*, Disarmament Fact Sheet #22 (1982).
- Ivan Illich, "The Delinking of Peace and Development," *Alternatives* 7:4 (1982): 409–416.
- Bjorn Hettne, "Peace and Development: Contradictions and Compatibilities," *Journal of Peace Research* 20:4 (1983): 329–342.

Mar. 27—Peace Research in the East and South

- G. I. Morozov and I. P. Blischenko, "The Methodology of Peace and Research in the USSR," in UNESCO, *UNESCO Yearbook on Peace and Conflict Studies, 1981* (Westport, CT: Greenwood Press, and Paris: UNESCO, 1982): 15–23.
- Julian Lider, "The Critique of Militarism in Soviet Studies," in Asbjorn Eide and Marek Thee (eds.), *Problems of Contemporary Militarism* (New York: St. Martin's Press, 1980): 173–191.
- Latin American Peace Research Council, "Latin America: Report from the Latin American Peace Research Council (CLAIP)," in UNESCO, *UNESCO Yearbook on Peace and Conflict Studies, 1981* (Westport, CT: Greenwood Press, and Paris: UNESCO, 1982): 296–306.
- Eboe Hutchful, "[Militarization] Trends in Africa," *Alternatives* 10:1 (1984): 115–137.

Apr. 3—Peace Research and Peace Movements
Paper outline due.
- Anatol Rapoport, "Peace Research and Peace Movements," *International Peace Research Newsletter* 3 (1983): 2–9.
- B. Welling Hall, "The Antinuclear Peace Movement: Toward an Evaluation of Effectiveness," *Alternatives* 9:4 (1984): 475–511.
- Herb Feith, "The Emergence of Peace Politics in Asia," *International Peace Research Newsletter* 1 (1984): 5–9.
- Eboe Hutchful, "The Peace Movement and the Third World," *Alternatives* 9:4 (1984): 593–603.
- Saul H. Mendlovitz, *The Struggle for a Just World Order: An Agenda of Inquiry and Praxis for the 1980s*, Working Paper No. 20 (New York: World Policy Institute, 1982).
- Charles Boasson, "Peace Researcher Quo Vadis?" *International Peace Research Newsletter* 12:1 (1984): 9–10.

Apr. 10—Peace Education
- Barbara Stanford, "Thinking Beyond the Limits," *Peace and Change* 10:2 (Summer 1984): 5–12.
- Christine Z. Cataldo, "Assertive Kindness and the Support of Early Prosocial Behavior," *Peace and Change* 10:2 (Summer 1984): 13–22.
- Mary E. Finn, "Peace Education and Teacher Education (A State of the Art Report)," *Peace and Change* 10:2 (Summer 1984): 53–70.
- Dan Fleming, "Nuclear War in Textbooks," *Peace and Change* 10:2 (Summer 1984): 71–78.

Apr. 18—Peace Education, cont'd
- William Eckhardt, "Peace Studies and Attitude Change: A Value Theory of Peace Studies," *Peace and Change* 10:2 (Summer 1984): 79–86.
- William Hazleton, "International Organizations and Conflict Resolution: Peace Education Through Stimulation," *Peace and Change* 10:2 (Summer 1984): 87–92.
- Olivia Frey, "The Pedagogy of Peace," *Peace and Change* 10:2 (Summer 1984): 93–100.

XXII

World Order Education and Teacher Training

1. Teaching About Human Rights*

Steven J. Haggbloom   *Spring 1988*
Psychology Dept., Arkansas State University,
State University, AR 72467

> *Some of the most disturbing and far-reaching problems of our society center in the area of human relationships and responsible citizenship. They will be resolved only as the capacity of individuals to deal with them is improved. This capacity is likely to be improved in a democratic society only as more people understand and become committed to the values and human rights delineated in the basic documents which constitute the legal foundation for government. . . . Formal education is a powerful and effective means by which our society can realize the promise of our human rights heritage. It is important that educational programs emphasize not only the rights but the responsibilities inherent in each of them. A major challenge for education is to teach these rights and responsibilities faithfully in every classroom.*
> —Phi Delta Kappa Commission on Education
> and Human Rights, 1974

The major purpose of this course will be to promote human rights education in the schools by familiarizing prospective educators with available human rights teaching units, classroom activities, and resources. The course

---

*Editor's Note: A newsletter for teachers of human rights, edited by Steven Haggbloom, is available from: Human Rights Internet, Harvard Law School, Cambridge, MA 02138.

will examine curriculum materials for all grade levels and for a very wide range of subject areas. Some of the "obvious" courses to include in instructional units on human rights are World History and U.S. History, Civics of Government, and Global Studies. In addition to these areas, the Honors course will examine curriculum materials for use in such nontraditional areas for human rights education as English, Literature, Art, Geography, Economics, and Math. These objectives will be accomplished through discussion and presentation (by students) of teaching units, "walking through" or role playing activities, and limited previewing of audio-visual resources.

There are several contemporary education trends that will be served by this course. First and foremost, there is a developing interest and emphasis on the part of both students and teachers on human rights education per se as a component of school curricula. This is evidenced by the fact that the California Legislature in 1985 enacted Assembly Bill 1273 requiring public schools to implement a model curriculum on human rights. Similar legislation is being considered in several other states. Responding to the increased demand for instructional materials, *Scholastic Update*, a magazine for secondary education students and teachers, devoted the entire October 1986 issue to international human rights. The demand for human rights education has been fueled by increased student interest due at least in part to a series of rock music concerts, billed as the "Conspiracy of Hope Tour," in 1986 and 1987, that focused young peoples' attention on human rights violations and concerns around the globe. The bicentennial of our constitution is also generating increased interest in human rights education by focusing attention on the fact that a concern for human rights is central to our national heritage.

This course will also serve three interrelated trends in contemporary education that are usually perceived as separate and often operate at cross purposes in competing for the same scarce resources, despite the fact that they all represent attempts to internationalize the perspective of American students and make them aware of the interdependence of the global community in which we live. These trends are multicultural education, global studies, and a revived emphasis on citizenship education. Human rights education can provide needed subject matter and a unifying theme for these educational objectives.

Text
Shiman, D. (1988). *Teaching About Human Rights*. Denver: University of Denver Center for Teaching International Relations.

Course Requirements and Evaluation Procedures
The major course requirements will be the preparation of teaching units. In one case, the unit will be developed from a model presented and discussed in class. In the second case, the unit will be developed by the student and presented in class.

Special Features of Course

Special features of this course include brainstorming sessions in which students will generate ideas for using various human rights teaching strategies and activities, role playing or demonstrating activities where this is appropriate, and the development by each student of a human rights teaching unit.

COURSE OUTLINE

Introduction

Purpose and goals of human rights education. Provisions of major human rights documents, treaties, and conventions. Resources (e.g., Human Rights Internet, Amnesty International).

- Gruhn, I.V. (1985). The nature of human rights. *Social Education* 49, pp. 446–447.
- Hahn, C. (1985). Human rights: An essential part of the social studies curriculum. *Social Education* 49, pp. 480–483.

Part I

Teaching units, classroom activities, and resources relating to specific human rights issues. Approximately one week of class time will be devoted to each of the topics listed below. Students will brainstorm about the ways in which the units, activities, and resources can be adapted to their own teaching specialties and grade level. Activities will be role played or demonstrated. The strengths and weaknesses of the unit will be discussed, and improvements will be entertained. Finally, a small team of students will have the responsibility to prepare a revision of the unit, taking into account the class ideas and discussion, for distribution to the entire class.

The Bill of Rights
- Cohen, W., Schwartz, M., & Sobul, D. (1970). *The Bill of Rights*, Vol. II: *A Teachers Handbook*. New York: Benziger Bros.

The United Nations Universal Declaration of Human Rights
- Tankard, A. (1973). *The Human Family, Human Rights and Peace*. Detroit: Wayne State Center for Teaching about Peace and War. (Note: This is a teaching unit on the Universal Declaration.)

General Human Rights Instruction for Elementary Grades
- Gesner, L. (1985). Children's rights and responsibilities: A teaching unit for elementary grades. *Social Education, 49*, pp. 500–503.
- Shiman, D. (1988). *Teaching About Human Rights*. Denver: University of Denver Center for Teaching International Relations.

General Human Rights Instruction for Secondary Grades
- Totten, S. (1985). Human rights: A unit. *The Social Studies, 76,* pp. 240–243.
- Shiman, D. (1988). *Teaching About Human Rights.* Denver: University of Denver Center for Teaching International Relations.

Apartheid
- Maxey, P.E. (1987). Secondary teaching strategies on South Africa. *Social Education, 51,* pp. 132–134.
- Pereira, C. (1987). Elementary teaching strategies: South Africa. *Social Education, 51,* pp. 128–131.
- Totten, S. (1985). Apartheid: A unit for secondary students. *Social Science Record, 22.*

Genocide
- Frelick, B. (1985). Teaching about genocide as a contemporary problem. *Social Education, 49,* pp. 510–515.
- Model Curriculum for Human Rights and Genocide (1985), California State Department of Education.

Torture
- Totten, S. (1985). Torture: A unit for secondary students. *Social Education, 49,* pp. 504–509.
- *Torture by Governments: A Seven Part Educational Guide for High Schools* (1984). New York: Amnesty International.

Censorship
- Amnesty International Education Project (1983). *Censorship.*

Political Prisoners
- Shiman, D. (1988). *Teaching About Human Rights.* Denver: University of Denver Center for Teaching International Relations.

Part II

The remainder of the term will be devoted to presentation and discussion of human rights teaching units developed by individual students. Students will have a choice between developing a unit appropriate for their own anticipated teaching area, developing a unit on a human rights issue they are especially interested in, or developing a unit around a particular resource, e.g., film, political cartoons, newspaper articles, Amnesty International, Urgent Action Appear, etc.

ANNOTATED BIBLIOGRAPHY

Branson, M.S., & Torney-Purta, J. (1982). *International Human Rights, Society, and the Schools.* Washington, D.C.: National Council for the Social

Studies. The titles of the seven chapters of this book attest to its comprehensive nature: International Human Rights: A Primer; International Human Rights and Civic Education; Socialization and Human Rights Research: Implications for Teachers; Human Rights in Elementary and Middle Schools; International Human Rights Education: The Challenge for Colleges and Universities; and Reading and "Righting": Books About Human Rights for Children and Youth.

Friedman, J.R., & Wiseberg, L.S. (eds.). (1981). *Teaching Human Rights.* Washington, D.C.: Human Rights Internet. This volume contains 27 syllabi for human rights courses and a "Bibliography of Human Rights Bibliographies." The topics of the syllabi include "Philosophical Approaches," "Social Science Approaches," "Courses in Literature," and "Special Topics."

Milgram, S. (1974). *Obedience to Authority.* New York: Harper and Row. Milgram presents a frightening account of his experiments on obedience to authority. The subjects were instructed to administer electric shocks of increasing severity to a protesting "victim." The results, and what they say about humanitarian values, are disillusioning.

Pettman, R. (1984). *Teaching Human Rights.* Australian Human Rights Commission. A year-long curriculum suitable for grades 4–7 with activities which allow students to experience for themselves the human rights under discussion, to analyze these in their complexity, and to act upon these experiences. Activities may be excerpted from the curriculum and applied individually.

Reardon, B. (1978). *Human Rights.* Philadelphia, PA: The World Affairs Council of Philadelphia. This curriculum includes "vocabulary warmups" and "review and discussion" sections, and presents a cogent view of the most salient issues inherent in the subject of human rights.

Tankard, A. (1973). *The Human Family, Human Rights and Peace.* Detroit: Wayne State Center for Teaching About Peace and War. This is a guide for teaching about the Universal Declaration of Human Rights.

2. International Development Education

Frank A. Stone   *Spring 1988*
School of Education, University of Connecticut, Storrs, CT 06268

This is a graduate-level seminar for professional educators and other people in related human services fields. The focus of our inquiry is "international" because we intend to have a global perspective addressing Third World conditions wherever they are encountered, in local communities of southern New England or overseas. By "development" is meant all efforts that have as their basic objective improving people's quality of life—not just some people but *all* people, with special emphasis on the poorest and most disadvantaged, who have thus far been bypassed by the developmental process. Education, as the term will be understood in this seminar, consists of formal school systems, nonformal learning, and the informal processes of enculturization, socialization, and acculturation. The three broad aims of this course are as follows:

1. Increasing the awareness and knowledge of educators from the United States and other societies regarding the role of education in cultural, economic, political, and social development.
2. Enhancing the practical understanding of all that is involved in providing effective international development education at home or abroad.
3. Teaching the competencies and skills that educators need in order to plan, organize, implement, and evaluate programs and projects designed to contribute to development through education.

More specific learning objectives include:

1. Comprehending the specialized terms employed by international development educators.
2. Familiarity with the provisions of the United Nations Declaration of the Rights of the Child.
3. Recognition of alternative conceptions about the optimum role of education in the development programs.
4. Awareness of eight influential contemporary theories of socio-economic development.
5. Knowledge of how demographic and population issues, food, hunger, and nutrition, human rights and social justice concerns, nonviolent conflict resolution, and war/peace studies pertain to international development education.
6. Knowing how to draft general situation profiles, make educational needs and resources assessments, write project plans and implementation designs, and make project evaluations for development education programs.
7. Being familiar with the organizations working in international development education.
8. Being able to discuss the role of women in development, and at least four case studies of applied educational development.

Textbook

Stone, Frank A. *Learning for Change: Approaches to International Development Education.* Storrs, CT: The Isaac N. Thut World Education Center, 1988.

Requirements

Please be regular in your attendance and participation in this seminar. The seminar process is supposed to be dynamic and interactive. Each person will be asked to take responsibility for making some presentations and facilitating some discussions. We will utilize instructional media and draw on the knowledge of informants. It is therefore vital that you be present for a minimum of twelve of our fourteen seminar meetings this semester. Four short writing projects will be part of the learning process in this seminar.

Writing Project One will be an analysis and critical review of one international development education journal such as:

Ceres: FAO Review on Agriculture and Development.
DEEP: Development Education Exchange Papers.
Development Forum (UN Division for Economic and Social Information/DPI
    and the United Nations University).
Horizons, United States Agency for International Development.
Ideas & Action, Freedom from Hunger Campaign/Action for Development, FAO/
    UN, Rome, Italy.
International Quarterly—the journal for and by overseas educators. International
    Schools Services, Princeton, N.J.
Kidma: Israel Journal of Development.
The IDRC Reports, International Development Research Centre, Ottawa,
    Canada.
Thai Development Newsletter.
The UNESCO Courier.
UNICEF News.
VITA News (Volunteers in Technical Assistance), Arlington, VA.

Your review should be approximately six pages long.

Writing Project Two will be a participant/observation report of a field visit to a development education project in southern New England. Please keep your report to six pages.

Writing Project Three will be a report of an oral history interview with an informant who can describe a situation in which a development education program or project has been implemented or ought to be undertaken. Please do not exceed eight pages in length.

Writing Project Four will be a report of at least one book or monograph specifically on international development education. It should be four to six pages long.

COURSE OUTLINE AND READINGS

Jan. 26—An Overview of This Seminar: The State of the World in 1988

• Stone, Foreword.

Unit One: An Orientation to the World of Development

Feb. 2—Introduction
The Concepts of "International," "Development," and "Education." The United Nations Declaration of the Rights of the Child. The role of ideologies in development education. What being an international development educator entails. The global crisis in education today.
• Stone, Introduction, pp. 1–28.

Feb. 9—A Spectrum of Perspectives on International Development and Education
Jagdish Bhagwati, P.T. Bauer, Gunnar Myrdal.
• Stone, chapter 2, pp. 29–49.

Feb. 16—A Spectrum of Perspectives on International Development and Education
Denis Goulet, Frederick H. Harbison, John Simmons, Guy Gran, Björn Hettne.

Feb. 23—Getting Acquainted with International Development Education Journals
Writing Project One, "An Analysis and Critical Review of One International Development Education Journal," will be due. Seminar reports are based on Writing Project One.

Unit Two: Teaching About Global Development Issues

Mar. 1—Demography and Population Concerns
Food, hunger, and nutrition.
• Stone, pp. 50–64.

Mar. 8—Human Rights and Social Justice—Conflict Resolution, War and Peace Studies—Irenics/Global Interdependence
• Stone, pp. 65–85.

Mar. 15—International Organizations that Work in the Field of Education for Development
• Stone, chapter 4.

Unit Three: Planning and Managing Educational Development Projects

Mar. 29—Getting Support for Developing Projects in Education
Obtaining and processing the information to make a case. Formulating a general prospectus. Compiling a "Guest List." Providing public information.

Presenting specific funding proposals. Writing Project Two, "A Participant/Observation Report of a Field Visit to a Development Education Project," will be due.
- Stone, chapter 5.

Apr. 5—Implementing and Evaluating Development Projects in Education

Unit Four: Case Studies of International Development Education

The Role of Women in Development
- Stone, chapter 6.

Apr. 19—The National Literacy Crusade of Nicaragua

Head Start: A Child Development Program in the United States. Writing Project Three, "A Report of an Oral History Interview with an Informant About International Development Education," will be due.
- Stone, chapter 7.

Apr. 26—Integrated Nonformal Education in Botswana—The Sarvodaya Shramadana Movement of Sri Lanka
- Stone, chapter 7.

May 3—Discussion of Collateral Reading About International Development Education

Writing Project Four, "A Report on a Book or Monograph About International Development Education," will be due. Seminar reports are based on Writing Project Four.

RECOMMENDED ADDITIONAL READING

Ahmed Manzoor, and Philip H. Coombs, eds. *Education for Rural Development: Case Studies for Planners.* New York: Praeger Publishers, 1975.

Bryant, Coralie, and Louise G. White. *Managing Devlopment in the Third World.* Boulder, CO: Westview Press, 1982.

Coombs, Philip H. *The World Crisis in Education: The View from the Eighties.* New York: Oxford University Press, 1985.

The Dutch Way: Information About the Broad System of Educational Development Assistance in the Netherlands. The Hague: NUFFIC, 1977.

Goodman, Louis J., and Ralph N. Love, eds. *Project Planning and Management: An Integrated Approach.* New York: Pergamon Press, 1980.

Goodwin, Crawford D., and Michael Nacht. *Decline and Renewal: Causes and Cures of Decay Among Foreign-Trained Intellectuals and Professionals in the Third World.* New York: Institute for International Education, 1986.

Financing Educational Development. Proceedings of an International Seminar Held in Mont Sainte Marie, Canada, 19–21 May 1982. Ottawa, Canada: International Development Research Centre, 1983.

Huston, Perdita. *Third World Women Speak Out.* New York: Praeger Publishers in Cooperation with the Overseas Development Council, 1979.

Jolly, Richard. *Disarmament and World Development.* Oxford, England, U.K.: Pergamon Press, 1978.

Kidron, Michael, and Ronald Segal. *The New State of the World Atlas, Revised and Updated.* New York: Simon and Schuster, Inc., 1987.

Shaeffer, Sheldon, and John A. Nkinyangi, eds. *Educational Research Environments in the Developing World.* Ottawa, Canada: International Development Research Centre, 1983.

Shepard, Mark. *Gandhi Today: A Report on Mahatma Ghandi's Successors.* Arcata, CA: Simple Productions, 1987.

Stockwell, Edward G., and Karen A. Laidlaw. *Third World Development: Problems and Prospects.* Chicago: Nelson-Hall, 1981.

Thomas, R. Murray, ed. *Politics and Education: Cases from Eleven Nations.* Oxford, England, U.K.: Pergamon Press, 1983.

van den Bor, Wout, ed. *The Art of Beginning: First Experiences and Problems of Western Expatriates in Developing Countries with Special Emphasis on Rural Development and Rural Education.* Wageningen, Netherlands: Centre for Agricultural Publishing and Documentation (PUDOC), 1983.

Worsley, Peter. *The Three Worlds: Culture and World Development.* Chicago: University of Chicago Press, 1984.

3. Education for International Understanding

Arnie Cooper   *Fall 1987*
Education Dept., Moorhead State University,
Moorhead, MN 56560

At the heart of a teacher education program that offers a pluralist perspective is a disciplined respect for human differences—differences of all sorts but particularly of ethnicity and culture. From this perspective, one seeks to understand and appreciate the multiplicity of cultural differences among people. The professional practice of teaching also requires a commitment to a global perspective as part of a pluralistic one. Education for International

Understanding is an effort to prepare future educators to understand the changing realities in a global world through a carefully developed and selected sequence of learning that requires knowledge of the differences and similarities of the world's people and how they confront problems.

Required Readings

Social Education, September, 1986. A special issue entitled "Images and Realities of Four World Regions."

Social Education, October, 1986. A special issue on Global Education.

Social Education, Feburary, 1987. A special issue on Apartheid in South Africa.

A packet of materials which consists of readings and exercises as well as classroom approaches to teaching global issues.

Assignments

Editor's Note: Due to its length, the Writing Awareness Assignment of this course could not be included in its entirety in this volume.

- Selecting Learning Materials.
- Your Community in the World.
- Writing Awareness Assignment: (a) An Insider Looking In; (b) An Outsider Looking In; (c) An Insider's Response to an Outsider's Perception.
- Two examinations.

COURSE SCHEDULE

It is the intent of your instructor to call upon the expertise of a number of guest lecturers who will offer insights on a variety of topics relevant to an understanding of global issues.

Introduction

Global Education: We Are the World

- *Social Education* (Oct. 1986): pp. 415, 416–423, 424–436, 437–446.

Global Education: The Road Ahead

- Secretary of Education, William J. Bennett, "America, the World, and Our Schools" (speech).

Examination #1

Images and Realities of Four World Regions: Textbooks as Global Educators

Selecting Learning Materials

- *Social Education* (Sept. 1986): pp. 340–344, 345–350, 351–356, 357–366, 367–375, 376–384.

Global Issues

Views of Development
- "The Story of Ranjit Singh."
- "A Second Look at Development."

Development: What's Your Choice?
- "The Situation in Talesh."

Food for All: Teaching Against Hunger
- "The Causes of Hunger."
- "Populations are Growing Rapidly."
- "The Great Scarcity Scare."

Food for All: Facts on Hand for the Teacher
- "The Hunger Cycle."
- World Map.
- "The Arithmetic of Poverty."
- "God to a Hungry Child."

Food for All: Putting Yourselves in Others' Shoes
- "Living on Less than $200 Per Year."
- "A Day in the Life of a Third World Teenager."

Law in a Global Age: Human Rights
- Universal Declaration of Human RIghts (UN, 1948).
- U.S. Bill of Rights (1791).

What Rights Are Right?
- "Rights in Other Countries."

Refugees and the Law: A Global Problem
- "Refugees Around the World."
- "Who Am I? A Refugee or an Immigrant."

Focus on South Africa: Apartheid—Roots and Definitions
- *Social Education* (Feb. 1987): pp. 106–108, 85–95, 124–127.

The Geography of Apartheid/Legislating Apartheid
- *Social Education* (Feb. 1987): pp. 118–119.

South Africa Exposed: Perspectives, Consitutional Change, and Education
- *Social Education* (Feb. 1987): pp. 96–100, 114–117, 120–123.

Review and Second Examination

ASSIGNMENTS

Selecting Learning Materials

One of the important tasks of teachers and other educators is the selection of learning materials. Quality materials alone will not ensure learning. Students learn from the teacher, from their peers, from mass media, and from other sources. Nonetheless, the impact of materials should not be minimized. Used as basic components in the curriculum, they play a major role in shaping what students learn.

The increasing volume of materials with an emphasis on global/ international sutdies is evident in the catalogs from publishers, the displays at conferences for educators, and the number and variety of such materials in curriculum resource centers and libraries. There are materials available to help achieve almost any goal or objective cited in curricular plans or course outlines. The major need is to identify what exists and to make judgments about its usefulness and appropriateness for your students and for your situation. This section of the planning guide provides some guidelines for selecting from among the increasing number of materials that emphasize global/international content and approaches.

> *Select a curriculum resource from the curriculum library and complete the following checklist:*
> - Title of materials.
> - Copyright date.
> - Author(s).
> - Publisher.
> - Format (textbook, filmstrip, etc.).
> - Evaluator.
> - What are the objectives of the class, unit, or course in which these materials might be used?
> - What are the expressed or implied objectives of these materials?
> - Is there agreement between the objectives of the materials and the objectives of the class, unit, or course? If not, how do you justify the possible use of these materials?

(Adapted from *Global Studies from American Schools* with the kind permission of the National Education Association and Harry Hutson.)

Directions

Answer the following questions in terms of the curricular material you choose.

Global Studies Considerations

1. To what extent do the materials emphasize that each person has a unique perspective on the world that may not be shared by others?
2. To what extent do the materials help students understand that the way we perceive ourselves and other persons influences how we behave toward others?
3. To what extent do the materials emphasize that there are basic needs, concerns, activities, and rights common to humanity?
4. To what extent do the materials encourage students to imagine what it would be like to live the life of persons in foreign cultures?
5. To what extent do the materials develop understanding of concepts such as "change," "growth," "ecology," "system," and "interdependence"?
6. To what extent do the materials build awareness of current trends and developments that are affecting the world as a whole now and in the future?
7. To what extent do the materials facilitate the analysis of problems such as overpopulation, pollution, poverty, racism, and war?
8. To what extent do the materials foster an understanding of how human organizations such as governments, churches, and corporations interact globally?
9. To what extent do the materials give recognition to the fact that the world's wealth is unequally distributed?
10. To what extent do the materials give recognition to the fact that the world's resources are finite and limited?
11. To what extent do the materials develop an understanding of how one's personal choices can affect others around the world?
12. To what extent do the materials help students to make comparisons and look for interrelationships across cultures, nations, or subgroups of societies?
13. To what extent do the materials encourage the appreciation of individual and group differences around the world?
14. To what extent do the materials encourage speculating, forecasting, scenario writing, and other ways of estimating how the world may be in the future?

Conclusions

15. To what extent are the materials generally teachable?
16. To what extent are the materials generally learnable?
17. To what extent are the materials suitable for students with special learning needs?
18. To what extent are the materials packaged in a suitable format?
19. To what extent do you recommend that these materials be purchased or used?

Our Community in the World

This activity is based on the research of Chadwick Alger and his associates at the Mershon Center of the Ohio State University. Complete the questions below for two separate organizations, institutions, or entities in your hometown.

Rationale for this assignment. The basic premise behind Our Community in the World type of project is that individuals and community organizations in local communities are making and carrying out foreign policy every day in the course of their normal transactions.

This is because these transactions have international dimensions not always recognized or articulated; these international dimensions may contribute to the enhancement or diminution of social welfare at home and abroad, without ever touching directly on governmental foreign policy transactions.

The export and import policies of businesses in your hometown may be an important source of international goodwill. The activities of local leadership training programs channeled through International Rotary may enhance leadership potentials in Third World countries. The activities of local churches and programs for youth, through scholarships, leadership training, and development aid programs, are channeled through international church bodies and may directly affect levels of living among the Third World poor.

1. What are the organization's foreign connections or concerns?
2. To what extent are they dependent on these foreign connections? To what extent interdependent?
3. How do they serve the global community?
4. How do they serve the local community? Other comments?

Locating Global Studies Resources in the Local Community

Students are usually surprised to learn that many people in their community have traveled abroad or are engaged in some form of transnational interaction. This inventory is intended to help teachers and students gather the kinds of data needed for a global studies directory of people, organizations, and other resources.

Use this checklist to identify possible global studies resources:
• The school library, resource room, media center, or center for materials.
• Parents and community members who may have global knowledge or interests based upon traveling, living, or working abroad.
• Fellow teachers and students who may have global knowledge or interests.

- Local businesses that have international connections.
- Local restaurants that serve international cuisine.
- Local stores that sell international products (grocery stores or gift shops, for example.)
- The local library and museums.
- Religious organizations with overseas mission or outreach activities.
- Newspaper accounts of global trends and international affairs.
- Local chapters of international organizations (Rotary, 4-H, Red Cross, etc.)
- International exchange and foreign study programs.
- Performing groups (dance, music, drama, athletics).
- Nearby landmarks where there have been points of international contact.
- Ethnic neighborhoods.
- Local traditions that have an international origin.
- Local events that have global implications.
- The home (foreign-made products, toys).
- Television (*The Global Papers, Big Blue Marble*, news specials).

Appendix

Professional Associations

PEACE STUDIES ASSOCIATION
Robin Crews, Executive Director
c/o Kansas Institute for Peace and Conflict Resolution
Bethel College
North Newton, KS 67117
USA

An organization of college and university academic programs established in 1987 to promote the study of peace, conflict, justice, and global security.

INTERNATIONAL PEACE RESEARCH ASSOCIATION
Elise Boulding, Secretary General
c/o Conflict Resolution Consortium
Box 372
University of Colorado
Boulder, CO 80309
USA

An international interdisciplinary research organization established in 1964 to examine the conditions of peace and the causes of war and other forms of violence.

CONSORTIUM FOR PEACE RESEARCH, EDUCATION, AND DEVELOPMENT
Maire Dugan, Executive Director
c/o Center for the Analysis and Resolution of Conflict
George Mason University
4400 University Drive
Fairfax, VA 22030
USA

An organization established in 1970 to promote research, education (kindergarten-university), and activism for peace, and especially to encourage dialogue between individuals and programs working in those three areas.

VICTORIAN ASSOCIATION OF PEACE STUDIES
GPO Box 1274L
Melbourne, Victoria 3001
AUSTRALIA

DUTCH-BELGIAN SOCIETY FOR PEACE AND CONFLICT RESEARCH
L. Desmet, Secretary
Vereniging voor Vredes-En Konfliktonderzoek
c/o Internationaal Vredescentrum
Kerkstraat 150
2000 Antwerp
BELGIUM

CANADIAN PEACE RESEARCH AND EDUCATION ASSOCIATION
M.V. Naidu, President
25 Dundana Avenue
Dundas, Ontario L9H 4E5
CANADA

CHILEAN PEACE RESEARCH ASSOCIATION
A. Varas Fernandez, Secretary General
Asociacion Chilena de Investigaciones Para La Paz
Casilla 80
Correo Miramontes
Santiago
CHILE

DANISH PEACE RESEARCH ASSOCIATION
M. Naur
Stensbjergves 18
Allerup
DENMARK

PEACE RESEARCH INFORMATION UNIT
K. H. Koppe, Director
German Society for Peace and Conflict Research
Deutsche Gesellschaft fur Friedens und Konfliktforschung
Theaterplatz 28
5300 Bonn 2 Bad Godesberg
FEDERAL REPUBLIC OF GERMANY

FINNISH PEACE RESEARCH ASSOCIATION
Raimo Vayrynen, President
Suomen Rauhantutk Musydistys R.Y.
Political Science Dept.
University of Tampere
Box 607
SF-33101 Tampere 10
FINLAND

FRENCH PEACE RESEARCH ASSOCIATION
Alain Joxe, Secretary General
nAssociation Francaise de Recherche sur la Paix
Maison des Sciences de l'Homme
54 Boulevard Raspail
75006 Paris
FRANCE

PEACE STUDIES ASSOCIATION OF JAPAN
S. Fukushima, President
Nihon Heiwa Gakkai

P.O. Box 5187
Tokyo International
JAPAN

LATIN AMERICAN PEACE RESEARCH COUNCIL
A. Cavalla, President
Consejo Latinamericano de Investigacion Para La Paz
Apartado Postal 20-105
Mexico D. F. 20
MEXICO

NEW ZEALAND FOUNDATION FOR PEACE STUDIES
L. C. Clements
P.O. Box 4110
29 Princess Street
Auckland 1
NEW ZEALAND

NORDIC COOPERATION COMMITTEE FOR INTERNATIONAL POLITICS,
    CONFLICT AND PEACE RESEARCH
Nordiska Samarbetskomitten fur Internationelli Politik,
    Inkl. Konflikt-och Fredskorskning
Swedish Institute for International Affairs
Lilla Nygatan 23, S-111
28 Stockholm
SWEDEN

COUNCIL ON PEACE RESEARCH IN HISTORY
Leonard Liggio
c/o Institute for Humane Studies
4400 University Drive
George Mason University
Fairfax, VA 22030
USA

NATIONAL CONFERENCE ON PEACEMAKING AND CONFLICT RESOLUTION
Joel Stronberg, Executive Director
George Mason University
Fairfax, VA 22030
USA

PEACE SCIENCE SOCIETY INTERNATIONAL
Walter Isard, Exective Director
B4 W Sibley Hall
Cornell University
Ithaca, NY 14853
USA

UNITED NATIONS PEACE STUDIES UNIT
Robin Ludwig
Department of Political Affairs
The United Nations
New York, NY 10017
USA

Undergraduate Academic Programs

This list includes: (1) undergraduate programs that offer majors, minors, and certificates in peace studies, conflict resolution, and closely-related fields; (2) programs that offer courses and extra-curricular activities without formal certification for the students; (3) faculty committees in the process of developing a coherent curriculum in this field; and (4) schools without a program structure that otherwise encourage independent concentrations in peace studies.

Undergraduate Programs in the United States and Canada

UNIVERSITY OF AKRON
Center for Peace Studies
Akron, OH 44325
Attn: Martha C. Leyden

ALMA COLLEGE
Peacemaking and Conflict Resolution Program
Alma, MI 48801
Attn: Verne Bechill

ALVERNO COLLEGE
Global Environment and Citizenship Division
3401 South 39th Street
Milwaukee, WI 53215
Attn: Stephen Sharkey

AMERICAN UNIVERSITY
Peace and Conflict Resolution Studies
School of International Service
Washington, DC 20016
Attn: Adrienne Kaufmann

AMHERST COLLEGE (see Five Colleges, Inc.)

ANNA MARIA COLLEGE
Peace and Justice Specialty
Paxton, MA 01612
Attn: Walter Noyalis

ANTIOCH UNIVERSITY
Peace Studies Concentration
Yellow Springs, OH 45387
Attn: Jill S. Beerman

AQUINAS COLLEGE
Conflict Resolution Program
Grand Rapids, MI 49506
Attn: Nancy Ann Flumerfelt

ARIZONA STATE UNIVERSITY
Peace and Multicultural Studies
Tempe, AZ 85287
Attn: Ann Hardt

ASSUMPTION COLLEGE
Peace Studies Committee

Worcester, MA 01602
Attn: Michael True

COLLEGE OF THE ATLANTIC
Peace Studies Faculty
Bar Harbour, ME 04609
Attn: John Buell

AUGSBURG COLLEGE
Program in Global Community
Center for Global Service and Education
Minneapolis, MN 55454
Attn: Joel Mugge

AURORA COLLEGE
Peace Studies Program
Psychology Department
347 South Gladstone
Aurora, IL 60506

AUSTIN COLLEGE
Contemporary Policy Studies
Sherman, TX 75090
Attn: Gerald Middents

BERKSHIRE COMMUNITY COLLEGE
Peace and World Order Studies
Pittsfield, MA 01201
Attn: Donald N. Lathrop

BETHEL COLLEGE
Peace Studies Department
North Newton, KS 67117
Attn: Robin Crews

BISCAYNE COLLEGE
Peace and Justice Education Program
16400 NW 32nd Street
Miami, FL 33050
Attn: P. Gerard Shaw

BLUFFTON COLLEGE
Peace and Conflict Studies Program
Department of English
Bluffton, OH 45817
Attn: Jeff Gundy

BOSTON COLLEGE
Peace and War Studies
Theology Department
Chestnut Hill, MA 02167
Attn: Robert J. Daly

BOSTON THEOLOGICAL INSTITUTE
Peace Education Program
210 Herrick Road
Chestnut Hill, MA 02167
Attn: Robert Melhorn

BRANDEIS UNIVERSITY
Peace Studies Program
Waltham, MA 02154
Attn: Seyom Brown

BRIAR CLIFF COLLEGE
Dean of Academic Affairs
Peace Studies Program
3303 Rebecca Street
Sioux City, IA 51104
Attn: Grace Ann White

BRIDGEWATER COLLEGE
International Peace Studies
Bridgewater, VA 22812
Attn: John Cooper

UNIVERSITY OF BRITISH COLUMBIA
Peace Studies Committee
Department of Political Science
Vancouver, British Columbia V6T 1Z2
CANADA
Attn: Michael Wallace

BRYN MAWR COLLEGE
Peace Studies Concentration
Political Science Department
Bryn Mawr, PA 19010
Attn: Marc Ross

UNIVERSITY OF CALGARY
Peace Studies Program
Faculty of General Studies
Calgary, Alberta T2N 1N4
CANADA
Attn: Dean R. G. Weyant

CALIFORNIA INSTITUTE OF INTEGRAL STUDIES
Peace/War and Global Studies
765 Ashbury Street
San Francisco, CA 94117
Attn: Ofer Zur

CALIFORNIA STATE UNIVERSITY AT FRESNO
Peace and Conflict Studies
School of Social Science
Fresno, CA 93740
Attn: Sudarshan Kapoor

CALIFORNIA STATE UNIVERSITY AT FULLERTON
Peace Studies Program
Religious Studies Department
Fullerton, CA 92634
Attn: George Saint-Laurent

CALIFORNIA STATE UNIVERSITY AT LONG BEACH
Peace Studies Committee

Department of Education
Long Beach, CA 90840
Attn: Carolyn M. Owen

CALIFORNIA STATE UNIVERSITY AT LOS ANGELES
Center for the Study of Armaments and Disarmament
Los Angeles, CA 90032
Attn: Richard Dean Burns

CALIFORNIA STATE UNIVERSITY AT SACRAMENTO
Peace and War Studies
Sacramento, CA 95819
Attn: Duane Campbell

UNIVERSITY OF CALIFORNIA AT BERKELEY
Peace and Conflict Studies
SAHS Department-Warren Hall
Berkeley, CA 94720
Attn: Sheldon Margen

UNIVERSITY OF CALIFORNIA AT IRVINE
Global Peace and Conflict Studies
Social Science Tower 531
Irvine, CA 92719
Attn: Julius Margolis

UNIVERSITY OF CALIFORNIA AT SANTA BARBARA
Global Peace and Security Program
6722 South Hall
Santa Barbara, CA 93106
Attn: John Ernest

UNIVERSITY OF CALIFORNIA AT SANTA CRUZ
Peace and Strategic Studies
Colwell College
Santa Cruz, CA 95064
Attn: Bruce Larkin

CALUMET COLLEGE
Peace and Justice Studies
Department of Philosophy
Whiting, IN 46394
Attn: Steven Schroeder

CARLOW COLLEGE
Peace Studies Program
Department of Communication
3333 Fifth Avenue
Pittsburgh, PA 15213
Attn: Brenda L. Carter

CATHOLIC UNIVERSITY
Peace and World Order Studies Program
Department of Religion
Washington, DC 20064
Attn: Joseph Komonchak

CENTRAL CONNECTICUT STATE UNIVERSITY
Peace Studies Committee
English Department
New Britain, CT 06117
Attn: Kevin Lynch

CHAPMAN COLLEGE
Peace and Justice Program
Orange, CA 92666
Attn: Barbara Mulch

CHRISTIAN BROTHERS COLLEGE
Peace Studies Program
Memphis, TN 38104
Attn: Gerard A. Vanderhaar

CLARKE COLLEGE
Justice and Peace Committee
Dubuque, IA 52001
Attn: Norman C. Freund

CLARK UNIVERSITY
Peace Studies Program
Cented 133
Worcester, MA 01610
Attn: Glen Gersmehl

CLEVELAND STATE UNIVERSITY
Peace and Conflict Resolution Studies
Department of Political Science
Cleveland, OH 44115
Attn: Robert B. Charlick

COLGATE UNIVERSITY
Peace Studies Program
Hamilton, NY 13346
Attn: Nigel Young

UNIVERSITY OF COLORADO AT BOULDER
Conflict and Peace Studies
Campus Box 331
Boulder, CO 80309
Attn: Howard Smokler

UNIVERSITY OF COLORADO AT BOULDER
Social Conflict Concentration
Campus Box 327
Boulder, CO 80309
Attn: Paul Wehr

UNIVERSITY OF CONNECTICUT AT STORRS
Peace Studies Committee
Storrs, CT 06268
Attn: Robert Luyster

UNIVERSITY OF CONNECTICUT AT WEST HARTFORD
War and Ethics Program
Undergraduate College

West Hartford, CT 06117
Attn: Robert L. Phillips

CONRAD GREBEL COLLEGE
Peace and Conflict Studies
University of Waterloo
Waterloo, Ontario N2L 3G6
CANADA
Attn: Conrad Brunk

DARTMOUTH COLLEGE
War/Peace Studies
English Department
Hanover, NH 03755
Attn: Peter A. Bien

UNIVERSITY OF DAYTON
Center for Peace and Justice Studies
Dayton, OH 45469
Attn: Phil Aaron

DE PAUW UNIVERSITY
Assistant Vice President
Conflict Resolution Studies
Greencastle, IN 46135
Attn: John B. White

DONNELLY COLLEGE
World Studies Program
1236 Sandersky Avenue
Kansas City, KS 66102
Attn: Martha Ann Linck

UNIVERSITY OF DUBUQUE
Peace Studies Concentration
2050 University Avenue
Dubuque, IA 52001
Attn: David Roberts

D'YOUVILLE COLLEGE
Peace Studies Project
320 Porter Avenue
Buffalo, NY 14201
Attn: Sr. Barbara Quinn

EARLHAM COLLEGE
Peace and Global Studies Program
Richmond, IN 47374
Attn: Tony Bing

EASTERN MENNONITE COLLEGE
Peace and Justice Studies
Religion Department
Harrisonburg, VA 22801
Attn: Ray Gingerich

EASTERN OREGON STATE COLLEGE
Peace Studies Committee

Sociology Department
LaGrande, OR 97850
Attn: John Millay

EDGEWOOD COLLEGE
Peace Education Program
855 Woodrow Street
Madison, WI 53711
Attn: Sr. Marie Stephen Reges

EVERGREEN STATE COLLEGE
Peace and Conflict Resolution Center
Cab 305
Olympia, WA 98505
Attn: Lillian Ford

FAIRFIELD UNIVERSITY
Peace and Justice Studies
Political Science Department
Fairfield, CT 06430
Attn: Kevin Cassidy

FIVE COLLEGES, INC.
Five College Program in Peace and World Security Studies
c/o Hampshire College
Amherst, MA 01002
Attn: Michael Klare
(Amherst, Hampshire, Mount Holyoke, and Smith Colleges and
the University of Massachusetts at Amherst)

FLORIDA STATE UNIVERSITY
Peace Studies Program
234 Williams Building
Tallahassee, FL 32306
Attn: John Carey

FORDHAM UNIVERSITY
Peace and Justice Studies Program
Political Science Department
Bronx, NY 10458
Attn: Martin Fergus

FRESNO PACIFIC COLLEGE
Conflict and Peacemaking Program
Fresno, CA 93702
Attn: Dalton Reimer

FRIENDS WORLD COLLEGE
Peace Studies and Conflict Resolution
Huntington, NY 11743
Attn: Arthur Meyer

GEORGE FOX COLLEGE
Center for Peace Learning
Newberg, OR 97132
Attn: Lon Fendall

GEORGETOWN UNIVERSITY
Center for Peace Studies
410 Maguire Building
Washington, DC 20057
Attn: Richard T. McSorley

GOSHEN COLLEGE
Peace Studies Program
Goshen, IN 46526
Attn: Don Blosser

GRAMBLING STATE UNIVERSITY
Center for Peace and Conflict Resolution
Sociology Department
Grambling, LA 71245
Attn: M. Francis Abraham

GUILFORD COLLEGE
World Peace and Justice Program
Greensboro, NC 27410
Attn: Cyrus Johnson

GUSTAVUS ADOLPHUS COLLEGE
Peace Education Program
St. Peter, MN 56082
Attn: Gregory Mason

HAMPSHIRE COLLEGE (see Five Colleges, Inc.)

HAVERFORD COLLEGE (see Bryn Mawr College)

UNIVERSITY OF HAWAII
Peace Studies Program
Institute for Peace
Honolulu, HI 96822
Attn: Ian Y. Lind

HOFSTRA UNIVERSITY
Peace Studies Committee
Political Science Department
New College
Hempstead, NY 11550
Attn: Linda Longmeyer

COLLEGE OF THE HOLY CROSS
Peace Studies Committee
Worcester, MA 01610
Attn: David O'Brien

UNIVERSITY OF IDAHO
Martin Institute of Human Behavior
Moscow, ID 83843
Attn: Sheila Burr

ILLINOIS COLLEGE
Peace Studies Committee
International Studies Program
Jacksonville, IL 62650
Attn: Richard Fry

INDIANA UNIVERSITY
Peace and Conflict Studies Committee
Sycamore Hall 230
Bloomington, IN 47405
Attn: James Hart

INDIANA UNIVERSITY AT FORT WAYNE
Peace Studies Committee
Sociology Department
Fort Wayne, IN 46807
Attn: Michael Nusbaumer

INDIANA UNIVERSITY-NORTHWEST
Peace Studies Committee
History Department
Gary, IN 46408
Attn: Ronald D. Cohen

IONA COLLEGE
Peace and Justice Studies
New Rochelle, NY 10801
Attn: Kathleen P. Designan

UNIVERSITY OF IOWA
Global Studies Program
Center for International Studies
405 Jefferson Building
Iowa City, IA 52242
Attn: James F. McCue

IOWA STATE UNIVERSITY
Peace Studies Committee
229 Spedding Hall
Ames, IA 50011
Attn: Bernard C. Gerstein

JOHN ABBOT COLLEGE
Peace Studies Program
Humanities Department
P.O. Box 2000
Ste. Anne de Bellevue, Quebec H9X 3L9
CANADA
Attn: Alan Silverman

JUNIATA COLLEGE
Peace and Conflict Studies
Huntingdon, PA 16652
Attn: Andrew Murray

KENT STATE UNIVERSITY
Center for Peaceful Change
Kent, OH 44242
Attn: William Keeney

LEWIS UNIVERSITY
Peace Education Committee
Philosophy Department

Romeoville, IL 60441
Attn: Marilyn Nissim-Sabat

UNIVERSITY OF LOWELL
Peace and Conflict Studies Program
Sociology Department
Lowell, MA 01854
Attn: John McDougall

LOYOLA MARYMOUNT UNIVERSITY
Peace Studies Program
Los Angeles, CA 90045
Attn: Michael A. Genovese

LOYOLA UNIVERSITY
Peace and Justice Studies Committee
Biological Sciences Department
New Orleans, LA 70118
Attn: E.L. Beard

McGILL UNIVERSITY
Peace Studies Group
McIntyre Medical Bldg.
3655 Drummond Street
Montreal H3G 1Y6
CANADA
Attn: Donald Gates

McMASTER DIVINITY COLLEGE
Peace Studies
Hamilton, Ontario L8S 4K1
CANADA
Attn: Paul R. Dekar

McMASTER UNIVERSITY
Peace Studies Committee
University Hall #B-118
1280 Main Street
West Hamilton, Ontario L8S 4K1
CANADA
Attn: Thomas Slee

UNIVERSITY OF MAINE
Peace Studies Committee
417 Chadbourne Hall
Orono, ME 04469
Attn: Emily Markides

MANCHESTER COLLEGE
Peace Studies Institute
North Manchester, IN 46962
Attn: Ken Brown

MANHATTEN COLLEGE
Peace Studies Institute
Riverdale, NY 10471
Attn: Raymond Antolik

UNIVERSITY OF MARYLAND
Program in Global and Transnational Problems
Government Department
College Park, MD 20742
Attn: Dennis C. Pirages

UNIVERSITY OF MASSACHUSETTS AT AMHERST (see Five Colleges, Inc.)

MESSIAH COLLEGE
Peacemaking Program
Grantham, PA 17027
Attn: Randy Basinger

UNIVERSITY OF MICHIGAN AT ANN ARBOR
Peace Studies Program
Political Science Department
Ann Arbor, MI 48109
Attn: Richard Mann

UNIVERSITY OF MISSOURI
Peace Studies Program
101 Professional Building
Columbia, MO 65211
Attn: Robbie Lieberman

MOLLOY COLLEGE
International Peace and Justice Studies
1000 Hempstead Avenue
Rockville Centre, NY 11570
Attn: Katherine Gee

MONMOUTH COLLEGE
Peace Studies Committee
West Long Branch, NJ 07764
Attn: Samuel Kim

MOREHOUSE COLLEGE
Peace Studies Committee
Political Science Department
Atlanta, GA 30314
Attn: Tobe Johnson

MORNINGSIDE COLLEGE
Peace Studies Committee
Religious Studies Department
Sioux City, SD 51106
Attn: Steve Plymel

MOUNT HOLYOKE COLLEGE (see Five Colleges, Inc.)

MOUNT HOOD COMMUNITY COLLEGE
Peace Studies Committee
Literature Department
26000 SE Stark St.
Gresham, OR 97030
Attn: Willene Lyon

NECCUM CONSORTIUM
Twelve College Peace Studies Program

51 Lawrence Street
Lawrence, MA 01841
Attn: Jacob L. Zar

UNIVERSITY OF NEVADA
Peace Studies Committee
Social Work Dept.
4505 S. Maryland Pkwy.
Las Vegas, NV 89154
Attn: Gerald Rubin

UNIVERSITY OF NEW HAMPSHIRE
Peace Studies Committee
Psychology Department
Durham, NH 03824
Attn: John A. Nevin

NEW YORK UNIVERSITY
Peace and Global Policy Studies
New York, NY 10003
Attn: Robert R. Holt

CITY UNIVERSITY OF NEW YORK
International Studies Program
Convent Avenue at 138th St.
New York, NY 10031
Attn: Sherry Baver

STATE UNIVERSITY OF NEW YORK AT BINGHAMTON
Peace Studies Education Center
School of Education and Human Development
Binghamton, NY 13901
Attn: Linda Rennie Forcey

STATE UNIVERSITY OF NEW YORK AT CORTLAND
Peace Studies Committee
Geology Department
Cortland, NY 13045
Attn: James E. Bugh

STATE UNIVERSITY OF NEW YORK AT OLD WESTBURY
Politics, Economics, and Society Program
Old Westbury, NY 11568
Attn: Angela Gilliam

STATE UNIVERSITY OF NEW YORK AT STONY BROOK
Peace Studies Resource Center
Center for Continuing Education
Stony Brook, NY 11794
Attn: Lester G. Paldy

UNIVERSITY OF NORTH CAROLINA
Peace, War, and Defense Studies
Hamilton Hall
Chapel Hill, NC 27514
Attn: James Leutze

UNIVERSITY OF NORTH DAKOTA
Center for Peace Studies
University Station, Box 8158
Grand Forks, ND 58202
Attn: Barry Vickrey

NORTHEASTERN UNIVERSITY
Peace Studies Committee
Philosophy Department
360 Huntingdon Avenue
Boston, MA 02115
Attn: Steve Nathanson

NORTHLAND COLLEGE
Studies in Conflict and Peacemaking
Ashland, WI 54806
Attn: Kent Shifferd

NORTHWESTERN UNIVERSITY
Peace Studies Center
Evanston, IL 60201
Attn: Paul Arnston

NORWICH UNIVERSITY
Peace Corps Program
Northfield, VT 05663
Attn: Richard E. May

UNIVERSITY OF NOTRE DAME
International Peace Studies
Notre Dame, IN 46556
Attn: Kathleen Maas Weitgert

OHIO STATE UNIVERSITY
Peace Studies Committee
Center for International Studies
Columbus, OH 43210
Attn: Stephen J. Summerhill

OHIO UNIVERSITY
Peace Studies Committee
History Department
Athens, OH 45701
Attn: R. H. Whealey

OREGON STATE UNIVERSITY
Peace Studies Program
Corvalis, OR 97331
Attn: Stan Shively

UNIVERSITY OF OREGON
Peace Studies Program
College of Arts and Sciences
Eugene, OR 97403
Attn: David Frank

PACIFIC UNIVERSITY
Peace and Conflict Studies

Forest Grove, OR 97116
Attn: Vernon L. Bates

UNIVERSITY OF PITTSBURGH
Peace and Conflict Resolution Committee
Pittsburgh, PA 15213
Attn: James Laulicht

PITZER COLLEGE
Peace Studies Committee
Claremont, CA. 91711
Attn: Thomas Ilgen

UNIVERSITY OF PORTLAND
University Peace Studies
College of Arts and Sciences
Portland, OR 97203
Attn: Matthew Baasten

PORTLAND STATE UNIVERSITY
Peace Studies Committee
International Studies Program
Portland, OR 92707
Attn: Mel Gurtov

QUINEBAUG VALLEY COMMUNITY COLLEGE
Peace Studies Committee
Danielson, CT 06239
Attn: John McClellan

RAMAPO COLLEGE
Peace Studies Committee
Psychology Department
Mahwah, NJ 07430
Attn: Roger N. Johnson

RENSSELAER POLYTECHNIC INSTITUTE
Science, Technology, and Values Program
Science and Technology Studies Department
Troy, NY 12181
Attn: Shirley S. Gorenstein

RICE UNIVERSITY
Peace Studies Committee
Sociology Department
Houston, TX 77251
Attn: Steven Kleinberg

ROCKFORD COLLEGE
Peace Studies Committee
5050 East State Street
Rockford, IL 61108
Attn: Justine Walhout

ROGER WILLIAMS COLLEGE
Peace Studies Committee
Counseling Center

Bristol, RI 02809
Attn: Nancy Hood

RUTGERS UNIVERSITY
Peace Studies Committee
Religion Department
New Brunswick, NJ 08903
Attn: Jim Johnson

COLLEGE OF SAINT BENEDICT
Peace Studies Program
St. Joseph, MN 56374
Attn: Phillip Durkee

SAINT BONAVENTURE UNIVERSITY
Peace Studies Program
St. Bonaventure, NY 14778
Attn: Barry Gan

SAINT JOHN'S UNIVERSITY
Peace Studies Program
Collegeville, MN 56321
Attn: Rene McGraw

SAINT JOSEPH'S COLLEGE
Justice and Peace Studies
Religious Studies Program
McAuley Hall, Room 106
West Hartford, CT 06117
Attn: J. Milburn Thompson

SAINT JOSEPH'S UNIVERSITY
Faith and Peace Institute
5600 City Avenue, Room 300 B/L
Philadelphia, PA 19131
Attn: Donald Clifford

COLLEGE OF SAINT MARY
Peace Studies Group
1901 South 72nd Street
Omaha, NE 68124
Attn: Patricia S. Hollins

SAINT MARY'S COLLEGE
Peace Studies Committee
Psychology Dept.
Notre Dame, IN 46556
Attn: Joseph Miller

SAINT MARY'S UNIVERSITY
Peace Studies Committee
San Antonio, TX 78284
Attn: Ann Semel

COLLEGE OF SAINT SCHOLASTICA
Peace Studies
Duluth, MN 55811
Attn: Mark Hanna

COLLEGE OF SAINT THOMAS
Justice and Peace Studies
Theology Department
Saint Paul, MN 55105
Attn: David W. Smith

SAINT XAVIER COLLEGE
Peace Studies Committee
History and Political Science Department
Chicago, IL 60655
Attn: Peter N. Kirstein

SALEM STATE COLLEGE
Peace Studies Institute
Salem, MA 01970
Attn: Ed Meagher

SAN FRANCISCO STATE UNIVERSITY
Global Peace Studies Committee
School of Humanities
San Francisco, CA 94132
Attn: Anatole Anton

SCHOOL FOR INTERNATIONAL TRAINING
World Issues Program
Brattleboro, VT 05301
Attn: Shaun Bennet

UNIVERSITY OF SCRANTON
Program in Peace and Justice
Scranton, PA 18510
Attn: William H. Osterle

SCRIPPS COLLEGE
Peace Studies Concentration
Claremont, CA 91711
Attn: James W. Gould

SEATTLE UNIVERSITY
Peace and Justice Center
Seattle, WA 98122
Attn: Bill Moyer

SETON HALL UNIVERSITY
Peace Studies Research Group
Judeo-Christian Studies Department
South Orange, NJ 07079
Attn: Lawrence Frizzell

SIENA COLLEGE
Peace Studies Program
Loudonville, NY 12211
Attn: Jean M. Stern

SMITH COLLEGE (see Five Colleges, Inc.)

UNIVERSITY OF SOUTHERN CALIFORNIA
Peace and Conflict Studies Program
208 Administration Building

Los Angeles, CA 90089
Attn: Joseph Kertes

SOUTHERN ILLINOIS UNIVERSITY
Peace Studies Program
Edwardsville, IL 62026
Attn: Ronald J. Glassop

SOUTHERN OREGON STATE COLLEGE
International Peace Studies Program
Ashland, OR 97520
Attn: Donald Rhodes

SOUTHWEST STATE UNIVERSITY
Peace Studies Committee
Marshall, MN 56258
Attn: Charles Reinhart

SPELMAN COLLEGE
Peace Studies Committee
Political Science Department
Atlanta, GA 30314
Attn: Jeanne Meadows

STANFORD UNIVERSITY
Peace Studies Group
Political Science Department
Stanford, CA 94305
Attn: Charles Dreckmeier

STOCKTON STATE COLLEGE
Peace and Conflict Resolution Program
Pomona, NJ 08240
Attn: Novella Keith

STONEHILL COLLEGE
Institute for Justice and Peace
North Easton, MA 02357
Attn: Peter H. Beisheim

SWARTHMORE COLLEGE
Peace Studies Program
Swarthmore, PA 19081
Attn: Marc Ross

SYRACUSE UNIVERSITY
Program in Nonviolent Conflict and Change
305 Sims V
Syracuse, NY 13244
Attn: Neil H. Katz

UNIVERSITY OF TORONTO
Peace and Conflict Studies Programme
University College
Toronto, Ontario M5S 1A1
CANADA
Attn: Anatol Rapaport

TUFTS UNIVERSITY
Peace and Justice Studies Program
Medford, MA 02155
Attn: Paul Joseph

VILLANOVA UNIVERSITY
Peace & Justice Education Center
Villanova, PA 19085
Attn: Daniel Regan

WALSH COLLEGE
Institute for Justice and Peace
Canton, OH 44720
Attn: Joseph Torma

WARREN WILSON COLLEGE
Peace Education Program
Swannanoa, NC 28778
Attn: Douglas E. Bartlett

UNIVERSITY OF WASHINGTON
Peace and Strategic Studies Committee
Psychology Department
Seattle, WA 98195
Attn: David Barash

WAYNE STATE UNIVERSITY
Peace and Conflict Studies
5229 Cass Avenue, Room 101
Detroit, MI 48202
Attn: Lillian Genser

WELLESLEY COLLEGE
Peace Studies Program
Wellesley, MA 02181
Attn: Craig Murphy

WESTCHESTER UNIVERSITY
Peace and Conflict Studies Program
Westchester, PA 19383
Attn: David Eldredge

WESTERN MICHIGAN STATE UNIVERSITY
Futures Studies Program
Religion Dept.
Kalamazoo, MI 49008
Attn: Rudolph J. Siebert

WESTERN WASHINGTON UNIVERSITY
Center for Global and Peace Education
Bellingham, WA 98225
Attn: Robert Kim

WEST VIRGINIA WESLEYAN COLLEGE
Peace Education Committee
Sociology Department
Buckhannon, WV 26201
Attn: Reginald Olson

WHEELING COLLEGE
Peace and Justice Studies Committee
Wheeling, WV 26003
Attn: James A. O'Brien

WHITMAN COLLEGE
Peace and World Order Studies Committee
Walla Walla, WA 99362
Attn: Patrick Henry

WHITWORTH COLLEGE
Peace Studies Program
Spokane, WA 99251
Attn: John C. Yoder

WICHITA STATE UNIVERSITY
Peace and War Studies
Campus Box 28
Wichita, KS 67208
Attn: Louis Goldman

WILLIAM PENN COLLEGE
Peace Studies Committee
201 Trueblood Avenue
Oskaloosa, IA 52577
Attn: Dale DeWild

WILLIAMS COLLEGE
World Order Studies Committee
Religion Department
Williamstown, MA 01267
Attn: William Darrow

WILMINGTON COLLEGE
Peace Studies Program
Pyle Center, Box 1243
Wilmington, OH 45177
Attn: Daniel Smith

UNIVERSITY OF WISCONSIN AT EAU CLAIRE
Peace Studies Committee
Eau Claire, WI 54701
Attn: Leonard Gambrell

UNIVERSITY OF WISCONSIN AT MADISON
Center for International Cooperation and Security Studies
1120 W. Johnson Street
Madison, WI 53715-1045
Attn: David Tarr

UNIVERSITY OF WISCONSIN AT MILWAUKEE
Peace Studies Committee
Milwaukee, WI 53201
Attn: Khalil A. Khavari

UNIVERSITY OF WISCONSIN AT PLATTEVILLE
Peace Studies Committee
Philosophy Department

Platteville, WI 53818
Attn: Ellsworth Hood

UNIVERSITY OF WISCONSIN AT STEVENS POINT
Peace Studies Program
History Department
Stevens Point, WI 54481
Attn: Charles Rumsey

WITTENBERG UNIVERSITY
Global Studies Program
Springfield, OH 45501
Attn: Lila Wagner

XAVIER UNIVERSITY
Peace Studies Committee
3800 Victory Parkway
Cincinnati, OH 45207
Attn: John Getz

YOUNGSTOWN STATE UNIVERSITY
Peace and Nonviolence Studies
Cushwa Hall, Room 8087
Youngstown, OH 44555

Undergraduate Programs Outside the United States and Canada

UNIVERSITY OF AARHUS
Peace Studies Center
Aarhus
DENMARK
Attn: Hans Henrik Holm

UNIVERSITY OF AUCKLAND
Centre for Peace Studies
Private Bag
Auckland
NEW ZEALAND
Attn: Bob White

UNIVERSITY OF BRADFORD
School of Peace Studies
Bradford, West Yorkshire BD7 1DP
ENGLAND, U.K.
Attn: James O'Connell

UNIVERSITY OF CANTERBURY
Peace Studies Programme
Continuing Education Department
Christchurch 1
NEW ZEALAND

FREE UNIVERSITY
Chair in Peace Studies
Koningslaan 31-33
Postbus 7161
1007 MC Amsterdam
THE NETHERLANDS

UNIVERSITY OF KENT
Center for the Analysis of Conflict
Canterbury, Kent CT2 7NX
ENGLAND, U.K.
Attn: Keith Webb

UNIVERSITY OF LANCASTER
Institute for Peace Studies
Department of Politics
Lancaster LA1 4YF
ENGLAND, U.K.
Attn: Paul Smoker

UNIVERSITY OF LONDON
Peace Studies Initiative
Institute of Education
20 Bedford Way
London WC1H 0AL
ENGLAND, U.K.
Attn: Thomas Daffern

MACQUARIE UNIVERSITY
Peace Studies Curriculum
School of History
Sidney 2019
AUSTRALIA
Attn: Dennis Phillips

MINDANAO STATE UNIVERSITY
Center for Peace Studies
Iligan City 8801
PHILIPPINES
Attn: Nagasura T. Madale

NOTRE DAME UNIVERSITY
Peace Education Centre
Cotobato City
Mindanao
PHILIPPINES
Attn: Ofelia Durante

ST. MARTIN'S COLLEGE
Centre for Peace Studies
Lancaster LA1 3JD
ENGLAND, U.K.

SHIKOKO GAKUIN UNIVERSITY
Center for Peace Studies
Zentsuji-Shi
Kagawa-Ken
JAPAN 765
Attn: Mitsuo Okomoto

UNIVERSITY OF ULSTER
Peace Studies Program
History Department

Coleraine, Derry B252 1SA
NORTHERN IRELAND, U.K.
Attn: A. Hepburn

UNITED WORLD COLLEGE
Peace Studies Program
St. Donat's Castle
Llantwit Major
South Glamorgan CF 6 9WF
WALES, U.K.
Attn: Colin Reid

UPPSALA UNIVERSITY
Peace and Conflict Research Department
P.O. Box 278
S-751 05, Uppsala
SWEDEN
Attn: Peter Wallensteen

Graduate and Professional Academic Programs

This list includes: (1) graduate programs that offer degrees (M.A. or Ph.D.) in peace studies and closely allied fields; (2) graduate programs that actively support peace studies within their curriculum and research, but offer degrees in a traditional discipline; and (3) programs in other fields that emphasize the methods of conflict resolution. For information on the numerous law schools with dispute resolution programs, contact the American Bar Association.

Graduate Programs in the United States

THE AMERICAN UNIVERSITY
Peace and Conflict Resolution Studies
School of International Service
Washington, DC 20016
Attn: Adrienne Kaufmann

ANTIOCH UNIVERSITY
Peace Studies Concentration
Yellow Springs, OH 45387
Attn: Dean Richard Kalish

ASSOCIATED MENNONITE BIBLICAL SEMINARIES
Peace Studies Program
3003 Benham Avenue
Elkhart, IN 46514

BETHANY THEOLOGICAL SEMINARY
Peace Studies Seminar
Butterfield & Meyers Roads
Oak Brook, IL 60521
Attn: Dale Brown

UNIVERSITY OF CALIFORNIA (serves all nine U.C. campuses)
Institute on Global Conflict and Cooperation
Mail Code Q-060

La Jolla, CA 92093
Attn: Allen Greb

UNIVERSITY OF CALIFORNIA AT SAN FRANCISCO
Health Science and Human Survival Program
School of Medicine
San Francisco, CA 94143
Attn: Christie W. Kiefer

CALIFORNIA INSTITUTE OF INTEGRAL STUDIES
East-West Psychology Program
765 Ashbury Street
San Francisco, CA 94117
Attn: Ofer Zur

CLAREMONT GRADUATE SCHOOL
Peace Studies Concentration
Scripps College
Humanities Building, Room 221
Claremont, CA 91711
Attn: James W. Gould

CLARK UNIVERSITY
International Development and Social Change
Worcester, MA 01610
Attn: Barbara P. Thomas

UNIVERSITY OF COLORADO
Concentration in Social Conflict
Department of Sociology
Boulder, CO 80309
Attn: Paul Wehr

COLUMBIA UNIVERSITY
International Security Policy Specialization
School of International and Public Affairs
New York, NY 10027
Attn: Ted Greenwood

COLUMBIA UNIVERSITY, TEACHERS COLLEGE
Program in Peace Education
Teachers College, Box 171
New York, NY 10027
Attn: Betty Reardon

CORNELL UNIVERSITY
Peace Studies Program
Center for International Studies
Ithaca, NY 14853
Attn: Richard Ned Lebow

UNIVERSITY OF DENVER
Center for the Teaching of International Relations
Graduate School of International Studies
Denver, CO 80208
Attn: Bruce Koranksi

UNIVERSITY OF DENVER
Graduate School of International Studies
Denver, CO 80208
Attn: Thomas Rowe

EARLHAM SCHOOL OF RELIGION
Peace and Justice Studies
Richmond, IN 47374
Attn: Patricia Washburn

EMORY UNIVERSITY LAW SCHOOL
Alternative Dispute Resolution
Atlanta, GA 30322
Attn: Jack Etheridge

GEORGE MASON UNIVERSITY
Center for the Analysis and Resolution of Conflict
Fairfax, VA 22030
Attn: Joseph Scimmeca

HARVARD LAW SCHOOL
Program on Negotiation
Cambridge, MA 02138
Attn: Lawrence E. Susskind

UNIVERSITY OF HAWAII
Conflict Resolution Specialization
Department of Political Science
Honolulu, HI 96822
Attn: Ted Becker

UNIVERSITY OF ILLINOIS
Family Mediation Program
Human Development Department
Urbana, IL 61801
Attn: Linda Girdner

INTERNATIONAL PEACE ACADEMY
777 United Nations Plaza
New York, NY 10017
Attn: Indar Jit Rikhye

MASSACHUSSETS INSTITUTE OF TECHNOLOGY
Defense and Arms Control Studies Program
Center for International Studies
Cambridge, MA 02139
Attn: Jack Ruina

UNIVERSITY OF MICHIGAN
World Security and Peace Research Program
Department of Political Science
Ann Arbor, MI 48109
Attn: J. David Singer

NEW YORK UNIVERSITY
New York City Peace Studies Consortium
East Building, Room 639
239 Greene Street

New York, NY. 10003
Attn: Betty Lall

CITY UNIVERSITY OF NEW YORK
Center on Violence & Human Survival
John Jay College
444 West 56th Street
New York, NY 10019
Attn: Charles Strozier

STATE UNIVERSITY OF NEW YORK AT BINGHAMTON
Peace Education Center
School of Education and Human Development
Binghamton, NY 13901
Attn: Linda Forcey

UNIVERSITY OF NOTRE DAME
Institute for International Peace Studies
Notre Dame, IN 46556
Attn: Robert C. Johansen

OKLAHOMA STATE UNIVERSITY
Program in Dispute Services
Psychology Department
Stillwater, OK 74078
Attn: Robert Helm

UNIVERSITY OF PENNSYLVANIA
Graduate Group in Peace Science
3718 Locust Walk
Philadelphia, PA 19104
Attn: Tony Smith

SCHOOL FOR INTERNATIONAL TRAINING
Admissions Office
Kipling Road
Brattleboro, VT 05301

SEATTLE UNIVERSITY
Theological and Religious Studies
Corpus/Sumore Programs
Seattle, WA 98122
Attn: Margaret K. Lead

STANFORD UNIVERSITY
Center for Arms Control and International Security
320 Galvez Way
Stanford, CA 94305

SYRACUSE UNIVERSITY
Program in Nonviolent Conflict and Change
305 Sims V
Syracuse, NY 13244
Attn: Neil Katz

SYRACUSE UNIVERSITY
Program on the Analysis and Resolution of Conflict
712 Ostrom

Syracuse, NY 13244
Attn: Louis Kriesberg

TUFTS UNIVERSITY
Center for Public Service
Medford, MA 02155
Attn: Patricia Watson

UNIVERSITY OF WASHINGTON
Committee on Conflict Studies
Graduate School of Social Science
268 Condon Hall
Seattle, WA 98105
Attn: R. L. Prosterman

Graduate Programs Outside the United States

AUSTRALIAN NATIONAL UNIVERSITY
Peace Research Centre
Research School for Pacific Studies
GPO Box 4
Canberra, ACT 2601
AUSTRALIA
Attn: Andrew Mack

UNIVERSITY OF BRADFORD
School of Peace Studies
Bradford, West Yorkshire BD7 1DP
ENGLAND, U.K.
Attn: Thomas Woodhouse

UNIVERSITY OF COPENHAGEN
Center of Peace and Conflict Research
Vandkunsten 5, DK 1467
Copenhagen K
DENMARK
Attn: Poul Holm Andreasen

UNIVERSITA DEGLI STUDI
International School on Disarmament and Conflict Research
Instituto de Fisica
P. le Aldo Moro 2
00185 Roma
ITALY

UNIVERSITY OF DELHI
Center for the Study of Developing Societies
Department of Political Science
Delhi, 110007
INDIA
Attn: Rajni Kothari

EUROPEAN UNIVERSITY CENTRE FOR PEACE STUDIES
(English is the working language of the "European Peace University")
A-7461 Burg Schlaining
AUSTRIA
Attn: Karl Kirnbaum

GOTHENBURG UNIVERSITY
Department of Peace and Development Research
Brogatan 4
413 01 Gothenburg
SWEDEN
Attn: Bjorn Hettne

STATE UNIVERSITY OF GRONINGEN
Polemological Institute
Heresingel 13
9711ER Groningen
THE NETHERLANDS
Attn: Hylke Tromp

UNIVERSITY OF HAIFA
Peace Studies Program
Haifa, 31 999
ISRAEL
Attn: Joseph D. Ben-Dak

INSTITUTE OF SOCIAL STUDIES
International Relations and Global Development Program
P.O. Box 90733
2509 LS, The Hague
THE NETHERLANDS
Attn: Godfried van Bentham van den Bergh

INTER-UNIVERSITY CENTER OF POSTGRADUATE STUDIES
Frana Bulica 4
YU-50000 Dubrovnik
YUGOSLAVIA
Attn: S. Korninger

IRISH SCHOOL OF ECUMENICS
Milltown Park
Dublin 6
IRELAND

UNIVERSITY OF KENT
Center for the Analysis of Conflict
Rutherford College
Canterbury, Kent CT2 7NX
ENGLAND, U.K.
Attn: Keith Webb

KYUNG-HEE UNIVERSITY
Office of Academic Affairs
Graduate Institute of Peace Studies
Kwangnung, Kyunggi-do
SOUTH KOREA

UNIVERSITY OF LANCASTER
Institute for Peace Studies
Department of Politics
LA1 4YF, Lancaster
ENGLAND, U.K.
Attn: Paul Smoker

LA TROBE UNIVERSITY
Peace Research Committee
Psychology Department
Bundoora, Victoria 3083
AUSTRALIA
Attn: Connie Peck

STATE UNIVERSITY OF LEIDEN
Center for the Study of Social Conflict
Stationsweg 46
2313 Leiden
THE NETHERLANDS

UNIVERSITY OF LUND
Department of Peace and Conflict Studies
POB 117
S-221 00 Lund
SWEDEN
Attn: Hakan Wiberg

MADURAI KAMARAJ UNIVERSITY
Ghandian Studies Department
Alagarkoil Road
Madurai 625 002
Tamilnadu State
INDIA
Attn: K. Arunachalam

NATIONAL INSTITUTE FOR HIGHER EDUCATION
Irish Peace Institute
Plassey Technological Park
Limerick
IRELAND

UNIVERSITY OF OSLO
Peace Research Seminar
International Summer School
P.O. Box 3, Blindern
0313 Oslo 3
NORWAY
Attn: Tord Hoivik

ST. MARTIN'S COLLEGE
Center for Peace Studies
Bowerham, Lancaster LA1 3JD
ENGLAND, U.K.
Attn: C. Reid

SEOUL NATIONAL UNIVERSITY
Peace and World Order Studies Program
International Relations Department
Seoul 151
SOUTH KOREA
Attn: Y. S. Ha

UNIVERSITY OF SYDNEY
Center for Peace and Conflict Studies

Department of Social Work and Social Policy
Sydney 2006
AUSTRALIA
Attn: Peter King

UNIVERSITY OF PEACE
P.O. Box 199, Escazu
COSTA RICA
Attn: Tapio Varis

UPPSALA UNIVERSITY
Department of Peace and Conflict Research
Ostra Agatan 53
S-753 22, Uppsala
SWEDEN
Attn: Peter Wallensteen

UNIVERSITY OF WOLLONGONG
Peace and War Studies
Science and Technology Program
P.O. Box 1144
Wollongong, NSW 2500
AUSTRALIA
Attn: Jim Falk

Research Institutes

Many of the undergraduate and graduate programs listed above, especially those in Europe and the United States, support research activities. This list of peace research institutes and associations around the world does not include those affiliated with an undergraduate or graduate program listed above.

AUSTRALIA (see the Australian National University and the University of Sydney)

AUSTRIA

AUSTRIAN INSTITUTE FOR PEACE RESEARCH
Osterreichisches Institut fur Friedensforschung
Burg, 7461 Stadschlaining
Burgenland

UNIVERSITATSZENTRUM FUR FRIEDENSFORSCHUNG
Schottenring 21
7A 1010 Vienna

BELGIUM

CENTER FOR PEACE RESEARCH
Centre de Recherche sur la Paix
College Jacques Leclerq
Place Montesquieu 1
B-1348 Louvain-La-Neuve

CENTER FOR POLEMOLOGY OF THE FREE UNIVERSITY OF BRUSSELS
Centrum voor Polemologie van Vrije Universiteit Brussel

Pleinlan 2
1050 Brussels

GROUPE DE RECHERCHE ET D'INFORMATION SUR LA PAIX
rue Van Hoorde, 33
B-1030 Brussels

CANADA

CANADIAN INSTITUTE FOR INTERNATIONAL PEACE AND SECURITY
307 Gilmour Street
Ottowa, Ontario L9H 4E5

CANADIAN PEACE RESEARCH INSTITUTE
119 Thomas Street
Oakville, Ontario L6J 3A7

PEACE RESEARCH INSTITUTE, DUNDAS
25 Dundana Avenue
Dundas, Ontario L9H 4E5

CZECHOSLOVAKIA

CHRISTIAN PEACE RESEARCH CONFERENCE
Jungmannova 9
11121 Prague 1

DENMARK (see the Universities of Aarhus and Copenhagen)

FEDERAL REPUBLIC OF GERMANY

BERGHOF STIFTUNG FUR KONFLIKTFORSCHUNG
Wilhelmstrasse 3E1
Leimenrode 29
8 Munchen

INSTITUTE FOR PEACE RESEARCH AND SECURITY POLICY
Institut fur Friedensforschung und Sicherheitspolitik
Universitat Hamburg
Falkenstein 1
D-2000 Hamburg 55

PEACE RESEARCH INSTITUTE FRANKFURT
Hessische Stiftung Friedens und Konfliktforschung
Leimenrode 29
6 Frankfurt am Main 1

STUDY GROUP FOR PEACE AND CONFLICT RESEARCH
Arbeitsgemeinschaft for Knoflikt und Friedensforschung
Marstallstrasse 6
D-6900 Heidelberg

STUDY GROUP FOR PEACE RESEARCH
Arbeitsgruppe Friedenforschung
Institut fur Politikwissenschaft
Universitat Tubingen
Brunnenstrasse 30
D-7400 Tubingen 1

STUDY GROUP ON WESTERN EUROPEAN PEACE POLITICS
Arbeitsgruppe Westeuropaische Freidenspolitik
Freie Universitat Berlin
Kiebitzweg 3
D-1000 Berlin

FINLAND

TAMPERE PEACE RESEARCH INSTITUTE
Rauhan-Ja Konfliktintotkimslaitos
Hameenkatu 13b A
Box 447
SF-33101 Tampere 10

FRANCE

CENTER FOR DOCUMENTATION AND RESEARCH ON PEACE AND CONFLICTS
Centre de Documentation et de Recherche sur la Paix et des Conflits
B.P. 1027
69201 Lyon, Cedex 01

INSTITUT FRANCAIS DE POLEMOLOGIE
Hotel National des Invalides
75007 Paris

INTERDISCIPLINARY CENTER FOR PEACE RESEARCH AND STRATEGIC
   STUDIES
Centre Interdisciplinaire de Recherches Sur La Paix et d'Etudes Strategiques
71 Boulevard Raspail
75006 Paris

UNESCO DIVISION OF HUMAN RIGHTS AND PEACE
United Nations Educational, Scientific, and Cultural Organization
Sector of the Social Sciences
7 Place de Fontenoy
75700 Paris

HUNGARY

CENTER FOR PEACE RESEARCH COORDINATION
Hungarian Academy of Sciences
Roosevelt-ter 9
1361 Budapest V

INDIA

CENTRE FOR STUDIES ON PEACE AND NON-VIOLENCE
Sri Venkateswara University
Tirupati 571 502

GANDHIAN INSTITUTE OF STUDIES
P.O. Box 116
Rajgat
Varanasi 221001

INSTITUTE OF GANDHIAN THOUGHT AND PEACE STUDIES
Gandhi Bhawan

University of Allahabad
Allahabad 211002
Utter Pradesh

INSTITUTE OF PEACE RESEARCH AND ACTION
5 Bank Enclave
Laxmi Nagar
Delhi 110092

PEACE RESEARCH CENTRE
Gujarat Vidyapith
Ashram Road
Ahmedabad 380014

ISRAEL & PALESTINE

MIDDLE EAST PEACE INSTITUTE
Box 1777
Tel Aviv

PALESTINIAN CENTER FOR THE STUDY OF NONVIOLENCE
Nuzha Building
P.O. Box 20317
Occupied Jerusalem
Via Israel

ITALY

ITALIAN PEACE RESEARCH INSTITUTE
Istituto Italiano per La Ricerca Sulla Pace
c/o Centro Comunitario Materdei
Largo S Gennaro a Materdei 3a
Napoli 80136

RESEARCH INSTITUTE FOR DISARMAMENT, DEVELOPMENT, AND PEACE
Istituto di Ricerche per Il Disarmo, Lo Sviluppo e La Pace
Via Tomacelli 103
00186 Rome

JAPAN (see also Shikoko Gakuin University)

ASAHI SHIMBUN PEACE RESEARCH INSTITUTE
Asahi Shimbun Tyoso Kenkyu-Situ Heiwa Mondai-Han
Asahi Shimbun, Yuroku-tyo 2-6-1
Tiyoda-ku
Tokyo

INSTITUTE FOR PEACE SCIENCE
Hiroshima University
1-1-89 Higashi-senda-machi
Hiroshima 730

INTERNATIONAL PEACE RESEARCH INSTITUTE MEIGAKU
Kamikurata 1518, Totsuka
Yokohama 244

JAPAN PEACE RESEARCH GROUP
Nihon Heiwa Kenkyu Kondankai

Faculty of Law
Chuo University
742-1, Higashinanano
Hachioji, Tokyo

JAPAN PEACE RESEARCH GROUP
Faculty of Law
University of Tokyo
Sunkyo-Ku, Tokyo 113

KOREA (see Kyung-Hee University and Seoul National University)

NETHERLANDS (also see the University of Leiden and the Free University)

INTERNATIONAL PEACE POLICY RESEARCH INSTITUTE
Neuhuyskade 40
2596 HL
The Hague

NETHERLANDS INSTITUTE FOR STUDIES ON PEACE AND SECURITY
Nederlands Instituut voor Vredesvaagstukken
Alexanderstraat 7
S-Gravenhage P.O. Box 85581
2508 CG S-Gravenhage

PEACE RESEARCH CENTER
Studiecentrum voor Vredesvaagstukken
Bijleveldsingel 70/72
6524 Ae Nijmegen

NEW ZEALAND

UNIVERSITY OF AUCKLAND
Centre for Peace Studies
Private Bag
Auckland

NIGERIA

PEACE RESEARCH INSTITUTE OF NIGERIA
Political Science Department
University of Nigeria
Nsukka

NORWAY

INTERNATIONAL PEACE RESEARCH INSTITUTE OSLO
Institutt for Fredsforskning
Fuglehauggt 11
N-0260 Oslo 2

PHILIPPINES (see Mindanao State University)

SOUTH AFRICA

CONFLICT AND PEACE STUDIES PROGRAM
Centre for Intergroup Studies

University of Cape Town
Rondebosch 7700

SPAIN

CENTRO DE INVESTICACION PARA LA PAZ
Alcala 117 - 6' derecha
28009 Madrid

CENTRO D'INFORMACIO I DOCUMENTARIO INTERNATIONALS A BARCELONA
Roger de Luria
125. ir. 1a
08037 Barcelona

SRI LANKA

PEACE AND CONFLICT RESEARCH GROUP
Department of Philosophy
University of Kelaniya
Kelaniya

SWEDEN (see also the Universities of Gothenburg, Lund, and Uppsala)

STOCKHOLM INTERNATIONAL PEACE RESEARCH INSTITUTE
Bergshamra
S-171 73 Solna

SWITZERLAND

GENEVA INTERNATIONAL PEACE RESEARCH INSTITUTE
41 Rue de Zurich
CH-1201 Geneva

UNITED NATIONS INSTITUTE FOR DISARMAMENT RESEARCH
Palais des Nations
CH-1211 Geneva 10

THAILAND

PEACE AND DEVELOPMENT EDUCATION PROGRAM
Faculty of Education
Chulalongkorn University
Phya Thai Road
Bangkok 10500

UNION OF SOVIET SOCIALIST REPUBLICS

SCIENTIFIC RESEARCH COUNCIL ON PEACE AND DISARMAMENT
USSR Academy of Sciences
Profsoyuznaya ul. 23
Moscow B-418, 117418

UNITED KINGDOM (see also the Universities of Bradford, Kent, and Lancaster)

ARMAMENT AND DISARMAMENT INFORMATION UNIT
Science Policy Research Unit
University of Sussex

Palmer
Brighton BN1 9RF

OXFORD RESEARCH GROUP
P.O. Box 4
Woodstock
Oxford OX7 1UZ

UNITED STATES OF AMERICA (see also the Five Colleges and the Universities of California, Cornell, Colgate, Colorado, New York, Notre Dame, Stanford, Syracuse, and others)

ALBERT EINSTEIN INSTITUTION
1430 Massachusetts Avenue
Cambridge, MA 02138

CENTER FOR COMMON SECURITY
Box 275
Williamstown, MA 01267

CENTER FOR PSYCHOLOGICAL STUDIES IN THE NUCLEAR AGE
Harvard University
1493 Cambridge Street
Cambridge, MA 02139

CENTER FOR WAR, PEACE, AND THE NEWS MEDIA
New York University
10 Washington Place
New York, NY 10003

DEPARTMENT FOR DISARMAMENT AFFAIRS
The United Nations
New York, NY 10017

INSTITUTE FOR DEFENSE AND DISARMAMENT STUDIES
2001 Beacon Street
Brookline, MA 02146

INSTITUTE FOR PEACE AND INTERNATIONAL SECURITY
91 Harvey Street
Cambridge, MA 02140

LENTZ PEACE RESEARCH LABORATORY
1115 Magnet
St. Louis, MO 63132

PROGRAM ON NON-VIOLENT SANCTIONS
Center for International Affairs
Harvard University
737 Cambridge Street
nbridge, MA 02138

ED STATES INSTITUTE OF PEACE
Street NW–Suite 700
ton, DC 20005

ORDER MODELS PROJECT
d Nations Plaza
NY 10017

About the
Essay Contributors

M. Francis Abraham is Professor of Sociology and Director of International Studies at Grambling State University, where he is currently working to establish a Martin Luther King–Gandhi Center for Peace and Conflict Resolution.

Elise Boulding is Professor Emerita at Dartmouth College and Secretary General-elect of the International Peace Research Association. She is also Chair of the University Peace Studies section of the Consortium on Peace Research, Education, and Development (COPRED), which she cofounded in 1970. Her most recent book is *Building a Global Civic Culture: Education for an Interdependent World* (Teachers College Press, 1988). She can now be reached c/o the Institute of Behavioral Science at the University of Colorado at Boulder.

Dale A. Bryan is Coordinator of the Peace and Justice Studies Program at Tufts University, and he directs the program's internship component. He also serves on the Executive Committee of the Peace Studies Association, and is a Professional Development Associate for Educators for Social Responsibility. He is currently a Ph.D. candidate in sociology at Brandeis University, with particular interest in social movements, organizations, and youth political participation.

Robin J. Crews is Chair of the Peace Studies Department at Bethel College, and Director of the Kansas Institute for Peace and Conflict Resolution. He is also Executive Director of the Peace Studies Association. His major interests include Gandhian nonviolence and the relationships among science, technology, and the arms race.

Michael T. Klare (coeditor) is Associate Professor and Director of the Five College Program in Peace and World Security Studies, based at Hampshire College. He has written and edited numerous books and articles on defense policy, including *Low-Intensity Warfare* (Pantheon, 1987) and *American Arms Supermarket* (University of Texas Press, 1985). He is currently on the Executive Committee of the Peace Studies Association and a board member of SANE/Freeze.

Dominic Careri Kulik and David Yaskulka founded and now direct the Center for Common Security, a peace research and education institute that leads workshops for students and other citizens on themes of leadership and global security. They are graduates of Williams College, where they organized and taught in the student-run nonviolence curriculum. In 1986–1987 they led workshops across the United States as the "Gaudino Project for Student Leadership and Nonviolent Alternatives."

George A. Lopez is Associate Professor of Government and International Studies and a Faculty Fellow at the Institute for International Peace Studies at the University of Notre Dame. He has served as Director of the Peace and Global Studies Program at Earlham College, and as a peace studies consultant to over thirty campuses over the past decade. He has written and edited numerous books on state violence, including *Development, Dependence and State Repression* (Greenwood Press, 1987).

Carol Rank is a doctoral candidate in education at the University of California at Berkeley. She is also a researcher at the U.C. Berkeley Peace and Conflict Studies Program, the International Peace Research Institute (Oslo, Norway), and the University of Bradford School of Peace Studies in England.

Betty Reardon is Coordinator of the Peace Education Program at Teachers College, Columbia University, and Director of the United Ministries in Education's Peacemaking in Education Program. She is author of *Sexism and the War System* (Teachers College Press, 1985) and is extensively involved in the international peace education movement.

Adele Simmons is President of Hampshire College and Vice President of The Five Colleges, Inc. She has served as Chair of the Board of the Carnegie Foundation for the Advancement of Teaching and of the American Association of Higher Education. She is on the board of the Union of Concerned Scientists and on the Executive Committee of the Committee on National Security.

Carolyn M. Stephenson is Assistant Professor of Political Science at the University of Hawaii at Manoa, where she serves as a member of the Executive Committee of the new Institute for Peace and head of its Research Committee. She was Director of Colgate University's Peace Studies Program from 1981 to 1984. She is editor of *Alternative Methods for International Security* (University Press of America, 1982) and is currently finishing a book on alternative international security systems.

Daniel C. Thomas (coeditor) is Coordinator of the National Curriculum Resources Project of the Five College Program in Peace and World Security Studies, based at Hampshire College. He is author of the *Guide to Careers and Graduate Education in Peace Studies* (Five Colleges, Inc., 1987). He is currently on the Executive Committee of the Peace Studies Association and has worked previously at the World Policy Institute in New York and the Institute for Defense and Disarmament Studies in Boston.

Nigel Young is the George Cooley Professor of Peace Studies and Director of the Peace Studies Program at Colgate University. He is Chair of the Section on Peace Movements of the International Peace Research Association, and former Deputy Director of the School of Peace Studies at the University of Bradford. He is author of numerous articles and books on social movements, including *War Resistance and the Nation-State* (University of California Press, 1988).